Information Security:
Theory and Practice

Information Security:
Theory and Practice

Edited by
Conner Casini

www.willfordpress.com

Published by Willford Press,
118-35 Queens Blvd., Suite 400,
Forest Hills, NY 11375, USA

ISBN: 978-1-68285-649-9

Cataloging-in-Publication Data

Information security : theory and practice / edited by Conner Casini.
    p. cm.
Includes bibliographical references and index.
ISBN 978-1-68285-649-9
1. Computer security. 2. Information technology--Security measures.
3. Data protection. I. Casini, Conner.
QA76.9.A25 I54 2019
005.8--dc23

For information on all Willford Press publications
visit our website at www.willfordpress.com

Contents

Preface

I am honored to present to you this unique book which encompasses the most up-to-date data in the field. I was extremely pleased to get this opportunity of editing the work of experts from across the globe. I have also written papers in this field and researched the various aspects revolving around the progress of the discipline. I have tried to unify my knowledge along with that of stalwarts from every corner of the world, to produce a text which not only benefits the readers but also facilitates the growth of the field.

The protection of confidentiality, integrity and availability of data, while ensuring policy implementation and organizational productivity is the primary focus of information security. An evaluation of the assets, threats, vulnerabilities, impacts and effectiveness of control measures is crucial for developing an effective risk management plan. The threats to information security can be in the form of software attacks, intellectual property thefts, sabotage and information extortion. Some common examples of software attacks are viruses, Trojan horses, phishing attacks and worms. This book is a compilation of chapters that discuss the most vital concepts and emerging trends in the field of information security. The various advancements in this field are glanced at and their applications as well as ramifications are looked at in detail. For all readers who are interested in information security, the case studies included in this book will serve as an excellent guide to develop a comprehensive understanding.

Finally, I would like to thank all the contributing authors for their valuable time and contributions. This book would not have been possible without their efforts. I would also like to thank my friends and family for their constant support.

Editor

SCPR: Secure Crowdsourcing-Based Parking Reservation System

Changsheng Wan,[1,2,3] Juan Zhang,[2] and Daoli Huang[3]

[1]School of Information Science and Engineering, Southeast University, Nanjing, Jiangsu 210096, China
[2]Nanjing University, Nanjing, Jiangsu 210093, China
[3]Key Lab of Information Network Security of Ministry of Public Security of China, Shanghai 201204, China

Correspondence should be addressed to Changsheng Wan; wan.changsheng@163.com

Academic Editor: Yacine Challal

The crowdsourcing-based parking reservation system is a new computing paradigm, where private owners can rent their parking spots out. Security is the main concern for parking reservation systems. However, current schemes cannot provide user privacy protection for drivers and have no key agreement functions, resulting in a lot of security problems. Moreover, current schemes are typically based on the time-consuming bilinear pairing and not suitable for real-time applications. To solve these security and efficiency problems, we present a novel security protocol with user privacy called SCPR. Similar to protocols of this field, SCPR can authenticate drivers involved in the parking reservation system. However, different from other well-known approaches, SCPR uses pseudonyms instead of real identities for providing user privacy protection for drivers and designs a novel pseudonym-based key agreement protocol. Finally, to reduce the time cost, SCPR designs several novel cryptographic algorithms based on the algebraic signature technique. By doing so, SCPR can satisfy a number of security requirements and enjoy high efficiency. Experimental results show SCPR is feasible for real world applications.

1. Introduction

As the amount of cars increases explosively, parking is becoming a precious resource in crowded urban areas such as New York and San Francisco [1]. To fully use parking spots that belong to "private owners (PO)," crowdsourcing-based parking reservation systems have been proposed [2, 3], where private owners can publish rental information to the "Service Provider (SP)," while other "Tenant Drivers (TD)" can download rental information from SP and make a reservation.

User privacy [4] is the basic concern for the above parking reservation system. Due to the openness of the website of SP, it is easy for malicious advertisers to download PO's private information (e.g., real identities such as user name or driver license) and annoy him by keeping on sending cheating advertisements. Moreover, during the reservation process, a terrorist may even trace the PO or the TD and establish a serious terrorist attack. Therefore, it is important to use pseudonyms instead of users' real identities in this parking reservation system, so that both cheating advertisements and terrorist attacks can be avoided. However, current crowdsourcing-based security protocols (i.e., [5–30]) are still based on real identities of PO and TD. So, to provide user privacy protection, it is urgent to develop a pseudonym-based security protocol for crowdsourcing-based parking reservation systems.

On the other hand, time cost is another serious concern for parking reservation systems. Due to the high speed of cars, the parking reservation system is a real-time application [11]. So the PO and the TD are seriously concerned about high time cost arising from running cryptographic operations. Therefore, to reduce time cost, it is desirable to use highly efficient cryptographic operations for designing security protocols for parking reservation systems. Unfortunately, current crowdsourcing-based security protocols are mainly based on the time-consuming bilinear pairing operations [5, 6]. So, to reduce time cost, it is important to develop a security protocol for crowdsourcing-based parking reservation systems without bilinear pairing.

Taking both user privacy and time cost into account, we shall design a pseudonym-based security protocol for crowdsourcing-based parking reservation systems without bilinear pairing. This security protocol should satisfy the following requirements.

(1) User Privacy. It should be guaranteed that real identities of the PO and the TD (e.g., user name or driver license) will not be extracted by an adversary. Without user privacy, the adversary may send cheating advertisements to the PO and the TD and trace them.

(2) Integrity of Rental Information. It should be guaranteed that the rental information will not be tampered by an adversary. Without integrity of rental information, the TD may download wrong rental information, resulting in parking failure.

(3) Authentication. It should be guaranteed that the PO and the TD are authenticated. Without authentication, an adversary may impersonate the TD or the PO, resulting in economic losses of the PO or the TD.

(4) Key Agreement. It should be guaranteed that the PO and the TD can negotiate a shared key for protecting subsequent transactions. Specifically, it should be guaranteed that the shared key will not be tampered or extracted by an adversary. Without key agreement, the subsequent transactions may be compromised by an adversary, resulting in reservation failure.

(5) Time Costs. It should be guaranteed that the time cost between the PO and the TD is low. Time cost is comprised of computation and communication costs. Computation cost is mainly consumed by cryptographic algorithms on the PO and the TD, while communication cost is mainly consumed by message-transmitting processes between the PO and the TD.

Obviously, designing a security protocol for crowdsourcing-based parking reservation systems is a nontrivial task, due to its complicated security and efficiency requirements as discussed above. Currently, requirement (3) has been well addressed in the literature. But, the other requirements (i.e., user privacy, integrity of rental information, key agreement, and time cost) have been largely neglected. More importantly, when considering this research topic, we find that there is no security primitive which can be directly deployed for satisfying all the above requirements. The detailed analysis for drawing this conclusion will be given in Section 2. This becomes a more urgent problem, with the deployment of parking reservation systems in real world. Motivated by this observation, we make three contributions, as described below.

(1) We discuss some security and efficiency issues in crowdsourcing-based parking reservation systems and then list a set of important requirements.

(2) We present a novel security protocol called SCPR that can fulfill all the above requirements. However, different from current crowdsourcing-based security protocols built on real identities, SCPR is based on pseudonyms. By doing so, the user privacy requirement can be fulfilled. Then, observing that the key agreement requirement is not fulfilled by current security protocols, we design a novel pseudonym-based key agreement protocol that can generate a shared key for protecting subsequent reservation transactions. Finally, observing that bilinear pairing operation is low efficient, we shall use algebraic signature [31] for designing the above security protocol. By doing so, the time cost of SCPR can be significantly reduced.

(3) We analyze the security of SCPR, showing it can fulfill requirements (1), (2), (3), and (4). And we evaluate the efficiency of SCPR, showing it can fulfill requirement (5).

The remainder of this paper is organized below. In Section 2, we discuss the related work. Then, in Section 3, we propose the SCPR protocol, followed by security analysis and efficiency evaluation in Sections 4 and 5, respectively. Finally, we draw our conclusions in Section 6.

2. Related Work

Due to its convenience, crowdsourcing has become more and more popular. For instance, [5] designed a crowdsourcing-based mobile-healthcare system. The paper [12] is a crowdsourcing-based city governance system. The paper [20] is a crowdsourcing-based system for enterprises. DYSWIS [25] introduced a crowdsourcing-based home network system. The papers [6, 21, 26] combined the cloud computing technique with crowdsourcing-based systems. The paper [27] introduced a location-based crowdsourcing scheme. The papers [18, 22] discussed the deployment of crowdsourcing technique in parking systems.

Security is the main concern for crowdsourcing-based systems. Recently, a lot of works have been focusing on this topic. For instance, [4, 7, 15, 29] analyzed the privacy-preserving and integrity of transmitted data. The paper [14] discussed the establishment of trust relationships in crowdsourcing-based systems. However, there are three issues with current works as shown below.

First, various applications may have different security requirements. For instance, in mobile-healthcare systems [5], privacy of transmitted data (personal health information) is the most important requirement, while in city governance systems [12], access control has vital significance. The security requirements of parking reservation systems are different from those of other crowdsourcing-based systems too, as discussed in Section 1. Therefore, it is desired to classify the security requirements for parking reservation systems.

Second, parking reservation systems have some special security requirements that have not been discussed by current works. For instance, in most of current protocols [5, 12, 20], real identities are used directly. However, for parking reservation systems, this may lead to a variety of security issues as discussed in Section 1. Therefore, it is desired to design a new security protocol for fulfilling those security requirements.

Third, current crowdsourcing-based parking reservation systems [18, 22] mainly focused on the data transmitting model and did not provide security protocols. For instance, [18] discussed the detailed transactions of parking reservation without designing security protocols for protecting the transactions, while [22] discussed several security issues of parking reservation systems without corresponding solutions. Therefore, it is desired to design security protocols for parking reservation systems.

At the same time, time cost is another serious concern for crowdsourcing-based systems [11, 28]. For instance, the crowdsourcing-based parking systems [18, 22] required the parking reservation protocols being executed quickly due to the high speed of cars, while the crowdsourcing-based video systems [9] required the time cost to be low due to the large amount of video data to be processed. However, current security protocols for crowdsourcing systems are mainly built on time-consuming bilinear maps. For instance, in [5, 6], both the TD and the PO have to run the pairing algorithm several times, resulting in high time cost. In Section 5, we will show that the pairing algorithm consumes much more time than other cryptographic algorithms. Therefore, it is desired to design security protocols for parking reservation systems using efficient cryptographic algorithms.

3. SCPR: The Protocol

3.1. Preliminaries. The algebraic signature [31] technique includes two processes.

The Signing Process. Given a set of secret keys $SK = \{sk_i \in Z_p, 1 \le i \le n\}$, the algebraic signature for a binary string $s = s_1 s_2 \cdots s_n$, where $s_i \in \{0, 1\}, 1 \le i \le n$, is generated as $\sigma = \sum_{i=1}^{n} s_i sk_i \mod p$.

The Verification Process. Given a binary string $s = s_1 s_2 \cdots s_n$, where $s_i \in \{0, 1\}, 1 \le i \le n$, and the corresponding algebraic signature σ, the verifier computes $\sigma' = \sum_{i=1}^{n} s_i sk_i \mod p$ and checks $\sigma' \overset{?}{=} \sigma$ to determine whether s is tampered by an attacker.

The above algebraic signature employs only several addition and modular multiplication operations. Therefore, it is highly efficient.

3.2. System Model. The system model of SCPR is shown in Figure 1, which includes three phases as illustrated below, and the notations in this paper are listed in Notations.

3.2.1. The Key-Distributing Phase. During the key-distributing phase, the SP first initializes SCPR by generating public and private system parameters. The public system parameters will be distributed to the PO and the TD, while the private system parameters will be hold by the SP. The initialization algorithm is illustrated below.

$\{SK_{SP}, PK_{SP}\} \leftarrow Init(n)$. This algorithm is run by the SP for initializing system parameters for SCPR. It takes as input the parameter of security level (i.e., n) and outputs a set of private system parameters (i.e., SK_{SP}) and the corresponding set of public system parameters (i.e., PK_{SP}).

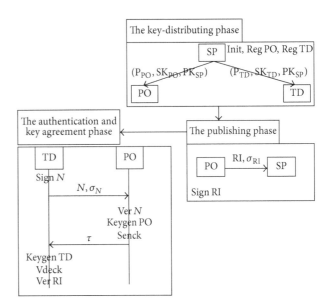

FIGURE 1: System model of SCPR.

Before publishing rental information, the PO sends a request to the SP. Upon receiving the request, the SP generates a pseudonym and a private key and distributes them to the PO over their preestablished secure channel, using the following RegPO algorithm.

$\{P_{PO}, SK_{PO}\} \leftarrow RegPO(RID_{PO}, SK_{SP}, PK_{SP})$. This algorithm is run by the SP for generating a pseudonym and a private key for the PO. It takes as inputs PO's real identity (i.e., RID_{PO}), the set of private system parameters (i.e., SK_{SP}), and the set of public system parameters (i.e., PK_{SP}) and outputs PO's pseudonym (i.e., P_{PO}) and a private key (i.e., SK_{PO}).

Before making a parking reservation, the TD sends a request to the SP. Upon receiving the request, the SP generates a pseudonym and a private key and distributes them to the TD over their preestablished secure channel, using the following RegTD algorithm.

$\{P_{TD}, SK_{TD}\} \leftarrow RegTD(RID_{TD}, SK_{SP}, PK_{SP})$. This algorithm is run by the SP for generating a pseudonym and a private key for the TD. It takes as inputs TD's real identity (i.e., RID_{TD}), the set of private system parameters (i.e., SK_{SP}), and the set of public system parameters (i.e., PK_{SP}) and outputs TD's pseudonym (i.e., P_{TD}) and a private key (i.e., SK_{TD}).

After the key-distributing phase, the PO holds the tuple $(P_{PO}, SK_{PO}, PK_{SP})$, and the TD holds the tuple $(P_{TD}, SK_{TD}, PK_{SP})$.

3.2.2. The Publishing Phase. When the PO wants to publish its rental information, it randomly generates a secret key (i.e., $SK_{RI} \in Z_p$) and signs the rental information using SK_{RI}. The signing algorithm is illustrated below.

$\sigma_{RI} \leftarrow SignRI(RI, SK_{RI})$. This algorithm is run by the SP for signing the rental information (i.e., RI). It takes as inputs RI and the secret key (i.e., SK_{RI}) and outputs a signature (i.e., σ_{RI}) for RI.

After the publishing phase, the PO holds SK_{RI}, and the SP gets the rental information (i.e., RI) and the signature (i.e., σ_{RI}).

3.2.3. The Authentication and Key Agreement Phase. The authentication and key agreement phase is carried out between the PO and the TD. During this phase, the TD and the PO authenticate each other and negotiate a shared key for protecting subsequent transactions. Then the PO sends SK_{RI} to the TD for checking the integrity of the rental information. The authentication and key agreement phase includes three steps as illustrated below.

Step 1. The TD establishes the authentication and key agreement phase by generating a nonce (i.e., N) and the corresponding signature (i.e., σ_N) using its own private key (i.e., SK_{TD}). Then, the TD sends N and σ_N to the PO for authentication. The signing algorithm for N is illustrated below.

$\{\sigma_N\} \leftarrow \text{Sign}N(N, P_{PO}, PK_{SP}, SK_{TD})$. This algorithm is run by the TD for generating a signature for the nonce. It takes as inputs the nonce (i.e., N), the PO's pseudonym (i.e., P_{PO}), the set of public system parameters (i.e., PK_{SP}), and the TD's private key (i.e., SK_{TD}) and outputs a signature (i.e., σ_N).

Step 2. When receiving N and σ_N from the TD, the PO checks them to authenticate the TD, using its private key (i.e., SK_{PO}) and the following VerN algorithm. If the verification succeeds, the PO generates the shared key (i.e., sk) from N using the following KeygenPO algorithm. Finally, the PO signs and encrypts SK_{RI} using sk and the following Senck algorithm and sends the signed and encrypted message to the TD. The VerN, KeygenPO, and Senck algorithms are illustrated below.

$\{T, F\} \leftarrow \text{Ver}N(N, \sigma_N, SK_{PO}, P_{TD}, PK_{SP})$. This algorithm is run by the PO for authenticating the TD. It takes as inputs the nonce (i.e., N), the signature (i.e., σ_N), PO's private key (i.e., SK_{PO}), TD's pseudonym (i.e., P_{TD}), and the set of public system parameters (i.e., PK_{SP}) and outputs T if the verification succeeds, or F otherwise.

$\{sk\} \leftarrow \text{KeygenPO}(N, SK_{PO}, P_{TD}, PK_{SP})$. This algorithm is run by the PO for generating the shared key. It takes as inputs the nonce (i.e., N), PO's private key (i.e., SK_{PO}), TD's pseudonym (i.e., P_{TD}), and the set of public system parameters (i.e., PK_{SP}) and outputs the shared key (i.e., sk).

$\{\tau\} \leftarrow \text{Senck}(PK_{SP}, sk, SK_{RI})$. This algorithm is run by the PO for signing and encrypting SK_{RI}. It takes as inputs the set of public system parameters (i.e., PK_{SP}), the shared key (i.e., sk), and the publishing key (i.e., SK_{RI}) and outputs a signed and encrypted message (i.e., τ).

Step 3. Upon getting τ from the PO, the TD first generates the shared key (i.e., sk) using the following KeygenTD algorithm. Then, it decrypts and verifies τ to extract SK_{RI} and to authenticate the PO, using the following Vdeck algorithm. Finally, the TD verifies RI and σ_{RI} downloaded from the SP to make sure it is not tamped by an adversary, using SK_{RI} and the following VerRI algorithm. The KeygenTD, Vdeck, and VerRI algorithms are illustrated below.

$\{sk\} \leftarrow \text{KeygenTD}(N, SK_{TD}, P_{PO}, PK_{SP})$. This algorithm is run by the TD for generating the shared key. It takes as inputs the nonce (i.e., N), TD's private key (i.e., SK_{TD}), PO's pseudonym (i.e., P_{PO}), and the set of public system parameters (i.e., PK_{SP}) and outputs the shared key (i.e., sk).

$\{SK_{RI}, \{T, F\}\} \leftarrow \text{Vdeck}(\tau, sk, PK_{SP})$. This algorithm is run by the TD for decrypting and verifying the publishing key and authenticating PO. It takes as inputs the data to be decrypted and verified (i.e., τ), the shared key (i.e., sk), and the set of public system parameters (i.e., PK_{SP}) and outputs the publishing key (i.e., SK_{RI}). Then, it outputs T if SK_{RI} can pass the verification and the PO is authenticated, or F otherwise.

$\{T, F\} \leftarrow \text{VerRI}(RI, \sigma_{RI}, SK_{RI}, PK_{SP})$. This algorithm is run by the TD for verifying the rental information downloaded from the SP. It takes as inputs the rental information (i.e., RI), the signature (i.e., σ_{RI}), the publishing key (i.e., SK_{RI}), and the set of public system parameters (i.e., PK_{SP}) and outputs T if RI can pass the verification, or F otherwise.

After the above three phases, the PO and the TD are both authenticated and a shared key (i.e., sk) is generated for protecting the subsequent transactions between them.

From this system model, it can be seen that the PO and the TD use pseudonyms instead of their real identities. Therefore, SCPR can satisfy requirement (1) described in Section 1 (i.e., user privacy). In Section 4, we will further analyze requirement (1).

From this system model, it can be seen that the rental information (i.e., RI) is signed. Therefore, SCPR can satisfy requirement (2) described in Section 1 (i.e., integrity of rental information). In Section 4, we will further analyze requirement (2).

From this system model, it can be seen that both the PO and the TD are authenticated, and a shared key is generated between them. Therefore, SCPR can satisfy requirements (3) and (4) described in Section 1 (i.e., authentication and key agreement). In Section 4, we will further analyze requirements (3) and (4).

3.3. Construction. The construction of SCPR is a tuple (Init, RegPO, RegTD, SignRI, VerRI, SignN, VerN, KeygenPO, KeygenTD, Senck, and Vdeck) of probabilistic polynomial time algorithms as illustrated below.

$\{SK_{SP}, PK_{SP}\} \leftarrow \text{Init}(n)$. The SP runs this algorithm for generating system parameters for SCPR as follows. First, the SP generates a group G with a prime order p and a generator g, where n is the security level determining the key length in bit, the length of p is n-bit, and g is a randomly picked element in G. Second, the SP randomly generates a set of private keys $SK_{SP} = \{skpo_x \in Z_p, sktd_x \in Z_p, 1 \le x \le n\}$. Third, for each $skpo_x \in SK_{SP}$ and $sktd_x \in SK_{SP}$, the SP computes $pkpo_x = g^{skpo_x} \in G$ and $pktd_x = g^{sktd_x} \in G$ and gets the set of public system parameters $PK_{SP} = \{G, p, g, pkpo_x, pktd_x, 1 \le x \le n\}$.

$\{P_{PO}, SK_{PO}\} \leftarrow \text{RegPO}(RID_{PO}, SK_{SP}, PK_{SP})$. The SP runs this algorithm for generating a pseudonym and a private key for the PO as follows. First, the SP generates PO's pseudonym as $P_{PO} = h_1(RID_{PO})$, where $h_1 : Z_p \rightarrow Z_p$ is a hash function. Second, the SP computes $a_1 \cdots a_n = h_2(P_{PO})$ and takes the algebraic signature $SK_{PO} = \sum_{x=1}^{n} a_x skpo_x \bmod p$ as the PO's private key, where $h_2 : Z_p \rightarrow \{0, 1\}^n$ is a hash function, and $a_1, \ldots, a_n \in \{0, 1\}$.

$\{P_{TD}, SK_{TD}\} \leftarrow \text{RegTD}(RID_{TD}, SK_{SP}, PK_{SP})$. The SP runs this algorithm for generating a pseudonym and a private key for the TD as follows. First, the SP generates TD's pseudonym as $P_{TD} = h_1(RID_{TD})$, where $h_1 : Z_p \to Z_p$ is a hash function. Second, the SP computes $b_1 \cdots b_n = h_2(P_{TD})$ and takes the algebraic signature $SK_{TD} = \sum_{x=1}^{n} b_x sktd_x \bmod p$ as the TD's private key, where $h_2 : Z_p \to \{0, 1\}^n$ is a hash function, and $b_1, \ldots, b_n \in \{0, 1\}$.

$\sigma_{RI} \leftarrow SignRI(RI, SK_{RI})$. The PO runs this algorithm for generating a signature for the rental information as $\sigma_{RI} = h_1(RI \mid SK_{RI})$, where $h_1 : Z_p \to Z_p$ is a hash function.

$\{\sigma_N\} \leftarrow SignN(N, P_{PO}, P_{SP}, SK_{TD})$. The TD runs this algorithm for generating a signature for the nonce as follows. First, the TD computes $PK_{PO} = \prod_{x=1}^{n} pkpo_x^{a_x} \in G$, where $a_1 \cdots a_n = h_2(P_{PO})$. Second, the TD computes $\sigma_N = h_1(N \mid H(PK_{PO}^{SK_{TD}}))$, where $h_2 : Z_p \to \{0, 1\}^n$, $H : G \to Z_p$, and $h_1 : Z_p \to Z_p$ are hash functions.

$\{T, F\} \leftarrow VerN(N, \sigma_N, SK_{PO}, P_{TD}, PK_{SP})$. The PO runs this algorithm for authenticating the TD as follows. First, the PO computes $PK_{TD} = \prod_{x=1}^{n} pktd_x^{b_x} \in G$, where $b_1 \cdots b_n = h_2(P_{TD})$. Second, the PO computes $\sigma'_N = h_1(N \mid H(PK_{TD}^{SK_{PO}}))$ and checks $\sigma'_N \overset{?}{=} \sigma_N$. If this equation holds, PO returns T. Otherwise, it returns F.

$\{sk\} \leftarrow KeygenPO(N, SK_{PO}, P_{TD}, PK_{SP})$. The PO runs this algorithm for generating the shared key as follows. First, the PO computes $PK_{TD} = \prod_{x=1}^{n} pktd_x^{b_x} \in G$, where $b_1 \cdots b_n = h_2(P_{TD})$, P_{TD} is the pseudonym of TD, and $pktd_x \in PK_{SP}$ ($x \in \{1, \ldots, n\}$) are distributed from the SP during the initialization phase. Second, the PO computes $sk = PK_{TD}^{SK_{PO}N} \in G$.

$\{\tau\} \leftarrow Senck(PK_{SP}, sk, SK_{RI})$. The PO runs this algorithm for signing and encrypting SK_{RI} as follows. First, the PO encrypts SK_{RI} as $c_1 = H(sk) \oplus SK_{RI} \bmod p$, where $H : G \to Z_p$ is a hash function. Second, the PO signs SK_{RI} as $c_2 = h_1(SK_{RI} \mid H(sk))$, where $H : G \to Z_p$ and $h_1 : Z_p \to Z_p$ are hash functions. Finally, the PO gets $\tau = (c_1, c_2)$.

$\{sk\} \leftarrow KeygenTD(N, SK_{TD}, P_{PO}, PK_{SP})$. The TD runs this algorithm for generating the shared key as follows. First, the TD computes $PK_{PO} = \prod_{x=1}^{n} pkpo_x^{a_x} \in G$, where $a_1 \cdots a_n = h_2(P_{PO})$, P_{PO} is the pseudonym of PO, and $pkpo_x \in PK_{SP}$ ($x \in \{1, \ldots, n\}$) are distributed from the SP during the initialization phase. Second, the TD computes $sk = PK_{PO}^{SK_{TD}N} \in G$.

$\{SK_{RI}, \{T, F\}\} \leftarrow Vdeck(\tau, sk, PK_{SP})$. The TD runs this algorithm for decrypting and verifying the publishing key as follows. First, the TD decrypts SK_{RI} as $SK_{RI} = c_1 \oplus H(sk) \bmod p$, where $H : G \to Z_p$ is a hash function. Second, the TD computes $c'_2 = h_1(SK_{RI} \mid H(sk))$ and checks $c'_2 \overset{?}{=} c_2$, where $H : G \to Z_p$ and $h_1 : Z_p \to Z_p$ are hash functions. If $c'_2 = c_2$, the TD returns (SK_{RI}, T). Otherwise, it returns F.

$\{T, F\} \leftarrow VerRI(RI, \sigma_{RI}, SK_{RI}, PK_{SP})$. The TD runs this algorithm for verifying the rental information as follows. First, the TD computes $\sigma'_{RI} = h_1(RI \mid SK_{RI})$, where $h_1 : Z_p \to Z_p$ is a hash function. Second, the TD checks $\sigma'_{RI} \overset{?}{=} \sigma_{RI}$. If this equation holds, TD returns T. Otherwise, it returns F.

From this construction, it can be seen that SCPR does not use bilinear map. In fact, it employs only a few modular exponentiations, which is quite efficient. We will further evaluate the efficiency of SCPR in Section 5. Note that, when computing PK_{PO} and PK_{TD}, there is no modular exponentiation, because $a_x \in \{0, 1\}$ and $b_x \in \{0, 1\}$. So our construction is highly efficient.

4. Security Analysis

In this section, we show that SCPR can fulfill the security requirements described in Section 1 (i.e., user privacy, key agreement, integrity of rental information, and authentication).

4.1. User Privacy. In SCPR, as the PO and the TD use pseudonyms generated from their real identities such as user name or driver license, this requirement is to ensure that the adversary cannot extract real identities from pseudonyms. From Section 3.3, it can be seen that the SP generates pseudonyms using a one-way hash function (see equations $P_{PO} = h_1(RID_{PO})$ and $P_{TD} = h_1(RID_{TD})$ in the RegPO and RegTD algorithms for details). So it is straightforward that the adversary cannot extract RID_{PO} and RID_{TD} from P_{PO} and P_{TD}, and SCPR can provide user privacy protection for the PO and the TD.

4.2. Key Agreement. In Section 3.3, the PO generates sk as $sk = PK_{TD}^{SK_{PO}N} = (g^{SK_{TD}})^{SK_{PO}N} = g^{SK_{TD}SK_{PO}N}$, and the TD generates sk as $sk = PK_{PO}^{SK_{TD}N} = (g^{SK_{PO}})^{SK_{TD}N} = g^{SK_{TD}SK_{PO}N}$ (see the KeygenPO and KeygenTD algorithms in Section 3.3 for details.). So if the PO and the TD run SCPR correctly, they both can get $sk = g^{SK_{TD}SK_{PO}N}$.

Then, we show that a potential adversary cannot extract sk in three steps. In Step 1, we describe a well-known mathematical problem that will not be efficiently solved. In Step 2, we describe the adversary. In Step 3, we show this potential adversary will not be able to extract *sk* efficiently. Otherwise, we will be able to use this adversary for solving the mathematical problem. So if this mathematical problem holds, the potential adversary does not exist. Our proof is described below.

Step 1 (the (t, ϵ)-CDH problem [32]). Given $g, g^a, g^b \in G$, where $a \in Z_p$ and $b \in Z_p$ are randomly distributed unknown numbers, there is no t-time algorithm, which has the nonnegligible probability ϵ in computing $g^{ab} \in G$.

Step 2 (the adversary). In the parking reservation system, the potential adversary is between the PO and the TD. It can compute public keys of the PO and the TD from pseudonyms: $PK_{PO} = g^{SK_{PO}} = \prod_{x=1}^{n} pkpo_x^{a_x}$ and $PK_{TD} = g^{SK_{TD}} = \prod_{x=1}^{n} pktd_x^{b_x}$, where $a_1 \cdots a_n = h_2(P_{PO})$ and $b_1 \cdots b_n = h_2(P_{TD})$. Moreover, the adversary can get N.

Step 3 (the proof). If this adversary can compute $sk = g^{SK_{TD}SK_{PO}N}$ from N, $PK_{PO} = g^{SK_{PO}} = \prod_{x=1}^{n} pkpo_x^{a_x}$, and $PK_{TD} = g^{SK_{TD}} = \prod_{x=1}^{n} pktd_x^{b_x}$ with the probability ϵ in time t, we can run this potential adversary with the set of parameters $(PK_{PO} = g^a, PK_{TD} = g^b, N)$ to get $sk = g^{SK_{PO}SK_{TD}N} = g^{abN} \Rightarrow g^{ab} = sk^{N^{-1}}$. That is to say, we can use this potential adversary for solving the CDH problem [32] in time t with the probability ϵ. As the CDH problem holds, this adversary does not exist. So the adversary cannot extract sk in SCPR.

Finally, we show that a potential adversary cannot tamper sk. Since sk is generated from N, P_{PO}, and P_{TD}, to tamper sk, the adversary has to tamper the pseudonyms or the nonce. The detailed proof can be illustrated in three steps too. Here, we just give a summarized example: If the adversary can tamper N to $M \neq N$ while still passing the VerN algorithm, it must be able to compute the signature $\sigma_M = h_1(M \mid H(\mathrm{PK}_{\mathrm{PO}}^{\mathrm{SK}_{\mathrm{TD}}})) = h_1(M \mid H(g^{\mathrm{SK}_{\mathrm{PO}}\mathrm{SK}_{\mathrm{TD}}}))$. Then, to compute σ_M, the adversary must be able to compute $g^{\mathrm{SK}_{\mathrm{PO}}\mathrm{SK}_{\mathrm{TD}}}$. As discussed above, since the adversary cannot compute $g^{\mathrm{SK}_{\mathrm{PO}}\mathrm{SK}_{\mathrm{TD}}}$ from $\mathrm{PK}_{\mathrm{PO}} = g^{\mathrm{SK}_{\mathrm{PO}}} = \prod_{x=1}^{n} \mathrm{pkpo}_x^{a_x}$ and $\mathrm{PK}_{\mathrm{TD}} = g^{\mathrm{SK}_{\mathrm{TD}}} = \prod_{x=1}^{n} \mathrm{pktd}_x^{b_x}$, it cannot tamper N to $M \neq N$.

4.3. Integrity of Rental Information.

In SCPR, as the rental information is signed using the symmetric key $\mathrm{SK}_{\mathrm{RI}}$, this requirement is to ensure that the adversary cannot tamper $\mathrm{SK}_{\mathrm{RI}}$ transmitted in the authentication and key agreement phase. Moreover, from the Senck and Vdeck algorithms illustrated in Section 3.3, we can see that $\mathrm{SK}_{\mathrm{RI}}$ is signed and encrypted using the negotiated shared key sk. So the integrity of rental information is to ensure that sk is secure. Since sk is secure as discussed in Section 4.2, SCPR can provide integrity protection for rental information.

4.4. Authentication.

In SCPR, as the PO and the TD communicate with each other using pseudonyms, authentication is to make sure that the pseudonyms are generated by the SP. Moreover, as $\mathrm{SK}_{\mathrm{PO}}$ and $\mathrm{SK}_{\mathrm{TD}}$ are algebraic signatures of pseudonyms (see the equations $\mathrm{SK}_{\mathrm{PO}} = \sum_{x=1}^{n} a_x \mathrm{skpo}_x \bmod p$, $\mathrm{sk}_{\mathrm{TD}} = \sum_{x=1}^{n} b_x \mathrm{sktd}_x \bmod p$, $a_1 \cdots a_n = h_2(\mathrm{P}_{\mathrm{PO}})$ and $b_1 \cdots b_n = h_2(\mathrm{P}_{\mathrm{TD}})$ in the RegPO and RegTD algorithms illustrated in Section 3.3 for details.), authentication is to prove that the PO and the TD really hold $\mathrm{SK}_{\mathrm{PO}}$ and $\mathrm{SK}_{\mathrm{TD}}$, respectively.

The proof of authentication is similar to that in Section 4.2, as illustrated by the following example. In the SignN and VerN algorithms, only when the PO and the TD hold the algebraic signatures (i.e., $\mathrm{SK}_{\mathrm{PO}}$ and $\mathrm{SK}_{\mathrm{TD}}$), they can compute $\mathrm{PK}_{\mathrm{PO}}^{\mathrm{SK}_{\mathrm{TD}}} = \mathrm{PK}_{\mathrm{TD}}^{\mathrm{SK}_{\mathrm{PO}}} = g^{\mathrm{SK}_{\mathrm{PO}}\mathrm{SK}_{\mathrm{TD}}}$. Therefore, the authentication can be reduced to the CDH problem too.

5. Efficiency Evaluation

There are many crowdsourcing-based systems (i.e., [5–30]). But, only [5, 6] aimed to design complete cryptographic algorithms and protocols [4], while other systems mainly focused on deploying crowdsourcing-based systems in multiple real world applications. So, in this section, we mainly compare SCPR with [5, 6].

Time cost is the major efficiency issue for parking reservation systems, which is comprised of computation and communication costs as discussed in Section 1. So we will first compare the computation cost of SCPR with those of [5, 6] in Section 5.1. Then, we shall compare the communication costs in Section 5.2. Finally, in Section 5.3, we will show the implementation of SCPR to make sure the newly designed protocol works well.

5.1. Comparison of Computation Costs.

Computation cost is the major measure of time cost, which is mainly consumed by cryptographic algorithms. So we first tested computation

TABLE 1: Basic algorithms (unit: μs).

T_{mm}	T_h	T_p	T_{me}
0.1	0.5	29540.2	577.8

T_{mm}: computation cost of modular multiplication, T_h: computation cost of hash function, T_p: computation cost of bilinear pairing, and T_{me}: computation cost of modular exponentiation.

costs of basic cryptographic algorithms. Then, we computed the computation costs of SCPR [5, 6].

To investigate the computation costs of basic cryptographic algorithms, we conducted the experiment on a computer with a CENTOS operating system and an Intel i7 processor. Cryptographic libraries used in this experiment include OPENSSL [33] and PBC [34]. Cryptographic group (i.e., G in Section 3) used in this experiment is the 160-bit elliptic curve [33]. Finally, we used the SHA1 hash function [33] and type F bilinear pairing parameter [34] in this experiment.

Table 1 lists the computation costs of basic cryptographic algorithms, in which the values are means of running basic cryptographic algorithms for 10,000 times. From Table 1, we can see the following.

(1) The computation costs of modular multiplication and hash function are much lower than those of modular exponentiation and bilinear pairing and can be omitted. This is because $T_h/T_p = 0.5/29540.2 \approx 1.7 \times 10^{-5}$, $T_h/T_{\mathrm{me}} = 0.5/577.8 \approx 8.7 \times 10^{-4}$, and $T_h/T_{\mathrm{mm}} = 0.5/0.1 = 5$. Therefore, in the following evaluation, we only take modular exponentiation and bilinear pairing into account.

(2) The computation cost of modular exponentiation is much lower than that of bilinear pairing. This is because $T_{\mathrm{me}}/T_p = 577.8/29540.2 \approx 2.0 \times 10^{-2}$. Therefore, by avoiding using bilinear pairing, SCPR can reduce the computation cost significantly.

Then, from Table 1, we computed the total computation costs of SCPR [5, 6]. The results are shown in Table 2 and Figure 2, where the values are total computation costs of modular exponentiation and bilinear pairing executed during the publishing phase and the authentication and key agreement phase. From Table 2 and Figure 2, we can see the following.

(1) On the PO's side, the computation costs of [5, 6] are around 10^1 to that of SCPR. This is because $(31.9n+2.9)/1.2 > (31.9 \times 1 + 2.9)/1.2 \approx 2.9 \times 10^1$ and $30.1/1.2 \approx 2.5 \times 10^1$.

(2) On the TD's side, the computation costs of [5, 6] are around $10^1 \sim 10^2$ to that of SCPR. This is because $(89.2n^2 + 59.1n)/1.2 > (89.2 + 59.1)/1.2 \approx 1.2 \times 10^2$ and $118.2/1.2 \approx 9.9 \times 10^1$.

(3) The total computation costs of [5, 6] are around 10^1 to that of SCPR. This is because $(89.2n^2+91n+2.9)/2.3 > (89.2 + 91 + 2.9)/2.3 \approx 8.0 \times 10^1$ and $148.3/2.3 \approx 6.4 \times 10^1$.

(4) On the TD's side, the computation cost of [6] will increase rapidly, when the number of attributes increases, as shown in Figure 2.

These three conclusions show that the computation cost of SCPR is much lower than those of [5, 6]. So SCPR can fulfill requirement (5) listed in Section 1.

TABLE 2: Comparison of computation costs (unit: ms).

	SCPR	[5]	[6]
T_{PO}	$2T_{me} = 1.2$	$T_p + T_{me} = 30.1$	$n(T_p + 4T_{me}) + 5T_{me} = 31.9n + 2.9$
T_{TD}	$2T_{me} = 1.2$	$4T_p = 118.2$	$(3T_p + T_{me})n^2 + 2nT_p = 89.2n^2 + 59.1n$
T_a	$4T_{me} = 2.3$	$5T_p + T_{me} = 148.3$	$(3T_p + T_{me})n^2 + n(3T_p + 4T_{me}) + 5T_{me} = 89.2n^2 + 91n + 2.9$

T_{PO}: computation cost of the PO, T_{TD}: computation cost of the TD, T_a: total computation cost on both the PO and the TD, and n: number of attributes in [5, 6].

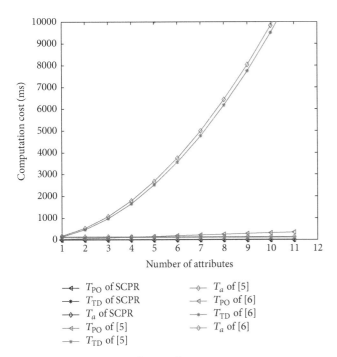

FIGURE 2: Evolution of computation costs.

6. Conclusion

In this paper, we have presented a security protocol for crowdsourcing-based parking reservation systems called SCPR. It can satisfy many security requirements that have not been addressed by current protocols, such as user privacy and key agreement. More importantly, to reduce the time cost, we designed several novel cryptographic algorithms for SCPR, which are quite light weight. Experimental results show SCPR is feasible for real world applications.

However, there are several more problems remaining to be solved. First, after the transaction is ended, the tenant driver and the private owner should be able to score the transaction. By doing so, the parking reservation system can provide differential services to users based on their reputation. Second, SCPR lacks a revocation method. These open issues are to be addressed in the future.

Notations

RID_{PO}, RID_{TD}:	Real identities of the PO and the TD, respectively
P_{PO}, P_{TD}:	Pseudonyms of the PO and the TD, respectively
PK_{SP}, SK_{SP}:	Public and private system parameters of SCPR
SK_{PO}, SK_{TD}:	Private keys of the PO and the TD, respectively
RI, σ_{RI}:	Rental information and its signature
SK_{RI}:	Secret key for signing and verifying RI
N, σ_N:	Nonce and its signature
sk:	The shared key negotiated between the PO and the TD
τ:	The signed and encrypted data for sk
G, g, p:	The cyclic group, its generator, and prime order
$h_1(), h_2(), H()$:	Hash functions.

5.2. Comparison of Communication Costs. During the publishing phase, the number of messages is one in SCPR [5, 6]. During the authentication and key agreement phase, both SCPR and [6] contain two messages, while [5] contains four messages. That is to say, SCPR and [6] contain fewer messages than [5]. So SCPR can fulfill requirement (5) listed in Section 1.

5.3. Implementation of SCPR. To make sure SCPR can work well, we implemented it. In the experiment, we use three computers, acting as the SP, the PO, and the TD, respectively. These three computers communicate with each other using 1 Gbps Ethernet. All the three computers have Intel i7 CPUs and are installed with CENTOS operating system. The cryptographic libraries used in the experiment are OPENSSL and PBC [33, 34] with the same parameters as those in Section 5.1. The Language used in our experiment is C, and the protocol for transmitting SCPR messages is TCP. Then, we get the total executing time of SCPR $\approx$ 2.4 ms. This is similar to the value computed in Table 2. Therefore, time cost is mainly consumed by cryptographic algorithms, and SCPR is feasible for real world applications.

Acknowledgments

This paper is supported by the NSFC (nos. 61101088 and 71402070), the NSF of Jiangsu province (no. BK20161099), and the Opening Project of Key Lab of Information Network Security of Ministry of Public Security (no. C16604).

References

[1] D. C. Shoup, "Cruising for parking," *Transport Policy*, vol. 13, no. 6, pp. 479–486, November 2006.

[2] R. Arnott and E. Inci, "An integrated model of downtown parking and traffic congestion," *Journal of Urban Economics*, vol. 60, no. 3, pp. 418–442, 2006.

[3] J. Kincaid, "Googles open spot makes parking a breeze, assuming everyone turns into a good samaritan," http://techcrunch.com/2010/07/09/google-parking-open-spot/.

[4] K. Yang, K. Zhang, J. Ren, and X. Shen, "Security and privacy in mobile crowdsourcing networks: challenges and opportunities," *IEEE Communications Magazine*, vol. 53, no. 8, pp. 75–81, August 2015.

[5] R. Lu, X. Lin, and X. Shen, "SPOC: a secure and privacy-preserving opportunistic computing framework for mobile-healthcare emergency," *IEEE Transactions on Parallel and Distributed Systems*, vol. 24, no. 3, pp. 614–624, March 2013.

[6] K. Yang, X. Jia, K. Ren, B. Zhang, and R. Xie, "DAC-MACS: effective data access control for multiauthority cloud storage systems," *IEEE Transactions on Information Forensics and Security*, vol. 8, no. 11, pp. 1790–1801, November 2013.

[7] D. Christin, A. Reinhardt, S. S. Kanhere, and M. Hollick, "A survey on privacy in mobile participatory sensing applications," *The Journal of Systems and Software*, vol. 84, no. 11, pp. 1928–1946, November 2011.

[8] Y. Wang, Z. Cai, G. Yin, Y. Gao, X. Tong, and G. Wu, "An incentive mechanism with privacy protection in mobile crowdsourcing systems," *Computer Networks*, vol. 102, pp. 157–171, June 2016.

[9] Ó. Figuerola Salas, V. Adzic, A. Shah, and H. Kalva, "Assessing internet video quality using crowdsourcing," in *Proceedings of the 2nd ACM international workshop on Crowdsourcing for multimedia*, pp. 23–28, the Association for Computing Machinery, Barcelona, Spain, October 2013.

[10] V. Goyal, O. Pandey, A. Sahai, and B. Waters, "Attribute-based encryption for fine-grained access control of encrypted data," in *Proceedings of the 13th ACM conference on Computer and communications security*, pp. 89–98, the Association for Computing Machinery, Alexandria, USA, November 2006.

[11] N. Nandan, A. Pursche, and X. Zhe, "Challenges in crowdsourcing real-time information for public transportation," in *Proceedings of the 15th IEEE International Conference on Mobile Data Management (MDM)*, pp. 67–72, IEEE, Brisbane, Australia, July 2014.

[12] G. Motta, L. You, D. Sacco, and T. Ma, "CITY FEED: a crowdsourcing system for city governance," in *Proceedings of the IEEE 8th International Symposium on Service Oriented System Engineering (SOSE)*, pp. 439–445, IEEE, Oxford, United Kingdom, April 2014.

[13] H. Zhou, J. Chen, J. Fan, Y. Du, and S. K. Das, "ConSub: incentive-based content subscribing in selfish opportunistic mobile networks," *IEEE Journal on Selected Areas in Communications*, vol. 31, no. 9, pp. 669–679, 2013.

[14] A. Tamilin, I. Carreras, E. Ssebaggala, A. Opira, and N. Conci, "Context-aware mobile crowdsourcing," in *Proceedings of the 2012 ACM Conference on Ubiquitous Computing*, pp. 717–720, the Association for Computing Machinery, Pittsburgh, Pennsylvania, September 2012.

[15] K. Parshotam, "Crowd computing: a literature review and definition," in *Proceedings of the South African Institute for Computer Scientists and Information Technologists Conference*, pp. 121–130, the Association for Computing Machinery, East London, South Africa, October 2013.

[16] N. Do, C. Cheng-Hsin, and N. Venkatasubramanian, "Crowd-MAC: a crowdsourcing system for mobile access," in *Proceedings of the 13th International Middleware Conference*, vol. 7662 of *Lecture Notes in Computer Science*, pp. 1–20, Springer Berlin Heidelberg, Montreal, Quebec, Canada, December 2012.

[17] E. Aubry, T. Silverston, A. Lahmadi, and O. Festor, "CrowdOut: a mobile crowdsourcing service for road safety in digital cities," in *Proceedings of he First International Workshop on Crowdsensing Methods, Techniques, and Applications*, pp. 86–91, IEEE, Budapest, Hungary, March 2014."

[18] B. Hoh, T. Yan, D. Ganesan, K. Tracton, T. Iwuchukwu, and J.-S. Lee, "CrowdPark: a crowdsourcing-based parking reservation system for mobile phones," University of Massachusetts at Amherst Tech. Report 1–14, IEEE, 2011.

[19] J. Shi, Z. Guan, C. Qiao, T. Melodia, D. Koutsonikolas, and G. Challen, "Crowdsourcing access network spectrum allocation using smartphones," in *Proceedings of the 13th ACM Workshop on Hot Topics in Networks*, pp. 1–7, ACM, Los Angeles, CA, USA, October 2014.

[20] M. Vukovic, "Crowdsourcing for Enterprises," in *Proceedings of 2009 IEEE Congress on Services (SERVICES)*, pp. 686–692, Los Angeles, CA, USA, July 2009.

[21] G. Chatzimilioudis and D. Zeinalipour-Yazti, "Crowdsourcing for Mobile Data Management," in *Proceedings of the 14th IEEE International Conference on Mobile Data Management (MDM)*, pp. 3-4, Milan, Italy, June 2013.

[22] X. Chen, E. Santos-Neto, and M. Ripeanu, "Crowdsourcing for on-street smart parking," in *Proceedings of the second ACM international symposium on Design and analysis of intelligent vehicular networks and applications*, pp. 1–8, ACM, Paphos, Cyprus, October 2012.

[23] X. Fang, J. Tang, D. Yang, and G. Xue, "Crowdsourcing to smartphones: incentive mechanism design for mobile phone sensing," in *Proceedings of the 18th annual international conference on Mobile computing and networking*, pp. 173–184, ACM, Istanbul, Turkey, August 2012.

[24] G. Chatzimilioudis, A. Konstantinidis, C. Laoudias, and D. Zeinalipour-Yazti, "Crowdsourcing with smartphones," in *Proceedings of the IEEE Internet Computing*, vol. 16, pp. 36–44, IEEE, June 2012.

[25] K. Kim, H. Nam, V. Singh, D. Song, and H. Schulzrinne, "DYSWIS: crowdsourcing a home network diagnosis," in *Proceedings of the 23rd International Conference on Computer Communication and Networks (ICCCN)*, pp. 1–10, IEEE, China, August 2014.

[26] C. L. V. Teo, *Hyrax: crowdsourcing mobile devices to develop proximity-based mobile clouds*, Carnegie Mellon University, Pittsburgh, PA, Pennsylvania, 2012.

[27] F. Alt, A. S. Shirazi, A. Schmidt, U. Kramer, and Z. Nawaz, "Location-based crowdsourcing: extending crowdsourcing to the real world," in *Proceedings of the 6th Nordic Conference on Human-Computer Interaction: Extending Boundaries*, pp. 13–22, ACM, Reykjavik, Iceland, October 2010.

[28] I. Boutsis and V. Kalogeraki, "On task assignment for real-time reliable crowdsourcing, distributed computing systems (icdcs)," in *Proceedings of the IEEE 34th International Conference on Distributed Computing Systems (ICDCS)*, pp. 1–10, IEEE, Madrid, Spain, June 2014.

[29] A. Faggiani, E. Gregori, L. Lenzini, V. Luconi, and A. Vecchio, "Smartphone-based crowdsourcing for network monitoring:

opportunities, challenges, and a case study," *IEEE Communications Magazine*, vol. 52, no. 1, pp. 106–113, 2014.

[30] R. K. Ganti, F. Ye, and H. Lei, "Mobile crowdsensing: current state and future challenges," *IEEE Communications Magazine*, vol. 49, no. 11, pp. 32–39, November 2011.

[31] T. J. E. Schwarz and E. L. Miller, "Store, forget, and check: using algebraic signatures to check remotely administered storage," in *Proceedings of the 26th IEEE International Conference on Distributed Computing Systems (ICDCS '06)*, p. 12, IEEE, July 2006.

[32] F. Bao, R. H. Deng, and H. Zhu, "Variations of diffie-hellman problem," in *Proceedings of the International Conference on Information and Communications Security*, vol. 2836 of *Lecture Notes in Computer Science*, pp. 301–312, Springer, Huhehaote, China, October 2003.

[33] Openssl.org, "openssl-1.0.1e.tar.gz," Feb 2013, http://www.openssl.org/source/.

[34] B. Lynn, "PBC Library Manual 0.5.11," 2006, http://crypto.stanford.edu/pbc/manual/.

Practical Implementation of an Adaptive Detection-Defense Unit against Link Layer DoS Attacks for Wireless Sensor Networks

Murat Dener[1] and Omer Faruk Bay[2]

[1]Graduate School of Natural and Applied Sciences, Gazi University, Besevler, Ankara, Turkey
[2]Department of Electronics and Computer, Gazi University, Besevler, Ankara, Turkey

Correspondence should be addressed to Murat Dener; muratdener@gazi.edu.tr

Academic Editor: Muhammad Khurram Khan

Wireless sensor networks (WSNs) have become a very popular subject in both industrial and academic fields of study due to the fact that they can operate on their own, do not require extra maintenance, and can be utilized in a wide variety of applications. In addition, the sensor nodes having limited hardware resources and power units cause certain security problems awaiting to be resolved. The Denial-of-Service (DoS) attacks, which cause disrupts in the communication of sensor nodes or abnormal situations, thus resulting in the decrease of the lifespan of the network, constitute a serious threat against the WSN security. Especially in military applications in which security is the most important design criterion, the WSN used in chemical and biological intrusion detection applications must be resistant against all forms of attacks. In this study, an adaptive detection-defense unit has been developed against the DoS attacks (packet collision, exhaustion, and unfairness) which occur in the data link layer. The developed unit has also been implemented on the TelosB nodes. Due to the new unit that was designed the lifespan of the nodes has been extended without the need for additional hardware by making them more secure against DoS attacks in the data link layer of the WSN.

1. Introduction

The WSN is exposed to a wide variety of security vulnerabilities due to the hardware limitations of the sensor nodes, wireless communication environment, real time processing needs, heterogenic structure, large number of nodes, need for measurability, mobility, the weight of the application environmental conditions, and cost [1]. Ensuring confidentiality, integrity, and availability, the primary goal of security is one of the most important problems to be solved in order to achieve time-critical and vital objectives [2]. When compared to the classical computer networks which are made up of personal or laptop computers that contain strong hardware and software nodes, the WSN displays many special characteristics [3]. Many of these unique features greatly make difficult the resolution of the security problem. One of the security requirements for WSNs is availability. Availability means being able to resume the services of the WSN even while under a Denial-of-Service (DoS) attack. DoS attacks are designed to interrupt services. It is a type of attack which

causes the system being unable to provide services to anyone due to an individual constantly attacking the system or an attack aimed at using all the resources that belong to that system. There is no taking over, taking charge, or technically "hacking" involved. The main goal is to force the victim site to use up all its resources so that it cannot provide services to anyone. DoS attacks can occur in each protocol layer of the WSN and can render the victim nodes ineffective. In addition to the DoS attacks, the weight of excessive communication or calculation can cause the battery of the node to finish earlier than expected. Being unable to maintain the availability of the WSN may cause serious results. For example, in a military observation application, if a couple of nodes do not work properly, enemy units can infiltrate through this part of the WSN which is not working as it should. Ensuring the availability principle means that the protocol is resistant against DoS attacks. Packet collision attack [4], exhaustion attack [5], unfairness attack [6] can be given as examples of DoS attacks which occur in the data link layer. Not being able to prevent any one of these attacks makes that protocol insecure. In this study, in order to establish the availability principle that is one of the WSN security requirements an Adaptive Detection and Defense Unit against packet collision, exhaustion, and unfairness attacks which occur in the data link layer has been developed and also implemented on the TelosB node. The second section describes related works. The third section describes the formation process of attacks. The fourth section defines the suggested unit and the fifth section further explains the adaptive system in the unit. The sixth section includes implementation practices; the seventh section provides experimental results from the study, and the last section presents the results of the study.

2. Related Works

The implementation of the suggested security protocols on the nodes is an important factor for the availability of the WSN. Therefore, it is important that the researchers increase their studies on the TinyOS operating system and the NesC programming language which are necessary to know in order for them to make applications on the nodes. When looking at the security solutions that are prevalent in the literature, only the TinySec [7], MiniSec [8], and SNEP [9] have software implementations on the sensor nodes. Even though the IEEE 802.15.4 [10] has been developed for the Wireless Personal Area Networks, it is also used in the WSN due to its low power exhaustion, low cost, and flexibility. These protocols are not able to provide the principle of availability which is one of the security needs of the WSN. In cases where the principle of availability is not provided, it means that this protocol is weak against DoS attacks.

TinySec supports two different security options: authenticated encryption (TinySec-AE) and authentication only (TinySec-Auth). With authenticated encryption, TinySec encrypts the data payload and authenticates the packet with a MAC. In authentication only mode, TinySec authenticates the entire packet with a MAC, but the data payload is not encrypted. TinySec provides data confidentiality, integrity, and authenticity with Skipjack + CBC-MAC. Minisec provides data confidentiality, integrity, and authenticity with Skipjack + OCB. SPINS have two security building blocks: SNEP and TESLA. SNEP provides semantic security, data authentication, replay protection, weak freshness, and low communication overhead. But, in these protocols there are no special tasks against link layer DoS attacks.

In addition, there are a couple of studies present in the literature which are aimed at preventing DoS attacks. These studies have not yet been implemented; only the simulations have been done. These are mapping protocols [11], FS-MAC [12], and G-MAC [13]. In mapping protocols several parameters are used to detect attacks. While under an attack and the enemy nodes occupy the area, it is very hard for a node to send a message. In order to overcome this situation, the jammed massages have been prioritized. The neighboring nodes receive the messages and prepare the lists of the jammed messages, thus allowing the designation of jammed areas. The FS-MAC has been created by adding a detection and defense unit to the IEEE 802.11 MAC protocol. The high number of packet collisions causes a packet collision attack,

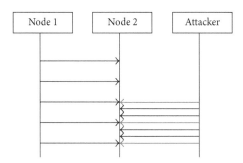

FIGURE 1: Packet collision and exhaustion attacks.

high number of RTS packets cause an exhaustion attack, and the waiting time causes an unfairness attack. A fuzzy logic has been used to designate the attack. The defensive method is that jammed nodes exposed to the attack wake up to sleep mode at short intervals until the attack ends. A central group method G-MAC is used against the DoS attacks. The nodes in the group use a gateway sensor to communicate with other nodes in the group. The packets obtained from other resources are neglected, thus allowing for avoidance from deceptive jammer attacks. In another study [14] that was conducted by Xu et al., four types of attack were designated and certain methods were developed to identify them. The first method is related to the signal strength, because during an attack there can be abnormal changes in the signal strength. The second method is the Carrier sense intervals. The Carrier sense intervals are widened during an attack. The other method is to control packet arrival rates. Of course these values are not enough by themselves. Without the presence of an attack on existing nodes in the network, under certain conditions, these ratios may show abnormal changes.

3. Formation of Attacks

This section describes formation of packet collision, exhaustion, and unfairness attacks. Figure 1 illustrates how packet collision and exhaustion attacks occur.

Node 1 sends a message to Node 2 after performing the detection operation in the environment. Since the CSMA is canceled at the attacking node, it continuously sends a message to Node 2 without waiting for the media to be empty. As a result a packet collision and exhaustion attack occur [15]. Packet collision attack occurs when the attacker node sends a message to the node in the environment once. In the event that the message sent by the attacker node is constant, exhaustion attack occurs.

Figure 2 shows how unfairness attack occurs.

Node 1 sends a message to Node 2 after performing the detection operation in the environment. Attacker node keeps Node 2 busy by sending a message. As a result a unfairness attack occurs [16]. In the CSMA based Medium Access Protocols, every node has the same amount of time for using up the media. Every node makes an effort to take over media and this is fairly distributed. The attacking node sends packets to the network by taking advantage of this rule. By doing this, instead of the nodes belonging to the channel using up the media, these attacking nodes take over.

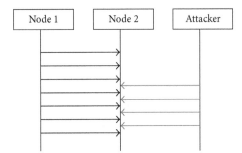

FIGURE 2: Unfairness attack.

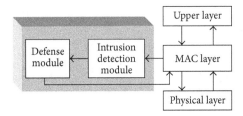

FIGURE 3: Structure of our proposed unit.

4. Proposed Method

This section describes the suggested adaptive detection-defense unit for packet collision, exhaustion, and unfairness attacks. Figure 3 shows the structure of our proposed unit. We improve the security of MAC layer through adding two special modules, intrusion detection module and intrusion defense module, into the original TinyOS operating system.

Detection module determines whether the intrusion exists or not. Then, if attacks are found, defense module is activated.

4.1. Packet Collision and Exhaustion Attack. The flowchart of the Adaptive Detection and Defense Unit that has been developed against the packet collision and exhaustion attacks is demonstrated in Figure 4.

The nodes in the environment send data, with a 0x11 message type, to the cluster head or base station every 60 ms. When this time period reaches 1 minute (60000 ms) the node attaches how many packets it has sent to the message packet and sends them through a 0x22 message type. The cluster head and base station which receives this message can determine to which node this packet belongs to. Then, it finds the number of packets received from this node. If there is no difference between the number of packets sent by that node and the number of packets received, it means that the network is operating in a healthy manner. If the packet disappeared during transfer, it means that a packet collision has occurred. Under normal circumstances, the average rate of packet delivery is very high with no attacks. The decreased rate of packet delivery lower than threshold value facilitates identifying attack scenarios for any types of attackers responsible for DoS attacks.

The cluster head or base station which detects this problem sends a warning message to that node and the node

which receives this message decreases its message sending frequency and continues to send messages. However, energy of the attacker node decreased or exhausted after a set period of time has been taken into consideration. To prevent the network from slow data transmission in this process, head of the clusters or base station transmits a message to enable the node to transmit data like previous time intervals if no packets are lost in a given time. This time interval will be decided by the adaptive system which is described in the next section.

As known within the literature [17], the Rate Limiting Technique is used for kinds of this attack. Rate Limiting Technique is demonstrated in Figure 5.

As can be seen in Figure 3, the amount of time in which the radio is active has been reduced. If the communication times of friendly nodes and the attacking times of attacker nodes do not overlap, the attacker will no longer be effective. One of the ways to reduce this possibility is to reduce the listening periods of the nodes. In other words, it is to sleep for a longer period of time during a listening/sleeping period and to be able to communicate in a shorter time. As a result the possibility of the attacker to make the attacking packets overlap with the communication times of the nodes is lowered. Due to this technique, the lifespan of the network increases considerably. By reducing the amount of data that is received and kept by the radio, the impact of the attack is reduced.

4.2. Unfairness Attack. The flowchart of the Adaptive Detection and Defense Unit that has been developed against the unfairness attack is demonstrated in Figure 6.

In the CSMA based Common Access Protocols, every node has the same amount of time for using up the media. For example, if five nodes will send data to the cluster head or base station, each one will be taking up % 20 of the media. Utilization rate of media = (the number of packets sent by x node/the total number of packets sent by the nodes) * 100. As can be seen by the formula above, every node will send an equal number of packets to the cluster head or base station (for example, 50) and according to the formula;

Utilization rate of media

$$= \left(\frac{50}{50} + 50 + 50 + 50 + 50\right) * 100 = \left(\frac{50}{250}\right) * 100 \quad (1)$$

$$= 20.$$

In other words, since the cluster head or base station is aware of the number of nodes that is in interaction with, it is able to calculate their rate of media usage while the nodes are sending messages every 1000 ms. If this rate is equal to that which is calculated by the cluster head or base station, it means that the network is operating in a healthy manner. However, if this value is below what it should be, it means that the media are being used by an attacker node. The cluster head or base stations which detect this problem send a message to the node and that node continues its message transmission by reducing the size of the packets. Size of the packets is decided by the adaptive system which is described in the next section. The small sized packets when compared to large size packets need lower transmission powers. The possibility of an error

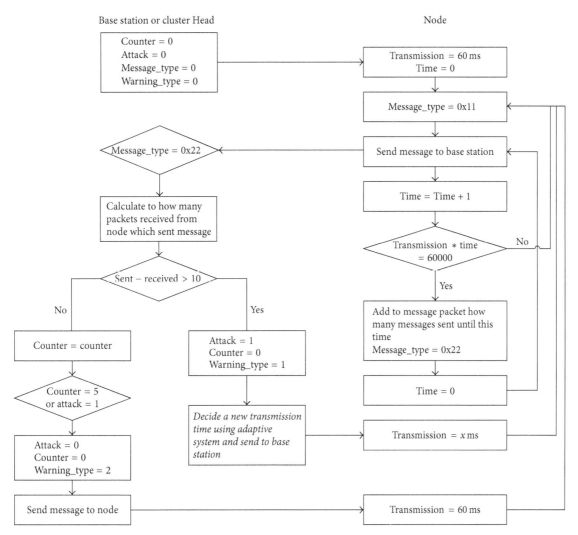

FIGURE 4: Flowchart of adaptive detection-defense unit for packet collision and exhaustion attacks.

FIGURE 5: Rate Limiting Technique.

occurring is quite low when compared to larger size packets. Due to the small sized packets, the nodes that belong to the network are able to increase the amount of time in which they will use the media. Once the cluster head or the base station determines that the attack is over, a message is sent to the nodes allowing them to return to their previous message sending types.

5. Adaptive System

This section describes adaptive system in detection and defense unit.

5.1. Packet Collision and Exhaustion Attack. The nodes initially transmit the packet of messages every 60 ms to detect

packet collision and exhaustion attacks. It is necessary to increase 60 ms in order to limit the speed at the moment of attack.

The developed adaptive system will decide the extent of increase. The system successfully computes the packet rate by increasing the transmission period every minute. This process is maintained as long as the successfully transmitted packet rate is increased. The process is finished whenever this rate is lower than the previous rate. Figure 7 illustrates the flowchart of how adaptive system reacts to packet collision and exhaustion attacks.

Table 1 shows an example of results from system operation during packet collision and exhaustion attacks.

As seen in Table 1, adaptive system computes the successfully transmitted packet rate, at the end of each minute during an attack. The frequency of packet transmission is adjusted to 1000 ms when this rate is detected to be 1000 ms maximum. While normally 997 packets are delivered, the fact that during an attack this number is being reduced to 60 packets can be explained by the following. When the attack occurs, the main objective is to reduce the number of packets lost. There are

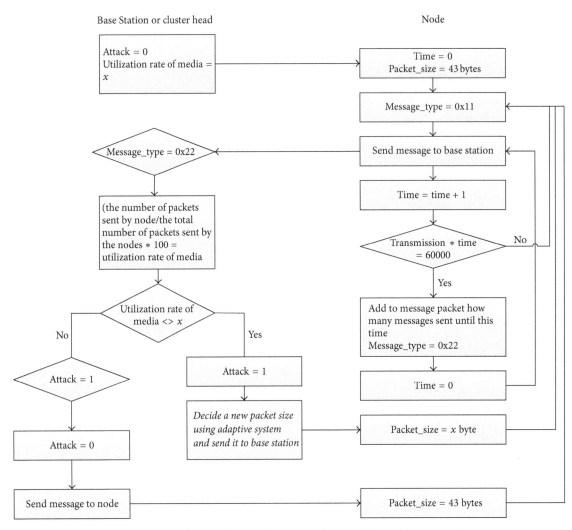

FIGURE 6: Flowchart of adaptive detection-defense unit for unfairness attack.

already samples from the 60 packets sent in 1 minute during an attack and the 997 packets that are normally delivered. Therefore, it is more efficient to use the value which allowed for the successful delivery of the most amount of packets when an attack took place.

5.2. Unfairness Attack. The nodes initially transmit message packets at 43 bytes. The size of message packet needs to be reduced during an attack. It is adaptive system that decides to what extent it should be reduced. The system computes the usage rate of medium by reducing the size of the packet each minute. This process carries on as long as use rate of medium is increased. The process is finished whenever this rate is equal to or less than the previous rate. Figure 8 illustrates the flowchart of how adaptive system reacts to an unfairness attack.

Table 2 shows an example of results from system operation during unfairness attacks.

As seen in the Table 2, adaptive system computes the usage rate of medium at the end of each minute during an attack. The size of the packet is adjusted to 19 bytes when this rate is detected to be 19 bytes maximum. Adaptive system

decides the value that needs to be used in order to increase the successfully transmitted packet rate and the usage rate of medium during attacks. The system is engaged in comparison for a certain period of time and then determines the values to be used at the end of this period. The developed adaptive detect-defense unit is resistant to the types of DoS attackers (constant jammer, deceptive jammer, reactive jammer, and random jammer) because of the operating form of the system.

6. Implementation

The architecture of the implemented application is given in Figure 9.

When you plug the TelosB node into the usb port of the computer, it acts as a base station. The sensor nodes in the medium transmit the data sensed to the base station. When base station receives a packet over the radio, it transmits it to the serial port of the computer. In Cygwin environment, the following encodings are used to transfer the sensed data to the PC via the serial port. With these codes, the Listen.java file, which is inside the TinyOS folder, runs.

cd tools/java

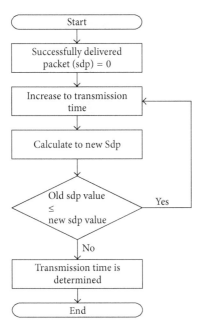

FIGURE 7: Flowchart of adaptive system for packet collision and exhaustion attacks.

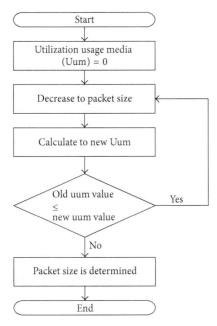

FIGURE 8: Flowchart of adaptive system for unfairness attack.

make

export MOTECOM=serial@COM3:telos

java net.tinyos.tools.Listen

In order to see the results, additions have been made to the Listen. java program within the TinyOS folder which enables the data received by the serial port to be transmitted to the computer. Through these additions, the data that comes to the serial port are inserted into the database. There are two

TABLE 1: Successfully delivered packets during an attack.

During an attack (ms)	Average delivered packets	Average packets lost	Successfully delivered packets (%)
60	997	120	87.96
80	749	90	87.98
100	558	65	88.35
120	497	57	88.53
150	398	36	90.95
200	298	26	91.28
250	237	20	91.56
300	199	14	92.96
400	148	10	93.24
500	118	7	94.07
600	100	5	95.00
750	79	3	96.20
800	74	2	97.30
1000	60	1	98.33
1200	50	1	98.00

TABLE 2: Utilization rate of media during an attack.

Packet size	Utilization rate of media (%)
43	53
41	56
37	60
33	65
29	69
27	70
25	74
22	77
19	80
17	80

important points in the additions. One of them is database connection and the other is query. Codes are given below.

```
Connection database=DriverManager.
getConnection("jdbc:" + "postgresql:
//localhost:5432/
postgres","postgres", "postgres");
Statement query=database.
createStatement();
query.executeUpdate("insert into table
(data,counter)values('"+data+"',
'"+counter+"')");
```

The following link can be used to access the Listen.java program:

http://w3.gazi.edu.tr/~muratdener/Listen_java.pdf

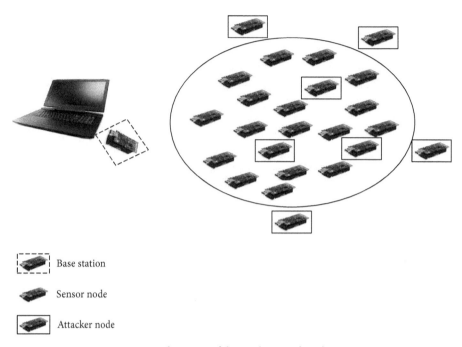

FIGURE 9: Architecture of the implemented application.

PostgreSQL has been used for the management of the database system. An interface has been written by using the Delphi program in order to see the results while looking at the data saved in the database. A total of 600 lines of NesC code were written in the present study during formation of attack nodes and adaptive detect-defense unit. There are 3 different code files available. These are for base station, sensor nodes, and attacker nodes. The base station and the sensor nodes operate according to Figures 4 and 6.

In attacker nodes, CSMA is deactivated to create packet collision and exhaustion attacks. The code that transmitted data to the medium with small packets is installed on the attacker node. In addition, the code that transmitted data to the medium with normal packets is installed on the attacker node to create unfairness attack. Attacker nodes operate according to Figures 1 and 2.

The following links can be used to access the NesC files of base station, sensor nodes, and attacker nodes.

http://w3.gazi.edu.tr/~muratdener/Base_Station.pdf

http://w3.gazi.edu.tr/~muratdener/Sensor_Node.pdf

http://w3.gazi.edu.tr/~muratdener/Attacker_Node.pdf

7. Experimental Results

To test our scheme we used TOSSIM—the simulator for TinyOS. It compiles directly from TinyOS code. Deriving the simulation from the same code that runs on real hardware greatly simplifies the development process. TOSSIM supports several realistic radiopropagation models and has been validated against real deployments for several applications. TOSSIM also incorporates TinyViz, a Javabased graphic user interface (GUI), that allows for visualization and control of

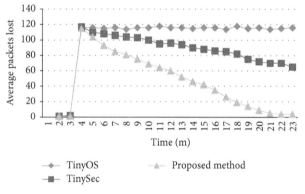

FIGURE 10: Results for packet collision and exhaustion attacks.

the simulation as it runs, inspecting debug messages, radio and UART packets, and so forth.

100 nodes are used as a network node; the base station is fixed. Each node is placed randomly within a 100×100 cell. Comparative performance analysis results are presented based on average packets lost and utilization rate of media themes. Average results are obtained under intense communication of network by running simulation 10 times.

(a) Figure 10 shows the comparative results of the proposed method, available TinyOS system, and TinySec protocol during packet collision and exhaustion attacks.

The loss of packets was 0 because no attacks occurred during the first 2 minutes. The attacker nodes began attacking between minute 2 and minute 3 and the 120 packets on average were lost. The developed adaptive detection and defense unit detected the attack after minute 3. The node that limited its rate upon receiving warning message of base station reduced its rate to minimize loss of packets

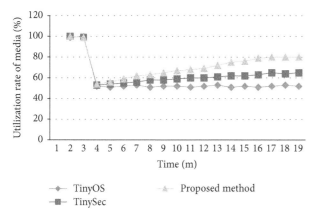

FIGURE 11: Results for unfairness attack.

for next periods. In TinySec protocol, because there is no special unit against collision and exhaustion attacks, it did not obtain same success with our proposed method. But, TinySec has other security solutions in its own protocol; this is reduced to average packet lost values. However, average loss of packets continues in TinyOS because TinyOS system does not provide the principle of availability. TinyOS system is still under attack and the frequency of packet transmission remains the same.

(b) Figure 11 shows the comparative results of the proposed method, available TinyOS system, and TinySec protocol during an unfairness attack.

The usage rate of the medium was 100% as no attacks occurred during the first 2 minutes. The attacker node began attacking between minute 2 and minute 3 and the use rate of the medium decreased to 50%. The developed adaptive detection and defense unit detected the attack after minute 3. The usage rate of the medium increased to 80% after the nodes received the warning message to reduce the size of packets. In TinySec protocol, because there is no special unit against unfairness attack, it did not obtain same success with our proposed method. But, TinySec has other security solutions in its own protocol; this is increased to utilization rate of media values. However, the usage rate of the medium remained at 53% in TinyOS because the size of the packets remained the same on TinyOS system that did not provide the principle of availability and the attack was carried on.

8. Conclusions

All security requirements must be provided because wireless sensor networks are used in very important applications such as military applications and health applications. Additionally, the sensor nodes having limited hardware resources and power units cause security vulnerabilities which await a resolution. It is therefore required to develop security protocols to fully cover such security threats.

Even if all of other conditions are provided, if the principle of availability which is one of the security needs of the WSN is not provided, the WSN will be defenseless against DoS attacks. This means that the WSN will not be able to perform its tasks during a packet collision, exhaustion, and unfairness

attacks. As known, if the principle of availability has not been established in the security application that is developed, the network will not be able to perform its tasks and stop working during DoS attacks. Even through the DoS attacks do not change the contents of the data in the network, the WSN that is victim to the attack will become disabled. The energy exhaustion of the nodes that constitute the WSN as well as the processor cycle increases. Due to this the lifespan of the network is reduced. As a result, security requirements need to be provided. In this study, an Adaptive Detection and Defense Unit against the packet collision, exhaustion, and unfairness attacks that occur in the data link layer have been carried out in order to provide the WSN security need of principle of availability.

Comparative performance analysis results are obtained in TOSSIM simulation platform based on average packets lost and utilization rate of media themes. Proposed method has better results than TinyOS system and TinySec protocol. Although TinySec is security protocol which provides data confidentially, integrity, and authentication, because it has no specific unit against link layer DoS attack, it did not show same success when compared to our method.

The developed unit is also implemented on the TelosB nodes. Due to the designed adaptive detection-defense unit, the lifespan of the nodes has been extended without the need for any further hardware by making the wireless sensor networks more secure against the DoS attacks that occur in the data link layer.

Competing Interests

The authors declare that there is no conflict of interests regarding the publication of this paper.

References

[1] E. Sharifi, M. Khandan, and M. Shamsi, "MAC protocols security in wireless sensor networks: a survey," *International Journal of Computer and Information Technology*, vol. 3, no. 1, pp. 105–109, 2014.

[2] G. Mahalakshmi and P. Subathra, "A survey on prevention approaches for denial of sleep attacks in wireless networks," *Journal of Emerging Technologies in Web Intelligence*, vol. 6, no. 1, pp. 106–110, 2014.

[3] P. Kour and L. C. Panwar, "A review on security challenges and attacks in wireless sensor networks," *International Journal of Science and Research*, vol. 3, no. 5, pp. 1360–1364, 2014.

[4] H. Ali, A. A. Mamun, and S. Anwar, "All possible security concern and solutions of WSN: a comprehensive study," *International Journal of Computer Science and Technology*, vol. 6, no. 4, pp. 64–74, 2015.

[5] D. Singla and C. Diwaker, "Analysis of security attacks in wireless sensor networks," *International Journal of Software and Web Sciences*, vol. 14, pp. 26–30, 2014.

[6] S. Ghildiyal, A. K. Mishra, A. Gupta, and N. Garg, "Analysis of Denial of Service (DOS) Attacks in wireless sensor networks," *International Journal of Research in Engineering and Technology*, vol. 3, no. 22, pp. 140–143, 2014.

[7] C. Karlof, N. Sastry, and D. Wagner, "TinySEC: a link layer security architecture for wireless sensor networks," in *Proceedings of the 2nd ACM Conference on Embedded Networked Sensor Systems (SENSYS '04)*, pp. 162–175, Baltimore, Md, USA, November 2004.

[8] M. Luk, G. Mezzour, A. Perrig, and V. Gligor, "MiniSec: a secure sensor network communication architecture," in *Proceedings of the 6th International Symposium on Information Processing in Sensor Networks (IPSN '07)*, pp. 479–488, Cambridge, Massachusetts, USA, April 2007.

[9] A. Perrig, R. Szewczyk, J. D. Tygar, V. Wen, and D. E. Culler, "SPINS: security protocols for sensor networks," *Wireless Networks*, vol. 8, no. 5, pp. 521–534, 2002.

[10] IEEE-TG15.4, *Part 15.4: Wireless Medium Access Control (MAC) and Physical Layer (PHY) Specifications for Low-Rate Wireless Personal Area Networks (LR-WPANs)*, IEEE Standard for Information Technology, 2003.

[11] A. Wood, J. Stankovic, and S. Son, "JAM: a jammed-area mapping service for sensor networks," in *Proceedings of the 24th IEEE Real-Time Systems Symposium (RTSS '03)*, pp. 286–297, Cancun, Mexico, December 2003.

[12] Q. Ren and Q. Liang, "Fuzzy logic-optimized secure media access control (FSMAC) protocol," in *Proceedings of the IEEE International Conference on Computational Intelligence for Homeland Security and Personal Safety (CIHSPS '05)*, pp. 37–43, April 2005.

[13] M. Brownfield, Y. Gupta, and N. Davis, "Wireless sensor network denial of sleep attack," in *Proceedings of the 6th Annual IEEE SMC Information Assurance Workshop (IAW '05)*, pp. 356–364, West Point, NY, USA, June 2005.

[14] W. Xu, W. Trappe, Y. Zhang, and T. Wood, "The feasibility of launching and detecting jamming attacks in wireless networks," in *Proceedings of the 6th ACM International Symposium on Mobile Ad Hoc Networking and Computing (MOBIHOC '05)*, pp. 46–57, Chicago, Ill, USA, May 2005.

[15] K. A. Basith and C. Balarengadurai, "Detection of DDoS attacks in IEEE 802.15.4—a review," *International Journal of Modern Sciences and Engineering Technology*, vol. 2, no. 6, pp. 103–111, 2015.

[16] S. Biswas and S. Adhikari, "A survey of security attacks, defenses and security mechanisms in wireless sensor network," *International Journal of Computer Applications*, vol. 131, no. 17, pp. 28–35, 2015.

[17] M. Panda, "Security threats at each layer of wireless sensor networks," *International Journal of Advanced Research in Computer Science and Software Engineering*, vol. 3, no. 11, pp. 61–67, 2013.

3

An SDN-Based Fingerprint Hopping Method to Prevent Fingerprinting Attacks

Zheng Zhao, Fenlin Liu, and Daofu Gong

Zhengzhou Science and Technology Institute, Zhengzhou 450002, China

Correspondence should be addressed to Fenlin Liu; liufenlin@vip.sina.com

Academic Editor: Roberto Di Pietro

Fingerprinting attacks are one of the most severe threats to the security of networks. Fingerprinting attack aims to obtain the operating system information of target hosts to make preparations for future attacks. In this paper, a fingerprint hopping method (FPH) is proposed based on software-defined networks to defend against fingerprinting attacks. FPH introduces the idea of moving target defense to show a hopping fingerprint toward the fingerprinting attackers. The interaction of the fingerprinting attack and its defense is modeled as a signal game, and the equilibriums of the game are analyzed to develop an optimal defense strategy. Experiments show that FPH can resist fingerprinting attacks effectively.

1. Introduction

Fingerprinting is a technique that is used to identify the operating system (OS) type and version of a target host and is an essential step for a successful network attack. With the OS information of the target host, the attacker can launch a better-targeted attack. Therefore, fingerprinting attacks are a significant threat to network security.

Fingerprinting attacks explore the OS of a target host based on the traffic from the target host. Different OS implementations and TCP/IP stacks exist; thus, different OS platforms communicate in different patterns, which means that some fields in packet headers are different and can be precisely distinguished by the fingerprinting attacker. The fingerprinting technique can be classified into two main classes: passive fingerprinting and active fingerprinting. A passive fingerprinting attacker sniffs and analyzes traffic from the target hosts and determines the OS type. Reconnaissance tools, such as p0f [1] and SinFP [2], can support this type of fingerprinting, whereas an active fingerprinting attacker sends a set of carefully constructed probes to the target host proactively and collects the response packets to determine the host OS type. Reconnaissance tools, such as Nmap [3] and Xprobe2 [4, 5], can be used in active fingerprinting. An attacker can collect much more OS information using active fingerprinting than passive fingerprinting, but active fingerprinting is more likely to be detected by a defender. In both passive and active fingerprinting, a set of packets sent from a target host is collected by the attacker; then, these packets are compared with a range of known OS signatures. If any signature is matched, the OS type can be obtained.

In fingerprinting attacks, a vital assumption is made by an attacker that the fingerprint of the target host is static. In fact, the static nature of the network gives the attacker a large advantage because they have relatively unlimited time and methods to explore the target. However, it is difficult for the defender to deal with every exploration because unknown attack methods always exist. However, if the fingerprint of a host is changed over time, an attacker will observe a dynamic fingerprint while the exploration space [6] of the attacker is enlarged. Thus, the attacker cannot accurately determine the target host OS. This is the idea behind moving target defense (MTD) [7–10]. MTD has recently been proposed to eliminate the asymmetric advantage of attackers, which shifts the attack surface [11] of the system to achieve an unpredictable network, effectively reducing the vulnerability exposure.

In this paper, a fingerprint hopping method (FPH) is proposed using MTD to enhance the host's ability to defend against fingerprinting attacks. First, a terminal-transparent architecture for FPH is constructed based on software-defined networks (SDN) [12]. Second, the interaction of a fingerprinting attack and defense is modeled as a signal game with consideration given to both active and passive fingerprinting. The equilibriums of the game are analyzed to obtain an optimal defense strategy. Third, an algorithm of selecting defense strategy is described. Experiments show that FPH can effectively defend against fingerprinting attacks.

2. Related Work

Honeypots are a traditional approach to defend against attackers that are attempting to fingerprint intranet hosts. Researchers use honeypots as a mechanism to deceive fingerprinting attackers and provide activity logs to defend against attacks. La et al. [13] proposed a game-based method for honeypot-enabled networks to defend against sophisticated attackers who attempt to deceive the defender by using different types of attacks. The equilibriums of both single and repeated games are analyzed to determine the optimal defense strategy. To make the best use of honeypot resources, HoneyMix [14], an SDN-based intelligent honeynet, has been proposed by Han et al., which takes advantage of SDN to achieve fine-grained flow control. HoneyMix forwards suspicious packets to a set of honeypots and replies to the attacker with the most desirable responses. Fan et al. [15] proposed a flexible general platform that supports deploying various types of honeypots. A dynamic configuration is used in virtual honeypot management to adapt to the changing network environment. However, these methods can only address attackers who try to communicate with a honeypot. If an attacker fingerprints the target host directly, these defense mechanisms will lose effectiveness. FPH is able to tackle the situation where an attacker has obtained the IP addresses of the target hosts and launched fingerprinting attack directly to the target hosts.

Packet scrubbing is a straightforward method that is used to avoid revealing intranet host information. Smart et al. [16] proposed a fingerprint scrubber to defend fingerprinting attacks. The scrubber removes identifiable information from all the packets in communication to prevent identification of the target host OS. However, this exhaustive defense method degenerates the communication performance because fingerprint scrubber modifies various fields in the packet header that are critical to performance and this method treats a benign sender and an attacker in the same way. Different from fingerprint scrubber, FPH tries to differentiate benign sender from attacker and utilizes game theory to get an optimal defense strategy to reduce the defense cost. Deceiving approaches are another way to defend against fingerprint attackers. These approaches distort the view of the attackers regarding the target host. Rahman et al. [17] proposed a game-theory approach named DeceiveGame to deceive fingerprinting attackers. Two types of senders are considered in this method, and the optimal strategy is obtained based on the equilibrium of the game. DeceiveGame scrubs fingerprint in outgoing packets and some fields of packets are randomized. However, FPH transforms the fingerprint in the packets into

another fingerprint so that the attacker will misjudge the OS of target host, which can steer attackers away from the target hosts or deceive them to launch an invalid attack. Albanese et al. [18] proposed a graph-based approach to deceive attackers who are performing target host fingerprinting. The fingerprint of the host changes by manipulating the responses of the attacker's probes, but in a static way. The fingerprint of a host is transformed to another one. Different from this method, FPH hops the fingerprints in real time to achieve a dynamic host fingerprint and brings more obfuscation to the fingerprinting attacks.

MTD-based defense methods change the system surface to increase the cost and complexity for the attackers. Fulp et al. [19] proposed a resilient configuration management that changes the configuration of the host based on an evolutionary algorithm. The vulnerability exposure is reduced, and the cost to the attacker increases. Unlike this method, instead of changing the terminal configuration, FPH transparently diversifies the responses to suspicious traffic, which can be easily deployed. Wang and Wu [20] proposed a sniffer reflector based on SDN to defend against reconnaissance attacks. This method builds a shadow network for suspicious traffic to obfuscate the attacker's view of the network. However, if a false alarm appears, normal communications will be influenced. FPH changes the packet fingerprint instead of its destination, which ensures normal communications even if a false alarm appears.

OF-RHM [21], a flexible IP hopping method based on SDN, has been proposed by Jafarian et al., which can randomly mutate an IP address to defend against scanning attacks. J. Sun and K. Sun [22] proposed a seamless IP randomization method to mitigate reconnaissance attacks. The host IP addresses mutate randomly to confuse attackers; then, legitimate communications are migrated seamlessly and kept alive. However, the above two methods lose their power when it comes to fingerprinting attack, as OS information still can leak even if real IP cannot be sniffed. FPH is able to change the external view of the OSes and limit the information obtained by an attacker. RRM [23, 24], a route hopping method, has been proposed by Duan et al., which can protect 90% of traffic flow from being sniffed. Instead of hopping routes in the network, FPH tries to change some attributes of the packets of outgoing traffic to defense fingerprinting attackers. Badishi et al. proposed a random port hopping method [25], which can repel DoS attacks by changing the communication port in an unpredictable way. This method randomizes the port of a packet, but attacker still can analyze the fingerprint through the IP header or TCP options. However, FPH hops the fingerprint in packets dynamically to confuse the attacker. DHC has been proposed in the literature [26], which changes multiple network configurations, including end information and the route, to resist sniffer attackers. But the fingerprint of hosts is not removed. FPH changes multiple fields in the packets and manipulates the attacker's view of the target host's OS.

Similar to proposed work, Kampanakis et al. [27] proposed a novel SDN-based OS hiding method against fingerprinting attack. Their method forges OS fingerprints to confuse attackers based on MTD technique. TCP sequence numbers as well as payload pattern in TCP, UDP, and ICMP

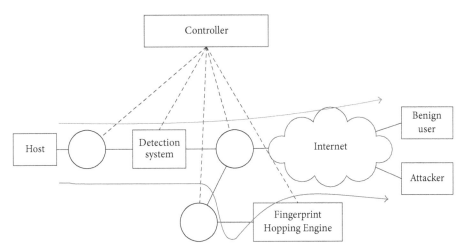

FIGURE 1: FPH architecture. (The blue line indicates the outgoing traffic route in a benign communication; the red line indicates the outgoing traffic route in a suspicious communication.)

are randomized for hiding the OS information. If illegitimate traffic is detected, a random sequence number or payload will be generated to respond to the opponent and a large overhead will be introduced to the attacker. However, a well-elaborated fingerprint hopping strategy may defend the fingerprinting attack with minor defense cost. FPH analyzes the fingerprinting attack and defense game and further provides optimal fingerprint hopping strategies for different situations based on the equilibriums of the game. Then, a strategy selection algorithm is proposed to maximize defense utility.

3. System Description of FPH

FPH monitors the traffic of each connection and identifies potential fingerprinting attackers based on the traffic pattern. If a communication is considered to have a fingerprinting behavior, the outgoing traffic of the communication will be rerouted and modified to hop their fingerprints. A flexible network configuration is needed to achieve traffic rerouting without communication interruption.

The powerful network management of SDN is used to construct a FPH system, as shown in Figure 1. It is a system that is transparent to the terminals because no terminal modifications are needed. The Controller, IDS, and Fingerprint Hopping Engine are the three main components of FPH. As the manager of the intranet, the Controller takes charge of route management. If fingerprint hopping is needed, the Controller generates corresponding flow entries and installs them on the switches to deliver packets from the protected host to the Fingerprint Hopping Engine. The IDS monitors the network traffic and detects the fingerprinting probes during communication. If any fingerprinting probes are detected, the IDS will inform the Controller to develop a strategy. The Fingerprint Hopping Engine is in charge of modifying fingerprints in response to fingerprinting probes and sending the response packets back to the network. It changes fingerprint in packets by modifying several fields in the packets, such as order of TCP options, the pattern of

initial sequence numbers, the initial window size, TTL value, and some application layer protocol fields.

FPH can detect suspicious packets from the Internet and hop the fingerprints of responses when suspicious packets appear. However, some benign communications also have a small number of packets that can be detected as suspicious. If FPH hops fingerprints for all packets in these communications, a heavy load will be placed on the Fingerprint Hopping Engine and a large delay will be introduced into these benign communications. Furthermore, with the knowledge of the strategy of the defender, the fingerprinting attacker will hide his identity to avoid detection by FPH. A sophisticated fingerprinting attacker will try to remain "normal" as a benign user to deceive the defender and carefully conduct fingerprinting to maximize the collection of fingerprint information. However, the defender hopes to allow only benign users to access the host on the intranet and randomly hop the fingerprints of the outgoing packets of any suspicious communication within an appropriate cost. To model this interaction, a fingerprinting attacker and defender game is formulated in the next section.

4. Fingerprint Attack and Defense Game

When an attacker fingerprints a remote host, two modes can be adopted by the attacker. One mode is the "Normal" mode through which the attacker communicates with the target host in a normal way. In the "Normal" mode, the attacker can obtain limited information about the target host, but the attacker is hard to be detected by the defender because he communicates with the target host as a benign user. On the other hand, the other mode is the "Suspicious" model. In this case, the attacker sends suspicious probes to the target host and much more information about the target OS can be obtained. However, the "Suspicious" mode is much more likely to be detected by the defender because it is one of the attack patterns.

Multiple attackers may present in the network at the same time. For each of them, the interaction with the defender of

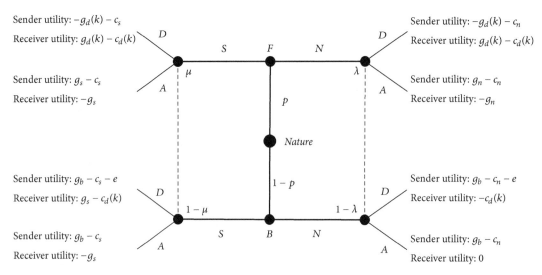

FIGURE 2: Extensive form of the fingerprinting attack and defense game.

the network can be modeled as a game. Here, we analyze each attacker-defender pair separately. There are two sender types, fingerprinting attacker and benign user. The fingerprint attacker tries to fingerprint the target host, and the benign user communicates with the host normally on the intranet. The two types of senders can communicate in two modes, Normal and Suspicious. The receiver is a defender of the intranet who monitors the network traffic and develops the defense strategy. When a fingerprinting behavior appears, the "defense" strategy is adopted to randomly hop the fingerprint of the protected host. Otherwise, an "Abstain" strategy is adopted to allow the sender to communicate with the intranet hosts.

4.1. Game Model. The interaction between the sender and receiver can be formulated as a game. Known from the interaction of the two players, the sender acts first (Normal or Suspicious); then, the receiver can observe the action and take action accordingly. Therefore, the game is a dynamic game. Moreover, the type of sender is private information to the receiver, and the game is an incomplete information game. By observing the actions of the sender, the receiver can infer the type of sender and selects an action (Defense or Abstain) based on the information regarding the sender type. This fingerprinting attack and defense can be modeled as a signaling game, and the definition is as follows.

Definition 1. The fingerprinting attack and defense game is a 5-tuple $(\Omega, \Theta, \Sigma, P, U)$.

Ω = {Sender, Receive} denotes the player set and consists of one sender and one receiver in the game.

$\Theta = \{F, B\}$ is the type space of the sender, where F denotes the fingerprinting attacker and B denotes the benign user.

$\Sigma = (M_S \times M_S) \times (A_R \times A_R)$ is the strategy combination space of the game. $M_S = \{S, N\}$ is the signal space of the sender, where S and N denote the Suspicious mode and Normal mode, respectively. $M_S \times M_S$ is the strategy space of the sender. For $(m_S, m_S') \in M_S \times M_S$ and m_S and m_S' are the signals

for F-type and B-type senders, respectively. $A_R = \{D, A\}$ is the action space of the receiver, where D and A denote the Defense and Abstain actions, respectively. $A_R \times A_R$ is the strategy space of the receiver. For $(a_R, a_R') \in A_R \times A_R$, a_R is the action for the signal S from the sender and a_R' is the action for signal N.

$P : \Theta \mapsto [0, 1]$ is the prior probability over the sender types or the belief of the defender regarding its opponent. $P = (p, 1 - p)$, where $p = \mathbb{P}(F)$, $1 - p = \mathbb{P}(B)$.

$U = (u_S, u_R)$. $u_S : \Theta \times M_S \times A_R \mapsto \mathbb{R}$ is the utility function of the sender, and $u_R : \Theta \times M_S \times A_R \mapsto \mathbb{R}$ is the utility function of the receiver.

The fingerprinting attack and defense game can be represented as the extensive form shown in Figure 2, where each branch represents a special situation with one type of sender. The nodes connected by the dotted line constitute an information set in which the defender cannot distinguish the nodes because the sender type is unknown. As seen in Figure 2, there are two information sets in this game. The left set is indicated as the S information set, and the right set is indicated as the N information set.

When the attacker fingerprints a host with probes, if the defender takes action A, the host OS information will be exposed. The attacker can benefit from this process under the risk of being detected by the defender. For the fingerprinting attacker, g_s and g_n are introduced to denote the benefit of the attacker given the signals S and N, respectively. c_s and c_n denote the cost of the attacker given the two signals, which is caused by the risk. Note that, for the attacker, a suspicious probe will obtain much more information than a normal probe and also increase the risk correspondingly. Therefore, it is assumed that $g_s > g_n$ and $c_s > c_n$. Considering a zero sum model, the more the attacker benefits (e.g., g_s), the more losses the defender suffers (e.g., $-g_s$).

For the defender, it is assumed that the fingerprint hopping space of the protected host is Ξ and the size of the hopping space is $k = |\Xi|$, which means that the defender can randomly select one of k different OS fingerprints to answer the attacker. If the defender replies to a fingerprinting attacker with Ξ, he will receive benefit $g_d(k)$ and pay cost $c_d(k)$. $g_d(k)$ and $c_d(k)$ increase with k because if the fingerprint space is larger, it will be more difficult for the attacker to discover the real fingerprint of the target host and the defender will take more resources, that is monotone increase function.

The utilities of both players in every situation are modeled as Utility = Benefit − Cost. In Figure 2, when the type of sender is F and (S, D) is played by the sender and receiver, the cost of the sender is c_s and the benefit is $-g_d(k)$, which is caused by the hopping fingerprint defense. Therefore, the utility of the sender is $-g_d(k) - c_s$. The receiver benefits $g_d(k)$, and the cost of the receiver is $c_d(k)$; therefore, the utility of the receiver is $g_d(k) - c_d(k)$ $(g_d(k) - c_d(k) > 0)$. When the type of the sender is F and (N, D) is played by the sender and receiver, the sender will obtain a hopping fingerprint, so he will obtain benefit $-g_d(k)$ and cost c_n. The receiver benefits $g_d(k)$ and cost $c_d(k)$; therefore, the utility of the receiver is $g_d(k) - c_d(k)$. When the type of sender is B and (S, A) is played by the sender and receiver, the sender achieves benefit g_b $(g_b > 0)$ because the benign user communicates with the target host successfully. In this case, the benefit of the receiver is $-g_s$ because the receiver responds to the sender with real fingerprint information that can be sniffed by a passive fingerprinting attacker. When the type of sender is B and (S, D) is played by the sender and receiver, the cost of the sender is $c_s + e$, where cost e is caused by the delay addition from hopping fingerprints. The benefit of the receiver is g_s because fingerprint information leakage is prevented using the hopping fingerprint. It is assumed that the utility of the receiver is $g_s - c_d(k) > 0$. When the type of sender is B and (N, A) is played by the sender and receiver, the utility of receiver is assumed to be 0 because the defender neither prevents fingerprint leakage nor takes a defensive measure. Other situations are easy to understand.

4.2. Equilibriums Analysis. As mentioned previously, the interaction between a fingerprinting attack and its defense has been modeled as a signaling game, where Perfect Bayesian Equilibrium (PBE) [28] is used to predict the outcome of the game. PBE describes the complete course of action of both players, which is an optimal strategy for all of the players of the game. None of the players can obtain a higher utility if they deviate from the PBE strategy. In the fingerprinting attack and defense game, a PBE is defined as a strategy combination; that is, PBE $\triangleq ((m_S, m'_S), (a_R, a'_R)) \in \sum$. (m_S, m'_S) describes the signals for both types of senders and (a_R, a'_R) describes the actions of the receiver as responses to the two potential signals sent by the sender. When the receiver observes a signal from the sender, the posterior probability of the sender type can be computed based on Bayes' rule. In the fingerprinting attack and defense game, the posterior probabilities are defined as (μ, λ), as shown in Figure 2, where

$$\mu = \mathbb{P}(F \mid S),$$

$$1 - \mu = \mathbb{P}(B \mid S),$$

$$\lambda = \mathbb{P}(F \mid N),$$

$$1 - \lambda = \mathbb{P}(B \mid N).$$

$$(1)$$

In the signal game, a pooling equilibrium means that both types of senders send the same signal. A separating equilibrium is a strategy in which different types of senders send different signals. In this section, all of the pooling equilibriums and separating equilibriums are analyzed for the fingerprinting attack and defense game.

4.2.1. Pooling PBE. There are two pooling strategies for the sender: (N, N) and (S, S). The pooling strategy (N, N) is examined first.

Theorem 2. *The fingerprinting attack and defense game has a pooling PBE $((N, N)(D, D))$ if $p \geq c_d(k)/(g_d(k) + g_n)$.*

Proof. The sender pooling strategy (N, N) means that the sender plays N in the game regardless of his type. Given the sender strategy (N, N), the information set N in Figure 2 is reached and the posterior probability about sender type can be calculated by Bayes' rule, as shown in

$$\lambda = \mathbb{P}(F \mid N) = \frac{\mathbb{P}(F)}{\mathbb{P}(F) + \mathbb{P}(B)} = \frac{p}{p + 1 - p} = p. \quad (2)$$

Using this posterior probability, the expected utility of the two actions of the receiver are shown in the following.

For action D, $E_{u_R}(D \mid N)$

$$= \mathbb{P}(F \mid N) \cdot u_R(F, N, D) + \mathbb{P}(B \mid N)$$

$$\cdot u_R(B, N, D) \quad (3)$$

$$= p(g_d(k) - c_d(k)) + (1 - p)(-c_d(k))$$

$$= pg_d(k) - c_d(k)$$

For action A, $E_{u_R}(A \mid N)$

$$= \mathbb{P}(F \mid N) \cdot u_R(F, N, A) + \mathbb{P}(B \mid N) \quad (4)$$

$$\cdot u_R(B, N, A) = p(-g_n) + (1 - p) \cdot 0 = -pg_n.$$

If $p \geq c_d(k)/(g_d(k) + g_n)$, $E_{u_R}(D \mid N) \geq E_{u_R}(A \mid N)$ can be obtained. In other words, D is the best response for the receiver given signal N. Thus, the utility of the sender is shown in the following.

For the F-type sender, $u_S(F, N, D) = -g_d(k) - c_n$

For the B-type sender, $u_S(B, N, D) = g_b - c_n - e$. $\quad (5)$

To ensure that the sender has no intention to deviate from signal N, we verified whether S can provide higher utility for a sender of any type. If S is the sender signal, the information set F in Figure 2 will be reached. The receiver observes the signal

S and the expected utilities of his two responses are shown as follows.

For action D, $E_{u_R}(D \mid S)$

$$= \mu(g_d(k) - c_d(k)) + (1 - \mu)(g_s - c_d(k)) \quad (6)$$

For action A, $E_{u_R}(A \mid S) = \mu(-g_s) + (1 - \mu)(-g_s)$.

D is better receiver response because $E_{u_R}(D \mid S) > 0 > E_{u_R}(A \mid S)$. Therefore, the utilities of senders of both types are shown in the following.

For the F-type sender, $u_S(F, S, D) = -g_d(k) - c_s$

$$\quad (7)$$

For the B-type sender, $u_S(B, S, D) = g_b - c_s - e$.

From (5) and (7), $u_S(F, N, D) > u_S(F, S, D)$ and $u_S(B, N, D) > u_S(B, S, D)$ can be obtained, which mean that the signal N can provide higher utility for both sender types. Therefore, the sender will not deviate from N; that is, $((N, N)(D, D))$ is a pooling PBE of the game if $p \geq c_d(k)/(g_d(k) + g_n)$. $\square$

Theorem 3. *The fingerprinting attack and defense game has a pooling PBE $((N, N)(D, A))$ if $p < c_d(k)/(g_d(k) + g_n)$.*

Using the same process, Theorem 3 can be proved. Theorems 2 and 3 show that the optimal strategy for a fingerprinting attacker is to appear normal, as a benign user. If the prior probability p is larger than a certain threshold, the defender will hop fingerprints for every packet, regardless of the signal of the opponent. Otherwise, the defender will play D for signal S and play A for signal N. It can also be proved that the pooling strategy (S, S) is not a part of PBE using the same process, and the details are omitted.

4.2.2. Separating PBE

Theorem 4. *The fingerprinting attack and defense game has no separating PBE.*

Proof. There are two possible separating strategies for the sender in this game: (S, N) and (N, S). (S, N) will be first discussed below.

Assuming that (S, N) is the strategy for the sender or that the F-type sender only sends signal S and the B-type sender only sends signal N, the utility of the sender is discussed as follows.

(1) If the sender is F-type, S is the signal of the sender according to the separating strategy. In this case, if the receiver plays D, he will obtain utility $g_d(k) - c_d(k)$. Otherwise, if the receiver plays A, he will obtain utility $-g_s$. $g_d(k) - c_d(k) > 0 > -g_s$, so the optimal action for the receiver is D; thus, the utility of the F-type sender is $-g_d(k) - c_s$.

(2) If the sender is B-type, N is the signal of the sender according to the separating strategy. In this case, if the receiver plays D, he will obtain utility $-c_d(k)$. Otherwise, if the receiver plays A, he will obtain utility 0. Obviously, A is the optimal action for the receiver because $-c_d(k) < 0$. Thus, the utility of the sender is $g_b - c_n$.

Given the receiver strategy (D, A), it is verified whether the sender will deviate from the separating strategy (S, N). If the F-type sender deviates from S to N, A is the receiver response and the sender will obtain utility $g_n - c_n$, which is larger than the utility when he plays S. Thus, the sender will deviate from signal S to N. Therefore, the separating strategy (S, N) is not part of a PBE.

For the other separating strategy for the sender (N, S), the same conclusion can be obtained using a similar process and the details are omitted.

In conclusion, the fingerprinting attack and defense game has no separating PBE. $\square$

4.3. Belief Model. In order to facilitate the analysis, the conclusions of Theorems 2 and 3 are obtained under an ideal condition that both the false positive rate (FP) and false negative rate (FN) of IDS are zero. In reality, small parts of suspicious probes cannot be detected by the IDS (FN > 0). It is also possible that a benign user can send a few suspicious packets in some special situations. With this knowledge, the fingerprinting attacker will send some suspicious probes to obtain more information about the target host OS. When the defender identifies suspicious packets from a sender, the belief of the defender about the sender type will be updated. Function $p(t)$ is defined as the belief of the defender instead of the constant p when t suspicious packets are received. Similar to the literature [17], $p(t)$ is formalized as

$$p(t) = \min\left(1, \frac{e^{(a_0 + \varphi(t))/G} - 1}{e - 1}\right). \quad (8)$$

In (8), a_0 is the initial value when no suspicious packet is detected. A larger a_0 indicates that the sender is more likely to be a fingerprinting attacker. G denotes the total fingerprint information obtained by a sender. $\varphi(t)$ is the fingerprint information gained for the sender in the communication, which can be calculated by (9), where r_i is the fingerprint information gain for the ith suspicious packet [17]. θ ($0 < \theta \leq 1$) represents the ratio of fingerprint information that can be reconnoitered by probes detected by IDS to that which can be reconnoitered by all probes sent by the attacker. It can be estimated by repeated tests on IDS using fingerprinting tools, such as Nmap. When a part of probes is not detected (FN > 0), some fingerprint information is leaked; that is $\theta < 1$. Note that $\varphi(0) = 0$.

$$\varphi(t) = \frac{1}{\theta}\sum_{i=1}^{t} r_i. \quad (9)$$

The exponential function is chosen as the belief function so that a unit increase of fingerprint information obtained by the sender leads to higher increase of suspiciousness with the increase of already obtained fingerprint information.

4.4. Fingerprint Hopping Space. Assuming that Ξ is the fingerprint hopping space for a protected host h and $k = |\Xi|$, fingerprint(h) $\in \Xi$, where fingerprint(h) is the real fingerprint of host h. In other words, the fingerprint hopping

```
Input: t, r_1, r_2, ..., r_t
Output: Strategy
StrategySelect
(01)  p* = c_d(k_m)/(g_d(k_m) + g_n)
(02)  φ(t) = 0
(03)  while communication is going on
(04)     if a new suspicious packet is detected by IDS
(05)        φ(t) = (1/θ) Σ_{i=1}^{t} r_i
(06)        Get p(t) using Eq. (8)
(07)     if p(t) ≥ p*
(08)        Select (D, D) as the strategy of the defender
(09)        Get k = k̃_o using Eq. (14)
(10)        Set up the strategy on the IDS and Fingerprint Hopping Engine
(11)     else
(12)        Select (D, A) as the strategy of the defender
(13)        k = k_m
(14)        Set up the strategy on the IDS and Fingerprint Hopping Engine
(15)  end while
(16)  return
```

ALGORITHM 1: Strategy selection algorithm.

space of h contains the real fingerprint of h because normal communication with h has exposed a part of its fingerprint. $g_d(k)$ and $c_d(k)$ are the benefit and cost of the defender, respectively, when the hopping space size is k. $g_d(k)$ and $c_d(k)$ are calculated by (10) and (11), respectively, where $u > 1$, $\beta > 0$, $k \in \mathbb{Z}^+$.

$$g_d(k) = \alpha \log_u k \qquad (10)$$

$$c_d(k) = \beta k - \beta. \qquad (11)$$

A logarithmic function is considered for $g_d(k)$ because the defender will benefit less with unit increase of k when the hopping space size is already large, as the addition of confusion to the attacker is less. Furthermore, $g_d(1) = 0$ should hold, which indicates that there should be no benefit for the defender if the hopping space size is 1; that is, $\Xi = \{fingerprint(h)\}$. Therefore, (10) is able to describe the property of the defender's benefit with respect to hopping space size. Other types of functions, such as exponential function and linear function, cannot reflect the relationship between defender's benefit and hopping space size. The cost function $c_d(k)$ reflects the penalty of memory consumption increased with the growth of hopping space size, which is defined as linear function, indicating fixed growth rate of hopping cost regardless of hopping space size. The defender's cost should be zero when the hopping space size is 1; that is, $c_d(1) = 0$. Other functions cannot describe the fixed growth rate of the hopping cost with the size of hopping space. As mentioned previously, when $p \geq c_d(k)/(g_d(k) + g_n)$, $((N, N)(D, D))$ is the equilibrium solution of the fingerprinting attack and defense game, and the expected utility of defender is shown in (3). Combined with (3), (10), and (11), (12) can be obtained.

$$E_{u_R} = p g_d(k) - c_d(k) = p\alpha \log_u k - (\beta k - \beta). \qquad (12)$$

If k is very small, the probability of successfully deducing the correct fingerprint by the attacker will be high; however,

if k is very large, the defender must bear a large defense cost. Thus, the defender will decide the value of k to maximize his expected utility. Equation (13) is obtained by deriving E_{u_R} with respect to k.

$$E'_{u_R} = \frac{p\alpha}{k \ln u} - \beta. \qquad (13)$$

When E'_{u_R} is zero, the maximum expected utility is found. Thus k_o can be obtained, as shown in (14). In practical application, $\tilde{k}_o$ is chosen as the optimal value shown in (15), where k_m is the minimum size of the fingerprint hopping space.

$$k_o = \frac{p\alpha}{\beta \ln u} \qquad (14)$$

$$\tilde{k}_o = \max(k_m, \lceil k_o \rceil). \qquad (15)$$

5. Strategy Selection Algorithm

With the updated belief, the defender should adjust his strategy to maximize his utility. A strategy selection algorithm is proposed to find the optimal strategy, as shown in Algorithm 1. In the algorithm, the belief threshold $p*$ is found with the initial size of the fingerprint hopping space k_m. When the IDS identifies a suspicious packet, the belief of the defender about the sender type will be updated. If the belief is smaller than threshold $p*$, strategy (D, A) will be played by the defender. Otherwise, (D, D) will be played.

6. FPH Design

A prototype system of FPH is designed based on SDN, as shown in Figure 3, which consists of the following three components: the Controller, IDS, and Fingerprint Hopping

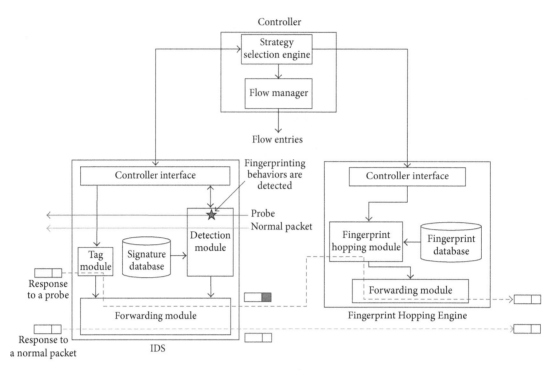

FIGURE 3: FPH design.

Engine. The green solid line and red solid line denote the paths of a normal packet and a fingerprinting probe, respectively. The green dash line and red dash line denote the paths of the responses of a normal packet and a fingerprinting probe, respectively. IDS monitors the packets in the communication. The Detection Module of IDS detects the fingerprinting behavior based on a Signature Database, which can be built through collecting the probe signatures of fingerprinting tools, such as Nmap. When a packet arrives, IDS will match the packet with the signatures in the database. If no signature is matched, the outgoing packets will be sent to network without modification. Otherwise, if any signature is matched, IDS will report to the Controller through the Controller Interface. When the defender strategizes to hop the fingerprint of a packet, the response packet will be tagged by the Tag Module of IDS. Then the tagged packet (red rectangle in Figure 3) will be forwarded to the network through Forwarding Module.

With the report message sent by the IDS, the Controller calculates the belief about the sender type and makes a strategy. If fingerprinting behaviors are detected, the Controller will set up flow entries to the Openflow switches through the Flow Manager to deliver the tagged response packets to the Fingerprint Hopping Engine. The Fingerprint Hopping Engine changes the fingerprint of these packets based on the size of the fingerprint hopping space informed by the Controller. Finally, the packets with the hopping fingerprints will be sent back to the network through the Forwarding Module of the Fingerprint Hopping Engine and the tag will be deleted.

To reroute the responses of suspicious packets, the tagging technique [29] is used to mark these responses. If the defender takes the Defense action, the IDS will be informed to add a tag to the responses of these suspicious packets and related flow entries will be installed on the switches to forward the packets with this tag to the Fingerprint Hopping Engine. The outgoing traffic routes of a protected host for a fingerprinting attacker and benign user are shown in Figure 4, in which the tagged packets are marked in red.

7. Experiments and Analysis

In this section, the security and performance of FPH are evaluated. The topology of the network, as shown in Figure 1, is constructed using Mininet [30] with a benign user, a fingerprinting attacker, and a target host. Openflow 1.0 [31] is applied and POX [32] is used as the Controller. In our experiments, all the evaluation examples are done on a machine with a 2.53 GHz Intel Xeon and 32 G RAM 64 bits.

7.1. Performance Evaluation. When FPH adopts hopping fingerprints to a suspicious communication, the Controller will set up related flow entries on the switches to forward the outgoing packets to the Fingerprint Hopping Engine. The Controller will also inform the Fingerprint Hopping Engine about the size of the hopping space. Due to these processes, network latency will be introduced. To evaluate the network delay, FPH is deployed based on Mininet and 10 repeated tests are conducted on a fingerprinting communication and a benign communication, which are created by Nmap and FTP, respectively. The result is shown in Figure 5, where the horizontal coordinates stand for the number of the tests in the experiment. When the communication is benign, the network delay is low, as seen in the figure, because the Defense action is not taken. FPH will not cause an additional delay for the benign user because the Defense action is only taken

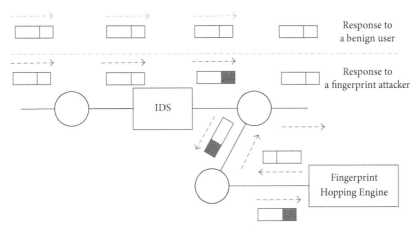

FIGURE 4: Fingerprint probe routes.

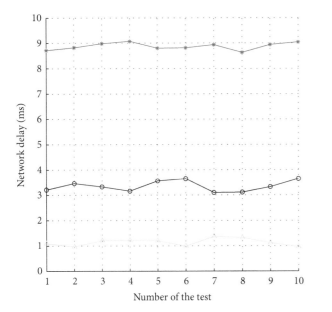

FIGURE 5: Network delay of FPH.

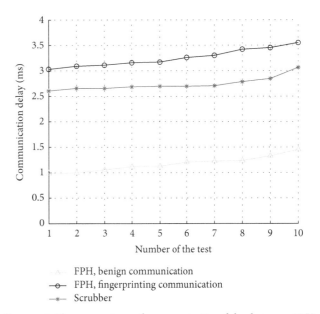

FIGURE 6: The comparison of communication delay between FPH and scrubber.

when the belief of the defender exceeds a certain threshold, which is unlikely to be reached by a benign user. The fingerprinting communication will cause the FPH Defense action, and the network delay of the suspicious communication will increase. A high delay is introduced for a packet that causes the Defense action because this packet has to wait in the network for the related flow entries to be set up. The average delay of the fingerprinting communication is much lower but still higher than that of the benign communication because the outgoing traffic of the fingerprinting communication will be sent to the Fingerprint Hopping Engine for modification.

Different from FPH, scrubber [16] is an exhaustive defense method, which degenerates the communication performance. In this experiment, the network delay introduced

to different types of communications by FPH and scrubber are compared. We focus on the fingerprint scrubbing method described in [16], which normalizes IP type-of-service and fragment bits in the IP header. We also implement a scrubber on SDN, so that all the experiments are conducted in the same condition. The delay of each packet in the communication is collected. The results are shown in Figure 6, where the communication delays are sorted in ascending order. For the scrubber, all the packets in the communication need to be modified regardless of the type of traffic. Compared with scrubber, FPH achieves much lower communication delay when the opponent is a benign sender, because no packet modification is required in the communication, which is a time-consuming operation. Therefore, FPH can achieve lower delay for a benign communication. However, for a fingerprinting communication, the communication delay of FPH is higher than that of scrubber. The reason is that, in

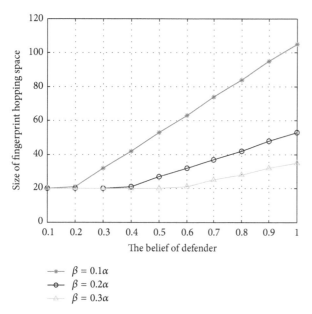

FIGURE 7: Fingerprint hopping space size versus defender belief.

TABLE 1: Output of the fingerprinting tools Nmap and p0f.

OS of the target host	Running FPH		No defense mechanism	
	Nmap	p0f	Nmap	p0f
Windows XP	N	N	Y	N
Windows 7	N	N	Y	Y
Windows 10	N	N	Y	YF
Ubuntu 10.10	N	NF	Y	Y
Ubuntu 11.10	N	N	Y	Y
Ubuntu 14.04	N	NF	Y	N

N: attacker fails to fingerprint the target host. NF: attacker falsely identifies the OS. Y: attacker succeeds to identify the OS. YF: attacker succeeds to identify the OS type but falsely identify the OS version.

FPH, not only does the outgoing traffic need to be modified to hop fingerprint, but also the incoming traffic needs to be monitored.

7.2. Evaluation of the Fingerprint Hopping Space. The optimal size of the hopping space, $\tilde{k}_o$, changes with the belief of the defender. Intuitively, if the defender has a stronger belief that the opponent is a fingerprinting attacker, he will adopt a larger hopping space to confuse the attacker. Otherwise, he will adopt a smaller hopping space to save defense costs. In the experiment, α and β in (10) and (11) are set to $\beta = 0.1\alpha$, $\beta = 0.2\alpha$, and $\beta = 0.3\alpha$, with $u = 1.1$ and $k_m = 20$. Then, the optimal size of the fingerprint hopping space can be obtained using (15), as shown in Figure 7. Due to the minimum size of the fingerprint hopping space, $\tilde{k}_o$ is a constant value when the belief value is small. When the belief value increases, $\tilde{k}_o$ grows linearly. As seen in the figure, a smaller β produces a larger hopping space because if the fingerprint hopping costs less, the defender can adopt a larger hopping space to obtain a greater benefit from making the attacker more confused.

7.3. Security Evaluation. In this experiment, Nmap (v7.40) and p0f (v3.09b) are used as active and passive fingerprinting tools to verify the security of FPH. The target host runs on a separate VM which is connected to the network generated by Mininet. The firewall of the target host is closed and we assume that false negative rate is 0; that is, $\theta = 1$. The attacker uses Nmap to actively fingerprint the target host, and p0f is employed to passively fingerprint the target host. The commands of the two tools are as follows.

Command for Nmap: nmap -O -v target_IP

Command for p0f: p0f -i target_interface

The results of the experiment are shown in Table 1. As can be seen, the security of FPH is verified on different OSes and OS versions. When no defense mechanism is adopted in the network, Nmap is able to fingerprint the target host precisely and p0f can also identify the OS of the host correctly for most cases. Windows 10 is falsely identified as Windows 7 or 8 by p0f, but the OS type is recognized correctly. Windows XP and Ubuntu 14.04 are not identified by p0f. This is because the feature database does not contain features that match the packets sent by target host. However, both the two fingerprinting tools fail to detect OS of the target host when FPH is adopted. Since the responses of the probes sent by Nmap are modified by FPH, the fingerprint observed by the attacker changes dynamically. As a result, Nmap cannot recognize the OS of target host through analyzing the responses. It also can be seen that, in some cases, p0f falsely identifies the target OS. The reason is that p0f fingerprints the target host using the attributes of single packet. FPH transforms the fingerprint in the packet into another fingerprint, so p0f misjudges the OS of target host, which will steer the attacker away from the target host or deceive them to launch an invalid attack.

8. Conclusions and Future Work

Fingerprinting is an essential step for network attacks, which enables the attacker to obtain the OS information of target host for attackers. In this paper, FPH is proposed based on SDN to provide a hopping fingerprint for attackers to resist fingerprinting attacks. Using the idea of MTD, FPH hops the fingerprint of the protected host to expand the exploration space of the attacker and disable the fingerprinting tools. The fingerprinting attack and defense game is modeled, and the equilibriums of the game are analyzed. An appropriate defense strategy is presented with sender type consideration. Experiments show that FPH can effectively defend against fingerprinting attacks. In this paper, the interactions of fingerprinting attack and defense are modeled as a series of one-shot games and the change of defender's belief is taken into consideration. However, we assume that only the defender has the knowledge of game history. In future work, a multistage game will be modeled for continuous interaction between the fingerprinting attack and defense. In addition, a more reasonable assumption that both the attacker and defender have knowledge of game history will be made and experiments where both attacker and defender adopt strategies derived based on this history will be conducted.

Competing Interests

The authors declare that there is no conflict of interests regarding the publication of this paper.

Acknowledgments

This work is supported by the National Natural Science Foundation of China (nos. 61401512, 61379151, 61272489, and 61302159) and The National Cryptography Development Fund of China (no. MMJJ201301005).

References

[1] M. Zalewski, "The new p0f: 2.0.8," September 2006, http://lcamtuf.coredump.cx/p0f.shtml.

[2] P. Auffret, "SinFP, unification of active and passive operating system fingerprinting," *Journal in Computer Virology*, vol. 6, no. 3, pp. 197–205, 2010.

[3] G. Lyon, "Nmap: a free network mapping and security scanning tool," 2014, http://nmap.org/.

[4] O. Arkin and F. Yarochkin, "Xprobe v2.0: a fuzzy approach to remote active operating system fingerprinting," Tech. Rep., 2002.

[5] F. V. Yarochkin, O. Arkin, M. Kydyraliev, S.-Y. Dai, Y. Huang, and S.-Y. Kuo, "Xprobe2++: low volume remote network information gathering tool," in *Proceedings of the IEEE/IFIP International Conference on Dependable Systems and Networks (DSN '09)*, pp. 205–210, Lisbon, Portugal, July 2009.

[6] R. Zhuang, S. A. DeLoach, and X. Ou, "Towards a theory of moving target defense," in *Proceedings of the 1st ACM Workshop on Moving Target Defense (MTD '14)—Co-located with 21st ACM Conference on Computer and Communications Security (CCS '14)*, pp. 31–40, Scottsdale, Ariz, USA, November 2014.

[7] A. Ghosh, D. Pendarakis, and W. Sanders, "Moving target defense co-chair's report-National Cyber Leap Year Summit 2009," Tech. Rep., Federal Networking and Information Technology Research and Development (NITRD) Program, 2009.

[8] T. Cyberspace, *Strategic Plan for the Federal Cybersecurity Research and Development Program*, Executive Office of the President National Science and Technology Council, Washington, DC, USA, 2011.

[9] S. Jajodia, A. K. Ghosh, V. Swarup, C. Wang, and X. S. Wang, *Moving Target Defense: Creating Asymmetric Uncertainty for Cyber Threats*, vol. 54, Springer Science & Business Media, 2011.

[10] S. Jajodia, A. K. Ghosh, V. Subrahmanian, V. Swarup, C. Wang, and X. S. Wang, *Moving Target Defense II. Application of Game Theory and Adversarial Modeling*, Advances in Information Security, Springer, Berlin, Germany, 2013.

[11] P. K. Manadhata, D. K. Kaynar, and J. M. Wing, *A Formal Model for a System's Attack Surface*, DTIC Document, 2007.

[12] N. McKeown, "Software-defined networking," *INFOCOM Keynote Talk*, vol. 17, no. 2, pp. 30–32, 2009.

[13] Q. D. La, T. Q. Quek, J. Lee, S. Jin, and H. Zhu, "Deceptive attack and defense game in honeypot-enabled networks for the internet of things," *IEEE Internet of Things Journal*, vol. 3, no. 6, pp. 1025–1035, 2016.

[14] W. Han, Z. Zhao, A. Doupé, and G.-J. Ahn, "HoneyMix: toward SDN-based intelligent honeynet," in *Proceedings of the ACM International Workshop on Security in Software Defined Networks and Network Function Virtualization*, pp. 1–6, 2016.

[15] W. Fan, D. Fernández, and Z. Du, "Versatile virtual honeynet management framework," *IET Information Security*, vol. 11, no. 1, pp. 38–45, 2017.

[16] M. Smart, G. R. Malan, and F. Jahanian, "Defeating TCP/IP stack fingerprinting," in *Proceedings of the 9th USENIX Security Symposium*, Denver, Colo, USA, August 2000.

[17] M. A. Rahman, M. H. Manshaei, and E. Al-Shaer, "A game-theoretic approach for deceiving remote operating system fingerprinting," in *Proceedings of the 1st IEEE International Conference on Communications and Network Security (CNS '13)*, pp. 73–81, October 2013.

[18] M. Albanese, E. Battista, S. Jajodia, and V. Casola, "Manipulating the attacker's view of a system's attack surface," in *Proceedings of the IEEE Conference on Communications and Network Security (CNS '14)*, pp. 472–480, San Francisco, Calif, USA, October 2014.

[19] E. W. Fulp, H. D. Gage, D. J. John, M. R. McNiece, W. H. Turkett, and X. Zhou, "An evolutionary strategy for resilient cyber defense," in *Proceedings of the 58th IEEE Global Communications Conference (GLOBECOM '15)*, San Diego, Calif, USA, December 2015.

[20] L. Wang and D. Wu, "Moving target defense against network reconnaissance with software defined networking," in *Proceedings of the International Conference on Information Security*, 2016.

[21] J. H. Jafarian, E. Al-Shaer, and Q. Duan, "OpenFlow random host mutation: transparent moving target defense using software defined networking," in *Proceedings of the 1st ACM International Workshop on Hot Topics in Software Defined Networks (HotSDN '12)*, pp. 127–132, Helsinki, Finland, August 2012.

[22] J. Sun and K. Sun, "DESIR: Decoy-Enhanced Seamless IP Randomization".

[23] Q. Duan, E. Al-Shaer, and H. Jafarian, "Efficient random route mutation considering flow and network constraints," in *Proceedings of the 1st IEEE International Conference on Communications and Network Security (CNS '13)*, October 2013.

[24] J. Jafarian, E. Al-Shaer, and Q. Duan, "Formal approach for route agility against persistent attackers," in *Computer Security—ESORICS 2013*, J. Crampton, S. Jajodia, and K. Mayes, Eds., pp. 237–254, Springer, Berlin, Germany, 2013.

[25] G. Badishi, A. Herzberg, and I. Keidar, "Keeping denial-of-service attackers in the dark," *IEEE Transactions on Dependable and Secure Computing*, vol. 4, no. 3, pp. 191–204, 2007.

[26] Z. Zhao, D. Gong, B. Lu, F. Liu, and C. Zhang, "SDN-based double hopping communication against sniffer attack," *Mathematical Problems in Engineering*, vol. 2016, Article ID 8927169, 13 pages, 2016.

[27] P. Kampanakis, H. Perros, and T. Beyene, "SDN-based solutions for Moving Target Defense network protection," in *Proceedings of the IEEE 15th International Symposium on a World of Wireless, Mobile and Multimedia Networks (WoWMoM '14)*, pp. 1–6, IEEE, Sydney, Australia, 2014.

[28] R. Gibbons, *Game Theory for Applied Economists*, Princeton University Press, Princeton, NJ, USA, 1992.

[29] Z. A. Qazi, C.-C. Tu, L. Chiang, R. Miao, V. Sekar, and M. Yu, "SIMPLE-fying middlebox policy enforcement using SDN,"

in *Proceedings of the ACM SIGCOMM 2013 conference on SIGCOMM (SIGCOMM '13)*, pp. 27–38, Hong Kong, China, August 2013.

[30] B. Lantz, B. Heller, and N. McKeown, "A network in a laptop: rapid prototyping for software-defined networks," in *Proceedings of the 9th ACM SIGCOMM Workshop on Hot Topics in Networks (HotNets '10)*, Monterey, Calif, USA, October 2010.

[31] N. McKeown, T. Anderson, H. Balakrishnan et al., "OpenFlow: enabling innovation in campus networks," *ACM SIGCOMM Computer Communication Review*, vol. 38, no. 2, pp. 69–74, 2008.

[32] M. McCauley, "About pox," 2013, http://www.noxrepo.org.

4

Cryptanalysis of Three Password-Based Remote User Authentication Schemes with Non-Tamper-Resistant Smart Card

Chenyu Wang and Guoai Xu

School of CyberSpace Security, Beijing University of Posts and Telecommunications, Beijing 100876, China

Correspondence should be addressed to Chenyu Wang; 2579005740@qq.com

Academic Editor: Alessandro Barenghi

Remote user authentication is the first step to guarantee the security of online services. Online services grow rapidly and numerous remote user authentication schemes were proposed with high capability and efficiency. Recently, there are three new improved remote user authentication schemes which claim to be resistant to various attacks. Unfortunately, according to our analysis, these schemes all fail to achieve some critical security goals. This paper demonstrates that they all suffer from offline dictionary attack or fail to achieve forward secrecy and user anonymity. It is worth mentioning that we divide offline dictionary attacks into two categories: (1) the ones using the verification from smart cards and (2) the ones using the verification from the open channel. The second is more complicated and intractable than the first type. Such distinction benefits the exploration of better design principles. We also discuss some practical solutions to the two kinds of attacks, respectively. Furthermore, we proposed a reference model to deal with the first kind of attack and proved its effectiveness by taking one of our cryptanalysis schemes as an example.

1. Introduction

These days an increasing number of online services (E-Health, E-Banking, and E-Shopping) have been provided for people's daily life with the rapid development of the Internet. Moreover, modern terminal equipment, like smartphones, smartwatches, and Google's Project Glass glasses, has become widespread. The growth of online services and terminal equipment makes the authentication process more important and difficult. Remote authentication is an essential part to guarantee both the claimed user and server are legitimate. In other words, authentication ensures that only the legitimate users can access the resources on the target server. And authentication protocols have been widely used for various fields, including cloud computing, E-Health, and wireless sensor [1–4].

In 1981, Lamport [5] designed the first authentication scheme based on password, while this scheme was pointed out as being insecure shortly: (1) the server having to maintain a password table and (2) high hash overhead. Therefore, many advanced schemes [6–8] were proposed with a lower overhead for the hash function to improve the computing performance of Lamport's scheme, while most of them still require a verification table.

To tackle this problem, Hwang et al. [9] developed a noninteractive password authentication scheme which discards the verification table but using smart card instead in 1990. The main drawback lies in the hardship of changing password. Because the password is related to the ID, for the sake of security, the ID has to be changed once the password is changed. However, it is not easy to change the ID. In 1991, Chang and Wu [10] also developed a scheme using smart card for storing sensitive information to help the authentication. Since then, smart cards have been applied to user authentication schemes widely, and some notable ones include [11–14]. Furthermore, these years many schemes used biometrics characteristic as an additional factor to provide the authentication [15–17].

From 1990 to 2004, numerous remote user authentication schemes with smart card were designed, while almost all were proved to be flawed. However after these years of research, remote user authentication has made great progress: on the one hand, the problem of maintaining the verification table was almost settled, and smart cards got widely used; on the other hand, the authentication schemes became more sophisticated to withstand the increasing new attacks or to meet more requirements (setting and changing the password freely, no verification table, etc.). Furthermore, ID protection was regarded as an important attribute to be noticed by researchers around 2000. In fact, in this period, most of the proposed schemes used a static user identity in the open communication channel, thus resulting in the ID theft problem. To deal with this problem, in 2004, Das et al. [18] designed a dynamic ID-based scheme, which became a landmark in the history of remote user authentication. The dynamic ID technique is able to conceal the real ID by using random numbers to generate a pseudo identity. As a good and new method to deal with ID theft, Das's scheme draws much attention. However, from then on, many authors raised concerns [19, 20] about Das's scheme and devised a variety of improved schemes. In 2005, Chien and Chen [21] criticized Das's scheme of its incapability of preserving user anonymity and proposed an enhanced one. In 2009, Wang et al. [22] also revealed that Das's scheme was completely insecure for its incapability of password-dependent goal, mutual authentication, and resistance of impersonation attack. In this period, most of the schemes (before or around 2004) assumed the smart cards are tamper resistant; that is, the parameters in the smart cards are unaccessible to adversaries.

Later, however, researchers demonstrated that the message stored in smart card can be easily extracted by reverse engineering techniques [23, 24] and power analysis [25, 26], which becomes another important landmark in remote user authentication area. Since then, most of schemes prefer to use non-tamper-resistant smart cards.

In 2010, Li et al. [27] proposed a password-authenticated key agreement scheme, while Tasi et al. [28] demonstrated it cannot be resistant to desynchronization attack and thus developed a new one. Unfortunately, in 2015 Wang et al. [29] showed Tsai's scheme suffers from smart card loss attack. Song [30] in 2010 revealed that the scheme [31] of Xu et al.'s is vulnerable to impersonation attack and thus designed a new one using symmetric key cryptosystem. Sandeep et al. [32], in the same year, also proved that Xu et al.'s scheme is not resistant to impersonation attack and offline dictionary attack and then devised a new enhanced one. Shortly after, however, Chen et al. [33] found that both the schemes of Song and Stood et al. are not secure: the scheme of Song cannot be resistant to smart card loss attack and offline dictionary attack; the scheme of Stood et al. fails to achieve mutual authentication. So Chen et al. designed an enhanced remote user authentication scheme. While this scheme was also proved by Kumari and Khan [34] it suffered from insider attack and impersonation attack. Li et al. [35], in 2013, reanalyzed Chen et al.'s scheme and then indicated that it cannot promise forward secrecy.

Till recent years, remote user authentication schemes display several distinctive features:

(1) Some attacks, including parallel session attacks, have stolen verifier attacks, and replay attacks are rarely mentioned, which means most schemes can resist these attacks.

TABLE 1: Security requirements.

1	Denial of Service (DoS) attack
2	Forgery attack (impersonation attack)
3	Replay attack
4	Stolen verifier attack
5	Parallel session attack
6	Password guessing attack
7	Smart card loss attack
8	Reflection attack
9	Insider attack

(2) Smart card loss attack and offline dictionary attack draw more and more attentions:

(i) Ma et al. [36] showed that the public key algorithm is required to resist offline dictionary attack (also called offline-password guessing attack). It is worth mentioning that we will show the following in later section: here the method is specifically applied to the offline dictionary attack using the verification from the open channel, while it is not applied to the offline dictionary attack using the verification from the smart card;

(ii) Wang et al. [29] demonstrated that there is an unavoidable trade-off between changing password locally and resisting smart card loss attack (including offline-password attack). As shown in [37], here the offline dictionary attack should be specific to the offline dictionary attack using the verification from the smart card, but not to offline dictionary attack using the verification from the open channel;

(iii) in [38], Wang gave an analysis to offline dictionary attack and proposed several security models.

(3) User anonymity and forward secrecy attract many discussions: Ma et al. [36] proved that public key algorithm is necessary to protect user anonymity; to achieve forward secrecy, the server side needs to conduct two exponentiation operations at least [36].

Although numerous user remote schemes were proposed, people are still confused about how to assess which scheme is better or whether a scheme is secure enough. Thus Madhusudhan and Mittal [39] tried to answer the question by giving nine security requirements and ten desirable attributes of a sound smart card-based authentication scheme, which we think is another landmark in the history of remote user authentication. Those security requirements and desirable attributes are shown in Tables 1 and 2. They have become an important criterion of an ideal remote authentication scheme. Most of remote user authentication schemes [4, 40–42] are designed and evaluated according to them, while none of the schemes could actually satisfy them simultaneously. Therefore, many researchers begin to pay more attention to

TABLE 2: Desirable attributes.

1	No password reveal
2	Password dependent
3	No verification table
4	Freely chosen password by the users
5	Forward secrecy
6	User anonymity
7	Mutual authentication
8	Efficiency for wrong password login
9	Smart-card revocation
10	Session key agreement

exploring the design principles and assessment criteria of authentication schemes. The most recent one is from Wang et al. [29, 37]. These two papers explored the relationship between the security requirements and desirable attributes and gave two significant tables to show the relationships. However, how to assess an authentication scheme is still an unsettled issue. Furthermore, in [11], D. Wang and P. Wang for the first time integrated "honeywords" and "fuzzy-verifiers" to settle a long-standing security-usability conflict (i.e., the trade-off between changing password locally and resisting smart card loss attack). It is a remarkable breakthrough in this area, and we will give more details in later section.

Throughout the history of two-factor authentication, it is easy to find the following: although there have been dozens of works endeavored to construct practical remote user authentication schemes, no one has succeeded in withstanding various attacks or satisfying various desirable attributes. The main reason is the chaos of some essential issue, for example, the sound assessment criterion, the reasonable classification, and definition of attacks in smart card-based scheme. Our work tries to give some inspiration on exploring better proposals.

1.1. Our Contributions. Most recently, Yeh [43] proved Chang et al.'s scheme [20] is vulnerable to replay attack, user impersonation attack, and so on and therefore proposed a new authentication scheme with user untraceability. In 2016, Kang et al. [44] showed that Djellali et al.'s scheme [45] suffers from offline dictionary attack, impersonation attack, and replay attack and then developed an enhanced scheme that achieves user anonymity with a Markov chain; and Kaul et al. [46] also designed an improved authentication scheme based on Kumari et al.'s scheme [34]. These schemes all claim to be resistant to various attacks, such as offline dictionary attack and impersonation attack. Unfortunately, according to our analysis, they fail to withstand those attacks as claimed. We summarize our contributions as follows:

(1) This paper demonstrates that the three schemes all suffer from offline dictionary attack, man-in-the-middle attack, and impersonation attack, as well as failing to preserve user anonymity or forward secrecy.

(2) Furthermore, we for the first time divide offline dictionary attacks into two categories: (1) the ones using the verification from smart cards and (2) the ones using the verification from the open channel.

The second is more complicated and intractable than the first type. We show that treating them with no difference arouses confusion and misleads the related research. Such distinction which benefits the exploration of better design principles is requisite and significant.

(3) Remarkably, we explore the solution to such two kinds of attacks and propose a reference model to settle the offline dictionary attack using the verification from the open channel and then use Yeh's scheme to check the effectiveness of our reference model; the result shows that our reference model actually works.

The remainder of this paper is organized as follows: in Section 2, the system architecture and the capacities of adversary are explained. In Section 3, we give a cryptanalysis of Yeh's scheme. We review Kang et al.'s scheme in Section 4 and Kaul et al.'s scheme in Section 5. Section 6 analyzes the two kinds of offline-password guessing attacks. And Section 7 gives a conclusion.

2. System Architecture and the Capacities of Adversary

In this section, we first list the notations used in the three schemes and then briefly introduce the system architecture and the capacities of the adversary in the schemes.

2.1. Notations and Abbreviations. The notations in the three schemes are shown in Notations and Abbreviations at the end of the paper.

2.2. System Architecture. Like many other smart card-based authentication methods, the three schemes involve a set of users and a single server. Users access the resources by mutual authentication with server. The authentication usually includes four basic phases: registration, login, authentication, and password change. Firstly, a user submits personal information to the server to register. Then the server issues the user a smart card with security parameters. The registration phase is only performed once unless the user reregisters for special reasons. After that, in the login phase, the user will send the access request. Then the server and the user authenticate each other in verification phase to finish the authentication. The phases of login and verification usually will be carried out many times. A sound two-factor authentication schemes should ensure that only the user who owns the smart card and submits the corresponding password can access the server successfully. As a realistic problem, the password change phase attracts more and more attention these years where the user can change his/her password locally or remotely.

2.3. The Capacities of Adversary. In the cryptanalysis of the two-factor authentication schemes, the adversary $\mathscr{A}$ is also supposed to have the following capacities [29, 47–49]:

(1) $\mathscr{A}$ can fully control the open communication channel; that is, $\mathscr{A}$ can modify, intercept, delete, and resend the eavesdropped messages over an open channel.

User/smart card	Channel	Server S
Choose $(\mathrm{ID}_i, \mathrm{PW}_i)$ Generate random number r_1, r_2	$\xrightarrow{(\mathrm{ID}_i, \mathrm{PW}_i, r_1, r_2)}$ $\xleftarrow[\ (N_i, M_i, r_1, h(\cdot))\ ]{\text{Smart card with}}$	Compute $\quad M_i = h(y \parallel r_2) \oplus h(\mathrm{PW}_i \parallel r_1)$ $\quad N_i = h(\mathrm{ID}_i \parallel x) \oplus h(\mathrm{PW}_i \parallel r_1)$ Store $h(h(y \parallel r_2))$ in table T
Input $(\mathrm{ID}_i', \mathrm{PW}_i')$ *Smart card* Generate random number r_3 Compute $\quad A = M_i \oplus h(\mathrm{PW}_i' \parallel r_1) = h(y \parallel r_2)$ $\quad D = r_3 \oplus h(A)$ $\quad B = N_i \oplus h(\mathrm{PW}_i' \parallel r_1) = h(\mathrm{ID}_i' \parallel x)$ $\quad N_i' = N_i \oplus h(h(A \parallel r_3))$ $\quad \mathrm{CID}_i = \mathrm{ID}_i' \oplus h(N_i \parallel h(A) \parallel r_3)$ $\quad C = h(N_i \parallel h(A) \parallel B \parallel r_3)$	$\xrightarrow{(D, \mathrm{CID}_i, N_i', C)}$	For each $h(h(y \parallel r_2))^*$ in table T Compute $\quad r_3^* = D \oplus h(h(y \parallel r_2))^*$ $\quad N_i^* = N_i' \oplus h(h(h(y \parallel r_2))^* \parallel r_3^*)$ $\quad \mathrm{ID}_i^* = \mathrm{CID}_i \oplus h(N_i^* \parallel h(h(y \parallel r_2))^* \parallel r_3^*)$ $\quad B^* = h(\mathrm{ID}_i^* \parallel x)$ $\quad C^* = h(N_i^* \parallel h(h(y \parallel r_2))^* \parallel B^* \parallel r_3^*)$ Check $C^* =?\ C$
Check the freshness of r_4 Compute $a' = h(B \parallel h(A) \parallel r_4)$ Check $a' =?\ a$ If it holds, U_i authenticate S	$\xleftarrow{(a, r_4)}$	Check the freshness of r_3 Generate a random number r_4 Compute $\quad a = h(B^* \parallel h(h(y \parallel r_2))^* \parallel r_4)$

FIGURE 1: The scheme of Yeh et al.

(2) $\mathscr{A}$ can enumerate all the items in $\mathscr{D}_{\mathrm{pw}} * \mathscr{D}_{\mathrm{id}}$ in polynomial time, where $\mathscr{D}_{\mathrm{pw}}$ and $\mathscr{D}_{\mathrm{id}}$ denote the password space and the identity space, respectively.

(3) $\mathscr{A}$ can acquire the password of a legitimate user by a malicious card reader or get the parameters in smart card but cannot achieve both.

(4) When evaluating forward secrecy, $\mathscr{A}$ can get the server's secret key.

3. Cryptanalysis of Yeh's Scheme

3.1. Review of Yeh's Scheme. This section gives a brief review of Yeh's [43] scheme with user untraceability (shown in Figure 1).

3.1.1. Registration Phase

Step 1 ($U_i \Rightarrow S$). U_i chooses ID_i, PW_i, and two random numbers r_1, r_2 and then sends $\{\mathrm{ID}_i, \mathrm{PW}_i, r_1, r_2\}$ to S via a secure channel.

Step 2 ($S \Rightarrow U_i$). S computes $M_i = h(y \parallel r_2) \oplus h(\mathrm{PW}_i \parallel r_1)$ and $N_i = h(\mathrm{ID}_i \parallel x) \oplus h(\mathrm{PW}_i \parallel r_1)$ and then sends U_i a smart card with security parameters $\{M_i, N_i, r_1, h(\cdot)\}$ via a secure channel and stores $h(h(y \parallel r_2))$ in a table.

3.1.2. Login Phase and Authentication Phase

Step 1 ($U_i \rightarrow S$). U_i inputs ID_i', PW_i'. The smart card generates a random number r_3, computes $A = M_i \oplus h(\mathrm{PW}_i' \parallel r_1) = h(y \parallel r_2)$, $D = r_3 \oplus h(A)$, $B = N_i \oplus h(\mathrm{PW}_i' \parallel r_1) = h(\mathrm{ID}_i' \parallel x)$, $N_i' = N_i \oplus h(h(A \parallel r_3))$, $\mathrm{CID}_i = \mathrm{ID}_i' \oplus h(N_i \parallel h(A) \parallel r_3)$, and $C = h(N_i \parallel h(A) \parallel B \parallel r_3)$, and then sends $\{D, \mathrm{CID}_i, N_i', C\}$ to S.

Step 2 ($S \rightarrow U_i$). S traverses the $h(h(y \parallel r_2))^*$ in table T, computes $r_3^* = D \oplus h(h(y \parallel r_2))^*$, $N_i^* = N_i' \oplus h(h(h(y \parallel r_2))^* \parallel r_3^*)$, $\mathrm{ID}_i^* = \mathrm{CID}_i \oplus h(N_i^* \parallel h(h(y \parallel r_2))^* \parallel r_3)$, $B^* = h(\mathrm{ID}_i^* \parallel x)$, and $C^* = h(N_i^* \parallel h(h(y \parallel r_2))^* \parallel B^* \parallel r_3^*)$, and then checks $C^* =?\ C$. If none of the value $h(h(y \parallel r_2))^*$ satisfies the equation, end the session. Otherwise, S examines the freshness of r_3 and whether $\{D, \mathrm{CID}_i, N_i', C\}$ has been received before. If one of the conditions is invalid, terminate the session. Otherwise, S generates a random number r_4, computes $a = h(B^* \parallel h(h(y \parallel r_2))^* \parallel r_4)$, and sends $\{a, r_4\}$ to U_i.

Step 3. The smart card firstly checks r_4, then computes $a' = h(B \parallel h(A) \parallel r_4)$, and checks whether a' equals a. If true, U_i authenticates S.

3.1.3. Password Change Phase.
If U_i wants to change the password, he/she inserts the smart card to the card reader and inputs ID_i, PW_i, and a new password $\mathrm{PW}_{i_{\mathrm{new}}}$. Then the smart card computes $M_{i_{\mathrm{new}}} = M_i \oplus h(\mathrm{PW}_i \parallel r_1) \oplus h(\mathrm{PW}_{i_{\mathrm{new}}} \parallel r_1)$ and $N_{i_{\mathrm{new}}} = N_i \oplus h(\mathrm{PW}_i \parallel r_1) \oplus h(\mathrm{PW}_{i_{\mathrm{new}}} \parallel r_1)$ and then replaces M_i and N_i with $M_{i_{\mathrm{new}}}$ and $N_{i_{\mathrm{new}}}$.

3.2. Cryptanalysis of Yeh's Schemes. In this section we show that Yeh's scheme cannot resist various attacks, such as password guessing attack, impersonation attack, and desynchronization attack.

3.2.1. Offline Dictionary Attack via Verification Value in Channel. Supposing the adversary $\mathscr{A}$ stole U_i's smart card and then got security parameters N_i, r_1, and M_i from the smart card, $\mathscr{A}$ also has $\{D_i, \mathrm{CID}_i, N_i', C\}$ through eavesdropping the open channel between U_i and S; then $\mathscr{A}$ can perform the attack by the following steps:

(1) Guess the value of PW_i to be PW_i^* from the password dictionary space $\mathscr{D}_{pw}$.

(2) Compute $A^* = M_i \oplus h(PW_i^* \parallel r_1) = h(y \parallel r_2)^*$; M_i and r_1 are extracted from the smart card.

(3) Compute $r_3^* = D \oplus h(A^*)$; D is eavesdropped from the open channel.

(4) Compute $B^* = N_i \oplus h(PW_i^* \parallel r_1)$; N_i and r_1 are extracted from the smart card.

(5) Compute $C^* = h(N_i \parallel h(A^*) \parallel B^* \parallel r_3^*)$; N_i is extracted from the smart card.

(6) Verify the correctness of PW_i^* by checking if $C^* =?$ C, C is from the open channel.

(7) Repeat Steps (1), (2), (3), (4), (5), and (6) until the correct value of PW_i^* is found.

The time complexity of the above attack is $\mathcal{O}(|\mathscr{D}_{pw}| * (3T_H + 3T_R))$. T_H is the running time for hash computation. T_R is the running time for exclusive-or operation. $|\mathscr{D}_{pw}|$ denotes the number of passwords in $\mathscr{D}_{pw}$, and $|\mathscr{D}_{pw}|$ is very limited in practice [49, 50]; usually $|\mathscr{D}_{pw}| \leq 10^6$; so the above attack is quite efficient.

Remark 1. The offline dictionary attack here uses the verification from the open channel. The inherent reason for this attack is that (1) the adversary can find a verification to check whether the guessing value is correct; (2) the password is the only unknown value to the adversary; that is, the adversary can get other parameters consisting of the verification, except the password or the identity. To such attack, the lightweight public key algorithm is the necessary condition, as explained in [36].

3.2.2. User Anonymity. Once the adversary $\mathscr{A}$ gets the password through "offline dictionary attack," he can get the user's ID by the following steps:

(1) Compute $A = M_i \oplus h(PW_i^* \parallel r_1) = h(y \parallel r_2)$; M_i and r_1 are from the smart card.

(2) Compute $r_3 = D \oplus h(A)$; D is from open channel.

(3) Compute $ID_i^* = CID_i \oplus h(N_i \parallel h(A) \parallel r_3)$; N_i is from smart card; CID_i is from open channel.

In computing ID_i, what the server knows more than the adversary is $h(h(y \parallel r_2))$, while, after getting the PW_i, the adversary can get $h(h(y \parallel r_2))$ by $M_i \oplus h(PW_i^* \parallel r_1)$, so in fact the adversary $\mathscr{A}$ has the same capacity as the server; thus $\mathscr{A}$ can get ID_i according to the way the server does.

3.2.3. User Impersonation Attack. With the PW_i^* and the ID_i^*, the adversary $\mathscr{A}$ can impersonate U_i as follows:

(1) Compute $A = M_i \oplus h(PW_i^* \parallel r_1) = h(y \parallel r_2)$; M_i and r_1 are from the smart card.

(2) Generate a random number r_3.

(3) Compute $D_a = r_3 \oplus h(A)$.

(4) Compute $B = N_i \oplus h(PW_i^* \parallel r_1) = h(ID_i^* \parallel x)$.

(5) Compute $N_a' = N_i \oplus h(h(A \parallel r_3))$; N_i is extracted from the smart card.

(6) Compute $CID_a = ID_i^* \oplus h(N_i \parallel h(A) \parallel r_3)$.

(7) Compute $C_a = h(N_i \parallel h(A) \parallel B \parallel r_3)$.

(8) Interrupt $\{D, CID_i, N_i', C\}$; send $\{D_a, CID_a, N_a', C_a\}$ to S to impersonate U_i.

As for the server S, it computes $r_3^* = D_a \oplus h(h(y \parallel r_2))^*$, $N_i^* = N_a' \oplus h(h(h(y \parallel r_2))^* \parallel r_3^*)$, $ID_i' = CID_a \oplus h(N_i^* \parallel h(h(y \parallel r_2))^* \parallel r_3^*)$, $B^* = h(ID_i^* \parallel x)$, and $C^* = h(N_i^* \parallel h(h(y \parallel r_2))^* \parallel B^* \parallel r_3^*)$ and then checks (1) $C^* =?$ C_a; (2) the freshness of r_3; and (3) whether $\{D_a, CID_a, N_a', C_a\}$ has ever been received before. All of them are satisfied, so $\mathscr{A}$ is authenticated by S successfully.

With PW_i, ID_i, and smart card, the adversary $\mathscr{A}$ has the same capacity as the legitimate user; that is, $\mathscr{A}$ can impersonate the user to the server successfully. The original reason for this attack is the offline dictionary attack.

3.2.4. Server Impersonation Attack. With the PW_i^*, $\mathscr{A}$ can impersonate S as follows:

(1) Compute $h(y \parallel r_2) = M_i \oplus h(PW_i^* \parallel r_1)$; M_i and r_1 are extracted the from smart card.

(2) Compute $B^* = N_i \oplus h(PW_i^* \parallel r_1) = h(ID_i^* \parallel x)$; N_i is extracted from the smart card.

(3) Generate a random number r_4; compute $a_a = h(B^* \parallel h(h(y \parallel r_2)) \parallel r_4^a)$.

(4) Interrupt $\{a, r_4\}$, and send $\{a_a, r_4^a\}$ to the user U_i to impersonate the server S.

On the user side, U_i computes $a' = h(B \parallel h(A) \parallel r_4^a)$, as $a' = a_a$; $\mathscr{A}$ is authenticated by the user U_i successfully.

In most cases, the capacity of legitimate user and remote server is the same; to be more precise, what the legitimate user knows can transform into what the remote server knows. So if the user impersonation attack can be performed, the server impersonation attack can be performed too.

3.2.5. Man-in-the-Middle Attack. With PW_i^* and ID_i^* that have been got from "password guessing attack" and "user anonymity," respectively, $\mathscr{A}$ can execute a man-in-the-middle attack as follows:

(1) Interrupt $\{D, CID_i, N_i', C\}$ that U_i sends to S.

(2) Compute $\{D_a, CID_a, N_a', C_a\}$ as in "user impersonation attack," and send them to S.

(3) Interrupt $\{a, r_4\}$ from S via an open channel.

(4) Compute $\{a_a, r_4^a\}$ as in "server impersonation attack," and send them to U_i.

Through above attack procedures, the adversary $\mathscr{A}$ can execute a man-in-the-middle attack without being noticed by U_i or S.

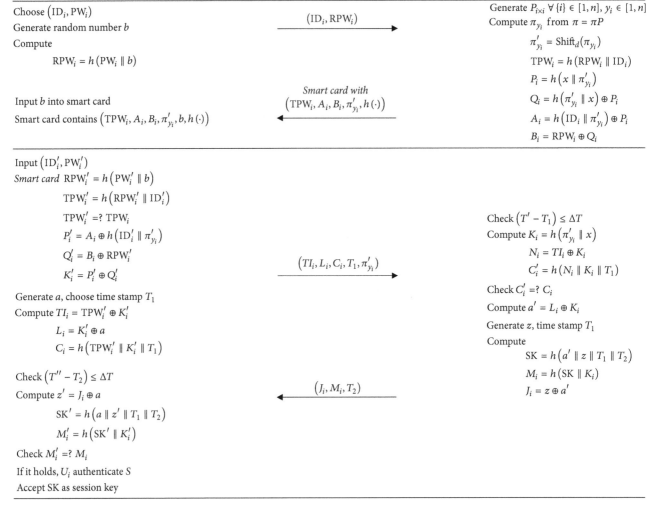

User/smart card	Channel	Server S
Choose $(\mathrm{ID}_i, \mathrm{PW}_i)$		Generate $P_{i \times i} \; \forall \{i\} \in [1, n], \; y_i \in [1, n]$
Generate random number b	$\xrightarrow{\;\;\;(\mathrm{ID}_i, \mathrm{RPW}_i)\;\;\;}$	Compute π_{y_i} from $\pi = \pi P$
Compute		$\pi'_{y_i} = \mathrm{Shift}_d(\pi_{y_i})$
$\quad \mathrm{RPW}_i = h(\mathrm{PW}_i \parallel b)$		$\mathrm{TPW}_i = h(\mathrm{RPW}_i \parallel \mathrm{ID}_i)$
		$P_i = h(x \parallel \pi'_{y_i})$
Input b into smart card	*Smart card with* $\xleftarrow{\;\;(\mathrm{TPW}_i, A_i, B_i, \pi'_{y_i}, h(\cdot))\;\;}$	$Q_i = h(\pi'_{y_i} \parallel x) \oplus P_i$
Smart card contains $(\mathrm{TPW}_i, A_i, B_i, \pi'_{y_i}, b, h(\cdot))$		$A_i = h(\mathrm{ID}_i \parallel \pi'_{y_i}) \oplus P_i$
		$B_i = \mathrm{RPW}_i \oplus Q_i$

User/smart card	Channel	Server S
Input $(\mathrm{ID}'_i, \mathrm{PW}'_i)$		
Smart card $\mathrm{RPW}'_i = h(\mathrm{PW}'_i \parallel b)$		
$\quad\quad \mathrm{TPW}'_i = h(\mathrm{RPW}'_i \parallel \mathrm{ID}'_i)$		
$\quad\quad \mathrm{TPW}'_i =? \; \mathrm{TPW}_i$		Check $(T' - T_1) \le \Delta T$
$\quad\quad P'_i = A_i \oplus h(\mathrm{ID}'_i \parallel \pi'_{y_i})$		Compute $K_i = h(\pi'_{y_i} \parallel x)$
$\quad\quad Q'_i = B_i \oplus \mathrm{RPW}'_i$		$N_i = TI_i \oplus K_i$
$\quad\quad K'_i = P'_i \oplus Q'_i$	$\xrightarrow{\;(TI_i, L_i, C_i, T_1, \pi'_{y_i})\;}$	$C'_i = h(N_i \parallel K_i \parallel T_1)$
Generate a, choose time stamp T_1		Check $C'_i =? \; C_i$
Compute $TI_i = \mathrm{TPW}'_i \oplus K'_i$		Compute $a' = L_i \oplus K_i$
$\quad\quad L_i = K'_i \oplus a$		Generate z, time stamp T_1
$\quad\quad C_i = h(\mathrm{TPW}'_i \parallel K'_i \parallel T_1)$		Compute
		$\quad SK = h(a' \parallel z \parallel T_1 \parallel T_2)$
Check $(T'' - T_2) \le \Delta T$		$M_i = h(SK \parallel K_i)$
Compute $z' = J_i \oplus a$	$\xleftarrow{\;\;(J_i, M_i, T_2)\;\;}$	$J_i = z \oplus a'$
$\quad\quad SK' = h(a \parallel z' \parallel T_1 \parallel T_2)$		
$\quad\quad M'_i = h(SK' \parallel K'_i)$		
Check $M'_i =? \; M_i$		
If it holds, U_i authenticate S		
Accept SK as session key		

FIGURE 2: The scheme of Kang et al.

In fact, man-in-the-middle attack usually is a result of "server impersonation attack" and "user impersonation attack," while offline dictionary attack is the original reason of these three attacks.

3.2.6. Desynchronization Attack. As there is no any verification in password change phase, an adversary $\mathcal{A}$ can execute desynchronization attack easily: stealing U_i's smart card and inputting a random ID_a, PW_a, and a new password $\mathrm{PW}_{a_{\mathrm{new}}}$. According to the scheme, M_i and N_i will be replaced by $M_{i_{\mathrm{new}}}$ and $N_{i_{\mathrm{new}}}$, respectively, where $M_{i_{\mathrm{new}}} = M_i \oplus h(\mathrm{PW}_a \parallel r_1) \oplus h(\mathrm{PW}_{a_{\mathrm{new}}} \parallel r_1)$ and $N_{i_{\mathrm{new}}} = N_i \oplus h(\mathrm{PW}_a \parallel r_1) \oplus h(\mathrm{PW}_{a_{\mathrm{new}}} \parallel r_1)$. As a result, even the legitimate user cannot login successfully.

Desynchronization attack often happens in password change phase where the user, without inputting the correct PW_i and ID_i, can change the password successfully. This results in the that legitimate user with correct old password cannot login successfully. So if a user wants to change the password, he should be authenticated firstly, and there are usually two ways: interacting with the remote server like the

authentication phase and interacting with the smart card. The second way requires a verification value from the smart card; thus such scheme is vulnerable to offline dictionary attack, but it helps detect wrong password input, which saves user's time. The first one requires costing more time to make the user change the password and detect wrong password input.

3.2.7. Insider Attack. In this scheme, the user U_i submits a pair of PW_i and ID_i to the server S without any transformation or protection; thus the server S can get the PW_i and ID_i and carries out an insider attack to impersonate the user U_i.

Insider attack is quite easy to deal with: do some transformation to the PW_i and ID_i, such as $h(\mathrm{PW}_i \parallel b)$ and $h(\mathrm{ID}_i \parallel b)$ (b is a random number).

4. Cryptanalysis of Kang et al.'s Scheme

4.1. Review of Kang et al.'s Scheme. This section gives a brief review of Kang et al.'s scheme [44] (Figure 2). As little relevance as password change phase, we omit it.

4.2. Registration Phase

Step 1 ($U_i \Rightarrow S$). U_i chooses ID_i, PW_i, and a random number b and computes $RPW_i = h(PW_i \parallel b)$ and then sends $\{ID_i, RPW_i\}$ to the server S via a secure channel.

Step 2 ($S \Rightarrow U_i$). S generates $P_{i\times i}$ and y_i, where $i \in [1, n]$, $y_i \in [1, n]$, and n is a small number, computes π_{y_i} from $\pi = \pi P$ and $\pi'_{y_i} = \text{Shift}_d(\pi_{y_i})$, computes $TPW_i = h(RPW_i \parallel ID_i)$, $P_i = h(x \parallel \pi'_{y_i})$, $Q_i = h(\pi'_{y_i} \parallel x) \oplus P_i$, $A_i = h(ID_i \parallel \pi'_{y_i}) \oplus P_i$, and $B_i = RPW_i \oplus Q_i$, and then issues the user U_i a smart card containing $\{TPW_i, A_i, B_i, \pi'_{y_i}, h(\cdot)\}$ via a secure channel.

Step 3. U_i inputs b into the smart card.

4.2.1. Login Phase and Authentication Phase

Step 1 ($U_i \rightarrow S$). U_i inserts his smart card and inputs ID'_i, PW'_i. The smart card computes $RPW'_i = h(PW'_i \parallel b)$ and $TPW'_i = h(RPW'_i \parallel ID'_i)$ and then checks $TPW'_i =? TPW_i$. If not satisfied, reject the request. Otherwise, the smart card computes $P'_i = A_i \oplus h(ID'_i \parallel \pi'_{y_i})$, $Q'_i = B_i \oplus RPW'_i$, and $K'_i = P'_i \oplus Q'_i$, generates a random number a and time stamp T_1, computes $TI_i = TPW'_i \oplus K'_i$, $L_i = K'_i \oplus a$, and $C_i = h(TPW'_i \parallel K'_i \parallel T_1)$, and finally sends $\{TI_i, L_i, C_i, T_1, \pi'_{y_i}\}$ to S.

Step 2 ($S \rightarrow U_i$). S firstly checks the freshness of T_1, then calculates $K_i = h(\pi'_{y_i} \parallel x)$, $N_i = TI_i \oplus K_i$, and $C'_i = h(N_i \parallel K_i \parallel T_1)$, and compares C'_i with C_i. If their values are not the same, reject the request; else generate a random number z and then compute $a' = L_i \oplus K_i$, and the session key $SK = h(a' \parallel z \parallel T_1 \parallel T_2)$, where T_2 is the time stamp, $M_i = h(SK \parallel K_i)$, and $J_i = z \oplus a'$. After that S sends $\{J_i, M_i, T_2\}$ to U_i.

Step 3. U_i firstly checks the freshness of T_2 and then computes $z' = J_i \oplus a$, $SK' = h(a \parallel z' \parallel T_1 \parallel T_2)$, and $M'_i = h(SK' \parallel K'_i)$ and verifies S through comparing M'_i with M_i. If the values of them are the same, U_i authenticates S, and accepts SK as the session key. Otherwise, end the session.

4.3. Cryptanalysis of Kang et al.'s Schemes

4.3.1. Offline Dictionary Attack via Verification Value in Channel.
Supposing the adversary $\mathscr{A}$ got U_i's smart card and then acquired security parameters TPW_i, A_i, b, and B_i from the smart card, $\mathscr{A}$ also has $\{TI_i, L_i, C_i, T_1, \pi'_{y_i}\}$ through eavesdropping the open channel between U_i and S; then $\mathscr{A}$ can perform the attack by the following steps:

(1) Guess PW_i to be PW^*_i and ID_i to be ID^*_i.

(2) Compute $RPW^*_i = h(PW^*_i \parallel b)$, $TPW^*_i = h(RPW^*_i \parallel ID^*_i)$, $P^*_i = A_i \oplus h(ID^*_i \parallel \pi'_{y_i})$, $Q^*_i = B_i \oplus RPW^*_i$, and $K^*_i = P^*_i \oplus Q^*_i$; TPW_i, A_i, b, B_i are extracted from the smart card.

(3) Compute $N_i = TI_i \oplus K^*_i$ and $C^*_i = h(N_i \parallel K^*_i \parallel T_1)$, and $\{TI_i, L_i, T_1, \pi'_{y_i}\}$ is from the channel.

(4) Verify the correctness of PW^*_i and ID^*_i by checking $C^*_i =? C_i$; C_i is from the channel.

(5) Repeat Steps (1), (2), (3), and (4) until the correct values of PW^*_i and ID^*_i are found.

The time complexity is $\mathcal{O}(|\mathscr{D}_{pw}| * 4(T_H + T_R))$, so the above attack is quite efficient. Once $\mathscr{A}$ has the PW_i, he/she also can carry out user impersonation attack, server impersonation attack, and man-in-the-middle attack. And as the methods to those attacks are similar to the methods in Yeh's schemes, it is unnecessary to go into details here.

4.3.2. Offline Dictionary Attack via Verification Value in Smart Card.
Supposing an adversary $\mathscr{A}$ got U_i's smart card and then acquired security parameters TPW_i, A_i, b, and B_i from the smart card, then $\mathscr{A}$ can perform the attack as follows:

(1) Guess the value of PW_i to be PW^*_i from the password dictionary space $\mathscr{D}_{pw}$ and ID_i to be ID^*_i from the identity dictionary space $\mathscr{D}_{id}$.

(2) Compute $RPW^*_i = h(PW^*_i \parallel b)$ and $TPW^*_i = h(RPW^*_i \parallel ID^*_i)$; b is from the smart card.

(3) Verify the correctness of PW^*_i and ID^*_i by checking whether $TPW^*_i =? TPW_i$; TPW_i is extracted from the smart card.

(4) Repeat Steps (1), (2), and (3) until the PW^*_i and ID^*_i are found.

Remark 2. The time complexity is $\mathcal{O}(|\mathscr{D}_{pw}| * 2T_H)$, so the above attack is quite efficient. This kind of offline dictionary attack above uses the verification from the smart card, while with the verification the user can change password locally. This is exactly what Wang et al. [29] demonstrated which is the trade-off between changing password locally and resisting offline-password attack. Luckily, in [11], D. Wang and P. Wang for the first time integrated "honeywords" and "fuzzy-verifiers" to settle such a long-standing security-usability conflict. So according to [11], we simply give an improved way to avoid such conflict. Let the verification $TPW_i = h((h(PW_i \parallel b) \parallel ID_i) \bmod n_0)$, where $2^4 \le n_0 \le 2^8$ and n_0 determines the capacity of the pool of the (ID, PW). So now there are $|\mathscr{D}_{pw}| * \mathscr{D}_{id} \setminus n_0 \approx 2^{32}$ candidates of (ID, PW) pair for adversary to guess when $n_0 = 2^8$ and $|\mathscr{D}_{pw}| = \mathscr{D}_{id} = 2^6$. For these candidates, the adversary can only guess the right one from online guessing, while there is also a way called "honeywords" to avoid such online dictionary guessing; "honeywords" in fact is a word list to timely detect whether the smart card is extracted.

4.3.3. Forward Secrecy.
Supposing $\mathscr{A}$ knew S's secret key x, then he can calculate the session key SK as follows:

(1) Interrupt $\{TI_i, L_i, C_i, T_1, \pi'_{y_i}\}$ that U_i sends to S.

(2) Compute $K_i = h(\pi'_{y_i} \parallel x)$; π'_{y_i} is from smart card.

(3) Compute $a' = L_i \oplus K_i$.

(4) Interrupt $\{J_i, M_i, T_2\}$ that S sends to U_i.

(5) Compute $z' = J_i \oplus a'$.

(6) Compute $SK = h(a' \parallel z' \parallel T_1 \parallel T_2)$; at this point the user $\mathscr{A}$ gets SK successfully.

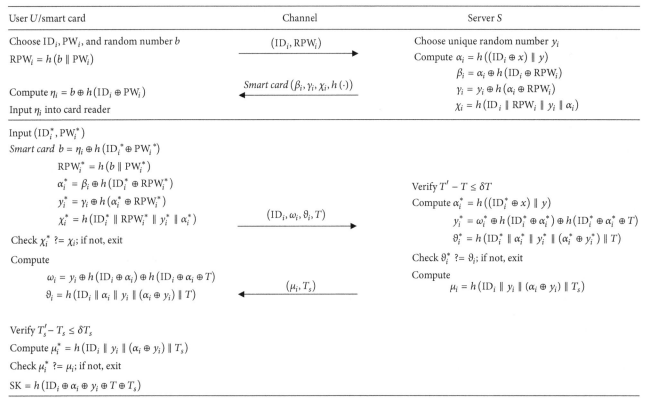

User U/smart card	Channel	Server S
Choose ID_i, PW_i, and random number b	(ID_i, RPW_i) $\longrightarrow$	Choose unique random number y_i
$RPW_i = h(b \parallel PW_i)$		Compute $\alpha_i = h((ID_i \oplus x) \parallel y)$
		$\beta_i = \alpha_i \oplus h(ID_i \oplus RPW_i)$
Compute $\eta_i = b \oplus h(ID_i \oplus PW_i)$	$\xleftarrow{\text{Smart card } (\beta_i, \gamma_i, \chi_i, h(\cdot))}$	$\gamma_i = y_i \oplus h(\alpha_i \oplus RPW_i)$
Input η_i into card reader		$\chi_i = h(ID_i \parallel RPW_i \parallel y_i \parallel \alpha_i)$
Input (ID_i^*, PW_i^*)		
Smart card $b = \eta_i \oplus h(ID_i^* \oplus PW_i^*)$		
$RPW_i^* = h(b \parallel PW_i^*)$		
$\alpha_i^* = \beta_i \oplus h(ID_i^* \oplus RPW_i^*)$		Verify $T' - T \le \delta T$
$y_i^* = \gamma_i \oplus h(\alpha_i^* \oplus RPW_i^*)$		Compute $\alpha_i^* = h((ID_i^* \oplus x) \parallel y)$
$\chi_i^* = h(ID_i^* \parallel RPW_i^* \parallel y_i^* \parallel \alpha_i^*)$	$\xrightarrow{(ID_i, \omega_i, \vartheta_i, T)}$	$y_i^* = \omega_i^* \oplus h(ID_i^* \oplus \alpha_i^*) \oplus h(ID_i^* \oplus \alpha_i^* \oplus T)$
Check χ_i^* ?= χ_i; if not, exit		$\vartheta_i^* = h(ID_i^* \parallel \alpha_i^* \parallel y_i^* \parallel (\alpha_i^* \oplus y_i^*) \parallel T)$
Compute		Check ϑ_i^* ?= ϑ_i; if not, exit
$\omega_i = y_i \oplus h(ID_i \oplus \alpha_i) \oplus h(ID_i \oplus \alpha_i \oplus T)$		Compute
$\vartheta_i = h(ID_i \parallel \alpha_i \parallel y_i \parallel (\alpha_i \oplus y_i) \parallel T)$	$\xleftarrow{(\mu_i, T_s)}$	$\mu_i = h(ID_i \parallel y_i \parallel (\alpha_i \oplus y_i) \parallel T_s)$
Verify $T_s' - T_s \le \delta T_s$		
Compute $\mu_i^* = h(ID_i \parallel y_i \parallel (\alpha_i \oplus y_i) \parallel T_s)$		
Check μ_i^* ?= μ_i; if not, exit		
$SK = h(ID_i \oplus \alpha_i \oplus y_i \oplus T \oplus T_s)$		

FIGURE 3: The scheme of Kaul et al.

In this scheme, the session key consists of a random number a from U_i, a random number z from S, and two open time stamps T_1 and T_2. The key parameters are the two random number, while, compared to the adversary, what the server only knows more is the secret key x, so once the adversary knows the secret key x, he can compute the random number a' chosen by U_i as the way the server does. On the other hand, in computing SK, what the user only knows more than the adversary is the random number a. While the adversary has known a now, thus the adversary also can compute the random number z chosen by the server as the user does. With a and z, the adversary gets sk. Furthermore, it proves that "more than two exponentiation operations conducted on the server side are necessary to achieve forward secrecy" [36].

5. Cryptanalysis of Kaul et al.'s Schemes

5.1. Review of Kaul et al.'s Scheme. This section gives a brief review of Kaul et al.'s scheme [46] (Figure 3), and password change phase is also omitted.

5.1.1. Registration Phase

Step 1 ($U_i \Rightarrow S$). U_i chooses ID_i, PW_i, and a random number b, then computes $RPW_i = h(b \parallel PW_i)$, and submits $S\{ID_i, RPW_i\}$ via a secure channel.

Step 2 ($S \Rightarrow U_i$). S chooses a unique random number y_i for U_i and computes $\alpha_i = h((ID_i \oplus x) \parallel y)$, $\beta_i = \alpha_i \oplus h(ID_i \oplus RPW_i)$,

$\gamma_i = y_i \oplus h(\alpha_i \oplus RPW_i)$, and $\chi_i = h(ID_i \parallel RPW_i \parallel y_i \parallel \alpha_i)$. Then S issues U_i a smart card with $\{\beta_i, \gamma, \chi_i, h(\cdot)\}$ via a secure channel.

Step 3. U_i enters η_i to the smart card.

5.1.2. Login Phase and Authentication Phase

Step 1 ($U_i \Rightarrow S$). User U_i inserts the smart card and inputs ID_i^* and PW_i^*. Smart card computes $b = \eta_i \oplus h(ID_i^* \oplus PW_i^*)$, $RPW_i^* = h(b \parallel PW_i^*)$, $\alpha_i^* = \beta_i \oplus h(ID_i^* \oplus RPW_i^*)$, $y_i^* = \gamma_i \oplus h(\alpha_i^* \oplus RPW_i^*)$, and $\chi_i^* = h(ID_i^* \parallel RPW_i^* \parallel y_i^* \parallel \alpha_i^*)$. If $\chi_i^* \ne \chi_i$, the smart card declines the request, otherwise it computes $\omega_i = y_i \oplus h(ID_i \oplus \alpha_i) \oplus h(ID_i \oplus \alpha_i \oplus T)$ and $\vartheta_i = h(ID_i \parallel \alpha_i \parallel y_i(\alpha_i \oplus y_i) \parallel T)$ and sends $\{ID, \omega_i, \vartheta_i, T\}$ to S.

Step 2 ($S \Rightarrow U_i$). Server S first checks whether $(T' - T) \le \delta T$, then computes $\alpha_i^* = h((ID_i^* \oplus x) \parallel y)$, $y_i^* = \omega_i^* \oplus h(ID_i^* \oplus \alpha_i^*) \oplus h(ID_i^* \oplus \alpha_i^* \oplus T)$, and $\vartheta_i^* = h(ID_i^* \parallel \alpha_i^* \parallel y_i^* \parallel (\alpha_i^* \oplus y_i^*) \parallel T)$, and further checks computed ϑ_i^* ?= ϑ_i. If the verification passed, it computes $\mu_i = h(ID_i \parallel y_i \parallel (\alpha_i \oplus y_i) \parallel T_s)$, where T_s is S's current time, and sends $\{\mu_i, T_s\}$ to U_i.

Step 3. Smart card first checks the freshness of T_s, then computes $\mu_i^* = h(ID_i \parallel y_i \parallel (\alpha_i \oplus y_i) \parallel T_s)$, and then verifies μ_i^* ?= μ_i to authenticate server.

Step 4. Both S and U_i accept the common session key SK = $h(ID_i \oplus \alpha_i \oplus y_i \oplus T \oplus T_s)$.

5.2. Cryptanalysis of Kaul et al.'s Schemes

5.2.1. User Anonymity. User anonymity preserves an adversary from acquiring user's privacy message including lifestyle, habit, and hobbies by analyzing the login history, communications, and services request. In an era of big data, user anonymity has a profound significance. A well-designed protocol needs to keep the identity notion not only unexposed, but also untraceable. The former requires that even if an adversary eavesdrops the message via the open channel, he still cannot know whose communication message it is; the latter requires that the adversary does not know whether the eavesdropped message is from the same user. In fact, the latter is more restrictive than the former. However, in this scheme the user identity ID_i was exposed in the open channel; the adversary just needs to eavesdrop the open channel to get the user ID_i. With the ID_i, every time the user logs in, the adversary can know. So the privacy of the user was revealed.

5.2.2. Offline Dictionary Attack via Verification Value in Channel. $\mathscr{A}$ who extracts η_i, β_i from smart card, and $\{ID, \omega_i, \vartheta_i, T\}$ can perform an offline dictionary attack as follows:

(1) Guess the value of PW_i to be PW_i^* from the password dictionary space $\mathscr{D}_{pw}$.

(2) Compute $b = \eta_i \oplus h(ID_i \oplus PW_i^*)$, $RPW_i^* = h(b \parallel PW_i^*)$, $\alpha_i^* = \beta_i \oplus h(ID_i^* \oplus RPW_i^*)$, $y_i^* = \omega_i^* \oplus h(ID_i^* \oplus \alpha_i^*) \oplus h(ID_i^* \oplus \alpha_i^* \oplus T)$, and $\vartheta_i^* = h(ID_i^* \parallel \alpha_i^* \parallel y_i^* \parallel (\alpha_i^* \oplus y_i^*) \parallel T)$, and η_i, β_i are from smart card and $\{ID, \omega_i, T\}$ is from the open channel.

(3) Verify the correctness of PW_i^* by checking whether ϑ_i^* ?= ϑ_i, and ϑ_i is from smart card.

(4) Repeat Steps (1), (2), and (3) until the correct PW_i^* is found.

The time complexity is $\mathcal{O}(|\mathscr{D}_{pw}| * (6T_H + 9T_R))$, so the above attack is quite efficient. With ID_i and PW_i, $\mathscr{A}$ can conduct further attack such as impersonation attack, man-in-the-middle attack, and getting session key by the ways described in Sections 3.2.3, 3.2.4, 3.2.5, and 4.3.3. Thus, the whole security of the system is compromised.

5.2.3. Offline Dictionary Attack via Verification Value in Smart Card. An adversary $\mathscr{A}$ who gets the smart card from U_i extracts security parameters β_i, γ, χ_i, η_i. Further as shown in the previous paragraph, $\mathscr{A}$ also can easily get ID_i. So now the adversary $\mathscr{A}$ can perform an offline dictionary attack by the following steps:

(1) Guess the value of PW_i to be PW_i^* from the password dictionary space $\mathscr{D}_{pw}$.

(2) Compute $b = \eta_i \oplus h(ID_i^* \oplus PW_i^*)$, $RPW_i^* = h(b \parallel PW_i^*)$, $\alpha_i^* = \beta_i \oplus h(ID_i^* \oplus RPW_i^*)$, $y_i^* = \gamma_i \oplus h(\alpha_i^* \oplus RPW_i^*)$, and $\chi_i^* = h(ID_i^* \parallel RPW_i^* \parallel y_i^* \parallel \alpha_i^*)$; β_i, γ, χ_i, and η_i are extracted from U_i's smart card.

(3) Verify the correctness of PW_i^* by checking whether χ_i^* ?= χ_i; χ_i is extracted from the smart card.

(4) Repeat Steps (1), (2), and (3) until the PW_i^* is found.

The time complexity is $\mathcal{O}(|\mathscr{D}_{pw}| * (5T_H + 5T_R))$, so the above attack is quite efficient.

6. A Deep Exploration to Offline Dictionary Attack

The scheme of Yeh, Kang et al., and Kaul et al. cannot resist offline-password guessing attacks, while this is exactly what most two-factor remote authentication schemes actually suffer from. As we mentioned before, such attack is also one of the original reasons for other attacks. In this section, we try to explain why it is so hard to avoid offline dictionary attack. Furthermore, we for the first time recommend distinguishing *offline dictionary attack via verification value in smart card* (hereafter called Attack I) from *offline dictionary attack via verification value in channel* (hereafter called Attack II). When talking about offline dictionary attack, most papers [36, 51, 52] ignore the difference between them and collectively call them as offline dictionary attack (offline-password guessing attack). Although the basic principles of these two attacks are the same, the key parameters transmitted in the insecure channel or in smart card, having no "camouflage" by random numbers or other special parameters only owned by the user or the server, the adversary can get a verification (usually it is the key parameter for the server or the user to verify the validity of the other one) to perform dictionary attack. Where the verifications come from is different, Attack I uses the verification from the smart card and Attack II from the channel. Do not overlook this little difference; this results in the quite slight difference in the corresponding solutions. Distinguishing them contributes to in-depth analysis of design principles. In this section, we analyze these two attacks thoroughly.

6.1. Solutions to Offline Dictionary Attack via Verification Value in Smart Card. In the schemes of Kang et al. and Kaul et al., to achieve better user-friendliness, that is, changing password locally and detecting the wrong password-inputting timely, a verification for a smart card to authenticate the user is stored in smart card. This results in $\mathscr{A}$ getting the key parameters ϑ_i and TPW_i in smart card, which leads to Attack I. What if there was no such verification parameters? Then the password change phase may be influenced, such as Yeh's scheme which changes password remotely and fails to detect wrong password input timely. In fact, [29] points out that "there is an unavoidable trade-off when achieving the password change locally and resisting offline dictionary attack." More specifically and accurately, the offline dictionary attack here should be specific to Attack I; it usually can be avoided by two ways:

(i) A new approach called "a fuzzy verifier" and "honeywords" [11], which is a new solution to such problem. This approach can greatly increase the cost of guessing password in respect of $\mathscr{A}$. And we have given a simple application case in Section 4.3.2.

(ii) Sacrificing certain performance (e.g., not providing the attribute of changing password locally). In other words, it is a problem of the trade-off between security and effectiveness. According to this principle, some schemes [43, 53, 54] just simply remove the authentication between the user and the smart card. Therefore, this scheme is secure to Attack II, while the cost is failing to detect the wrong password input timely (costing more time).

Obviously, Attack II is not included in the above situation. So just collectively calling the two attacks as offline dictionary attack will result in confusion and making the problem more complicated.

6.2. Solutions to Offline Dictionary Attack via Verification Value in Channel. In Yeh's scheme, if we regard the parameters in smart card as opened, then the key parameters (i.e., the verification refers to the parameters used to verify the validity of the participants, and we use $Veri\_Vau$ to represent it) $C = f(PW_i, ID_i, r_3)$, where $f()$ refers to a series of cryptographic operations in the protocol, and $f(PW_i, ID_i, r_3)$ means that those cryptographic operations are actually only related to PW_i, ID_i, r_3. On the face of it, the $Veri\_Vau$ C is protected by the random number r_3. While with in-depth examination, it is clear that r_3 can be computed by PW_i. So in fact, the $Veri\_Vau = C = f(PW_i, ID_i)$. Then if an adversary guesses the PW_i and ID_i to be PW_i^* and ID_i^*, he/she can use $Veri\_Vau$ to check the correct guessed value and thus carry out an offline dictionary attack, that is, Attack II.

Typically, only when the $Veri\_Vau$ was "camouflaged" by random numbers or other special parameters which only the user and the server can get can the scheme resist Attack II, such as [11, 14, 55]. So how can we conceal the $Veri\_Vau$ and those sensitive parameters?

Naturally, someone may think of a symmetric cryptography way: if the message transmitted in the open channel is encrypted, then only the one owning the key can read the message. It seems a good solution. However, it is far from practical: how can the key be distributed and stored? Especially to the users, where can they store that private key securely? Furthermore, with the number of servers accessed increasing, the number of the keys which the user needs to store increases too; for the servers, the storage of those keys is also a big problem; it will consume a lot of storage space, and once the storage space is leaked, the security of the system will run down. Anyway, symmetric cryptography is beyond our consideration. In this work, we focus on what Ma et al. [36] advised, that is, the public key algorithm to deal with Attack II. And here is our brief explanation about the necessary public-key algorithm (for more detail please refer to [36]).

Getting a verification ($Veri\_Vau$) by the adversary in open channel is the main reason for Attack II. So a well-designed scheme has to protect the $Veri\_Vau$ in the open channel. Then how can we protect them? *On the one hand*, the parameters in the smart card can be captured by the adversary. So if we do not consider a symmetric cryptography, the only way is to use random numbers as a camouflage to protect the $Veri\_Vau$. What is more, the random number cannot be exposed to the open channel and cannot be computed only with PW_i and ID_i. *On the other hand*, the

server needs to know the random number to compute the $Veri\_Vau$. So based on the two points, the public key algorithm is a necessary approach. Moreover, smart cards always have limited memory and computing power; thus the lightweight public key operations are good choices.

However, many schemes though equipped with a public key algorithm still fail to resist Attack II, such as [52, 56, 57]. The inherent reason is the incorrectness of deploying the public key algorithm. So how can we correctly apply the public key algorithm to a authentication protocol? We will give one of the solutions, although it is not the only one, but it actually is one of the many effective solutions. Furthermore, we will give an reference model of such solution (see Figure 4) and use Yeh's scheme as an example to verify its feasibility.

As we all know, the nature of a authentication protocol is to provide a secure mutual authentication. And the basis for authentication in a password-based scheme with smart card is "what you know" and "what you have." To a user, the PW_i and ID_i are what they know; the smart card is what they have. While as the parameters in the card can be extracted by the adversary and the card itself can easily be stolen, so it seems that the smart card acts as an assistant. To a server, the long term key x is what they know. The verifier table is what they have. Similarly, the verifier table actually also acts as an assistant.

So when the server authenticates the user, the user has to prove that he really knows PW_i and ID_i and has the corresponding smart card, while, in order to prevent inside attack and eavesdropping attack, the user cannot tell the server the value of PW_i directly. Then a good way to solve such conflict is to negotiate an intermediate parameter Mid_Vau as a key evidence of authentication, where $Mid\_Vau = f(PW_i, ID_i, x)$. This step is finished in registration phase and the related auxiliary parameters are stored in the smart card. So if a user has the corresponding smart card, then he/she can computes the Mid_Vau as $f(PW_i, ID_i)$. Therefore, with the Mid_Vau, we can verify not only whether the user knows about the PW_i and ID_i, but also whether the user has the corresponding smart card. However, as $Mid\_Vau = f(PW_i, ID_i)$ in helping with the smart card, if $Veri\_Vau = f(Mid\_Vau)$, then once the adversary gets the smart card, he/she can guess the PW_i and ID_i to be PW_i^* and ID_i^*, respectively, then intercept the $Veri\_Vau$ to check the correctness of the guessed value, and thus carry out Attack II. Take Yeh's scheme as an example, in this scheme, the $Mid\_Vau = h(ID_i \parallel x)$. To U_i, $Mid\_Vau = N_i \oplus h(PW_i \parallel r_1)$, where N_i and r_1 are from smart card, $Veri\_Vau = f(Mid\_Vau) = f(PW_i, ID_i)$, and thus an adversary with the card conducts Attack II successfully.

Therefore, besides the Mid_Vau, there should be other key parameters which only S and U_i can compute. As PW_i, ID_i, and smart card have been used for Mid_Vau, it makes no sense to use them again. Thus now, to a user, he/she has no more things which can be used as evidence. The one good choice seems to initiate a challenge for the server to respond. Actually, the challenge is a random number, and the transmission and response to the challenge require the help of a public key algorithm. All in all, the other key parameters which consist of $Veri\_Vau$ should be equipped with a public key algorithm; then the $Veri\_Vau$ should be $f(Mid\_Vau, Pub\_Vau)$,

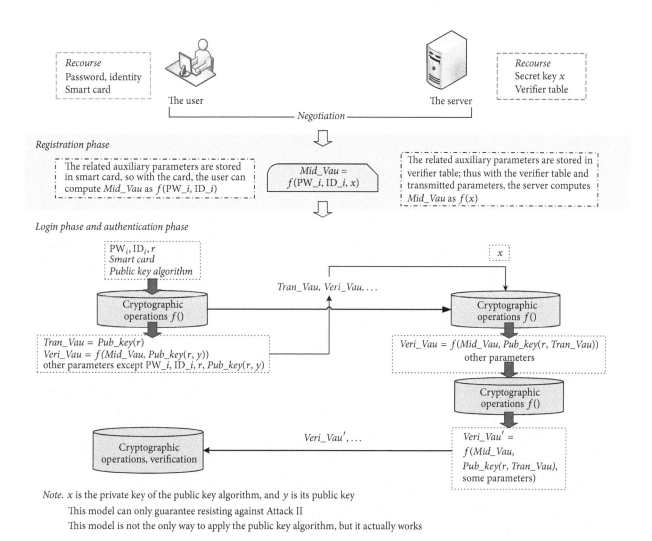

Note. x is the private key of the public key algorithm, and y is its public key

This model can only guarantee resisting against Attack II

This model is not the only way to apply the public key algorithm, but it actually works

FIGURE 4: The reference model to employ a public key algorithm securely.

where the *Pub_Vau* refers to the parameters deploying a public key algorithm. To U_i, with the knowledge of the random number r, *Pub_Vau* = *Pub_key*(r, y), where y is the public key and *Pub_key*(r, y) refer to a series of public key operations; to S, with the knowledge of private key x, *Pub_Vau* = *Pub_key*$(x, Tran\_Vau)$, where *Tran_Vau* = *Pub_key*(r). All in all, to resist Attack II, the *Veri_Vau* should satisfy *Veri_Vau* = $f(Mid\_Vau, Pub\_Vau)$; the *Mid_Vau*, PW_i, ID_i, r, and *Pub_Vau* cannot be exposed to the open channel; furthermore, *Tran_Vau* should be transmitted to the server. When U_i authenticates S, if only considering resisting Attack II, S only requires proving that it knows about the *Mid_Vau* and *Pub_Vau*. Furthermore, the parameters transmitted in the open channel follow the same principles as above.

Now, we take Yeh's scheme as an example to check the effectiveness of our reference model. And we select the Computational Diffie-Hellman problem to construct the public key algorithm. In Yeh et al.'s scheme, the *Mid_Vau* has been designed well, so we only need to apply the Computational Diffie-Hellman problem to this scheme. The definition of the Computational Diffie-Hellman problem is as follows.

g is the generator of a cyclic group Z_p^*; then, given g^β and g^α where $\beta, \alpha \in Z_p^*$, it is hard to compute α, β within a polynomial time.

According to this, we can design a lightweight public key algorithm for the user and the server: S selects a larger prime p, a generator g of cyclic group Z_p^*, and a secret key x and computes the public key $Y = g^x \bmod p$. Then if U_i selects a random number r_1, it computes $M_1 = g^{r_1} \bmod p$ and $M_2 = Y^{r_1} \bmod p$ and sends M_1 to S. S can compute M_2 as $M_1^x \bmod p$. Here, $M_1 = Tran\_Vau$ and $M_2 = Pub\_Vau$; even the adversary intercepts the M_1; he/she still cannot compute the M_2. So then S only needs to prove that it knows about the M_2. Furthermore, to U_i, $M_1 = Pub\_key(r)$ and $M_2 = Pub\_key(r, Y)$; to S, $M_2 = Pub\_key(x, Tran\_Vau)$; it also follows the principles mentioned above. In short, we improve Yeh's scheme as shown in Figure 5.

In the improved scheme, *Veri_Vau* = $C = f(Mid\_Vau, Pub\_Vau)$; even the adversary guesses the PW_i and ID_i to be PW_i^* and ID_i^*, while without *Pub_Vau*, he/she cannot find a verification to check the correctness of the guessed value

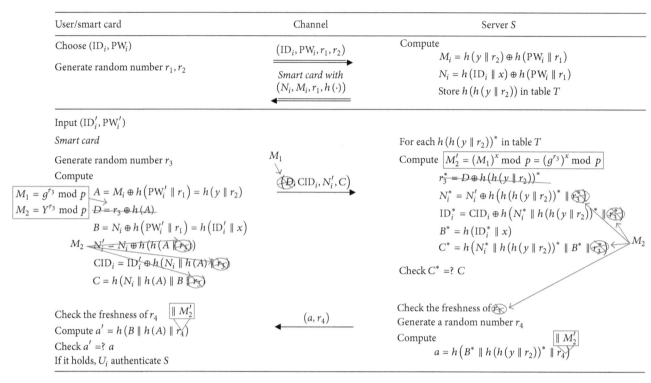

FIGURE 5: Improving Yeh et al.'s scheme to resist Attack II.

and thus fails to perform Attack II. It should be noted that we only improve Yeh's scheme to be secure to Attack II, and the reference model can only be applied to resisting Attack II.

It is generally accepted that public key algorithm is necessary for resisting offline dictionary attack, while, according to our analysis, the offline dictionary attack here should be specific to Attack II, and Attack I is not included in it: the public key algorithm consists of a private key and a public key. In Attack II, the vulnerability takes place in the authentication between the server and the smart card. So the public key algorithm acts on the server and the smart card. Usually the server takes the responsibility to keep private key x, while, in Attack I, the vulnerability takes place in the authentication between the user and the smart card. But it makes no sense to both of them to own such private key for two reasons at least:

(i) *To the users*: he always uses the password as the unique parameter to get authenticated, and the private key plays the same role as the password. Moreover, the private key is too long for the user to remember or preserve.

(ii) *Smart card*: as we have stated before, the parameters in the smart card can be easily obtained by an adversary.

7. Conclusion

In this paper, we demonstrated that the schemes of Yeh, Kang et al., and Kaul et al. all suffer from various attacks, such as offline dictionary attack and impersonation attack. Furthermore, we showed that offline dictionary attack is the

original reason of many other attacks. Remarkably, we divide offline dictionary attacks into two categories: (1) the ones using the verification from smart cards and (2) the ones using the verification from the open channel. The solution to the first type involves the trade-off between the security and effectiveness, or "a fuzzy verifier" + "honeywords" as suggested in [11]. While the solution to the second is using a public key algorithm as advised by Ma et al. [36], this solution is not applicable to the first type. Furthermore, even many schemes using a public key algorithm still suffer from Attack II. The original reason is incorrectly deploying the public key algorithms. Thus, we proposed a reference model to guide the protocol designers to deploy the public key algorithms correctly. Our reference model is not the only way to deal with such problem, but it really is one of them. We hope that this work provides new insights into future research.

Notations and Abbreviations

U_i:	ith user
S:	Remote server
$\mathscr{A}$:	Malicious adversary
ID_i:	Identity of U_i
PW_i:	Password of U_i
x:	The secret key of S
y:	The secret number of S
$h(\cdot)$:	Collision-free one-way hash function
$\oplus$:	The bitwise XOR operation
$\|$:	The string concatenation operation
$\rightarrow$:	An insecure channel
$\Rightarrow$:	A secure channel.

Acknowledgments

The authors thank Dr. Wang Ding at Peking University for invaluable help. This research is supported by the National Natural Science Foundation of China (NSFC) under Grant no. 61401038 and 2016 Guangdong Provincial Science and Technology Department Frontier and Key Technology Innovation Project under Grant no. 2016B010110002.

References

[1] Z. Xia, Y. Zhu, X. Sun, Z. Qin, and K. Ren, "Towards Privacy-preserving Content-based Image Retrieval in Cloud Computing," *IEEE Transactions on Information Forensics and Security*, vol. 11, no. 11, pp. 2594–2608, 2016.

[2] Z. Fu, K. Ren, J. Shu, X. Sun, and F. Huang, "Enabling personalized search over encrypted outsourced data with efficiency improvement," *IEEE Transactions on Parallel and Distributed Systems*, vol. 27, no. 9, pp. 2546–2559, 2016.

[3] Z. Fu, X. Sun, S. Ji, and G. Xie, "Towards efficient content-aware search over encrypted outsourced data in cloud," in *Proceedings of the 35th Annual IEEE International Conference on Computer Communications (INFOCOM '16)*, pp. 1–9, San Francisco, Calif, USA, April 2016.

[4] Q. Jiang, J. Ma, F. Wei, Y. Tian, J. Shen, and Y. Yang, "An untraceable temporal-credential-based two-factor authentication scheme using ecc for wireless sensor networks," *Journal of Network & Computer Applications*, vol. 76, pp. 37–48, 2016.

[5] L. Lamport, "Password authentication with insecure communication," *Communications of the ACM*, vol. 24, no. 11, pp. 770–772, 1981.

[6] A. Shimizu, "Dynamic password authentication method using a one-way function," *Systems and Computers in Japan*, vol. 22, no. 7, pp. 32–40, 1991.

[7] S.-P. Shieh, W.-H. Yang, and H.-M. Sun, "An authentication protocol without trusted third party," *IEEE Communications Letters*, vol. 1, no. 3, pp. 87–89, 1997.

[8] T. Hwang, "Password authentication using public-key encryption," in *Proceedings of IEEE Int. Carnahan Conf. Security Technol.*, pp. 141–144, 1983.

[9] T. Hwang, Y. Chen, and C. J. Laih, "Non-interactive password authentications without password tables," in *Proceedings of IEEE Region 10 Conference on Computer and Communication Systems Conference*, pp. 429–431, Hong Kong.

[10] C.-C. Chang and T.-C. Wu, "Remote password authentication with smart cards," *IEE Proceedings E: Computers and Digital Techniques*, vol. 138, no. 3, pp. 165–168, 1991.

[11] D. Wang and P. Wang, "Two Birds with One Stone: Two-Factor Authentication with Security Beyond Conventional Bound," *IEEE Transactions on Dependable and Secure Computing*, pp. 1-1.

[12] X. Huang, Y. Xiang, A. Chonka, J. Zhou, and R. H. Deng, "A generic framework for three-factor authentication: Preserving security and privacy in distributed systems," *IEEE Transactions on Parallel and Distributed Systems*, vol. 22, no. 8, pp. 1390–1397, 2011.

[13] D. He, S. Zeadally, B. Xu, and X. Huang, "An Efficient Identity-Based Conditional Privacy-Preserving Authentication Scheme for Vehicular Ad Hoc Networks," *IEEE Transactions on Information Forensics and Security*, vol. 10, no. 12, pp. 2681–2691, 2015.

[14] D. Wang, N. Wang, P. Wang, and S. Qing, "Preserving privacy for free: Efficient and provably secure two-factor authentication scheme with user anonymity," *Information Sciences*, vol. 321, Article ID 11496, pp. 162–178, 2015.

[15] V. Odelu, A. K. Das, and A. Goswami, "A Secure Biometrics-Based Multi-Server Authentication Protocol Using Smart Cards," *IEEE Transactions on Information Forensics and Security*, vol. 10, no. 9, pp. 1953–1966, 2015.

[16] C. Yuan, X. Sun, and R. Lv, "Fingerprint liveness detection based on multi-scale LPQ and PCA," *China Communications*, vol. 13, no. 7, pp. 60–65, 2016.

[17] D. He and D. Wang, "Robust Biometrics-Based Authentication Scheme for Multiserver Environment," *IEEE Systems Journal*, vol. 9, no. 3, pp. 816–823, 2015.

[18] M. L. Das, A. Saxena, and V. P. Gulati, "A dynamic ID-based remote user authentication scheme," *IEEE Transactions on Consumer Electronics*, vol. 50, no. 2, pp. 629–631, 2004.

[19] M. Khan and S. Kim, "Cryptanalysis and security enhancement of a more efficient & secure dynamic id-based remote user authentication scheme," *Computer Communications*, vol. 34, no. 3, pp. 305–309, 2011.

[20] Y.-F. Chang, W.-L. Tai, and H.-C. Chang, "Untraceable dynamic-identity-based remote user authentication scheme with verifiable password update," *International Journal of Communication Systems*, vol. 27, no. 11, pp. 3430–3440, 2014.

[21] H.-Y. Chien and C.-H. Chen, "A remote authentication scheme preserving user anonymity," in *19th International Conference on Advanced Information Networking and Applications, AINA 2005*, pp. 245–248, twn, March 2005.

[22] Y.-Y. Wang, J.-Y. Liu, F.-X. Xiao, and J. Dan, "A more efficient and secure dynamic ID-based remote user authentication scheme," *Computer Communications*, vol. 32, no. 4, pp. 583–585, 2009.

[23] T. H. Kim, C. Kim, and I. Park, "Side channel analysis attacks using AM demodulation on commercial smart cards with SEED," *Journal of Systems and Software*, vol. 85, no. 12, pp. 2899–2908, 2012.

[24] K. Nohl, D. Evans, S. Starbug, and H. Plötz, "Reverse-engineering a cryptographic rfid tag," in *Proceedings of USENIX Security*, pp. 185–193, San Jose, CA, USA.

[25] T. S. Messerges, E. A. Dabbish, and R. . Sloan, "Examining smart-card security under the threat of power analysis attacks," *Institute of Electrical and Electronics Engineers. Transactions on Computers*, vol. 51, no. 5, pp. 541–552, 2002.

[26] A. Moradi, A. Barenghi, T. Kasper, and C. Paar, "On the vulnerability of FPGA bitstream encryption against power analysis attacks: Extracting keys from Xilinx Virtex-II FPGAs," in *18th ACM Conference on Computer and Communications Security, CCS'11*, pp. 111–123, usa, October 2011.

[27] X. Li, W. Qiu, D. Zheng, K. Chen, and J. Li, "Anonymity enhancement on robust and efficient password-authenticated key agreement using smart cards," *IEEE Transactions on Industrial Electronics*, vol. 57, no. 2, pp. 793–800, 2010.

[28] J. L. Tsai, N. W. Lo, and T. C. Wu, "Novel anonymous authentication scheme using smart cards," *IEEE Transactions on Industrial Informatics*, vol. 9, no. 4, pp. 2004–2013, 2013.

[29] D. Wang, D. He, P. Wang, and C.-H. Chu, "Anonymous Two-Factor Authentication in Distributed Systems: Certain Goals Are Beyond Attainment," *IEEE Transactions on Dependable and Secure Computing*, vol. 12, no. 4, pp. 428–442, 2015.

[30] R. Song, "Advanced smart card based password authentication protocol," *Computer Standards and Interfaces*, vol. 32, no. 5-6, pp. 321–325, 2010.

[31] J. Xu, W.-T. Zhu, and D.-G. Feng, "An improved smart card based password authentication scheme with provable security," *Computer Standards and Interfaces*, vol. 31, no. 4, pp. 723–728, 2009.

[32] K. S. Sandeep, K. S. Anil, and S. Kuldip, "An improvement of xu et al.'s authentication scheme using smart cards," in *Proceedings of the ACM 3th Bangalore Conference*, vol. 1, pp. 240–245, Bangalore, India, 2010.

[33] B.-L. Chen, W.-C. Kuo, and L.-C. Wuu, "Robust smart-card-based remote user password authentication scheme," *International Journal of Communication Systems*, vol. 27, no. 2, pp. 377–389, 2014.

[34] S. Kumari and M. K. Khan, "Cryptanalysis and improvement of a robust smart-card-based remote user password authentication scheme," *International Journal of Communication Systems*, vol. 27, no. 12, pp. 3939–3955, 2014.

[35] X. Li, J. Niu, M. Khurram Khan, and J. Liao, "An enhanced smart card based remote user password authentication scheme," *Journal of Network and Computer Applications*, vol. 36, no. 5, pp. 1365–1371, 2013.

[36] C.-G. Ma, D. Wang, and S.-D. Zhao, "Security flaws in two improved remote user authentication schemes using smart cards," *International Journal of Communication Systems*, vol. 27, no. 10, pp. 2215–2227, 2014.

[37] D. Wang, Q. Gu, H. Cheng, and P. Wang, "The request for better measurement: A comparative evaluation of two-factor authentication schemes," in *Proceedings of 11th ACM Asia Conference on Computer and Communications Security, ASIA CCS*, pp. 475–486, China, June 2016.

[38] Y. Wang, "Password protected smart card and memory stick authentication against off-line dictionary attacks," *IFIP Advances in Information and Communication Technology*, vol. 376, pp. 489–500, 2012.

[39] R. Madhusudhan and R. C. Mittal, "Dynamic ID-based remote user password authentication schemes using smart cards: a review," *Journal of Network and Computer Applications*, vol. 35, no. 4, pp. 1235–1248, 2012.

[40] X. Li, Y. Xiong, J. Ma, and W. Wang, "An enhanced and security dynamic identity based authentication protocol for multi-server architecture using smart cards," *Journal of Network & Computer Applications*, vol. 35, no. 2, pp. 763–769, 2012.

[41] D. He, S. Zeadally, N. Kumar, and W. Wu, "Efficient and Anonymous Mobile User Authentication Protocol Using Self-Certified Public Key Cryptography for Multi-Server Architectures," *IEEE Transactions on Information Forensics and Security*, vol. 11, no. 9, pp. 2052–2064, 2016.

[42] S. Kumari, M. K. Khan, X. Li, and F. Wu, "Design of a user anonymous password authentication scheme without smart card," *International Journal of Communication Systems*, vol. 29, no. 3, pp. 441–458, 2016.

[43] K.-H. Yeh, "A lightweight authentication scheme with user untraceability," *Frontiers of Information Technology and Electronic Engineering*, vol. 16, no. 4, pp. 259–271, 2015.

[44] D. Kang, J. Jung, J. Mun, D. Lee, Y. Choi, and D. Won, "Efficient and robust user authentication scheme that achieve user anonymity with a markov chain," *Security & Communication Networks*, 2016.

[45] B. Djellali, K. Belarbi, A. Chouarfia, and P. Lorenz, "User authentication scheme preserving anonymity for ubiquitous devices," *Security and Communication Networks*, vol. 8, no. 17, pp. 3131–3141, 2015.

[46] S. D. Kaul and A. K. Awasthi, "Security Enhancement of an Improved Remote User Authentication Scheme with Key Agreement," *Wireless Personal Communications*, pp. 1–17, 2016.

[47] Q. Jiang, J. Ma, and F. Wei, "On the security of a privacy-aware authentication scheme for distributed mobile cloud computing services," *IEEE Systems Journal*, 2016.

[48] X. Huang, Y. Xiang, E. Bertino, J. Zhou, and L. Xu, "Robust multi-factor authentication for fragile communications," *IEEE Transactions on Dependable and Secure Computing*, vol. 11, no. 6, pp. 568–581, 2014.

[49] D. Wang, Z. Zhang, P. Wang, J. Yan, and X. Huang, "Targeted Online Password Guessing," in *Proceedings of ACM CCS 16*, pp. 1242–1254, Vienna, Austria, October 2016.

[50] D. Wang and P. Wang, "On the implications of zipfs law in passwords," *Proceedings of ESORICS*, pp. 111–131, 2016.

[51] S. H. Islam, "Design and analysis of an improved smartcard-based remote user password authentication scheme," *International Journal of Communication Systems*, vol. 29, no. 11, pp. 1708–1719, 2016.

[52] D. Wang, C. Ma1, and P. Wu, "Secure password-based remote user authentication scheme with non-tamper resistant smart cards," in *Proceedings of DBSec*, vol. 7371, pp. 114–121, France, Paris, 2012.

[53] H. Zhu, "Cryptanalysis and Improvement of a Mobile Dynamic ID Authenticated Key Agreement Scheme Based on Chaotic Maps," *Wireless Personal Communications*, vol. 85, no. 4, pp. 2141–2156, 2015.

[54] J. Wei, W. Liu, and X. Hu, "Secure and efficient smart card based remote user password authentication scheme," *International Journal of Network Security*, vol. 18, no. 4, pp. 782–792, 2016.

[55] Q. Jiang, J. Ma, and Y. Tian, "Cryptanalysis of smart-card-based password authenticated key agreement protocol for session initiation protocol of Zhang et al.," *International Journal of Communication Systems*, vol. 28, no. 7, pp. 1340–1351, 2015.

[56] K. Marimuthu and R. Saravanan, "A secure remote user mutual authentication scheme using smart cards," *Journal of Information Security & Applications*, vol. 19, no. (4-5), pp. 282–294, 2014.

[57] T. Maitra, M. Obaidat, R. Amin, S. Islam, S. Chaudhry, and D. Giri, "A robust elgamal-based password-authentication protocol using smart card for client-server communication," *International Journal of Communication Systems*, 2016.

5

Remotely Exploiting AT Command Attacks on ZigBee Networks

Ivan Vaccari, Enrico Cambiaso, and Maurizio Aiello

National Research Council (CNR), IEIIT Institute, Via De Marini 6, 16149 Genova, Italy

Correspondence should be addressed to Enrico Cambiaso; enrico.cambiaso@iciit.cnr.it

Academic Editor: Wojciech Mazurczyk

Internet of Things networks represent an emerging phenomenon bringing connectivity to common sensors. Due to the limited capabilities and to the sensitive nature of the devices, security assumes a crucial and primary role. In this paper, we report an innovative and extremely dangerous threat targeting IoT networks. The attack is based on Remote AT Commands exploitation, providing a malicious user with the possibility of reconfiguring or disconnecting IoT sensors from the network. We present the proposed attack and evaluate its efficiency by executing tests on a real IoT network. Results demonstrate how the threat can be successfully executed and how it is able to focus on the targeted nodes, without affecting other nodes of the network.

1. Introduction

The Internet is today adopted for a wide range of different purposes and by several kinds of entities, ranging from banking and stock market sectors adoption to personal use for social networking and web surfing. The Internet is indeed populated by billions of devices of different nature. In the last years, we have seen the appearance of several categories of always connected devices: smartphones, tablets, smartwatches, and healthcare devices are today only a few kinds of components of the global network. We are today experiencing a new emerging trend related to the evolution of common "analog" sensors, making them connect to each other, creating a "parallel" network based on machine-to-machine communications.

In this context, the term Internet of Things (IoT) represents a general concept relative to the ability of common sensors to collect data from the real world and hence share the retrieved information across a network, by communicating with other connected devices. IoT networks are today deployed for different purposes. The most known and adopted ones are the home automation/domotics and the industrial (Industry 4.0) contexts: while in a domotic context IoT networks are used to provide connectivity to common and security devices (light bulbs, internal cameras, fire sensors, etc.), in an Industry 4.0 scenario, IoT is used to monitor, control, inform, and automate production

processes. In order to communicate on the network, IoT devices support different communication protocols, such as Industrial Ethernet [1], Wi-Fi [2], ZigBee [3], and Z-Wave [4].

Our research, presented in this paper, investigates security aspects of IoT networks. We focus on ZigBee, a communication protocol ensuring low power consumption and characterized by low data transmission rates. During our study, we found important security issues related to a ZigBee based system and, potentially, to other IoT protocols. We identified the possibility of sending Remote AT Commands, where AT means "attention," to a connected sensor, in order to reconfigure the device, for instance, by making it join a different malicious network and hence forward captured data to the enemy. We evaluate the possibility of perpetrating a successful attack by setting up a network laboratory composed of XBee devices (XBee is one of the most adopted ZigBee radio modules in the Do-It-Yourself (DIY) scenario [5]). We describe the exposure to Remote AT Commands threats by focusing on evaluating efficiency and performance characteristics of this innovative attack.

The focus of our work is on the proposal of an innovative cyberattack. This may result in an unconventional and not needed activity. Nevertheless, especially in the research field, it is well known that offence research is as needed as defense research, in order to properly master a field and better prepare to counter cyber-criminal activities [6, 7].

The remaining of the paper focuses on the presentation of the innovative discovered threat and it is structured as follows. Section 2 reports the structure of the ZigBee protocol. Section 3 reports related work on the topic, while Section 4 reports our contribution on Remote AT Command exploitation. Then, Section 5 exposes the adopted testbed and obtained results by executing the attack on a controlled environment. Finally, Section 7 concludes the paper and reports possible extensions of the work.

2. The ZigBee Protocol

ZigBee is a wireless standard introduced by the ZigBee Alliance in 2004. It is based on the IEEE 802.15.4 standard, used in the Wireless Personal Area Networks (WPAN) context [8]. ZigBee is designed for embedded systems, often characterized by extremely low power consumption and low-rate transfers requirements [9]. The protocol is indeed able to minimize battery replacement frequency (up to 2 years) and to provide a communication rate up to 250 kbps, for a coverage radius up to 1000 meters. Figure 1 depicts the ZigBee stack protocol.

The physical layer of the IEEE 802.15.4 standard manages modulation and demodulation operations. Particularly, ZigBee supports three different frequencies:

(i) 2.4 GHz with support to 16 different channels, providing a maximum communication rate of 250 kbps (used worldwide)

(ii) 868 MHz with support to 1 channel and a maximum data rate of 20 kbps (used in Europe)

(iii) 915 MHz with support to 10 channels and 40 kbps of communication rate (used in US)

Since they work on the same frequency, in case of 2.4 GHz adoption, there may be interferences with existent Wi-Fi networks [10].

The MAC layer, also implemented in IEEE 802.15.4, takes care of ensuring a reliable and secure communication, by implementing a Carrier Sense Multiple Access with Collision Avoidance (CSMA/CA) to control access to the physical level [11].

The network layer of the ZigBee protocol implements instead network topologies, new devices management, and security handling. Particularly, ZigBee supports three different network topologies:

(i) A star topology, where each node communicates with a central node

(ii) A tree topology, where central nodes of different networks are connected with a bus network

(iii) A mesh topology, where all the nodes are connected to each other

Mesh networks are the most interesting ones: in this case, ZigBee implements ad hoc routing algorithms to automatically rearrange communications if a node of the network is disconnected [12].

The Application Framework layer represents the user interface and it is composed of three main components:

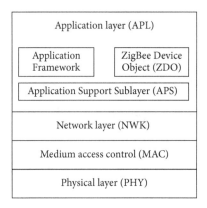

FIGURE 1: The ZigBee stack protocol.

(i) Application Support Sublayer (APS), providing an interface between network and application layers; moreover, it controls and manages data sent and received by other protocol layers to ensure proper packet transmission and encryption

(ii) ZigBee Device Objects (ZDO), an application object responsible for the initialization procedures of the APS and the ZigBee network layer to perform discovery of services and new nodes in the network

(iii) Application Framework (AF), an execution environment for "application objects," each ones identified by an endpoint address from 1 to 254 (0 is reserved for ZigBee Device Object (ZDO), 255 for broadcast messages): application objects are usually implemented by different manufacturers. In order to enhance products interoperability, the ZigBee Alliance has published different application profiles. The most common ones are home automation, smart energy, light link, and green power [8]

2.1. ZigBee Node Types. ZigBee supports different kind of devices with different functionalities:

(i) ZigBee end-device (ZED): it represents the sensor, usually in sleep mode most of the time and periodically waking up in order to communicate with the other nodes of the network.

(ii) ZigBee router (ZR): it is an optional node used to route packets on the network.

(iii) ZigBee coordinator (ZC): it is a ZigBee router with gateway functions used to manage the network.

While on the same network it is common to have several different ZED nodes and different routers, a single coordinator is found.

2.2. ZigBee Security. As many other wireless networks, like Wi-Fi [13] or ad hoc wireless sensor network [14, 15], security assumes a crucial role in the ZigBee protocol. The encryption algorithm used in ZigBee is Advanced Encryption Standard (AES) with a 128-bit key. Such algorithm, considered extremely secure and reliable, guarantees confidentiality and authenticity on wireless communications [16].

ZigBee provides two different security profiles [17]: Standard Security, the basic security profile, rarely adopted because of its exposure to attacks, and High Security, mostly used since it guarantees greater security during communications. Particularly, while considering the standard security profile, the network key is shared in clear text (unencrypted), it is encrypted with the link key in case of high security profile adoption. The link key is one of the security keys adopted by ZigBee:

(i) Master key is usually hardcoded on the device or shared out-of-band. It is needed in order to retrieve the other keys but it is never directly sent on the network.

(ii) Network key is a key shared by all the devices connected to the same network. It is generated by the Trust Center and it can be sent on the network as plain text or in encrypted form, depending on the adopted security profile.

(iii) Link key is a key generated using the master key and adopted for communications between two different devices on the same network.

In a ZigBee network, if communication is unencrypted, an attacker may access all information of the network and may even sniff/capture exchanged packets. Otherwise, if communication is encrypted, a malicious user may only perform attacks that do not require access to the network, such as denial of service or jamming, since it is very difficult to retrieve the ZigBee adopted network key and hence decrypt exchanged packets.

3. Related Work

Because of the wide adoption of the ZigBee protocol, one of the most important concerns is related to ZigBee based networks protection. Many security experts have studied the protocol and identified several threats able to target such systems. In this context, an important contribution is provided by Wright, the creator of Killerbee, a framework including a set of tools able to exploit the ZigBee protocol analyzing network traffic and processing the recovered packets [18]. Although such software is extremely dangerous, its specific hardware requirements (such as Atmel AVR USB Stick or TelosB mote models) limit the execution of properly equipped attackers. Thanks to Killerbee, it is possible to execute several attacks against a ZigBee network: for instance, it is possible to retrieve the network key when sent as clear text. Such retrieval requires the attacker to be located in proximity of the network nodes, in order to sniff the key exchange. Killerbee also includes other threats such as replay [19] or manipulation/injection [20].

Other attacks focus on denial of service (DoS) activities, executed in order to disconnect a node from the network. DoS attacks are popular on the Internet [7] and they are extending to last generation fields such as mobile [21], SDN [22], and IoT [23]. Considering such kind of threats

perpetrated against a ZigBee system, several attacks target battery powered sensors in order to reduce the lifetime of the device. In this context, the ZigBee end-device sabotage attack [24] is executed by keeping sensors active when a broadcast message is sent every time the device wakes up from the sleep status. In this way, a sensor under attack is forced to reply the malicious user, hence delaying the next sleep and discharging the batteries quickly. A similar threat, the ghost attack proposed by Shila, reduces the lifetime of the targeted device by sending several crafted bogus messages to the victim [25]. Vidgren et al. demonstrate instead how it is possible to discharge the batteries of a sensor if the attacker knows the adopted sensor polling rate [26]. Pacheco et al. investigate instead DDoS attacks feasibility against IoT environments [27]. Another DoS attack proposed by Vidgren et al. exploits the ZigBee frame counter. Such counter is commonly used by different network protocols to prevent threats such as replay attacks. Concerning ZigBee frame counter exploitation, a malicious user could send a parameter containing the maximum allowed frame counter value (sized 4 bytes), hence forcing the victim to set the counter to the received value. If Message Integrity Check [28] is not implemented by the victim, each packet received after the malicious one will be discarded by the victim since it will present a lower frame counter [26].

Another attack, known as same-nonce attack [29], can be carried out only if the Trust Center, a device providing reliability during the key exchange stage, provides the same-nonce encrypt with the same network key for two consecutive times. In a ZigBee network, coordinators have role of Trust Center. In this scenario, an attacker may retrieve part of the plain text simply calculating the XOR between the two sniffed packets. Although this situation rarely happens, it is possible to force this behavior by causing a power failure, for example, by discharging batteries of a Trust Center. In this case, Trust Center resets the nonce to its default value and it is possible to send a packet with the same nonce [26].

Considering other threats, ZigBee networks are also vulnerable to attacks known as Sinkhole and Wormhole, proposed by Karnain and Zakaria [30]. During a Sinkhole attack, a malicious node attracts the network packets with the aim of creating confusion in the routing phase. Instead, during a Wormhole attack, the malicious user receives packets at one point in the network and then replays these packets in other areas to interfere with all network functionality. Also, while Krivtsova et al. propose the broadcast storm attack clogging the network by sending numerous broadcast packets [31], Yang et al. introduced two attacks against ZigBee, known as Absolute Slot Number (ASN) and time synchronization tree attack. Considering that the time is split into different slots/ASNs of fixed length, during an ASN attack, since current ASN value is sent during communication, the legitimate nodes may get an incorrect ASN value from the attacker that sends on the network a broadcast message with a wrong ASN value. In this way, a node would not be able to communicate on the network since the wrong ASN packet would lead to a communication interruption. In time synchronization tree attack, the malicious user may send bogus DAG Information Objects (DIO) packets [32] to the neighbors with the aim of desynchronizing their connections with the network [32]. A Sybil attack, proposed by Lee et al., is launched by an attacker that acquires multiple identities on the network. The aim of this attack is to convince the other devices that the malicious node is a legitimate node. In this way, a malicious node may, for example, access all services of the network or identify itself as a ZigBee router [33]. Another type of attack is performed if the enemy can physically access a ZigBee device. Indeed, the malicious user may perform a firmware dump in order to extrapolate the network key stored/hardcoded in the device [34].

Other attacks focus instead on specific version of ZigBee. In this context, a particular version of the ZigBee protocol, called ZigBee Light Link, used, for instance, by Philips Hue bulbs [35], has been exploited different times. Indeed, Gent found that the adopted ZigBee network key can be retrieved if an attacker can sniff the reinitialization process accomplished by the bulbs after a reset and if he knows the ZigBee Light Link master key [36]. Another attack on ZigBee Light Link is proposed by Ronen et al., creating a worm that automatically infects adjacent bulbs, building a custom infected firmware, and being deployed as a fake OTA update [37].

Many works focus instead on ZigBee protection. For instance, a solution to detect the Sybil attack is proposed by Marian and Mircea, presenting an interesting protection system using RSSI derived metrics to detect a Sybil attack by computing the location of a node and then classifying it as malicious or not [38]. Al Baalbaki et al. introduced instead an Anomaly Behavior Analysis System (ABAS) for the ZigBee protocol based on network traffic analysis. After detection is triggered, ABAS can classify the attack as known or unknown using information like packets origin or destination [39]. Another protection algorithm proposed by Jokar and Leung and known as HANIDPS implements machine learning based intrusion detection and prevention system. HANIDPS analyzes the network traffic and compares it with a normal in order to detect a running threat [40]. A similar approach may analyze energy consumption [41] to identify running attacks. Cui et al. proposed instead a fuzzing method based on finite state machines. A fuzzy test is implemented by injecting different testing cases into the system in order to detect vulnerabilities [42]. A defense against impulsive noise is proposed by Jia and Meng, implementing a system using a noise filtering processing activity in two steps: while during the first step an estimate of the noise is computed, in the second one, a noise cancellation is accomplished, in order to state if the estimate is suspect or not [43].

During our research work, we have studied security aspects of ZigBee based IoT networks by initially studying the protocol, thus analyzing the major threats affecting it, hence studying possible protection systems and approaches. During our study, we have discovered the proposed threat and, to the best of our knowledge, we noticed that a vulnerability analysis focused on AT Command exploitation is still missing. Nevertheless, this vulnerability should be considered extremely innovative and particularly dangerous, since it allows malicious users to retrieve/forward sensitive information or manipulate nodes functionality. Our work focuses on the proposal of the innovative Remote AT Command attack,

explained in the next section, by illustrating the proposed threat and evaluating its efficiency.

4. Remote Control Exploitability

In order to properly investigate ZigBee security, we have studied the protocol and analyzed communication flows, considering the different types of packets supported by ZigBee. While, at first, we focused on packets containing data sent from the coordinator to the end-device, later, we have also analyzed other packets exchanged in the network. In this context, we found that, at the MAC layer, it is possible to send Remote AT Commands. By working at such lower layer, received packets are not processed at the application layer; hence, it may not be possible to access the packet content to avoid interpretation, except from the device manufacturer.

During our research work, we identified a particular vulnerability affecting AT Commands capabilities implemented in IoT sensor networks. Our work focuses on the exploitation of such weakness. AT Commands are specific packets, historically adopted by old generation modems to interface with the device, today used by radio modules such as XBee [44], ESP8266 (more information is available at http://esatjournals.net/ijret/2017v06/i01/IJRET20170601027.pdf), or ETRX3 [45] to configure parameters like connection type, network identifier, device name on the network, or destination address for a communication. AT Commands are today supported by many devices of different nature, providing different functionalities and hence commands. For instance, modules that provide connectivity support AT Command packets for network parameters configuration, while other modules may use these packets to alter light intensity of light bulbs.

For our research, as previously mentioned, we focused on XBee modules. Such modules, widely adopted around the world, especially in DIY contexts, implement two different AT Command packets, related to request and response operations, respectively. Concerning XBee modules, these packets can be sent remotely: we talk in this case of Remote AT Commands. Such packets belong to the (IEEE 802.15.4) MAC layer and they are interpreted by the (XBee) module automatically. Therefore, by being such interpretation demanded to the device firmware, and being such firmware provided by the manufacturer, Digi International, it is not possible to avoid implicit Remote AT Commands interpretation. In order to execute the proposed attack, the AT Command functionality of XBee has to be exploited. XBee supports several AT Command packets (more information is available at https://www.sparkfun.com/datasheets/Wireless/Zigbee/XBee-Datasheet.pdf). Particularly, for our aim, we have used ATID commands to target sensors (in general, other commands/approaches may be used for different purposes: e.g., to make the sensor join a different network, to forward (sensitive) data to a different malicious receiver, and to disable data encryption). ATID is used by XBee modules to set the network identifier. During the proposed Remote AT Command attack, the malicious user sends an ATID packet with a bogus identifier in order to make it join a different (inexistent, in our case) network.

In order to maliciously exploit Remote AT Command, it is assumed that the attacker is connected to the network of the target. In this case, the enemy may, for instance, disconnect an end-device from the ZigBee network and make it join a different (malicious) network and hence forward potentially sensitive data to third malicious parties. Given the nature of IoT end-devices, often associated with a critical data and operations, it may be obvious how a Remote AT Command attack represents a serious threat for the entire infrastructure.

5. Testbed

In this section, we report information about the tests we have conducted in order to validate the success and the efficiency of a Remote AT Command attack. In order to accomplish the tests, we have built a ZigBee test network, depicted in Figure 2.

The network is composed of a single ZigBee coordinator, two end-devices representing common sensors on the network, and a malicious user/node connected to the ZigBee network. As can be deduced from the figure, the attacker sends Remote AT Command packets only to one sensor and not to each device on the network. This implementation allows us to monitor the effects of the attack on the two sensors, hence evaluating the possibility of carrying out a successful attack without affecting targeted nodes. Indeed, we expect that, during a Remote AT Command attack, only the targeted sensor is affected by the threat, while other nodes keep working correctly (unless their behavior depends on the targeted sensor).

Considering the described scenario, we will now detail at first adopted hardware, hence reporting information about testbed configuration, finally exposing the obtained results.

5.1. Testbed Configuration. Different devices have been used to create ZigBee network to implement AT Command attack. For our aim, network components are composed as reported in the following:

(i) *Coordinator*, composed of a Raspberry Pi 3 equipped with an XBee USB Board and an XBee Series 2

(ii) *Targeted sensor*, composed of an Arduino UNO R3, equipped with an XBee Shield and an XBee Series 2

(iii) *Not targeted sensor*, composed of an Arduino UNO R3, equipped with an XBee Shield and an XBee Series 2

(iv) *Attacker*, composed of a Raspberry Pi 3 equipped with an XBee USB Board and an XBee Series 2

As the reader may notice, end-devices/sensors share the same hardware. Hence, our evaluation allows us to identify the efficiency of the attack on the targeted node, and simultaneously the possibility of avoiding side effects on other nodes (this is not possible, e.g., for jamming attacks).

Moreover, since XBee series 2 modules have low computational capacity, we adopted Arduino microcontrollers to generate and elaborate information, hence using XBee modules only for network communications. In order to

guarantee the sleep status of end-devices, a PIN Hibernation has been implemented [46] by connecting the 7th PIN of the XBee Shield to an Arduino digital PIN. In order to implement PIN Hibernation, $D7$ value, a PIN used to send and receive serial data, has been disabled (through XCTU XBee programming software). In order to test this vulnerability, the innovative attack is implemented and tested with this configuration: the attack was performed on only one sensor because by monitoring the network traffic is possible to verify the efficiency of this threat.

5.2. Network Nodes Implementation. Every 35 seconds, sensors are programmed to send a packet to the coordinator. Each packet contains a random generated number. After the message has been sent, the sensor device enters in sleep mode in order to reduce power consumption. Since the content of the message is not meaningful to us, the "random number" solution allows us to generate data to be transmitted on the network without requiring environmental sensors.

Figures 3 and 4 monitor the network traffic of the various XBee modules. Although we stated that a single packet is sent every 35 seconds, sending is relative to application layer packets, while the capture is relative to the entire ZigBee network stack. Although such capture includes additional (lower layers) packets (including, for instance, wake-up commands containing network node information and synchronization packets), it is representative of the network behavior of the sensor (e.g., we can see that, after the attack, no packets are sent by the victim node), while a capture focused on application layer packets/messages would produce single peaks missing useful information.

Data is received by the coordinator and shown to the user through an HTML based graphical interface, also reporting if sensors are correctly communicating with the coordinator. This environment is representative of a wide range of network types. For instance, sensors installed on a specific area/farm/company could be monitored through a similar approach, or industry machines and fire prevention systems may be part of a network system similar to the proposed one.

6. Results

Network traffic was analyzed from an external ZigBee device capturing data on the same channel used by the targeted network. From sniffed traffic, we are able to extrapolate communication flows of single hosts of the network.

Figures 3(a) and 3(b) report the network traffic flow of both targeted and not targeted sensors during a running attack. Traffic was monitored for 120 seconds and it is split into two phases: during the first 50 seconds, the attacker acts in a "passive" way, by scanning the ZigBee spectrum in order to identify the devices connected to the network and define the target. Instead, on the second "active" phase, the attacker sends Remote AT Command packets to the targeted sensor in order to perform the attack. Particularly, for our aim, the passive behavior is not intended as a "listen only" behavior. Instead, during this phase, the attacker does not send any malicious packet on the network. Therefore, we expect that

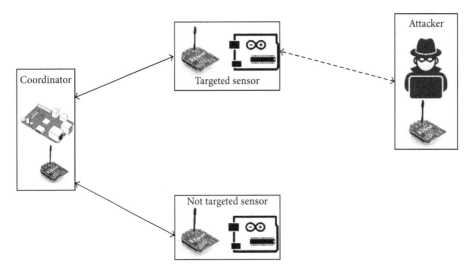

FIGURE 2: Test network.

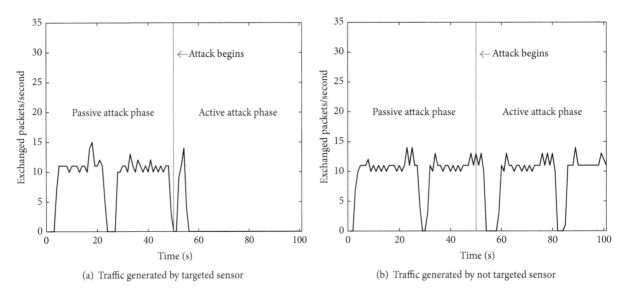

(a) Traffic generated by targeted sensor

(b) Traffic generated by not targeted sensor

FIGURE 3: Network traffic captured during attack execution.

detecting a malicious behavior during the passive phase is particularly difficult.

Figure 3(a) reports the traffic flow of the targeted sensor. By analyzing the graph, it is possible to notice that while the sensor is correctly working during the passive phase, a few seconds after the attack is (actively) performed, the device is disconnected from the network and its communication with the coordinator is interrupted. Therefore, the attack is successful on the targeted sensor.

Instead, Figure 3(b) reports the status of the nontargeted sensor during the attack. Particularly, it is possible to notice that the connection is maintained alive for the entire considered period. Indeed, since this sensor is not directly targeted by the attacker, Remote AT Commands are not received/interpreted; hence, the network parameters of the sensor are not altered by the attacker and communication capability of the sensor is maintained and not even

disturbed. This represents an important characteristic of the proposed threat, since it is able to only affect the targeted device, by making the attack not directly visible to the other sensors/devices. Such stealth behavior makes the attack more difficult to detect. Moreover, considering that device communication interruption may be related to external factors (e.g., battery drain, wireless noise, and malfunctioning device), the proposed attack should be considered a serious threat.

Figure 4 shows instead the captured attack traffic during the considered period.

By analyzing the passive phase of the attack, as previously mentioned, the enemy performs a scan of the network in order to identify each device connected to the network and choose the targeted device. Instead in the active attack phase, Remote AT Command packets are sent to the targeted sensor with the aim of disconnecting it from the network (by reconfiguring it). If we analyze the attack traffic flow, it

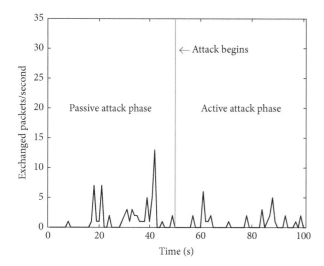

FIGURE 4: Traffic generated by attacker sensor.

is very difficult to distinguish a passive (hence, potentially legitimate) behavior from an active (malicious) one. Hence, detection of a running threat may require packet inspection or data flows interpretation (not easy to accomplish in case of encrypted traffic).

Although our testbed focuses on two network sensors/devices, the proposed Remote AT Commands attack is particularly scalable, due to the (minimum) requirements for the attacker (a single packet is sent to the victim to reconfigure it). Particularly, the time required to send such packet is minimal, so in case of multiple targeted sensors, the attack success is guaranteed. Of course, in case of extremely large amounts of targeted sensors, the effectiveness of the attack depends on the scan time: the attack is successful if the minimum "sleep time" of each sensor is larger than the average time required to target all the sensors.

7. Conclusion and Future Work

The proposed paper is focused on Internet of Things (IoT) environments security, by analyzing the possibility of carrying out a successful attack against a targeted node/sensor/device. During our work, we found a novel vulnerability affecting IoT devices: by exploiting a particular type of packet, Remote AT Command, it is possible to remotely reconfigure/program network nodes as the attacker wishes, hence compromising data communication security of the network.

By focusing on the ZigBee (wireless) protocol, we have described and implemented the proposed attack with the aim of interrupting the communication capabilities of a targeted device of the network. For our tests, we targeted XBee modules [44], able to communicate through the ZigBee protocol. Results show that the attack is successful and it is able to target a single node without affecting the other nodes of the network. Moreover, since the number of packets sent by the attacker is minimum, it is not easy to detect a running attack, without doing deep packet inspection. The attack is

therefore particularly dangerous, since it may compromise the security of an IoT network with minimum effort for the attacker. By comparing the effects of the proposed attack to other network based threats, they can be assimilated to denial of service, man-in-the-middle (traffic sniffing), or traffic redirection activities, in function of the strategy adopted by the attacker.

Future work on the topic may concern additional tests of the attack in large scale networks composed of different nodes, in order to identify the limits of the threat, in function of the sleeping/polling times adopted by the nodes. Considering instead the design of defense systems, additional extensions of the work may be directed to the implementation of efficient protection techniques able to defend an IoT system from a Remote AT Command attack. Since detection of a running threat may not be immediate, in order to protect a remote device from a Remote AT Command attack, it may be preferred to directly work on the (potentially vulnerable) nodes. In this context, three different approaches can be adopted, working at different levels:

(i) Firmware level: creation of a modified version of the firmware, implementing Remote AT Commands filtering or allowing AT Commands elaboration at the application layer

(ii) Device configuration level: providing to the user the ability to configure a device with disabled support to Remote AT Commands

(iii) External level: demanding protection capabilities to an external application program.

Each approach provides an efficient solution to protect the device. Nevertheless, some approaches may not be adopted (e.g., device configuration, if not available). Suggested implementations provide a possible protection for this innovative threat.

The first proposed solution (firmware level protection) requires a device firmware upgrade to allow total AT Command packet management, such as the ability to process only packets received by the coordinator or secure devices. Such solution would provide the user with the possibility of configuring the device in order to avoid implicit Remote AT Commands interpretation.

Since modifying a firmware may not be easy, and the source code must be open source, it is suggested to have simpler but equally effective solutions. The second solution (device configuration level protection) implements the ability to disable Remote AT Command support of the module, by implementing a specific setting able to disable automatic Remote AT Command interpretation (e.g., packets discard). In this way, the proposed threat would be ineffective.

The last proposed solution (external level protection) is the most interesting; the main purpose is to implement protection logics on the Arduino device by implementing a function at application layer. The aim of the function is to verify if the XBee module may be communicating on the network. In this case, just before the sensor is ready to communicate on the network, an internal check is accomplished.

Although the mentioned approaches may protect IoT modules and network sensors from this innovative attack, by ensuring data transmission security, their design implementation and evaluation are on the scope of further work on the topic.

Acknowledgments

This work has been supported by the following research projects: (i) My Health-My Data (MHMD) project has received funding from the European Union's Horizon 2020 Research and Innovation Programme under Grant agreement no. 732907; (ii) Advanced Networked Agents for Security and Trust Assessment in CPS/IoT Architectures (ANASTACIA) project has received funding from the European Union's Horizon 2020 Research and Innovation Programme under Grant agreement no. 731558.

References

[1] J. S. Rinaldi and P. S. Marshall, "Industrial ethernet," *ISA Press Release*, Article ID 945541, p. 04, 2004.

[2] L. Li, H. Xiaoguang, C. Ke, and H. Ketai, "The applications of WiFi-based Wireless Sensor Network in Internet of Things and Smart Grid," in *Proceedings of the 6th IEEE Conference on Industrial Electronics and Applications (ICIEA '11)*, pp. 789–793, IEEE, Beijing, China, June 2011.

[3] C. Fan, Z. Wen, F. Wang, and Y. Wu, "A middleware of internet of things(iot) based on Zigbee and RFID," in *Proceedings of the IET International Conference on Communication Technology and Application, ICCTA 2011*, pp. 732–736, October 2011.

[4] Z. W. Alliance, "The internet of things is powered by z-wave.(2016)," *Z-Wave Alliance*, vol. 28, p. 2016, 2016.

[5] R. Faludi, *Building Wireless Sensor Networks: with ZigBee, XBee, Arduino, and Processing*, O'Reilly Media, Inc., 2010.

[6] P. Farina, E. Cambiaso, G. Papaleo, and M. Aiello, "Are mobile botnets a possible threat? the case of SlowBot Net," *Computers & Security*, vol. 58, pp. 268–283, 2016.

[7] E. Cambiaso, G. Papaleo, G. Chiola, and M. Aiello, "Slow DoS attacks: definition and categorisation," *International Journal of Trust Management in Computing and Communications*, vol. 1, no. 3/4, p. 300, 2013.

[8] C. M. Ramya, M. Shanmugaraj, and R. Prabakaran, "Study on ZigBee technology," in *Proceedings of the 3rd International Conference on Electronics Computer Technology (ICECT '11)*, pp. 297–301, IEEE, Kanyakumari, India, April 2011.

[9] A. Dementyev, S. Hodges, S. Taylor, and J. Smith, "Power consumption analysis of Bluetooth Low Energy, ZigBee and ANT sensor nodes in a cyclic sleep scenario," in *Proceedings of the IEEE International Wireless Symposium (IWS '13)*, April 2013.

[10] M. A. Sarijari, M. S. Abdullah, A. Lo, and R. A. Rashid, "Experimental studies of the ZigBee frequency agility mechanism in home area networks," in *Proceedings of the 39th Annual IEEE Conference on Local Computer Networks, LCN 2014*, pp. 711–717, September 2014.

[11] P. Baronti, P. Pillai, V. W. C. Chook, S. Chessa, A. Gotta, and Y. F. Hu, "Wireless sensor networks: a survey on the state of the art and the 802.15.4 and ZigBee standards," *Computer Communications*, vol. 30, no. 7, pp. 1655–1695, 2007.

[12] J. Li, X. Zhu, N. Tang, and J. Sui, "Study on ZigBee network architecture and routing algorithm," in *Proceedings of the 2nd International Conference on Signal Processing Systems (ICSPS '10)*, vol. 2, pp. V2-389–V2-393, Dalian, China, July 2010.

[13] S. Gold, "Cracking wireless networks," *Network Security*, vol. 2011, no. 11, pp. 14–18, 2011.

[14] E. Cayirci and C. Rong, *Security in Wireless Ad Hoc and Sensor Networks*, John Wiley & Sons, 2008.

[15] L. Caviglione and F. Davoli, "Peer-to-peer middleware for bandwidth allocation in sensor networks," *IEEE Communications Letters*, vol. 9, no. 3, pp. 285–287, 2005.

[16] L. Caviglione, M. Gaggero, E. Cambiaso, and M. Aiello, "Measuring the Energy Consumption of Cyber Security," *IEEE Communications Magazine*, vol. 55, no. 7, pp. 58–63, 2017.

[17] G. Dini and M. Tiloca, "Considerations on security in Zig-Bee networks," in *Proceedings of the 2010 IEEE International Conference on Sensor Networks, Ubiquitous, and Trustworthy Computing, SUTC 2010, 2010 IEEE International Workshop on Ubiquitous and Mobile Computing, UMC 2010*, pp. 58–65, June 2010.

[18] J. Wright, *Killerbee: practical zigbee exploitation framework*, 2009.

[19] B. Stelte and G. D. Rodosek, "Thwarting attacks on ZigBee - Removal of the KillerBee stinger," in *Proceedings of the 2013 9th International Conference on Network and Service Management, CNSM 2013 and its three collocated Workshops - ICQT 2013, SVM 2013 and SETM 2013*, pp. 219–226, October 2013.

[20] A. Biswas, A. Alkhalid, T. Kunz, and C.-H. Lung, "A lightweight defence against the Packet in Packet attack in ZigBee networks," in *Proceedings of the 2012 IFIP Wireless Days, WD 2012*, November 2012.

[21] R. H. Jhaveri, S. J. Patel, and D. C. Jinwala, "DoS attacks in mobile ad hoc networks: A survey," in *Proceedings of the 2012 2nd International Conference on Advanced Computing and Communication Technologies, ACCT 2012*, pp. 535–541, January 2012.

[22] R. Kandoi and M. Antikainen, "Denial-of-service attacks in OpenFlow SDN networks," in *Proceedings of the 14th IFIP/IEEE International Symposium on Integrated Network Management, IM 2015*, pp. 1322–1326, May 2015.

[23] H. Suo, J. Wan, C. Zou, and J. Liu, "Security in the internet of things: a review," in *Proceedings of the International Conference on Computer Science and Electronics Engineering (ICCSEE '12)*, pp. 648–651, Hangzhou, China, March 2012.

[24] O. Olawumi, K. Haataja, M. Asikainen, N. Vidgren, and P. Toivanen, "Three practical attacks against ZigBee security: Attack scenario definitions, practical experiments, countermeasures, and lessons learned," in *Proceedings of the 2014 14th International Conference on Hybrid Intelligent Systems, HIS 2014*, pp. 199–206, December 2014.

[25] D. M. Shila, "Ghost-in-the-wireless: Energy depletion attack on zigbee".

[26] N. Vidgren, K. Haataja, J. L. Patiño-Andres, J. J. Ramírez-Sanchis, and P. Toivanen, "Security threats in ZigBee-enabled systems: Vulnerability evaluation, practical experiments, countermeasures, and lessons learned," in *Proceedings of the 46th Annual Hawaii International Conference on System Sciences, HICSS 2013*, pp. 5132–5138, January 2013.

[27] L. A. B. Pacheco, J. J. C. Gondim, P. A. S. Barreto, and E. Alchieri, "Evaluation of distributed denial of service threat in the internet of things," in *Proceedings of the 15th IEEE International Sympo-*

sium on Network Computing and Applications, NCA 2016, pp. 89–92, November 2016.

[28] H. Li, Z. Jia, and X. Xue, "Application and analysis of ZigBee security services specification," in *Proceedings of the 2nd International Conference on Networks Security, Wireless Communications and Trusted Computing, NSWCTC 2010*, pp. 494–497, April 2010.

[29] N. Sastry and D. Wagner, "Security considerations for IEEE 802.15.4 networks," in *Proceedings of the 3rd ACM Workshop on Wireless Security (WiSe '04)*, pp. 32–42, ACM, October 2004.

[30] M. A. B. Karnain and Z. B. Zakaria, "A review on ZigBee security enhancement in smart home environment," in *Proceedings of the 2nd IEEE International Conference on Information Science and Security, ICISS 2015*, December 2015.

[31] I. Krivtsova, I. Lebedev, M. Sukhoparov et al., "Implementing a broadcast storm attack on a mission-critical wireless sensor network," *Lecture Notes in Computer Science (including subseries Lecture Notes in Artificial Intelligence and Lecture Notes in Bioinformatics): Preface*, vol. 9674, pp. 297–308, 2016.

[32] W. Yang, Q. Wang, Y. Wan, and J. He, "Security Vulnerabilities and Countermeasures for Time Synchronization in IEEE802.15.4e Networks," in *Proceedings of the 3rd IEEE International Conference on Cyber Security and Cloud Computing, CSCloud 2016 and 2nd IEEE International Conference of Scalable and Smart Cloud, SSC 2016*, pp. 102–107, June 2016.

[33] G. Lee, J. Lim, D.-K. Kim, S. Yang, and M. Yoon, "An approach to mitigating sybil attack in wireless networks using ZigBee," in *Proceedings of the 2008 10th International Conference on Advanced Communication Technology*, pp. 1005–1009, February 2008.

[34] L. Jun and Y. Qing, "Take unauthorized control over zigbee devices," 2015, https://media.defcon.org/defcon23/defcon23presentations/defcon-23-li-jun-yang-qing-i-am-a-newbie-yet-i-can-hack-zigbee.pdf.

[35] J. Wang, "Zigbee light link and its applicationss," *IEEE Wireless Communications Magazine*, vol. 20, no. 4, pp. 6-7, 2013.

[36] A. Gent, "A lightbulb worm?" in *Blackhat*, 2016, https://www.blackhat.com/docs/us-16/materials/us-16-oflynn-a-lightbulb-worm-wp.pdf.

[37] E. Ronen, A. Shamir, A. Weingarten, and C. OFlynn, "IoT Goes Nuclear: Creating a ZigBee Chain Reaction," in *Proceedings of the 2017 IEEE Symposium on Security and Privacy (SP)*, pp. 195–212, San Jose, CA, USA, May 2017.

[38] S. Marian and P. Mircea, "Sybil attack type detection in Wireless Sensor networks based on received signal strength indicator detection scheme," in *Proceedings of the 10th Jubilee IEEE International Symposium on Applied Computational Intelligence and Informatics, SACI 2015*, pp. 121–124, May 2015.

[39] B. Al Baalbaki, J. Pacheco, C. Tunc, S. Hariri, and Y. Al-Nashif, "Anomaly Behavior Analysis System for ZigBee in smart buildings," in *Proceedings of the 12th IEEE/ACS International Conference of Computer Systems and Applications, AICCSA 2015*, November 2015.

[40] P. Jokar and V. Leung, "Intrusion Detection and Prevention for ZigBee-Based Home Area Networks in Smart Grids," *IEEE Transactions on Smart Grid*, pp. 1-1.

[41] L. Caviglione, M. Gaggero, J.-F. Lalande, W. Mazurczyk, and M. Urbański, "Seeing the unseen: Revealing mobile malware hidden communications via energy consumption and artificial intelligence," *IEEE Transactions on Information Forensics and Security*, vol. 11, no. 4, pp. 799–810, 2016.

[42] B. Cui, S. Liang, S. Chen, B. Zhao, and X. Liang, "A novel fuzzing method for Zigbee based on finite state machine," *International Journal of Distributed Sensor Networks*, vol. 2014, Article ID 762891, 2014.

[43] J. Jia and J. Meng, "A novel approach for impulsive noise mitigation in ZigBee communication system," in *Proceedings of the 2014 Global Information Infrastructure and Networking Symposium, GIIS 2014*, September 2014.

[44] R. Piyare and S. r. Lee, "Performance analysis of xbee zb module based wireless sensor networks," *International Journal of Scientific & Engineering Research*, vol. 4, pp. 1615–1621.

[45] A. T. C. Dictionary, "Etrx2 and etrx3 series zigbee modules at-command dictionary".

[46] P. Manual, "Xbee/xbee-pro rf modules," http://store.express-inc.com/pdf/xa-a.pdf.

6

Vague Sets Security Measure for Steganographic System Based on High-Order Markov Model

Chun-Juan Ouyang,[1,2] Ming Leng,[1,2] Jie-Wu Xia,[1,2] and Huan Liu[1,2]

[1]*Key Laboratory of Watershed Ecology and Geographical Environment Monitoring of NASG, Jinggangshan University, Ji'an 343009, China*
[2]*School of Electronics and Information Engineering, Jinggangshan University, Ji'an 343009, China*

Correspondence should be addressed to Chun-Juan Ouyang; oycj001@163.com

Academic Editor: Yushu Zhang

Security measure is of great importance in both steganography and steganalysis. Considering that statistical feature perturbations caused by steganography in an image are always nondeterministic and that an image is considered nonstationary, in this paper, the steganography is regarded as a fuzzy process. Here a steganographic security measure is proposed. This security measure evaluates the similarity between two vague sets of cover images and stego images in terms of n-order Markov chain to capture the interpixel correlation. The new security measure has proven to have the properties of boundedness, commutativity, and unity. Furthermore, the security measures of zero order, first order, second order, third order, and so forth are obtained by adjusting the order value of n-order Markov chain. Experimental results indicate that the larger n is, the better the measuring ability of the proposed security measure will be. The proposed security measure is more sensitive than other security measures defined under a deterministic distribution model, when the embedding is low. It is expected to provide a helpful guidance for designing secure steganographic algorithms or reliable steganalytic methods.

1. Introduction

Security of the steganographic system is the fundamental issue in the field of the information hiding. Image steganography is the technique of hiding information in digital image and trying to conceal the existence of the secret information. The image with and the image without hidden information are called stego image and cover image, respectively [1]. Steganography and steganalysis are in a hide-and-seek game [2]. They try to defeat each other and also develop with each other. In recent years, steganalysis researches have made much head-way [3, 4], and many attempts have been made to build up secure steganographic algorithms [5–8]. Up until now, there is no standard security measure for steganographic system. The security of the steganography always depends on the encryption of the steganography, which contradicts Kerckhoffs' principle [9]. Hence, it is very necessary to study the security measure which can provide guidance for

designing the high-secure steganography and steganalytic algorithms with high performance.

Now, the study of the security measure becomes one of the hotspots in the steganography research field. Researchers have put forward their views from different viewing angles. From the point of view of information theory, Cachin [10] proposed a security measure in terms of the relative entropy between the probability mass functions (PMF) of the cover images and the stego images. Sullivan et al. [11] employed the divergence distance of the empirical matrices to define the security measure. They modeled the sequence of image pixels as first-order Markov chain which could capture one adjacent pixel dependency. Furthermore, Zhang et al. [12] models the images pixels as n-order Markov chain to provide the security measure. Based on game theory, Liu et al. [13] presented that the counterwork relationship is modeled between steganography side and attack side. In [14], Schöttle and Böhme studied adaptive steganography while taking the knowledge of the steganalyst into account. Liu and Tang [15] also provided the security for the adaptive steganography. In [16], Chandramouli et al. proposed an alternative security measure based on steganalyzer's ROC (Receiver Operating Characteristic) performance. From the point of feature space, Pevný and Fridrich [17] provided the MMD (Maximum Mean Discrepancy) by employing a high-dimensional feature space set as the covers models.

The security measures mentioned above all assume that accurate statistical estimations can be obtained from the finite data samples. However, an image is a nonstationary process; its local statistical correlation will change when image is changed slightly. So the statistical features change is nondeterministic after steganography processing. Meanwhile, for a steganographic system, the warden is lack of the knowledge of the cover distribution. Thus, the distribution estimates of the cover and stego image are not stable. So the security measures defined under the deterministic statistical model are hard to apply due to the lack of the accurate distribution.

To address this problem, we regard the steganography as a fuzzy and indeterministic process. The goal of this paper is to provide a practical security measure in terms of the vague sets similarity measure between cover images and the stego images. Particularly, the sequence of image pixels is modeled as an *n-order* Markov chain to capture the interpixel correlations. The main contributions of this work are as follows:

(1) We derive a security measure for a steganographic system which is different from the deterministic ones. The existing security measures are defined by evaluating the difference between cover images and stego images. In contrast, the new security measure is defined by evaluating the similarity between cover images and their stego version.

(2) The *n-order* security measure based on vague sets similarity measure is proven to have the properties of the boundedness, commutativity, and unity. The properties guarantee the security measure is indeed a real distance which indeed satisfies the symmetry and triangle inequality. The boundedness guarantees the new benchmark can measure the steganographic security.

(3) Simulation results verify the effectiveness of the new security measure by benchmarking several popular steganographic schemes. When embedding rate is low, the new security measure is more sensitive to reveal the statistical features change than other security measures. Thus, the proposed security measure can provide a better guidance for the design of steganography and steganalysis.

The rest of the paper is organized as follows. Section 2 gives a review of the two security measures with the deterministic statistical distribution model and introduces the *n-order* Markov chain model. The *n-order* secure measure based on vague sets similarity measure is presented in detail in Section 3. Experimental results are provided in Section 4 to demonstrate the effectiveness and the superiority of the

proposed security measure. We draw our conclusions in Section 5.

2. Steganographic Security and Cover Model

2.1. Security Measure Based on Kullback-Leibler (K-L) Divergence. Suppose C is the set of all the covers, and it is an assumption that the selections of the covers and stegos from the set C can be described by the random variables c and s on C with the probability mass functions (PMF) P_c and P_s, respectively. Cachin [10] quantified the security of a steganographic system in terms of the Kullback-Leibler (K-L) divergence (sometimes called relative entropy); that is,

$$D\left(P_c \parallel P_s\right) = \sum_{x \in X} P_c\left(x\right) \log \frac{P_c\left(x\right)}{P_s\left(x\right)}, \qquad (1)$$

where X is the set of possible pixel values. A steganographic system is called perfectly secure if (1) is zero or ε-secure if $0 \le D(P_c \parallel P_s) \le \varepsilon$ is satisfied. The K-L divergence provides a simple yet convenient method for measuring the difference between cover images and stego images.

In fact, we have little information about the PMF involved due to the large dimensionality of the set C. So the security measure is usually defined with simplified cover models, such as independent and identically distributed (i.i.d.) ones. The security measure of K-L divergence calculates the difference from the view of the first-order statistical features (such as one-dimensional histogram feature).

2.2. Security Measure Based on Divergence Distance. To account for the dependence of the pixels, Sullivan et al. [11] employed the first-order Markov chain model to capture the interpixel correlation. The divergence distance was used to quantify the statistical feature perturbations introduced by a steganography between the two empirical matrices of cover images and stego images. Suppose C and S are two random sequences of the cover image pixels and the stego image pixels, respectively, obtained by a given scanning method. Let M^c and M^s be the empirical matrixes of C and S, respectively. The divergence distance is given by

$$D\left(M^c, M^s\right) = \sum_{i,j \in R} M_{ij}^c \log\left(\frac{M_{ij}^c}{\sum_j M_{ij}^c} \frac{\sum_j M_{ij}^s}{M_{ij}^s}\right), \qquad (2)$$

where $M_{ij}^c / \sum_j M_{ij}^c$ and $M_{ij}^s / \sum_j M_{ij}^s$ are the transition probabilities of cover images and stego images, respectively. The transition probability is commonly calculated by the ratio of the total number to the pixel changes from value i to value j over the total number of possible pixel changes (e.g., for an 8-bit image, the total possible pixel changes number is 256×256). The constant R is the range of all possible pixel values. Thus, the divergence distance provides the difference between cover images and their stego version from the view of the second-order statistical features (such as two-dimensional histogram feature and difference histogram feature).

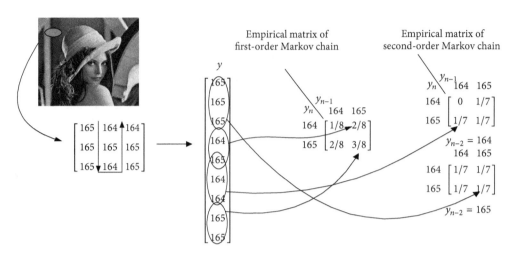

FIGURE 1: The generating process of the empirical matrixes of first-order and second-order Markov chain.

The two security measures mentioned above are defined based on the Shannon information theory under the assumption that the image data statistical distribution is deterministic. Most of the security measures proposed later are also defined under the same assumption. However, the image data shows the sceneries in the aspects of gray, texture, shape, and so forth. There are many a kind of indeterministic factors (such as noise) in a steganography process. Therefore, the security measures with the deterministic statistical distribution model cannot measure the security accurately.

2.3. n-Order Markov Chain Model. The weakness of the above two security measure lies in the fact that the image model such as i.i.d and first-order Markov are too simple to capture interpixel dependency. Therefore, here we model the sequence of image pixels as an n-order Markov chain. The n-order Markov chain is a random sequence indexing the image pixels scanned by a given mode. For instance, when $n = 2$, the second-order Markov chain accounting for two adjacent pixels' correlation meets the following condition:

$$P\left(Y_m \mid Y_{m-1}, Y_{m-2}, \ldots, Y_1\right) = P\left(Y_m \mid Y_{m-1}, Y_{m-2}\right). \quad (3)$$

There are at least two reasons for us to select n-order Markov chain model. First, the model is flexible. When $n = 0$, it turns out to be the i.i.d model, in which the image pixels are assumed to be unrelated. When $n = 1$, the first-order Markov chain can capture only one adjacent pixel dependence. Furthermore, the n-order Markov chain can capture more interpixel relationships among the pixels when $n \geq 2$. Second, compared with the Markov random field model [9], the Markov chain model, though simple, is able to calculate the statistical estimation of the image samples. For n-order Markov chain, it is easy to calculate the realistic statistical estimates using the empirical matrixes. In the following, we construct the empirical matrixes of the first-order and second-order Markov chain.

Let $\{Y_n, \ n = 1, 2, \ldots, L\}$ be an n-order Markov chain on the finite set ω, where Y_n is the n-indexed set of pixels obtained by a row, column, zigzag, or Hilbert scanning

method. ω is the possible gray scale values. When $n = 1$, the first-order Markov chain source is defined by the transition matrixes $T_{i_1,i_2} = P(Y_n = i_1 \mid Y_{n-1} = i_2)$ and marginal probabilities $p_{i_1} = P(Y_n = i_1)$. For a realization, $y = (y_1, y_2, \ldots, y_L)^T$. Let η_{i_1,i_2} be the number of transitions from values i_1 to i_2 in y. The empirical matrixes are $M_1(y) = \eta_{i_1,i_2}(y)/(L - 1)$. That is, the i_1, i_2 element represent the proportion of spatially adjacent pixel pairs with the grayscale value of i_1 followed by i_2. Thus the empirical matrixes provide an estimation of the transition matrixes and marginal probabilities. The empirical matrixes are similar to the concurrence matrixes of the image. It can be recognized as a matrix form of the two-dimensional normalized histogram for estimating the joint probability mass function (PMF) of a source image. Similarly, when $n = 2$, we can get the empirical matrixes of the second-order Markov chain, denoted by $M_2(y) = \eta_{i_1,i_2,i_3}(y)/(L - 1)$. $\eta_{i_1,i_2,i_3}(y)$ is the number of transitions from values i_1 to i_3 via i_2 in y. For an 8-bit image, the size of the empirical matrixes $M_2(y)$ is $256 \times 256 \times 256$. The element of the empirical matrixes represents the proportion of spatially adjacent pixel group with a grayscale value of i_1 followed by i_2 and i_3. A simple example of generating the empirical matrixes of first-order and second-order Markov chain is shown in Figure 1.

In Figure 1, the small block is derived from the standard image "Lena." Its size is 3×3, including pixels 164 and 165. The example image pixels are scanned vertically. The size of the empirical matrixes of first-order Markov chain in Figure 1 is 2×2. The element represents the proportion of spatially adjacent pixel pairs with (164, 164), (164, 165), (165, 164), and (165, 165). The right-hand side of Figure 1 demonstrates the procedure of the empirical matrixes of second-order Markov chain. Its size is $2 \times 2 \times 2$, in which the element represents the proportion of spatially adjacent pixel groups with (164, 164, 164), (164, 165, 164), (165, 164, 164), (165, 165, 164), and so forth.

Since the cover sources are strongly correlated, the probabilities of two adjacency samples are equal or nearly equal. As a result, in the empirical matrixes, the masses are more

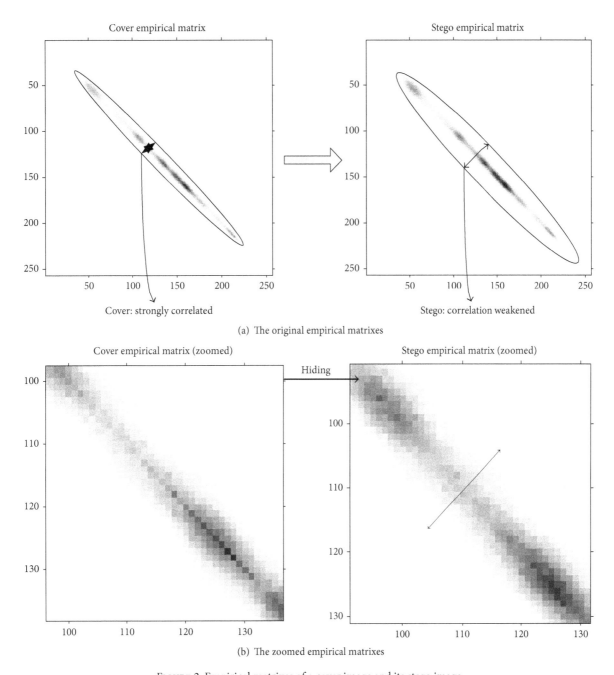

(a) The original empirical matrixes

(b) The zoomed empirical matrixes

FIGURE 2: Empirical matrixes of a cover image and its stego image.

concentrated near the main diagonal in a correlated source. In [18], Harmsen and Pearlman considered that information hiding can be viewed as adding the additive noise to the cover image. The secret information (additive noise) is uncorrelated after hiding, and its empirical matrixes spread evenly over the main diagonal. Thus we see that hiding weakens the dependencies among the cover samples, which is illustrated in Figure 2(a). Figure 2(b) is part of the zoomed empirical matrixes. According to the above analysis, the steganography tends to spread the density of the pixels pairs away from the main diagonal of the empirical matrixes. This property may shed some light on designing of the security measure for a steganographic system. Thus, in Section 3, we will propose an *n-order* security measure in terms of the vague sets similarity

measure by modeling the sequence of images pixels as an *n-order* Markov chain.

3. Security Measure Based on Vague Sets Similarity Measure

The vague sets similarity measure [19, 20] describes the matching degree of two vague sets. In a practical steganographic system, there are many indeterministic factors introduced by steganography. In this work, we regard the responding probability distribution sets of the cover samples and the stego samples as two discrete vague sets. Then a new security measure is proposed below in terms of vague sets similarity measure to measure the similarity between cover images and stego images.

3.1. Vague Sets. Roughly speaking, a fuzzy set is a class with fuzzy boundaries. The fuzzy set A is a class of objects X along with a grade of membership function $\mu_A(x)$, $x \in X$. It assigns a single value to each object. This single value combines the evidence for x $\in$ X and the evidence against $x \in X$. And it is only a measure of the pros/cons evidence. However, in many practical applications we often require pros and cons evidence simultaneously. Gau and Buehrer [21] advanced the concept of vague sets. The vague sets theory adopts a true membership function t_A and a false membership function f_A to record the lower bounds on μ_A. These lower bounds are used to create a subinterval on [0, 1], namely, $[t_A(x_i), 1 - f_A(x_i)]$, to generalize $\mu_A(x_i)$ of fuzzy sets, where $t_A(x_i) \leq \mu_A(x_i) \leq 1 - f_A(x_i)$. Vague sets expand the value of the membership function to a subinterval of [0, 1] instead of a single value; thus it has stronger ability to reveal the indeterminacy than the fuzzy set theory. The related definitions of vague sets are as follows.

Definition 1 (vague sets). Let X be the universe of discourse, $X = \{x_1, x_2, \ldots, x_n\}$. $V(x)$ denotes all the vague sets of X, $\forall A \in V(x)$. The vague set A is characterized by a true membership function t_A and a false membership function f_A:

$$t_A : X \longrightarrow [0, 1],$$
$$f_A : X \longrightarrow [0, 1], \tag{4}$$

where $t_A(x_i)$ is the lower bound on the grade of membership of x_i derived from the evidence for x_i. $f_A(x_i)$ is a lower bound on the negation of x_i derived from the evidence against x_i, satisfying $t_A(x_i) + f_A(x_i) \leq 1$. The grade of membership of x_i is bounded to a subinterval $[t_A(x_i), 1 - f_A(x_i)]$ of [0, 1]. When X is discrete, a vague set A can be written as

$$A = \sum_{i=1}^{n} \frac{[t_A(x_i), 1 - f_A(x_i)]}{x_i}, \quad x_i \in X. \tag{5}$$

Definition 2. Let X be the universe of discourse, $X = \{x_1, x_2, \ldots, x_n\}$. A and B are two vague sets of X. The entropy of the vague set A, $E(A)$, is defined as

$$E(A)$$
$$= -\frac{1}{n \ln 2} \sum_{i=1}^{n} [t_A(x_i) \ln t_A(x_i) + f_A(x_i) \ln f_A(x_i)]. \tag{6}$$

Definition 3. Let X be the universe of discourse, $X = \{x_1, x_2, \ldots, x_n\}$. A and B are two vague sets of X. The partial entropy of vague set A against vague set B, $E_B(A)$, is defined as

$$E_B(A) = -\sum_{i=1}^{n} [t_B(x_i) \ln t_A(x_i) + f_B(x_i) \ln f_A(x_i)]. \tag{7}$$

3.2. The n-Order Security Measure Based on Vague Sets Similarity Measure. As discussed in Section 2.3, the *n*-order

Markov chain model can capture sufficient inherent correlations. Additionally, the changes in image statistical features, introduced by steganography, are indeterministic. Therefore, in the new security measure, we model the sequence of the image pixels as an *n-order* Markov chain. Simultaneously, the empirical matrixes of the *n-order* Markov chain of cover images and stego images are regarded as two vague sets. Then the *n*-order security measure based on the vague sets similarity measure is defined as follows.

Suppose C and S are *n*-order Markov chain sequence of cover images and stego images, respectively, and then scan them by a given mode (such as horizontal, vertical, zigzag, and Hilbert mode). *MC* and *MS* represent the corresponding empirical matrixes. $m_{i_1,i_2,\ldots,i_{n+1}}$, the element of empirical matrixes, denotes the joint probability distribution from pixels i_1 to i_{n+1} via the states of $i_2, i_3, \ldots$ and i_n. The $i_1, i_2, \ldots, i_{n+1}$ is the image pixel value, $i \in [0, 255]$. G denotes the set of all possible values of $m_{i_1,i_2,\ldots,i_{n+1}}$. Let $M_{i_1,i_2,\ldots,i_{n+1}}$ be the universe of discourse composed of $m_{i_1,i_2,\ldots,i_{n+1}}$. Then MC and MS are two vague sets on $M_{i_1,i_2,\ldots,i_{n+1}}$. That is,

$$MC = \frac{\sum_{i=0}^{255} \left[t_{MC}\left(m_{i_1,i_2\cdots i_{n+1}}\right), 1 - f_{MC}\left(m_{i_1,i_2\cdots i_{n+1}}\right) \right]}{m_{i_1,i_2\cdots i_{n+1}}},$$
$$m_{i_1,i_2\cdots i_{n+1}} \in M_{i_1,i_2\cdots i_{n+1}},$$
$$MS = \frac{\sum_{i=0}^{255} \left[t_{MS}\left(m_{i_1,i_2\cdots i_{n+1}}\right), 1 - f_{MS}\left(m_{i_1,i_2\cdots i_{n+1}}\right) \right]}{m_{i_1,i_2\cdots i_{n+1}}}, \tag{8}$$
$$m_{i_1,i_2\cdots i_{n+1}} \in M_{i_1,i_2\cdots i_{n+1}}.$$

Definition 4. Let $M_{i_1,i_2,\ldots,i_{n+1}}$ be the universe of discourse. MC and MS are two vague sets of $M_{i_1,i_2,\ldots,i_{n+1}}$. The similarity measure $T_n(MC, MS)$ between the vague sets MC and MS is defined as the *n-order* secure measure for a steganographic system; that is,

$$T_n(MC, MS) = \frac{m \ln 2 (E(MC) + E(MS))}{E_{MC}(MS) + E_{MS}(MC)}, \tag{9}$$

where $E(MC)$ and $E(MS)$ denote the entropy of the vague set MC and MS, respectively; $E_{MC}(MS)$ stands for the partial entropy of vague set MS against vague set MC; $E_{MS}(MC)$ is the partial entropy of vague set MC against vague set MS. $E(MC)$ and $E_{MC}(MS)$ can be written as

$$E(MC) = -\frac{1}{m \ln 2}$$
$$\cdot \sum_{i_1,i_2\cdots i_{n+1} \in G} \left[t_{MC}\left(m_{i_1,i_2\cdots i_{n+1}}\right) \ln t_{MC}\left(m_{i_1,i_2\cdots i_{n+1}}\right) \right.$$
$$\left. + f_{MC}\left(m_{i_1,i_2\cdots i_{n+1}}\right) \ln f_{MC}\left(m_{i_1,i_2\cdots i_{n+1}}\right) \right], \tag{10}$$
$$E_{MS}(MC)$$
$$= - \sum_{i_1,i_2\cdots i_{n+1} \in G} \left[t_{MS}\left(m_{i_1,i_2\cdots i_{n+1}}\right) \ln t_{MC}\left(m_{i_1,i_2\cdots i_{n+1}}\right) \right.$$
$$\left. + f_{MS}\left(m_{i_1,i_2\cdots i_{n+1}}\right) \ln f_{MC}\left(m_{i_1,i_2\cdots i_{n+1}}\right) \right].$$

Similarly, $E(MS)$ and $E_{MC}(MS)$ can be written as

$$E(MS) = -\frac{1}{m \ln 2}$$
$$\cdot \sum_{i_1, i_2 \cdots i_{n+1} \in G} \left[t_{MS}\left(m_{i_1, i_2 \cdots i_{n+1}}\right) \ln t_{MS}\left(m_{i_1, i_2 \cdots i_{n+1}}\right) \right.$$
$$\left. + f_{MS}\left(m_{i_1, i_2 \cdots i_{n+1}}\right) \ln f_{MS}\left(m_{i_1, i_2 \cdots i_{n+1}}\right) \right], \quad (11)$$

$$E_{MC}(MS)$$
$$= - \sum_{i_1, i_2 \cdots i_{n+1} \in G} \left[t_{MC}\left(m_{i_1, i_2 \cdots i_{n+1}}\right) \ln t_{MS}\left(m_{i_1, i_2 \cdots i_{n+1}}\right) \right.$$
$$\left. + f_{MC}\left(m_{i_1, i_2 \cdots i_{n+1}}\right) \ln f_{MS}\left(m_{i_1, i_2 \cdots i_{n+1}}\right) \right].$$

Moreover, a steganographic system is called perfectly secure if $T_n(MC, MS) = 1$ or ε-secure if $T_n(MC, MS) = \varepsilon$, $\varepsilon \in (0, 1)$. $T_n(MC, MS) = 0$.

Theorem 5. *Let $T_n(MC, MS)$ be the n-order secure measure of a steganographic system based on vague set similarity measure. Then $T_n(MC, MS)$ satisfies the following.*

(1) Boundedness is

$$0 \leq T_n(MC, MS) \leq 1. \quad (12)$$

(2) Commutativity is

$$T_n(MC, MS) = T_n(MS, MC). \quad (13)$$

(3) Unity is

$$T_n(MC, MS) = 1 \Longleftrightarrow$$
$$MC = MS. \quad (14)$$

$T_n(MC, MS)$ *provides a security measure for a steganographic system in terms of the similarity between cover images and stego images. $T_n(MC, MS)$ is limited in a finite interval of $[0, 1]$, where 1 denotes "perfectly secure," while 0 denotes "definitely unsecure." However, other security measures under the deterministic statistical model calculate the difference between cover images and stego images. The values range in an infinite interval $[0, \infty)$. The property of the boundedness guarantees the proposed security measure can measure a steganographic algorithm quantitatively. Hence, it has stronger ability to reveal the statistical changes of the cover images. When $n = 0$, the image pixels distribution is said to be i.i.d., and $T_0(MC, MS)$ is called the zero-order security measure. When $n = 1$, the sequence of image pixels is considered to be a first-order Markov chain, and $T_1(MC, MS)$ is defined as the first-order security measure. Thus, a different order security measure can be obtained by adjusting the value of n.*

4. Experimental Results and Discussion

In this section, we report experimental results that demonstrate the capability of the new security measure. First of all

in Section 4.1 the image databases used for the experiment are described. Afterwards, in Section 4.2, we benchmark several different steganographic methods with *n-order* security measure based on vague sets, with particular attention to the effectiveness of low embedding rate. Finally, we compare the proposed security measure with previously used benchmarks designed under the deterministic statistical model.

4.1. Image Database. For the experimental validation we used two image databases. The first one is BOWS2 [22] image database including 10000 grayscale images with fixed size 512×512. The other one is NRCS Photo Gallery [23]. We selected 1500 images from NRCS Photo Gallery. All images were converted into grayscale and central cropped to a size of 512×512 for experimental purposes. The images in our experiments show a wide range of scenarios including house, manmade objects, and animal. Some images are shown in Figure 3.

4.2. Verification of the Effectiveness of the Proposed Security Measure. To evaluate the performance of the proposed method for measuring the security of the steganographic algorithms, the new security measure with different orders is used to measure the security of different steganographic algorithms with different embedding rates. First, we select some spatial-domain steganographic algorithms, including LSBM (least significant bit matching) [24], LSB ± 2, HUGO [25] (highly undetectable steganography). We use 2000 images from BOWS2 image database; all the images are grayscale with the fixed size 512×512. As discussed in Section 2.3, first-order and second-order Markov chain models have captured sufficient interpixel correlations. Additionally, considering the computation complexity, we use the zero-order, first-order, and second-order security measure based on vague sets to measure the LSBM, LSBM2, and HUGO steganographic methods with the embedding rate ranging from 0.1 bpp (bits per pixel) to 1 bpp in a step size of 0.1 bpp. The average measure results for zero-order, first-order, and second-order security measure of 2000 images with different embedding rates are depicted in Figure 4.

In Figure 4, all curves indicate that the value of security measure gradually decreases with an increase in the embedding rate for the same steganographic algorithm. It is consistent with the definition of the security measure based on vague sets. Its value is limited in an interval of $[0, 1]$, where 1 denotes "perfectly secure" for the steganographic system. Hence the value of the *n*-order security measure satisfies monotonic decreasing property; that is, the higher the security of the stego images, the larger the value of the security measure. Furthermore, as is evident in Figure 4, the values of the same order security measure are different for different stego schemes with the same embedding rate. Note that LSB ± 2 obtains the lowest value in Figure 4, implying that it is most unsecure among the three hiding methods under the same condition. On the contrary, HUGO gains the highest value. All the measure results are coincident with the theoretical analysis of the three embedding schemes.

Furthermore, in order to evaluate the measuring ability of different order security measures, we compare the security

(a) Some images of BOWS2

(b) Some images of NRCS

Figure 3: Some images of image database.

for the same steganographic algorithm using different order security measures. Figure 6 shows the average measure results of zero-order, first-order, and second-order security measure for LSBM, LSB ± 2, and HUGO, respectively. In fact, all the data in Figure 5 is derived from Figure 4. As demonstrated in Figure 5, for the same steganographic method, the values of the zero-order, first-order, and second-order security measure are different at the same embedding rate. It is demonstrated that the value of the first-order security measure is smaller than that of the zero-order measure but larger than that of the second-order measure for the same steganographic method with the same embedding rate. The experiments show that the second-order security measure provides the largest measure interval to reveal the security change of the cover images with the embedding rate ranging from 0.1 bpp to 1 bpp. So we can conclude that second-order security measure can provide more obvious statistical distributed changes caused by steganography.

To further verify the effectiveness of the proposed security measure. We used it to benchmark JPEG steganographic algorithms schemes on different database. And we focus on low payloads to see if any of the test steganographic schemes becomes distinguishable by using the vague sets security measure with finite image sample.

We selected 1500 images from NRCS Photo Gallery. All images were converted into grayscale and central cropped to a size of 512 × 512 for experimental purposes. The images were embedded with pseudorandom payloads with 5%, 10%, 15%, and 20% bpac (bits per nonzero AC coefficient). The tested stego schemes include F3, F5 without shrinkage (nsF5) [26], Model Based Steganography without deblocking (MB1) [27], and Model Based Steganography with deblocking (MB2)

[28]. The cover images were single-compressed JPEGs with quality factor 70. The measure results using zero-order, first-order, and second-order security measure based on vague sets are showed in Table 1. The data in Table 1 indicates that, for the same steganography, the larger the embedding rate, the lower the value of the same security measure. It also exhibited that, for the same steganography, the higher the order of the security measure, the smaller the value of the security measure, suggesting that second-order security measure can get a value lower than the other two security measures under the same condition.

The data in Table 1 also shows, according to the same order security measure, the MB2 is the least statistically detectable, followed by MB1 and nsF5, while F3 is the most detectable. All the measure results are coincident with the theoretical security among adopted stego algorithms. In a word, the experimental results indicate that the proposed security measure is effective for measuring the security for different steganographic methods on different image database. Meanwhile, the greater the order, the stronger the measure ability of the security measure.

4.3. Comparison with Security Measure under Deterministic Statistical Model. To show the superiority of the proposed security measure $T_n(MC, MS)$, we compare it with two security measures under the deterministic statistical model. One is the Kullback-Leibler (K-L) divergence between the probability mass functions (PMF) proposed by Anderson [9], denoted by $D(P_c \parallel P_s)$. The other, denoted as $D(M_c, M_s)$, is the divergence distance between the two empirical matrices proposed by Cachin [10]. To be unbiased, the zero-order measure $T_0(MC, MS)$ is compared with $D(P_c \parallel P_s)$ when

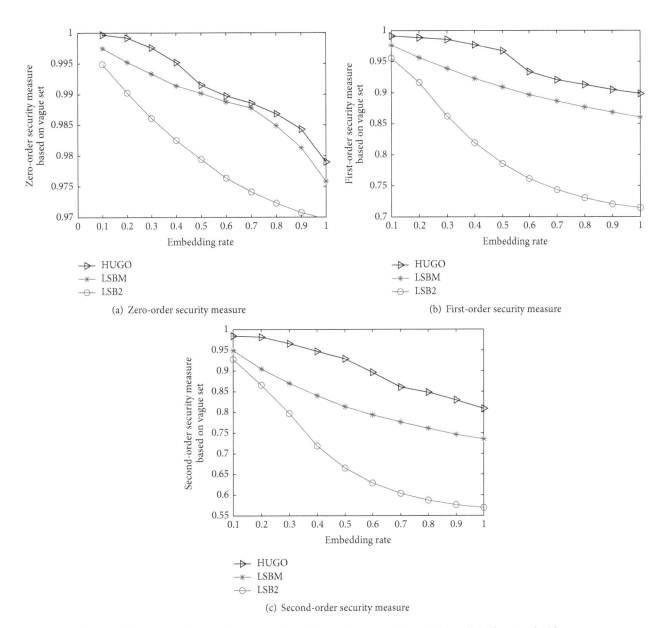

FIGURE 4: The same order security measure for different steganographic methods with different embedding rate.

$D(P_c \parallel P_s)$ is used under the assumption that the image model is i.i.d. Similarly, the first-order measure $T_1(MC, MS)$ is compared with $D(M_c, M_s)$ since their image pixel sequences are all modeled as the first-order Markov chain. In the experiments, the same 2000 images from BOWS2 are adopted. $T_0(MC, MS)$, $D(P_c \parallel P_s)$, $T_1(MC, MS)$, and $D(M_c, M_s)$ are used to measure the security of the HUGO with the embedding rate ranging from 0.05 bpp to 1 bpp in a step size of 0.05 bpp. Figures 6(a) and 6(b) show the average measure of $T_0(MC, MS)$ and $D(P_c \parallel P_s)$ with different embedding rates, respectively. The average measure values of $T_1(MC, MS)$ and $D(M_c, M_s)$ are also illustrated in Figures 7(a) and 7(b), respectively.

Looking at Figures 6 and 7, we see that the value of security measure based on vague sets decreases as the embedding rate increases, whereas the value of security measure under the deterministic distribution model increases as the embedding rate increases. All the curves in Figures 6 and 7 indicate that both the security measure models are effective in measuring the security of the steganography. In order to show the superiority of the proposed security measure, we define $\delta = \Delta y / y$ as the sensitivity of, where Δy is the security measure variation of a given embedding rate change range, and y is the total security measure variation of the embedding rate change. Obviously, Figures 6(b) and 7(b) demonstrate that δ of security measure is very small when embedding rate is lower than 0.5 bpp. So its corresponding

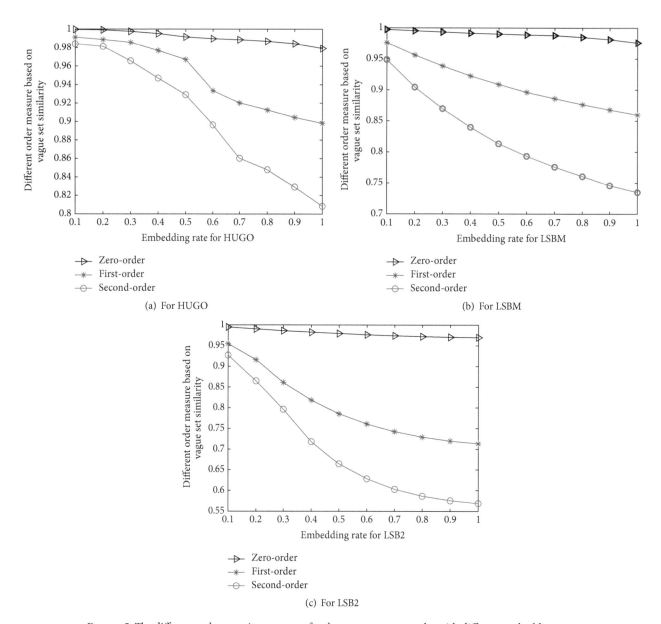

FIGURE 5: The different order security measures for the same steganography with different embedding rate.

security measure is not sensitive to the statistical distribution change. Hence, the new security measure can reveal more obvious statistical change than the security measures under deterministic statistical distribution model when embedding rate is low.

5. Conclusions

Vague sets similarity measure is a simple yet effective tool for measuring the similarity between two vague sets. In this work, a novel security measure for a steganographic system in terms of the vague sets similarity measure is proposed to measure the similarity between cover images and stego images. Particularly, in the new security measure, the sequence of image pixels is modeled as an *n-order*

Markov chain to capture sufficient interpixel dependencies. The proposed security measure is proven to have such properties as boundedness, commutativity, and unity. Various order security measures can be obtained by adjusting the value of *n*. Experimental results confirm the effectiveness of the proposed security measure for evaluating different steganographic algorithms. Meanwhile, the security measure with a higher order always has a better measure ability. Additionally, when the embedding rate is low, the *n-order* security measure based on vague sets is more sensitive than other security measures under the deterministic distribution model. Considering the computational complexity and steganalytic ability, two issues should be tackled in our further research. One is how to use the *n-order* security measure to design reliable steganalytic methods by extracting the statistical feature from the empirical matrixes. The other is

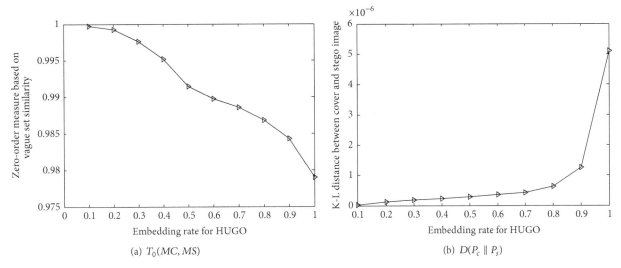

(a) $T_0(MC, MS)$

(b) $D(P_c \parallel P_s)$

FIGURE 6: $T_0(MC, MS)$ and $D(P_c \parallel P_s)$ for HUGO with different embedding rates.

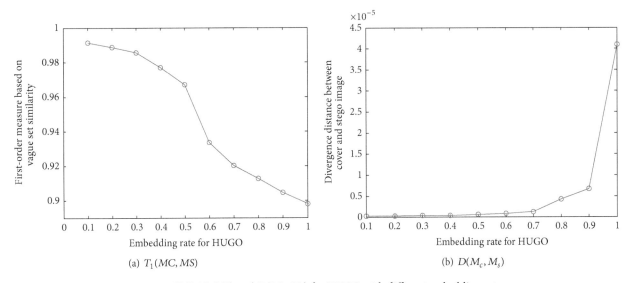

(a) $T_1(MC, MS)$

(b) $D(M_c, M_s)$

FIGURE 7: $T_1(MC, MS)$ and $D(M_c, M_s)$ for HUGO with different embedding rates.

how to use the new security measure to design highly secure steganographic algorithms.

Appendix

Proof of Theorem 5. (1)

$$E_{MC}(MS) + E_{MS}(MC) - m \ln 2 \left(E(MC) + E(MS) \right)$$

$$= - \sum_{i_1, i_2 \cdots i_{n+1} \in G} \left[t_{MC}\left(m_{i_1, i_2 \cdots i_{n+1}}\right) \ln t_{MS}\left(m_{i_1, i_2 \cdots i_{n+1}}\right) \right.$$

$$+ f_{MC}\left(m_{ij}\right) \ln f_{MS}\left(m_{i_1, i_2 \cdots i_{n+1}}\right) \Big]$$

$$- \sum_{i_1, i_2 \cdots i_{n+1} \in G} \left[t_{MS}\left(m_{i_1, i_2 \cdots i_{n+1}}\right) \ln t_{MC}\left(m_{i_1, i_2 \cdots i_{n+1}}\right) \right.$$

$$+ f_{MS}\left(m_{ij}\right) \ln f_{MC}\left(m_{i_1, i_2 \cdots i_{n+1}}\right) \Big]$$

$$+ \sum_{i_1, i_2 \cdots i_{n+1} \in G} \left[t_{MC}\left(m_{i_1, i_2 \cdots i_{n+1}}\right) \ln t_{MC}\left(m_{i_1, i_2 \cdots i_{n+1}}\right) \right.$$

$$+ f_{MC}\left(m_{i_1, i_2 \cdots i_{n+1}}\right) \ln f_{MC}\left(m_{i_1, i_2 \cdots i_{n+1}}\right) \Big]$$

$$+ \sum_{i_1, i_2 \cdots i_{n+1} \in G} \left[t_{MS}\left(m_{i_1, i_2 \cdots i_{n+1}}\right) \ln t_{MS}\left(m_{i_1, i_2 \cdots i_{n+1}}\right) \right.$$

$$+ f_{MS}\left(m_{i_1, i_2 \cdots i_{n+1}}\right) \ln f_{MS}\left(m_{i_1, i_2 \cdots i_{n+1}}\right) \Big]$$

$$= \sum_{i_1, i_2 \cdots i_{n+1} \in G} \left[t_{MC}\left(m_{i_1, i_2 \cdots i_{n+1}}\right) \ln \frac{t_{MC}\left(m_{i_1, i_2 \cdots i_{n+1}}\right)}{t_{MS}\left(m_{i_1, i_2 \cdots i_{n+1}}\right)} \right.$$

$$+ f_{MC}\left(m_{i_1, i_2 \cdots i_{n+1}}\right) \ln \frac{f_{MC}\left(m_{i_1, i_2 \cdots i_{n+1}}\right)}{f_{MS}\left(m_{i_1, i_2 \cdots i_{n+1}}\right)} \Big]$$

TABLE 1: Different order vague sets security measure for different steganography methods.

Steganography method	Embedding rate (bpac)	Zero-order	First-order	Second-order
F3	5%	0.9768	0.9662	0.9569
	10%	0.9755	0.9647	0.9569
	15%	0.9714	0.9608	0.9498
	20%	0.9683	0.9584	0.9477
nsF5	5%	0.9865	0.9736	0.9593
	10%	0.9847	0.9711	0.9542
	15%	0.9840	0.9687	0.9531
	20%	0.9818	0.9656	0.9515
MB1	5%	0.9994	0.9879	0.9785
	10%	0.9991	0.9866	0.9699
	15%	0.9965	0.9849	0.9673
	20%	0.9959	0.9837	0.9656
MB2	5%	0.9999	0.9868	0.9687
	10%	0.9996	0.9842	0.9624
	15%	0.9987	0.9922	0.9617
	20%	0.9982	0.9818	0.9609

$$+ \sum_{i_1,i_2\cdots i_{n+1}\in G}\left[t_{MS}\left(m_{i_1,i_2\cdots i_{n+1}}\right)\ln\frac{t_{MS}\left(m_{i_1,i_2\cdots i_{n+1}}\right)}{t_{MC}\left(m_{i_1,i_2\cdots i_{n+1}}\right)}\right.$$
$$\left. + f_{MS}\left(m_{i_1,i_2\cdots i_{n+1}}\right)\ln\frac{f_{MS}\left(m_{i_1,i_2\cdots i_{n+1}}\right)}{f_{MC}\left(m_{i_1,i_2\cdots i_{n+1}}\right)}\right]. \tag{A.1}$$

Since the inequality satisfies $\ln x \geq (1 - 1/x)$, we have

$$E_{MC}(MS) + E_{MS}(MC) - m\ln 2\left(E(MC) + E(MS)\right)$$
$$\geq \sum_{i_1,i_2\cdots i_{n+1}\in G}\left[t_{MC}\left(m_{i_1,i_2\cdots i_{n+1}}\right)\right.$$
$$\cdot\left(1 - \frac{t_{MS}\left(m_{i_1,i_2\cdots i_{n+1}}\right)}{t_{MC}\left(m_{i_1,i_2\cdots i_{n+1}}\right)}\right) + f_{MC}\left(m_{i_1,i_2\cdots i_{n+1}}\right)$$
$$\left.\cdot\left(1 - \frac{f_{MS}\left(m_{i_1,i_2\cdots i_{n+1}}\right)}{f_{MC}\left(m_{i_1,i_2\cdots i_{n+1}}\right)}\right)\right]$$
$$+ \sum_{i_1,i_2\cdots i_{n+1}\in G}\left[t_{MS}\left(m_{i_1,i_2\cdots i_{n+1}}\right)\right.$$
$$\cdot\left(1 - \frac{t_{MC}\left(m_{i_1,i_2\cdots i_{n+1}}\right)}{t_{MS}\left(m_{i_1,i_2\cdots i_{n+1}}\right)}\right) + f_{MS}\left(m_{i_1,i_2\cdots i_{n+1}}\right)$$
$$\left.\cdot\left(1 - \frac{f_{MC}\left(m_{i_1,i_2\cdots i_{n+1}}\right)}{f_{MS}\left(m_{i_1,i_2\cdots i_{n+1}}\right)}\right)\right]$$

$$\geq \sum_{i_1,i_2\cdots i_{n+1}\in G}\left[t_{MC}\left(m_{i_1,i_2\cdots i_{n+1}}\right) - t_{MS}\left(m_{i_1,i_2\cdots i_{n+1}}\right)\right.$$
$$\left. + f_{MC}\left(m_{i_1,i_2\cdots i_{n+1}}\right) - f_{MS}\left(m_{i_1,i_2\cdots i_{n+1}}\right)\right]$$
$$+ \sum_{i_1,i_2\cdots i_{n+1}\in G}\left[t_{MS}\left(m_{i_1,i_2\cdots i_{n+1}}\right) - t_{MC}\left(m_{i_1,i_2\cdots i_{n+1}}\right)\right.$$
$$\left. + f_{MS}\left(m_{i_1,i_2\cdots i_{n+1}}\right) - f_{MC}\left(m_{i_1,i_2\cdots i_{n+1}}\right)\right] = 0. \tag{A.2}$$

Hence $E_{MC}(MS) + E_{MS}(MC) - m\ln 2(E(MC) + E(MS)) \geq 0$, such that $E_{MC}(MS) + E_{MS}(MC) \geq m\ln 2(E(MC)+E(MS))$.

Since $t_{MC}(m_{i_1,i_2\cdots i_{n+1}}), t_{MS}(m_{i_1,i_2\cdots i_{n+1}}), f_{MC}(m_{i_1,i_2\cdots i_{n+1}})$, and $f_{MS}(m_{i_1,i_2\cdots i_{n+1}})$ are all in the range of $[0,1]$ and $0 \times \ln 0 = 0$, $E(MC), E(MS), E_{MC}(MS)$, and $E_{MS}(MC)$ are all positive. Hence $0 \leq T_n(MC, MS) \leq 1$.

(2) According to the definition of the n-order security measure, $T_n(MC, MS)$ is described as

$$T_n(MC, MS) = \frac{m\ln 2\left(E(MC) + E(MS)\right)}{E_{MC}(MS) + E_{MS}(MC)}. \tag{A.3}$$

And it can also be described as

$$T_n(MS, MC) = \frac{m\ln 2\left(E(MS) + E(MC)\right)}{E_{MS}(MC) + E_{MC}(MS)}. \tag{A.4}$$

Hence $T_n(MC, MS) = T_n(MS, MC)$.

(3) From the proving procedure of property (1), we have

$$E_{MC}(MS) + E_{MS}(MC) - m\ln 2(E(MC) + E(MS)) \geq 0, \tag{A.5}$$

$$\begin{aligned}
&E_{MC}(MS) + E_{MS}(MC) - m\ln 2(E(MC) + E(MS)) \\
&= \sum_{i_1,i_2\cdots i_{n+1}\in G}\left[t_{MC}\left(m_{i_1,i_2\cdots i_{n+1}}\right)\ln\frac{t_{MC}\left(m_{i_1,i_2\cdots i_{n+1}}\right)}{t_{MS}\left(m_{i_1,i_2\cdots i_{n+1}}\right)} \right. \\
&\quad\left. + f_{MC}\left(m_{i_1,i_2\cdots i_{n+1}}\right)\ln\frac{f_{MC}\left(m_{i_1,i_2\cdots i_{n+1}}\right)}{f_{MS}\left(m_{i_1,i_2\cdots i_{n+1}}\right)} \right] \\
&\quad + \sum_{i_1,i_2\cdots i_{n+1}\in G}\left[t_{MS}\left(m_{i_1,i_2\cdots i_{n+1}}\right)\ln\frac{t_{MS}\left(m_{i_1,i_2\cdots i_{n+1}}\right)}{t_{MC}\left(m_{i_1,i_2\cdots i_{n+1}}\right)} \right. \\
&\quad\left. + f_{MS}\left(m_{i_1,i_2\cdots i_{n+1}}\right)\ln\frac{f_{MS}\left(m_{i_1,i_2\cdots i_{n+1}}\right)}{f_{MC}\left(m_{i_1,i_2\cdots i_{n+1}}\right)} \right].
\end{aligned} \tag{A.6}$$

If and only if

$$\begin{aligned}
t_{MC}\left(m_{i_1,i_2\cdots i_{n+1}}\right) &= t_{MS}\left(m_{i_1,i_2\cdots i_{n+1}}\right), \\
f_{MC}\left(m_{i_1,i_2\cdots i_{n+1}}\right) &= f_{MS}\left(m_{i_1,i_2\cdots i_{n+1}}\right).
\end{aligned} \tag{A.7}$$

Namely, when $MC = MS$ and $MC = MS$, such that $E_{MC}(MS) + E_{MS}(MC) - m\ln 2(E(MC) + E(MS)) = 0$.
Hence $T_n(MC, MS) = 1 \Leftrightarrow MC = MS$. $\qquad\square$

Acknowledgments

This work was supported by the National Natural Foundation of China (nos. 61462046, 61363014), the Science and Technology Research Projects of Jiangxi Province Education Department (nos. GJJ16079, GJJ160750), the Natural Science Foundation of Jiangxi Province (nos. 20151BAB207026, 20161BAB202050, and 20161BAB202049), Jinggangshan University Doctoral Scientific Research Foundation (nos. JZB1311, JZB15016), and Key Laboratory of Watershed Ecology and Geographical Environment Monitoring of NASG (nos. WE2015012, WE2016013).

References

[1] B. Li, J. He, J. Huang, and Y. Q. Shi, "A survey on image steganography and steganalysis," *Journal of Information Hiding and Multimedia Signal Processing*, vol. 2, no. 2, pp. 142–172, 2011.

[2] X.-P. Zang, Z.-X. Qian, and S. Li, "Prospect of digital steganography research," *Journal of Applied Sciences-Electronics and Information Engineering*, vol. 34, no. 5, pp. 475–489, 2016.

[3] J. Fridrich and J. Kodovský, "Rich models for steganalysis of digital images," *IEEE Transactions on Information Forensics and Security*, vol. 7, no. 3, pp. 868–882, 2012.

[4] V. Holub and J. Fridrich, "Low-complexity features for JPEG steganalysis using undecimated DCT," *IEEE Transactions on Information Forensics and Security*, vol. 10, no. 2, article A1, pp. 219–228, 2015.

[5] V. Sedighi, R. Cogranne, and J. Fridrich, "Content-adaptive steganography by minimizing statistical detectability," *IEEE Transactions on Information Forensics and Security*, vol. 11, no. 2, pp. 221–234, 2016.

[6] N. Zhou, H. Li, D. Wang, S. Pan, and Z. Zhou, "Image compression and encryption scheme based on 2D compressive sensing and fractional Mellin transform," *Optics Communications*, vol. 343, pp. 10–21, 2015.

[7] L. Guo, J. Ni, and Y. Q. Shi, "Uniform embedding for efficient JPEG steganography," *IEEE Transactions on Information Forensics and Security*, vol. 9, no. 5, pp. 814–825, 2014.

[8] N. Zhou, S. Pan, S. Cheng, and Z. Zhou, "Image compression-encryption scheme based on hyper-chaotic system and 2D compressive sensing," *Optics and Laser Technology*, vol. 82, pp. 121–133, 2016.

[9] R. Anderson, "Why information security is hard - An economic perspective," in *Proceedings of the 17th Annual Computer Security Applications Conference, ACSAC 2001*, pp. 358–365, usa, December 2001.

[10] C. Cachin, "An information-theoretic model for steganography," *Information and Computation*, vol. 192, no. 1, pp. 41–56, 2004.

[11] K. Sullivan, U. Madhow, S. Chandrasekaran, and B. S. Manjunath, "Steganalysis for Markov cover data with applications to images," *IEEE Transactions on Information Forensics and Security*, vol. 1, no. 2, pp. 275–287, 2006.

[12] Z. Zhang, G. J. Wang, W. Jun et al., "Steganalysis of spread spectrum image steganography based on high-order markov chain mode," *ACTA Electronica Sinica*, vol. 38, no. 11, pp. 2578–2584, 2010.

[13] G.-J. Liu, Y.-W. Dai, Y.-X. Zhao, and Z.-Q. Wang, "Modeling steganographic counterwork by game theory," *Journal of Nanjing University of Science and Technology*, vol. 32, no. 2, pp. 199–204, 2008.

[14] P. Schöttle and R. Böhme, "Game theory and adaptive steganography," *IEEE Transactions on Information Forensics and Security*, vol. 11, no. 4, pp. 760–773, 2016.

[15] J. Liu and G.-M. Tang, "Game research on large-payload and adaptive steganographic counterwork," *Acta Electronica Sinica*, vol. 42, no. 10, pp. 1963–1969, 2014.

[16] R. Chandramouli, M. Kharrazi, and N. Memon, "Image steganography and steganalysis: concepts and practice," in *Proceedings of the IWDW'03*, vol. 2939, pp. 35–49, 2003.

[17] T. Pevný and J. Fridrich, "Benchmarking for steganography," in *Information Hiding. 10th International Workshop*, pp. 251–267, Santa Barbara, Calif, USA, 2008.

[18] J. J. Harmsen and W. A. Pearlman, "Steganalysis of additive noise modelable information hiding," in *Proceedings of the IST/SPIE 15th Annu. Symp. Electronic Imaging Science Technology*, pp. 21–24, San Jose, Calif, USA, January 2003.

[19] F. Li and Z.-Y. Xu, "Measures of similarity between vague sets," *Journal of Software*, vol. 12, no. 6, pp. 922–927, 2001.

[20] S. Y. Quan, "The vague set similarity measure based on Meaning of Information," *Computer Engineering and Applications*, vol. 43, no. 25, pp. 87–89, 2007.

[21] W. L. Gau and D. J. Buehrer, "Vague sets," *IEEE Transactions on Systems, Man and Cybernetics*, vol. 23, no. 2, pp. 610–614, 1993.

[22] P. Bas, T. Filler, and T. Pevny, "Break our steganographic system—the ins and outs of organizing BOSS," in *Proceedings of the 13th International Workshop on Information Hiding*, pp. 59–70, Berlin, Germany, 2011.

[23] United States Department of Agriculture, Natural resources conservation service photo gallery, [DB/OL] http://photogallery .nrcs.usda.gov, 2002.

[24] T. Sharp, "An implementation of key-based digital signal steganography," in *Proceedings of the Information Hiding Workshop*, vol. 2137, pp. 13–26, 2001.

[25] T. Pevný, T. Filler, and P. Bas, "Using high-dimensional image models to perform highly undetectable steganography," *Lecture Notes in Computer Science (including subseries Lecture Notes in Artificial Intelligence and Lecture Notes in Bioinformatics)*, vol. 6387, pp. 161–177, 2010.

[26] J. Fridrich, D. Soukal, and M. Goljan, "Maximum likelihood estimation of length of secret message embedded using ±K steganography in spatial domain," in *Proceedings of SPIE-IS and T Electronic Imaging - Security, Steganography, and Watermarking of Multimedia Contents VII*, vol. 5681, pp. 595–606, January 2005.

[27] P. Sallee, "Model-Based Steganography," in *Digital Watermarking*, T. Kalker, Ed., vol. 2939 of *Lecture Notes in Computer Science*, pp. 154–167, Springer, Berlin, Heidelberg, 2004.

[28] P. Sallee, "Model-based methods for steganography and steganalysis," *International Journal of Image and Graphics*, vol. 5, no. 1, pp. 167–189, 2005.

7

Protecting Privacy in Shared Photos via Adversarial Examples Based Stealth

Yujia Liu, Weiming Zhang, and Nenghai Yu

University of Science and Technology of China, Hefei, China

Correspondence should be addressed to Weiming Zhang; zhangwm@ustc.edu.cn

Academic Editor: Lianyong Qi

Online image sharing in social platforms can lead to undesired privacy disclosure. For example, some enterprises may detect these large volumes of uploaded images to do users' in-depth preference analysis for commercial purposes. And their technology might be today's most powerful learning model, deep neural network (DNN). To just elude these automatic DNN detectors without affecting visual quality of human eyes, we design and implement a novel *Stealth algorithm*, which makes the automatic detector blind to the existence of objects in an image, by crafting a kind of *adversarial examples*. It is just like all objects disappear after wearing an *"invisible cloak"* from the view of the detector. Then we evaluate the effectiveness of *Stealth algorithm* through our newly defined measurement, named *privacy insurance*. The results indicate that our scheme has considerable success rate to guarantee privacy compared with other methods, such as mosaic, blur, and noise. Better still, *Stealth algorithm* has the smallest impact on image visual quality. Meanwhile, we set a user adjustable parameter called *cloak thickness* for regulating the perturbation intensity. Furthermore, we find that the processed images have transferability property; that is, the adversarial images generated for one particular DNN will influence the others as well.

1. Introduction

With the pervasiveness of cameras, especially smartphone cameras, coupled with the almost ubiquitous availability of Internet connectivity, it is extremely easy for people to capture photos and share them on social networks. For example, according to the statistics, around 300 million photos are uploaded onto Facebook every day [1]. Unfortunately, when users are eager to share photos online, they also hand over their privacy inadvertently [2]. Many companies are adept at analyzing the information from photos which users upload to social networks [3]. They collect massive amounts of data and use advanced algorithms to explore users' preferences and then perform more accurate advertising [4]. The owner's life behind each photo is like being peeped.

Recently, we may shudder at a news report about fingerprint information leakage from the popular two-fingered pose in photos [5]. The researchers are able to copy fingerprints according to photos taken by a digital camera as far as three metres away from the subject. Another shocking news is that a new crop of digital marketing firms emerge. They aim at searching, scanning, storing, and repurposing images uploaded to popular photo-sharing sites, to facilitate marketers to send targeted ads [6, 7] or conduct market research [8]. These behaviors of large-scale continuous accessing users' private information will, no doubt, make the photo owners very disturbed.

Moreover, shared photos may contain information about location, events, and relationships, such as family members or friends [9, 10]. This will inadvertently bring security threats to others. After analyzing more than one million online photos collected from 9987 randomly selected users on Twitter, we find that people are fairly fond of sharing photos containing people's portrait on social platforms, as shown in Table 1. We test on 9987 users and take 108.7 images on average from each person. The result shows that about 53.4% of the photos contain people's portrait and 97.9% of the users have shared one or more photos containing people's portrait, which shows great risks of privacy disclosure. In addition to portrait, photos containing other objects may reveal privacy as well, such as road signs and air tickets.

TABLE 1: Some statistics on photos from Twitter.

Number of randomly collected users	9987
Number of collected photos per user	108.7
Photos containing people's portrait	53.4%
Users sharing photos containing portrait	97.9%

Traditional methods of protecting personal information in images are mosaic, blur, partial occlusion, and so on [11, 12]. These approaches are usually very violent and destructive. A more elegant way is to use a fine-grained access control mechanism, which enforces the visibility of each part of an image, according to the access control list for every accessing user [13]. More flexibly, a portrait privacy preserving photo capturing and sharing system can give users, who are photographed, the selection to choose appearing (select the "tagged" item) in the photo or not (select the "invisible" item) [14].

These processing methods can be good ways to shield people's access. But for many companies which push large-scale advertising, they usually use automated systems rather than manual work to detect user uploaded images. For instance, Figure 1 shows the general process of obtaining privacy through online photos. First, a user shares a photo on the social network unguardedly. Then this photo is collected by astute companies and put into their own automatic detection system. Based on the detection results from a simple photo, the user's privacy information might be at their fingertips. The traditional processing methods (mosaic, blur, etc.) will not only greatly reduce image quality undesirably, but also not work well to the automatic detection system based on DNN, as shown in the later experimental results (Figure 6). Users' purpose of sharing photos is to show their life to other people, but not to give detection machine any opportunity to pry into their privacy. Therefore, we need a technique to deal with images, so that the automatic detection system is unable to work well, but humans cannot be aware of the subtle changes in images.

From Figure 1, we can see, whether for commercial or wicked purposes, the basic model of infringing image privacy follows the same patterns: first, the system gives object proposals, that is, to find where objects may exist in the picture and outline bounding boxes of all possible objects; then the system identifies the specific category of each proposal.

With regard to the detection process, the most advanced algorithm is based on deep neural networks. The unparalleled accuracy turns them into the darling of artificial intelligence (AI). DNNs are able to reach near-human-level performance in language processing [15], speech recognition [16], and some vision tasks [17–19], such as classification, detection, and segmentation.

Although they dominate the AI field, recent studies have shown that DNNs are vulnerable to *adversarial examples* [20], which are well designed to mislead DNNs to give an incorrect classification result. But, for humans, the processed images still remain visually indistinguishable with the original ones. Since adversarial examples have a great deal of resistance on

the *classification task*, then for the more complex *detection task*, can we produce adversarial examples with a similar effect? Even if the classification result is incorrect, knowing the existence of an object (not knowing its specific category) is a kind of privacy leakage to some extent. So disenabling the detection machine to see anything is both meaningful and challenging.

As we mentioned above, the detection process is divided into two steps, region proposal and proposal box classification. If we can successfully break through either of these two and visual quality of the original image does not deteriorate, then we are able to produce a new kind of adversarial examples specifically for detection task. A successful resistance involves two cases. One is failing in object proposal, that is, proposing nothing for the next step; and the other is going wrong in recognition on the given right proposal boxes. Our work focuses on the first case. It makes DNNs turn a blind eye to the objects in images; in other words, DNNs will fail to give any boxes of possible objects. Intuitively, our approach is implemented as if objects in an image are wearing an *"invisible cloak."* Therefore, we call it *Stealth algorithm*. Furthermore, we define *cloak thickness* to evaluate the strength of perturbation and *privacy insurance* to measure the capacity of privacy preservation, and their interconnections are also discussed. In addition, we find the *cloak* can be shared; that is, adversarial examples which we make specially for one DNN can also resist other DNN detectors.

In previous work, adversarial examples were usually used to attack various detection systems, such as face recognition [21, 22], malicious code detection [23], and spam filtering [24], all of which are aggressive behaviors out of malice. But, in our work, adversarial examples are made to protect users' privacy. It is an unusually positive and helpful use. Overall, this paper makes the following contributions:

(i) We realize the privacy protection for image content by means of resisting automatic detection machine based on deep neural networks.

(ii) We propose the *Stealth algorithm* of manufacturing adversarial examples for detection task. And this algorithm makes the DNN detection system unable to give object bounding boxes.

(iii) We put forward two new definitions, *cloak thickness* and *privacy insurance*. Measured by them, our experiment shows that *Stealth algorithm* far outdoes several common methods of disturbing image, no matter in effectiveness or in image visual quality.

(iv) We conduct some experiments to show that adversarial examples produced by *Stealth algorithm* have satisfactory transferability property.

The rest of the paper is organized as follows. In Section 2, we review the related work. In Section 3, we introduce several DNN-based detectors and highlight the Faster RCNN detection framework, which we use in our algorithm. In Section 4, we illustrate the approach we design to process an image into an adversarial one for eluding a DNN detector. Then, in Section 5, we evaluate our approach in multiple

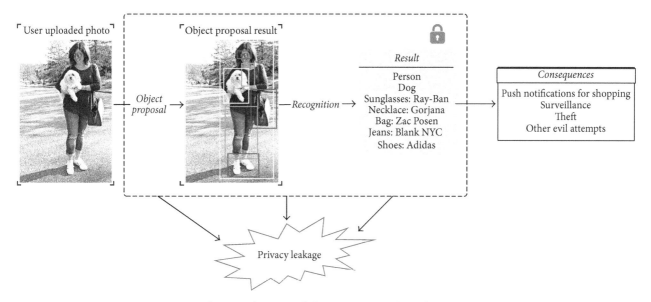

FIGURE 1: The general process of obtaining privacy through online photos.

aspects. Finally, in Section 6, we make conclusions and discuss the future work.

2. Related Work

Over the past few years, many researchers are committed to studying the limitation of deep learning and it is found to be quite vulnerable to some well-designed inputs. Many algorithms spring up in classification tasks to generate this kind of adversarial input. Christian et al. [25] first discovered that there is a huge difference between DNN and human vision. Adding an almost imperceptible interference into the original image (e.g., a dog seen in human eyes) would cause DNN to misclassify it into a completely unrelated category (maybe an ostrich). Then the fast gradient sign method was presented by Ian Goodfellow et al. [20], which can be very efficient in calculating the interference to an image for a particular DNN model. An iterative algorithm of generating adversarial perturbation by Papernot et al. [26] followed it, which is based on a precise understanding of the mapping between inputs and outputs of DNNs by constructing adversarial saliency maps, and the algorithm can choose any category as the target to mislead the classifier. Nguyen et al. [27], along the opposite line of thinking, synthesized a kind of "fooling images." They are totally unrecognizable to human eyes, but DNNs classify them into a specified category with high confidence. More interestingly, Moosavi-Dezfooli et al. [28] found that there exists a universal perturbation vector that can fool a DNN on all the natural images. Adversarial examples have also been found by Ian Goodfellow et al. [20] to have the transferability property. It means an adversarial image designed to mislead one model is very likely to mislead another as well. That is to say, it might be possible for us to craft adversarial perturbation in circumstance of not having access to the underlying DNN model. Papernot et al.

[29, 30] then put forward such a black-box attack based on cross-model transfer phenomenon. Attackers do not need to know the network architecture, parameters, or training data. Kurakin et al. [31] have also shown that, even in the physical world scenarios, DNNs are vulnerable to adversarial examples. Followed by an ingenious face recognition deceiving system by Sharif et al. [32], it enables the subjects to dodge face recognition when they just wear printed paper eye glasses frame.

It can be seen that most of the previous studies on the confrontation against DNNs are usually for classification task. Our work is about the detection task, which is another basic task in computer vision. It is quite distinct from classification, since the returned values of detection are usually both several bounding boxes indicating object positions and labels for categories. Also, its implementation framework is more complicated than classification. Higher dimensions of the result, continuity of the bounding box coordinates, and more complex algorithm make deceiving DNNs on detection become more challenging work.

Viewed from another aspect, Ilia et al. [13] proposed an approach that can prevent unwanted individuals from recognizing users in a photo. When another user attempts to access a photo, the designed system determines which faces the user does not have permission to view and presents the photo with the restricted faces blurred out. Zhang et al. [14] presented a portrait privacy preserving photo capturing and sharing system. People who do not want to be captured in a photo will be automatically erased from the photo by the technique of image inpainting or blurring.

Previous work is to protect the privacy on the level of human vision, whereas these methods have proven less effective for computer vision. In this article, we attempt to design a privacy protection method for computer vision, and meanwhile it ensures human visual quality. This method can

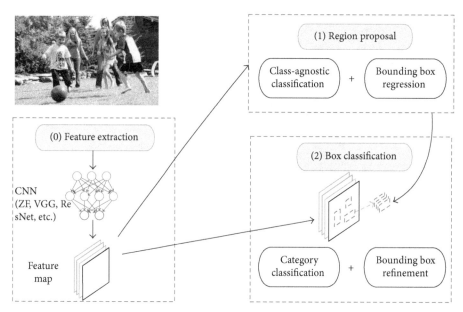

FIGURE 2: Faster RCNN detection architecture.

be applied in conjunction with the above-mentioned photo-sharing system by Zhang et al. [14] in the future work. And it will allow users to choose whether their purpose of privacy protection is against computer vision or human vision.

3. Object Detectors Based on DNNs

Object detection frameworks based on DNNs have been emerging in recent years, such as RCNN [33], Fast RCNN [34], Faster RCNN [18], Multibox [35], R-FCN [36], SSD [37], and YOLO [38]. These methods generally have excellent performance, many of which have even been put into practical applications. In order to avoid the practitioners hesitating to choose detection frameworks, some researchers have made some detailed test and evaluation on the speed and accuracy of Faster RCNN, R-FCN, and SSD, which are prominent on detection task [39]. Results reflect, in general, that Faster RCNN exhibits optimal performance on the trade-off between speed and accuracy. So we choose to resist the detection system employing the *Faster RCNN* framework, as shown in Figure 2.

Technically, it integrates RPN (region proposal network) and Fast RCNN together. The proposal obtained by RPN is directly connected to the ROI (region of interest) pooling layer [34], which is an end-to-end object detection framework implemented with DNNs. First of all, images are processed to extract features by one kind of DNN (ZF-net, VGG-net, ResNet, etc.). And then the detection happens in the following two stages: *region proposal* and *box classification*. At the stage of region proposal, the features are used for predicting class-agnostic bounding box proposals (object or not object). At the second stage, which is box classification, the same features and corresponding box proposals are used to predict a specific class and bounding box refinement.

Here, we do some explanation of the notations. $\mathbf{X} \in \mathbb{R}^m$ is an input image composed of m pixels, and κ is the number of classes that can be detected. The trained models

of the two processes in detection, region proposal, and box classification are f_{rp} and f_{cl}, respectively. And of course there is a feature extraction process f_{feat} before both of them at the very beginning.

In the process of feature extraction, some translation-invariant reference boxes, called anchors, are generated based on the extracted features, denoted by

$$f_{\mathrm{feat}}(\mathbf{X}) = \begin{pmatrix} x_{a1} & y_{a1} & w_{a1} & h_{a1} \\ x_{a2} & y_{a2} & w_{a2} & h_{a2} \\ \vdots & \vdots & \vdots & \vdots \\ x_{ar} & y_{ar} & w_{ar} & h_{ar} \end{pmatrix} = \mathbf{A}(\mathbf{X}). \quad (1)$$

The value r represents the number of anchors. $x_{ai}, y_{ai}, w_{ai}, h_{ai}$ $(i = 1, 2, \ldots, r)$ are, respectively, the vertical and horizontal coordinates of the upper left corner of the anchors and its width and height. Each anchor corresponds to a nearby ground truth box, which can be denoted by

$$b_{\mathrm{gt}}(\mathbf{X}) = \begin{pmatrix} x_{\mathrm{gt1}} & y_{\mathrm{gt1}} & w_{\mathrm{gt1}} & h_{\mathrm{gt1}} \\ x_{\mathrm{gt2}} & y_{\mathrm{gt2}} & w_{\mathrm{gt2}} & h_{\mathrm{gt2}} \\ \vdots & \vdots & \vdots & \vdots \\ x_{\mathrm{gtr}} & y_{\mathrm{gtr}} & w_{\mathrm{gtr}} & h_{\mathrm{gtr}} \end{pmatrix}. \quad (2)$$

Then, in the region proposal stage, f_{rp} predict r region proposals, which are parameterized relative to r anchors.

$$f_{\mathrm{rp}}(\mathbf{X}) = \begin{pmatrix} x_1 & y_1 & w_1 & h_1 & \bigg| & p_1 \\ x_2 & y_2 & w_2 & h_2 & \bigg| & p_2 \\ \vdots & \vdots & \vdots & \vdots & \bigg| & \vdots \\ x_r & y_r & w_r & h_r & \bigg| & p_r \end{pmatrix} \quad (3)$$

$$= \left(\mathbf{B}(\mathbf{X}) \,\big|\, \mathbf{P}(\mathbf{X}) \right).$$

x_i, y_i, w_i, h_i ($i = 1, 2, \ldots, r$) are, respectively, the vertical and horizontal coordinates of the upper left corner of the region proposal and its width and height. The value p_i is the probability of it being an object (only two classes: object versus background). For convenience, we let $\mathbf{B(X)}$ be the first four columns, which contain the location and size information of all the bounding boxes and let $\mathbf{P(X)}$ be the last column containing their probability information.

The region proposal function is followed by a function for box classification $f_{\text{cl}} \colon \mathbb{R}^m \times \mathbb{R}^{r \times 5} \to \mathbb{R}^{n \times (4+\kappa)}$. Here, except the image $\mathbf{X}$, the above partial result $\mathbf{B(X)}$ is also as one of inputs.

$$f_{\text{cl}}\left(\mathbf{X}, \mathbf{B}\left(\mathbf{X}\right)\right)$$

$$= \left(\begin{array}{cccc|cccc} \tilde{x}_1 & \tilde{y}_1 & \tilde{w}_1 & \tilde{h}_1 & p_{11} & p_{12} & \cdots & p_{1\kappa} \\ \tilde{x}_2 & \tilde{y}_2 & \tilde{w}_2 & \tilde{h}_2 & p_{21} & p_{22} & \cdots & p_{2\kappa} \\ \vdots & \vdots & \vdots & \vdots & \vdots & \vdots & \ddots & \vdots \\ \tilde{x}_n & \tilde{y}_n & \tilde{w}_n & \tilde{h}_n & p_{n1} & p_{n2} & \cdots & p_{n\kappa} \end{array} \right) \quad (4)$$

$$= \left(\ \widetilde{\mathbf{B}}\left(\mathbf{X}, \mathbf{B}\left(\mathbf{X}\right)\right) \ \middle| \ \widetilde{\mathbf{P}}\left(\mathbf{X}, \mathbf{B}\left(\mathbf{X}\right)\right) \ \right).$$

The value n is the number of final bounding boxes results ($n \leq r$). And similarly, $\tilde{x}_i, \tilde{y}_i, \tilde{w}_i, \tilde{h}_i$ ($i = 1, 2, \ldots, n$) represent their location and size information. $p_{i1}, p_{i2}, \ldots, p_{i\kappa}$ are, respectively, the probability of each box result belonging to each class (κ classes in total). We also let $\widetilde{\mathbf{B}}(\mathbf{X}, \mathbf{B}(\mathbf{X}))$ and $\widetilde{\mathbf{P}}(\mathbf{X}, \mathbf{B}(\mathbf{X}))$ be the two parts of the result matrix. In short, Faster RCNN framework is the combination of region proposal and box classification.

4. Stealth Algorithm for Privacy

4.1. Motivation and Loss Function. Our *Stealth algorithm* is aimed at the first stage, region proposal. The processing method which directs at the first stage could be the simplest and most effective, because if the detector does not give any proposal boxes, the next stage (box classification) will be even more impossible to succeed. In a word, we deceive a DNN detector from the source.

Our aim is to find a small perturbation $\delta\mathbf{X}$, $\mathbf{X}^{\text{st}} = \mathbf{X} + \delta\mathbf{X}$, s.t.

$$\Pr\left[\mathbf{P}\left(\mathbf{X}^{\text{st}}\right) < \left(\mathbf{th_{rp}}\right)_r \mid \mathbf{P}(\mathbf{X}) \geq \left(\mathbf{th_{rp}}\right)_r, \delta\mathbf{X} < \varepsilon \right] > \eta_{\text{rp}}$$

$$\text{where,} \ \left(\mathbf{th_{rp}}\right)_r = \text{th}_{\text{rp}} \times \begin{pmatrix} 1 \\ 1 \\ \vdots \\ 1 \end{pmatrix}_{r \times 1}. \quad (5)$$

Here th_{rp} is a threshold, according to which the detection machine decides each box to be retained or not. Formula (5) expresses that we want to add some small perturbations, so that in region proposal stage any object proposals cannot be detected with considerable probability η_{rp}. In other words, at this stage, all the boxes with low scores (probability of being an object) will be discarded by the system.

Likewise, we can also interfere with the subsequent box classification stage, which can be expressed as

$$\Pr\left[\max\left(\widetilde{\mathbf{P}}\left(\mathbf{X}^{\text{st}}, \mathbf{B}\left(\mathbf{X}^{\text{st}}\right)\right)\right) < \left(\mathbf{th_{cl}}\right)_n \mid \max\left(\widetilde{\mathbf{P}}\left(\mathbf{X}, \mathbf{B}\left(\mathbf{X}\right)\right)\right) \geq \left(\mathbf{th_{cl}}\right)_n, \delta\mathbf{X} < \varepsilon \right] > \eta_{\text{cl}},$$

$$\text{where,} \ \left(\mathbf{th_{cl}}\right)_n = \text{th}_{\text{cl}} \times \begin{pmatrix} 1 \\ 1 \\ \vdots \\ 1 \end{pmatrix}_{n \times 1}, \quad \max\left(\widetilde{\mathbf{P}}\left(\mathbf{X}, \mathbf{B}\left(\mathbf{X}\right)\right)\right) \triangleq \begin{pmatrix} \max\{p_{11}, p_{12}, \ldots, p_{1\kappa}\} \\ \max\{p_{21}, p_{22}, \ldots, p_{1\kappa}\} \\ \vdots \\ \max\{p_{n1}, p_{n2}, \ldots, p_{n\kappa}\} \end{pmatrix}. \quad (6)$$

Some other bounding boxes will be discarded, because the probability that they belong to any class among the κ classes is less than the threshold th_{cl} with great probability.

On the surface, formula (5) and formula (6) are two modification methods. But in the detection framework Faster RCNN, its two tasks (region proposal and box classification) share the convolution layers; that is, the two functions (f_{rp} and f_{cl}) regard the same deep features as their input. We modify the image for purpose of resisting either of the two stages, which may mislead the other function inadvertently. Therefore, we just choose to deal with the image as formula (5). This operation will obviously defeat the region proposal stage, and it will be even very likely to defeat the following box classification process in formula (6). A more straightforward explanation is that, in the view of the detection machine, our algorithm makes the objects in the image no longer resemble *an object*, let alone *an object of a certain class*. The image seems to be wearing an invisible cloak. So, in the machine's eyes, an image including a lot of content looks completely empty, which lives up to our expectation.

We are more concerned about the region proposal stage, and its loss function in Faster RCNN framework is

$$\mathscr{L}\left(\mathbf{T}\left(\mathbf{A}\left(\mathbf{X_i}\right), \mathbf{B}\left(\mathbf{X_i}\right)\right), \mathbf{T}\left(\mathbf{A}\left(\mathbf{X_i}\right), b_{\text{gt}}\left(\mathbf{X_i}\right)\right), \mathbf{P}\left(\mathbf{X_i}\right),$$

$$\phi\left(\mathbf{X_i}\right); \theta\right) = \lambda \cdot \mathbf{P}\left(\mathbf{X_i}\right) \ell_{\text{box}}\left(\mathbf{T}\left(\mathbf{A}\left(\mathbf{X_i}\right), \mathbf{B}\left(\mathbf{X_i}\right)\right), \quad (7)$$

$$\mathbf{T}\left(\mathbf{A}\left(\mathbf{X_i}\right), b_{\text{gt}}\left(\mathbf{X_i}\right)\right)\right) + \mu \cdot \ell_{\text{prb}}\left(\mathbf{P}\left(\mathbf{X_i}\right), \phi\left(\mathbf{X_i}\right)\right).$$

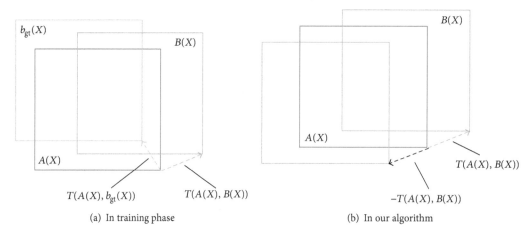

(a) In training phase　　　　　　　　　　　　　　(b) In our algorithm

FIGURE 3: Region proposal process in the training phase and in our algorithm.

Here $\mathbf{T}(\mathbf{A}(\mathbf{X_i}), \mathbf{B}(\mathbf{X_i}))$ represents a certain distance between anchors and the predicted region proposals, and $\mathbf{T}(\mathbf{A}(\mathbf{X_i}), b_{\text{gt}}(\mathbf{X_i}))$ is that between anchors and ground truth boxes (in Figure 3, we represent it as a vector). In training phase, the goal of the neural network is to make $\mathbf{T}(\mathbf{A}(\mathbf{X_i}), \mathbf{B}(\mathbf{X_i}))$ closer to $\mathbf{T}(\mathbf{A}(\mathbf{X_i}), b_{\text{gt}}(\mathbf{X_i}))$, as shown in Figure 3(a). More specifically,

$$
\mathbf{T}(\mathbf{A}(\mathbf{X}), \mathbf{B}(\mathbf{X}))
$$

$$
= \begin{pmatrix} \dfrac{(x_1 - x_{a1})}{w_{a1}} & \dfrac{(y_1 - y_{a1})}{h_{a1}} & \log\left(\dfrac{w_1}{w_{a1}}\right) & \log\left(\dfrac{h_1}{h_{a1}}\right) \\ \dfrac{(x_2 - x_{a2})}{w_{a2}} & \dfrac{(y_2 - y_{a2})}{h_{a2}} & \log\left(\dfrac{w_2}{w_{a2}}\right) & \log\left(\dfrac{h_2}{h_{a2}}\right) \\ \vdots & \vdots & \vdots & \vdots \\ \dfrac{(x_r - x_{ar})}{w_{ar}} & \dfrac{(y_r - y_{ar})}{h_{ar}} & \log\left(\dfrac{w_r}{w_{ar}}\right) & \log\left(\dfrac{h_r}{h_{ar}}\right) \end{pmatrix} \quad (8)
$$

$$
\triangleq \left(\dfrac{(\mathbf{x} - \mathbf{x}_a)}{\mathbf{w}_a} \quad \dfrac{(\mathbf{y} - \mathbf{y}_a)}{\mathbf{h}_a} \quad \log\left(\dfrac{\mathbf{w}}{\mathbf{w}_a}\right) \quad \log\left(\dfrac{\mathbf{h}}{\mathbf{h}_a}\right) \right).
$$

Similarly,

$$
\mathbf{T}\left(\mathbf{A}(\mathbf{X}), b_{\text{gt}}(\mathbf{X})\right)
$$

$$
\triangleq \left(\dfrac{(\mathbf{x}_{\text{gt}} - \mathbf{x}_a)}{\mathbf{w}_a} \quad \dfrac{(\mathbf{y}_{\text{gt}} - \mathbf{y}_a)}{\mathbf{h}_a} \quad \log\left(\dfrac{\mathbf{w}_{\text{gt}}}{\mathbf{w}_a}\right) \quad \log\left(\dfrac{\mathbf{h}_{\text{gt}}}{\mathbf{h}_a}\right) \right). \quad (9)
$$

And $\phi(\mathbf{X_i})$ in the loss function is the probability of the ground truth object labels ($\phi(\mathbf{X_i}) \in \{0, 1\}$: 1 represents the box is an object and 0 represents not). θ is the parameter of the trained model. At the region proposal stage, the total loss $\mathscr{L}$ is composed of two parts, box regression loss ℓ_{box} (smooth $L1$ loss) and binary classification loss ℓ_{prb} (log loss). λ and μ are the weights balancing the two losses.

4.2. Algorithm Details. Here we elaborate on our *Stealth algorithm* of generating adversarial examples in our experiment. Algorithm 1 shows our *Stealth* idea. It takes a benign image $\mathbf{X}$, a trained feature extraction and detection model

f_{feat} and f_{rp}, iteration number Γ, and a user-defined cloak thickness τ as input. Users can control how much privacy to protect as needed, by adjusting the parameter τ to change the interference intensity added to an image. It outputs a new adversarial example $\mathbf{X}^{\text{st}}$ against detection. In general, the algorithm employs two basic steps over multiple iterations: (1) Get the anchors $\mathbf{A}(\mathbf{X_i})$ on the basis of the features extracted from DNN. $\mathbf{X_i}$ is the temporary image in the ith iteration. (2) Compute the forward prediction $f_{\text{rp}}(\mathbf{X_i})$. This indicates the position of the prediction boxes. (3) Get the adversarial perturbation $\delta \mathbf{X_i}$ based on backpropagation of the loss. The loss function $\mathscr{L}$ is the same as that of Faster RCNN, but we change one of its independent variables. In other words, we replace $\mathbf{T}(\mathbf{A}(\mathbf{X_i}), b_{\text{gt}}(\mathbf{X_i}))$ with $-\mathbf{T}(\mathbf{A}(\mathbf{X_i}), \mathbf{B}(\mathbf{X_i}))$, as shown in Figure 3(b). We compute the backpropagation value of the total loss function:

$$
\nabla_{\mathbf{X_i}} \mathscr{L} \left(\mathbf{T}\left(\mathbf{A}(\mathbf{X_i}), \mathbf{B}(\mathbf{X_i})\right), \right.
$$
$$
\left. -\mathbf{T}\left(\mathbf{A}(\mathbf{X_i}), \mathbf{B}(\mathbf{X_i})\right), \mathbf{P}(\mathbf{X_i}), \phi(\mathbf{X_i}); \theta \right) \quad (10)
$$

as the perturbation $\delta \mathbf{X_i}$ in one iteration. The role of backpropagation and loss function in the training process is to adjust the network so that the current output moves closer to the ground truth. Here we substitute the reverse of the direction towards which the box should be adjusted ($-\mathbf{T}(\mathbf{A}(\mathbf{X_i}), \mathbf{B}(\mathbf{X_i}))$) for the ground truth b_{gt}. An intuitive understanding is that we try to track the adjustment on region proposal by DNN detector. If it is found that the DNN wants to move the proposals in a certain direction, then we add some small and well-designed perturbations onto the original image. These perturbations may cause the proposals to move in the opposite direction and consequently counteract their generation.

The original image and that processed by the *Stealth algorithm* will have totally different results through the DNN detector, as shown in Figure 4. The original image can be detected and labeled correctly, while as for the processed image no objects are detected by the DNN detector; that is, no information has been perceived at all. Even better, in human eyes, there is little difference between the adversarial image and the original image.

Input: Image $\mathbf{X}$, model f_{feat}, f_{rp}, iteration number Γ, invisible cloak thickness τ.
Output: Adversarial image $\mathbf{X}^{\text{st}}$.
Initialize: $\mathbf{X_0} \Leftarrow \mathbf{X}$, $i \Leftarrow 0$.
while $i < n$ **do**
  $\mathbf{A}(\mathbf{X_i}) \Leftarrow f_{\text{feat}}(\mathbf{X_i})$,
  $(\mathbf{B}(\mathbf{X_i}), \mathbf{P}(\mathbf{X_i})) \Leftarrow f_{\text{rp}}(\mathbf{X_i})$,
  $\delta \mathbf{X_i} \Leftarrow -\dfrac{\tau}{n} \cdot (\nabla_{\mathbf{X_i}} \mathscr{L}(\mathbf{T}(\mathbf{A}(\mathbf{X_i}), \mathbf{B}(\mathbf{X_i})), -\mathbf{T}(\mathbf{A}(\mathbf{X_i}), \mathbf{B}(\mathbf{X_i})), \mathbf{P}(\mathbf{X_i}), \phi(\mathbf{X_i}); \theta))$,
  $\mathbf{X_{i+1}} \Leftarrow \mathbf{X_i} + \delta \mathbf{X_i}$,
  $i \Leftarrow i + 1$,
end while
$\mathbf{X}^{\text{st}} \Leftarrow \mathbf{X_i}$,
return $\mathbf{X}^{\text{st}}$.

ALGORITHM 1: Stealth algorithm for detection system.

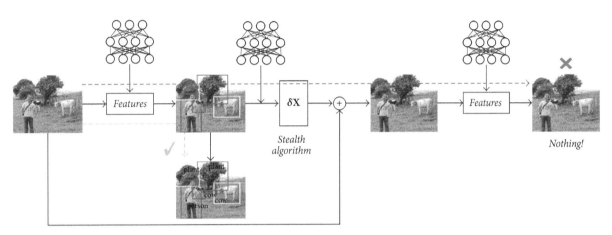

FIGURE 4: The original and processed image through a DNN detector.

4.3. Privacy Metric. To measure the effectiveness of our algorithm quantitatively, we define a variable PI, named *privacy insurance*. It can be interpreted as how much privacy the algorithm can protect. We let O_k be the total number of bounding boxes of the kth class ($1 \leq k \leq \kappa$), which are detection results based on all original images, including both correct and wrong results. And we let V_k be the number of just correct boxes of each class detected on adversarial ones and PI be the average of all PI_k values.

$$\text{PI}_k = \begin{cases} 1 - \dfrac{V_k}{O_k} & O_k \neq 0 \\ 0 & O_k = 0, \end{cases} \quad 1 \leq k \leq \kappa$$

$$\text{PI} = \frac{\sum_{k=1}^{\kappa} \text{PI}_k}{\sum_{k=1}^{\kappa} \delta(O_k, 0)}, \tag{11}$$

$$\text{where, } \delta(O_k, 0) = \begin{cases} 1 & O_k \neq 0 \\ 0 & O_k = 0, \end{cases} \quad 1 \leq k \leq \kappa.$$

We can observe from the above definition that PI means the success rate of our detection resistance actually, and it also indicates how much privacy owned by users can be preserved.

Normally, mAP (mean average precision) is usually used to measure the validity of a detector. But here our PI value

is a more appropriate evaluation index. Suppose there are κ classes in the dataset, each with an independent *privacy insurance* value PI_k ($k = 1, 2, \ldots, \kappa$), because the model itself has some errors when detecting original images; that is, the accuracy is not 100%. And the major concern of our algorithm is to resist the detection model. Consider such a case: the machine's judgment itself on the original image is wrong. And after dealing with it by the algorithm, the judgment is still wrong, but it has two different wrong forms. Then this processing of resisting detection is successful theoretically. But calculating the difference of mAP value between pre- and postprocessing cannot reflect that this case is a successful one. On the contrary, PI can evaluate the validity of our work at all cases, of course including the above one.

5. Experiment and Evaluation

In order to illustrate the effectiveness of our *Stealth algorithm*, we will evaluate it from four aspects: (i) We clarify whether the processed images by our algorithm can resist DNNs effectively. We show the result of performing on nearly 5000 images in PASCAL VOC 2007 test dataset to confirm that. (ii) We compare our algorithm with other ten methods of modifying images for resisting detection. Results indicate that our method works best and has minimal impact on

FIGURE 5: (a) Original images; (b) original results; (c) adversarial perturbations (×20 to show more clearly); (d) processed images; (e) new results.

image visual quality. (iii) We explore the relations among cloak thickness, visual quality, and *privacy insurance* in the algorithm. (iv) We illustrate the transferability of our *Stealth algorithm* on different DNNs.

5.1. Some Experimental Setups. We test our algorithm on the PASCAL VOC 2007 dataset [40]. This dataset consists of 9963 images and is equally split into the trainval (training and validation) set and test set. And it contains 20 categories, which are common objects in life, including people, several kinds of animals, vehicles, and indoor items. Each image contains one or more objects, and the objects vary considerably in scale. As for DNNs, we use two nets trained by Faster RCNN on the deep learning framework Caffe [41]. One is the fast version of ZF-net [42] with 5 convolution layers and 3 fully connected layers, and the other is the widely used VGG-16 net [43] with 13 convolution layers and 3 fully connected layers. In addition, our implementation is completed on a machine with 64 GB RAM, Intel Core i7-5960X CPU, and two Nvidia GeForce GTX 1080 GPU cards.

5.2. Effectiveness and Comparison. Here we first illustrate the effectiveness through several samples and compare with other trivial methods. In the next subsection, we will then introduce the results of larger-scale experiments. As shown in Figure 5, one can observe that images processed by our algorithm can dodge detection successfully. And humans can hardly notice the slight changes. Consequently, we have generated a kind of machine-harm but human-friendly images. For most images in our experimental dataset, the machine cannot see where objects are (the first two rows in Figure 5), let alone identifying what specific category they belong to. For a small number of images, even if the machine is really aware that

there may be some objects in the image, it cannot locate them exactly or classify them correctly (the last row in Figure 5). In short, in the vast majority of cases, the machine will give the wrong answer. To give a quantitative analysis, we introduce a new measurement, *cloak thickness*, which will be explained in detail in Section 5.3.

In addition, we show the other ten trivial but interesting ways of modifying images to interfere with detection machines in Figure 6. We use PSNR (Peak Signal to Noise Ratio) to evaluate the visual quality of the processed images. These methods include both global and local modification. Local processing here is on the location of objects, rather than a random location.

(i) Whether global mosaic in Figure 6(b), local mosaic in Figure 6(c), global blur (Gaussian blur here) in Figure 6(d), or local blur in Figure 6(e), compared to other ways, their PSNR value is a bit larger. This indicates that although the perturbation is not very considerable, the image gets disgustingly murky. People usually cannot endure viewing such images on the Web. Sadly, although people cannot bear it, the machine can still detect most objects correctly. Thus some smoothing filters (like mosaic or Gaussian blur) are unable to resist DNN-based detector. We think DNNs could compensate for the homogeneous loss of information; that is, once a certain pixel is determined, a small number of surrounding pixels are not very critical.

(ii) As shown in Figures 6(f) and 6(g), an image with large Gaussian noise has poor quality judged by its low PSNR value. But the machine is also able to draw an almost correct conclusion. This shows that

FIGURE 6: Images processed by diverse methods of disturbing are detected by the detection framework based on Faster RCNN. Each two horizontal images compose a pair, respectively, representing processed images and the results from the detector.

adding Gaussian noise is not a good way to deceive the detector, either.

(iii) As for a large area of occlusion on key objects, whether black occlusion in Figure 6(h) or white occlusion in Figure 6(i), they both make the quality deteriorate drastically. In spite of a large amount of information loss, the detection result is still almost accurate surprisingly.

(iv) From Figure 6(j), we can see that adjusting the image brightness to a fairly low level cannot resist the detector, either. It causes the greatest damage to the image simultaneously so that human eyes cannot see anything in the image at all. But the detector gives rather accurate results.

(v) In order to make the machine unaware of the existence of objects in the image, another natural idea is to make objects become transparent in front of the machine. So we try to change its transparency and hide it in another image, as shown in Figure 6(k). And yet it still does not work.

(vi) On the contrary, from Figure 6(l), we can see that our *Stealth algorithm* substantially has the smallest damage to image quality and it is also resistant to detection effectively. In order to better illustrate its effectiveness, we have carried out other larger-scale experiments which will be described next.

5.3. Privacy Insurance. In order to depict the degree of privacy protection in our algorithm, we define a parameter, *cloak thickness* τ, to weight the trap-door between privacy and visual quality. Users can tune this parameter to determine the adversarial disturbance intensity on each pixel. For a specific τ, the modification to each pixel is obviously uneven. What we need to do is multiplying τ by the gradient value of DNN backpropagation. This is equivalent to expanding the gradient of each pixel by τ times simultaneously, and it is considered as the final modification added to the image. Greater gradient value of pixel means further distance away from our target, so we need to add more adversarial interference on this pixel. Certainly, different τ values also influence the results. The added interference is proportional to τ value. The greater τ, the thicker the *cloak* the image is wearing, and the machine will be more blind to it. But, of course, the visual quality will go down.

We test on nearly 5000 images and calculate the PI using ZF-net and VGG-net, and the results can be found in Table 2. The 20 classes include airplane, bicycle, bird, boat, bottle, bus, car, cat, chair, cow, dining table, dog, horse, motorbike, person, potted plant, sheep, sofa, train, and tv monitor. Except for very few classes, the PI values of the vast majority are fairly high. This roughly means that we have successfully protected the users' most information in images.

Assume that a user shares many pictures and then tries to protect his privacy by using different methods of perturbing images. We test the PI values of all these methods, as shown in Figure 7. We can see from it that our *Stealth algorithm* can protect most privacy, and mosaic comes second, but it

nevertheless has destructive effects on image. Other methods not only fail to protect privacy, but also cause terrible visual quality of images that users cannot put up with. Of course, users can get more insurance for their privacy by increasing the *cloak thickness* τ, but they may have to face the risk of image quality deteriorating, as shown in Figure 8. From this figure, we can find $\tau = 0.3 \times 10^3$ could be an appropriate value, at which we can not only get a satisfactory *privacy insurance* but also ensure the visual effects. Even if the value of *cloak thickness* is fairly large (e.g., $\tau = 1.2 \times 10^3$), the PSNR is still greater than any other methods. The *Stealth algorithm*'s modification to a pixel is related to the current value of the pixel, so it does not seem so abrupt after the processing.

From the above experimental results, we can see our algorithm works well, but the fact that there exist classes with low PI value (e.g., Class 8 "cat," Class 12 "dog," and Class 14 "motorbike") is worth thinking about. Here we present some illustrations and thoughts on this question. The extracted feature of each region proposal corresponds to a point in a high dimensional space. The correctness of the judgment is related to the classification boundary. Our work is to change positions of these corresponding points by adding perturbation to an image, so that the points can cross the boundary and jump to another class (from be-object class to not-object class).

Our algorithm is independent of the specific class of the object. That is to say, to offset the generation of region proposal, we use the same number of iterations (Γ) and multiple times (τ) when we superimpose the gradient disturbance for all classes. In the abstract high dimensional space, features of different classes occupy different subspaces, which are large or small. So perturbations with the same iterations and multiple times are bound to cause a problem where features of some classes are successfully counteracted, while some few other classes may fail. The reason for failure may be that the number of iterations is insufficient or the magnitude of modification is not enough for these classes. For each region proposal feature in the detector, Figure 9 gives a vivid illustration of the following four cases.

Case 1. The region proposal features of some classes are successfully counteracted after the image is processed. In other words, the corresponding feature point jumps from be-object subspace to not-object subspace. In this case, our algorithm can be deemed a success.

Case 2. Region proposal features of some classes are counteracted partly. So the feature point jumps to a be-object subspace, but features in this subspace are not strong enough to belong to any specific class. That is to say, these proposals will be discarded in the following classification stage for their scores of each class are lower than our set threshold. In this case, the final result is that objects cannot be detected, so it is an indirect success.

Case 3. The feature point jumps from one object class to another. Result is that the detector will give a bounding box approximately, but its label might be incorrect. This case is just a weak success.

TABLE 2: Privacy insurance of each category after using *Stealth algorithm* on ZF-net and VGG-net.

PI_k	1	2	3	4	5	6	7	8	9	10	11	12	13	14	15	16	17	18	19	20	PI
ZF	0.99	0.75	0.87	1.00	0.84	0.97	0.85	0.47	0.86	0.85	0.98	0.23	0.74	0.34	0.70	0.95	0.90	1.00	0.99	0.96	**0.82**
VGG	1.00	0.70	0.87	0.87	1.00	0.73	0.85	0.31	0.92	0.95	0.99	0.95	0.92	0.39	0.93	0.94	0.98	0.99	0.95	0.80	**0.85**

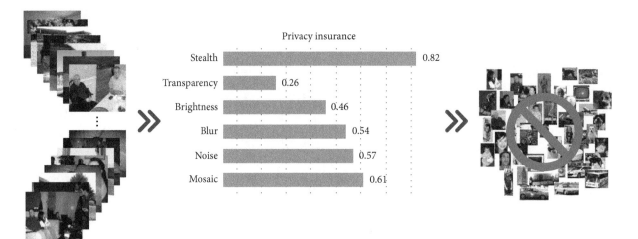

FIGURE 7: Different ways of fooling detection machine. Assume that the user shares many pictures and then tries to protect their privacy by different methods of image scrambling. Obviously our veil algorithm can protect the most privacy. Mosaic comes second, but it has destructive effects on image itself.

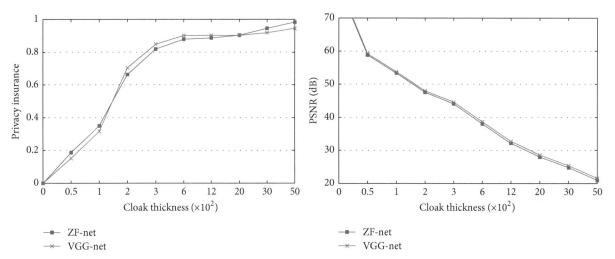

FIGURE 8: Privacy insurance versus PSNR with different cloak thickness.

Case 4. The feature point only jumps within an object class subspace. Its range might be larger than others or its position is farther away from the boundary of not-object class subspace. It is kind of equivalent to saying that the trained detector has better robustness for this specific class. An adversarial algorithm may fail when encountering this case.

The classes with low PI value after our *Stealth algorithm* may fall into Case 4. The iteration and multiple times which we set are not enough to make the proposal feature jump out of its original subspace. However, in order to ensure a good vision quality, we should not set them very high. It is a trade-off between human vision and machine vision.

5.4. Transferability of Cloak. The *Stealth* interference generated for one particular DNN also has an impact on another DNN, even if their network architectures are quite different. We call it the transferability of different *cloaks*. When we put

the adversarial images generated for ZF-net, which is with a slightly larger *cloak thickness*, onto the VGG-net for detection, we can calculate that its *privacy insurance,* PI, is 0.66. And, at this time, the visual quality is still satisfactory. There may exist some subtle regular pattern only when seeing it from a very close distance, but it is much better than mosaic, blur, and other methods for human eyes. Likewise, we detect the VGG adversarial images on ZF-net, and the PI value is 0.69.

So far we have been focusing on the white-box scenario: the user knows the internals, including network architecture and parameters of the system. To some extent, the transferability here leads to the implementation of a black-box system. We do not need to know the details of network. What we only need to know is that the detection system we try to deceive is based on some kind of DNN. Then we can generate an adversarial example for the image to be uploaded against our local DNN. According to the above experimental results, the generated images on local machine are very likely to deceive the detection system of online social network.

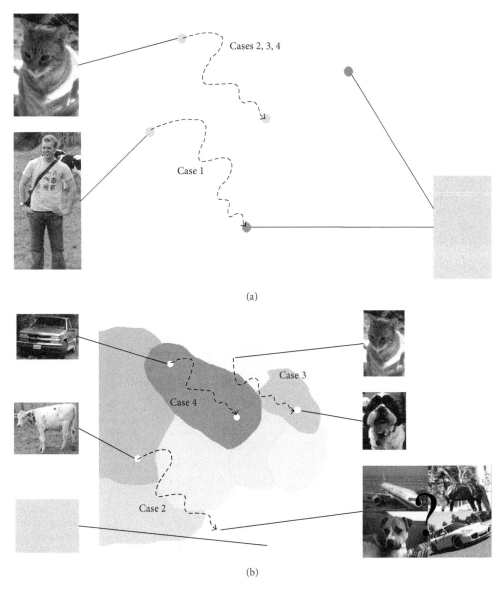

FIGURE 9: An intuitive understanding of adversarial images for detection task in the high dimensional space. (a) Different cases that feature point moves between the be-object class and not-object class in the high dimensional feature space. (b) Different cases that feature point moves among different specific classes. Each subspace with a color represents a specific class. The subspace in the be-object region but not belonging to any specific class represents its score of belonging to any class which is lower than our set threshold.

6. Conclusion and Future Work

In this paper, we propose the *Stealth algorithm* of elaborating adversarial examples to resist the automatic detection system based on the Faster RCNN framework. Similar to misleading the classification task in previous work, we also add some interference to cheat the computer vision of ignoring the existence of objects contained in images. Users can process images to be uploaded onto social networks through our algorithm, thus avoiding the tracking of online detection system, so as to meet the goal of minimizing privacy disclosure. In effect, it is like objects in images wearing an invisibility *cloak* and everything disappearing in machine's view. As a comparison, we conduct experiments of modifying images with several other trivial but intriguing methods (e.g., mosaic, blur, noise, low brightness, and transparency). The result shows our *Stealth* scheme is the most effective and has minimal impact on image visual quality. It can guarantee both high image fidelity to human and invisibility to machine with high probability. We define a user adjustable parameter to determine the adversarial disturbance intensity on each pixel, that is, *cloak thickness*, and a measurement to indicate how much privacy can be protected, that is, *privacy insurance*. And we have further explored the relation between them. In addition, we find the adversarial examples crafted by our *Stealth algorithm* have transferability property; that is, the interference generated for one particular DNN also has an impact on another DNN.

One of our further researches will be a theoretical analysis about the transferability property between different network models. And, according to it, we will try to find a method of crafting adversarial examples with good generalization performance on many different DNNs. Even if its fooling performance on any one of DNN models will not be as good as the specific adversarial example, it can maximize the average performance on all models. Furthermore, it is evident that our algorithm is a global processing on images. So another ongoing study should be conducted to only add partial adversarial perturbation to achieve the same deceiving effect. That is to say, we try to modify only part of pixels, instead of processing the image globally. But this requirement may lead to significant changes on a few pixels, which will cause an uncomfortable visual effect. So we should try to find out some ways to make the processed image look more natural.

Acknowledgments

This work was supported in part by the Natural Science Foundation of China under Grants U1636201 and 61572452. Yujia Liu, Weiming Zhang, and Nenghai Yu are with CAS Key Laboratory of Electromagnetic Space Information, University of Science and Technology of China, Hefei 230026, China.

References

[1] Zephoria, "The Top 20 Valuable Facebook Statistics," 2017, https://zephoria.com/top-15-valuable-facebook-statistics/.

[2] B. Krishnamurthy and C. E. Wills, "On the leakage of personally identifiable information via online social networks," in *Proceedings of the 2nd ACM SIGCOMM Workshop on Online Social Networks, WOSN '09*, pp. 7–12, 2009.

[3] B. Henne and M. Smith, "Awareness about photos on the web and how privacy-privacy-tradeoffs could help," *Lecture Notes in Computer Science (including subseries Lecture Notes in Artificial Intelligence and Lecture Notes in Bioinformatics): Preface*, vol. 7862, pp. 131–148, 2013.

[4] M. Hardt and S. Nath, "Privacy-aware personalization for mobile advertising," in *Proceedings of the 2012 ACM Conference on Computer and Communications Security, (CCS '12)*, pp. 662–673, October 2012.

[5] "Japan researchers warn of fingerprint theft from 'peace' sign," 2017, https://phys.org/news/2017-01-japan-fingerprint-theft-peace.html./.

[6] W. Meng, X. Xing, A. Sheth, U. Weinsberg, and W. Lee, "Your online interests-Pwned! A pollution attack against targeted advertising," in *Proceedings of the 21st ACM Conference on Computer and Communications Security, (CCS '14)*, pp. 129–140, November 2014.

[7] A. Reznichenko and P. Francis, "Private-by-design advertising meets the real world," in *Proceedings of the 21st ACM Conference on Computer and Communications Security, CCS ('14)*, pp. 116–128, November 2014.

[8] Icondia, "Smile Marketing Firms Are Mining Your Selfies," 2016, http://www.icondia.com/wp-content/uploads/2014/11/Image-Mining.pdf

[9] N. E. Bordenabe, K. Chatzikokolakis, and C. Palamidessi, "Optimal geo-indistinguishable mechanisms for location privacy," in *Proceedings of the 21st ACM Conference on Computer and Communications Security, CCS 2014*, pp. 251–262, November 2014.

[10] M. E. Andrés, N. E. Bordenabe, K. Chatzikokolakis, and C. Palamidessi, "Geo-indistinguishability: differential privacy for location-based systems," in *Proceedings of the ACM SIGSAC Conference on Computer and Communications Security (CCS '13)*, pp. 901–914, ACM, Berlin, Germany, November 2013.

[11] M. J. Wilber, V. Shmatikov, and S. Belongie, "Can we still avoid automatic face detection?" in *Proceedings of the IEEE Winter Conference on Applications of Computer Vision, (WACV '16)*, March 2016.

[12] I. Polakis, P. Ilia, F. Maggi et al., "Faces in the distorting mirror: revisiting photo-based social authentication," in *Proceedings of the 21st ACM Conference on Computer and Communications Security, CCS ('14)*, pp. 501–512, November 2014.

[13] P. Ilia, I. Polakis, E. Athanasopoulos, F. Maggi, and S. Ioannidis, "Face/off: preventing privacy leakage from photos in social networks," in *Proceedings of the 22nd ACM SIGSAC Conference on Computer and Communications Security, (CCS '15)*, pp. 781–792, October 2015.

[14] L. Zhang, K. Liu, X.-Y. Li, C. Liu, X. Ding, and Y. Liu, "Privacy-friendly photo capturing and sharing system," in *Proceedings of the 2016 ACM International Joint Conference on Pervasive and Ubiquitous Computing, UbiComp 2016*, pp. 524–534, September 2016.

[15] R. Collobert and J. Weston, "A unified architecture for natural language processing: deep neural networks with multitask learning," in *Proceedings of the 25th International Conference on Machine Learning*, pp. 160–167, ACM, July 2008.

[16] A. Hannun, C. Case, J. Casper, B. Catanzaro et al., "Deep speech: scaling up end-to-end speech recognition," 2014, https://arxiv.org/abs/1412.5567.

[17] A. Krizhevsky, I. Sutskever, and G. E. Hinton, "Imagenet classification with deep convolutional neural networks," in *Proceedings of the 26th Annual Conference on Neural Information Processing Systems (NIPS '12)*, pp. 1097–1105, Lake Tahoe, Nev, USA, December 2012.

[18] S. Ren, K. He, R. Girshick, and J. Sun, "Faster R-CNN: towards real-time object detection with region proposal networks," in *Advances in Neural Information Processing Systems*, pp. 91–99, 2015.

[19] J. Long, E. Shelhamer, and T. Darrell, "Fully convolutional networks for semantic segmentation," in *Proceedings of the IEEE Conference on Computer Vision and Pattern Recognition (CVPR '15)*, pp. 3431–3440, IEEE, Boston, Mass, USA, June 2015.

[20] J. Ian Goodfellow, S. Jonathon, and S. Christian, "Explaining and harnessing adversarial examples," 2014, https://arxiv.org/abs/1412.6572.

[21] Y. Sun, Y. Chen, X. Wang, and X. Tang, "Deep learning face representation by joint identification-verification," in *Advances in neural information processing systems*, pp. 1988–1996, 2014.

[22] B. B. Zhu, J. Yan, Q. Li et al., "Attacks and design of image recognition CAPTCHAs," in *Proceedings of the 17th ACM Conference on Computer and Communications Security, CCS'10*, pp. 187–200, October 2010.

[23] G. E. Dahl, J. W. Stokes, L. Deng, and D. Yu, "Large-scale malware classification using random projections and neural networks," in *Proceedings of the 2013 38th IEEE International*

Conference on Acoustics, Speech, and Signal Processing, ICASSP 2013, pp. 3422–3426, May 2013.

[24] T. S. Guzella and W. M. Caminhas, "A review of machine learning approaches to Spam filtering," *Expert Systems with Applications*, vol. 36, no. 7, pp. 10206–10222, 2009.

[25] S. Christian, Z. Wojciech, I. Sutskever et al., "Intriguing properties of neural networks," 2013, https://arxiv.org/abs/1312.6199.

[26] N. Papernot, P. McDaniel, J. Somesh, M. Fredrikson, Z. Berkay Celik, and S. Ananthram, "The limitations of deep learning in adversarial settings," in *Security and Privacy (EuroS&P), 2016 IEEE European Symposium on IEEE*, pp. 372–387.

[27] A. Nguyen, J. Yosinski, and J. Clune, "Deep neural networks are easily fooled: High confidence predictions for unrecognizable images," in *Proceedings of the IEEE Conference on Computer Vision and Pattern Recognition, CVPR 2015*, pp. 427–436, June 2015.

[28] S.-M. Moosavi-Dezfooli, A. Fawzi, and P. Frossard, "Universal adversarial perturbations," 2016, https://arxiv.org/abs/1610.08401.

[29] N. Papernot, P. McDaniel, S. Jha, M. Fredrikson, Z. B. Celik, and A. Swami, "Practical black-box attacks against deep learning systems using adversarial examples," 2016, https://arxiv.org/abs/1602.02697.

[30] N. Papernot, P. McDaniel, and I. Goodfellow, "Transferability in machine learning: from phenomena to black-box attacks using adversarial samples," 2016, https://arxiv.org/abs/1605.07277.

[31] A. Kurakin, I. Goodfellow, and S. Bengio, "Adversarial examples in the physical world," 2016, https://arxiv.org/abs/1607.02533.

[32] M. Sharif, S. Bhagavatula, L. Bauer, and M. K. Reiter, "Accessorize to a crime: Real and stealthy attacks on state-of-the-art face recognition," in *Proceedings of the 23rd ACM Conference on Computer and Communications Security, (CCS '16)*, pp. 1528–1540, October 2016.

[33] R. Girshick, J. Donahue, T. Darrell, and J. Malik, "Rich feature hierarchies for accurate object detection and semantic segmentation," in *Proceedings of the 27th IEEE Conference on Computer Vision and Pattern Recognition (CVPR '14)*, pp. 580–587, Columbus, Ohio, USA, June 2014.

[34] R. Girshick, "Fast R-CNN," in *Proceedings of the 15th IEEE International Conference on Computer Vision (ICCV '15)*, pp. 1440–1448, December 2015.

[35] S. Christian, R. Scott, and E. Dumitru, "Scalable, high-quality object detection," 2014, https://arxiv.org/abs/1412.1441.

[36] Y. Li, H. Kaiming, S. Jian et al., "R-fcn: Object detection via region-based fully convolutional networks," *Advances in Neural Information Processing Systems*, pp. 379–387, 2016.

[37] W. Liu, D. Anguelov, D. Erhan et al., "SSD: single shot multibox detector," *Lecture Notes in Computer Science (including subseries Lecture Notes in Artificial Intelligence and Lecture Notes in Bioinformatics): Preface*, vol. 9905, pp. 21–37, 2016.

[38] J. Redmon, S. Divvala, R. Girshick, and A. Farhadi, "You only look once: Unified, real-time object detection," in *Proceedings of the 2016 IEEE Conference on Computer Vision and Pattern Recognition, CVPR 2016*, pp. 779–788, July 2016.

[39] H. Jonathan, R. Vivek, and S. Chen, "Speed/accuracy trade-offs for modern convolutional object detectors," 2016, https://arxiv.org/abs/1611.10012.

[40] M. Everingham, L. van Gool, C. K. I. Williams, J. Winn, and A. Zisserman, "The pascal visual object classes (VOC) challenge," *International Journal of Computer Vision*, vol. 88, no. 2, pp. 303–338, 2010.

[41] Y. Jia, E. Shelhamer, J. Donahue et al., "Caffe: convolutional architecture for fast feature embedding," in *Proceedings of the ACM International Conference on Multimedia*, pp. 675–678, ACM, Orlando, Fla, USA, November 2014.

[42] M. D. Zeiler and R. Fergus, "Visualizing and understanding convolutional networks," in *Computer Vision—ECCV 2014: 13th European Conference, Zurich, Switzerland, September 6–12, 2014, Proceedings, Part I*, vol. 8689 of *Lecture Notes in Computer Science*, pp. 818–833, Springer, 2014.

[43] K. Simonyan and A. Zisserman, "Very deep convolutional networks for large-scale image recognition," 2014, https://arxiv.org/abs/1409.1556.

8

A Policy-Based Framework for Preserving Confidentiality in BYOD Environments: A Review of Information Security Perspectives

Chalee Vorakulpipat, Soontorn Sirapaisan, Ekkachan Rattanalerdnusorn, and Visut Savangsuk

National Electronics and Computer Technology Center, 112 Thailand Science Park, Phahonyothin Road, Khlong 1, Khlong Luang, Pathum Thani 12120, Thailand

Correspondence should be addressed to Chalee Vorakulpipat; chalee.vorakulpipat@nectec.or.th

Academic Editor: Alexandre Viejo

Today, many organizations allow their employees to bring their own smartphones or tablets to work and to access the corporate network, which is known as a bring your own device (BYOD). However, many such companies overlook potential security risks concerning privacy and confidentiality. This paper provides a review of existing literature concerning the preservation of privacy and confidentiality, with a focus on recent trends in the use of BYOD. This review spans a large spectrum of information security research, ranging from management (risk and policy) to technical aspects of privacy and confidentiality in BYOD. Furthermore, this study proposes a policy-based framework for preserving data confidentiality in BYOD. This framework considers a number of aspects of information security and corresponding techniques, such as policy, location privacy, centralized control, cryptography, and operating system level security, which have been omitted in previous studies. The main contribution is to investigate recent trends concerning the preservation of confidentiality in BYOD from the perspective of information security and to analyze the critical and comprehensive factors needed to strengthen data privacy in BYOD. Finally, this paper provides a foundation for developing the concept of preserving confidentiality in BYOD and describes the key technical and organizational challenges faced by BYOD-friendly organizations.

1. Introduction

Bring your own device (BYOD) policies that include smartphones and tablets have played an important role in technological enhancements over the past decade. Today, many organizations employ a BYOD policy and allow their employees to freely use BYOD. Some companies view this as an opportunity to implement new technology without investing their own resources on devices [1]. Often, employees simply bring their devices to work because they own those devices and use them to play games or watch videos while at work. On many occasions, those employees who do use these devices for work do so without prior authorization from their employer, and, in the majority of cases, there are no workplace rules regarding the use of such devices. However, many employers overlook security concerns regarding potential leaks of private or confidential information. For instance, if an employee loses his/her smartphone which may contain confidential organizational data such as email and trade secrets, there is potential of that data leaking in an unauthorized fashion to the public. This can be detrimental to the organization's reputation and profitability [2]. In light of such issues, security management can be addressed in various manners, depending on the organization's policies. An organization may allow devices to be used freely, in a limited manner with some restrictions, or not at all. A security policy may state clear guidelines regarding BYOD but not contain technical guidelines that employees can implement. Factors such as access control, intrusion detection, protocol vulnerability and threat assessment, cryptography, device and OS security, and security management should be taken into account while implementing BYOD security. A framework that addresses these factors could provide a guideline for implementing mechanisms to control BYOD at an organization level.

The objective of this study is to provide a guiding framework for BYOD control, with an emphasis on preserving confidentiality and privacy. This paper is divided into five sections. Following this introduction, related studies are discussed regarding BYOD and security. Then, the proposed framework and an analysis of this framework are presented, respectively. The final section provides a conclusion and suggestions for further study.

2. Related Research

2.1. BYOD Overview and Comparison. The use of mobile devices, including laptops, smartphones, and tablets, is common in workplaces, and the implementation of BYOD controls would significantly reduce security breaches associated with BYOD [3]. However, trends in how employees prefer to use mobile devices have been evolving. Traditionally, companies would configure mobile devices for their employees to work within the office or on site. Because the company would have full control over these devices and the network infrastructure, they could ensure that the devices complied with company security policies. Security measures would be in place, so that the company could manage risks and control any damage that might result from policy violations. It has been reported that companies spend large portions of their budgets for such a provision of mobile devices. This strategy is known as corporate owned, personally enabled (COPE) [4], here is your own device (HYOD), choose your own device (CYOD) [5], or use what you are told (UWYT) [6]. Unlike conventional schemes, some companies have adopted a new policy, which supports the use of employees' personal mobile devices in the office and working environments and is called bring your own device (BYOD). Some employees prefer this option and have begun to bring their own devices to work with them wherever they go. This working style results in increased flexibility and agility and less frustration, as employees can work anywhere with familiar devices. Some employees and executives believe that they can enhance productivity through the integration of work and lifestyles. Regardless of the additional work required to support the use of BYOD, this policy can reduce the corporate costs of hardware provision.

A summary of the differences between HYOD and BYOD is presented in Table 1, and detailed information can be found in the work of Singh [6].

2.2. Risks and Concerns. Despite the fact that both companies and their employees can benefit from various aspects of BYOD, there are also risks and concerns accompanying the adoption of BYOD.

Often, the use of BYOD results in conflicts between usability and security [5, 7]. Typically, users tend to value usability over security, because they simply want to do their jobs effectively without worrying about cumbersome security measures. Hence, while the use of BYOD can result in higher employee satisfaction, it can also increase certain security risks and concerns, such as the following aspects.

(i) Network Access Controls. Mobile devices that can remotely connect to corporate networks from anywhere at anytime can place the corporate network and corresponding data at risk. Without proper protection, adversaries may be able to intercept corporate information or even impersonate legitimate employees and illegally gain access to networks and services.

(ii) Vulnerabilities and Exploitation. Devices that are centrally managed by an organization are generally better protected as their security profiles must meet stricter standards. This means these devices are in a more controlled environment and not as susceptible to exploitation. On the other hand, devices owned by individual employees may or may not comply with regulations and standards, hence leading to uncontrollable vulnerabilities. When vulnerable devices connect to a corporate network, they present new exploitable security holes concerning the whole network.

(iii) Corporate Applications. Companies may offer certain applications and services for which they wish to allow access only to employees with sufficient privileges and appropriate roles. Traditional measures of who can access such resources may not be sufficient. Companies may need to consider, for instance, which devices can access these resources where and when.

(iv) Device Policies. The security posture of organizational owned devices is more straightforward to design and implement using a security guideline or template. Devices that are employee-owned and are not managed centrally by the organization may not meet the security standards required and thus place organizational data at risk.

(v) Data Protection. In BYOD scenarios, company data such as corporate emails, classified documents, and project photos can be stored together with users' private data. Protection measures regarding data leakage in the event of lost or stolen devices must be in place to protect corporate data. Storage encryption and remote data wiping should be considered as a line of defense in order to prevent data from falling into the wrong hands.

In 2014, the well-known security company Symantec conducted an experiment to investigate what would happen to lost mobile devices in the real world, by intentionally "losing" devices incites with high traffic. This project was called the "Honey Stick Project" [8]. In the experiment, Symantec loaded mobile phones with dummy information, including bank accounts, HR salaries, personal photos, and other documents, and installed tracking software to monitor what would happen after the phones were found. The phones were left without security protection, such as screen locks, so that their finders could do virtually anything they wanted with the phones. The phones were dropped in six Canadian cities: Vancouver, Calgary, Toronto, Ottawa, Montreal, and Halifax. The major findings of the investigation were as follows:

(i) 93% of people accessed the phones.

(ii) 63% of people viewed corporate emails.

TABLE 1: Differences between HYOD and BYOD.

	HYOD (employer's devices)	BYOD (employee's devices)
Information security governance	(i) Standardized devices (ii) Tightly coupled (iii) Focus on corporate control (iv) Fully controllable	(i) Diverse devices (ii) Loosely coupled (iii) Focus on flexibility and agility (iv) Partially controllable, require user awareness
Operations	(i) Full centralized management (ii) Standard hardware (iii) Standard software (iv) Acceptable use policy	(i) User is responsible for their own devices (ii) Hardware of their choice (iii) Standard and user's software (iv) Acceptable use policy and BYOD policy
Personnel	(i) Lesser level of employee technical ability (ii) Central support (iii) Lower cost for personnel training due to standard devices	(i) Higher level of employee technical ability (ii) Central support and self-service (iii) Higher cost for personnel training due to diverse devices
Information and data flow	(i) Centrally provisioned and secured information (ii) Easier to comply with rules and audit (iii) Easier to implement access control to limit information leakage	(i) Centrally provisioned, distributed security (ii) Harder to comply with rules and audit (iii) Harder to implement access control to limit information leakage (iv) Remote information wiping is required
Application	(i) Standard and corporate applications (ii) Controllable vulnerabilities and data leakage	(i) Standard, corporate, and user's applications (ii) Harder to control vulnerabilities and data leakage, sandboxed or container management (iii) Focus on open standards
System	(i) Centralized control of access to applications, systems, and information	(i) Centralized control of infrastructure, distributed control of applications and information

(iii) 83% of people viewed personal data.

(iv) 50% of people viewed private photos.

(v) 55% of people tried to return the phones.

Apparently, in the absence of proper protection measures, once mobile devices are lost, it is very likely that information on those phones will be exposed, which could result in serious data leakages.

2.3. Location-Based Service. Advances in location detecting technology for mobile devices have accelerated the development of and demand for location-based services (LBS) [9, 10]. LBS are services that leverage a user's geographical location in order to deliver personalized information. In order to better understand LBS, let us consider the following scenarios.

(i) Alice Is Currently Staying in Thailand. When she types the keywords "famous sightseeing" into the input box of a search engine, the search engine will return results for "famous sightseeing" in Thailand, such as the Grand Palace, Doi Inthanon, and Phuket. Other locations, such as the Forbidden City or Big Ben, are excluded from the search results, because they are not located in Thailand.

(ii) Bob Is Visiting His Friend at NECTEC. He wants to know the locations of the nearest big shopping malls in the area, so he opens a map application on his mobile phone and searches for "big shopping malls." The app returns Future Park Rangsit as the first result, based on his present location, rather than Siam Paragon or Central World.

(iii) Kate Uses a Social Network App on Her Mobile Phone. It has a feature called "Shake and meet new friends." When she shakes her phone, the app sends a request for a list of users who are currently staying nearby and then shows Kate a list of users that are close to her location. Then, she can begin to chat with these new friends.

These customized services are made possible by modern positioning technologies, especially on mobile devices. There are several common techniques that are used to locate positions of mobile devices. Global positioning system (GPS) is a navigation system that provides location and time data for a client to a GPS receiver, through communications with four or more GPS satellites. Other similar technologies can be used in a similar manner, such as GLONASS, IRNSS, and BeiDou-2. Furthermore, cellular triangulation uses raw radio measurements to determine the locations of devices relative to tower bases, and the WiFi positioning system (WiPS) is mainly used for indoor positioning systems.

LBS can be utilized in a BYOD environment to track devices and enforce location-based policies. For instance, a policy may allow employees to use their mobile devices in corporate locations without screen locking, but once employees leave such areas, the devices can be locked, and employees must enter a passcode in order to unlock their device. In the case of lost or forgotten devices, devices' locations can be used to help locate and retrieve those devices.

2.4. Operating System Level. To secure BYOD at an operating system (OS) level, the White House in the United States (US) suggests that virtualization, walled gardens, and limited separation should be included in a BYOD policy to allow access to personal and corporate data on the same device [11], which was also confirmed in [12, 13]. Virtualization is employed as a virtual desktop solution or thin client, which allows computing resources to be accessed remotely on personal devices without data being stored or apps being processed [12, 14]. Therefore, mobile device management (MDM) may not be required, because data processing takes place on a corporate server. In addition, a virtualization-based technique called virtual machine (VM) is used to separate an enterprise space from a personal space. A hypervisor or virtual machine monitor (VMM) is implemented to create a VM. Either a Type-1 or Type-2 hypervisor can be selected [12]. However, the criteria of selection are based on separation levels, performance, and OS kernels. For example, a Type-1 hypervisor provides the best separation between personal space and corporate space, but the performance is poorer. A Type-2 hypervisor is more flexible, but the OS security can be compromised. Nevertheless, it is clear that mobile visualization faces some practical challenges. For example, hardware level virtualization requires the support of mobile device vendors, whereas software level virtualization is not fully secure against malware [15]. A study that considers OS-level virtualization for containers describes the two crucial drawbacks of additional resource constraints and severe performance limitations [16]. Despite this, it has been suggested that, in order to minimize user reactance and enable seamless, transparent personas, the use of universal standards are required for VMs (instead of limiting reliance on vendors), such as TCP/IP and loosely coupled architectures [15].

Regarding walled gardens or walled sandboxes, corporate data and apps are processed within a separate secure partition or secure application on the personal device, and this can ensure the separation between personal and corporate data [11]. A secure application can provide MDM services in the form of cloud-based software-as-a-service, in order to synchronize emails, calendars, and contacts [11]. To apply a walled garden in a BYOD enterprise architecture, internal services can be either logically or physically separated when accessed by personal devices and corporate-owned devices [17]. In fact, physical separation reduces the risk of data leakage [17]. Sensitive information storage methods usually employ a walled garden approach. For example, in cancer research, private personal information is simply moved to a walled garden, from where it is securely combined with public datasets [18]. Furthermore, tutors at the Open University can provide online courses using a secure messaging service via a walled garden [19]. In terms of app development, walled gardens are used to separate app developer areas from manufacturer areas and in most cases are associated with licensing issues [20]. Today, mobile device platforms (e.g., iOS and Android) operate within a strict walled garden, which results in severe limitations for organization-based applications [21]. The introduction of a cross-platform message delivery system is highly recommended [21].

While the separation between personal data and corporate data ensures security, it can inhibit seamless operations. A limited separation allows personal and corporate data to be processed on the same device, while enforcing policies to ensure that minimum security requirements are met [11, 22, 23]. The combination of policies, practices, and technical controls must be implemented successfully in order to be accepted by mobile device users [24]. An organization must provide MDM solutions for limited separation implementation to ensure security and privacy. For example, the data on a mobile device can be remotely wiped when a user violates the BYOD policy. Because of this, limited separation can be confronted with both technical and management issues. Limited separation may be the least expensive solution, owing to (a) the lack of requirements; (b) the ease of implementation, because it can work with existing infrastructures; and (c) the existence of this function in the two well-known operating systems iOS and Android [25].

In addition, trusted boot in mobile devices has recently become increasingly important for improving the security of the boot sequence. This falls into the following two categories of (a) secure boot where the boot sequence is evaluated and aborted if a suspicious component attempts to be loaded and (b) trusted boot where a log is maintained during the boot process for later audit [26]. Secure boot has been criticized for locking down devices, resulting in limited functionality. On the other hand, trusted boot lacks the enforcement of run-time verification [26]. Therefore, a software-only approach cannot fully secure software applications on mobile devices against cyberattacks, especially for operating systems with end-user access, which can be hacked [27]. A number of studies have proposed a dedicated security hardware-assisted solution, to customize trusted boot and thus to tackle the above problems [26–28]. Using a phone-centric approach, a trusted boot technique can protect data once the device has been switched on [29].

3. Proposed Framework

3.1. Policy. An organization must have a clear policy regarding BYOD use, whether that is to support its use fully, partially, or not at all [30]. This choice will depend on the level of security required in the organization. In addition, business requirements and productivity should also be considered. If an organization chooses to fully support BYOD, then that organization must accept security risks, and the adoption of BYOD policies is highly recommended. Many control mechanisms must be implemented to support these policies. A top-down approach is generally used to distribute BYOD policies to employees. The corresponding mechanisms should be ready to employ prior to announcing the policy. However, if an organization does not allow BYOD, then that organization will avoid the associated security risks and BYOD policies or control mechanisms may not be required. Furthermore, the scope of the use of BYOD covered in the policy must be clearly defined. For example, a CIO should be able to decide whether or not the policy will cover a scenario in which a device is used at home to connect to the corporate network or where a device is used in an organization but does not connect to the corporate network or is offline.

3.2. Registration.

If an organization allows the use of BYOD, then it is important to know the identities of devices and their owners. A device owner is required to register their identification (e.g., employee number, name, and email) and device identification (e.g., International Mobile Station Equipment Identity (IMEI)). This registration process can be automatic. The registration system can link device identification data to personal information stored in the organization's database system (such as a human research database). The registration process is the most important aspect of BYOD. The impact of a lack of registration may be equivalent to that of a lack of log storage.

3.3. Provision.

If an organization fully supports BYOD use, then devices must be configured so as not to allow unauthorized users to gain access to the corporate network. There are several possible controls. For example, all devices must be protected by a passcode, to prevent unauthorized use. Failure to enter this correctly would be reported to the administrator or would result in the suspension of the use of BYOD. In addition, inappropriate use, such as jailbreaking or rooting a device that may result in an increase of vulnerability, should not be allowed, be closely monitored, or be allowed on a case-by-case basis (e.g., in the case of research purposes). Moreover, in some organizations, policies may limit the use of certain functions in BYOD, such as cameras. A mechanism to disable these functions can be implemented. For example, the camera app icon can be disabled or hidden.

3.4. Centralized Control.

BYOD control mechanisms essentially involve data sanitization, compliance control, and centralized configuration control [31]. Moreover, all activities can be monitored and detected by an administrator. A dashboard is employed to signal misuses of BYOD. This helps to ensure that BYOD policy is followed. In terms of the preservation of confidential data, the administrator can force a factory reset to wipe all data or force selective wiping through a designated channel, such as Google Cloud Messaging for Android or another cloud-based system [31]. This mechanism helps to protect an organization's information assets in cases of lost or stolen BYOD devices. It is important that a communication channel through which a user can send a request to the administrator to wipe data exists. An appropriate authentication method is required to identify users. This is similar to an authentication method for mobile banking transactions.

As mentioned, all such controls are completely centralized, and an agent connecting to the centralized control must be installed on the device.

3.5. Monitoring and Tracking.

Besides the monitoring of activities related to access to the corporate network, the monitoring and tracking of locations are necessary. This is crucial when a device is an asset of an organization. Organizations sometimes place restrictions on the use of devices (either BYOD or organization-owned devices), where a user cannot use or bring the device outside of designated areas. A mechanism for tracking the locations of users could ensure that users do not bring devices outside of specific locations. This can be underpinned by GPS or a mobile network. Moreover, not only should information regarding physical locations be monitored and tracked, but rather contextual information (e.g., time-based, behavioral-based, and statistical-based information) should also be considered to control access [32]. Issues regarding privacy concerns may be raised, but monitoring and tracking systems can only be active during specific times, such as when a user borrows an organization-owned device for ad hoc work, or when a user is connecting to the corporate network using their BYOD device during working hours.

3.6. Location Privacy.

Information regarding the locations of users' devices is legally collected for tracking purposes. This implies that user locations are also known to the company. If this location data is not stored under proper protection and is accessed by adversaries or malicious attackers, then the attackers may learn user identities, corporate interests, working routines, and so on and use this information for their own benefit. Hence, it is essential that location privacy is considered, in order to protect the privacy of users. The risks of location data exposure can be mitigated through several approaches. Location perturbation [33] is the simplest technique for preserving anonymity, by providing a dummy location back to the system. For instance, a random position in the legitimate range is reported back instead of the exact location of the user, as long as the user is still in the permitted area. Spatial cloaking [34–36], also referred to as location cloaking or location blurring, is a technique used to blur the user's exact location with a bigger area, called a "cloaked region." It is reported that location privacy depends strongly on the size of the cloaked region. The bigger the cloaked region, the more strongly the location privacy protected, and vice versa. For example, if a user is currently located at the NECTEC building, a larger fuzzy area name, such as Thailand Science Park or even the Khlong Luang District, can be employed as a cloaked region to disguise the user's location. An approach called k-anonymity [37–43] is used to blend the exact location of the user with other locations of users nearby that are impossible or difficult to distinguish. This approach uses a similar idea as spatial cloaking to blur the real location of the user but uses locations from a group of k users instead of a cloaked region. For instance, if Alice is currently located at NECTEC, while Bob, Charlie, and Dave are located at other buildings nearby, then Alice can hide her real location by reporting the locations of all of these users, including hers, back to the system.

3.7. Password and Challenge Response. Passwords represent one authentication technique [44–46] that has been widely employed in many application domains over a longtime. In parlance of security terminology, this is categorized as a "something you know" authentication method. This leverages a concept where a service provider shares a secret with its users. The provider may share secrets with either a single individual or a group of users. Only valid users know this secret and use it to validate their identities and prove that they are who they claim to be. The password authentication scheme does not increase the cost of implementation, because it does not require special hardware or software. The protection it provides is as strong as its length, complexity, and difficulty to guess. A good password should be of reasonable length, mix various types of characters, and be difficult to guess for other people.

One major weakness of the password method is that if a password is discovered by an adversary by guessing, intercepting, brute force, or other means, then they can impersonate the identity of the user. To prevent password exposure through interception, guessing, or brute force attacks, a technique called a challenge-response mechanism can be introduced to reduce the risks posed by adversaries. Instead of simply relying on the password alone, a service provider will send a challenge value to a user, and the user then computes the response value and replies with this. The challenge-response authentication scheme is deployed in many well-known protocols, such as CHAP, CRAM-MD5, SCRAM, and Session Initialization Protocol. It can also be implemented as a solution to prevent bots from carrying out brute force attacks or accessing services, for example, using CAPTCHA or re-CAPTCHA. As a response to password guessing and cracking techniques becoming more sophisticated, the one-time password (OTP) technique has been introduced to solve the resulting problems. In practice, this has proved to be a considerably efficient authentication method, owing to the fact that it is volatile, unique, and only usable for a short period of time.

3.8. Public-Key Cryptography. Public-key cryptography [47, 48], also referred to as asymmetric cryptography, is a cryptographic algorithm that uses a pair of generated keys. These consist of a public key, which can be distributed widely in public spaces, and a private key, which is only accessible to the owner. The strength of the public-key cryptography system is a reflection of the difficulty of calculating the private key from its corresponding public key. Cryptographic algorithms are usually based on complex mathematical problems, such as integer factorization, discrete logarithm, and elliptic curve problems. One of the most widely employed public-key cryptography systems is RSA (Rivest-Shamir-Adleman), which is based on the practical difficulty of factoring products of two large prime numbers.

The private key-public key pair is used to encrypt and decrypt a message. If the private key is used to encrypt the message, then the message must be decrypted using the public key. In this manner, the message is guaranteed to originate from the real author only if it can be decrypted using the author's public key. Similarly, if the public key is used to encrypt the message, then the private key is used to decrypt it. This ensures that only the owner of the private key can view a message that is encrypted using their public key. A secure channel is not required for the exchange of public keys. However, the authenticity and the integrity of a public key are usually assured through a digital certificate issued by a "certificate authority (CA)" [49]. Today, certificateless signatures (CLSs) are used as a security model for managing the key escrow problem of identity-based signatures, with an emphasis on public-key replacements and strong unforgeability [50].

Owing to the computational complexity of public-key cryptography, it is commonly employed for small chunks of data, such as the exchange of a session key (symmetric key) that is used to secure a communication channel. The use of public-key cryptography can strengthen the security of BYOD communications. In the context of mobile commerce, cryptography algorithms and standards are taken into account for the purpose of energy-aware consumption [51].

3.9. Cryptographic Hash Function. The cryptographic hash function [52] is a mathematical algorithm that generates a fixed size bit string from data of an arbitrary size. It inherits the property of a one-way function, which means that it is impossible to recover the original input data from an output hash string. A slight change in the input data can significantly alter the output string (avalanche effect). Despite this irreversibility property, it is theoretically possible to find other input data that can produce the same output hash string. This is called hash collision. However, in practice, it is infeasible and impractical to carry out a collision attack on a good cryptographic hash function, because it is extremely difficult to find inputs that produce the same hash string from an infinite pool of data within a limited time.

Because of the uniqueness and irreversibility properties, cryptographic hash functions are widely employed in information security applications, especially in preserving user privacy and data integrity [53, 54]. The privacy of the user is achieved by applying cryptographic hash functions to sensitive information, such as usernames and passwords for accounts or personal identification numbers. Cryptographic hash functions are also used to create identification mechanisms or to summarize messages, which is similar to fingerprinting a person. Hence, this technique is also often called message digest or checksum.

This method can be used to verify the validity of data [55]. For example, a user can download a program installer from the internet and verify its hash value to check whether the installer is complete and has not been corrupted or altered by a malicious attacker. Another use case is cryptographic hash functions in PGP [56, 57], where a sender wants to send a message to the intended receivers, and the receivers want to verify the authenticity of the message. To ensure the integrity of the message and reduce computational costs, a digest of the message is computed and signed using the sender's private key, which is called the "signature," instead of signing the whole message. The sender then sends the message, along with the signature, to the receivers. The receivers can verify the authenticity of the message by using the sender's public key to decrypt the signature and compare it with the message digest computed from the message by themselves.

Although cryptographic hash functions have been proven to be useful in practice for many cryptographic applications, obsolete algorithms such as MD5 are discouraged and should be avoided [58, 59]. For security reasons, stronger algorithms, such as algorithms from the SHA-2 family, should be used instead.

3.10. Virtualization, Walled Garden, Limited Separation, and Trusted Boot. System architecture security in BYOD situations addresses operating system level approaches, which include virtualization, walled gardens, limited separation, and trusted boots. The first three approaches are connected to business objectives. Therefore, prior to their implementation, information asset classification must be carried out, to determine personal as well as corporate data. In a policy-based framework, the implementation should also involve an information owner, who should be the best qualified person to verify the accuracy of personal and corporate data, as well as business objectives. Although a number of existing studies only suggest that the three technical approaches of virtualization, walled gardens, and limited separation should be included in a policy-based framework, it is presently also highly recommended that trusted boot should be considered for inclusion in a BYOD policy. This is because trusted boot techniques can help to achieve lower-level protection [60]. This means that lower-level programs can ensure the security of higher-level programs that are to be activated [61]. Either a software-only approach or a hardware-assisted solution can be chosen to implement trusted boot, depending on the level of security required.

4. Framework Analysis

A framework analysis reveals a number of factors that should be addressed in the implementation of BYOD controls. A summary of this analysis can be divided into categories based on technical specifications, as depicted in Table 2. The technical specifications adapted from [10] include network structures, secure communication channels, location-based functions, identity preservation, sensitive information preservation, platform dependency, multiple device management, provisioning, and policy enforcement.

Meanings and explanations of each technical specification topic listed in Table 2 are provided as follows.

(i) Network Structure. These are networks that are used for the transmission of data and control communications between management systems and mobile devices. Some large companies may have strict policies, clearly stating that all communication traffic must pass through their own corporate trusted or secured network, and all information must be stored under their autonomous sites.

(ii) Secure Communication Channel. These are mechanisms used to secure communications between management sys-

tems and mobile devices or between mobile devices and other mobile devices. This ensures that adversaries cannot easily intercept valuable information from a network.

(iii) Location-Based Function. The location information of mobile devices and users can be utilized for more than just viewing locations on a map. For instance, this information can be used to restrict the use of devices within given areas or to require that device holders must enter a passcode to unlock devices when using them outside of certain areas.

(iv) Identity Preservation. The identities of users should be appropriately protected, in order to avoid the risks associated with leakages of identity data. The cryptographic hash function method can be used to generate fingerprints of user accounts, so that the possibility of account information being accessed is reduced. To further protect identity data, techniques of blurring identities, such as k-anonymity and area cloaking, can also greatly help to protect identities.

(v) Sensitive Information Preservation. Sensitive information, such as account information, corporate emails, prototype photos, or project documents, should be stored securely and protected by reasonable measures. Besides passwords and challenge-response mechanisms, data encryption can strongly prevent unauthorized individuals from accessing sensitive information. Another layer of protection can be provided by remote wiping, which enables users to clear important data on their devices remotely, hence preventing valuable information from falling into the wrong hands when devices are lost.

(vi) Platform Dependency. Major mobile operating systems have their own mobile device management platforms, such as Find My iPhone for iOS and Android Device Manager for Android. There are also similar services provided by third-party developers, as standalone applications or as parts of features of their applications. However, from a corporate aspect, devices need to be manageable by both the owner of the device and the company. Thus, it is necessary to have a central platform for device management.

(vii) Security Architecture. Common security architectures and models are not sufficient to secure BYOD devices and enable the seamless execution of processes. The four techniques of virtualization, walled gardens, limited separation, and trusted boot should be considered, because all of these techniques not only focus on technical issues but also address business objectives and management issues.

(viii) Multiple Device Management. Owing to the rapid development and high popularity of smart devices, many people may own multiple mobile devices, such as smart phones, tablets, and smart wearable devices. A unified platform is crucial for the management of mobile devices in a company, so that each individual, as well as the company, can manage devices effectively and comply with policies.

(ix) Provisioning. It is very common that a considerable amount of people enter and leave job positions at an office.

TABLE 2: A comparative analysis of device management frameworks.

Technical specification	Typical personal device management framework	The proposed framework
Network structure	Public network	Corporate network, trusted network, and secured network
Secure communication channel	SSL/TLS, proprietary	SSL/TLS, VPN
Location-based function	Location tracking	Location tracking and location-based policy enforcement
Identity preservation	Unknown, proprietary	k-Anonymity, area cloaking, one-way hash, and public-key cryptographic
Sensitive information preservation	Unknown, optional	Passcode locking, data/storage encryption, and remote wiping/selective wiping
Platform dependency	Platform dependent, vendor specific	Platform independent
Security architecture	Operating system security in general	Emphasis on virtualization, walled garden, limited separation, and trusted boot
Multiple device management	Managed individually	Managed individually or centrally by company
Provisioning	Not provided	Corporate network connection, corporate email, and other corporate applications
Policy enforcement	Not provided	Role-based policy enforcing and location-based policy enforcing

The tasks involved in device provisioning are nontrivial. WiFi connection settings, setting up corporate email accounts, corporate application installations, and so on are tasks that consume time and human resources. A central management platform and corporate application store can automate these processes and greatly reduce the human effort that is required for these tasks.

(x) Policy Enforcement. In order for policies issued by a company to be effective, they must be suitably enforced such that employees comply. The proposed framework can help to enforce policies by providing tools to set policies for mobile devices based on the rolls and locations of the users.

An experiment is conducted to validate the framework in a real environment. To obtain a better understanding of the metrics used for framework validation, let us consider the real scenario described as follows. Dave is an employee in an organization that takes data security and the privacy of the organization seriously. This organization has issued and enforced a BYOD policy, with which every staff member must comply. The provisioning of devices must be carried out prior to letting staff begin using mobile devices for work, such as setting up corporate email and configuring WiFi setting. There are some mandatory requirements for Dave before he can use mobile devices provided by either the company or himself for work. These devices must connect to the centralized controller, so that the organization can detect if there are any suspicious activities that do not comply with

their policy and also Dave can manage these devices remotely. The communication channel between the devices and the controller must be secured, in order to prevent malicious attackers or adversaries from intercepting confidential data or exploiting vulnerabilities and illegally accessing the devices. It is also crucial and common to use a VPN to establish a secure tunnel from the devices to the corporate network before accessing some internal services. When Dave is working at an external site, keeping track of location information can benefit both the organization and Dave. The positions of the devices can be used to determine which services and functionalities are open to Dave. Dave can also use location information as concrete evidence to prove that he is really on a business trip. If any devices are lost or stolen, then Dave can track their current or last-known locations, increasing the chance of retrieving the devices. More importantly, there should be a way to enable Dave to lock the devices or even to wipe all corporate data remotely, because confidential data can be considerably important and has the potential to result in catastrophic damage to an organization if it falls into the wrong hands.

In order to comply with the BYOD policy and satisfy the requirements explained above, an implementation of the framework is achieved through a centralized mobile device management platform, which has the necessary features and can manage devices remotely and straightforwardly. The platform supports the two most commonly used mobile operating systems, Android and iOS. WSO2 is used as the

TABLE 3: Implementation of the proposed framework.

Features implementation		Proposed framework
Network structure	Accessing within corporate network	+
	Accessing from public network	+
Secure communication channel	SSL/TLS	+
	VPN	−
Location-based function	Location tracking	+
	Location-based policy enforcing	*
Identities preserving	Identities blurring/hiding	−
Sensitive information preserving	Passcode locking	+
	Data encryption	−
	Remote wiping	+
Platform dependency	Support major mobile OSes	+
	Central management platform	+
Security architecture	Virtualization, walled garden, and limit separation	+
	Trusted boot	+
Multiple devices management	Individual management	+
	Central management	+
Provisioning	Network connection	+
	Corporate email	+
	Corporate apps	+
Policy enforcing	Role-based enforcing	+
	Location-based enforcing	*

+: the feature is implemented.
−: the feature is not implemented.
*: the feature can possibly be implemented in the future.

main tool for developing the BYOD control mechanism for the Android platform, while the iOS platform also has its own mobile device management platform.

Although the underlying implementations are different for the different operating system platforms, they share common features that provide similar functionalities. The results of using these implementations to achieve the goals of the proposed framework are summarized and discussed in Table 3.

VPN functionality is not integrated into the platform directly. However, owing to the enterprise store capability allowing an administrator to upload corporate-specific applications that only company staff can access and download, a VPN application can be deployed through the corporate store, along with other internal applications. Because the communication channel for transmitting sensitive data from mobile devices to the platform is secured using an SSL/TLS tunnel, and organizations usually have concerns regarding accountability, hiding employees' identities is not necessary (because the company already knows who uses which devices), and it is practically impossible for other parties to intercept identity information. Typically, accessing configuration data for applications on these devices is impossible without rooting or jailbreaking devices, although other data stored on shared partitions can be accessed publicly. However, full storage encryption is possible, and users can enable this feature manually.

5. Conclusions

A policy-based framework for a BYOD environment should consider the key concepts of information security and privacy. The features in the framework described in this paper should be accordingly implemented in line with a company's information security and privacy policies. An organization must clearly define the allowed scope for use of BYOD and decide the extent to which the organization will support the use of BYOD. Because a BYOD policy is strongly linked to information security, it is necessary that an information security policy must first be implemented to determine the overall requirements. Thus, a BYOD policy must be based on an organization's information security policies. A mechanism for satisfying technical requirements, including network structure, secure communication channels, location-based functions, identity preservation, preservation of sensitive information, security architecture, platform dependency, multiple device management, provisioning, and policy enforcement, must be balanced effectively and must be based on the organization's information security policies. Furthermore, security levels (regarding privacy and confidentiality) should be determined based on business objectives. Thus, different organizations that adopt the same framework may operate at different levels of security. The recommendations for the further study can be established based on this paper. The proposed framework can be further studied in conjunction with other existing mobile device management techniques to improve effectiveness and ensure validity and reliability of the solution. Ultimately, when the proposed framework is deployed in various ways in new organizational settings, the study of organization environment such as organization history and business objectives should be conducted first. It is hoped that the present review will contribute to the ongoing debate on BYOD policy and its future evolution.

Competing Interests

The authors declare that they have no competing interests.

References

[1] A. M. French, C. J. Guo, and J. P. Shim, "Current status, issues, and future of bring your own device (BYOD)," *Communications of the Association for Information Systems,* vol. 35, pp. 191–197, 2014.

[2] D. Sangroha and V. Gupta, "Exploring security theory approach in BYOD environment," *Smart Innovation, Systems and Technologies,* vol. 28, no. 2, pp. 259–266, 2014.

[3] N. Zahadat, P. Blessner, T. Blackburn, and B. A. Olson, "BYOD security engineering: a framework and its analysis," *Computers & Security,* vol. 55, pp. 81–99, 2015.

[4] J. Holleran, "Building a better BYOD strategy," *Risk Management,* vol. 61, pp. 12–14, 2014.

[5] A. Ghosh, P. K. Gajar, and S. Rai, "Bring your own device (BYOD): security risks and mitigating strategies," *Journal of Global Research in Computer Science,* no. 4, pp. 62–70, 2013.

[6] N. Singh, "BYOD genie is out of the bottle-'devil or angel'," *Journal of Business Management Social Sciences Research,* vol. 1, pp. 1–12, 2012.

[7] B. Tokuyoshi, "The security implications of BYOD," *Network Security,* vol. 2013, no. 4, pp. 12–13, 2013.

[8] Symantec, *The Symantec Smartphone Honey Stick Project,* Symantec, Cupertino, Calif, USA, 2012.

[9] S. Teerakanok, C. Vorakulpipat, S. Kamolphiwong, and S. Siwamogsatham, "Preserving user anonymity in context-aware location-based services: a proposed framework," *ETRI Journal,* vol. 35, no. 3, pp. 501–511, 2013.

[10] S. Teerakanok, M. Pattaranantakul, C. Vorakulpipat, S. Kamolphiwong, and S. Siwamogsatham, "A privacy-preserving framework for location-based service: a review of structural design and analysis," *IETE Technical Review,* vol. 31, pp. 422–439, 2014.

[11] The White House, "Bring Your Own Device," 2012, https://www.whitehouse.gov/digitalgov/bring-your-own-device.

[12] J. M. Chang, P.-C. Ho, and T.-C. Chang, "Securing bYOD," *IT Professional,* vol. 16, no. 5, pp. 9–11, 2014.

[13] S. Earley, R. Harmon, M. R. Lee, and S. Mithas, "From BYOD to BYOA, phishing, and botnets," *IT Professional,* vol. 16, no. 5, pp. 16–18, 2014.

[14] Y. Dong, J. Mao, H. Guan, J. Li, and Y. Chen, "A virtualization solution for BYOD with dynamic platform context switching," *IEEE Micro,* vol. 35, no. 1, pp. 34–43, 2015.

[15] A. Hovav and F. F. Putri, "This is my device! Why should I follow your rules? Employees' compliance with BYOD security policy," *Pervasive and Mobile Computing,* vol. 32, pp. 35–49, 2016.

[16] L. Xu, Z. Wang, and W. Chen, "The study and evaluation of ARM-based mobile virtualization," *nternational Journal of Distributed Sensor Networks,* vol. 11, no. 7, pp. 1–10, 2015.

[17] Centre for the Protection of National Infrastructure and CESG, "BYOD Guidance: Enterprise Considerations," 2014, https://www.gov.uk/government/publications/byod-guidance-enterprise-considerations/byod-guidance-enterprise-considerations.

[18] F. M. De La Vega, Y. Wu, T. Shmaya et al., "Abstract LB-308: a novel data safe haven approach to bring analyses to the International Cancer Genome Consortium data," *Cancer Research,* vol. 75, no. 15, pp. LB-308–LB-308, 2015.

[19] H. Farley and A. Pike, "Engaging prisoners in education: reducing risk and recidivism," *Journal of the International Corrections and Prisons Association,* vol. 1, pp. 65–73, 2016.

[20] A. Bhardwaj, K. Pandey, and R. Chopra, "Android and iOS security—an analysis and comparison report," *International Journal of Information Security and Cybercrime,* vol. 5, no. 1, pp. 32–44, 2016.

[21] D. Jaramillo, R. Newhook, and R. Smart, "Cross-platform, secure message delivery for mobile devices," in *Proceedings of the IEEE SoutheastCon,* Jacksonville, Fla, USA, April 2013.

[22] L. Rafferty, B. Kroese, and P. C. K. Hung, "Toy computing background," in *Mobile Services for Toy Computing,* P. C. K. Hung, Ed., pp. 9–38, 2015.

[23] CIO Council, "A Toolkit to Support Federal Agencies Implementing Bring Your Own Device (BYOD) Programs," 2012, https://cio.gov/wp-content/uploads/downloads/2012/09/byod-toolkit.pdf.

[24] A. Cormack, "BYOD toolkit," 2012, https://community.jisc.ac.uk/blogs/regulatory-developments/article/byod-toolkit.

[25] J. Booker, S. Peng, S. Meduri, and J. German, "Bring Your Own Device: An Interactive Report," 2015, http://apps.pittsburghpa.gov/cis/BYOD_interactive.pptx.pdf.

[26] J. González, M. Hölzl, P. Riedl, P. Bonnet, and R. Mayrhofer, "A practical hardware-assisted approach to customize trusted boot for mobile devices," in *Proceedings of the in International Conference on Information Security,* Hong Kong, China, October 2014.

[27] M. Baentsch, P. Buhler, L. Garcés-Erice et al., "IBM secure enterprise desktop," *IBM Journal of Research and Development,* vol. 58, no. 1, Article ID 6717139, 2014.

[28] V. Chandra and R. Aitken, "Mobile hardware security," in *Proceedings of the IEEE Hot Chips 26 Symposium (HCS '14),* pp. 1–40, IEEE, Cupertino, Calif, USA, August 2014.

[29] A. B. Garba, J. Armarego, and D. Murray, "Bring your own device organisational information security and privacy," *ARPN Journal of Engineering and Applied Sciences,* vol. 10, no. 3, pp. 1279–1287, 2015.

[30] Azzurri Communications, *Azzurri's BYOD Matrix,* Azzurri Communications, Surrey, UK, 2014.

[31] C. Vorakulpipat, C. Polprasert, and S. Siwamogsatham, "Managing mobile device security in critical infrastructure sectors," in *Proceedings of the 7th International Conference on Security of Information and Networks (SIN'14),* pp. 65–68, Scotland, UK, September 2014.

[32] D. Kang, J. Oh, and C. Im, "Context based smart access control on BYOD environments," *Information Security Applications,* vol. 8909, pp. 165–176, 2015.

[33] R. Dewri, "Local differential perturbations: location privacy under approximate knowledge attackers," *IEEE Transactions on Mobile Computing,* vol. 12, no. 12, pp. 2360–2372, 2013.

[34] P.-Y. Li, W.-C. Peng, T.-W. Wang, W.-S. Ku, J. Xu, and J. A. Hamilton Jr., "A cloaking algorithm based on spatial networks for location privacy," in *Proceedings of the IEEE International*

Conference on Sensor Networks, Ubiquitous, and Trustworthy Computing (SUTC '08), pp. 90–97, IEEE, Taichung, Taiwan, June 2008.

[35] C.-Y. Chow, M. F. Mokbel, and X. Liu, "Spatial cloaking for anonymous location-based services in mobile peer-to-peer environments," *GeoInformatica*, vol. 15, no. 2, pp. 351–380, 2011.

[36] T. C. Li and W. T. Zhu, "Protecting user anonymity in location-based services with fragmented cloaking region," in *Proceedings of the 2012 IEEE International Conference on Computer Science and Automation Engineering (CSAE'12)*, pp. 227–231, Zhangjiajie, China, May 2012.

[37] B. Gedik and L. Liu, "Protecting location privacy with personalized k-anonymity: architecture and algorithms," *IEEE Transactions on Mobile Computing*, vol. 7, no. 1, pp. 1–18, 2008.

[38] L. Sweeney, "k-Anonymity: a model for protecting privacy," *International Journal of Uncertainty, Fuzziness and Knowledge-Based Systems*, vol. 10, no. 5, pp. 557–570, 2002.

[39] G. Zhong and U. Hengartner, "A distributed k-anonymity protocol for location privacy," in *Proceedings of the 7th Annual IEEE International Conference on Pervasive Computing and Communications (PerCom'09)*, Galveston, Tex, USA, March 2009.

[40] S. Wang and X. S. Wang, "AnonTwist: nearest neighbor querying with both location privacy and k-anonymity for mobileusers," in *Proceedings of the International Conference on Mobile Data Management, System, Services, and Middleware*, Taipei, Taiwan, 2009.

[41] T. Hashem, L. Kulik, and R. Zhang, "Privacy preserving group nearest neighbor queries," in *Proceedings of the 13th International Conference on Extending Database Technology (EDBT '10)*, Lausanne, Switzerland, March 2010.

[42] A. Masoumzadeh and J. Joshi, "An alternative approach to k-anonymity for location-based services," in *Proceedings of the International Conference on Mobile Web Information System*, Niagara Falls, Canada, 2011.

[43] R.-H. Hwang and F.-H. Huang, "SocailCloaking: a distributedarchitecture for k-anonymity location privacy protection," in *Proceedings of the International Conference on Computing, Networking and Communications ((ICNC'14)*, Honolulu, Hawaii, USA, February 2014.

[44] L. Lamport, "Password authentication with insecure communication," *Communications of the ACM*, vol. 24, no. 11, pp. 770–772, 1981.

[45] B. Ross, C. Jackson, N. Miyake, D. Boneh, and J. C. Mitchell, "Stronger password authentication using browser extensions," in *Proceedings of the Usenix Security Symposium*, Baltimore, Md, USA, 2005.

[46] M. Sandirigama and A. Shimizu, "Simple and secure password authentication protocol (SAS)," *IEICE Transactions on Communications*, vol. 83, no. 6, pp. 1363–1365, 2000.

[47] M. E. Hellman, "An overview of public key cryptography," *IEEE Communications Magazine*, vol. 16, no. 5, pp. 42–49, 1978.

[48] W. Diffie and M. E. Hellman, "New directions in cryptography," *IEEE Transactions on Information Theory*, vol. 22, no. 6, pp. 644–654, 1976.

[49] B. A. Forouzan, *Cryptography and Network Security*, McGraw-Hill Higher Education, New Delhi, India, 2008.

[50] Y.-C. Chen and R. Tso, "A survey on security of certificateless signature schemes," *IETE Technical Review*, vol. 33, no. 2, pp. 115–121, 2016.

[51] F. Hamad, L. Smalov, and A. James, "Energy-aware security in M-commerce and the internet of things," *IETE Technical Review*, vol. 26, no. 5, pp. 357–362, 2009.

[52] B. Schneier, *One-Way Hash Functions, in Applied Cryptography*, John Wiley & Sons, Indianapolis, Ind, USA, 2015.

[53] A. H. M. Ragab and N. A. Ismail, "An efficientmessage digest algorithm (MD) for data security," in *Proceedings of the IEEE Region 10 International Conference on Electricaland Electronic Technology*, Singapore, 2001.

[54] A. Habib, D. Xu, M. Atallah, B. Bhargava, and J. Chuang, "A tree-based forward digest protocol to verify data integrity in distributed media streaming," *IEEE Transactions on Knowledge and Data Engineering*, vol. 17, no. 7, pp. 1010–1013, 2005.

[55] Q. Wang, C. Wang, K. Ren, W. Lou, and J. Li, "Enabling public auditability and data dynamics for storage security in cloud computing," *IEEE Transactions on Parallel and Distributed Systems*, vol. 22, no. 5, pp. 847–859, 2011.

[56] D. Kumar, D. Kashyap, K. K. Mishra, and A. K. Misra, "Security Vs cost: an issue of multi-objective optimization for choosing PGP algorithms," in *Proceedings of the 2010 International Conference on Computer and Communication Technology (ICCCT'10)*, pp. 532–535, Uttar Pradesh, India, September 2010.

[57] W. Stallings, *Network and Internetwork Security: Principles and Practice*, Prentice Hall, Englewood Cliffs, NJ, USA, 1995.

[58] T. Xie and D. Feng, "How to find weak input differences for MD5 collision attacks," *IACR Cryptology ePrint Archive*, vol. 2009, p. 223, 2009.

[59] V. Klima, "Finding MD5 collisions on a notebook PC using multi-message modifications," *IACR Cryptology ePrint Archive*, vol. 2005, p. 102, 2005.

[60] C. Huang, C. Hou, H. Dai, Y. Ding, S. Fu, and M. Ji, "Research on Linux trusted boot method based on reverse integrity verification," *Scientific Programming*, vol. 2016, Article ID 4516596, 12 pages, 2016.

[61] Y. Inamura, T. Nakayama, and A. Takeshita, "Trusted mobile platform technology for secure terminals," *NTT DoCoMo Technical Journal*, vol. 7, pp. 25–39, 2005.

9

Efficient KDM-CCA Secure Public-Key Encryption via Auxiliary-Input Authenticated Encryption

Shuai Han,[1,2] Shengli Liu,[1,2,3] and Lin Lyu[1,2]

[1]*Department of Computer Science and Engineering, Shanghai Jiao Tong University, Shanghai 200240, China*
[2]*State Key Laboratory of Cryptology, P.O. Box 5159, Beijing 100878, China*
[3]*Westone Cryptologic Research Center, Beijing 100070, China*

Correspondence should be addressed to Shengli Liu; slliu@sjtu.edu.cn

Academic Editor: Muhammad Khurram Khan

KDM[$\mathscr{F}$]-CCA security of public-key encryption (PKE) ensures the privacy of key-dependent messages $f(\mathsf{sk})$ which are closely related to the secret key sk, where $f \in \mathscr{F}$, even if the adversary is allowed to make decryption queries. In this paper, we study the design of KDM-CCA secure PKE. To this end, we develop a new primitive named *Auxiliary-Input Authenticated Encryption* (AIAE). For AIAE, we introduce two related-key attack (RKA) security notions, including *IND-RKA* and *weak-INT-RKA*. We present a generic construction of AIAE from tag-based hash proof system (HPS) and one-time secure authenticated encryption (AE) and give an instantiation of AIAE under the Decisional Diffie-Hellman (DDH) assumption. Using AIAE as an essential building block, we give two constructions of efficient KDM-CCA secure PKE based on the DDH and the Decisional Composite Residuosity (DCR) assumptions. Specifically, (i) our first PKE construction is the first one achieving KDM[$\mathscr{F}_{\mathrm{aff}}$]-CCA security for the set of affine functions and compactness of ciphertexts simultaneously. (ii) Our second PKE construction is the first one achieving KDM[$\mathscr{F}_{\mathrm{poly}}^d$]-CCA security for the set of polynomial functions and almost compactness of ciphertexts simultaneously. Our PKE constructions are very efficient; in particular, they are pairing-free and NIZK-free.

1. Introduction

For public-key encryption (PKE) schemes, Chosen-Ciphertext Attack (CCA) security is the de facto security notion. In the CCA security model, the adversary sees the public key and gets challenge ciphertexts, which are encryptions of messages of its choices. It is also allowed to make decryption queries and obtain the decrypted messages for ciphertexts (but not the challenge ciphertexts) of its choices. CCA security considers whether the challenge ciphertexts can protect the security of messages. Observe that the adversary does not know the secret keys; thus it is not able to submit messages that are closely related to the secret keys. Thus, there is a corner that is not covered by CCA security, that is, the security of messages which are closely dependent on the secret keys. It was Goldwasser and Micali [1] who first pointed out this problem. In 2002, the security of such key-dependent messages (KDM) was formalized by Black et al. [2]. Up to now, KDM-security has found many applications, such as anonymous credential systems [3] and hard disk encryption [4].

KDM[$\mathscr{F}$]-security means KDM-security for a set $\mathscr{F}$ of functions. Loosely speaking, in the n-KDM[$\mathscr{F}$]-security model, the adversary obtains public keys $(\mathsf{pk}_1, \ldots, \mathsf{pk}_n)$ of n users and has access to an encryption oracle. Each time, the adversary submits a function f in the function set $\mathscr{F}$, the encryption oracle will encrypt $f(\mathsf{sk}_1, \ldots, \mathsf{sk}_n)$ or a dummy message (say 0) and output the challenge ciphertext to the adversary. The n-KDM[$\mathscr{F}$]-CPA security stipulates that the adversary cannot distinguish the two cases, and the n-KDM[$\mathscr{F}$]-CCA security demands the indistinguishability of the two cases even if the adversary is also allowed to make decryption queries. KDM-CCA is obviously stronger than KDM-CPA security notion. Moreover, the KDM-security is stronger when the function set $\mathscr{F}$ is larger.

KDM[$\mathscr{F}$]-CPA Security. In 2008, Boneh et al. (BHHO) [4] proposed the first KDM[$\mathscr{F}_{\text{aff}}$]-CPA secure PKE construction for the affine function set $\mathscr{F}_{\text{aff}}$, from the Decisional Diffie-Hellman (DDH) assumption. Soon after, the BHHO scheme was generalized by Brakerski and Goldwasser [5], who presented KDM[$\mathscr{F}_{\text{aff}}$]-CPA secure PKE constructions under the Quadratic Residuosity (QR) assumption or the Decisional Composite Residuosity (DCR) assumption. However, these schemes suffer from incompact ciphertext, which contains $O(\lambda)$ group elements (λ denotes the security parameter throughout the paper).

Applebaum et al. [6] proved that a variant of the Regev scheme [7] is KDM[$\mathscr{F}_{\text{aff}}$]-CPA secure and enjoys compact ciphertexts, that is, encompassing only $O(1)$ group elements.

Brakerski et al. [8] provided a KDM[$\mathscr{F}_{\text{poly}}^d$]-CPA secure PKE scheme for the polynomial function set $\mathscr{F}_{\text{poly}}^d$, which contains all polynomials whose degrees are at most d. The drawback of the scheme is incompact ciphertext, which contains $O(\lambda^{d+1})$ group elements.

Barak et al. [9] presented a KDM-CPA secure PKE for the set of Boolean circuits whose sizes are a priori bounded, which is a very large function set. Nevertheless, their scheme is neither practical nor flexible.

In 2011, Malkin et al. [10] proposed the first efficient KDM[$\mathscr{F}_{\text{poly}}^d$]-CPA secure PKE. The ciphertext of their PKE construction is almost compact and consists of only $O(d)$ group elements.

KDM[$\mathscr{F}$]-CCA Security. The first approach to KDM-CCA security was proposed by Camenisch, Chandran, and Shoup (CCS) [11]. The CCS approach follows the Naor-Yung paradigm [12], and the building blocks are a PKE scheme with CCA security, a PKE scheme with KDM-CPA security, and a noninteractive zero-knowledge (NIZK) proof system which proves that the two PKE schemes encrypt the same message.

The Groth-Sahai proofs [13] are the only practical NIZK. To obtain efficient KDM-CCA secure PKE, we have to employ an efficient PKE scheme with KDM-CPA security and the Groth-Sahai proofs if we follow the CCS approach [11]. Unfortunately, the existing efficient PKE schemes with KDM-CPA security, like [6, 10], are not compatible with the Groth-Sahai proofs, since the underlying groups of their schemes are not pairing-friendly ones.

Galindo et al. [14] proposed a KDM-CCA secure PKE scheme from the Matrix Decisional Diffie-Hellman assumption. Their scheme enjoys compact ciphertexts, but the KDM-CCA security of their scheme is constrained (more precisely, in their KDM-CCA security model, the adversary is only allowed to have access to the encryption oracle for a number of times linear in the secret key's size).

In order to achieve both KDM-CCA security and efficiency for PKE, Hofheinz [15] developed another approach, making use of a novel primitive named "lossy algebraic filter." The PKE scheme proposed by Hofheinz enjoys the security of KDM[$\mathscr{F}_{\text{circ}}$]-CCA and the compactness of ciphertexts simultaneously, but the function set $\mathscr{F}_{\text{circ}}$ is made up of constant functions and selection functions $f(\text{sk}_1, \ldots, \text{sk}_n) = \text{sk}_i$.

In fact, it is a challenging job to enlarge the KDM-CCA function set $\mathscr{F}$ while keeping the efficiency of the PKE scheme. Recently, Lu et al. [16] designed the first PKE achieving both KDM[$\mathscr{F}_{\text{aff}}$]-CCA security and compact ciphertexts. Their construction is referred to as the LLJ scheme in this paper. The essential building block in their scheme is "authenticated encryption" ($\overline{\text{AE}}$). The so-called INT-$\mathscr{F}_{\text{aff}}$-RKA security of $\overline{\text{AE}}$ turns out to be critical to the KDM[$\mathscr{F}_{\text{aff}}$]-CCA security of the LLJ scheme. Unfortunately, their security reduction of the INT-$\mathscr{F}_{\text{aff}}$-RKA security of $\overline{\text{AE}}$ to the underlying DDH assumption is flawed. Roughly speaking, the problem of their security reduction is that there is no efficient way for the DDH adversary to convert the forgery provided by the INT-$\mathscr{F}_{\text{aff}}$-RKA adversary to a decision bit for solving the DDH problem, since it has no trapdoor. See our conference version [17] for details. The failure of $\overline{\text{AE}}$'s INT-$\mathscr{F}_{\text{aff}}$-RKA security reduction directly affects the validity of LLJ's KDM[$\mathscr{F}_{\text{aff}}$]-CCA security proof.

To construct efficient KDM[$\mathscr{F}_{\text{poly}}^d$]-CCA secure PKE schemes, the CCS approach [11] is the unique way, to the best of our knowledge. However, the only efficient KDM[$\mathscr{F}_{\text{poly}}^d$]-CPA secure PKE [10] is incompatible with the Groth-Sahai NIZK proofs [13]; thus the CCS approach must adopt a general inefficient NIZK.

Our Contribution. In this work, we focus on the design of efficient PKE schemes possessing KDM[$\mathscr{F}_{\text{aff}}$]-CCA security and KDM[$\mathscr{F}_{\text{poly}}^d$]-CCA security, respectively.

(i) We develop a new primitive named *"Auxiliary-Input Authenticated Encryption"* (AIAE). We introduce new related-key attack (RKA) security notions for it, called *IND-$\mathscr{F}'$-RKA* and *weak-INT-$\mathscr{F}'$-RKA*.

    (a) We show a general paradigm for constructing such an AIAE from a one-time secure AE and a *tag-based hash proof system* (HPS) that is universal$_2$, extracting, and key-homomorphic.

    (b) We present an instantiation of tag-based HPS under the DDH assumption. Following our paradigm, we immediately obtain a DDH-based AIAE for the set of restricted affine functions.

(ii) Using AIAE as an essential building block, we design the first PKE scheme enjoying KDM[$\mathscr{F}_{\text{aff}}$]-CCA security and compactness of ciphertexts simultaneously. Specifically, the ciphertext of our scheme contains only $O(1)$ group elements.

(iii) Furthermore, we design the first PKE scheme enjoying KDM[$\mathscr{F}_{\text{poly}}^d$]-CCA security and almost compactness of ciphertexts simultaneously. More precisely, the number of group elements contained in a ciphertext is independent of the security parameter λ.

In Table 1, we list the existing PKE schemes which either achieve KDM-CCA security or are KDM-secure for the set $\mathscr{F}_{\text{poly}}^d$ of polynomial functions.

TABLE 1: Comparison among PKE schemes achieving either KDM-CCA security or security against the set $\mathcal{F}_{\text{poly}}^d$ of polynomial functions. Here, we denote by λ the security parameter and by $\mathcal{F}_{\text{circ}}$, $\mathcal{F}_{\text{aff}}$, and $\mathcal{F}_{\text{poly}}^d$ the set of selection functions, the set of affine functions, and the set of polynomial functions of bounded degree d, respectively. "CCA" indicates that the scheme is KDM-CCA secure. By the symbol "**?**", we mean that the security proof is not rigorous. $\mathbb{G}$, $\mathbb{Z}_{N^2}$, $\mathbb{Z}_{N^3}$, $\mathbb{Z}_{N^s}$, and $\mathbb{Z}_{\overline{N}}$ are the underlying groups, where $s \geq 1$.

Scheme	Set	CCA?	Free of pairing?	The size of ciphertext	Assumption
BHHO08 [4] + CCS09 [11]	$\mathcal{F}_{\text{aff}}$	$\sqrt{}$	—	$(6\lambda + 13)\|\mathbb{G}\|$	DDH
BGK11 [8]	$\mathcal{F}_{\text{poly}}^d$	—	$\sqrt{}$	$(\lambda^{d+1})\|\mathbb{G}\|$	DDH or LWE
MTY11 [10]	$\mathcal{F}_{\text{poly}}^d$	—	$\sqrt{}$	$(d + 2)\|\mathbb{Z}_{N^s}\|$	DCR
Hof13 [15]	$\mathcal{F}_{\text{circ}}$	$\sqrt{}$	—	$6\|\mathbb{Z}_{N^3}\| + 49\|\mathbb{G}\|$	DDH & DCR
LLJ15 [16]	$\mathcal{F}_{\text{aff}}$	**?**	$\sqrt{}$	$3\|\mathbb{Z}_{N^2}\| + 3\|\mathbb{Z}_{N^s}\| + \|\mathbb{Z}_{\overline{N}}\|$	DDH & DCR
Our scheme in Section 4	$\mathcal{F}_{\text{aff}}$	$\sqrt{}$	$\sqrt{}$	$9\|\mathbb{Z}_{N^2}\| + 9\|\mathbb{Z}_{N^s}\| + 2\|\mathbb{Z}_{\overline{N}}\|$	DDH & DCR
Our scheme in Section 5	$\mathcal{F}_{\text{poly}}^d$	$\sqrt{}$	$\sqrt{}$	$9\|\mathbb{Z}_{N^2}\| + (8d^9 + 1)\|\mathbb{Z}_{N^s}\| + 2\|\mathbb{Z}_{\overline{N}}\|$	DDH & DCR

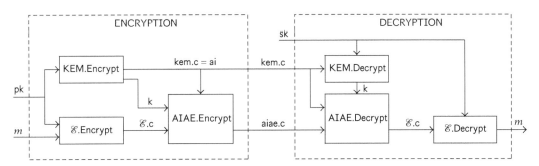

FIGURE 1: Our approach of PKE construction.

Overview of Our Construction. In the construction of our KDM-CCA secure PKE schemes, we adopt a key encapsulation mechanism (KEM) + data encapsulation mechanism (DEM) approach [18] and employ three building blocks: KEM, $\mathcal{E}$, and AIAE, as shown in Figure 1.

(i) KEM and $\mathcal{E}$ share the same pair of public and secret keys.

(ii) A key k is encapsulated by KEM.Encrypt, and an encapsulation kem.c is generated by KEM.Encrypt along the way.

(iii) The message m is encrypted by $\mathcal{E}$.Encrypt, and the resulting $\mathcal{E}$-ciphertext is $\mathcal{E}$.c.

(iv) The key k generated by KEM is used by AIAE.Encrypt to encrypt $\mathcal{E}$.c with auxiliary input ai := kem.c, and the resulting AIAE-ciphertext is aiae.c.

(v) The ciphertext of our PKE scheme is (kem.c, aiae.c).

Following this approach, we design KDM[$\mathcal{F}_{\text{aff}}$]-CCA and KDM[$\mathcal{F}_{\text{poly}}^d$]-CCA secure PKE schemes, respectively, by constructing specific building blocks.

Differences to Conference Version. This paper constitutes an extended full version of [17]. The new results in this paper are as follows.

(i) In contrast to presenting a concrete construction of AIAE in the conference paper, we give a general

paradigm for constructing AIAE from a one-time secure authenticated encryption (AE) and a *tag-based hash proof system* (HPS) in this paper.

(a) In Section 3.2, we show that the resulting AIAE is IND-RKA secure and weak-INT-RKA secure, as long as the underlying tag-based HPS is universal$_2$, extracting, and key-homomorphic.

(b) In Section 3.3, we give an instantiation of tag-based HPS based on the DDH assumption. Following our paradigm, we obtain a DDH-based AIAE scheme in Section 3.4.

We view the specific AIAE proposed in the conference paper as an instantiation of the general paradigm presented in this paper.

(ii) In this paper, we provide the full proofs of the theorems regarding the KDM[$\mathcal{F}_{\text{aff}}$]-CCA security and KDM[$\mathcal{F}_{\text{poly}}^d$]-CCA security of our PKEs. Compared with the conference paper, we add the proofs of Lemmas 16, 18, 25, 26, and 29, and the proof of indistinguishability between Hybrids 2 and 3 in Section 5.3.

2. Preliminaries

Throughout this paper, denote by $\lambda \in \mathbb{N}$ the security parameter. $y \leftarrow_\$ \mathcal{Y}$ means choosing an element y from set $\mathcal{Y}$ uniformly. $y \leftarrow_\$ \mathcal{A}(x; r)$ means executing algorithm $\mathcal{A}$ with

Proc. INITIALIZE:	**Proc.** ENCRYPT$(f \in \mathscr{F}, i \in [n])$:	**Proc.** DECRYPT$(\text{pke.c}, i \in [n])$:
$\text{pars} \leftarrow_\$ \text{ParGen}(1^\lambda)$.	$m_1 := f(\text{sk}_1, \ldots, \text{sk}_n)$.	If $(\text{pke.c}, i) \in \mathcal{Q}_{\mathscr{ENC}}$,
For $i \in [n]$,	$m_0 := 0^{|m_1|}$.	$\qquad$ Output $\perp$.
$\qquad (\text{pk}_i, \text{sk}_i) \leftarrow_\$ \text{KeyGen}(\text{pars})$.	$\text{pke.c} \leftarrow_\$ \text{Encrypt}(\text{pk}_i, m_\beta)$.	Output $\text{Decrypt}(\text{sk}_i, \text{pke.c})$.
$\beta \leftarrow_\$ \{0, 1\}$.	$\mathcal{Q}_{\mathscr{ENC}} := \mathcal{Q}_{\mathscr{ENC}} \cup \{(\text{pke.c}, i)\}$.	**Proc.** FINALIZE(β'):
Output $(\text{pars}, \text{pk}_1, \ldots, \text{pk}_n)$.	Output pke.c.	Output $(\beta' = \beta)$.

FIGURE 2: n-KDM$[\mathscr{F}]$-CCA security game.

input x and randomness r and assigning output to y. We sometimes abbreviate this to $y \leftarrow_\$ \mathscr{A}(x)$. "PPT" is short for probabilistic polynomial-time. For integers $n < m$, we denote $[n] := \{1, 2, \ldots, n\}$ and $[n, m] := \{n, n+1, \ldots, m\}$. For a security notion YY and a primitive XX, the advantage of a PPT adversary $\mathscr{A}$ is typically denoted by $\text{Adv}_{XX,\mathscr{A}}^{YY}(\lambda)$ and we denote $\text{Adv}_{XX}^{YY}(\lambda) := \max_{\text{PPT} \mathscr{A}} \text{Adv}_{XX,\mathscr{A}}^{YY}(\lambda)$. Let $\text{negl}(\cdot)$ denote an unspecified negligible function.

Games. We will use games in our security definitions and proofs. Typically, a game G begins with an INITIALIZE procedure and ends with a FINALIZE procedure. In the game, there might be other procedures PROC$_1$, ..., PROC$_n$ which perform as oracles. All procedures are presented with pseudocode, all sets are initialized as empty sets, and all variables are initialized as empty strings. In the execution of a game G with an adversary $\mathscr{A}$, firstly $\mathscr{A}$ calls INITIALIZE and obtains its output; then $\mathscr{A}$ makes arbitrary oracle queries to PROC$_i$ according to their specifications and obtains their outputs; finally $\mathscr{A}$ calls FINALIZE. In the end of the execution, if FINALIZE outputs b, then we write this as $\text{G}^{\mathscr{A}} \Rightarrow b$. The statement $a \overset{\text{G}}{=} b$ means that, in game G, a is computed as b or a equals b.

2.1. Public-Key Encryption. There are four PPT algorithms $\text{PKE} = (\text{ParGen}, \text{KeyGen}, \text{Encrypt}, \text{Decrypt})$ in a public-key encryption (PKE) scheme:

(i) $\text{ParGen}(1^\lambda)$ outputs a public parameter pars. We assume that pars implicitly defines a secret key space $\mathscr{SK}$ and a message space $\mathscr{M}$.

(ii) $\text{KeyGen}(\text{pars})$ takes pars as input and outputs a public key pk and a secret key sk.

(iii) $\text{Encrypt}(\text{pk}, m)$ takes pk and a message $m \in \mathscr{M}$ as input and outputs a ciphertext pke.c.

(iv) $\text{Decrypt}(\text{sk}, \text{pke.c})$ takes sk and a ciphertext pke.c as input and outputs either a message m or a symbol $\perp$ indicating the failure of the decryption.

We require PKE to have perfect correctness; that is, for all possible $\text{pars} \leftarrow_\$ \text{ParGen}(1^\lambda)$ and all $m \in \mathscr{M}$, we have

$$\Pr[(\text{pk}, \text{sk})$$

$$\leftarrow_\$ \text{KeyGen}(\text{pars}) : \text{Decrypt}(\text{sk}, \text{Encrypt}(\text{pk}, m)) \quad (1)$$

$$= m] = 1.$$

Definition 1 (KDM$[\mathscr{F}]$-CCA security). Let $n \in \mathbb{N}$ and let $\mathscr{F}$ denote a set of functions from $(\mathscr{SK})^n$ to $\mathscr{M}$. A scheme PKE is n-KDM$[\mathscr{F}]$-CCA secure, if for any PPT adversary $\mathscr{A}$, we have $\text{Adv}_{\text{PKE},\mathscr{A}}^{\text{kdm-cca}}(\lambda) := |\Pr[n\text{-KDM}[\mathscr{F}]\text{-CCA}^{\mathscr{A}} \Rightarrow 1] - 1/2| \le \text{negl}(\lambda)$, where n-KDM$[\mathscr{F}]$-CCA is the security game shown in Figure 2.

2.2. Authenticated Encryption. There are three PPT algorithms $\text{AE} = (\text{AE.ParGen}, \text{AE.Encrypt}, \text{AE.Decrypt})$ in an authenticated encryption (AE) scheme:

(i) $\text{AE.ParGen}(1^\lambda)$ generates a system parameter pars_{AE}. We require pars_{AE} to be an implicit input to other algorithms and assume that pars_{AE} implicitly defines a key space $\mathscr{K}_{\text{AE}}$ and a message space $\mathscr{M}$.

(ii) $\text{AE.Encrypt}(\text{k}, m)$ takes a key $\text{k} \in \mathscr{K}_{\text{AE}}$ and a message $m \in \mathscr{M}$ as input and outputs a ciphertext ae.c.

(iii) $\text{AE.Decrypt}(\text{k}, \text{ae.c})$ takes a key $\text{k} \in \mathscr{K}_{\text{AE}}$ and a ciphertext ae.c as input and outputs a message $m \in \mathscr{M}$ or a symbol $\perp$.

We require AE to have perfect correctness; that is, for all possible $\text{pars}_{\text{AE}} \leftarrow_\$ \text{AE.ParGen}(1^\lambda)$, all keys $\text{k} \in \mathscr{K}_{\text{AE}}$, and all $m \in \mathscr{M}$,

$$\Pr[\text{AE.Decrypt}(\text{k}, \text{AE.Encrypt}(\text{k}, m)) = m] = 1. \quad (2)$$

Definition 2 (one-time security). A scheme AE is one-time secure (OT-secure), that is, IND-OT and INT-OT secure, if for any PPT $\mathscr{A}$, both $\text{Adv}_{\text{AE},\mathscr{A}}^{\text{ind-ot}}(\lambda) := |\Pr[\text{IND-OT}^{\mathscr{A}} \Rightarrow 1] - 1/2| \le \text{negl}(\lambda)$ and $\text{Adv}_{\text{AE},\mathscr{A}}^{\text{int-ot}}(\lambda) := \Pr[\text{INT-OT}^{\mathscr{A}} \Rightarrow 1] \le \text{negl}(\lambda)$, where IND-OT and INT-OT are the security games presented in Figure 3.

2.3. Key Encapsulation Mechanism. There are three PPT algorithms $\text{KEM} = (\text{KEM.KeyGen}, \text{KEM.Encrypt}, \text{KEM.Decrypt})$ in a key encapsulation mechanism (KEM):

(i) $\text{KEM.KeyGen}(1^\lambda)$ generates a public key pk and a secret key sk.

(ii) $\text{KEM.Encrypt}(\text{pk})$ takes pk as input and outputs a key k together with a ciphertext kem.c.

(iii) $\text{KEM.Decrypt}(\text{sk}, \text{kem.c})$ takes sk and a ciphertext kem.c as input and outputs either a key k or a symbol $\perp$.

```
Proc. INITIALIZE:                           Proc. INITIALIZE:
pars_AE ←_$ AE.ParGen(1^λ), k ←_$ 𝒦_AE.      pars_AE ←_$ AE.ParGen(1^λ), k ←_$ 𝒦_AE.
β ←_$ {0, 1}.                                Output pars_AE.
Output pars_AE.

Proc. ENCRYPT(m_0, m_1):    // one query     Proc. ENCRYPT(m):       // one query
If |m_0| ≠ |m_1|, Output ⊥.                  ae.c ←_$ AE.Encrypt(k, m).
ae.c ←_$ AE.Encrypt(k, m_β).                 Output ae.c.
Output ae.c.

                                             Proc. FINALIZE(ae.c*):
Proc. FINALIZE(β'):                          If ae.c* = ae.c, Output 0.
Output (β' = β).                             Output (AE.Decrypt(k, ae.c*) ≠ ⊥).
```

(a)   (b)

FIGURE 3: IND-OT (a) and INT-OT (b) security games.

We require KEM to have perfect correctness; that is, for all possible $(pk, sk) ←_\$ \text{KEM.KeyGen}(1^\lambda)$, we have

$$\Pr\big[(k, \text{kem.c})$$
$$←_\$ \text{KEM.Encrypt}(pk) : \text{KEM.Decrypt}(sk, \text{kem.c}) \quad (3)$$
$$= k\big] = 1.$$

2.4. Tag-Based Hash Proof System: Universal$_2$, Extracting, and Key-Homomorphism. Tag-based hash proof system (HPS) was first defined in [19]. The definition is similar to extended HPS [20], but the universal$_2$ property is slightly different.

Definition 3 (tag-based hash proof system). A tag-based hash proof system THPS = (THPS.Setup, THPS.Pub, THPS.Priv) is comprised of three PPT algorithms:

(i) THPS.Setup(1^λ) outputs a parameterized instance pars$_{THPS}$, which implicitly defines $(\mathcal{K}, \mathcal{C}, \mathcal{V}, \mathcal{T}, \mathcal{HK}, \mathcal{PK}, \Lambda_{(\cdot)}, \mu)$, where $\mathcal{K}, \mathcal{C}, \mathcal{V}, \mathcal{T}, \mathcal{HK}, \mathcal{PK}$ are all finite sets with $\mathcal{V} \subseteq \mathcal{C}$, $\Lambda_{(\cdot)} : \mathcal{C} \times \mathcal{T} \rightarrow \mathcal{K}$ is a set of hash functions indexed by hk $\in \mathcal{HK}$, and $\mu : \mathcal{HK} \rightarrow \mathcal{PK}$ is a function. We assume that μ is efficiently computable, and there are PPT algorithms sampling hk $←_\$ \mathcal{HK}$ uniformly, sampling $C ←_\$ \mathcal{C}$ uniformly, sampling $C ←_\$ \mathcal{V}$ uniformly with a witness w, and checking membership in $\mathcal{C}$.

(ii) THPS.Pub(pk, C, w, t) takes a projection key pk $= \mu(hk) \in \mathcal{PK}$, an element $C \in \mathcal{V}$ with a witness w, and a tag $t \in \mathcal{T}$ as input and outputs a hash value $K = \Lambda_{hk}(C, t) \in \mathcal{K}$.

(iii) THPS.Priv(hk, C, t) takes a hashing key hk $\in \mathcal{HK}$, an element $C \in \mathcal{C}$, and a tag $t \in \mathcal{T}$ as input and outputs a hash value $K = \Lambda_{hk}(C, t) \in \mathcal{K}$ without knowing a witness.

We require THPS to be *projective*; that is, for all pars$_{THPS}$ $←_\$$ THPS.Setup(1^λ), all hk $\in \mathcal{HK}$ and pk $= \mu(hk) \in \mathcal{PK}$, all $C \in \mathcal{V}$ with all witnesses w and all $t \in \mathcal{T}$, it holds that

$$\text{THPS.Pub}(pk, C, w, t) = \Lambda_{hk}(C, t)$$
$$= \text{THPS.Priv}(hk, C, t). \quad (4)$$

Tag-based HPS is associated with a subset membership problem. Informally speaking, it asks to distinguish the uniform distribution over $\mathcal{V}$ from the uniform distribution over $\mathcal{C} \setminus \mathcal{V}$.

Definition 4 (SMP). The Subset Membership Problem (SMP) related to THPS is hard, if for any PPT adversary $\mathcal{A}$, one has

$$\text{Adv}^{smp}_{THPS, \mathcal{A}}(\lambda) := \big|\Pr[\mathcal{A}(pars_{THPS}, C) = 1]$$
$$- \Pr[\mathcal{A}(pars_{THPS}, C') = 1]\big| \leq negl(\lambda), \quad (5)$$

where pars$_{THPS}$ $←_\$$ THPS.Setup(1^λ), $C ←_\$ \mathcal{V}$, and $C' ←_\$ \mathcal{C} \setminus \mathcal{V}$.

Definition 5 (universal$_2$). THPS is called (strongly) universal$_2$, if for all possible pars$_{THPS}$ $←_\$$ THPS.Setup(1^λ), all pk $\in \mathcal{PK}$, all $C \in \mathcal{C}$, all $C' \in \mathcal{C} \setminus \mathcal{V}$, all $t, t' \in \mathcal{T}$ with $t \neq t'$, and all $K, K' \in \mathcal{K}$, it holds that

$$\Pr\big[\Lambda_{hk}(C', t') = K' \mid \mu(hk) = pk, \Lambda_{hk}(C, t) = K\big]$$
$$= \frac{1}{|\mathcal{K}|}, \quad (6)$$

where the probability is over hk $←_\$ \mathcal{HK}$.

The key difference between tag-based HPS and extended HPS lies in the definition of the universal$_2$ property [19]. Extended HPS requires (6) to hold for $(C, t) \neq (C', t')$, while tag-based HPS requires (6) to hold only for $t \neq t'$. Hence, any (universal$_2$) extended HPS is also a (universal$_2$) tag-based HPS, but not vice versa. Tag-based HPS is essentially a weaker variant of extended HPS and admits more efficient constructions.

Dodis et al. [21] defined an extracting property for extended HPS, which requires the hash value $\Lambda_{hk}(C, t)$ to be uniformly distributed over $\mathcal{K}$ for any $C \in \mathcal{C}$ and $t \in \mathcal{T}$, as long as hk is randomly chosen from $\mathcal{HK}$. Besides, Xagawa [22] considered a key-homomorphic property for extended HPS, which stipulates that $\Lambda_{hk+\Delta}(C, t) = \Lambda_{hk}(C, t) \cdot \Lambda_{\Delta}(C, t)$ holds for any hk, $\Delta \in \mathcal{HK}, C \in \mathcal{C}$, and $t \in \mathcal{T}$. Here we adapt these notions to tag-based HPS.

Definition 6 (extracting). THPS is called extracting, if for all pars$_{\text{THPS}} \leftarrow_\$ $ THPS.Setup(1^λ), all $C \in \mathcal{C}$, all $t \in \mathcal{T}$, and all $K \in \mathcal{K}$, it holds that

$$\Pr\left[\Lambda_{hk}(C, t) = K\right] = \frac{1}{|\mathcal{K}|}, \tag{7}$$

where hk $\leftarrow_\$ \mathcal{HK}$.

Definition 7 (key-homomorphism). THPS is called key-homomorphic, if for all pars$_{\text{THPS}} \leftarrow_\$ $ THPS.Setup(1^λ), which defines $(\mathcal{K}, \mathcal{C}, \mathcal{V}, \mathcal{T}, \mathcal{HK}, \mathcal{PK}, \Lambda_{(\cdot)}, \mu)$, one has the following:

(i) Both $(\mathcal{HK}, +)$ and $(\mathcal{K}, \cdot)$ are groups.

(ii) For all $C \in \mathcal{C}$ and all $t \in \mathcal{T}$, the mapping $\Lambda_{(\cdot)}(C, t) : \mathcal{HK} \rightarrow \mathcal{K}$ is a group homomorphism. That is, for all hk, b $\in \mathcal{HK}$ and all $a \in \mathbb{Z}$, it holds that $\Lambda_{a \cdot hk + b}(C, t) = (\Lambda_{hk}(C, t))^a \cdot \Lambda_b(C, t)$.

2.5. DCR, DDH, DL, and IV$_d$ Assumptions.

Suppose that GenN(1^λ) is a PPT algorithm generating $(p, q, N, \overline{N})$, where p, q are safe primes of λ-bit, $N = pq$, and $\overline{N} = 2N + 1$ is a prime. We define the following:

(i) $\mathbb{QR}_{\overline{N}} := \{a^2 \bmod \overline{N} \mid a \in \mathbb{Z}_{\overline{N}}\}$.

Then $\mathbb{QR}_{\overline{N}}$ is a cyclic group of order N. For $s \in \mathbb{N}$ and $T = 1 + N$, we define

(i) $\mathbb{QR}_{N^s} := \{a^2 \bmod N^s \mid a \in \mathbb{Z}_{N^s}^*\}$,

(ii) $\mathbb{SCR}_{N^s} := \{a^{2N^{s-1}} \bmod N^s \mid a \in \mathbb{Z}_{N^s}^*\}$,

(iii) $\mathbb{RU}_{N^s} := \{T^r \bmod N^s \mid r \in [N^{s-1}]\}$.

Then $\mathbb{SCR}_{N^s}$ is a cyclic group of order $\phi(N)/4$, and $\mathbb{QR}_{N^s} = \mathbb{SCR}_{N^s} \otimes \mathbb{RU}_{N^s}$, where $\otimes$ represents the internal direct product.

Damgård and Jurik [23] showed that the discrete logarithm $d\log_T(u) \in [N^{s-1}]$ of an element $u \in \mathbb{RU}_{N^s}$ can be efficiently computed from u and N. Observe that $\mathbb{Z}_{N^s}^* = \mathbb{Z}_2 \otimes \mathbb{Z}_2' \otimes \mathbb{SCR}_{N^s} \otimes \mathbb{RU}_{N^s}$; thus for any $v = v(\mathbb{Z}_2) \cdot v(\mathbb{Z}_2') \cdot v(\mathbb{SCR}_{N^s}) \cdot T^x \in \mathbb{Z}_{N^s}^*$, we have $v^{\phi(N)} = T^{x \cdot \phi(N)} \in \mathbb{RU}_{N^s}$ and

$$\frac{d\log_T\left(v^{\phi(N)}\right)}{\phi(N)} \bmod N^{s-1} = x. \tag{8}$$

Definition 8 (DCR assumption). The Decisional Composite Residuosity (DCR) assumption holds for GenN and $\mathbb{QR}_{N^s}$, if for any PPT $\mathcal{A}$, it holds that

$$\begin{aligned}
\mathsf{Adv}^{\text{dcr}}_{\text{GenN}, \mathcal{A}}(\lambda) \\
:= |\Pr[\mathcal{A}(N, u) = 1] - \Pr[\mathcal{A}(N, v) = 1]| \\
\le \mathsf{negl}(\lambda),
\end{aligned} \tag{9}$$

where $(p, q, N, \overline{N}) \leftarrow_\$ $ GenN(1^λ), $u \leftarrow_\$ \mathbb{QR}_{N^s}$, and $v \leftarrow_\$ \mathbb{SCR}_{N^s}$.

The Interactive Vector (IV$_d$) assumption is implied by the DCR assumption, as shown in [5]. Here we recall the IV$_d$ assumption according to [16].

Definition 9 (IV$_d$ assumption). The IV$_d$ assumption holds for GenN and $\mathbb{QR}_{N^s}$, if for any PPT $\mathcal{A}$, it holds that

$$\begin{aligned}
\mathsf{Adv}^{\text{iv}_d}_{\text{GenN}, \mathcal{A}}(\lambda) \\
:= \left|\Pr\left[\mathcal{A}^{\text{CHAL}^b_{\text{IV}_d}}(N, g_1, \ldots, g_d) = b\right] - \frac{1}{2}\right| \\
\le \mathsf{negl}(\lambda),
\end{aligned} \tag{10}$$

where $(p, q, N, \overline{N}) \leftarrow_\$ $ GenN(1^λ), $g_1, \ldots, g_d \leftarrow_\$ \mathbb{SCR}_{N^s}$, $b \leftarrow_\$ \{0, 1\}$, and $\mathcal{A}$ is allowed to query the oracle $\text{CHAL}^b_{\text{IV}_d}(\cdot)$ adaptively. Each time, $\mathcal{A}$ can submit $(\delta_1, \ldots, \delta_d)$ to the oracle, and $\text{CHAL}^b_{\text{IV}_d}(\delta_1, \ldots, \delta_d)$ selects $r \leftarrow_\$ [[N/4]]$ randomly: if $b = 0$, the oracle outputs $(g_1^r, \ldots, g_d^r)$ to $\mathcal{A}$; otherwise it outputs $(g_1^r T^{\delta_1}, \ldots, g_d^r T^{\delta_d})$ to $\mathcal{A}$, where $T = 1 + N$.

Definition 10 (DDH assumption). The DDH assumption holds for GenN and $\mathbb{QR}_{\overline{N}}$, if for any PPT $\mathcal{A}$, it holds that

$$\begin{aligned}
\mathsf{Adv}^{\text{ddh}}_{\text{GenN}, \mathcal{A}}(\lambda) := |\Pr[\mathcal{A}(N, p, q, g_1, g_2, g_1^x, g_2^x) = 1] \\
- \Pr[\mathcal{A}(N, p, q, g_1, g_2, g_1^x, g_2^y) = 1]| \le \mathsf{negl}(\lambda),
\end{aligned} \tag{11}$$

where $(p, q, N, \overline{N}) \leftarrow_\$ $ GenN(1^λ), $g_1, g_2 \leftarrow_\$ \mathbb{QR}_{\overline{N}}$, $x, y \leftarrow_\$ \mathbb{Z}_N \setminus \{0\}$.

Definition 11 (DL assumption). The Discrete Logarithm (DL) assumption holds for GenN and $\mathbb{SCR}_{N^s}$, if for any PPT $\mathcal{A}$, it holds that

$$\begin{aligned}
\mathsf{Adv}^{\text{dl}}_{\text{GenN}, \mathcal{A}}(\lambda) := \Pr[\mathcal{A}(N, p, q, g, g^x) = x] \\
\le \mathsf{negl}(\lambda),
\end{aligned} \tag{12}$$

where $(p, q, N, \overline{N}) \leftarrow_\$ $ GenN(1^λ), $g \leftarrow_\$ \mathbb{SCR}_{N^s}$, $x \leftarrow_\$ [\phi(N)/4]$.

2.6. Collision-Resistant Hashing

Definition 12 (collision-resistant hashing). Let $\mathcal{H} = \{H : \mathcal{X} \rightarrow \mathcal{Y}\}$ be a set of hash functions. $\mathcal{H}$ is said to be *collision-resistant*, if for any PPT $\mathcal{A}$, one has

$$\mathsf{Adv}^{\mathrm{cr}}_{\mathcal{H}, \mathcal{A}}(\lambda) := \Pr\left[H \longleftarrow_\$ \mathcal{H}, (x, x') \longleftarrow_\$ \mathcal{A}(H) : x \right.$$
$$\left. \neq x' \wedge H(x) = H(x')\right] \leq \mathsf{negl}(\lambda). \tag{13}$$

3. Auxiliary-Input Authenticated Encryption

Our PKE constructions in Sections 4 and 5 will resort to a new primitive AIAE. To serve the KDM-CCA security of our PKE construction in Figure 1, our AIAE should satisfy the following properties.

(i) AIAE must take an auxiliary input ai in both the encryption and decryption algorithms.

(ii) AIAE must have IND-$\mathcal{F}$-RKA security and weak-INT-$\mathcal{F}$-RKA security. Compared to the INT-$\mathcal{F}$-RKA security proposed in [16], the weak-INT-$\mathcal{F}$-RKA security imposes a special rule to determine whether the adversary's forgery is successful or not.

In the following, we present the syntax of *AIAE* and define its *IND-$\mathcal{F}$-RKA Security* and *Weak-INT-$\mathcal{F}$-RKA Security*. We also show a general paradigm of AIAE from tag-based HPS and give an instantiation of AIAE under the DDH assumption.

3.1. Auxiliary-Input Authenticated Encryption

Definition 13 (AIAE). There are three PPT algorithms AIAE = (AIAE.ParGen, AIAE.Encrypt, AIAE.Decrypt) in an AIAE scheme:

(i) The parameter generation algorithm AIAE.ParGen(1^λ) generates a system parameter pars$_{\mathsf{AIAE}}$. We require pars$_{\mathsf{AIAE}}$ to be an implicit input to other algorithms and assume that pars$_{\mathsf{AIAE}}$ implicitly defines a key space $\mathcal{K}_{\mathsf{AIAE}}$, a message space $\mathcal{M}$, and an auxiliary-input space $\mathcal{A}\mathcal{I}$.

(ii) The encryption algorithm AIAE.Encrypt(k, m, ai) takes a key k $\in \mathcal{K}_{\mathsf{AIAE}}$, a message m $\in \mathcal{M}$, and an auxiliary input ai $\in \mathcal{A}\mathcal{I}$ as input and outputs a ciphertext aiae.c.

(iii) The decryption algorithm AIAE.Decrypt(k, aiae.c, ai) takes a key k $\in \mathcal{K}_{\mathsf{AIAE}}$, a ciphertext aiae.c, and an auxiliary input ai $\in \mathcal{A}\mathcal{I}$ as input and outputs a message m $\in \mathcal{M}$ or a symbol $\perp$.

We require AIAE to have perfect correctness; that is, for all possible pars$_{\mathsf{AIAE}} \longleftarrow_\$ $ AIAE.ParGen(1^λ), all keys k $\in \mathcal{K}_{\mathsf{AIAE}}$, all messages m $\in \mathcal{M}$, and all auxiliary-inputs ai $\in \mathcal{A}\mathcal{I}$,

$$\Pr\left[\mathsf{AIAE.Decrypt}\left(\mathsf{k}, \mathsf{AIAE.Encrypt}\left(\mathsf{k}, m, \mathsf{ai}\right), \mathsf{ai}\right)\right.$$
$$\left. = m\right] = 1. \tag{14}$$

In fact, AIAE is a generalization of traditional AE, and traditional AE can be viewed as AIAE with $\mathcal{A}\mathcal{I} = \emptyset$.

Definition 14 (RKA security). Denote by $\mathcal{F}$ a set of functions from $\mathcal{K}_{\mathsf{AIAE}}$ to $\mathcal{K}_{\mathsf{AIAE}}$. A scheme AIAE is IND-$\mathcal{F}$-RKA secure and weak-INT-$\mathcal{F}$-RKA secure, if for any PPT $\mathcal{A}$,

$$\mathsf{Adv}^{\mathrm{ind\text{-}rka}}_{\mathsf{AIAE}, \mathcal{A}}(\lambda) := \left| \Pr\left[\mathsf{IND\text{-}}\mathcal{F}\text{-}\mathsf{RKA}^{\mathcal{A}} \Longrightarrow 1\right] - \frac{1}{2}\right|$$
$$\leq \mathsf{negl}(\lambda),$$
$$\mathsf{Adv}^{\mathrm{weak\text{-}int\text{-}rka}}_{\mathsf{AIAE}, \mathcal{A}}(\lambda) := \Pr\left[\mathsf{weak\text{-}INT\text{-}}\mathcal{F}\text{-}\mathsf{RKA}^{\mathcal{A}} \Longrightarrow 1\right]$$
$$\leq \mathsf{negl}(\lambda), \tag{15}$$

where IND-$\mathcal{F}$-RKA and weak-INT-$\mathcal{F}$-RKA are the security games presented in Figure 4.

3.2. Generic Construction of AIAE from Tag-Based HPS and OT-Secure AE. Our construction of AIAE needs the following ingredients.

(i) A tag-based hash proof system THPS = (THPS.Setup, THPS.Pub, THPS.Priv), where the hash value space is $\mathcal{K}$, the tag space is $\mathcal{T}$, and the hashing key space is $\mathcal{H}\mathcal{K}$.

(ii) A (traditional) authenticated encryption scheme AE = (AE.ParGen, AE.Encrypt, AE.Decrypt), where the message space is $\mathcal{M}$ and the key space is $\mathcal{K}$.

(iii) A set of hash functions $\mathcal{H} = \{H : \{0,1\}^* \rightarrow \mathcal{T}\}$.

We present our AIAE construction AIAE = (AIAE.ParGen, AIAE.Encrypt, AIAE.Decrypt) in Figure 5, whose key space is $\mathcal{K}_{\mathsf{AIAE}} := \mathcal{H}\mathcal{K}$, message space is $\mathcal{M}$, and auxiliary-input space is $\mathcal{A}\mathcal{I} := \{0,1\}^*$.

By the perfect correctness of AE, it is routine to check that AIAE has perfect correctness.

Theorem 15. *If (i)* THPS *is universal$_2$, extracting, key-homomorphic and has a hard subset membership problem, (ii)* AE *is one-time secure, and (iii)* $\mathcal{H}$ *is collision-resistant, then the scheme* AIAE *in Figure 5 is IND-$\mathcal{F}_{raff}$-RKA and weak-INT-$\mathcal{F}_{raff}$-RKA secure. Here* $\mathcal{F}_{raff} := \{f_{(a,b)} : \mathsf{hk} \in \mathcal{H}\mathcal{K} \mapsto a \cdot \mathsf{hk} + b \in \mathcal{H}\mathcal{K} \mid a \in \mathbb{Z}^*_{|\mathcal{K}|}, b \in \mathcal{H}\mathcal{K}\}$ *is the set of restricted affine functions.*

Proof of Theorem 15 (IND-$\mathcal{F}_{raff}$-RKA Security). Denote by $\mathcal{A}$ a PPT adversary who is against the IND-$\mathcal{F}_{raff}$-RKA security and queries ENCRYPT oracle for at most Q_e times. We show the IND-$\mathcal{F}_{raff}$-RKA security through a series of games. For an event E, we denote by $\Pr_j[\mathsf{E}]$, $\Pr_{j'}[\mathsf{E}]$, and $\Pr_{j''}[\mathsf{E}]$ the probability of E occurring in games G_j, G'_j, and G''_j, respectively.

Game G_1. It is the original IND-$\mathcal{F}_{raff}$-RKA game. Denote the event $\beta' = \beta$ by Succ. According to the definition, $\mathsf{Adv}^{\mathrm{ind\text{-}rka}}_{\mathsf{AIAE}, \mathcal{A}}(\lambda) = |\Pr_1[\mathsf{Succ}] - 1/2|$.

Proc. INITIALIZE:

$\text{pars}_{\text{AIAE}} \leftarrow_\$ \text{AIAE.ParGen}(1^\lambda).$

$k \leftarrow_\$ \mathcal{K}_{\text{AIAE}}.$

$\beta \leftarrow_\$ \{0,1\}.$

Output $\text{pars}_{\text{AIAE}}.$

Proc. ENCRYPT$(m_0, m_1, \text{ai}, f \in \mathcal{F})$:

If $|m_0| \neq |m_1|$, Output $\perp$.

$\text{aiae.c} \leftarrow_\$ \text{AIAE.Encrypt}(f(k), m_\beta, \text{ai}).$

Output aiae.c.

Proc. FINALIZE(β'):

Output $(\beta' = \beta).$

Proc. INITIALIZE:

$\text{pars}_{\text{AIAE}} \leftarrow_\$ \text{AIAE.ParGen}(1^\lambda),\ k \leftarrow_\$ \mathcal{K}_{\text{AIAE}}.$

Output $\text{pars}_{\text{AIAE}}.$

Proc. ENCRYPT$(m, \text{ai}, f \in \mathcal{F})$:

$\text{aiae.c} \leftarrow_\$ \text{AIAE.Encrypt}(f(k), m, \text{ai}).$

$Q_{\mathcal{ENC}} := Q_{\mathcal{ENC}} \cup \{(\text{ai}, f, \text{aiae.c})\}.$

$Q_{\mathcal{AF\text{-}F}} := Q_{\mathcal{AF\text{-}F}} \cup \{(\text{ai}, f)\}.$

Output aiae.c.

Proc. FINALIZE$(\text{ai}^*, f^* \in \mathcal{F}, \text{aiae.c}^*)$:

If $(\text{ai}^*, f^*, \text{aiae.c}^*) \in Q_{\mathcal{ENC}}$, Output 0.

// Special rule

If there exists $(\text{ai}, f) \in Q_{\mathcal{AF\text{-}F}}$ such that

$\text{ai} = \text{ai}^*$ but $f \neq f^*$, Output 0.

Output $(\text{AIAE.Decrypt}(f^*(k), \text{aiae.c}^*, \text{ai}^*) \neq \perp).$

(a)   (b)

FIGURE 4: IND-$\mathcal{F}$-RKA (a) and weak-INT-$\mathcal{F}$-RKA (b) security games. We note that, in the weak-INT-$\mathcal{F}$-RKA game, there is a special rule (as shown in the shadow) of outputting 0 in FINALIZE.

AIAE.ParGen(1^λ):	AIAE.Encrypt$(\text{hk}, m, \text{ai})$:	AIAE.Decrypt$(\text{hk}, \langle C, \chi \rangle, \text{ai})$:
$\text{pars}_{\text{THPS}} \leftarrow_\$ \text{THPS.Setup}(1^\lambda).$	$C \leftarrow_\$ \mathcal{V}$ with witness w.	If $C \notin \mathcal{C}$, Output $\perp$.
$\text{pars}_{\text{AE}} \leftarrow_\$ \text{AE.ParGen}(1^\lambda).$	$t := \mathsf{H}(C, \text{ai}) \in \mathcal{T}.$	$t := \mathsf{H}(C, \text{ai}) \in \mathcal{T}.$
$\mathsf{H} \leftarrow_\$ \mathcal{H}.$	$\kappa := \Lambda_{\text{hk}}(C, t) \in \mathcal{K}.$	$\kappa := \Lambda_{\text{hk}}(C, t) \in \mathcal{K}.$
$\text{pars}_{\text{AIAE}} := (\text{pars}_{\text{THPS}}, \text{pars}_{\text{AE}}, \mathsf{H}).$	$\chi \leftarrow_\$ \text{AE.Encrypt}(\kappa, m).$	$m/\perp \leftarrow \text{AE.Decrypt}(\kappa, \chi).$
Output $\text{pars}_{\text{AIAE}}.$	Output $\langle C, \chi \rangle.$	Output $m/\perp.$

FIGURE 5: Generic construction of AIAE from THPS and AE.

As for the ℓth ($\ell \in [Q_e]$) ENCRYPT query $(m_{\ell,0}, m_{\ell,1}, \text{ai}_\ell, f_\ell)$, where $f_\ell = \langle a_\ell, b_\ell \rangle \in \mathcal{F}_{\text{raff}}$, the challenger prepares the challenge ciphertext as follows:

(i) pick $C_\ell \leftarrow_\$ \mathcal{V}$ together with witness w_ℓ,

(ii) compute $t_\ell := \mathsf{H}(C_\ell, \text{ai}_\ell) \in \mathcal{T}$,

(iii) compute $\kappa_\ell := \Lambda_{a_\ell \cdot \text{hk} + b_\ell}(C_\ell, t_\ell) \in \mathcal{K}$,

(iv) invoke $\chi_\ell \leftarrow_\$ \text{AE.Encrypt}(\kappa_\ell, m_{\ell,\beta})$,

and it outputs the challenge ciphertext $\langle C_\ell, \chi_\ell \rangle$ to $\mathcal{A}$.

Game $\mathsf{G}_{1,j}$, $j \in [Q_e + 1]$. It is identical to G_1, except that, for the first $j-1$ times of ENCRYPT queries, that is, $\ell \in [j-1]$, the challenger chooses $\kappa_\ell \leftarrow_\$ \mathcal{K}$ randomly for the AE scheme.

Clearly $\mathsf{G}_{1,1}$ is identical to G_1; thus $\text{Pr}_1[\text{Succ}] = \text{Pr}_{1,1}[\text{Succ}].$

Game $\mathsf{G}'_{1,j}$, $j \in [Q_e]$. It is identical to $\mathsf{G}_{1,j}$, except that, for the jth ENCRYPT query, the challenger samples $C_j \leftarrow_\$ \mathcal{C} \setminus \mathcal{V}$ uniformly.

The difference between $\mathsf{G}_{1,j}$ and $\mathsf{G}'_{1,j}$ lies in the distribution of C_j. In game $\mathsf{G}_{1,j}$, C_j is uniformly chosen from $\mathcal{V}$; in game $\mathsf{G}'_{1,j}$, C_j is uniformly chosen from $\mathcal{C} \setminus \mathcal{V}$. Any difference between $\mathsf{G}_{1,j}$ and $\mathsf{G}'_{1,j}$ results in a PPT adversary solving the subset membership problem related to THPS; thus we have that $|\text{Pr}_{1,j}[\text{Succ}] - \text{Pr}_{1,j'}[\text{Succ}]| \leq \text{Adv}^{\text{smp}}_{\text{THPS}}(\lambda).$

Game $\mathsf{G}''_{1,j}$, $j \in [Q_e]$. It is identical to $\mathsf{G}'_{1,j}$, except that, for the jth ENCRYPT query, the challenger chooses $\kappa_j \leftarrow_\$ \mathcal{K}$ randomly.

Lemma 16. *For all* $j \in [Q_e]$, $Pr_{1,j'}[\text{Succ}] = Pr_{1,j''}[\text{Succ}].$

Proof. For game $\mathsf{G}'_{1,j}$ and game $\mathsf{G}''_{1,j}$, the difference between them lies in the computation of κ_j in the jth ENCRYPT query. In $\mathsf{G}'_{1,j}$, κ_j is properly computed, while in $\mathsf{G}''_{1,j}$, it is chosen from $\mathcal{K}$ uniformly.

We analyze the information about the key hk that is used in game $\mathsf{G}'_{1,j}$.

(i) For the ℓth ($\ell \in [j-1]$) query, ENCRYPT does not use hk at all since κ_ℓ is randomly chosen from $\mathcal{K}$.

(ii) For the ℓth ($\ell \in [j+1, Q_e]$) query, ENCRYPT can use pk $= \mu(\mathsf{hk})$ to compute κ_ℓ:

$$\kappa_\ell = \Lambda_{a_e \cdot \mathsf{hk} + b_e}(C_\ell, t_\ell): \quad C_\ell \longleftarrow_\$ \mathscr{V} \text{ with witness } w_\ell$$

$$= (\Lambda_{\mathsf{hk}}(C_\ell, t_\ell))^{a_e} \cdot \Lambda_{b_e}(C_\ell, t_\ell):$$

via key-homomorphism (16)

$$= (\mathsf{THPS.Pub}(\mathsf{pk}, C_\ell, w_\ell, t_\ell))^{a_e} \cdot \Lambda_{b_e}(C_\ell, t_\ell):$$

via projective property.

(iii) For the jth query, ENCRYPT uses $\Lambda_{\mathsf{hk}}(C_j, t_j)$ to compute κ_j:

$$\kappa_j = \Lambda_{a_j \cdot \mathsf{hk} + b_j}(C_j, t_j): \quad C_j \longleftarrow_\$ \mathscr{C} \setminus \mathscr{V}$$

$$= (\Lambda_{\mathsf{hk}}(C_j, t_j))^{a_j} \cdot \Lambda_{b_j}(C_j, t_j): \tag{17}$$

via key-homomorphism.

Since $C_j \in \mathscr{C} \setminus \mathscr{V}$, by the universal$_2$ property of THPS, $\Lambda_{\mathsf{hk}}(C_j, t_j)$ is uniformly distributed over $\mathscr{K}$ conditioned on pk $= \mu(\mathsf{hk})$. Then as long as $a_j \in \mathbb{Z}^*_{|\mathscr{K}|}$, $\kappa_j = (\Lambda_{\mathsf{hk}}(C_j, t_j))^{a_j} \cdot \Lambda_{b_j}(C_j, t_j)$ is also randomly distributed over $\mathscr{K}$. Consequently, $\mathsf{G}''_{1,j}$ is essentially the same as $\mathsf{G}''_{1,j}$, and $\Pr_{1,j'}[\mathsf{Succ}] = \Pr_{1,j''}[\mathsf{Succ}]$. $\square$

Now, we show that game $\mathsf{G}''_{1,j}$ is computationally indistinguishable from game $\mathsf{G}_{1,j+1}$, $j \in [Q_e]$. Note that the divergence between $\mathsf{G}''_{1,j}$ and $\mathsf{G}_{1,j+1}$ lies in the distribution of C_j in the jth ENCRYPT query. In game $\mathsf{G}''_{1,j}$, C_j is uniformly chosen from $\mathscr{C} \setminus \mathscr{V}$; in game $\mathsf{G}_{1,j+1}$, C_j is uniformly chosen from $\mathscr{V}$. Any difference between these two games results in a PPT adversary solving the subset membership problem related to THPS; thus we have that $|\Pr_{1,j''}[\mathsf{Succ}] - \Pr_{1,j+1}[\mathsf{Succ}]| \leq \mathsf{Adv}^{\mathsf{smp}}_{\mathsf{THPS}}(\lambda)$.

Game G_2. It is identical to G_{1,Q_e+1}, except that when answering ENCRYPT queries, the challenger invokes $\chi_\ell \leftarrow_\$ \mathsf{AE.Encrypt}(\kappa_\ell, 0^{|m_{\ell,0}|})$.

In game G_{1,Q_e+1}, the challenger computes $\chi_\ell \leftarrow_\$ \mathsf{AE.Encrypt}(\kappa_\ell, m_{\ell,\beta})$; in game G_2, the challenger computes $\chi_\ell \leftarrow_\$ \mathsf{AE.Encrypt}(\kappa_\ell, 0^{|m_{\ell,0}|})$. Since each κ_ℓ is chosen from $\mathscr{K}$ uniformly at random, $\ell \in [Q_e]$, by a standard hybrid argument, any difference between G_{1,Q_e+1} and G_2 results in a PPT adversary against the IND-OT security of AE, so that $|\Pr_{1,Q_e+1}[\mathsf{Succ}] - \Pr_2[\mathsf{Succ}]| \leq Q_e \cdot \mathsf{Adv}^{\mathsf{ind\text{-}ot}}_{\mathsf{AE}}(\lambda)$.

Finally, in game G_2, since the challenge ciphertexts are encryptions of $0^{|m_{\ell,0}|}$, hence β is perfectly hidden to $\mathscr{A}$. So $\Pr_2[\mathsf{Succ}] = 1/2$.

Summing up, we proved the IND-$\mathscr{F}_{\mathsf{raff}}$-RKA security.

This completes the proof of Theorem 15 (IND-$\mathscr{F}_{\mathsf{raff}}$-RKA security).

Proof of Theorem 15 (Weak-INT-$\mathscr{F}_{\mathsf{raff}}$-RKA Security). Denote by $\mathscr{A}$ a PPT adversary who is against the weak-INT-$\mathscr{F}_{\mathsf{raff}}$-RKA security and queries ENCRYPT oracle for at most Q_e times. Similarly, the proof goes through a series of games, which are defined analogously, just like those games of the previous proof.

Game G_0. It is the original weak-INT-$\mathscr{F}_{\mathsf{raff}}$-RKA game.

As for the ℓth ($\ell \in [Q_e]$) ENCRYPT query $(m_\ell, \mathsf{ai}_\ell, f_\ell)$, the challenger computes the challenge ciphertext $\langle C_\ell, \chi_\ell \rangle$ in similar steps as the previous proof and outputs $\langle C_\ell, \chi_\ell \rangle$ to $\mathscr{A}$. Moreover, the challenger will put $(\mathsf{ai}_\ell, f_\ell, \langle C_\ell, \chi_\ell \rangle)$ to a set $\mathcal{Q}_{\mathscr{ENC}}$, put $(\mathsf{ai}_\ell, f_\ell)$ to a set $\mathcal{Q}_{\mathscr{AF\text{-}F}}$, and put $(C_\ell, \mathsf{ai}_\ell, t_\ell)$ to a set $\mathcal{Q}_{\mathscr{TAG}}$. In the end, the adversary outputs a forgery $(\mathsf{ai}^*, f^*, \langle C^*, \chi^* \rangle)$, where $f^* = \langle a^*, b^* \rangle$, and the challenger invokes the FINALIZE procedure as follows:

(i) If $(\mathsf{ai}^*, f^*, \langle C^*, \chi^* \rangle) \in \mathcal{Q}_{\mathscr{ENC}}$, output 0.

(ii) If $\exists (\mathsf{ai}_\ell, f_\ell) \in \mathcal{Q}_{\mathscr{AF\text{-}F}}$ such that $\mathsf{ai}_\ell = \mathsf{ai}^*$ but $f_\ell \neq f^*$, output 0.

(iii) If $C^* \notin \mathscr{C}$, output 0.

(iv) Compute $t^* := \mathsf{H}(C^*, \mathsf{ai}^*) \in \mathscr{T}$ and $\kappa^* := \Lambda_{a^* \cdot \mathsf{hk} + b^*}(C^*, t^*) \in \mathscr{K}$.

Output $(\mathsf{AE.Decrypt}(\kappa^*, \chi^*) \neq \bot)$.

Denote the event that FINALIZE outputs 1 by Forge. According to the definition, $\mathsf{Adv}^{\mathsf{weak\text{-}int\text{-}rka}}_{\mathsf{AIAE}, \mathscr{A}}(\lambda) = \Pr_0[\mathsf{Forge}]$.

Game G_1. It is identical to G_0, except that the following rule is added to the procedure FINALIZE by the challenger:

(i) If $\exists (C_\ell, \mathsf{ai}_\ell, t_\ell) \in \mathcal{Q}_{\mathscr{TAG}}$ such that $t_\ell = t^*$ but $(C_\ell, \mathsf{ai}_\ell) \neq (C^*, \mathsf{ai}^*)$, output 0.

Since $t_\ell = \mathsf{H}(C_\ell, \mathsf{ai}_\ell)$ and $t^* = \mathsf{H}(C^*, \mathsf{ai}^*)$, any difference between G_0 and G_1 implies a hash collision of H. So $|\Pr_0[\mathsf{Forge}] - \Pr_1[\mathsf{Forge}]| \leq \mathsf{Adv}^{\mathsf{cr}}_{\mathscr{H}}(\lambda)$.

Game $\mathsf{G}_{1,j}$, $j \in [Q_e + 1]$. It is identical to G_1, except that, for the first $j-1$ times of ENCRYPT queries, that is, $\ell \in [j-1]$, the challenger chooses $\kappa_\ell \leftarrow_\$ \mathscr{K}$ uniformly for the AE scheme.

Clearly, $\mathsf{G}_{1,1}$ is identical to G_1; thus $\Pr_1[\mathsf{Forge}] = \Pr_{1,1}[\mathsf{Forge}]$.

Game $\mathsf{G}'_{1,j}$, $j \in [Q_e]$. It is identical to $\mathsf{G}_{1,j}$, except that, for the jth ENCRYPT query, the challenger samples $C_j \leftarrow_\$ \mathscr{C} \setminus \mathscr{V}$ uniformly.

The difference between $\mathsf{G}_{1,j}$ and $\mathsf{G}'_{1,j}$ lies in the distribution of C_j. In game $\mathsf{G}_{1,j}$, C_j is uniformly chosen from $\mathscr{V}$; in game $\mathsf{G}'_{1,j}$, C_j is uniformly chosen from $\mathscr{C} \setminus \mathscr{V}$. Any difference between these two games results in a PPT adversary solving the subset membership problem related to THPS. We emphasize that the PPT adversary (simulator) is able to check the occurrence of Forge in an efficient way, because the key hk can be chosen by the simulator itself. Consequently, the difference between $\mathsf{G}_{1,j}$ and $\mathsf{G}'_{1,j}$ can be reduced to the subset membership problem smoothly.

Lemma 17. *For all $j \in [Q_e]$, $|Pr_{1,j}[\mathsf{Forge}] - Pr_{1,j'}[\mathsf{Forge}]| \le$* $\mathsf{Adv}_{\mathsf{THPS}}^{smp}(\lambda)$.

Proof. To bound the difference between $\mathsf{G}_{1,j}$ and $\mathsf{G}_{1,j}'$, we build an efficient adversary $\mathcal{B}$ solving the subset membership problem. Given $(\mathsf{pars}_{\mathsf{THPS}}, C)$, where $\mathsf{pars}_{\mathsf{THPS}} \leftarrow_\$$ $\mathsf{THPS.Setup}(1^\lambda)$, $\mathcal{B}$ aims to distinguish $C \leftarrow_\$ \mathcal{V}$ from $C \leftarrow_\$$ $\mathscr{C} \setminus \mathcal{V}$.

$\mathcal{B}$ simulates $\mathsf{G}_{1,j}$ or $\mathsf{G}_{1,j}'$ for $\mathcal{A}$. Firstly, $\mathcal{B}$ invokes $\mathsf{pars}_{\mathsf{AE}} \leftarrow_\$ \mathsf{AE.ParGen}(1^\lambda)$, picks $\mathsf{H} \leftarrow_\$ \mathcal{H}$ randomly, and sends $\mathsf{pars}_{\mathsf{AIAE}} := (\mathsf{pars}_{\mathsf{THPS}}, \mathsf{pars}_{\mathsf{AE}}, \mathsf{H})$ to $\mathcal{A}$. Next, $\mathcal{B}$ chooses $\mathsf{hk} \leftarrow_\$ \mathcal{HK}$.

As for the ℓth ($\ell \in [Q_e]$) ENCRYPT query $(m_\ell, \mathsf{ai}_\ell, f_\ell)$, where $f_\ell = \langle a_\ell, b_\ell \rangle \in \mathcal{F}_{\mathrm{raff}}$, $\mathcal{B}$ prepares the challenge ciphertext $\langle C_\ell, \chi_\ell \rangle$ in the following way.

(i) If $\ell \in [j-1]$, $\mathcal{B}$ computes $\langle C_\ell, \chi_\ell \rangle$ just like that in both $\mathsf{G}_{1,j}$ and $\mathsf{G}_{1,j}'$. That is, $\mathcal{B}$ chooses $C_\ell \leftarrow_\$ \mathcal{V}$ with witness w_ℓ, chooses $\kappa_\ell \leftarrow_\$ \mathcal{K}$ randomly, and invokes $\chi_\ell \leftarrow_\$ \mathsf{AE.Encrypt}(\kappa_\ell, m_\ell)$.

(ii) If $\ell \in [j+1, Q_e]$, $\mathcal{B}$ computes $\langle C_\ell, \chi_\ell \rangle$ just like that in both $\mathsf{G}_{1,j}$ and $\mathsf{G}_{1,j}'$. That is, $\mathcal{B}$ chooses $C_\ell \leftarrow_\$$ $\mathcal{V}$ with witness w_ℓ, computes $t_\ell := \mathsf{H}(C_\ell, \mathsf{ai}_\ell)$ and $\kappa_\ell := \Lambda_{a_\ell \cdot \mathsf{hk} + \mathsf{b}_\ell}(C_\ell, t_\ell)$, and invokes $\chi_\ell \leftarrow_\$$ $\mathsf{AE.Encrypt}(\kappa_\ell, m_\ell)$.

(iii) If $\ell = j$, $\mathcal{B}$ embeds its own challenge C to C_j, that is, $C_j := C$. Then it computes $t_j := \mathsf{H}(C_j, \mathsf{ai}_j)$, $\kappa_j := \Lambda_{a_j \cdot \mathsf{hk} + \mathsf{b}_j}(C_j, t_j)$, and invokes $\chi_j \leftarrow_\$$ $\mathsf{AE.Encrypt}(\kappa_j, m_j)$.

$\mathcal{B}$ outputs the challenge ciphertext $\langle C_\ell, \chi_\ell \rangle$ to $\mathcal{A}$. Moreover, $\mathcal{B}$ puts $(\mathsf{ai}_\ell, f_\ell, \langle C_\ell, \chi_\ell \rangle)$ to $Q_{\mathcal{ENC}}$, $(\mathsf{ai}_\ell, f_\ell)$ to $Q_{\mathcal{AF\text{-}F}}$, and $(C_\ell, \mathsf{ai}_\ell, t_\ell)$ to $Q_{\mathcal{TAG}}$.

Obviously, $\mathcal{B}$ simulates $\mathsf{G}_{1,j}$ in the case of $C \leftarrow_\$ \mathcal{V}$ and simulates $\mathsf{G}_{1,j}'$ in the case of $C \leftarrow_\$ \mathscr{C} \setminus \mathcal{V}$.

Finally, $\mathcal{A}$ sends a forgery $(\mathsf{ai}^*, f^*, \langle C^*, \chi^* \rangle)$ to $\mathcal{B}$, with $f^* = \langle a^*, b^* \rangle \in \mathcal{F}_{\mathrm{raff}}$. Then $\mathcal{B}$ decides whether FINALIZE outputs 1 or not with the help of hk.

(i) If $(\mathsf{ai}^*, f^*, \langle C^*, \chi^* \rangle) \in Q_{\mathcal{ENC}}$, $\mathcal{B}$ outputs 0 (to its own challenger).

(ii) If $\exists (\mathsf{ai}_\ell, f_\ell) \in Q_{\mathcal{AF\text{-}F}}$ such that $\mathsf{ai}_\ell = \mathsf{ai}^*$ but $f_\ell \ne f^*$, $\mathcal{B}$ outputs 0.

(iii) If $C^* \notin \mathscr{C}$, $\mathcal{B}$ outputs 0.

(iv) $\mathcal{B}$ computes $t^* := \mathsf{H}(C^*, \mathsf{ai}^*) \in \mathcal{T}$.

(v) If $\exists (C_\ell, \mathsf{ai}_\ell, t_\ell) \in Q_{\mathcal{TAG}}$ such that $t_\ell = t^*$ but $(C_\ell, \mathsf{ai}_\ell) \ne (C^*, \mathsf{ai}^*)$, $\mathcal{B}$ outputs 0.

(vi) $\mathcal{B}$ computes $\kappa^* := \Lambda_{a^* \cdot \mathsf{hk} + \mathsf{b}^*}(C^*, t^*) \in \mathcal{K}$ and outputs $(\mathsf{AE.Decrypt}(\kappa^*, \chi^*) \ne \bot)$.

With the help of hk, $\mathcal{B}$ is able to perfectly simulate FINALIZE, just like that in both $\mathsf{G}_{1,j}$ and $\mathsf{G}_{1,j}'$. Moreover, $\mathcal{B}$ outputs 1 to its own challenger if and only if the event Forge occurs.

As a result, we have that $|Pr_{1,j}[\mathsf{Forge}] - Pr_{1,j'}[\mathsf{Forge}]| \le$ $\mathsf{Adv}_{\mathsf{THPS}, \mathcal{B}}^{smp}(\lambda)$. $\quad\square$

Game $\mathsf{G}_{1,j}''$, $j \in [Q_e]$. It is identical to $\mathsf{G}_{1,j}'$, except that, for the jth ENCRYPT query, the challenger chooses $\kappa_j \leftarrow_\$ \mathcal{K}$ randomly.

Lemma 18. *For all $j \in [Q_e]$, $Pr_{1,j'}[\mathsf{Forge}] \le Pr_{1,j''}[\mathsf{Forge}] +$* $\mathsf{Adv}_{\mathsf{AE}}^{int\text{-}ot}(\lambda)$.

Proof. For game $\mathsf{G}_{1,j}'$ and game $\mathsf{G}_{1,j}''$, the difference between them lies in the computation of κ_j in the jth ENCRYPT query. In $\mathsf{G}_{1,j}'$, κ_j is properly computed; in $\mathsf{G}_{1,j}''$, κ_j is chosen from $\mathcal{K}$ uniformly.

We consider the information about the key hk that is used in $\mathsf{G}_{1,j}'$.

(i) For the ℓth ($\ell \in [j-1]$) query, ENCRYPT does not use hk at all since κ_ℓ is randomly chosen from $\mathcal{K}$.

(ii) For the ℓth ($\ell \in [j+1, Q_e]$) query, similar to the proof of Lemma 16, ENCRYPT can use $\mathsf{pk} = \mu(\mathsf{sk})$ to compute κ_ℓ.

(iii) For the jth query, similar to the proof of Lemma 16, ENCRYPT uses $\Lambda_{\mathsf{hk}}(C_j, t_j)$ to compute κ_j:

$$\kappa_j = \Lambda_{a_j \cdot \mathsf{hk} + \mathsf{b}_j}(C_j, t_j): \quad C_j \leftarrow_\$ \mathscr{C} \setminus \mathcal{V}$$

$$= \left(\Lambda_{\mathsf{hk}}(C_j, t_j)\right)^{a_j} \cdot \Lambda_{\mathsf{b}_j}(C_j, t_j): \tag{18}$$

$$\text{via key-homomorphism.}$$

(iv) The FINALIZE procedure, which defines the event Forge, uses $\Lambda_{\mathsf{hk}}(C^*, t^*)$ to compute κ^*:

$$\kappa^* = \Lambda_{a^* \cdot \mathsf{hk} + \mathsf{b}^*}(C^*, t^*)$$

$$= \left(\Lambda_{\mathsf{hk}}(C^*, t^*)\right)^{a^*} \cdot \Lambda_{\mathsf{b}^*}(C^*, t^*): \tag{19}$$

$$\text{via key-homomorphism.}$$

We divide the event Forge into the following two subevents:

(i) Subevent: $\mathsf{Forge} \wedge t_j \ne t^*$. Let us first consider the event $t_j \ne t^*$. We show that

$$\Pr_{1,j'}\left[t_j \ne t^*\right] = \Pr_{1,j''}\left[t_j \ne t^*\right]. \tag{20}$$

By the fact that $C_j \in \mathscr{C} \setminus \mathcal{V}$ and by the universal$_2$ property of THPS, $\Lambda_{\mathsf{hk}}(C_j, t_j)$ is uniformly distributed over $\mathcal{K}$ conditioned on $\mathsf{pk} = \mu(\mathsf{hk})$. Then as long as $a_j \in \mathbb{Z}_{|\mathcal{K}|}^*$, $\kappa_j = (\Lambda_{\mathsf{hk}}(C_j, t_j))^{a_j} \cdot \Lambda_{\mathsf{b}_j}(C_j, t_j)$ is also randomly distributed over $\mathcal{K}$. Hence, $\mathsf{G}_{1,j}'$ is the same as $\mathsf{G}_{1,j}''$ before $\mathcal{A}$ queries FINALIZE, and consequently, $t_j \ne t^*$ occurs with the same probability in $\mathsf{G}_{1,j}'$ and $\mathsf{G}_{1,j}''$.

Next we consider the event Forge conditioned on $t_j \ne t^*$. We show that

$$\Pr_{1,j'}\left[\mathsf{Forge} \mid t_j \ne t^*\right] = \Pr_{1,j''}\left[\mathsf{Forge} \mid t_j \ne t^*\right]. \tag{21}$$

Since $t_j \neq t^*$ and $C_j \in \mathscr{C} \setminus \mathscr{V}$, by the universal$_2$ property of THPS, $\Lambda_{\mathsf{hk}}(C_j, t_j)$ is uniformly distributed over $\mathscr{K}$ conditioned on $\mathsf{pk} = \mu(\mathsf{hk})$ and $\Lambda_{\mathsf{hk}}(C^*, t^*)$. With a similar argument, κ_j is also randomly distributed over $\mathscr{K}$. Hence, $\mathsf{G}'_{1,j}$ is the same as $\mathsf{G}''_{1,j}$ when $t_j \neq t^*$, and consequently, the probability that Forge occurs in $\mathsf{G}'_{1,j}$ and $\mathsf{G}''_{1,j}$ conditioned on $t_j \neq t^*$ is the same.

In conclusion, we have that

$$\Pr_{1,j'} \left[\mathsf{Forge} \wedge t_j \neq t^* \right] = \Pr_{1,j''} \left[\mathsf{Forge} \wedge t_j \neq t^* \right]$$

$$\leq \Pr_{1,j''} \left[\mathsf{Forge} \right]. \tag{22}$$

(ii) Subevent: $\mathsf{Forge} \wedge t_j = t^*$. By the new rule added in game G_1, Forge and $t_j = t^*$ will imply $(C_j, \mathsf{ai}_j) = (C^*, \mathsf{ai}^*)$. In addition, Forge and $\mathsf{ai}_j = \mathsf{ai}^*$ will imply that $f_j = f^*$, due to the special rule in the weak-INT-$\mathscr{F}_{\mathsf{raff}}$-RKA game (see Figure 4). Then it is straightforward to check that $\Lambda_{\mathsf{hk}}(C_j, t_j) = \Lambda_{\mathsf{hk}}(C^*, t^*)$ and

$$\kappa_j = \left(\Lambda_{\mathsf{hk}} \left(C_j, t_j \right) \right)^{a_j} \cdot \Lambda_{\mathsf{b}_j} \left(C_j, t_j \right)$$

$$= \left(\Lambda_{\mathsf{hk}} \left(C^*, t^* \right) \right)^{a^*} \cdot \Lambda_{\mathsf{b}^*} \left(C^*, t^* \right) = \kappa^*. \tag{23}$$

Since $C_j \in \mathscr{C} \setminus \mathscr{V}$, by the universal$_2$ property of THPS, $\Lambda_{\mathsf{hk}}(C_j, t_j)$ ($= \Lambda_{\mathsf{hk}}(C^*, t^*)$) is uniformly distributed over $\mathscr{K}$ conditioned on $\mathsf{pk} = \mu(\mathsf{hk})$. Then as long as a_j (which equals $a^*) \in \mathbb{Z}_{|\mathscr{K}|}^*$, κ_j (which equals κ^*) is also randomly distributed over $\mathscr{K}$. Also in this subevent, $(\mathsf{ai}^*, f^*, C^*) = (\mathsf{ai}_j, f_j, C_j)$ implies $\chi^* \neq \chi_j$; thus the probability of $\mathsf{AE.Decrypt}(\kappa^*, \chi^*) \neq \perp$ is bounded by $\mathsf{Adv}_{\mathsf{AE}}^{\mathsf{int\text{-}ot}}(\lambda)$. So we have the following claim. We present the full description of the reduction in Appendix A.

Claim 19. One has $\Pr_{1,j'}[\mathsf{Forge} \wedge t_j = t^*] \leq \mathsf{Adv}_{\mathsf{AE}}^{\mathsf{int\text{-}ot}}(\lambda)$.

Combining the above two subevents together, Lemma 18 follows. □

Now, we show that game $\mathsf{G}''_{1,j}$ is computationally indistinguishable from game $\mathsf{G}_{1,j+1}$, $j \in [Q_e]$. Note that the divergence between $\mathsf{G}''_{1,j}$ and $\mathsf{G}_{1,j+1}$ lies in the distribution of C_j in the jth ENCRYPT query. In game $\mathsf{G}''_{1,j}$, C_j is uniformly chosen from $\mathscr{C} \setminus \mathscr{V}$; in game $\mathsf{G}_{1,j+1}$, C_j is uniformly chosen from $\mathscr{V}$. Similar to Lemma 17, any difference between these two games results in a PPT adversary solving the subset membership problem related to THPS; thus we have that $|\Pr_{1,j''}[\mathsf{Forge}] - \Pr_{1,j+1}[\mathsf{Forge}]| \leq \mathsf{Adv}_{\mathsf{THPS}}^{\mathsf{smp}}(\lambda)$.

Finally, in game G_{1,Q_e+1}, note that the challenger does not use hk to compute κ_ℓ at all; thus hk is uniformly random to $\mathscr{A}$. Consequently, in the FINALIZE procedure, we have

$$\kappa^* = \left(\Lambda_{\mathsf{hk}} \left(C^*, t^* \right) \right)^{a^*} \cdot \Lambda_{\mathsf{b}^*} \left(C^*, t^* \right). \tag{24}$$

By the extracting property of THPS, $\Lambda_{\mathsf{hk}}(C^*, t^*)$ is uniformly random over $\mathscr{K}$. Therefore, as long as $a^* \in \mathbb{Z}_{|\mathscr{K}|}^*$, κ^* is uniformly random over $\mathscr{K}$ as well. Hence, the probability of

$\mathsf{AE.Decrypt}(\kappa^*, \chi^*) \neq \perp$ is bounded by $\mathsf{Adv}_{\mathsf{AE}}^{\mathsf{int\text{-}ot}}(\lambda)$, and we have $\Pr_{1,Q_e+1}[\mathsf{Forge}] \leq \mathsf{Adv}_{\mathsf{AE}}^{\mathsf{int\text{-}ot}}(\lambda)$.

In all, we proved the weak-INT-$\mathscr{F}_{\mathsf{raff}}$-RKA security.

This completes the proof of Theorem 15 (weak-INT-$\mathscr{F}_{\mathsf{raff}}$-RKA security).

Remark 20. We emphasize that the special rule in the weak-INT-$\mathscr{F}$-RKA game (cf. Figure 4) plays an essential role in proving Lemma 18. Below is the reason.

Without this special rule, the adversary is allowed to submit f^* ($= \langle a^*, b^* \rangle$) which is different from f_j ($= \langle a_j, b_j \rangle$), even if $\mathsf{ai}^* = \mathsf{ai}_j$ holds. In this case, we cannot expect to employ the INT-OT security of the underlying AE scheme to show that the second subevent ($\mathsf{Forge} \wedge t_j = t^*$) occurs with only a negligible probability. To demonstrate the problem clearly, suppose that the adversary $\mathscr{A}$ submits $f_j = \langle a_j, b_j \rangle$ in the jth ENCRYPT query and submits $f^* = \langle a^*, b^* \rangle = \langle a_j, b_j + \Delta \rangle$ in the FINALIZE procedure, where Δ is a constant. Then we have

$$\kappa^* = \left(\Lambda_{\mathsf{hk}} \left(C_j, t_j \right) \right)^{a_j} \cdot \Lambda_{\mathsf{b}_j + \Delta} \left(C_j, t_j \right)$$

$$= \left(\Lambda_{\mathsf{hk}} \left(C_j, t_j \right) \right)^{a_j} \cdot \Lambda_{\mathsf{b}_j} \left(C_j, t_j \right) \cdot \Lambda_\Delta \left(C_j, t_j \right) \tag{25}$$

$$= \kappa_j \cdot \Lambda_\Delta \left(C_j, t_j \right),$$

where the second equality follows from the key-homomorphism of THPS. Thus, κ^* and κ_j are *closely related but may not be equal*; in particular, the quotient κ^*/κ_j ($= \Lambda_\Delta(C_j, t_j)$) is a constant.

Consequently, it is hard for us to show that the subevent $\mathsf{Forge} \wedge t_j = t^*$ occurs with a negligible probability. The reason is as follows. To show that it is infeasible for any PPT adversary $\mathscr{A}$, who obtains $\chi_j \leftarrow_\$ \mathsf{AE.Encrypt}(\kappa_j, m_j)$ in the jth ENCRYPT query, to generate an AE-ciphertext χ^* satisfying $\mathsf{AE.Decrypt}(\kappa^*, \chi^*)$ ($= \mathsf{AE.Decrypt}(\kappa_j \cdot \Lambda_\Delta(C_j, t_j), \chi^*)$) $\neq \perp$, it seems that INT-RKA security of AE is required to some extent. We definitely cannot require INT-RKA security for the underlying AE scheme, since we are constructing (weak) INT-RKA secure (AI)AE scheme AIAE. As a result, it is hard to prove Lemma 18 without our special rule in the weak-INT-$\mathscr{F}$-RKA game.

3.3. Tag-Based HPS from the DDH Assumption.

Qin et al. [19] gave a construction of tag-based HPS from the d-LIN assumption. Here we construct a key-homomorphic THPS$_{\mathsf{DDH}}$ under the DDH assumption in Figure 6. With a routine check, the projective property of THPS$_{\mathsf{DDH}}$ follows.

Theorem 21. THPS$_{\mathsf{DDH}}$ *in Figure 6 is universal$_2$, extracting, and key-homomorphic. Moreover, the subset membership problem related to* THPS$_{\mathsf{DDH}}$ *is hard under the DDH assumption for* GenN *and* $\mathbb{QR}_{\overline{N}}$.

Proof of Theorem 21.

Universal$_2$. Suppose that $C = (g_1^{w_1}, g_2^{w_2}) \in \mathscr{C}$, $C' = (g_1^{w_1'}, g_2^{w_2'}) \in \mathscr{C} \setminus \mathscr{V}$, and $t, t' \in \mathscr{T}$ with $t \neq t'$. For $\mathsf{hk} = (k_1, k_2, k_3,$

$$\text{pars}_{\text{THPS}} \leftarrow_\$ \text{THPS.Setup}(1^\lambda):$$

$(p, q, N, \overline{N}) \leftarrow_\$ \text{GenN}(1^\lambda)$,

   i.e., p, q are safe primes, $N := pq, \overline{N} := 2N + 1$ is a prime.

$g_1, g_2 \leftarrow_\$ \mathbb{QR}_{\overline{N}}$.

Output $\text{pars}_{\text{THPS}} := (N, p, q, \overline{N}, g_1, g_2)$, which implicitly defines $(\mathscr{K}, \mathscr{C}, \mathscr{V}, \mathscr{T}, \mathscr{HK}, \mathscr{PK}, \Lambda_{(\cdot)}, \mu)$:

$\mathscr{K} := \mathbb{QR}_{\overline{N}}$. $\mathscr{C} := \mathbb{QR}_{\overline{N}}^2 \setminus \{(1,1)\}$. $\mathscr{V} := \{(g_1^w, g_2^w) \mid w \in \mathbb{Z}_N \setminus \{0\}\}$.

$\mathscr{T} := \mathbb{Z}_N$. $\mathscr{HK} := (\mathbb{Z}_N)^4$. $\mathscr{PK} := \mathbb{QR}_{\overline{N}}^2$.

For $\text{hk} = (k_1, k_2, k_3, k_4) \in \mathscr{HK}, C = (c_1, c_2) \in \mathscr{C}, t \in \mathscr{T}, \Lambda_{\text{hk}}(C, t) := c_1^{k_1 + k_3 t} c_2^{k_2 + k_4 t} \in \mathscr{K}$.

For $\text{hk} = (k_1, k_2, k_3, k_4) \in \mathscr{HK}, \text{pk} = \mu(\text{hk}) := (g_1^{k_1} g_2^{k_2}, g_1^{k_3} g_2^{k_4}) \in \mathscr{PK}$.

$K \leftarrow \text{THPS.Pub}(\text{pk}, C, w, t):$	$K \leftarrow \text{THPS.Priv}(\text{hk}, C, t):$
Parse $\text{pk} = (h_1, h_2) \in \mathscr{PK}$.	Parse $\text{hk} = (k_1, k_2, k_3, k_4) \in \mathscr{HK}$ and $C = (c_1, c_2) \in \mathscr{C}$.
Output $K := h_1^w h_2^{wt}$.	Output $K := c_1^{k_1 + k_3 t} c_2^{k_2 + k_4 t}$.

FIGURE 6: Construction of THPS_{DDH}.

$k_4) \leftarrow_\$ (\mathbb{Z}_N)^4$, we analyze the distribution of $\Lambda_{\text{hk}}(C', t')$ conditioned on $\text{pk} = \mu(\text{hk})$ and $\Lambda_{\text{hk}}(C, t)$.

Denote $d := d\log_{g_1} g_2 \in \mathbb{Z}_N$. Firstly $\text{pk} = \mu(\text{hk}) = (g_1^{k_1} g_2^{k_2}, g_1^{k_3} g_2^{k_4}) = (g_1^{k_1 + dk_2}, g_1^{k_3 + dk_4})$, which may leak the values of $k_1 + dk_2$ and $k_3 + dk_4$.

Next

$$\Lambda_{\text{hk}}(C, t) = (g_1^{w_1})^{k_1 + k_3 t} \cdot (g_2^{w_2})^{k_2 + k_4 t}$$
$$= g_1^{\overbrace{(w_1 k_1 + w_2 dk_2) + t \cdot (w_1 k_3 + w_2 dk_4)}^{\triangleq X}}, \quad (26)$$

which may further leak the value of X.

Similarly,

$$\Lambda_{\text{hk}}(C', t') = (g_1^{w_1'})^{k_1 + k_3 t'} \cdot (g_2^{w_2'})^{k_2 + k_4 t'}$$
$$= g_1^{\underbrace{(w_1' k_1 + w_2' dk_2) + t' \cdot (w_1' k_3 + w_2' dk_4)}_{\triangleq Y}}. \quad (27)$$

By the fact that $C' = (g_1^{w_1'}, g_2^{w_2'}) \notin \mathscr{V}$, we have $w_1' \neq w_2'$. Then as long as $t \neq t'$, Y is independent of $k_1 + dk_2$, $k_3 + dk_4$, and X, and consequently, Y is uniformly distributed over $\mathbb{Z}_N$.

Therefore, conditioned on $\text{pk} = \mu(\text{hk})$ and $\Lambda_{\text{hk}}(C, t)$, $\Lambda_{\text{hk}}(C', t') (= g_1^Y)$ is randomly distributed over $\mathscr{K} = \mathbb{QR}_{\overline{N}}$.

Extracting. Suppose that $C = (g_1^{w_1}, g_2^{w_2}) \in \mathscr{C}$ and $t \in \mathscr{T}$. For $\text{hk} = (k_1, k_2, k_3, k_4) \leftarrow_\$ (\mathbb{Z}_N)^4$, we analyze the distribution of $\Lambda_{\text{hk}}(C, t)$.

By (26), $\Lambda_{\text{hk}}(C, t) = g_1^X$ with $X = (w_1 k_1 + w_2 dk_2) + t \cdot (w_1 k_3 + w_2 dk_4)$. Since $C = (g_1^{w_1}, g_2^{w_2}) \in \mathscr{C}$, we have $(w_1, w_2) \neq (0, 0)$. Then when (k_1, k_2, k_3, k_4) is randomly chosen from $(\mathbb{Z}_N)^4$, X is uniformly distributed over $\mathbb{Z}_N$. Consequently, $\Lambda_{\text{hk}}(C, t)$ is randomly distributed over $\mathscr{K} = \mathbb{QR}_{\overline{N}}$.

Key-Homomorphism. For all $\text{hk} = (k_1, k_2, k_3, k_4) \in (\mathbb{Z}_N)^4$, all $a \in \mathbb{Z}$, all $b = (b_1, b_2, b_3, b_4) \in (\mathbb{Z}_N)^4$, all $C = (c_1, c_2) \in \mathscr{C}$, and

all $t \in \mathscr{T}$, we have $a \cdot \text{hk} + b = a \cdot (k_1, k_2, k_3, k_4) + (b_1, b_2, b_3, b_4) = (ak_1 + b_1, ak_2 + b_2, ak_3 + b_3, ak_4 + b_4)$. Then it follows that

$$\Lambda_{a \cdot \text{hk} + b}(C, t) = c_1^{(ak_1 + b_1) + (ak_3 + b_3)t} \cdot c_2^{(ak_2 + b_2) + (ak_4 + b_4)t}$$
$$= \left(c_1^{k_1 + k_3 t} c_2^{k_2 + k_4 t}\right)^a \cdot \left(c_1^{b_1 + b_3 t} c_2^{b_2 + b_4 t}\right) \quad (28)$$
$$= \Lambda_{\text{hk}}(C, t)^a \cdot \Lambda_b(C, t).$$

Subset Membership Problem. The subset membership problem related to THPS_{DDH} requires that $(\text{pars}_{\text{THPS}} = (N, p, q, \overline{N}, g_1, g_2), C = (g_1^w, g_2^w))$ is computationally indistinguishable from $(\text{pars}_{\text{THPS}} = (N, p, q, \overline{N}, g_1, g_2), C' = (g_1^{w_1}, g_2^{w_2}))$, where $C \leftarrow_\$ \mathscr{V}$ and $C' \leftarrow_\$ \mathscr{C} \setminus \mathscr{V}$. It trivially holds under the DDH assumption for GenN and $\mathbb{QR}_{\overline{N}}$.   □

3.4. Instantiation: AIAE_{DDH} from DDH-Based THPS_{DDH} and OT-Secure AE. When plugging the THPS_{DDH} (cf. Figure 6) into the paradigm in Figure 5, we immediately obtain an AIAE scheme AIAE_{DDH} under the DDH assumption, as shown in Figure 7. The key space is $\mathscr{K}_{\text{AIAE}} = (\mathbb{Z}_N)^4$.

By combining Theorem 15 with Theorem 21, we have the following corollary regarding the RKA security of AIAE_{DDH}.

Corollary 22. *If (i) the DDH assumption holds for GenN and $\mathbb{QR}_{\overline{N}}$, (ii) AE is one-time secure, and (iii) $\mathscr{H}$ is collision-resistant, then the scheme AIAE_{DDH} in Figure 7 is IND-$\mathscr{F}_{\text{raff}}$-RKA and weak-INT-$\mathscr{F}_{\text{raff}}$-RKA secure. Here $\mathscr{F}_{\text{raff}} := \{f_{(a,b)} : (k_1, k_2, k_3, k_4) \in (\mathbb{Z}_N)^4 \mapsto (ak_1 + b_1, ak_2 + b_2, ak_3 + b_3, ak_4 + b_4) \in (\mathbb{Z}_N)^4 \mid a \in \mathbb{Z}_N^*, b = (b_1, b_2, b_3, b_4) \in (\mathbb{Z}_N)^4\}$.*

Remark 23. Our AIAE_{DDH} enjoys the following property: $\kappa = c_1^{k_1 + k_3 t} \cdot c_2^{k_2 + k_4 t}$ will be randomly distributed over $\mathbb{QR}_{\overline{N}}$, as long as any element k_j in $\mathbf{k} = (k_1, k_2, k_3, k_4)$ is uniformly chosen. As a result, the one-time security of AE will guarantee that $\text{AIAE.Decrypt}(\mathbf{k}, \text{aiae.c}, \text{ai}) = \perp$ holds for any $(\text{aiae.c}, \text{ai})$ except with probability $\text{Adv}_{\text{AE}}^{\text{int-ot}}(\lambda) \leq \text{Adv}_{\text{AIAE}_{\text{DDH}}}^{\text{weak-int-rka}}(\lambda)$. This

AIAE.ParGen(1^λ):
$(p, q, N, \overline{N}) \leftarrow_\$ \mathsf{GenN}(1^\lambda)$,
$\quad$ i.e., p, q are safe primes, $N := pq$, $\overline{N} := 2N + 1$ is a prime.
$g_1, g_2 \leftarrow_\$ \mathbb{QR}_{\overline{N}}$. $\mathrm{pars}_{\mathsf{AE}} \leftarrow_\$ \mathsf{AE.ParGen}(1^\lambda)$. $\mathsf{H} \leftarrow_\$ \mathscr{H}$.
Output $\mathrm{pars}_{\mathsf{AIAE}} := (N, p, q, \overline{N}, g_1, g_2, \mathrm{pars}_{\mathsf{AE}}, \mathsf{H})$.

AIAE.Encrypt(k, m, ai):	AIAE.Decrypt(k, $\langle c_1, c_2, \chi \rangle$, ai):
Parse k $= (k_1, k_2, k_3, k_4) \in (\mathbb{Z}_N)^4$.	Parse k $= (k_1, k_2, k_3, k_4) \in (\mathbb{Z}_N)^4$.
$w \leftarrow_\$ \mathbb{Z}_N \setminus \{0\}$. $(c_1, c_2) := (g_1^w, g_2^w) \in \mathbb{QR}_{\overline{N}}^2$.	If $(c_1, c_2) \notin \mathbb{QR}_{\overline{N}}^2 \vee (c_1, c_2) = (1, 1)$,
$t := \mathsf{H}(c_1, c_2, \mathrm{ai}) \in \mathbb{Z}_N$.	$\quad$ Output $\perp$.
$\kappa := c_1^{k_1 + k_3 t} \cdot c_2^{k_2 + k_4 t} \in \mathbb{QR}_{\overline{N}}$.	$t := \mathsf{H}(c_1, c_2, \mathrm{ai}) \in \mathbb{Z}_N$.
$\chi \leftarrow_\$ \mathsf{AE.Encrypt}(\kappa, m)$.	$\kappa := c_1^{k_1 + k_3 t} \cdot c_2^{k_2 + k_4 t} \in \mathbb{QR}_{\overline{N}}$.
Output $\langle c_1, c_2, \chi \rangle$.	Output $\mathsf{AE.Decrypt}(\kappa, \chi)$.

FIGURE 7: Construction of $\mathsf{AIAE}_{\mathsf{DDH}}$ from AE and $\mathsf{THPS}_{\mathsf{DDH}}$.

fact will be used in the security proof of the PKE schemes presented in Sections 4 and 5.

4. PKE with n-KDM[$\mathscr{F}_{\mathrm{aff}}$]-CCA Security

Denote by $\mathsf{AIAE}_{\mathsf{DDH}}$ = ($\mathsf{AIAE.ParGen}$, $\mathsf{AIAE.Encrypt}$, $\mathsf{AIAE.Decrypt}$) the DDH-based AIAE scheme in Figure 7, where the key space is $(\mathbb{Z}_N)^4$. We need two other building blocks, following the approach in Figure 1.

> KEM: to be compatible with this $\mathsf{AIAE}_{\mathsf{DDH}}$, we have to design a KEM encapsulating a key tuple $(k_1, k_2, k_3, k_4) \in (\mathbb{Z}_N)^4$.
>
> $\mathscr{E}$: to support the set $\mathscr{F}_{\mathrm{aff}}$ of affine functions, we have to construct a special public-key encryption $\mathscr{E}$, so that after a computationally indistinguishable change, $\mathscr{E}$.Encrypt can serve as an entropy filter for the affine function set.

The proposed PKE scheme PKE = (ParGen, KeyGen, Encrypt, Decrypt) is presented in Figure 8, in which the shadowed parts highlight algorithms of KEM and $\mathscr{E}$.

The correctness of PKE is guaranteed by the correctness of $\mathsf{AIAE}_{\mathsf{DDH}}$, $\mathscr{E}$, and KEM.

Theorem 24. *If (i) the DCR assumption holds for* GenN *and* $\mathbb{QR}_{N^s}$, *(ii)* $\mathsf{AIAE}_{\mathsf{DDH}}$ *is IND-$\mathscr{F}_{\mathrm{raff}}$-RKA and weak-INT-$\mathscr{F}_{\mathrm{raff}}$-RKA secure, and (iii) the DL assumption holds for* GenN *and* $\mathbb{SCR}_{N^s}$, *then the proposed scheme* PKE *in Figure 8 is n-KDM[$\mathscr{F}_{\mathrm{aff}}$]-CCA secure.*

Proof of Theorem 24. Denote by $\mathscr{A}$ a PPT adversary who is against the n-KDM[$\mathscr{F}_{\mathrm{aff}}$]-CCA security, querying ENCRYPT oracle for at most Q_e times and DECRYPT oracle for at most Q_d times. The theorem is proved through a series of games. A rough description of differences between adjacent games is summarized in Table 2.

In the proof, G_1-G_2 deals with the n-user case; G_3-G_4 is used to eliminate the utilization of the $(\bmod N)$ part of

$(x_j, y_j)_{j=1}^4$ in the ENCRYPT oracle; the aim of G_5-G_6 is to use $(x_j, y_j)_{j=1}^4 \bmod N$ to hide a base key $\mathsf{k}^* = (k_1^*, \ldots, k_4^*)$ of $\mathsf{AIAE}_{\mathsf{DDH}}$ in the ENCRYPT oracle; G_7-G_8 is used to eliminate the utilization of $(x_j, y_j)_{j=1}^4 \bmod N$ in the DECRYPT oracle; in G_9-G_{10}, the IND-$\mathscr{F}_{\mathrm{raff}}$-RKA security of $\mathsf{AIAE}_{\mathsf{DDH}}$ leads to the n-KDM[$\mathscr{F}_{\mathrm{aff}}$]-CCA security, because $\mathsf{k}^* = (k_1^*, \ldots, k_4^*)$ now is concealed by $(x_j, y_j)_{j=1}^4 \bmod N$ perfectly.

Game G_0. It is the n-KDM[$\mathscr{F}_{\mathrm{aff}}$]-CCA game. Denote the event $\beta' = \beta$ by Succ. According to the definition, $\mathsf{Adv}_{\mathsf{PKE}, \mathscr{A}}^{\mathrm{kdm\text{-}cca}}(\lambda) = |\mathrm{Pr}_0[\mathsf{Succ}] - 1/2|$.

For the ith user, $i \in [n]$, let $\mathsf{pk}_i = (h_{i,1}, \ldots, h_{i,4})$ and $\mathsf{sk}_i = (x_{i,1}, y_{i,1}, \ldots, x_{i,4}, y_{i,4})$ denote the corresponding public key and secret key, respectively.

Game G_1. It is identical to G_0, except the way of answering the DECRYPT query ($\langle \mathrm{ai}, \mathrm{aiae.c} \rangle$, $i \in [n]$). More precisely, the challenger outputs $\perp$ if $\langle \mathrm{ai}, \mathrm{aiae.c} \rangle = \langle \mathrm{ai}_\ell, \mathrm{aiae.c}_\ell \rangle$ for some $\ell \in [Q_e]$, where $\langle \mathrm{ai}_\ell, \mathrm{aiae.c}_\ell \rangle$ is the challenge ciphertext of the ℓth ENCRYPT oracle query (f_ℓ, i_ℓ).

Case 1 ($\langle \mathrm{ai}, \mathrm{aiae.c} \rangle, i$) = ($\langle \mathrm{ai}_\ell, \mathrm{aiae.c}_\ell \rangle, i_\ell$). DECRYPT will output $\perp$ in G_0 since ($\langle \mathrm{ai}_\ell, \mathrm{aiae.c}_\ell \rangle, i_\ell$) $\in \mathcal{Q}_{\mathscr{E}\mathcal{N}\mathscr{C}}$ is prohibited by DECRYPT.

Case 2 ($\langle \mathrm{ai}, \mathrm{aiae.c} \rangle = \langle \mathrm{ai}_\ell, \mathrm{aiae.c}_\ell \rangle$ but $i \neq i_\ell$). We show that, in G_0, DECRYPT will output $\perp$, due to $e_{\ell,1} u_{\ell,1}^{x_{i,1}} u_{\ell,2}^{y_{i,1}} \notin \mathbb{RU}_{N^2}$, with overwhelming probability. Recall that $u_{\ell,1} = g_1^{r_\ell}$, $u_{\ell,2} = g_2^{r_\ell}$, $e_{\ell,1} = h_{i_\ell,1}^{r_\ell} T^{k_{\ell,1}}$, so

$$\begin{aligned} e_{\ell,1} u_{\ell,1}^{x_{i,1}} u_{\ell,2}^{y_{i,1}} &= h_{i_\ell,1}^{r_\ell} T^{k_{\ell,1}} \cdot (g_1^{r_\ell})^{x_{i,1}} (g_2^{r_\ell})^{y_{i,1}} \\ &= \left(h_{i_\ell,1} h_{i,1}^{-1} \right)^{r_\ell} T^{k_{\ell,1}} \quad \bmod N^2, \end{aligned} \tag{29}$$

where $h_{i_\ell,1}$ and $h_{i,1}$ are parts of public keys of i_ℓth user and ith user, respectively, and are uniformly random over $\mathbb{SCR}_{N^s}$.

$\text{pars} \leftarrow_\$ \text{ParGen}(1^\lambda):$	$(\text{pk}, \text{sk}) \leftarrow_\$ \text{KeyGen}(\text{pars}):$
$\text{pars}_{\text{AIAE}} \leftarrow_\$ \text{AIAE.ParGen}(1^\lambda)$, where	$x_1, y_1, x_2, y_2, x_3, y_3, x_4, y_4 \leftarrow_\$ \left[\!\left[\dfrac{N^2}{4}\right]\!\right].$
$\quad \text{pars}_{\text{AIAE}} = (N, p, q, \overline{N}, \overline{g}_1, \overline{g}_2, \text{pars}_{\text{AE}}, H),$	
$\quad N = pq, \ \overline{N} = 2N + 1, \ \overline{g}_1, \overline{g}_2 \in \mathbb{QR}_{\overline{N}}.$	$(h_1, h_2, h_3, h_4) := (g_1^{-x_1} g_2^{-y_1}, g_2^{-x_2} g_3^{-y_2},$
$\text{pars}'_{\text{AIAE}} := (N, \overline{N}, \overline{g}_1, \overline{g}_2, \text{pars}_{\text{AE}}, H).$	$\quad g_3^{-x_3} g_4^{-y_3}, g_4^{-x_4} g_5^{-y_4}) \bmod N^s.$
$g_1, g_2, g_3, g_4, g_5 \leftarrow_\$ \mathbb{SCR}_{N^s}.$	$\text{pk} := (h_1, h_2, h_3, h_4).$
Output $\text{pars} := (\text{pars}'_{\text{AIAE}}, g_1, g_2, g_3, g_4, g_5).$	$\text{sk} := (x_1, y_1, x_2, y_2, x_3, y_3, x_4, y_4).$
	Output $(\text{pk}, \text{sk}).$
$\langle ai, aiae.c \rangle \leftarrow_\$ \text{Encrypt}(\text{pk}, m): \quad m \in [N^{s-1}]$	$m/\bot \leftarrow \text{Decrypt}(\text{sk}, \langle ai, aiae.c \rangle):$
$\mathbin{/\!/} (k, ai) \leftarrow_\$ \text{KEM.Encrypt}(\text{pk}):$	$\mathbin{/\!/} k/\bot \leftarrow \text{KEM.Decrypt}(\text{sk}, ai):$
$k = (k_1, k_2, k_3, k_4) \leftarrow_\$ (\mathbb{Z}_N)^4.$	Parse $ai := (u_1, \dots, u_5, e_1, \dots, e_4).$
$r \leftarrow_\$ \left[\!\left[\dfrac{N}{4}\right]\!\right].$	If $e_1 u_1^{x_1} u_2^{y_1}, e_2 u_2^{x_2} u_3^{y_2}, e_3 u_3^{x_3} u_4^{y_3},$
$(u_1, u_2, u_3, u_4, u_5) := (g_1^r, g_2^r, g_3^r, g_4^r, g_5^r)$	$\quad e_4 u_4^{x_4} u_5^{y_4} \in \mathbb{RU}_{N^2}$
$\quad \bmod N^2.$	$\quad (k_1, k_2, k_3, k_4) := (d \log_T(e_1 u_1^{x_1} u_2^{y_1}),$
$(e_1, e_2, e_3, e_4) := (h_1^r T^{k_1}, h_2^r T^{k_2}, h_3^r T^{k_3},$	$\quad\quad d \log_T(e_2 u_2^{x_2} u_3^{y_2}), d \log_T(e_3 u_3^{x_3} u_4^{y_3}),$
$\quad h_4^r T^{k_4}) \bmod N^2.$	$\quad\quad d \log_T(e_4 u_4^{x_4} u_5^{y_4})) \bmod N.$
$ai := (u_1, \dots, u_5, e_1, \dots, e_4).$	$\quad k := (k_1, k_2, k_3, k_4).$
$\mathbin{/\!/} \mathscr{E}.c \leftarrow_\$ \mathscr{E}.\text{Encrypt}(\text{pk}, m):$	Else, Output $\bot.$
$\tilde{r}_1, \tilde{r}_2, \tilde{r}_3, \tilde{r}_4 \leftarrow_\$ \left[\!\left[\dfrac{N}{4}\right]\!\right].$	$\mathscr{E}.c/\bot \leftarrow \text{AIAE.Decrypt}(k, aiae.c, ai).$
$(\tilde{u}_1, \tilde{u}_2, \tilde{u}_3, \tilde{u}_4, \tilde{u}_5, \tilde{u}_6, \tilde{u}_7, \tilde{u}_8) := (g_1^{\tilde{r}_1}, g_2^{\tilde{r}_1},$	$\mathbin{/\!/} m/\bot \leftarrow \mathscr{E}.\text{Decrypt}(\text{sk}, \mathscr{E}.c):$
$\quad g_2^{\tilde{r}_2}, g_3^{\tilde{r}_2}, g_3^{\tilde{r}_3}, g_4^{\tilde{r}_3}, g_4^{\tilde{r}_4}, g_5^{\tilde{r}_4}) \bmod N^s.$	Parse $\mathscr{E}.c := (\tilde{u}_1, \dots, \tilde{u}_8, \tilde{e}, t).$
$\tilde{e} := h_1^{\tilde{r}_1} h_2^{\tilde{r}_2} h_3^{\tilde{r}_3} h_4^{\tilde{r}_4} T^m \bmod N^s.$	If $\tilde{e} \tilde{u}_1^{x_1} \tilde{u}_2^{y_1} \tilde{u}_3^{x_2} \tilde{u}_4^{y_2} \tilde{u}_5^{x_3} \tilde{u}_6^{y_3} \tilde{u}_7^{x_4} \tilde{u}_8^{y_4} \in \mathbb{RU}_{N^s}$
$t := g_1^m \bmod N \in \mathbb{Z}_N.$	$\quad m := d \log_T(\tilde{e} \tilde{u}_1^{x_1} \tilde{u}_2^{y_1} \tilde{u}_3^{x_2} \tilde{u}_4^{y_2} \tilde{u}_5^{x_3} \tilde{u}_6^{y_3}$
$\mathscr{E}.c := (\tilde{u}_1, \dots, \tilde{u}_8, \tilde{e}, t).$	$\quad\quad \tilde{u}_7^{x_4} \tilde{u}_8^{y_4}) \bmod N^{s-1}.$
$aiae.c \leftarrow_\$ \text{AIAE.Encrypt}(k, \mathscr{E}.c, ai).$	If $t = g_1^m \bmod N$, Output $m.$
Output $\langle ai, aiae.c \rangle.$	Else, Output $\bot.$

FIGURE 8: Construction of PKE from AIAE_{DDH}. The shadowed parts highlight algorithms of KEM and $\mathscr{E}$. Here p, q in $\text{pars}_{\text{AIAE}}$ are not provided in $\text{pars}'_{\text{AIAE}}$, since they are not used in AIAE.Encrypt and AIAE.Decrypt of AIAE_{DDH}.

So $h_{i_\ell, 1} h_{i, 1}^{-1} \neq 1$; hence $e_{\ell, 1} u_{\ell, 1}^{x_{i, 1}} u_{\ell, 2}^{y_{i, 1}} \notin \mathbb{RU}_{N^2}$, except with negligible probability $2^{-\Omega(\lambda)}$.

Thus G_0 and G_1 are the same except with probability at most $Q_d \cdot 2^{-\Omega(\lambda)}$ according to the union bound, and $|\Pr_0[\text{Succ}] - \Pr_1[\text{Succ}]| \leq Q_d \cdot 2^{-\Omega(\lambda)}$.

Game G_2. It is identical to G_1, except the way the challenger samples the secret keys $\text{sk}_i = (x_{i,1}, y_{i,1}, \dots, x_{i,4}, y_{i,4})$, $i \in [n]$. In game G_2, the challenger first chooses $(x_1, y_1, \dots, x_4, y_4)$ and $(\overline{x}_{i,1}, \overline{y}_{i,1}, \dots, \overline{x}_{i,4}, \overline{y}_{i,4})$ randomly from $[\lfloor N^2/4 \rfloor]$; next it computes $(x_{i,1}, y_{i,1}, \dots, x_{i,4}, y_{i,4}) := (x_1, y_1, \dots, x_4, y_4) + (\overline{x}_{i,1}, \overline{y}_{i,1}, \dots, \overline{x}_{i,4}, \overline{y}_{i,4}) \bmod \lfloor N^2/4 \rfloor$ for $i \in [n]$.

Obviously, the secret keys $\text{sk}_i = (x_{i,1}, y_{i,1}, \dots, x_{i,4}, y_{i,4})$ are uniformly distributed. Hence G_2 is identical to G_1, and $\Pr_1[\text{Succ}] = \Pr_2[\text{Succ}]$.

Game G_3. It is identical to G_2, except the way the challenger responds to the ℓth ($\ell \in [Q_e]$) ENCRYPT query (f_ℓ, i_ℓ). In game G_3, instead of using the public key $\text{pk}_{i_\ell} = (h_{i_\ell, 1}, \dots, h_{i_\ell, 4})$, the challenger uses the secret key $\text{sk}_{i_\ell} = (x_{i_\ell, 1}, y_{i_\ell, 1}, \dots, x_{i_\ell, 4}, y_{i_\ell, 4})$ to prepare $(e_{\ell, 1}, \dots, e_{\ell, 4})$ and $\tilde{e}_\ell$ in the following way:

(i)

$$(e_{\ell, 1}, \dots, e_{\ell, 4})$$
$$:= \left(u_{\ell, 1}^{-x_{i_\ell, 1}} u_{\ell, 2}^{-y_{i_\ell, 1}} T^{k_{\ell, 1}}, \dots, u_{\ell, 4}^{-x_{i_\ell, 4}} u_{\ell, 5}^{-y_{i_\ell, 4}} T^{k_{\ell, 4}} \right) \quad (30)$$
$$\bmod N^2,$$

(ii)

$$\tilde{e}_\ell$$
$$:= \tilde{u}_{\ell, 1}^{-x_{i_\ell, 1}} \tilde{u}_{\ell, 2}^{-y_{i_\ell, 1}} \tilde{u}_{\ell, 3}^{-x_{i_\ell, 2}} \tilde{u}_{\ell, 4}^{-y_{i_\ell, 2}} \tilde{u}_{\ell, 5}^{-x_{i_\ell, 3}} \tilde{u}_{\ell, 6}^{-y_{i_\ell, 3}} \tilde{u}_{\ell, 7}^{-x_{i_\ell, 4}} \tilde{u}_{\ell, 8}^{-y_{i_\ell, 4}} T^{m_\beta} \quad (31)$$
$$\bmod N^s.$$

Note that for $j \in [4]$,

$$e_{\ell, j} \overset{G_2}{=} h_{i_\ell, j}^r T^{k_{\ell, j}} = \left(g_j^{-x_{i_\ell, j}} g_{j+1}^{-y_{i_\ell, j}} \right)^r T^{k_{\ell, j}}$$
$$\overset{G_3}{=} u_{\ell, j}^{-x_{i_\ell, j}} u_{\ell, j+1}^{-y_{i_\ell, j}} T^{k_{\ell, j}} \quad \bmod N^2,$$

TABLE 2: Brief description of the security proof of Theorem 24.

	Changes between adjacent games	Assumptions
G_0	The original n-KDM-CCA security game.	—
G_1	DECRYPT: reject if $\langle \text{ai}, \text{aiae.c} \rangle = \langle \text{ai}_\ell, \text{aiae.c}_\ell \rangle$ for some $\ell \in [Q_e]$.	$G_0 \approx_s G_1$
G_2	INITIALIZE: sample secret keys with $(x_{i,1}, y_{i,1}, \ldots, x_{i,4}, y_{i,4}) := (x_1, y_1, \ldots, x_4, y_4) + (\overline{x}_{i,1}, \overline{y}_{i,1}, \ldots, \overline{x}_{i,4}, \overline{y}_{i,4})$.	$G_1 = G_2$
G_3	ENCRYPT(f_ℓ, i_ℓ): use the secret keys to run KEM.Encrypt and $\mathscr{E}$.Encrypt	$G_2 = G_3$
G_4	ENCRYPT(f_ℓ, i_ℓ): when ENCRYPT oracle encrypts affine function of secret keys, $\mathscr{E}$.c is computed with $(\widetilde{u}_{\ell,j})_{j\in[8]} := (g_1^{\widetilde{r}_{\ell,1}} T^{\delta_1}, \ldots, g_5^{\widetilde{r}_{\ell,4}} T^{\delta_8})$ instead of $(g_1^{\widetilde{r}_{\ell,1}}, \ldots, g_5^{\widetilde{r}_{\ell,4}})$. ENCRYPT does not use $(x_j, y_j)_{j=1}^4 \bmod N$ any more if $(\delta_j)_{j\in[8]}$ is carefully chosen.	$G_3 \approx_c G_4$ by IV$_5$
G_5	ENCRYPT(f_ℓ, i_ℓ): kem.ct $(= \text{ai})$ of KEM.Encrypt is computed with $(u_{\ell,j})_{j\in[5]} := ((g_j^{r^*} T^{\alpha_j})^{r_\ell})_{j\in[5]}$ instead of $(g_j^{r_\ell})_{j\in[5]}$. Now KEM.Encrypt encapsulates four keys $(k_{\ell,j} - r_\ell \cdot (\alpha_j x_{i,j} + \alpha_{j+1} y_{i,j}))_{j=1}^4 \bmod N$ but $(k_{\ell,j})_{j=1}^4$ is the key used in AIAE.Encrypt.	$G_4 \approx_c G_5$ by IV$_5$
G_6	ENCRYPT(f_ℓ, i_ℓ): sample $k_{\ell,j} := r_\ell k_j^* + s_{\ell,j}$ for $j \in [4]$. Now KEM.Encrypt encapsulates four keys $(r_\ell(k_j^* - \alpha_j x_j - \alpha_{j+1} y_j) - r_\ell(\alpha_j \overline{x}_{i,j} + \alpha_{j+1} \overline{y}_{i,j}) + s_{\ell,j})_{j=1}^4$ but $(r_\ell k_j^* + s_{\ell,j})_{j=1}^4$ is the key used in AIAE.Encrypt.	$G_5 = G_6$
G_7	DECRYPT: use $\phi(N)$ and secret keys to answer decryption queries.	$G_6 = G_7$
G_8	DECRYPT: add an additional rejection rule. Reject if $\text{Bad}' := (\exists u_j \notin \mathbb{SCR}_{N^2})$ or $\widetilde{\text{Bad}} := (\forall u_j \in \mathbb{SCR}_{N^2}) \wedge (\exists \widetilde{u}_j \notin \mathbb{SCR}_{N^s})$ happens. Bad' and $\widetilde{\text{Bad}}$ can be detected by using $\phi(N)$. Now only the $(\bmod \, \phi(N)/4)$ part of secret keys and $\phi(N)$ are used in DECRYPT. The randomness of $(\alpha_j x_j + \alpha_{j+1} y_j)_{j=1}^4 \bmod N$ perfectly hides $(k_1^*, \ldots, k_4^*)$ in ENCRYPT, thus $(k_1^*, \ldots, k_4^*)$ is uniform. $(r_\ell k_j^* + s_{\ell,j})_{j=1}^4$ is the key used in AIAE.Encrypt. Bad' may lead to a fresh successful forgery for AIAE$_{\text{DDH}}$.	$G_7 = G_8$ if neither Bad' nor $\widetilde{\text{Bad}}$ happens. $\Pr[\text{Bad}'] = \text{negl}$ due to weak INT-$\mathscr{F}_{\text{raff}}$-RKA security of AIAE$_{\text{DDH}}$
G_9	INITIALIZE: sample an independent random tuple $(\overline{k}_1^*, \ldots, \overline{k}_4^*)$. ENCRYPT$(f_\ell, i_\ell)$: use $(r_\ell \overline{k}_j^* + s_{\ell,j})_{j=1}^4$ in AIAE.Encrypt.	$G_8 = G_9$ to the adversary
G_{10}	ENCRYPT: encrypt zeros instead of the affine function of secret keys. $\widetilde{\text{Bad}}$ happens with negligible probability, since $t \neq g_1^m \bmod N$ in DECRYPT. Adversary $\mathscr{A}$ wins with probability $1/2$.	$G_9 \approx_c G_{10}$ by IND-$\mathscr{F}_{\text{raff}}$-RKA security of AIAE$_{\text{DDH}}$. $\Pr[\widetilde{\text{Bad}}] = \text{negl}$

$$\widetilde{e}_\ell \overset{G_2}{=} h_{i_\ell,1}^{\widetilde{r}_{\ell,1}} \cdots h_{i_\ell,4}^{\widetilde{r}_{\ell,4}} T^{m_\beta}$$

$$= \left(g_1^{-x_{i_\ell,1}} g_2^{-y_{i_\ell,1}} \right)^{\widetilde{r}_{\ell,1}} \cdots \left(g_4^{-x_{i_\ell,4}} g_5^{-y_{i_\ell,4}} \right)^{\widetilde{r}_{\ell,4}} T^{m_\beta}$$

$$\overset{G_3}{=} \widetilde{u}_{\ell,1}^{-x_{i_\ell,1}} \widetilde{u}_{\ell,2}^{-y_{i_\ell,1}} \cdots \widetilde{u}_{\ell,7}^{-x_{i_\ell,4}} \widetilde{u}_{\ell,8}^{-y_{i_\ell,4}} T^{m_\beta} \quad \bmod N^s. \tag{32}$$

Thus, G_3 is the same as G_2, and $\Pr_2[\text{Succ}] = \Pr_3[\text{Succ}]$.

Game G_4. It is identical to G_3, except the way the challenger responds to the ℓth $(\ell \in [Q_e])$ ENCRYPT query (f_ℓ, i_ℓ). In game G_4, in the case of $\beta = 1$, $(\widetilde{u}_{\ell,1}, \ldots, \widetilde{u}_{\ell,8})$ and $\widetilde{e}_\ell$ are computed without the use of $(x_1, y_1, \ldots, x_4, y_4) \bmod N$:

(i)

$$(\widetilde{u}_{\ell,1}, \ldots, \widetilde{u}_{\ell,8}) := \left(g_1^{\widetilde{r}_{\ell,1}} T^{\sum_{i=1}^n a_{i,1}}, g_2^{\widetilde{r}_{\ell,1}} T^{\sum_{i=1}^n b_{i,1}}, \right.$$

$$g_2^{\widetilde{r}_{\ell,2}} T^{\sum_{i=1}^n a_{i,2}}, g_3^{\widetilde{r}_{\ell,2}} T^{\sum_{i=1}^n b_{i,2}}, g_3^{\widetilde{r}_{\ell,3}} T^{\sum_{i=1}^n a_{i,3}}, g_4^{\widetilde{r}_{\ell,3}} T^{\sum_{i=1}^n b_{i,3}},$$

$$\left. g_4^{\widetilde{r}_{\ell,4}} T^{\sum_{i=1}^n a_{i,4}}, g_5^{\widetilde{r}_{\ell,4}} T^{\sum_{i=1}^n b_{i,4}} \right) \quad \bmod N^s,$$

$$\tag{33}$$

(ii)

$$\widetilde{e}_\ell := h_{i_\ell,1}^{\widetilde{r}_{\ell,1}} \cdots h_{i_\ell,4}^{\widetilde{r}_{\ell,4}} T^{\sum_{i=1}^n \sum_{j=1}^4 (a_{i,j}(\overline{x}_{i,j}-\overline{x}_{i_\ell,j})+b_{i,j}(\overline{y}_{i,j}-\overline{y}_{i_\ell,j}))+c}$$

$$\bmod N^s, \tag{34}$$

where $f_\ell = (\{a_{i,1}, b_{i,1}, \ldots, a_{i,4}, b_{i,4}\}_{i\in[n]}, c) \in \mathscr{F}_{\text{aff}}$.
Note that

$$\widetilde{e}_\ell \overset{G_4}{=} \prod_{j=1}^4 h_{i_\ell,j}^{\widetilde{r}_{\ell,j}} \cdot T^{\sum_{i=1}^n \sum_{j=1}^4 (a_{i,j}(\overline{x}_{i,j}-\overline{x}_{i_\ell,j})+b_{i,j}(\overline{y}_{i,j}-\overline{y}_{i_\ell,j}))+c}$$

$$= \prod_{j=1}^4 h_{i_\ell,j}^{\widetilde{r}_{\ell,j}} \cdot T^{\sum_{i=1}^n \sum_{j=1}^4 (a_{i,j}(x_{i,j}-x_{i_\ell,j})+b_{i,j}(y_{i,j}-y_{i_\ell,j}))+c}$$

$$= \prod_{j=1}^{4} \left(g_j^{-x_{i_\ell,j}} g_{j+1}^{-y_{i_\ell,j}} \right)^{\tilde{r}_{e,j}} \cdot T^{m_1 - \sum_{i=1}^{n} \sum_{j=1}^{4} (a_{i,j} x_{i_\ell,j} + b_{i,j} y_{i_\ell,j})}$$

$$= \prod_{j=1}^{4} \left(g_j^{\tilde{r}_{e,j}} T^{\sum_{i=1}^{n} a_{i,j}} \right)^{-x_{i_\ell,j}} \left(g_{j+1}^{\tilde{r}_{e,j}} T^{\sum_{i=1}^{n} b_{i,j}} \right)^{-y_{i_\ell,j}} \cdot T^{m_1}$$

$$= \tilde{u}_{\ell,1}^{-x_{i_\ell,1}} \tilde{u}_{\ell,2}^{-y_{i_\ell,1}} \cdots \tilde{u}_{\ell,7}^{-x_{i_\ell,4}} \tilde{u}_{\ell,8}^{-y_{i_\ell,4}} T^{m_1} \quad \bmod N^s,$$

$$\tag{35}$$

where the third equality follows from $m_1 = \sum_{i=1}^{n}(a_{i,1}x_{i,1} + b_{i,1}y_{i,1} + \cdots + a_{i,4}x_{i,4} + b_{i,4}y_{i,4}) + c$.

We analyze the difference between G_3 and G_4 via the following lemma.

Lemma 25. *One has* $|\Pr_3[\mathsf{Succ}] - \Pr_4[\mathsf{Succ}]| \le \mathsf{Adv}_{\mathsf{GenN}}^{iv_5}(\lambda)$.

Proof. According to the last line of (35), the way that $\tilde{e}_\ell$ is computed from $(\tilde{u}_{\ell,1}, \ldots, \tilde{u}_{\ell,8})$ is the same in G_3 and G_4. Therefore the only divergence between G_3 and G_4 lies in $(\tilde{u}_{\ell,1}, \ldots, \tilde{u}_{\ell,8})$.

We show that any difference between G_3 and G_4 results in a PPT adversary $\mathcal{B}_1$ solving the IV_5 problem. $\mathcal{B}_1$ is provided with $(N, g_1, \ldots, g_5)$ and has access to its $\mathsf{CHAL}_{IV_5}^b$ oracle. $\mathcal{B}_1$ simulates game G_3 or game G_4 for $\mathcal{A}$. Firstly, $\mathcal{B}_1$ prepares pars and generates $(\mathsf{pk}_i, \mathsf{sk}_i)$, $i \in [n]$, as in G_3 and G_4. As for the ℓth ($\ell \in [Q_e]$) ENCRYPT query (f_ℓ, i_ℓ) from $\mathcal{A}$, where $f_\ell = (\{a_{i,1}, b_{i,1}, \ldots, a_{i,4}, b_{i,4}\}_{i\in[n]}, c) \in \mathcal{F}_{\mathsf{aff}}$, $\mathcal{B}_1$ proceeds as follows: it queries its own $\mathsf{CHAL}_{IV_5}^b$ oracle with $(\sum_{i=1}^{n} a_{i,1}, \sum_{i=1}^{n} b_{i,1}, *, *, *)$, $(*, \sum_{i=1}^{n} a_{i,2}, \sum_{i=1}^{n} b_{i,2}, *, *)$, $(*, *, \sum_{i=1}^{n} a_{i,3}, \sum_{i=1}^{n} b_{i,3}, *)$, $(*, *, *, \sum_{i=1}^{n} a_{i,4}, \sum_{i=1}^{n} b_{i,4})$, where the symbol "$*$" denotes dummy messages. Then $\mathcal{B}_1$ obtains its challenges $(\tilde{u}_{\ell,1}, \tilde{u}_{\ell,2}, \tilde{*}, \tilde{*}, \tilde{*})$, $(\tilde{*}, \tilde{u}_{\ell,3}, \tilde{u}_{\ell,4}, \tilde{*}, \tilde{*})$, $(\tilde{*}, \tilde{*}, \tilde{u}_{\ell,5}, \tilde{u}_{\ell,6}, \tilde{*})$, $(\tilde{*}, \tilde{*}, \tilde{*}, \tilde{u}_{\ell,7}, \tilde{u}_{\ell,8})$ and neglects "$\tilde{*}$" terms. According to the definition of $\mathsf{CHAL}_{IV_5}^b$ oracle, $(\tilde{u}_{\ell,1}, \ldots, \tilde{u}_{\ell,8})$ is one of the following:

Case 1 ($b = 0$). $(g_1^{\tilde{r}_{e,1}}, g_2^{\tilde{r}_{e,1}}, g_2^{\tilde{r}_{e,2}}, g_3^{\tilde{r}_{e,2}}, g_3^{\tilde{r}_{e,3}}, g_4^{\tilde{r}_{e,3}}, g_4^{\tilde{r}_{e,4}}, g_5^{\tilde{r}_{e,4}})$.

Case 2 ($b = 1$). $(g_1^{\tilde{r}_{e,1}} T^{\sum_{i=1}^{n} a_{i,1}}, g_2^{\tilde{r}_{e,1}} T^{\sum_{i=1}^{n} b_{i,1}}, g_2^{\tilde{r}_{e,2}} T^{\sum_{i=1}^{n} a_{i,2}}, g_3^{\tilde{r}_{e,2}} T^{\sum_{i=1}^{n} b_{i,2}}, g_3^{\tilde{r}_{e,3}} T^{\sum_{i=1}^{n} a_{i,3}}, g_4^{\tilde{r}_{e,3}} T^{\sum_{i=1}^{n} b_{i,3}}, g_4^{\tilde{r}_{e,4}} T^{\sum_{i=1}^{n} a_{i,4}}, g_5^{\tilde{r}_{e,4}} T^{\sum_{i=1}^{n} b_{i,4}})$.

Next $\mathcal{B}_1$ uses the obtained $(\tilde{u}_{\ell,1}, \ldots, \tilde{u}_{\ell,8})$ and the secret keys to compute $\tilde{e}_\ell$ via (35) for $\mathcal{A}$. In the meantime, $\mathcal{B}_1$ can also simulate DECRYPT for $\mathcal{A}$ since it knows the secret keys. Finally, $\mathcal{B}_1$ outputs 1 if the event Succ occurs.

In Case 1, $\mathcal{B}_1$ simulates game G_3 perfectly for $\mathcal{A}$; in Case 2, $\mathcal{B}_1$ simulates game G_4 perfectly for $\mathcal{A}$. Any difference between $\Pr_3[\mathsf{Succ}]$ and $\Pr_4[\mathsf{Succ}]$ results in $\mathcal{B}_1$'s advantage over the IV_5 problem. Thus Lemma 25 follows. $\qquad\square$

Game G_5. It is identical to G_4, except for the following differences. In the INITIALIZE procedure of game G_5, the challenger picks $r^* \leftarrow_\$ [\lfloor N/4 \rfloor]$ and $\alpha_1, \ldots, \alpha_5 \leftarrow_\$ \mathbb{Z}_N$ randomly. As for the ℓth ($\ell \in [Q_e]$) ENCRYPT query (f_ℓ, i_ℓ), the challenger computes $(u_{\ell,1}, \ldots, u_{\ell,5})$ as follows:

(i) $(u_{\ell,1}, \ldots, u_{\ell,5}) := ((g_1^{r^*} T^{\alpha_1})^{r_e}, \ldots, (g_5^{r^*} T^{\alpha_5})^{r_e}) \bmod N^2$.

The only difference between G_4 and G_5 is the distribution of $(u_{\ell,1}, \ldots, u_{\ell,5})$. In game G_4, $(u_{\ell,1}, \ldots, u_{\ell,5}) = (g_1^{r_e}, \ldots, g_5^{r_e}) \bmod N^2$, while in game G_5, $(u_{\ell,1}, \ldots, u_{\ell,5}) = ((g_1^{r^*} T^{\alpha_1})^{r_e}, \ldots, (g_5^{r^*} T^{\alpha_5})^{r_e}) \bmod N^2$. Just like Lemma 25, any difference between G_4 and G_5 results in a PPT adversary solving IV_5 problem by invoking $\mathcal{A}$. Therefore, $|\Pr_4[\mathsf{Succ}] - \Pr_5[\mathsf{Succ}]| \le \mathsf{Adv}_{\mathsf{GenN}}^{iv_5}(\lambda)$.

Game G_6. It is identical to G_5, except for the following differences. In the INITIALIZE procedure of game G_6, the challenger picks $\mathsf{k}^* = (k_1^*, k_2^*, k_3^*, k_4^*)$ randomly. As for the ℓth ($\ell \in [Q_e]$) ENCRYPT query (f_ℓ, i_ℓ), the challenger computes $\mathsf{k}_\ell = (k_{\ell,1}, k_{\ell,2}, k_{\ell,3}, k_{\ell,4})$ and $(e_{\ell,1}, \ldots, e_{\ell,4})$ in a different way:

(i) Pick $\mathsf{s}_\ell = (s_{\ell,1}, s_{\ell,2}, s_{\ell,3}, s_{\ell,4}) \leftarrow_\$ (\mathbb{Z}_N)^4$ and $r_\ell \leftarrow_\$ [\lfloor N/4 \rfloor]$ randomly, and compute $\mathsf{k}_\ell = (k_{\ell,1}, k_{\ell,2}, k_{\ell,3}, k_{\ell,4}) := (r_\ell k_1^* + s_{\ell,1}, \ldots, r_\ell k_4^* + s_{\ell,4})$.

(ii)

$$(e_{\ell,1}, \ldots, e_{\ell,4}) := \left(h_{i_\ell,1}^{r^* r_e} T^{r_e \cdot (k_1^* - \alpha_1 x_{i_\ell,1} - \alpha_2 y_{i_\ell,1}) + s_{\ell,1}}, \ldots, \right.$$
$$\left. h_{i_\ell,4}^{r^* r_e} T^{r_e \cdot (k_4^* - \alpha_4 x_{i_\ell,4} - \alpha_5 y_{i_\ell,4}) + s_{\ell,4}} \right).$$
$$\tag{36}$$

Clearly k_ℓ is uniformly random over $(\mathbb{Z}_N)^4$, just like that in game G_5. In the meantime, for $j \in [4]$, we have

$$e_{\ell,j} \overset{G_5}{=} u_{\ell,j}^{-x_{i_\ell,j}} u_{\ell,j+1}^{-y_{i_\ell,j}} T^{k_{\ell,j}}$$

$$= \left(g_j^{r^*} T^{\alpha_j} \right)^{-r_e \cdot x_{i_\ell,j}} \left(g_{j+1}^{r^*} T^{\alpha_{j+1}} \right)^{-r_e \cdot y_{i_\ell,j}} T^{k_{\ell,j}}$$

$$= \left(g_j^{-x_{i_\ell,j}} g_{j+1}^{-y_{i_\ell,j}} \right)^{r^* r_e} T^{k_{\ell,j} - r_e \cdot (\alpha_j x_{i_\ell,j} + \alpha_{j+1} y_{i_\ell,j})}$$

$$\overset{G_6}{=} h_{i_\ell,j}^{r^* r_e} T^{r_e \cdot (k_j^* - \alpha_j x_{i_\ell,j} - \alpha_{j+1} y_{i_\ell,j}) + s_{\ell,j}} \quad \bmod N^2.$$
$$\tag{37}$$

Thus, G_6 is the same as G_5, and $\Pr_5[\mathsf{Succ}] = \Pr_6[\mathsf{Succ}]$.

Game G_7. It is identical to G_6, except the way the challenger answers the DECRYPT oracle queries $(\langle \mathsf{ai}, \mathsf{aiae.c}\rangle, i \in [n])$. In game G_7, it uses $\mathsf{sk}_i = (x_{i,1}, y_{i,1}, \ldots, x_{i,4}, y_{i,4})$ and $\phi(N) = (p-1)(q-1)$ to decrypt $\langle \mathsf{ai}, \mathsf{aiae.c}\rangle$, where $\mathsf{ai} = (u_1, \ldots, u_5, e_1, \ldots, e_4)$. More precisely, it computes $\mathsf{k} = (k_1, \ldots, k_4)$ and m in the following way:

(i)

$$(\alpha_1', \ldots, \alpha_5')$$

$$:= \left(\frac{d \log_T \left(u_1^{\phi(N)} \right)}{\phi(N)}, \ldots, \frac{d \log_T \left(u_5^{\phi(N)} \right)}{\phi(N)} \right)$$

$$\bmod N,$$

$$\left(\gamma_1', \ldots, \gamma_4'\right) := \left(\frac{d\log_T\left(e_1^{\phi(N)}\right)}{\phi(N)}, \ldots, \frac{d\log_T\left(e_4^{\phi(N)}\right)}{\phi(N)}\right)$$

$$\mod N,$$

$$\mathsf{k} = (k_1, \ldots, k_4)$$

$$:= \left(\alpha_1' x_{i,1} + \alpha_2' y_{i,1} + \gamma_1', \ldots, \alpha_4' x_{i,4} + \alpha_5' y_{i,4} + \gamma_4'\right)$$

$$\mod N, \tag{38}$$

(ii)

$$\mathscr{C}.c = (\tilde{u}_1, \ldots, \tilde{u}_8, \tilde{e}, t) \,/\, \bot \longleftarrow \mathsf{AIAE.Decrypt}\,(\mathsf{k}, \mathsf{aiae.c}, \mathsf{ai})\,, \tag{39}$$

(iii)

$$\left(\tilde{\alpha}_1, \ldots, \tilde{\alpha}_8\right)$$

$$:= \left(\frac{d\log_T\left(\tilde{u}_1^{\phi(N)}\right)}{\phi(N)}, \ldots, \frac{d\log_T\left(\tilde{u}_8^{\phi(N)}\right)}{\phi(N)}\right)$$

$$\mod N^{s-1}, \tag{40}$$

$$\tilde{\gamma} := \frac{d\log_T\left(\tilde{e}^{\phi(N)}\right)}{\phi(N)} \mod N^{s-1},$$

$$m$$

$$:= \tilde{\alpha}_1 x_{i,1} + \tilde{\alpha}_2 y_{i,1} + \tilde{\alpha}_3 x_{i,2} + \tilde{\alpha}_4 y_{i,2} + \tilde{\alpha}_5 x_{i,3} + \tilde{\alpha}_6 y_{i,3}$$

$$+ \tilde{\alpha}_7 x_{i,4} + \tilde{\alpha}_8 y_{i,4} + \tilde{\gamma} \mod N^{s-1}.$$

According to (8), for $j \in [4]$, we have that

$$k_j \stackrel{\mathsf{G}_6}{=} d\log_T\left(e_j u_j^{x_{i,j}} u_{j+1}^{y_{i,j}}\right)$$

$$= \frac{d\log_T\left(e_j u_j^{x_{i,j}} u_{j+1}^{y_{i,j}}\right)^{\phi(N)}}{\phi(N)} \mod N$$

$$= \frac{d\log_T\left(u_j^{\phi(N)\cdot x_{i,j}}\right)}{\phi(N)} + \frac{d\log_T\left(u_{j+1}^{\phi(N)\cdot y_{i,j}}\right)}{\phi(N)}$$

$$+ \frac{d\log_T\left(e_j^{\phi(N)}\right)}{\phi(N)}$$

$$\stackrel{\mathsf{G}_7}{=} \underbrace{\frac{d\log_T\left(u_j^{\phi(N)}\right)}{\phi(N)}}_{\alpha_j'} \cdot x_{i,j} + \underbrace{\frac{d\log_T\left(u_{j+1}^{\phi(N)}\right)}{\phi(N)}}_{\alpha_{j+1}'} \cdot y_{i,j}$$

$$+ \underbrace{\frac{d\log_T\left(e_j^{\phi(N)}\right)}{\phi(N)}}_{\gamma_j'},$$

$$m \stackrel{\mathsf{G}_6}{=} d\log_T\left(\tilde{e}\tilde{u}_1^{x_{i,1}} \tilde{u}_2^{y_{i,1}} \tilde{u}_3^{x_{i,2}} \tilde{u}_4^{y_{i,2}} \tilde{u}_5^{x_{i,3}} \tilde{u}_6^{y_{i,3}} \tilde{u}_7^{x_{i,4}} \tilde{u}_8^{y_{i,4}}\right)$$

$$\mod N^{s-1}$$

$$\stackrel{\mathsf{G}_7}{=} \underbrace{\frac{d\log_T\left(\tilde{u}_1^{\phi(N)}\right)}{\phi(N)}}_{\tilde{\alpha}_1} \cdot x_{i,1} + \cdots + \underbrace{\frac{d\log_T\left(\tilde{u}_8^{\phi(N)}\right)}{\phi(N)}}_{\tilde{\alpha}_8}$$

$$\cdot y_{i,4} + \underbrace{\frac{d\log_T\left(\tilde{e}^{\phi(N)}\right)}{\phi(N)}}_{\tilde{\gamma}}. \tag{41}$$

Hence G_7 is essentially the same as G_6, and $\mathrm{Pr}_6[\mathsf{Succ}] = \mathrm{Pr}_7[\mathsf{Succ}]$.

Game G_8. It is identical to G_7, except the way of answering the DECRYPT oracle queries ($\langle \mathsf{ai}, \mathsf{aiae.c}\rangle, i \in [n]$). More precisely, a rejection rule is added in DECRYPT:

(i) If $\alpha_1' \neq 0 \vee \cdots \vee \alpha_5' \neq 0 \vee \tilde{\alpha}_1 \neq 0 \vee \cdots \vee \tilde{\alpha}_8 \neq 0$, output $\bot$.

Denote by Bad the event that $\mathscr{A}$ ever queries the DECRYPT oracle with ($\langle \mathsf{ai}, \mathsf{aiae.c}\rangle, i \in [n]$), satisfying

$$e_1 u_1^{x_{i,1}} u_2^{y_{i,1}}, \ldots, e_4 u_4^{x_{i,4}} u_5^{y_{i,4}} \in \mathbb{RU}_{N^2} \tag{42}$$

$$\wedge \mathsf{AIAE.Decrypt}\,(\mathsf{k}, \mathsf{aiae.c}, \mathsf{ai}) \neq \bot$$

$$\wedge \tilde{e}\tilde{u}_1^{x_{i,1}} \tilde{u}_2^{y_{i,1}} \tilde{u}_3^{x_{i,2}} \tilde{u}_4^{y_{i,2}} \tilde{u}_5^{x_{i,3}} \tilde{u}_6^{y_{i,3}} \tilde{u}_7^{x_{i,4}} \tilde{u}_8^{y_{i,4}} \in \mathbb{RU}_{N^s} \tag{43}$$

$$\wedge t = g_1^m \mod N$$

$$\wedge \left(\alpha_1' \neq 0 \vee \cdots \vee \alpha_5' \neq 0 \vee \tilde{\alpha}_1 \neq 0 \vee \cdots \vee \tilde{\alpha}_8 \neq 0\right). \tag{44}$$

Obviously, G_8 is identical to G_7 unless Bad occurs. Thus, $|\mathrm{Pr}_7[\mathsf{Succ}] - \mathrm{Pr}_8[\mathsf{Succ}]| \leq \mathrm{Pr}_8[\mathsf{Bad}]$.

To show the computational indistinguishability of G_7 and G_8, we must prove that $\mathrm{Pr}_8[\mathsf{Bad}]$ is negligible. To this end, Bad is divided into two subevents:

(i) Bad': $\mathscr{A}$ ever queries the DECRYPT oracle with ($\langle \mathsf{ai}, \mathsf{aiae.c}\rangle, i \in [n]$), satisfying

Conditions $(42), (43) \wedge \left(\alpha_1' \neq 0 \vee \cdots \vee \alpha_5' \neq 0\right). \tag{45}$

(ii) $\widetilde{\mathsf{Bad}}$: $\mathscr{A}$ ever queries the DECRYPT oracle with ($\langle \mathsf{ai}, \mathsf{aiae.c}\rangle, i \in [n]$), satisfying

Conditions $(42), (43) \wedge \left(\alpha_1' = \cdots = \alpha_5' = 0\right)$

$$\wedge \left(\tilde{\alpha}_1 \neq 0 \vee \cdots \vee \tilde{\alpha}_8 \neq 0\right). \tag{46}$$

Obviously, $\mathrm{Pr}_8[\mathsf{Bad}] \leq \mathrm{Pr}_8[\mathsf{Bad}'] + \mathrm{Pr}_8[\widetilde{\mathsf{Bad}}]$. We will defer the analysis of $\mathrm{Pr}_8[\widetilde{\mathsf{Bad}}]$ to subsequent games. Through the following lemma, we provide the analysis of $\mathrm{Pr}_8[\mathsf{Bad}']$.

Lemma 26. *One has* $\mathrm{Pr}_8[\mathsf{Bad}'] \leq 2Q_d \cdot \mathsf{Adv}_{\mathsf{AIAE}_{\mathsf{DDH}}}^{weak\text{-}int\text{-}rka}(\lambda)$.

Proof. In DECRYPT of game G_8, the challenger will reply $\perp$ to $\mathscr{A}$ unless $\alpha_1' = \cdots = \alpha_5' = 0$ and $\widetilde{\alpha}_1 = \cdots = \widetilde{\alpha}_8 = 0$. Consequently, the $(\bmod\, \phi(N)/4)$ part of sk_i, that is, $(x_{i,1}, y_{i,1}, \ldots, x_{i,4}, y_{i,4}) \bmod \phi(N)/4$, $i \in [n]$, and the value of $\phi(N)$, is enough for answering DECRYPT queries. In particular, the values of $(x_1, y_1, \ldots, x_4, y_4) \bmod N$ are not necessary in DECRYPT.

Bad$'$ is further divided into the following two subevents:

(i) Bad$'$-1: $\mathscr{A}$ ever queries the DECRYPT oracle with $(\langle ai, aiae.c \rangle,\ i \in [n])$, satisfying

$$\text{Conditions } (42), (43) \wedge \left(\alpha_1' \neq 0 \vee \cdots \vee \alpha_5' \neq 0 \right)$$
$$\wedge \left(\exists j \in [4], \frac{\alpha_j'}{\alpha_j} \neq \frac{\alpha_{j+1}'}{\alpha_{j+1}} \bmod N \right). \tag{47}$$

(ii) Bad$'$-2: $\mathscr{A}$ ever queries the DECRYPT oracle with $(\langle ai, aiae.c \rangle,\ i \in [n])$, satisfying

$$\text{Conditions } (42), (43) \wedge \left(\alpha_1' \neq 0 \vee \cdots \vee \alpha_5' \neq 0 \right)$$
$$\wedge \left(\frac{\alpha_1'}{\alpha_1} = \cdots = \frac{\alpha_5'}{\alpha_5} \bmod N \right). \tag{48}$$

Recall that $(\alpha_1, \ldots, \alpha_5)$ are chosen in INITIALIZE.

We will consider the two subevents in game G_8 separately via the following two claims.

Claim 27. One has $\Pr_8[\text{Bad}'\text{-1}] \leq Q_d \cdot \text{Adv}_{\text{AIAE}_{\text{DDH}}}^{\text{weak-int-rka}}(\lambda)$.

Proof. In game G_8, the values of $(x_1, y_1, \ldots, x_4, y_4) \bmod N$ are not needed in DECRYPT, and the computation of $t_\ell = g_1^{m_\beta} \bmod N$ in ENCRYPT only makes use of $(x_1, y_1, \ldots, x_4, y_4) \bmod \phi(N)/4$. Thus the only information about $(x_1, y_1, \ldots, x_4, y_4) \bmod N$ leaked to $\mathscr{A}$ is through the computation of $(e_{\ell,1}, \ldots, e_{\ell,4})$ in ENCRYPT, which may leak the values of $(\alpha_1 x_1 + \alpha_2 y_1)$, $(\alpha_2 x_2 + \alpha_3 y_2)$, $(\alpha_3 x_3 + \alpha_4 y_3)$, $(\alpha_4 x_4 + \alpha_5 y_4) \bmod N$: for $j \in [4]$,

$$e_{\ell,j} = h_{i_\ell,j}^{r^* r_\ell} T^{r_\ell \cdot (k_j^* - \alpha_j x_{i_\ell,j} - \alpha_{j+1} y_{i_\ell,j}) + s_{\ell,j}} \bmod N^2$$

$$= h_{i_\ell,j}^{r^* r_\ell} T^{\underbrace{r_\ell \cdot (k_j^* - \alpha_j x_j - \alpha_{j+1} y_j}_{\triangleq \widehat{k}_j} - \alpha_j \overline{x}_{i_\ell,j} - \alpha_{j+1} \overline{y}_{i_\ell,j}) + s_{\ell,j}} \tag{49}$$

$$\bmod N^2.$$

If Bad$'$-1 occurs, for concreteness, say that $\alpha_1'/\alpha_1 \neq \alpha_2'/\alpha_2 \bmod N$, then

$$k_1 = \alpha_1' x_{i,1} + \alpha_2' y_{i,1} + \gamma_1'$$
$$= \alpha_1' x_1 + \alpha_2' y_1 + \alpha_1' \overline{x}_{i,1} + \alpha_2' \overline{y}_{i,1} + \gamma_1' \bmod N, \tag{50}$$

where k_1 is independent of $(\alpha_1 x_1 + \alpha_2 y_1) \bmod N$, thus uniformly distributed over $\mathbb{Z}_N$ from $\mathscr{A}$'s view. By Remark 23, for $k = (k_1, k_2, k_3, k_4)$ where $k_1 \leftarrow_{\$} \mathbb{Z}_N$, the probability

of AIAE.Decrypt$(k, aiae.c, ai)$ $\neq\perp$ is upper bounded by $\text{Adv}_{\text{AIAE}_{\text{DDH}}}^{\text{weak-int-rka}}(\lambda)$.

Then $\Pr_8[\text{Bad}'\text{-1}] \leq Q_d \cdot \text{Adv}_{\text{AIAE}_{\text{DDH}}}^{\text{weak-int-rka}}(\lambda)$ by a union bound. $\qquad\square$

Claim 28. One has $\Pr_8[\text{Bad}'\text{-2}] \leq Q_d \cdot \text{Adv}_{\text{AIAE}_{\text{DDH}}}^{\text{weak-int-rka}}(\lambda)$.

Proof. Similar to the discussion in the proof for the previous claim, in game G_8, the only information about $(x_1, y_1, \ldots, x_4, y_4) \bmod N$ and $k^* = (k_1^*, k_2^*, k_3^*, k_4^*)$ involved is through ENCRYPT, which uses the value of $\widehat{k}_1 := (k_1^* - \alpha_1 x_1 - \alpha_2 y_1)$, $\widehat{k}_2 := (k_2^* - \alpha_2 x_2 - \alpha_3 y_2)$, $\widehat{k}_3 := (k_3^* - \alpha_3 x_3 - \alpha_4 y_3)$, $\widehat{k}_4 := (k_4^* - \alpha_4 x_4 - \alpha_5 y_4) \bmod N$ via computing $(e_{\ell,1}, \ldots, e_{\ell,4})$ (see (49)) and also uses $k_\ell = r_\ell \cdot (k_1^*, k_2^*, k_3^*, k_4^*) + (s_{\ell,1}, \ldots, s_{\ell,4})$ as the encryption key of AIAE.Encrypt.

Note that because of the randomness of $(x_1, y_1, \ldots, x_4, y_4) \bmod N$, $(\widehat{k}_1, \widehat{k}_2, \widehat{k}_3, \widehat{k}_4)$ are uniformly distributed and independent of $(k_1^*, k_2^*, k_3^*, k_4^*)$. Therefore it is possible to construct an algorithm to simulate DECRYPT and ENCRYPT of game G_8 without $k^* = (k_1^*, k_2^*, k_3^*, k_4^*)$ and $(x_1, y_1, \ldots, x_4, y_4) \bmod N$. The algorithm can also simulate AIAE.Encrypt as long as it has access to a weak-INT-$\mathscr{F}_{\text{raff}}$-RKA encryption oracle of the AIAE$_{\text{DDH}}$ scheme.

More precisely, we construct a PPT adversary $\mathscr{B}_2(\text{pars}_{\text{AIAE}})$, which has access to ENCRYPT$_{\text{AIAE}}$ oracle, against the weak-INT-$\mathscr{F}_{\text{raff}}$-RKA security of the AIAE$_{\text{DDH}}$ scheme, where $\text{pars}_{\text{AIAE}} = (N, p, q, \ldots)$. $\mathscr{B}_2$ does not choose $k^* = (k_1^*, k_2^*, k_3^*, k_4^*)$ in INITIALIZE any more, and it implicitly sets k^* to be the encryption key used by its weak-INT-$\mathscr{F}_{\text{raff}}$-RKA challenger. $\mathscr{B}_2$ does not choose $(x_1, y_1, \ldots, x_4, y_4) \bmod N$ either, and instead, it chooses $\widehat{k} = (\widehat{k}_1, \widehat{k}_2, \widehat{k}_3, \widehat{k}_4)$ uniformly from $(\mathbb{Z}_N)^4$. $\mathscr{B}_2$ picks $(x_1, y_1, \ldots, x_4, y_4) \bmod \phi(N)/4$ and $(\overline{x}_{i,1}, \overline{y}_{i,1}, \ldots, \overline{x}_{i,4}, \overline{y}_{i,4}) \in [\lfloor N^2/4 \rfloor]$, $i \in [n]$, randomly. To simulate ENCRYPT, $\mathscr{B}_2$ can use $(\overline{x}_{i_\ell,j}, \overline{y}_{i_\ell,j}, \widehat{k}_j)_{j=1}^4$ to compute $(e_{\ell,j})_{j=1}^4$ via (49) and use $(\overline{x}_{i,j}, \overline{y}_{i,j})_{j=1}^4$, $i \in [n]$, to compute $\widetilde{e}_\ell$. Note that $\mathscr{B}_2$ is able to compute $t_\ell = g_1^{m_\beta} \bmod N$, even if $\beta = 1$, because it knows the $(\bmod\, \phi(N)/4)$ part of sk_i, that is, $(x_j, y_j)_{j=1}^4 \bmod \phi(N)/4$ and $(\overline{x}_{i,j}, \overline{y}_{i,j})_{j=1}^4 \bmod \phi(N)/4$, $i \in [n]$. Then $\mathscr{B}_2$ submits $(\mathscr{E}.c_\ell, a\hat{i}_\ell, \langle r_\ell, s_\ell = (s_{\ell,1}, \ldots, s_{\ell,4}) \rangle)$ to its own ENCRYPT$_{\text{AIAE}}$ oracle and obtains aiae.c_ℓ. The final ciphertext is $\langle a\hat{i}_\ell, \text{aiae}.c_\ell \rangle$. According to the weak-INT-$\mathscr{F}_{\text{raff}}$-RKA security game, the ENCRYPT$_{\text{AIAE}}$ oracle will encrypt $\mathscr{E}.c_\ell$ with the auxiliary input ai_ℓ under the transformed key $k_\ell = r_\ell \cdot k^* + s_\ell$; that is, the ENCRYPT$_{\text{AIAE}}$ oracle behaves as AIAE.Encrypt$(k_\ell, \mathscr{E}.c_\ell, ai_\ell)$. Thus $\mathscr{B}_2$'s simulation of ENCRYPT is identical to G_8. For DECRYPT, $\mathscr{B}_2$ answers decryption queries with the $(\bmod\, \phi(N)/4)$ part of all the secret keys and $\phi(N) = (p-1)(q-1)$, just like G_8.

Suppose that $\mathscr{A}$ ever queries the DECRYPT oracle with $(\langle ai, aiae.c \rangle,\ i \in [n])$, such that Bad$'$-2 occurs. For concreteness, say that $r := \alpha_1'/\alpha_1 = \cdots = \alpha_5'/\alpha_5 \neq 0 \bmod N$, then for $j \in [4]$,

$$k_j = \alpha_j' x_{i,j} + \alpha_{j+1}' y_{i,j} + \gamma_j' = r \cdot \left(\alpha_j x_{i,j} + \alpha_{j+1} y_{i,j} \right) + \gamma_j'$$
$$\bmod N$$

$$= r \cdot k_j^* - r \cdot \left(k_j^* - \alpha_j x_{i,j} - \alpha_{j+1} y_{i,j} \right) + \gamma_j' \mod N$$

$$= r \cdot k_j^* - r$$

$$\cdot \left(\underbrace{k_j^* - \alpha_j x_j - \alpha_{j+1} y_j}_{= \hat{k}_j} - \alpha_j \overline{x}_{i,j} - \alpha_{j+1} \overline{y}_{i,j} \right)$$

$$+ \gamma_j' \mod N$$

$$= r \cdot k_j^* \underbrace{- r \cdot \left(\hat{k}_j - \alpha_j \overline{x}_{i,j} - \alpha_{j+1} \overline{y}_{i,j} \right) + \gamma_j'}_{\triangleq s_j}$$

$$= r \cdot k_j^* + s_j \mod N.$$

$$(51)$$

Thus $\mathsf{k} = (k_1, \ldots, k_4) = r \cdot \mathsf{k}^* + \mathsf{s}$, where $\mathsf{s} := (s_1, \ldots, s_4)$. $\mathcal{B}_2$ can compute $\langle r, \mathsf{s} = (s_1, \ldots, s_4) \rangle$ as above using $(\overline{x}_{i,j}, \overline{y}_{i,j}, \hat{k}_j)_{j=1}^4$ and outputs $(\mathsf{ai}, \langle r, \mathsf{s} \rangle, \mathsf{aiae.c})$ to its weak-INT-$\mathcal{F}_{\mathrm{raff}}$-RKA challenger as a forgery. We analyze the success probability of $\mathcal{B}_2$ as follows.

(i) Firstly, a valid decryption query from $\mathcal{A}$ satisfies $\langle \mathsf{ai}, \mathsf{aiae.c} \rangle \neq \langle \mathsf{ai}_\ell, \mathsf{aiae.c}_\ell \rangle$ for all $\ell \in [Q_e]$; thus $(\mathsf{ai}, \langle r, \mathsf{s} \rangle, \mathsf{aiae.c}) \neq (\mathsf{ai}_\ell, \langle r_\ell, \mathsf{s}_\ell \rangle, \mathsf{aiae.c}_\ell)$ will hold for all $\ell \in [Q_e]$; that is, $\mathcal{B}_2$ always outputs a fresh forgery.

(ii) Secondly, if $\mathsf{ai} = \mathsf{ai}_\ell$ for some $\ell \in [Q_e]$, then it is easy to have that $\alpha_1' = \alpha_1 \cdot r_\ell, \ldots, \alpha_5' = \alpha_5 \cdot r_\ell$ and thus $r = r_\ell$. Furthermore for $j \in [4]$, it clearly holds that $\gamma_j' = r_\ell \cdot (\hat{k}_j - \alpha_j \overline{x}_{i,j} - \alpha_{j+1} \overline{y}_{i,j}) + s_{\ell,j}$ (cf. (49)); thus $s_j = -r \cdot (\hat{k}_j - \alpha_j \overline{x}_{i,j} - \alpha_{j+1} \overline{y}_{i,j}) + \gamma_j' = s_{\ell,j}$ and $\mathsf{s} = \mathsf{s}_\ell$. That is, if $\mathsf{ai} = \mathsf{ai}_\ell$ for some $\ell \in [Q_e]$, then it holds that $\langle r, \mathsf{s} \rangle = \langle r_\ell, \mathsf{s}_\ell \rangle$. Obviously it satisfies the special rule required for the weak-INT-$\mathcal{F}_{\mathrm{raff}}$-RKA security.

(iii) Finally, if $\mathsf{Bad}'\text{-}2$ occurs in this decryption query, then $\mathsf{AIAE.Decrypt}(\mathsf{k}, \mathsf{aiae.c}, \mathsf{ai}) \neq \bot$, where $\mathsf{k} = r \cdot \mathsf{k}^* + \mathsf{s}$, will imply that $\mathcal{B}_2$'s forgery is successful.

By a union bound, we have that $\Pr_8[\mathsf{Bad}'\text{-}2] \leq Q_d \cdot \mathsf{Adv}_{\mathsf{AIAE}_{\mathrm{DDH}}, \mathcal{B}_2}^{\mathrm{weak\text{-}int\text{-}rka}}(\lambda)$. $\square$

In conclusion, Lemma 26 follows from the above two claims.

This completes the proof of Lemma 26.

Game G_9. It is identical to G_8, except for the following differences. In the INITIALIZE procedure of game G_9, the challenger picks an independent $\overline{\mathsf{k}}^* = (\overline{k}_1^*, \overline{k}_2^*, \overline{k}_3^*, \overline{k}_4^*) \leftarrow_\$ (\mathbb{Z}_N)^4$ besides $\mathsf{k}^* = (k_1^*, k_2^*, k_3^*, k_4^*)$. As for the ℓth ($\ell \in [Q_e]$) ENCRYPT oracle query (f_ℓ, i_ℓ), the challenger employs a different key for $\mathsf{AIAE}_{\mathrm{DDH}}$ in the computation of $\mathsf{aiae.c}_\ell$:

(i) $\overline{\mathsf{k}}_\ell := (r_\ell \overline{k}_1^* + s_{\ell,1}, \ldots, r_\ell \overline{k}_4^* + s_{\ell,4})$;

(ii) $\mathsf{aiae.c}_\ell \leftarrow_\$ \mathsf{AIAE.Encrypt}(\overline{\mathsf{k}}_\ell, \mathscr{E}.c_\ell, \mathsf{ai}_\ell)$.

We stress that the challenger still employs $\mathsf{k}^* = (k_1^*, k_2^*, k_3^*, k_4^*)$ in the computation of $(e_{\ell,1}, \ldots, e_{\ell,4})$.

In G_8, the only place that involves the value of $(x_1, y_1, \ldots, x_4, y_4) \mod N$ is in the computation of $(e_{\ell,1}, \ldots, e_{\ell,4})$ in the ENCRYPT oracle. Specifically, for $j \in [4]$,

$$e_{\ell,j} = h_{i_\ell,j}^{r^* r_\ell} T^{r_\ell \cdot (k_j^* - \alpha_j x_{i_\ell,j} - \alpha_{j+1} y_{i_\ell,j}) + s_{\ell,j}} \mod N^2$$

$$= h_{i_\ell,j}^{r^* r_\ell} T^{r_\ell \cdot (k_j^* - \alpha_j x_j - \alpha_{j+1} y_j - \alpha_j \overline{x}_{i_\ell,j} - \alpha_{j+1} \overline{y}_{i_\ell,j}) + s_{\ell,j}} \tag{52}$$

$$\mod N^2.$$

Note that the computation of $t_\ell = g_1^{m_\beta} \mod N$ in the ENCRYPT oracle only involves $(x_1, y_1, \ldots, x_4, y_4) \mod \phi(N)/4$. Moreover, observe that neither $\mathsf{k}^* = (k_1^*, k_2^*, k_3^*, k_4^*)$ nor $(x_1, y_1, \ldots, x_4, y_4) \mod N$ is used in DECRYPT. Hence, $\mathsf{k}^* = (k_1^*, k_2^*, k_3^*, k_4^*)$ is perfectly hidden by $(x_1, y_1, \ldots, x_4, y_4) \mod N$.

Therefore, the challenger could always employ another $\overline{\mathsf{k}}^* = (\overline{k}_1^*, \ldots, \overline{k}_4^*)$ in the computation of $\overline{\mathsf{k}}_\ell$ and utilize $\overline{\mathsf{k}}_\ell$ in the $\mathsf{AIAE}_{\mathrm{DDH}}$'s encryption in the ENCRYPT oracle, as in G_9.

Then game G_8 and game G_9 are essentially the same from $\mathcal{A}$'s view, so $\Pr_8[\mathsf{Succ}] = \Pr_9[\mathsf{Succ}]$ and $\Pr_8[\widetilde{\mathsf{Bad}}] = \Pr_9[\widetilde{\mathsf{Bad}}]$.

Game G_{10}. It is identical to G_9, except the way the challenger answers the ℓth ($\ell \in [Q_e]$) ENCRYPT oracle query (f_ℓ, i_ℓ). More precisely, in game G_{10}, the challenger computes $\mathsf{aiae.c}_\ell$ in the following way:

(i) $\mathsf{aiae.c}_\ell \leftarrow_\$ \mathsf{AIAE.Encrypt}(\overline{\mathsf{k}}_\ell, 0^{\lambda.\mathscr{M}}, \mathsf{ai}_\ell)$.

Observe that, in G_9 and G_{10}, $\overline{\mathsf{k}}^*$ is employed only in the $\mathsf{AIAE}_{\mathrm{DDH}}$ encryption, where it uses $\overline{\mathsf{k}}_\ell = r_\ell \cdot \overline{\mathsf{k}}^* + \mathsf{s}_\ell$ as the encryption key with $\mathsf{s}_\ell = (s_{\ell,1}, \ldots, s_{\ell,4})$. Any difference between G_9 and G_{10} results in a PPT adversary against the IND-$\mathcal{F}_{\mathrm{raff}}$-RKA security of the $\mathsf{AIAE}_{\mathrm{DDH}}$ scheme. Therefore, $|\Pr_9[\mathsf{Succ}] - \Pr_{10}[\mathsf{Succ}]| \leq \mathsf{Adv}_{\mathsf{AIAE}_{\mathrm{DDH}}}^{\mathrm{ind\text{-}rka}}(\lambda)$ and $|\Pr_9[\widetilde{\mathsf{Bad}}] - \Pr_{10}[\widetilde{\mathsf{Bad}}]| \leq \mathsf{Adv}_{\mathsf{AIAE}_{\mathrm{DDH}}}^{\mathrm{ind\text{-}rka}}(\lambda)$.

Finally in G_{10}, the challenger always computes the $\mathsf{AIAE}_{\mathrm{DDH}}$ encryption of $0^{\lambda.\mathscr{M}}$ in the ENCRYPT oracle, so β is perfectly hidden from $\mathcal{A}$'s view. Thus, $\Pr_{10}[\mathsf{Succ}] = 1/2$.

To complete the proof of Theorem 24, we only need to prove the following lemma.

Lemma 29. *One has* $\Pr_{10}[\widetilde{\mathsf{Bad}}] \leq (Q_d + 1) \cdot 2^{-\Omega(\lambda)} + \mathsf{Adv}_{\mathsf{GenN}}^{dl}(\lambda)$.

Proof. In G_{10}, neither DECRYPT nor ENCRYPT uses the values of $(x_1, y_1, \ldots, x_4, y_4) \mod \phi(N)/4$. The only information leaked about them lies in the public keys pk_i, $i \in [n]$, which reveal the values of $(w_1 x_1 + w_2 y_1)$, $(w_2 x_2 + w_3 y_2)$, $(w_3 x_3 + w_4 y_3)$, $(w_4 x_4 + w_5 y_4) \mod \phi(N)/4$, where we denote $w_j := d \log_g g_j \mod \phi(N)/4$ for some base $g \in \mathbb{SCR}_{N^s}$, $j \in [5]$.

$\widetilde{\text{Bad}}$ is further divided into the following disjoint two subevents:

(i) $\widetilde{\text{Bad}}$-1: $\mathscr{A}$ ever queries the DECRYPT oracle with ($\langle$ai, aiae.c$\rangle$, $i \in [n]$), satisfying

Conditions $(42), (43) \wedge \left(\alpha_1' = \cdots = \alpha_5' = 0 \right) \wedge (\widetilde{\alpha}_1$

$$\neq 0 \vee \cdots \vee \widetilde{\alpha}_8 \neq 0) \wedge \left(\frac{\widetilde{\alpha}_1}{w_1} \neq \frac{\widetilde{\alpha}_2}{w_2} \vee \frac{\widetilde{\alpha}_3}{w_2} \neq \frac{\widetilde{\alpha}_4}{w_3} \vee \frac{\widetilde{\alpha}_5}{w_3} \right) \quad (53)$$

$$\neq \frac{\widetilde{\alpha}_6}{w_4} \vee \frac{\widetilde{\alpha}_7}{w_4} \neq \frac{\widetilde{\alpha}_8}{w_5} \Bigg).$$

(ii) $\widetilde{\text{Bad}}$-2: $\mathscr{A}$ ever queries the DECRYPT oracle with ($\langle$ai, aiae.c$\rangle$, $i \in [n]$), satisfying

Conditions $(42), (43) \wedge \left(\alpha_1' = \cdots = \alpha_5' = 0 \right) \wedge (\widetilde{\alpha}_1$

$$\neq 0 \vee \cdots \vee \widetilde{\alpha}_8 \neq 0) \wedge \left(\frac{\widetilde{\alpha}_1}{w_1} = \frac{\widetilde{\alpha}_2}{w_2} \wedge \frac{\widetilde{\alpha}_3}{w_2} = \frac{\widetilde{\alpha}_4}{w_3} \wedge \frac{\widetilde{\alpha}_5}{w_3} \right) \quad (54)$$

$$= \frac{\widetilde{\alpha}_6}{w_4} \wedge \frac{\widetilde{\alpha}_7}{w_4} = \frac{\widetilde{\alpha}_8}{w_5} \Bigg).$$

We will analyze the two subevents in game G_{10} separately via the following two claims.

Claim 30. One has $\Pr_{10}[\widetilde{\text{Bad}}\text{-}1] \leq Q_d \cdot 2^{-\Omega(\lambda)}$.

Proof. If $\widetilde{\text{Bad}}$-1 occurs, for concreteness, say that $\widetilde{\alpha}_1/w_1 \neq \widetilde{\alpha}_2/w_2$, then

$$\begin{aligned} g_1^m &= g_1^{\widetilde{\alpha}_1 x_{i,1} + \widetilde{\alpha}_2 y_{i,1} + \cdots} \\ &= g_1^{\widetilde{\alpha}_1 x_1 + \widetilde{\alpha}_2 y_1 + \widetilde{\alpha}_1 \overline{x}_{i,1} + \widetilde{\alpha}_2 \overline{y}_{i,1} + \cdots \bmod \phi(N)/4} \quad \bmod N, \end{aligned} \quad (55)$$

and $(\widetilde{\alpha}_1 x_1 + \widetilde{\alpha}_2 y_1) \bmod \phi(N)/4$ is independent of $(w_1 x_1 + w_2 y_1) \bmod \phi(N)/4$. Thus g_1^m is uniformly distributed over $\mathbb{SCR}_{N^s}$ from $\mathscr{A}$'s view, and $t = g_1^m \bmod N$ will not hold except with negligible probability $2^{-\Omega(\lambda)}$.

Then according to a union bound, $\Pr_{10}[\widetilde{\text{Bad}}\text{-}1] \leq Q_d \cdot 2^{-\Omega(\lambda)}$. $\square$

Claim 31. One has $\Pr_{10}[\widetilde{\text{Bad}}\text{-}2] \leq \mathsf{Adv}^{\mathrm{dl}}_{\mathrm{GenN}}(\lambda) + 2^{-\Omega(\lambda)}$.

Proof. In game G_{10}, if $\widetilde{\text{Bad}}$-2 occurs, then we can construct a PPT adversary $\mathscr{B}_3(N, p, q, g, h)$ to compute the discrete logarithm of h based on g, where $g, h \in \mathbb{SCR}_{N^s}$. With (N, p, q, g, h), $\mathscr{B}_3$ simulates INITIALIZE as follows. $\mathscr{B}_3$ picks z_j, z_j' uniformly from $[\phi(N)/4]$ and sets $g_j := g^{z_j} h^{z_j'}$ for $j \in [5]$. Then g_j is uniformly distributed over $\mathbb{SCR}_{N^s}$. Next, $\mathscr{B}_3$ samples secret keys and computes public keys just the same way as INITIALIZE in G_{10}. Since $\mathscr{B}_3$ knows all the secret keys together with $\phi(N) = (p-1)(q-1)$, $\mathscr{B}_3$ can perfectly simulates ENCRYPT and DECRYPT the same way as G_{10} does. Furthermore, z_j' is hidden by z_j perfectly from $\mathscr{A}$' view. If we denote $w := d\log_g h \bmod \phi(N)/4$, then for $j \in [5]$, $w_j = d\log_g g_j = z_j + w z_j' \bmod \phi(N)/4$.

If $\widetilde{\text{Bad}}$-2 occurs in DECRYPT, for concreteness, say that $\widetilde{\alpha}_1/w_1 = \widetilde{\alpha}_2/w_2 \neq 0 \bmod \phi(N)/4$, that is, $g_1^{\widetilde{\alpha}_2} = g_2^{\widetilde{\alpha}_1} \neq 1$, then $\mathscr{B}_3$ can compute w by solving the equation $w_1 \widetilde{\alpha}_2 = w_2 \widetilde{\alpha}_1 \bmod \phi(N)/4$, or equivalently,

$$z_1 \widetilde{\alpha}_2 + w z_1' \widetilde{\alpha}_2 = z_2 \widetilde{\alpha}_1 + w z_2' \widetilde{\alpha}_1 \bmod \frac{\phi(N)}{4}. \quad (56)$$

Since z_j' is hidden from the point of view of $\mathscr{A}$, $(z_1' \widetilde{\alpha}_2 - z_2' \widetilde{\alpha}_1) \bmod \phi(N)/4$ is multiplicative invertible except with negligible probability $2^{-\Omega(\lambda)}$. Thus $\mathscr{B}_3$ will succeed in computing the discrete logarithm of h based on g and output $w = (z_1' \widetilde{\alpha}_2 - z_2' \widetilde{\alpha}_1)^{-1} \cdot (z_2 \widetilde{\alpha}_1 - z_1 \widetilde{\alpha}_2) \bmod \phi(N)/4$ to its challenger. Clearly, we have $\Pr_{10}[\widetilde{\text{Bad}}\text{-}2] \leq \mathsf{Adv}^{\mathrm{dl}}_{\mathrm{GenN}, \mathscr{B}_3}(\lambda) + 2^{-\Omega(\lambda)}$. $\square$

In conclusion, Lemma 29 follows from the above two claims.

This completes the proof of Lemma 29.

In all, we proved the n-KDM$[\mathscr{F}_{\mathrm{aff}}]$-CCA security.

This completes the proof of Theorem 24.

5. PKE with n-KDM$[\mathscr{F}^d_{\mathrm{poly}}]$-CCA Security

5.1. The Basic Idea. We extend the construction of n-KDM$[\mathscr{F}_{\mathrm{aff}}]$-CCA secure PKE to that of n-KDM$[\mathscr{F}^d_{\mathrm{poly}}]$-CCA secure PKE. We allow adversaries to submit polynomial function in $\mathscr{F}^d_{\mathrm{poly}}$ in the form of *modular arithmetic circuit* (MAC) [10], which is a polynomial-sized circuit computing $f \in \mathscr{F}^d_{\mathrm{poly}}$. We stress that there is no a priori bound on the size of modular arithmetic circuits. The only requirement is that the degree d of the polynomials is a priori bounded. We still follow the approach in Figure 1 in our PKE construction. Indeed, we use the same $\mathsf{AIAE}_{\mathrm{DDH}}$ and KEM as those in the previous n-KDM$[\mathscr{F}_{\mathrm{aff}}]$-CCA secure PKE in Figure 8. We only need to construct a new $\mathscr{E}$ to serve as an entropy filter for the polynomial function set. Moreover, the new $\mathscr{E}$ should employ the same pair of public and secret keys with KEM. That is, we have $\mathsf{sk}_i = (x_{i,1}, y_{i,1}, \ldots, x_{i,4}, y_{i,4})$ and $\mathsf{pk}_i = (h_{i,1}, \ldots, h_{i,4})$ with $h_{i,1} = g_1^{-x_{i,1}} g_2^{-y_{i,1}}, \ldots, h_{i,4} = g_4^{-x_{i,4}} g_5^{-y_{i,4}} \bmod N^s$, for $i \in [n]$.

5.2. Reducing Polynomials of $8n$ Variables to Polynomials of 8 Variables

How to Reduce $8n$-Variable Polynomial f_ℓ. In the n-KDM$[\mathscr{F}^d_{\mathrm{poly}}]$-CCA security game, the adversary is allowed to query the ENCRYPT oracle with ($f_\ell, i_\ell \in [n]$) for $\ell \in [Q_e]$. Note that the function f_ℓ is a polynomial in the n secret keys $(x_{i,j}, y_{i,j})_{i \in [n], j \in [4]}$; thus f_ℓ has $8n$ variables and is of degree at most d. The bad news is that f_ℓ contains as many as $\binom{8n+d}{8n} = \Theta(d^{8n})$ monomial functions. Note that this number can be exponentially large.

The good news is that we found an efficient way to greatly reduce the number of monomials from $\Theta(d^{8n})$ to $\Theta(d^8)$. In particular, the polynomial $f_\ell((x_{i,j}, y_{i,j})_{i \in [n], j \in [4]})$ can always be changed to a polynomial $f_\ell'((x_{i_\ell,j}, y_{i_\ell,j})_{j \in [4]})$ of 8 variables, consisting of at most $\binom{8+d}{8} = \Theta(d^8)$ monomial functions. Now this number is polynomial in λ.

The efficient method for reducing the $8n$-variable polynomial f_ℓ is as follows. In the INITIALIZE procedure, sk_i could be computed as $x_{i,j} := x_j + \overline{x}_{i,j}$ and $y_{i,j} := y_j + \overline{y}_{i,j} \bmod \lfloor N^2/4 \rfloor$ for $i \in [n]$ and $j \in [4]$. By using $(\overline{x}_{i,j}, \overline{y}_{i,j})_{i\in[n],j\in[4]}$, $(x_{i,j}, y_{i,j})_{i\in[n],j\in[4]}$ could be represented as shifts of $(x_{i_\ell,j}, y_{i_\ell,j})_{j\in[4]}$; that is,

$$x_{i,j} = x_{i_\ell,j} + \overline{x}_{i,j} - \overline{x}_{i_\ell,j},$$
$$y_{i,j} = y_{i_\ell,j} + \overline{y}_{i,j} - \overline{y}_{i_\ell,j}. \tag{57}$$

Consequently, f_ℓ in $8n$ variables $(x_{i,j}, y_{i,j})_{i\in[n],j\in[4]}$ can be reduced to f'_ℓ in 8 variables $(x_{i_\ell,j}, y_{i_\ell,j})_{j\in[4]}$; that is,

$$f_\ell\left(\left(x_{i,j}, y_{i,j}\right)_{i\in[n],j\in[4]}\right) = f_\ell\left(\left(\underbrace{x_{i_\ell,j} + \overline{x}_{i,j} - \overline{x}_{i_\ell,j}}_{x_{i,j}},\right.\right.$$

$$\left.\left.\underbrace{y_{i_\ell,j} + \overline{y}_{i,j} - \overline{y}_{i_\ell,j}}_{y_{i,j}}\right)_{i\in[n],j\in[4]}\right) = f'_\ell\left(\left(x_{i_\ell,j},\right.\right. \tag{58}$$

$$\left.\left. y_{i_\ell,j}\right)_{j\in[4]}\right) = \sum_{0\le c_1+\cdots+c_8\le d} a_{(c_1,\ldots,c_8)}$$

$$\cdot x_{i_\ell,1}^{c_1} y_{i_\ell,1}^{c_2} x_{i_\ell,2}^{c_3} y_{i_\ell,2}^{c_4} x_{i_\ell,3}^{c_5} y_{i_\ell,3}^{c_6} x_{i_\ell,4}^{c_7} y_{i_\ell,4}^{c_8}.$$

The degree of the resulting polynomial f'_ℓ is still upper bounded by d. Moreover, the coefficients $a_{(c_1,\ldots,c_8)}$ of f'_ℓ are completely determined by the shifts $(\overline{x}_{i,j}, \overline{y}_{i,j})_{i\in[n],j\in[4]}$.

How to Determine Coefficients $a_{(c_1,\ldots,c_8)}$ for f'_ℓ Efficiently with Only $(\overline{x}_{i,j}, \overline{y}_{i,j})_{i\in[n],j\in[4]}$. In order to compute the coefficients $a_{(c_1,\ldots,c_8)}$ of f'_ℓ, we can repeat the following procedure:

(i) Choose $(x_{i_\ell,j}, y_{i_\ell,j})_{j\in[4]}$ uniformly.

(ii) Feed modular arithmetic circuit (which functions as f_ℓ) with $(x_{i_\ell,j} + \overline{x}_{i,j} - \overline{x}_{i_\ell,j}, y_{i_\ell,j} + \overline{y}_{i,j} - \overline{y}_{i_\ell,j})_{i\in[n],j\in[4]}$ as input. We stress that $(\overline{x}_{i,j}, \overline{y}_{i,j})_{i\in[n],j\in[4]}$ are always the ones chosen in INITIALIZE.

(iii) Record the output of the circuit.

Repeating the above procedure about $\binom{8+d}{8} = \Theta(d^8)$ times, all the coefficients $a_{(c_1,\ldots,c_8)}$ can be extracted through solving a linear system of equations:

$$f_\ell\left(\left(x_{i_\ell,j} + \overline{x}_{i,j} - \overline{x}_{i_\ell,j}, y_{i_\ell,j} + \overline{y}_{i,j} - \overline{y}_{i_\ell,j}\right)_{i\in[n],j\in[4]}\right)$$

$$= \sum_{0\le c_1+\cdots+c_8\le d} a_{(c_1,\ldots,c_8)} \tag{59}$$

$$\cdot x_{i_\ell,1}^{c_1} y_{i_\ell,1}^{c_2} x_{i_\ell,2}^{c_3} y_{i_\ell,2}^{c_4} x_{i_\ell,3}^{c_5} y_{i_\ell,3}^{c_6} x_{i_\ell,4}^{c_7} y_{i_\ell,4}^{c_8}.$$

The overall time complexity for computing the coefficients $a_{(c_1,\ldots,c_8)}$ is polynomial in λ.

5.3. How to Design $\mathscr{E}$: A Warmup. To illustrate the ideas behind our construction, we take a simple case as consideration: construct $\mathscr{E}$ for a concrete type of monomial function; that is,

$$f'_\ell\left(\left(x_{i_\ell,j}, y_{i_\ell,j}\right)_{j\in[4]}\right)$$

$$= a \cdot x_{i_\ell,1} y_{i_\ell,1} x_{i_\ell,2} y_{i_\ell,2} x_{i_\ell,3} y_{i_\ell,3} x_{i_\ell,4} y_{i_\ell,4}. \tag{60}$$

Algorithms $\mathscr{E}$.Encrypt and $\mathscr{E}$.Decrypt are shown in Figure 9.

Security Proof. Now we sketch the proof of KDM-CCA security for this concrete type of monomial functions, that is, $a \cdot x_{i_\ell,1} y_{i_\ell,1} x_{i_\ell,2} y_{i_\ell,2} x_{i_\ell,3} y_{i_\ell,3} x_{i_\ell,4} y_{i_\ell,4}$. The proof is similar to that for Theorem 24 (cf. Table 2). The only difference lies in games G_3-G_4, which are related to the building block $\mathscr{E}$. Next, we will replace G_3-G_4 with the following hybrids (i.e., Hybrid 1–Hybrid 3), as shown in Figure 10. Concretely, the $\mathscr{E}$.Encrypt part of ENCRYPT is changed in a computationally indistinguishable way, so that it can serve as an entropy filter for this concrete monomial function, reserving the entropy of $(x_1, y_1, \ldots, x_4, y_4) \bmod N$.

Suppose that the adversary submits $(f_\ell, i_\ell \in [n])$ to the ENCRYPT oracle. Our purpose is to eliminate the use of $(x_j, y_j)_{j=1}^4 \bmod N$ in the computation of $\mathscr{E}$.Encrypt$(\mathsf{pk}_{i_\ell}, f_\ell((x_{i,j}, y_{i,j})_{i\in[n],j\in[4]}))$, so the entropy of $(x_j, y_j)_{j=1}^4 \bmod N$ is reserved.

Hybrid 0. In the INITIALIZE procedure, the secret keys are computed as $x_{i,j} := x_j + \overline{x}_{i,j}$ and $y_{i,j} := y_j + \overline{y}_{i,j} \bmod \lfloor N^2/4 \rfloor$ for $i \in [n]$, $j \in [4]$. This hybrid is identical to G_2 in the proof of Theorem 24.

Hybrid 1. Using $(\overline{x}_{i,j}, \overline{y}_{i,j})_{i\in[n],j\in[4]}$, reduce $(f_\ell, i_\ell \in [n])$ to $(f'_\ell, i_\ell \in [n])$, and calculate the coefficient a of f'_ℓ, such that

$$f'_\ell\left(\left(x_{i_\ell,j}, y_{i_\ell,j}\right)_{j\in[4]}\right)$$

$$= a \cdot x_{i_\ell,1} y_{i_\ell,1} x_{i_\ell,2} y_{i_\ell,2} x_{i_\ell,3} y_{i_\ell,3} x_{i_\ell,4} y_{i_\ell,4}. \tag{61}$$

Hybrid 2. Implement $\mathscr{E}$.Encrypt using $\mathsf{sk}_{i_\ell} = (x_{i_\ell,j}, y_{i_\ell,j})_{j\subset[4]}$. This hybrid corresponds to G_3 in the proof of Theorem 24.

(i) Invoke $\mathscr{E}$.Encrypt to set up table.

(ii) Invoke $\mathscr{E}$.Decrypt to compute $\widehat{v}_0, \ldots, \widehat{v}_8$ from table.

(iii) Employ $\widehat{v}_8$ rather than $\widetilde{v}_8$ in the computation of $\widetilde{e}$, that is, $\widetilde{e} := \widehat{v}_8 \cdot T^{f'_\ell((x_{i_\ell,j}, y_{i_\ell,j})_{j\in[4]})} \bmod N^s$, and compute $t := g_1^{f'_\ell((x_{i_\ell,j}, y_{i_\ell,j})_{j\in[4]})} \bmod N$.

Clearly, $\widehat{v}_0, \ldots, \widehat{v}_8$ computed via $\mathscr{E}$.Decrypt are the same as $\widetilde{v}_0, \ldots, \widetilde{v}_8$ computed via $\mathscr{E}$.Encrypt. Therefore, this is just a conceptual change.

Hybrid 3. This hybrid corresponds to G_4 in the proof of Theorem 24.

(i) table is computed similarly as that in $\mathscr{E}$.Encrypt, except for a small difference. More precisely, in table,

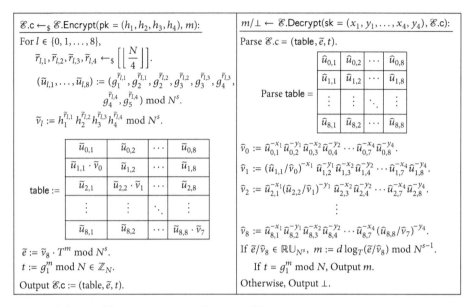

FIGURE 9: $\mathscr{E}$ designed for a concrete type of monomial functions $a \cdot x_{i_\ell,1} y_{i_\ell,1} x_{i_\ell,2} y_{i_\ell,2} x_{i_\ell,3} y_{i_\ell,3} x_{i_\ell,4} y_{i_\ell,4}$.

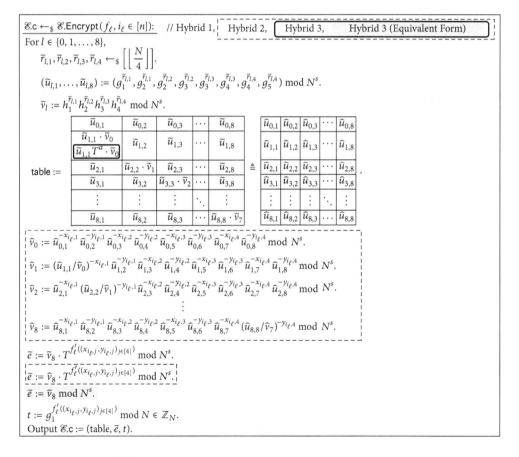

FIGURE 10: Security proof of $\mathscr{E}$.Encrypt as an entropy filter for concrete monomials $a \cdot x_{i_\ell,1} y_{i_\ell,1} x_{i_\ell,2} y_{i_\ell,2} x_{i_\ell,3} y_{i_\ell,3} x_{i_\ell,4} y_{i_\ell,4}$.

the entry located in row 1 and column 1 is now computed as $\hat{u}_{1,1} = (\tilde{u}_{1,1}T^a) \cdot \tilde{v}_0$ rather than $\hat{u}_{1,1} = \tilde{u}_{1,1} \cdot \tilde{v}_0$. By the IV_5 assumption, this difference is computationally undetectable (see Appendix B for a formal analysis).

(ii) Invoke $\mathscr{E}$.Decrypt to compute $\hat{v}_0, \ldots, \hat{v}_8$ from table.

(iii) Compute $\tilde{e} := \hat{v}_8 \cdot T^{f_\ell'((x_{i_\ell,j}, y_{i_\ell,j})_{j\in[4]})} \bmod N^s$, and $t := g_1^{f_\ell'((x_{i_\ell,j}, y_{i_\ell,j})_{j\in[4]})} \bmod N$.

Through a routine calculation, we have $\hat{v}_0 = \tilde{v}_0, \hat{v}_1 = \tilde{v}_1 \cdot T^{-ax_{i_\ell,1}}, \hat{v}_2 = \tilde{v}_2 \cdot T^{-ax_{i_\ell,1}y_{i_\ell,1}}, \ldots, \hat{v}_8 = \tilde{v}_8 \cdot T^{-ax_{i_\ell,1}y_{i_\ell,1}\cdots x_{i_\ell,4}y_{i_\ell,4}} = \tilde{v}_8 \cdot T^{-f_\ell'((x_{i_\ell,j}, y_{i_\ell,j})_{j\in[4]})}$; hence $\tilde{e} = \hat{v}_8 \cdot T^{f_\ell'((x_{i_\ell,j}, y_{i_\ell,j})_{j\in[4]})} = \tilde{v}_8$.

Consequently, Hybrid 3 can be implemented in an equivalent way.

Hybrid 3 (Equivalent Form). (i) table is computed similarly as that in $\mathscr{E}$.Encrypt, except for a small difference. More precisely, the entry located in row 1 and column 1 in table is now computed as $\hat{u}_{1,1} = (\tilde{u}_{1,1}T^a) \cdot \tilde{v}_0$ rather than $\hat{u}_{1,1} = \tilde{u}_{1,1} \cdot \tilde{v}_0$.

(ii) Compute $\tilde{e} := \tilde{v}_8 \bmod N^s$, and $t := g_1^{f_\ell'((x_{i_\ell,j}, y_{i_\ell,j})_{j\in[4]}) \bmod \phi(N)/4} \bmod N$.

Now $(x_1, y_1, \ldots, x_4, y_4) \bmod N$ is not used in $\mathscr{E}$.Encrypt any more.

After these computationally indistinguishable changes, the $\mathscr{E}$.Encrypt part of the ENCRYPT oracle reserves the entropy of $(x_1, y_1, \ldots, x_4, y_4) \bmod N$.

Similarly, we can change the DECRYPT oracle in a computationally indistinguishable way, so that $(x_j, y_j)_{j=1}^4 \bmod N$ is not involved at all. More precisely, DECRYPT uses only the $(\bmod \phi(N)/4)$ part of secret key and $\phi(N)$. This change corresponds to G_7-G_8 in the proof of Theorem 24. Loosely speaking, $\phi(N)$ is used to ensure that all entries in table are elements in $\mathbb{SCR}_{N^s}$. If this is not the case, DECRYPT rejects immediately. Consequently, the DECRYPT oracle leaks nothing about $(x_1, y_1, \ldots, x_4, y_4) \bmod N$. We can also show the computational indistinguishability of this change, through a similar analysis as that of $\Pr[\mathsf{Bad}]$ in the proof of Theorem 24.

5.4. The General $\mathscr{E}$ Designed for $\mathscr{F}_{\text{poly}}^d$. In Section 5.3, we presented the construction of $\mathscr{E}$ for a concrete type of monomial functions. Generally, a polynomial function f_ℓ' of degree d might contain as many as $\binom{8+d}{8} = \Theta(d^8)$ monomials. In order to construct a general $\mathscr{E}$ for the set $\mathscr{F}_{\text{poly}}^d$ of polynomial functions, we must handle all types of monomial functions. To this end, we generate a table for each type of nonconstant monomial and associate it with a $\tilde{v}$, which is named as a *title*. Algorithms $\mathscr{E}$.Encrypt and $\mathscr{E}$.Decrypt are shown in Figure 11.

Neglecting the coefficients of monomials, there are $\binom{8+d}{8} - 1$ types of nonconstant monomial functions whose degrees are at most d. For each nonconstant monomial type $x_{i_\ell,1}^{c_1} y_{i_\ell,1}^{c_2} x_{i_\ell,2}^{c_3} y_{i_\ell,2}^{c_4} x_{i_\ell,3}^{c_5} y_{i_\ell,3}^{c_6} x_{i_\ell,4}^{c_7} y_{i_\ell,4}^{c_8}$, we can associate it with a degree tuple $c = (c_1, \ldots, c_8)$. Let $\mathscr{S}$ denote the set of all such degree tuples, that is, $\mathscr{S} := \{c = (c_1, \ldots, c_8) \mid 1 \le c_1 + \cdots + c_8 \le d\}$.

For each degree tuple $c = (c_1, \ldots, c_8) \in \mathscr{S}$, which corresponds to the monomial $x_{i_\ell,1}^{c_1} y_{i_\ell,1}^{c_2} x_{i_\ell,2}^{c_3} y_{i_\ell,2}^{c_4} x_{i_\ell,3}^{c_5} y_{i_\ell,3}^{c_6} x_{i_\ell,4}^{c_7} y_{i_\ell,4}^{c_8}$, we generate $\mathsf{table}^{(c)}$ and $\tilde{v}^{(c)}$ by invoking the algorithm TableGen shown in Figure 11. Finally in $\tilde{e}$, T^m is hidden by the product of all the titles.

Meanwhile, with the help of the secret key $\mathsf{sk} = (x_1, y_1, \ldots, x_4, y_4)$, we can recover $\hat{v}^{(c)} = \tilde{v}^{(c)}$ from $\mathsf{table}^{(c)}$ by invoking the algorithm CalculateV in Figure 11. Thus, the titles $(\tilde{v}^{(c)})_{c\in\mathscr{S}}$ could always be extracted from $(\mathsf{table}^{(c)})_{c\in\mathscr{S}}$ one by one, and finally m is recovered.

Security Proof. We sketch the proof of KDM$[\mathscr{F}_{\text{poly}}^d]$-CCA security for the set of polynomial functions. The proof is also similar to that for Theorem 24 (cf. Table 2). The only difference lies in games G_3-G_4. Next, we will replace G_3-G_4 with the following hybrids (Hybrid 1–Hybrid 3). Specifically, the $\mathscr{E}$.Encrypt part of ENCRYPT is changed in a computationally indistinguishable way, so that it can serve as an entropy filter for polynomial functions of degree at most d, reserving the entropy of $(x_1, y_1, \ldots, x_4, y_4) \bmod N$.

Suppose that the adversary submits $(f_\ell, i_\ell \in [n])$ to the ENCRYPT oracle. Our purpose is to eliminate the use of $(x_j, y_j)_{j=1}^4 \bmod N$ in the computation of $\mathscr{E}$.Encrypt$(\mathsf{pk}_{i_\ell}, f_\ell((x_{i,j}, y_{i,j})_{i\in[n], j\in[4]}))$, so the entropy of $(x_j, y_j)_{j=1}^4 \bmod N$ is reserved.

Hybrid 0. In the INITIALIZE procedure, the secret keys are computed as $x_{i,j} := x_j + \overline{x}_{i,j}$ and $y_{i,j} := y_j + \overline{y}_{i,j} \bmod \lfloor N^2/4 \rfloor$ for $i \in [n]$, $j \in [4]$. This hybrid is identical to G_2 in the proof of Theorem 24.

Hybrid 1. Using $(\overline{x}_{i,j}, \overline{y}_{i,j})_{i\in[n], j\in[4]}$, reduce $(f_\ell, i_\ell \in [n])$ to $(f_\ell', i_\ell \in [n])$, and compute the coefficients $a_{(c_1, \ldots, c_8)}$ of f_ℓ', as discussed in Section 5.2. Then

$$f_\ell'\left((x_{i_\ell,j}, y_{i_\ell,j})_{j\in[4]}\right)$$

$$= \sum_{(c_1,\ldots,c_8)\in\mathscr{S}} a_{(c_1,\ldots,c_8)} \tag{62}$$

$$\cdot x_{i_\ell,1}^{c_1} y_{i_\ell,1}^{c_2} x_{i_\ell,2}^{c_3} y_{i_\ell,2}^{c_4} x_{i_\ell,3}^{c_5} y_{i_\ell,3}^{c_6} x_{i_\ell,4}^{c_7} y_{i_\ell,4}^{c_8} + \delta,$$

where δ is the constant term $a_{(0,\ldots,0)}$ of f_ℓ'.

Hybrid 2. Implement $\mathscr{E}$.Encrypt using $\mathsf{sk}_{i_\ell} = (x_{i_\ell,j}, y_{i_\ell,j})_{j\in[4]}$. This hybrid corresponds to G_3 in the proof of Theorem 24.

(i) For each $c = (c_1, \ldots, c_8) \in \mathscr{S}$

(1) invoke $(\mathsf{table}^{(c)}, \tilde{v}^{(c)}) \leftarrow_\$ \mathsf{TableGen}(\mathsf{pk}_{i_\ell}, c)$,

(2) invoke $\hat{v}^{(c)} \leftarrow \mathsf{CalculateV}(\mathsf{sk}_{i_\ell}, \mathsf{table}^{(c)}, c)$.

(ii) Employ $(\hat{v}^{(c)})_{c\in\mathscr{S}}$ rather than $(\tilde{v}^{(c)})_{c\in\mathscr{S}}$ in the computation of $\tilde{e}$, that is, $\tilde{e} := \prod_{c\in\mathscr{S}} \hat{v}^{(c)} \cdot T^{f_\ell'((x_{i_\ell,j}, y_{i_\ell,j})_{j\in[4]})} \bmod N^s$, and compute $t := g_1^{f_\ell'((x_{i_\ell,j}, y_{i_\ell,j})_{j\in[4]})} \bmod N$.

$\mathscr{E}.c \leftarrow_\$ \mathscr{E}.\mathsf{Encrypt}(\mathsf{pk}, m)$:

For each $\mathsf{c} = (c_1, \dots, c_8) \in \mathscr{S}$

$\quad (\mathsf{table}^{(\mathsf{c})}, \widetilde{v}^{(\mathsf{c})}) \leftarrow_\$ \mathsf{TableGen}(\mathsf{pk}, \mathsf{c})$.

$\widetilde{e} := \prod_{\mathsf{c} \in \mathscr{S}} \widetilde{v}^{(\mathsf{c})} \cdot T^m \bmod N^s$.

$t := g_1^m \bmod N \in \mathbb{Z}_N$.

Output $\mathscr{E}.c := ((\mathsf{table}^{(\mathsf{c})})_{\mathsf{c} \in \mathscr{S}}, \widetilde{e}, t)$.

$m/\bot \leftarrow \mathscr{E}.\mathsf{Decrypt}(\mathsf{sk}, \mathscr{E}.c)$:

Parse $\mathscr{E}.c := ((\mathsf{table}^{(\mathsf{c})})_{\mathsf{c} \in \mathscr{S}}, \widetilde{e}, t)$.

For each $\mathsf{c} = (c_1, \dots, c_8) \in \mathscr{S}$

$\quad \widehat{v}^{(\mathsf{c})} \leftarrow \mathsf{CalculateV}(\mathsf{sk}, \mathsf{table}^{(\mathsf{c})}, \mathsf{c})$.

If $\widetilde{e} \cdot (\prod_{\mathsf{c} \in \mathscr{S}} \widehat{v}^{(\mathsf{c})})^{-1} \in \mathbb{RU}_{N^s}$

$\quad m := d\log_T(\widetilde{e} \cdot (\prod_{\mathsf{c} \in \mathscr{S}} \widehat{v}^{(\mathsf{c})})^{-1}) \bmod N^{s-1}$.

$\quad$ If $t = g_1^m \bmod N$, Output m.

Otherwise, Output $\bot$.

(a)

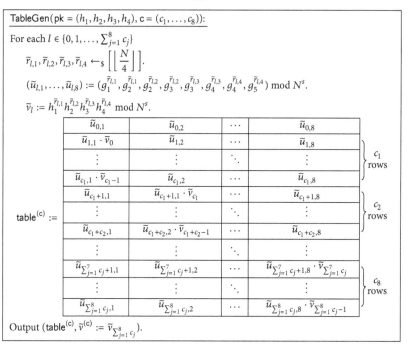

(b)

$\mathsf{CalculateV}(\mathsf{sk} = (x_1, y_1 \dots, x_4, y_4), \mathsf{table}^{(\mathsf{c})}, \mathsf{c} = (c_1, \dots, c_8))$:

Parse $\mathsf{table}^{(\mathsf{c})} = \{\boxed{\widehat{u}_{l,1} \mid \widehat{u}_{l,2} \mid \cdots \mid \widehat{u}_{l,8}}\}_{l \in \{0, 1, \dots, \sum_{j=1}^8 c_j\}}$.

$\widehat{v}_0 := \widehat{u}_{0,1}^{-x_1} \widehat{u}_{0,2}^{-y_1} \widehat{u}_{0,3}^{-x_2} \widehat{u}_{0,4}^{-y_2} \widehat{u}_{0,5}^{-x_3} \widehat{u}_{0,6}^{-y_3} \widehat{u}_{0,7}^{-x_4} \widehat{u}_{0,8}^{-y_4}$.

For each $l \in \{1, \dots, c_1\}$

$\quad \widehat{v}_l := (\widehat{u}_{l,1}/\widehat{v}_{l-1})^{-x_1} \widehat{u}_{l,2}^{-y_1} \widehat{u}_{l,3}^{-x_2} \widehat{u}_{l,4}^{-y_2} \widehat{u}_{l,5}^{-x_3} \widehat{u}_{l,6}^{-y_3} \widehat{u}_{l,7}^{-x_4} \widehat{u}_{l,8}^{-y_4}$.

For each $l \in \{c_1 + 1, \dots, c_1 + c_2\}$

$\quad \widehat{v}_l := \widehat{u}_{l,1}^{-x_1} (\widehat{u}_{l,2}/\widehat{v}_{l-1})^{-y_1} \widehat{u}_{l,3}^{-x_2} \widehat{u}_{l,4}^{-y_2} \widehat{u}_{l,5}^{-x_3} \widehat{u}_{l,6}^{-y_3} \widehat{u}_{l,7}^{-x_4} \widehat{u}_{l,8}^{-y_4}$.

$\quad\quad\quad\quad\quad\quad\quad \vdots$

For each $l \in \{\sum_{j=1}^7 c_j + 1, \dots, \sum_{j=1}^8 c_j\}$

$\quad \widehat{v}_l := \widehat{u}_{l,1}^{-x_1} \widehat{u}_{l,2}^{-y_1} \widehat{u}_{l,3}^{-x_2} \widehat{u}_{l,4}^{-y_2} \widehat{u}_{l,5}^{-x_3} \widehat{u}_{l,6}^{-y_3} \widehat{u}_{l,7}^{-x_4} (\widehat{u}_{l,8}/\widehat{v}_{l-1})^{-y_4}$.

Output $\widehat{v}^{(\mathsf{c})} := \widehat{v}_{\sum_{j=1}^8 c_j}$.

(c)

FIGURE 11: (a) $\mathscr{E}.\mathsf{Encrypt}$ (left) and $\mathscr{E}.\mathsf{Decrypt}$ (right) of $\mathscr{E}$ designed for $\mathcal{F}_{\mathrm{poly}}^d$; (b) $\mathsf{TableGen}$, which generates $\mathsf{table}^{(\mathsf{c})}$ together with a title $\widetilde{v}^{(\mathsf{c})}$; (c) $\mathsf{CalculateV}$, which calculates a title $\widehat{v}^{(\mathsf{c})}$ from $\mathsf{table}^{(\mathsf{c})}$ using secret key.

Clearly, for each $c = (c_1, \ldots, c_8) \in \mathcal{S}$, $\widehat{v}^{(c)}$ computed via CalculateV is the same as $\widetilde{v}^{(c)}$ computed via TableGen. Therefore, this change is just conceptual.

Hybrid 3. This hybrid corresponds to G_4 in the proof of Theorem 24.

(i) For each $c = (c_1, \ldots, c_8) \in \mathcal{S}$

    (1) $\mathsf{table}^{(c)}$ is computed by $(\mathsf{table}^{(c)}, \widetilde{v}^{(c)}) \leftarrow_\$ \mathsf{TableGen}(\mathsf{pk}_{i_\ell}, c)$, except for a small difference; more precisely, in $\mathsf{table}^{(c)}$, the entry located in row 1 and column $j := \min\{i \mid 1 \le i \le 8, c_i \ne 0\}$ is now computed as $\widehat{u}_{1,j} = (\widetilde{u}_{1,j} T^{a_{(c_1,\ldots,c_8)}}) \cdot \widetilde{v}_0$ rather than $\widehat{u}_{1,j} = \widetilde{u}_{1,j} \cdot \widetilde{v}_0$; by the IV_5 assumption, this difference is computationally undetectable,

    (2) extract $\widehat{v}^{(c)}$ from the (modified) $\mathsf{table}^{(c)}$ by invoking $\widehat{v}^{(c)} \leftarrow \mathsf{CalculateV}(\mathsf{sk}_{i_\ell}, \mathsf{table}^{(c)}, c)$.

(ii) Compute $\widetilde{e} := \prod_{c \in \mathcal{S}} \widehat{v}^{(c)} \cdot T^{f'_\ell((x_{i_\ell,j}, y_{i_\ell,j})_{j \in [4]})} \bmod N^s$, and $t := g_1^{f'_\ell((x_{i_\ell,j}, y_{i_\ell,j})_{j \in [4]})} \bmod N$.

Through a routine calculation, for each $c = (c_1, \ldots, c_8) \in \mathcal{S}$, we have

$$\widehat{v}^{(c)} = \widetilde{v}^{(c)} \cdot T^{-a_{(c_1,\ldots,c_8)} x_{i_\ell,1}^{c_1} y_{i_\ell,1}^{c_2} x_{i_\ell,2}^{c_3} y_{i_\ell,2}^{c_4} x_{i_\ell,3}^{c_5} y_{i_\ell,3}^{c_6} x_{i_\ell,4}^{c_7} y_{i_\ell,4}^{c_8}}. \tag{63}$$

Hence,

$$\begin{aligned}
\widetilde{e} &= \prod_{c \in \mathcal{S}} \widehat{v}^{(c)} \cdot T^{f'_\ell((x_{i_\ell,j}, y_{i_\ell,j})_{j \in [4]})} \\
&= \prod_{c \in \mathcal{S}} \widetilde{v}^{(c)} \cdot \prod_{c \in \mathcal{S}} T^{-a_{(c_1,\ldots,c_8)} x_{i_\ell,1}^{c_1} y_{i_\ell,1}^{c_2} x_{i_\ell,2}^{c_3} y_{i_\ell,2}^{c_4} x_{i_\ell,3}^{c_5} y_{i_\ell,3}^{c_6} x_{i_\ell,4}^{c_7} y_{i_\ell,4}^{c_8}} \\
&\quad \cdot T^{f'_\ell((x_{i_\ell,j}, y_{i_\ell,j})_{j \in [4]})} = \prod_{c \in \mathcal{S}} \widetilde{v}^{(c)} \cdot T^\delta.
\end{aligned} \tag{64}$$

Consequently, Hybrid 3 can be implemented in an equivalent way.

Hybrid 3 (Equivalent Form). (i) For each $c = (c_1, \ldots, c_8) \in \mathcal{S}$

    $\mathsf{table}^{(c)}$ is computed by $(\mathsf{table}^{(c)}, \widetilde{v}^{(c)}) \leftarrow_\$ \mathsf{TableGen}(\mathsf{pk}_{i_\ell}, c)$, except for a small difference. More precisely, in $\mathsf{table}^{(c)}$, the entry located in row 1 and column $j := \min\{i \mid 1 \le i \le 8, c_i \ne 0\}$ is now computed as $\widehat{u}_{1,j} = (\widetilde{u}_{1,j} T^{a_{(c_1,\ldots,c_8)}}) \cdot \widetilde{v}_0$ rather than $\widehat{u}_{1,j} = \widetilde{u}_{1,j} \cdot \widetilde{v}_0$.

    (ii) Compute $\widetilde{e} := \prod_{c \in \mathcal{S}} \widetilde{v}^{(c)} \cdot T^\delta \bmod N^s$, and $t := g_1^{f'_\ell((x_{i_\ell,j}, y_{i_\ell,j})_{j \in [4]}) \bmod \phi(N)/4} \bmod N$.

Now $(x_1, y_1, \ldots, x_4, y_4) \bmod N$ is not used in $\mathcal{E}.\mathsf{Encrypt}$ any more.

After these computationally indistinguishable changes, the $\mathcal{E}.\mathsf{Encrypt}$ part of the ENCRYPT oracle reserves the entropy of $(x_1, y_1, \ldots, x_4, y_4) \bmod N$.

With a similar argument as that in Section 5.3, we can change the DECRYPT oracle in a computationally indistinguishable way, so that $(x_j, y_j)_{j=1}^4 \bmod N$ is not employed at all.

Appendix

A. Proof of Claim 19

We build a PPT adversary $\mathcal{B}$ against the INT-OT security of AE. Suppose that the INT-OT challenger picks a key $\widehat{\kappa} \leftarrow_\$ \mathcal{K}$ randomly. $\mathcal{B}$ is given $\mathsf{pars}_{\mathsf{AE}}$ and has access to the oracle $\mathrm{ENCRYPT}_{\mathsf{AE}}(\cdot) = \mathsf{AE}.\mathsf{Encrypt}(\widehat{\kappa}, \cdot)$ for one time.

Firstly, $\mathcal{B}$ prepares $\mathsf{pars}_{\mathsf{AIAE}}$ in the same way as in $\mathsf{G}'_{1,j}$. That is, invoke $\mathsf{pars}_{\mathsf{THPS}} \leftarrow_\$ \mathsf{THPS}.\mathsf{Setup}(1^\lambda)$, pick $\mathsf{H} \leftarrow_\$ \mathcal{H}$ randomly, and set $\mathsf{pars}_{\mathsf{AIAE}} := (\mathsf{pars}_{\mathsf{THPS}}, \mathsf{pars}_{\mathsf{AE}}, \mathsf{H})$. $\mathcal{B}$ sends $\mathsf{pars}_{\mathsf{AIAE}}$ to $\mathcal{A}$. Besides, $\mathcal{B}$ chooses $\mathsf{hk} \leftarrow_\$ \mathcal{HK}$.

As for the ℓth ($\ell \in [Q_e]$) ENCRYPT query $(m_\ell, \mathsf{ai}_\ell, f_\ell)$, where $f_\ell = \langle a_\ell, b_\ell \rangle \in \mathcal{F}_{\mathsf{raff}}$, $\mathcal{B}$ prepares the challenge ciphertext $\langle C_\ell, \chi_\ell \rangle$ in the following way.

    (i) If $\ell \in [j-1]$, $\mathcal{B}$ computes $\langle C_\ell, \chi_\ell \rangle$ just like that in $\mathsf{G}'_{1,j}$. That is, $\mathcal{B}$ picks $C_\ell \leftarrow_\$ \mathcal{V}$ with witness w_ℓ, chooses $\kappa_\ell \leftarrow_\$ \mathcal{K}$, and invokes $\chi_\ell \leftarrow_\$ \mathsf{AE}.\mathsf{Encrypt}(\kappa_\ell, m_\ell)$.

    (ii) If $\ell \in [j+1, Q_e]$, $\mathcal{B}$ computes $\langle C_\ell, \chi_\ell \rangle$ just like that in $\mathsf{G}'_{1,j}$. That is, $\mathcal{B}$ picks $C_\ell \leftarrow_\$ \mathcal{V}$ with witness w_ℓ, computes $t_\ell := \mathsf{H}(C_\ell, \mathsf{ai}_\ell)$ and $\kappa_\ell := \Lambda_{a_\ell \cdot \mathsf{hk} + b_\ell}(C_\ell, t_\ell)$, and invokes $\chi_\ell \leftarrow_\$ \mathsf{AE}.\mathsf{Encrypt}(\kappa_\ell, m_\ell)$.

    (iii) If $\ell = j$, $\mathcal{B}$ does not use the key hk at all, and instead, it will resort to its own $\mathrm{ENCRYPT}_{\mathsf{AE}}(\cdot)$ oracle. More precisely, $\mathcal{B}$ picks $C_j \leftarrow_\$ \mathcal{C} \setminus \mathcal{V}$ randomly and computes $t_j := \mathsf{H}(C_j, \mathsf{ai}_j)$. Then $\mathcal{B}$ implicitly sets $\kappa_j = \widehat{\kappa}$ as the key used by its challenger and queries its $\mathrm{ENCRYPT}_{\mathsf{AE}}(\cdot)$ oracle with m_j and gets the challenge χ_j.

    According to the $\mathrm{ENCRYPT}_{\mathsf{AE}}(\cdot)$ oracle, we have $\chi_j \leftarrow_\$ \mathsf{AE}.\mathsf{Encrypt}(\widehat{\kappa}, m_j)$. As discussed in the proof of Lemma 18, κ_j is uniformly random in $\mathsf{G}'_{1,j}$. Therefore, the simulation of $\mathcal{B}$ is the same as that in $\mathsf{G}'_{1,j}$.

$\mathcal{B}$ outputs the challenge ciphertext $\langle C_\ell, \chi_\ell \rangle$ to $\mathcal{A}$. Moreover, $\mathcal{B}$ puts $(\mathsf{ai}_\ell, f_\ell, \langle C_\ell, \chi_\ell \rangle)$ to $Q_{\mathcal{ENC}}$, $(\mathsf{ai}_\ell, f_\ell)$ to $Q_{\mathcal{AF\text{-}F}}$, and $(C_\ell, \mathsf{ai}_\ell, t_\ell)$ to $Q_{\mathcal{TAG}}$.

Finally, $\mathcal{A}$ sends a forgery $(\mathsf{ai}^*, f^*, \langle C^*, \chi^* \rangle)$ to $\mathcal{B}$, with $f^* = \langle a^*, b^* \rangle \in \mathcal{F}_{\mathsf{raff}}$. $\mathcal{B}$ prepares its own forgery with respect to the AE scheme as follows.

    (i) If $(\mathsf{ai}^*, f^*, \langle C^*, \chi^* \rangle) \in Q_{\mathcal{ENC}}$, $\mathcal{B}$ aborts the game.

    (ii) If $\exists (\mathsf{ai}_\ell, f_\ell) \in Q_{\mathcal{AF\text{-}F}}$ such that $\mathsf{ai}_\ell = \mathsf{ai}^*$ but $f_\ell \ne f^*$, $\mathcal{B}$ aborts the game.

    (iii) If $C^* \notin \mathcal{C}$, $\mathcal{B}$ aborts the game.

    (iv) $\mathcal{B}$ computes $t^* := \mathsf{H}(C^*, \mathsf{ai}^*) \in \mathcal{T}$.

    (v) If $\exists (C_\ell, \mathsf{ai}_\ell, t_\ell) \in Q_{\mathcal{TAG}}$ such that $t_\ell = t^*$ but $(C_\ell, \mathsf{ai}_\ell) \ne (C^*, \mathsf{ai}^*)$, $\mathcal{B}$ aborts the game.

    (vi) If $t^* \ne t_j$, $\mathcal{B}$ aborts the game. If $t^* = t_j$, $\mathcal{B}$ outputs χ^* to its INT-OT challenger.

We analyze $\mathcal{B}$'s success probability. As discussed in the proof of Lemma 18, the subevent $\mathsf{Forge} \wedge t_j = t^*$ will imply that $(\mathsf{ai}^*, f^*, C^*) = (\mathsf{ai}_j, f_j, C_j)$, $\chi^* \neq \chi_j$, $\kappa^* = \kappa_j$, and $\mathsf{AE.Decrypt}(\kappa^*, \chi^*) \neq \bot$. Since $\mathcal{B}$ implicitly sets $\kappa_j = \widehat{\kappa}$ as the key used by its challenger, then $\chi^* \neq \chi_j$, $\kappa^* = \kappa_j$, and $\mathsf{AE.Decrypt}(\kappa^*, \chi^*) \neq \bot$ implies that $\chi^* \neq \chi_j$ and $\mathsf{AE.Decrypt}(\widehat{\kappa}, \chi^*) \neq \bot$; that is, the χ^* output by $\mathcal{B}$ is a fresh forgery.

In summary, $\mathcal{B}$ perfectly simulates $\mathsf{G}'_{1,j}$ for $\mathcal{A}$ and outputs a fresh forgery as long as the subevent $\mathsf{Forge} \wedge t_j = t^*$ occurs. Thus, we have that $\Pr_{1,j'}[\mathsf{Forge} \wedge t_j = t^*] \leq \mathsf{Adv}^{\mathsf{int\text{-}ot}}_{\mathsf{AE},\mathcal{B}}(\lambda)$. This completes the proof of Claim 19.

B. Proof of Indistinguishability between Hybrids 2 and 3 in Section 5.3

To show the indistinguishability between Hybrids 2 and 3, we build a PPT adversary $\mathcal{B}^{\mathrm{CHAL}^b_{\mathrm{IV}_5}}(N, g_1, \ldots, g_5)$ to solve the IV_5 problem. Firstly, $\mathcal{B}$ generates secret and public keys in INITIALIZE as Hybrid 0 does. When $\mathcal{A}$ submits an encryption query $(f_\ell, i_\ell \in [n])$, $\mathcal{B}$ reduces $(f_\ell, i_\ell \in [n])$ to $(f'_\ell, i_\ell \in [n])$ as Hybrid 1 does and obtains the coefficient a. Then $\mathcal{B}$ simulates $\mathcal{E}.\mathsf{Encrypt}$ as follows.

(i) For the 0th row of table, $\mathcal{B}$ computes $(\widetilde{u}_{0,1}, \ldots, \widetilde{u}_{0,8})$ and $\widetilde{v}_0$ as in Hybrids 2 and 3.

(ii) For the 1st row, $\mathcal{B}$ queries its own $\mathrm{CHAL}^b_{\mathrm{IV}_5}$ oracle with $(a, 0, *, *, *)$ and obtains its challenge $(\widetilde{u}^*_{1,1}, \widetilde{u}^*_{1,2}, \widetilde{*}, \widetilde{*}, \widetilde{*})$; that is,

Case ($b = 0$): $(\widetilde{u}^*_{1,1}, \widetilde{u}^*_{1,2}) = (g_1^{\widetilde{r}_{1,1}}, g_2^{\widetilde{r}_{1,1}}) = (\widetilde{u}_{1,1}, \widetilde{u}_{1,2})$ or

Case ($b = 1$): $(\widetilde{u}^*_{1,1}, \widetilde{u}^*_{1,2}) = (g_1^{\widetilde{r}_{1,1}} T^a, g_2^{\widetilde{r}_{1,1}}) = (\widetilde{u}_{1,1} T^a, \widetilde{u}_{1,2})$.

$\mathcal{B}$ sets $\widehat{u}_{1,1} := \widetilde{u}^*_{1,1} \cdot \widetilde{v}_0$, which is $\widehat{u}_{1,1} = \widetilde{u}_{1,1} \cdot \widetilde{v}_0$ if $b = 0$ and $\widehat{u}_{1,1} = \widetilde{u}_{1,1} T^a \cdot \widetilde{v}_0$ if $b = 1$. Then $\mathcal{B}$ generates the remaining elements $(\widetilde{u}_{1,3}, \ldots, \widetilde{u}_{1,8})$ in the 1st row of table using its public keys and sets the 1st row of table to be

$$\boxed{\widehat{u}_{1,1} = \widetilde{u}^*_{1,1} \cdot \widetilde{v}_0 \mid \widetilde{u}^*_{1,2} \mid \widetilde{u}_{1,3} \mid \cdots \mid \widetilde{u}_{1,8}}. \qquad (\text{B.1})$$

$\mathcal{B}$ also computes $\widetilde{v}^*_1$ from $(\widetilde{u}^*_{1,1}, \widetilde{u}^*_{1,2}, \widetilde{u}_{1,3}, \ldots, \widetilde{u}_{1,8})$ via $\widetilde{v}^*_1 := \widetilde{u}^{*-x_{i_\ell,1}}_{1,1} \widetilde{u}^{*-y_{i_\ell,1}}_{1,2} \widetilde{u}^{-x_{i_\ell,2}}_{1,3} \cdots \widetilde{u}^{-y_{i_\ell,4}}_{1,8}$, which equals

Case ($b = 0$): $\widetilde{v}^*_1 = \widetilde{v}_1$ or

Case ($b = 1$): $\widetilde{v}^*_1 = \widetilde{v}_1 T^{-a \cdot x_{i_\ell,1}}$.

(iii) For the 2nd row, $\mathcal{B}$ queries its own $\mathrm{CHAL}^b_{\mathrm{IV}_5}$ oracle with $(0, a \cdot x_{i_\ell,1}, *, *, *)$; remember that $\mathcal{B}$ has the secret keys and obtains its challenge $(\widetilde{u}^*_{2,1}, \widetilde{u}^*_{2,2}, \widetilde{*}, \widetilde{*}, \widetilde{*})$; that is,

Case ($b = 0$): $(\widetilde{u}^*_{2,1}, \widetilde{u}^*_{2,2}) = (g_1^{\widetilde{r}_{2,1}}, g_2^{\widetilde{r}_{2,1}}) = (\widetilde{u}_{2,1}, \widetilde{u}_{2,2})$ or

Case ($b = 1$): $(\widetilde{u}^*_{2,1}, \widetilde{u}^*_{2,2}) = (g_1^{\widetilde{r}_{2,1}}, g_2^{\widetilde{r}_{2,1}} T^{a \cdot x_{i_\ell,1}}) = (\widetilde{u}_{2,1}, \widetilde{u}_{2,2} T^{a \cdot x_{i_\ell,1}})$.

$\mathcal{B}$ sets $\widehat{u}_{2,2} := \widetilde{u}^*_{2,2} \cdot \widetilde{v}^*_1$; that is, $\widehat{u}_{2,2} = \widetilde{u}_{2,2} \cdot \widetilde{v}_1$ if $b = 0$ and $\widehat{u}_{2,2} = (\widetilde{u}_{2,2} T^{a \cdot x_{i_\ell,1}})(\widetilde{v}_1 T^{-a \cdot x_{i_\ell,1}}) = \widetilde{u}_{2,2} \cdot \widetilde{v}_1$ if $b = 1$.

Thus $\widehat{u}_{2,2} = \widetilde{u}_{2,2} \cdot \widetilde{v}_1$ in both cases. Then $\mathcal{B}$ generates the remaining elements $(\widetilde{u}_{2,3}, \ldots, \widetilde{u}_{2,8})$ in the 2nd row of table using its public keys and sets the 2nd row of table to be

$$\boxed{\widetilde{u}^*_{2,1} \mid \widehat{u}_{2,2} = \widetilde{u}^*_{2,2} \cdot \widetilde{v}^*_1 \mid \widetilde{u}_{2,3} \mid \cdots \mid \widetilde{u}_{2,8}}. \qquad (\text{B.2})$$

$\mathcal{B}$ also computes $\widetilde{v}^*_2$ from $(\widetilde{u}^*_{2,1}, \widetilde{u}^*_{2,2}, \widetilde{u}_{2,3}, \ldots, \widetilde{u}_{2,8})$ via $\widetilde{v}^*_2 := \widetilde{u}^{*-x_{i_\ell,1}}_{2,1} \widetilde{u}^{*-y_{i_\ell,1}}_{2,2} \widetilde{u}^{-x_{i_\ell,2}}_{2,3} \cdots \widetilde{u}^{-y_{i_\ell,4}}_{2,8}$, which equals

Case ($b = 0$): $\widetilde{v}^*_2 = \widetilde{v}_2$ or

Case ($b = 1$): $\widetilde{v}^*_2 = \widetilde{v}_2 T^{-a \cdot x_{i_\ell,1} y_{i_\ell,1}}$.

(iv) For the 3rd row, $\mathcal{B}$ queries its own $\mathrm{CHAL}^b_{\mathrm{IV}_5}$ oracle with $(*, a \cdot x_{i_\ell,1} y_{i_\ell,1}, 0, *, *)$ and obtains its challenge $(\widetilde{*}, \widetilde{u}^*_{3,3}, \widetilde{u}^*_{3,4}, \widetilde{*}, \widetilde{*})$; that is,

Case ($b = 0$): $(\widetilde{u}^*_{3,3}, \widetilde{u}^*_{3,4}) = (g_2^{\widetilde{r}_{3,2}}, g_3^{\widetilde{r}_{3,2}}) = (\widetilde{u}_{3,3}, \widetilde{u}_{3,4})$ or

Case ($b = 1$): $(\widetilde{u}^*_{3,3}, \widetilde{u}^*_{3,4}) = (g_2^{\widetilde{r}_{3,2}} T^{a \cdot x_{i_\ell,1} y_{i_\ell,1}}, g_3^{\widetilde{r}_{3,2}}) = (\widetilde{u}_{3,3} T^{a \cdot x_{i_\ell,1} y_{i_\ell,1}}, \widetilde{u}_{3,4})$.

$\mathcal{B}$ sets $\widehat{u}_{3,3} := \widetilde{u}^*_{3,3} \cdot \widetilde{v}^*_2$; similarly, it is easy to check that $\widehat{u}_{3,3} = \widetilde{u}_{3,3} \cdot \widetilde{v}_2$ in both cases. Then $\mathcal{B}$ generates the remaining elements in the 3rd row of table using its public keys and sets the 3rd row of table to be

$$\boxed{\widetilde{u}_{3,1} \mid \widetilde{u}_{3,2} \mid \widehat{u}_{3,3} = \widetilde{u}^*_{3,3} \cdot \widetilde{v}^*_2 \mid \widetilde{u}^*_{3,4} \mid \widetilde{u}_{3,5} \mid \cdots \mid \widetilde{u}_{3,8}}. \qquad (\text{B.3})$$

$\mathcal{B}$ also computes $\widetilde{v}^*_3$ from $(\widetilde{u}_{3,1}, \widetilde{u}_{3,2}, \widetilde{u}^*_{3,3}, \widetilde{u}^*_{3,4}, \widetilde{u}_{3,5}, \ldots, \widetilde{u}_{3,8})$ via $\widetilde{v}^*_3 := \widetilde{u}^{-x_{i_\ell,1}}_{3,1} \widetilde{u}^{-y_{i_\ell,1}}_{3,2} \widetilde{u}^{*-x_{i_\ell,2}}_{3,3} \widetilde{u}^{*-y_{i_\ell,2}}_{3,4} \widetilde{u}^{-x_{i_\ell,3}}_{3,5} \cdots \widetilde{u}^{-y_{i_\ell,4}}_{3,8}$, which equals

Case ($b = 0$): $\widetilde{v}^*_3 = \widetilde{v}_3$ or

Case ($b = 1$): $\widetilde{v}^*_3 = \widetilde{v}_3 T^{-a \cdot x_{i_\ell,1} y_{i_\ell,1} x_{i_\ell,2}}$.

(v) For the 4~8th rows, $\mathcal{B}$ computes table similarly as above.

(vi) Finally, $\mathcal{B}$ computes $\widehat{v}_0, \ldots, \widehat{v}_8$ from table, just as in Hybrids 2 and 3 (also as the original $\mathcal{E}.\mathsf{Decrypt}$ algorithm), and computes $\widetilde{e} := \widehat{v}_8 \cdot T^{f'_\ell((x_{i_\ell,j}, y_{i_\ell,j})_{j\in[4]})} \bmod N^s$, $t := g_1^{f'_\ell((x_{i_\ell,j}, y_{i_\ell,j})_{j\in[4]})} \bmod N$ using the secret keys.

If $b = 0$, $\mathcal{B}$ perfectly simulates Hybrid 2. If $b = 1$, $\mathcal{B}$ perfectly simulates Hybrid 3. Any difference between Hybrids 2 and 3 results in $\mathcal{B}$'s advantage over the IV_5 problem.

Acknowledgments

This work was supported by the National Natural Science Foundation of China Grant nos. 61672346 and 61373153.

References

[1] S. Goldwasser and S. Micali, "Probabilistic encryption," *Journal of Computer and System Sciences*, vol. 28, no. 2, pp. 270–299, 1984.

[2] J. Black, P. Rogaway, and T. Shrimpton, "Encryption-scheme security in the presence of key-dependent messages," in *Selected Areas in Cryptography*, K. Nyberg and H. M. Heys, Eds., vol. 2595 of *Lecture Notes in Computer Science*, pp. 62–75, Springer, 2003.

[3] J. Camenisch and A. Lysyanskaya, "An efficient system for non-transferable anonymous credentials with optional anonymity revocation," in *Advances in Cryptology*, B. Pfitzmann, Ed., vol. 2045 of *Lecture Notes in Computer Science*, pp. 93–118, Springer, 2001.

[4] D. Boneh, S. Halevi, M. Hamburg, and R. Ostrovsky, "Circular-secure encryption from decision Diffie-Hellman," in *Advances in Cryptology*, D. Wagner, Ed., vol. 5157 of *Lecture Notes in Computer Science*, pp. 108–125, Springer, 2008.

[5] Z. Brakerski and S. Goldwasser, "Circular and leakage resilient public-key encryption under subgroup indistinguishability (or: quadratic residuosity strikes back)," in *Advances in Cryptology*, T. Rabin, Ed., vol. 6223 of *Lecture Notes in Computer Science*, pp. 1–20, Springer, 2010.

[6] B. Applebaum, D. Cash, C. Peikert, and A. Sahai, "Fast cryptographic primitives and circular-secure encryption based on hard learning problems," in *Advances in Cryptology*, S. Halevi, Ed., vol. 5677 of *Lecture Notes in Computer Science*, pp. 595–618, Springer, 2009.

[7] O. Regev, "On lattices, learning with errors, random linear codes, and cryptography," in *Proceedings of the 37th Annual ACM Symposium on Theory of Computing (STOC '05)*, H. N. Gabow and R. Fagin, Eds., pp. 84–93, ACM, 2005.

[8] Z. Brakerski, S. Goldwasser, and Y. T. Kalai, "Black-box circular-secure encryption beyond affine functions," in *Theory of Cryptography*, Y. Ishai, Ed., vol. 6597 of *Lecture Notes in Computer Science*, pp. 201–218, Springer, 2011.

[9] B. Barak, I. Haitner, D. Hofheinz, and Y. Ishai, "Bounded key-dependent message security," in *Advances in Cryptology*, H. Gilbert, Ed., vol. 6110 of *Lecture Notes in Computer Science*, pp. 423–444, Springer, 2010.

[10] T. Malkin, I. Teranishi, and M. Yung, "Efficient circuit-size independent public key encryption with KDM security," in *Advances in Cryptology*, K. G. Paterson, Ed., vol. 6632 of *Lecture Notes in Computer Science*, pp. 507–526, Springer, 2011.

[11] J. Camenisch, N. Chandran, and V. Shoup, "A public key encryption scheme secure against key dependent chosen plaintext and adaptive chosen ciphertext attacks," in *Advances in Cryptology*, A. Joux, Ed., vol. 5479 of *Lecture Notes in Computer Science*, pp. 351–368, Springer, 2009.

[12] M. Naor and M. Yung, "Public-key cryptosystems provably secure against chosen ciphertext attacks," in *Proceedings of the 22nd Annual ACM Symposium on Theory of Computing (STOC '90)*, H. Ortiz, Ed., pp. 427–437, May 1990.

[13] J. Groth and A. Sahai, "Efficient non-interactive proof systems for bilinear groups," in *Advances in Cryptology*, N. P. Smart, Ed., vol. 4965 of *Lecture Notes in Computer Science*, pp. 415–432, Springer, 2008.

[14] D. Galindo, J. Herranz, and J. Villar, "Identity-based encryption with master key-dependent message security and leakage-resilience," in *European Symposium on Research in Computer Security*, S. Foresti, M. Yung, and F. Martinelli, Eds., vol. 7459 of *Lecture Notes in Computer Science*, pp. 627–642, 2012.

[15] D. Hofheinz, "Circular chosen-ciphertext security with compact ciphertexts," in *Advances in Cryptology*, T. Johansson and P. Q. Nguyen, Eds., vol. 7881 of *Lecture Notes in Computer Science*, pp. 520–536, Springer, 2013.

[16] X. Lu, B. Li, and D. Jia, "KDM-CCA security from RKA secure authenticated encryption," in *Advances in Cryptology. Part I*, E. Oswald and M. Fischlin, Eds., vol. 9056 of *Lecture Notes in Computer Science*, pp. 559–583, Springer, 2015.

[17] S. Han, S. Liu, and L. Lyu, "Efficient KDM-CCA secure public-key encryption for polynomial functions," in *Annual International Conference on the Theory and Applications of Cryptology and Information Security*, J. H. Cheon and T. Takagi, Eds., vol. 10032 of *Lecture Notes in Computer Science*, pp. 307–338, Springer, 2016.

[18] R. Cramer and V. Shoup, "Design and analysis of practical public-key encryption schemes secure against adaptive chosen ciphertext attack," *SIAM Journal on Computing*, vol. 33, no. 1, pp. 167–226, 2003.

[19] B. Qin, S. Liu, and K. Chen, "Efficient chosen-ciphertext secure public-key encryption scheme with high leakage-resilience," *IET Information Security*, vol. 9, no. 1, pp. 32–42, 2015.

[20] R. Cramer and V. Shoup, "Universal hash proofs and a paradigm for adaptive chosen ciphertext secure public-key encryption," in *Advances in Cryptology*, L. R. Knudsen, Ed., vol. 2332 of *Lecture Notes in Computer Science*, pp. 45–64, Springer, 2002.

[21] Y. Dodis, E. Kiltz, K. Pietrzak, and D. Wichs, "Message authentication, revisited," in *Advances in Cryptology*, D. Pointcheval and T. Johansson, Eds., vol. 7237 of *Lecture Notes in Computer Science*, pp. 355–374, Springer, 2012.

[22] K. Xagawa, "Message authentication codes secure against additively related-key attacks," in *Proceedings of the Symposium on Cryptography and Information Security (SCIS '13)*, 2013.

[23] I. Damgård and M. Jurik, "A generalisation, a simplification and some applications of Paillier's probabilistic public-key system," in *Public Key Cryptography*, K. Kim, Ed., vol. 1992 of *Lecture Notes in Computer Science*, pp. 119–136, Springer, 2001.

10

Data Placement for Privacy-Aware Applications over Big Data in Hybrid Clouds

Xiaolong Xu,[1,2,3,4] **Xuan Zhao,**[3] **Feng Ruan,**[5] **Jie Zhang,**[3] **Wei Tian,**[1,2]
Wanchun Dou,[3] **and Alex X. Liu**[4]

[1]*School of Computer and Software, Nanjing University of Information Science and Technology, Nanjing, China*
[2]*Jiangsu Engineering Centre of Network Monitoring, Nanjing University of Information Science and Technology, Nanjing, China*
[3]*State Key Laboratory for Novel Software Technology, Nanjing University, Nanjing, China*
[4]*Department of Computer Science and Engineering, Michigan State University, East Lansing, MI, USA*
[5]*School of Information and Control, Nanjing University of Information Science and Technology, Nanjing, China*

Correspondence should be addressed to Wanchun Dou; douwc@nju.edu.cn

Academic Editor: Md Z. A. Bhuiyan

Nowadays, a large number of groups choose to deploy their applications to cloud platforms, especially for the big data era. Currently, the hybrid cloud is one of the most popular computing paradigms for holding the privacy-aware applications driven by the requirements of privacy protection and cost saving. However, it is still a challenge to realize data placement considering both the energy consumption in private cloud and the cost for renting the public cloud services. In view of this challenge, a cost and energy aware data placement method, named CEDP, for privacy-aware applications over big data in hybrid cloud is proposed. Technically, formalized analysis of cost, access time, and energy consumption is conducted in the hybrid cloud environment. Then a corresponding data placement method is designed to accomplish the cost saving for renting the public cloud services and energy savings for task execution within the private cloud platforms. Experimental evaluations validate the efficiency and effectiveness of our proposed method.

1. Introduction

The rapid development of science and technology makes the network information increase exponentially, and the continuous accumulation of network data brings opportunities and challenges for big data. Big data gives plenty of benefits to humanity in many fields including network, health care, transportation, finance, military, and politics. Recommendation service, prediction service, and computing service can be realized through big data storage and analysis [1–3]. As huge amount of data could lead to system crash with the traditional data storage techniques, it is essential to realize the big data storage [4, 5]. Distributed file systems and databases are beneficial to big data storage. The emergence and development of cloud computing contributes to the big data storage, access, and processing, as cloud computing provides ubiquitous and various resources, to respond the explosive growth of data accumulation.

Cloud computing is a powerful technology that can provide humorous cloud services for the customers everywhere through the Internet, which aggregates geodistributed resources, to accomplish higher throughput and computing ability [6]. The customers could benefit from the public cloud services, as they are not necessary to build the infrastructure and manage the data center [7]. Currently, data privacy issues have received a lot of attention due to the increasing concern of the privacy and the data value protections, since the individuals often suffer heavy blows from privacy leaks [8, 9]. How to protect data and improve the security level of private data has become a hot topic of cloud computing [10]. Generally, it is an effective way to place these datasets in the private cloud; thus hybrid cloud for big data storage should be taken into consideration for privacy-aware applications [11, 12].

TABLE 1: Key terms and descriptions for cost, access time, and energy analysis in hybrid cloud.

Notation	Description
V	All the available VM instances $V = \{v_1, v_2, \ldots, v_M\}$
v_m	mth $(1 \leq w \leq W)$ VM in V
D	The dataset need to be placed $D = \{d_1, d_2, \ldots, d_W\}$
d_w	wth $(1 \leq w \leq W)$ dataset in D
l_w^m	The binary variable to judge whether d_w is placed on v_m
$r_{m',w}$	The data access time for $v_{m'}$ $(1 \leq m' \leq M)$ extracting the d_w
T	The tasks need to be performed, $T = \{t_1, t_2, \ldots, t_N\}$
t_n	nth $(1 \leq n \leq N)$ task in T
I_n^m	The binary variable to judge whether t_n is place on v_m
$c_{n,w}$	The time cost for the task t_n to extract the dataset d_w
F_m	The binary variable to judge whether v_m is on public cloud
O	The total access time of public datasets
O'	The access time for obtaining the datasets in private cloud
PE	The baseline power consumed by the active PMs
VE	The power consumed by the active VMs is calculated by
IE	The power consumed by the VMs in the idle mode
TE	The power consumed by the switches due to data access
E	The total power consumption to perform the tasks

Nowadays, an increasing number of applications, especially for the scientific workflows, for example, weather forecasting flows, are deployed in the hybrid cloud.

Data placement has a direct impact on the data access efficiency and the cost for data storage, as the locations of big data could affect the overhead for the service renting and the access time for data extraction. Therefore, reasonable and efficient data placement methods are essential to the performance of big data processing [13–15]. For the data placement in hybrid clouds, the payment of public cloud services and the energy consumption generated in the private cloud are key factors to determine the locations of the datasets for the execution of the privacy-aware applications.

With the above observations, it is still a challenge to realize data placement for privacy-aware applications over big data in the hybrid cloud, considering the cost saving in the public cloud and the energy saving in the private cloud. In view of this challenge, we design an efficient data placement method to deal with the above challenge. Our main contributions are threefold. Firstly, we undergo cost, access time, and energy analysis over big data in hybrid cloud. Secondly, a corresponding cost and energy aware data placement method, named CEDP, is designed to address the resource provisioning problem for the privacy-aware applications over big data in the hybrid cloud. Finally, a sequence of experimental analysis is conducted to validate the efficiency and the effectiveness of our proposed method.

The rest of this paper is organized as follows. In Section 2, formalized concepts are presented for cost, access time, and energy analysis over big data in hybrid cloud. Section 3 specifies our proposed method. The comparison analysis and performance evaluation are described in Section 4. Section 5 presents the related work, and Section 6 concludes the paper and gives outlook for the future work.

2. Cost, Access Time, and Energy Analysis over Big Data in Hybrid Cloud

In this section, cost and access time for data placement in the public cloud are analyzed. Besides, the access time and the energy consumption analysis for data placement in the private cloud are also presented. Table 1 specifies the key terms and description for cost, access time, and energy analysis over big data in the hybrid cloud.

2.1. Cost and Access Time Analysis in Public Cloud. In the cloud environment, the datasets and the tasks both need to be hosted in the form of VMs. Suppose there are M VM instances that are available for hosting tasks and datasets across the public clouds and the private cloud data centers, denoted as $V = \{v_1, v_2, \ldots, v_M\}$. Suppose there are W datasets that need to be stored in the hybrid cloud platforms, denoted as $D = \{d_1, d_2, \ldots, d_W\}$.

Let l_w^m be a binary variable to judge whether d_w $(1 \leq w \leq W)$ is placed on v_m $(1 \leq m \leq M)$, which is measured by

$$l_w^m = \begin{cases} 1, & d_w \text{ is placed on } v_m \\ 0, & \text{Otherwise.} \end{cases} \quad (1)$$

The reserved datasets need to be extracted from one VM to another. When the VM $v_{m'}$ $(1 \leq m' \leq M)$ needs to extract d_w, the data access time is denoted as $r_{m',w}$, which is calculated by

$$r_{m',w} = \begin{cases} l_w^m \cdot \dfrac{|d_w|}{\sum_{i=1}^{\kappa_{m,m'}} bw_i}, & i > 0 \\ 0, & i = 0, \end{cases} \quad (2)$$

where $\kappa_{m,m'}$ is the number of links between v_m and $v_{m'}$, $|d_w|$ represents the data size of d_w, and bw_i $(0 \leq i \leq \kappa_{m,m'})$ is the bandwidth of the ith link.

Suppose there are N tasks that need to be performed in the hybrid cloud environment, denoted as $T = \{t_1, t_2, \ldots, t_N\}$. The tasks are executed on the VMs whether in the public cloud or in the private cloud. Thus, these tasks have placement relationships with the VM instances. Let I_n^m be the binary variable to judge whether t_n $(1 \leq n \leq N)$ is placed on v_m, which is measured by

$$I_n^m = \begin{cases} 1, & t_n \text{ is placed on } v_m \\ 0, & \text{Otherwise.} \end{cases} \tag{3}$$

Thus, the time cost for the nth $(1 \leq n \leq N)$ task t_n to extract the dataset d_w, denoted as $c_{n,w}$, is calculated by

$$c_{n,w} = \sum_{m'=1}^{M} I_n^{m'} \cdot r_{m',w}. \tag{4}$$

As big data is now expanding explosively in both academia and industry, the execution of one task may need several datasets for supporting. For the data extraction in the public cloud, we mainly focus on the bandwidth cost for the data transferring.

Let F_m be the binary variable to judge whether v_m is placed on the public cloud, which is measured by

$$F_m = \begin{cases} 1, & v_m \text{ is placed on public cloud} \\ 0, & \text{Otherwise.} \end{cases} \tag{5}$$

The datasets could be extracted by the tasks in both public cloud and private cloud. The access time by the tasks in the public cloud is calculated by

$$O_{\text{pub}} = \sum_{n=1}^{N} \sum_{w=1}^{W} \sum_{m=1}^{M} \sum_{m'=1}^{M} F_{m'} \cdot F_m \cdot I_n^m \cdot r_{m',w} \cdot G_n^w, \tag{6}$$

where G_n^w is a binary variable to judge whether d_w is necessary for the execution of t_n.

$$G_n^w = \begin{cases} 1, & t_n \text{ requires } d_w \text{ for execution} \\ 0, & \text{Otherwise.} \end{cases} \tag{7}$$

The access time for the datasets in the public cloud by the tasks in the private cloud is calculated by

$$O_{\text{pri}} = \sum_{n=1}^{N} \sum_{w=1}^{W} \sum_{m=1}^{M} \sum_{m'=1}^{M} F_{m'} \cdot (1 - F_m) \cdot I_n^m \cdot r_{m',w} \cdot G_n^w. \tag{8}$$

Then the total access time for extracting the datasets from the public cloud is calculated by

$$\begin{aligned} O &= O_{\text{pub}} + O_{\text{pri}} \\ &= \sum_{n=1}^{N} \sum_{w=1}^{W} \sum_{m=1}^{M} \sum_{m'=1}^{M} F_{m'} \cdot F_m \cdot I_n^m \cdot r_{m',w} \cdot G_n^w \\ &\quad + \sum_{n=1}^{N} \sum_{w=1}^{W} \sum_{m=1}^{M} \sum_{m'=1}^{M} F_{m'} \cdot (1 - F_m) \cdot I_n^m \cdot r_{m',w} \cdot G_n^w \\ &= \sum_{n=1}^{N} \sum_{w=1}^{W} \sum_{m=1}^{M} \sum_{m'=1}^{M} F_{m'} \cdot I_n^m \cdot r_{m',w} \cdot G_n^w. \end{aligned} \tag{9}$$

The bandwidth cost for the data transferring in the public cloud is calculated by

$$C = \sum_{n=1}^{N} \sum_{w=1}^{W} \sum_{m=1}^{M} \sum_{m'=1}^{M} F_{m'} \cdot I_n^m \cdot r_{m',w} \cdot G_n^w \cdot \theta_m, \tag{10}$$

where θ_m is the expenditure of v_m for data transferring per unit time.

2.2. Access Time and Energy Consumption Analysis in Private Cloud.

For a private cloud data center, the cloud providers need to take into account the time cost and the power consumption while allocating the datasets. The access time for obtaining the datasets in private cloud is calculated by

$$\begin{aligned} O' = \sum_{n=1}^{N} \sum_{w=1}^{W} \sum_{m=1}^{M} \sum_{m'=1}^{M} (1 - F_{m'}) \cdot (1 - F_m) \cdot I_n^m \cdot r_{m',w} \\ \cdot G_n^w. \end{aligned} \tag{11}$$

Suppose there are Q PMs denoted as $P = \{p_1, p_2, \ldots, p_Q\}$ that are available to host the private datasets. And the tasks in the private clouds are also deployed on the PMs in P.

The energy consumption in the private cloud for the execution of the privacy-aware applications mainly refers to the energy consumed by the PM base power, active VMs, and the unused VMs, and the energy consumption due to data transferring. The PMs in the sleep mode also consume a certain amount of power, but it is far less than the energy consumed by the active PMs in the order of magnitude, that could be neglected [16, 17].

The baseline power consumed by the active PMs is calculated by

$$\text{PE} = \sum_{q=1}^{Q} \alpha_q \cdot \eta_q, \tag{12}$$

where α_q $(1 \leq q \leq Q)$ and η_q are the baseline power consumption rate and the total running time for p_q.

The power consumed by the active VMs is calculated by

$$\text{VE} = \sum_{m=1}^{M} (1 - F_m) \cdot \beta_m \cdot \delta_m, \tag{13}$$

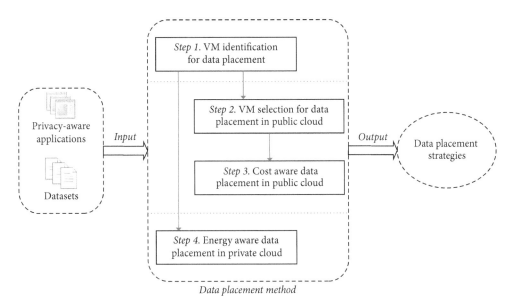

FIGURE 1: Specification of our proposed method.

where β_m, δ_m are the power consumption rate and the running time for v_m, respectively.

The power consumed by the VMs in the idle mode is calculated by

$$\mathrm{IE} = \sum_{m=1}^{M} \left(1 - F_m \right) \cdot \beta_m' \cdot \delta_m', \qquad (14)$$

where β_m' and δ_m' are the power rate and the idle time of v_m, respectively.

The power consumed by the switches due to data access is calculated by

$$\mathrm{TE} = \sum_{n=1}^{N} \sum_{w=1}^{W} \sum_{m=1}^{M} \left(1 - F_m \right) \cdot c_{n,w} \cdot G_n^w \cdot \theta_{n,w} \cdot \gamma, \qquad (15)$$

where θ_m is the number of switches between t_n and d_w, and γ is the active power rate for each switch.

Then the total power consumption to perform the tasks with data extraction processes is calculated by

$$E = \mathrm{PE} + \mathrm{VE} + \mathrm{IE} + \mathrm{TE}. \qquad (16)$$

Then the objectives for data placement over big data in the hybrid cloud are min E and min C.

3. Cost and Energy Aware Data Placement Method for Privacy-Aware Applications

In this section, a cost and energy aware data placement method is proposed for privacy-aware applications over big data in the hybrid environment. In this method, we aim to reduce the cost for renting cloud services and achieve energy savings in the private cloud.

3.1. Method Overview. In this paper, a cost and energy aware data placement method is proposed to address the challenges of data placement problem for the privacy-aware applications in the hybrid cloud environment.

Figure 1 shows the specification of our proposed method. The input of our method is the privacy-aware applications with task distribution in the hybrid cloud, and the datasets that need to be placed in the hybrid cloud. Our method consists of four main steps, i.e., VM identification for data placement, VM selection for data placement in public cloud, cost aware data placement in public cloud, and energy aware data placement in private cloud.

For each dataset, the VMs that need to access it are identified in Step 1. Then in the public cloud, we choose available VMs to host the datasets, which need to be placed in the public cloud, through Step 2. For the VMs obtained by Step 2, we conduct cost aware data placement through Step 3, so that the optimal data placement strategies with minimum cost are designed for the datasets that need to be placed in the public cloud. For the datasets with privacy preservation requirements, they are necessary to place in the private cloud. Energy aware data placement are designed in Step 4 to achieve energy savings while allocating VMs to store these datasets. The ultimate output of our method is the data placement strategies.

3.2. VM Identification for Data Placement. In the hybrid cloud, both the datasets and the tasks combined in the privacy-aware applications physical resources from cloud platforms for hosting, which could be responded by the VMs. Generally, the resource capacity of PMs and the resource requirements from tasks and datasets are specified by the amount of the resource units, that is, the VM instances [16]. For many public cloud vendors, such as Amazon, they provide many types of VM instances, including CPU-intensive instances and I/O optimized instances.

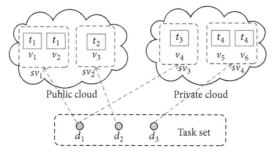

FIGURE 2: An example of special VM identification with tasks ($t_1{\sim}t_4$) and datasets ($d_1{\sim}d_3$) deployed on VMs ($v_1{\sim}v_6$) in the hybrid cloud.

Input: The dataset D
Output: The special VM set VS
(1) **for** $i = 1$ to $|D|$ **do**
(2)   **for** $j = 1$ to N **do**
(3)   **if** t_j requires v_i for execution **then**
(4)   Add t_j to r_i
(5)   flag $= 1, k = 1$
(6)   **while** flag $== 1$ && $k \leq M$ **do**
(7)   **if** $I_n^k == 1$ **then**
(8)   Add v_k to vs_i
(9)   flag $= 0$
(10)   **else** $k = k + 1$
(11)   **end if**
(12)   **end while**
(13)   **end if**
(14)   **end for**
(15)   Classify the VMs in vs_i as several special VMs
(16) **end for**
(17) **Return** SV

ALGORITHM 1: Special VM identification for data access.

Definition 1 (resource requirement of t_n). The resource requirement of t_n mainly refers to the VM instance type and the number of VM instances, which is denoted as $r_n = \{vt_n, cou_n\}$, where vt_n and cou_n are the VM instance type and the required total amount of VM instances of t_n, respectively.

To satisfy the requirements of a dataset that needs to be stored, one or more VM instances with the same specification are requested, and these instances could be regarded as a special VM.

Definition 2 (special VM). For the VM instances that deployed to perform the same task or store the same dataset, it could be treated as a special VM.

Currently, in the big data era, large-scale datasets could be shared for multiple tasks, and one task may need several different datasets for execution. To place the dataset efficiently, the special VMs that rented for hosting the tasks, which require the datasets for execution, should be identified. For the dataset d_w in D, the special VM set is denoted as sv_w; then D has a corresponding special VM set $SV = \{sv_1, sv_2, \ldots, sv_W\}$.

Figure 2 shows an example of special VM identification. In this example, there are three datasets (i.e., d_1, d_2, and d_3) that need to be stored in the hybrid cloud. d_1 needs to be accessed by tasks t_1 and t_3, d_2 needs to be accessed by t_2, and d_3 needs to be accessed by t_4. t_1 requires v_1 and v_2 for execution, t_2 requires v_3 for execution, t_4 requires v_5 and v_6 for execution. In this example, the two VM instances v_1 and v_2 occupied by t_1 could treated as a special VM sv_1, v_3 is treated as sv_2, v_4 is treated as special VM sv_3, and v_5 and v_6 are treated as special VM sv_4.

The VMs identified according to the task distribution and the dataset access requirements should be specified as the special VMs. For the dataset d_w, the corresponding special VMs are put in the VM set sv_w. Then all special VM sets for all datasets are recorded as $SV = \{sv_1, sv_2, \ldots, sv_W\}$.

Algorithm 1 specifies the key idea of special VM identification for data access. The input is the dataset D. This algorithm should traverse all the datasets (Line (1)) and all the tasks (Line (2)). For each dataset, we find the VMs of the tasks that need to access the dataset (Lines (3) to (12)). Finally, the output is the special VM set SV.

3.3. VM Selection for Data Placement in Public Cloud. The datasets should be placed on the VMs, thus the available

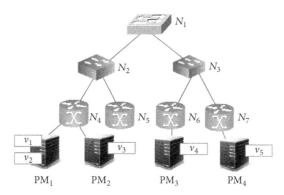

FIGURE 3: An example of VM distribution in a FatTree-based data center network with core switch N_1, aggregation switches N_2 and N_3, and edge switches $N_4 \sim N_7$.

VMs on the cloud should be identified to store the datasets. For the PMs and VMs in the private cloud, the resource scheduler could be aware of the map relationship between PMs and VMs. However, in the public cloud, the resource scheduler can only select the available VMs that cloud vendors provided.

In the public cloud platforms, when renting VMs for storing the datasets. We would like to choose the VM instances with lowest cost. Generally, the more the renting time of bandwidth is, the more cost the users need to pay. Thus, the access time for tasks extracting the datasets should be taken into consideration. FatTree is a typical network topology for cloud datacenters. For most VMs connected to different switches, the data access time is almost the same. In this section, we conduct VM selection process, to select the VMs that could store the datasets in the public cloud. And these VMs should be sorted by the distances between the selected VMs and the VM for holding tasks, identified in Algorithm 1.

Figure 3 shows an example of VM distribution in a FatTree-based data center network. There are seven switches (i.e., $N_1 \sim N_7$), distributed as a tree network. In these switches, N_1 is the core switch, N_2 and N_3 are the aggregation switches, and the switches $N_4 \sim N_7$ are edge switches. There are three PMs (i.e., $PM_1 \sim PM_3$) connected to the edge switches. In this example, there are five running VMs distributed on these PMs, where v_1 and v_2 are placed on PM_1, v_3 is placed on PM_2, v_4 is placed on PM_3, and v_5 is placed on PM_4.

The data access time is a key objective that users take into consideration, which is closely relevant to the distances between the VMs where the task hosts and the datasets locates. The distance calculation relies on the locations on the FatTree network. The distance between two VMs on the same PM is 0. For example, as shown in Figure 3, v_1 and v_2 are placed on the same PM; the distance between v_1 and v_2 is 0. The distance between two VMs on different PMs depends on the number of links between these two VMs. For example, the distance between v_1 and v_3 is 2. Furthermore, if the PMs are connected to two different edge switches, but they have the same aggregation switch, the distance is double than the distance between two VMs connected to the same edge switch. For example, the distance between v_4 and v_5 is 4.

Besides, if the VMs are connected to the different aggression switch, the distance of them is triple than the distance of VMs connected to the same edge switch. For example, the distance between v_1 and v_4 is 6, and the distance between v_3 and v_4 is also 6.

Based on the process of distance calculation, the identified VMs, which are available for hosting the datasets, could be sorted by the increasing order of the distance values. The datasets placed in the public cloud also be accessed by the tasks deployed in the private cloud. In the private cloud datacenter, the network is also built based on FatTree; thus the data access between VMs in these two kinds of cloud platforms needs to access the core switch, the aggregation switch, and the core switch in both public and private cloud, which is an edge-to-edge communication across clouds and platforms. So, in this section, we mainly focus on the access time within the public cloud platform.

For the dataset d_w, which is arranged to store in the public cloud, there are several tasks in the public cloud should access d_w; the special VMs in sv_w should be updated by removing the special VMs in private clouds. The corresponding VMs are selected to hold d_w, which are put in the VM set cv_w. For all the datasets, the VM set list is denoted as $CV = \{cv_1, cv_2, \ldots, cv_W\}$.

Algorithm 2 specifies the key process of VM selection for data placement. The input is the VM node set SV. This algorithm traverses all the VM set in SV (Line (1)), and, for each VM set, the VMs in the private cloud removed (Line (2)). For each VM in the VM set, we select the VMs in the public cloud and calculate the distances between the selected VM and the VM in the VM set (Lines (3) to (12)). Then the selected VMs are put in the VM set CV, and it is sorted in the increasing order of distance (Line (13)). The final output is the identified VM set CV.

3.4. Cost Aware Data Placement in Public Cloud. After the processing of VM selection in Algorithm 2, the VMs that could be allocated to store the datasets in public cloud are obtained. As, in the public cloud, the cost and the access time are closely relevant, especially, in the FatTree network, in this section, we mainly focus on the cost for the public cloud services.

Input: The VM set VS
Output: The identified VM set CV
(1) **for** $i = 1$ to $|VS|$ **do**
(2)   Remove the VMs in private cloud from vs_i
(3)   **for** $j = 1$ to vs_i **do**
(4)   **for** $k = 1$ to M **do**
(5)   **if** v_k is in the public cloud **then**
(6)   **if** v_k is not in cv_i **then**
(7)   Add v_k to cv_i
(8)   Calculate the distance between v_k to $vs_{i,j}$
(9)   **end if**
(10)   **end if**
(11)   **end for**
(12)   **end for**
(13)   Sort the VMs in cv_i in the increasing order of distance
(14) **end for**
(15) **Return** CV

ALGORITHM 2: VM selection for data placement.

The cost mainly depends on the service time and the unit payment fee for VM renting. As we know there are different VM instances provided by the cloud vendors, and the cost for these VM instances are various; thus, to achieve cost efficiency, we should select the optimal data placement strategy with minimum cost for the datasets that need to be placed in the public cloud.

Definition 3 (data placement strategy of d_w). The dataset placement strategy of d_w consists of the VM instances that need to rent for storing d_w, denoted as s_w.

For all the datasets in D, the relevant data placement strategy set is denoted as $S = \{s_1, s_2, \ldots, s_W\}$. After the processing by Algorithm 1, we get the special VMs for each dataset access, which are used to hold the tasks that need to access the dataset. Although the datasets in the public cloud could be accessed by the tasks both running in the public cloud and the private cloud, the datasets only can use the public cloud services for storing, due to the resource limit in the private cloud. The VMs that could be employed to respond the resource requirements could be achieved by Algorithm 2.

Then for each dataset in the public cloud, we try to select the suitable data placement policy, to save the cost expenditure for cloud service renting. As there are multiple data placement policies for each dataset, the placement policy with the minimum cost, calculated by formula (10), is selected as the final data placement strategy.

Algorithm 3 specifies the key idea of cost aware data placement. The input for this algorithm is the dataset D that need to be placed in the hybrid cloud. The special VMs for each dataset are identified by Algorithm 1 (Line (1)). Then we traverse all the datasets (Line (2)) and select the datasets that need to be placed in the public cloud (Line (3)). The VM instances are selected to respond to the resource requirements of each dataset in public cloud (Line (5)). Then multiple iterations are undergoing to find the data placement

policy with lowest cost (Lines (7) to (16)). The output of this algorithm is the data placement strategy S.

3.5. Energy Aware Data Placement in Private Cloud. After the data placement in Section 3.4, the data placement strategies for the datasets that need to be placed in the public cloud are all designed. For the privacy-aware applications of users, some tasks contained in them are deployed in their own datacenter, that is, the private cloud constructed by themselves. In this scenario, the resource scheduler could know the specification of the task distribution and the map relationship between VMs and PMs. Similar to the network topology of the public cloud, the private cloud data center also constructed based on the FatTree network. Thus, when allocating VMs to store the datasets in the private cloud, the access time is not a key issue to take care of. In the private cloud, we mainly focus on reducing the energy consumption due to data access and task execution.

In Section 2, the energy consumption is specified as the energy consumed by the running PMs, the active VMs, the idle VMs, and the switches due to data transferring. The energy consumed due to data access could be specified as the following three scenarios:

(1) The datasets could be placed on the PMs that the tasks located which need to access the datasets. In this case, the energy consumption of switches due to data transferrin could be neglected. For example, the VMs v_1 and v_2 in Figure 4 share the data storage of PM_1; thus there are no data transferring through any switch.

(2) The datasets also could be placed on the VMs which are connected to the same edge switches with the tasks which need to access the datasets. Then the data access only across one switch, and the energy for data transferring only occurs in this switch. For example, the VMs v_1 and v_3 are placed on PM_1 and

---

Input: The dataset D
Output: The dataset placement strategy $S = \{s_1, s_2, \ldots, s_W\}$
(1) **Algorithm** 1 Special VM identification for data access
(2) **for** $i = 1$ to $|D|$ **do**
(3)   **if** d_i needs to be placed in public cloud **then**
(4)   Update vs_i and r_i
(5)   Get the VM instances by **Algorithm** 2
(6)   Classify CV as special VMs, denoted as sv_i
(7) $C = \text{MAXCV}, j = 1$
(8)   **while** $j \leq |sv_i|$ **do**
(9)   **if** $sv_{i,j}$ can hold d_i **then**
(10)   Calculate the total cost TC by (10)
(11)   **if** TC $< C$ **then**
(12) $C = \text{TC}$
(13)   **else** $j = j + 1$
(14)   **end if**
(15)   **end if**
(16)   **end while**
(17)   Update s_i with cost C
(18)   **end if**
(19) **end for**
(20) **Return** S

ALGORITHM 3: Cost aware data placement.

PM$_2$ separately, and the data transferring between these two VMs only employs the switch N_4.

(3) The datasets also cloud be placed on the PMs with the different switches to the PMs that hosted the tasks need to access the datasets. In this situation, whether the datasets placed on which PM, the energy consumed due to data transferring is same, as the data access use five switches, that is, two edge switches, two aggregation switches, and one core switch. For example, in Figure 4, the energy consumption due to data access between v_1 and v_4, will use the edge switch N_4, the aggregation switch N_2, the core switch N_1, the aggregation switch N_3, and the edge switch N_6.

From the above analysis, the occupation of the VMs which are near to the VMs the task hosts, which need to acccess the dataset, will cause fewer energy consumption. Besides, for the energy consumption for PM running, the main idea to save the energy consumption is to make full use of the running PMs and try best to reduce the number of running PMs. If the VMs are placed on the PMs with the tasks, it can achieve energy saving from the perspective of both data access and PM running. Thus, the PMs are sorted in the decreasing order of the distances between the VM to host the tasks and the VM identified for hosting the dataset. Then, we select the PM through multiple iterations; at last we select the PM to host the dataset with the minimum energy consumption, calculated by formula (16).

The data placement strategy for the datasets in the private cloud could be improved as $s_w = \{nm_w, pm_w\}$, where nm_w and pm_w are the amount of VM instances and the VM location of d_w, respectively.

Algorithm 4 shows the key idea of energy aware data placement in private cloud. In this algorithm; the input is the dataset D. The special VMs for hosting the tasks in the private cloud are identified by Algorithm 1 (Line (1)). Then all the datasets are traversed to check whether the dataset needs to place in the private cloud (Line (2) and Line (3)). For each dataset, we traverse the PM list, to select the PMs that can hold it (Lines (4) to (8)). The PM list is sorted in the decreasing order of VM distance between the VMs selected by Algorithm 1 and the PMs (9). We find the PM with energy consumption for data placement through multiple iterations (Lines (10) to (20)). The final output of this algorithm is the updated data placement strategy set S.

4. Experimental Evaluation

In this section, we use the cloud simulator CloudSim to simulate the hybrid cloud environment and the data placement method CEDP.

4.1. Experimental Context. In this paper, 4 different scales datasets with VM distributions and task distributions are generated to validate our proposed method. Besides, the bid datasets are also provided with 4 different scales. The above datasets are stored in the Google disk (https://drive.google .com/open?id=0B0T819XffFKrQVFoOHM2TU1zZHM). Our method is validated on the physical node, equipped with the processor (Intel Core i5-5300U CPU @2.30 GHz) and 8.00 GB memory.

The parameters used in our simulation are specified in Table 2. We use 4 types of PMs (150 PMs for each type) to construct our private cloud platform. And the energy consumption rate settings are similar to our previous work in [16–18].

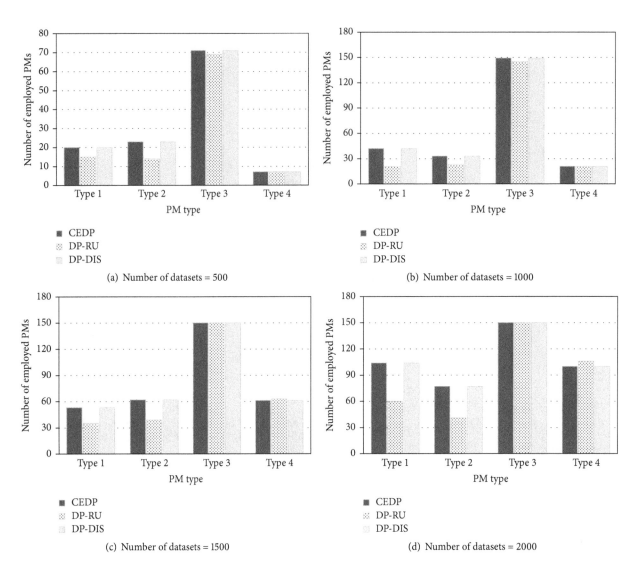

FIGURE 4: Comparison of the number of employed PMs by CEDP, DP-RU, and DP-DIS with 4 different scales of datasets placed in private cloud.

TABLE 2: Parameter Settings.

Parameter	Domain
Number of hosts in private cloud	600
PM type	4
PM baseline energy consumption (W)	$\{86, 93.7, 192, 342\}$
Number of VMs for each type of PM	$\{6, 8, 18, 34\}$
VM type in public cloud	4
Cost for each type of VM (cents/h)	$\{2, 2.5, 3, 3.5\}$
Number of datasets	$\{500, 1000, 1500, 2000\}$
Unit cost for data access (cents/GB·time)	1.5
Bandwidth (MB)	80
Switch power (W)	300
Data size for each dataset (GB)	$[1, 50]$

Input: The dataset D
Output: The dataset placement strategy $S = \{s_1, s_2, \ldots, s_W\}$
(1)   **Algorithm** 1 Special VM identification for data access
(2)   **for** $i = 1$ to $|D|$ **do**
(3)   **if** d_i needs to be placed in private cloud **then**
(4)   **for** $j = 1$ to Q **do**
(5)   **if** p_j can hold d_i **then**
(6)   Add p_j to cp_i
(7)   **end if**
(8)   **end for**
(9)   Sort cp_i in the decreasing order of VM distance between the VM in svi and the VM in cp_i
(10)   Calculate the energy consumption ec_1 after allocating d_i to $cp_{i,1}$ by (16)
(11) $MC = ec_1$, num = 2
(12)   **while** num $\leq |cp_i|$ **do**
(13)   Calculate the energy consumption ec_{num} after allocating d_i to $cp_{i,num}$ by Eq. (16)
(14)   **if** $ec_{num} < MC$ **then**
(15) $MC = ec_{num}$
(16)   **end if**
(17)   num = num + 1
(18)   **end while**
(19)   Update s_i according to MC and the relevant PM
(20)   **end if**
(21)   **end for**
(22)   **Return** S

ALGORITHM 4: Energy aware data placement in private cloud.

We use 4 datasets with different scale of datasets that need to be placed in the hybrid cloud. And 20% of them are privacy-aware data, which should be placed in the private cloud. For the public cloud, there are 4 types of VMs that are presented for data placement.

4.2. Performance Evaluation. The performance evaluation is conducted from two aspects, that is, the public cloud and the private cloud. For the private cloud, we mainly focus on the energy consumption and the access time. However, for the public cloud, we mainly validate the method performance through the comparison analysis on cost for VMs renting. As our work is the first to privatize a data placement policy for privacy-aware applications over big data in hybrid cloud, two benchmark methods are employed for comparison analysis. On is a resource utilization aware data placement method, named DP_RU, which aims to optimize the resource utilization for the cloud datacenters. The other is a distance-aware data placement method, named DP_DIS, which aims to place the datasets near the tasks which needs to access them.

(1) Evaluation on Energy Consumption in Private Cloud. The energy consumption is closely relevant to the number of the employed PMs. Figure 4 shows the comparison of the employed PMs by CEDP, DP_RU, and DP_DIS with 4 different scales of datasets for data placement in private cloud. In Figure 4, it is intuitive that our proposed method employs the same number of PMs with DP_DIS. It is because that our

method considers the data access time, which also depends on the distance between the tasks and the datasets. From Figure 4, we can find that, in most cases, DP_RU applies fewer PMs than CEDP and DP_DIS, because DP_RU is a greedy algorithm to achieve high resource usage, regardless of the data access time.

Although we employ more PMs than DP_RU, it does not mean DP_DIS is more energy efficient than CEDP, as the data access processes also consume a certain amount of energy.

Figure 5 shows the comparison of the total energy consumption with different scale of datasets by using CEDP, DP_RU, and DP_DIS. As shown in Figure 5, CEDP and DP_DIS achieve the same energy consumption after data placement in the private cloud. And these two methods achieve better energy efficiency than DP_RU, although DP_RU employs fewer PMs than CEDP. We can detect that there is more energy consumed by the switches due to data access.

(2) Evaluation on Access Time in Private Cloud. As the applications need big data for processing, the tasks need to access the placed data frequently. The access time is a key attribute to measure the quality of cloud service. Figure 6 (including 4 subfigures) shows the comparison of the access time by CEDP, DP_RU, and DP_DIS with different scale of datasets placed in private cloud. For these 4 datasets, there are 100, 200, 300, and 400 privacy-aware datasets, separately. To

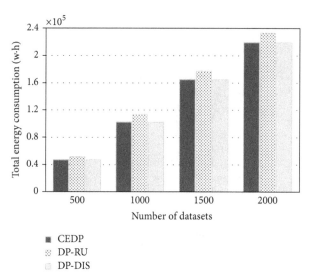

FIGURE 5: Comparison of total energy consumption with different scale of datasets by using CEDP, DP-RU, and DP-DIS.

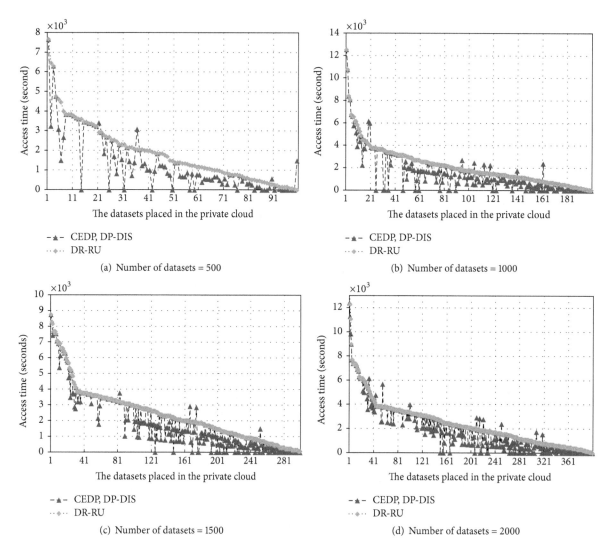

FIGURE 6: Comparison of access time by CEDP, DP-RU, and DP-DIS with different scale of datasets placed in private cloud.

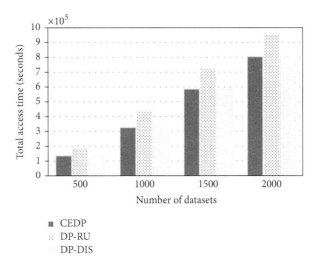

FIGURE 7: Comparison of total access time with different scale of datasets by using CEDP, DP-RU, and DP-DIS.

better show the comparison analysis, we sort the experimental results in the decreasing order of access time, achieved by DR_RU. From Figure 6, we can find that our method CEDP obtains optimal access time than DP_RU, in most cases. For example, in Figure 6(c), when the total number of datasets is 1500, there are 300 privacy-aware datasets that should be placed in the private cloud, where there are 296 datasets that could obtain better access time by CEDP among 300 datasets than DP_RU. Obsolutely, there are still some accidental cases that DP_RU achieves better access time than CEDP. As there are multiple datasets that could be provided for the same task, a dataset has been placed in advance, and there are no spare PMs that connected to the same edge switch or the aggression switch. Our proposed method CEDP is a global optimization method that can achieve better time efficiency than DP_RU from a global perspective. Therefore, for some of the datasets, it is reasonable that there are some accidental cases. Overall, CEDP could obtain time efficiency than DP_RU.

Figure 7 shows the comparison of total overall access time with different scale of datasets by using CEDP, DP_RU, and DP_DIS. It is intuitive from Figure 7 that CEDP could get the same access time as DP_DIS, and both of them are superior compared to DP_RU. For example, when the number of datasets is 2000 and CEDP and DP_DIS get the overall time near 8×10^5 seconds, whereas DP_RU achieves near 9.5×10^5 seconds overall access time. CEDP and DP_DIS are both distance-aware data methods; thus they are time-sensitive.

(3) Evaluation on Cost in Public Cloud. For the performance evaluation in the public cloud, the cost for VMs renting is one of the most key metrics. The renting fee is closely relevant to the VM instance type. Thus, we analyze the number of employed VMs for data placement in public cloud. Four figures in Figure 8 show the comparison analysis of the number of employed VMs by CEDP, DP-RU, and DP-DIS with different scale of datasets placed in public cloud. From Figure 8, we can find that CEDP employs cheaper VM instances (i.e., type 1 and type 2) than DP_RU and DP-DIS. Besides, CEDP employs fewer expensive VM instances (i.e.,

type 3 and type 4) than DP_RU and DP_DIS. For example, in Figure 8(a), CEDP employs over 100 VM instances with type 1 and type 2, whereas DP_RU and DP_DIS both employ less than 50. But CEDP employs fewer VMs with respect to type 3 and type 4 VMs.

Then we conduct the statistics of total cost for these 3 methods. Figure 9 shows the comparison of total cost with different scale of datasets by using CEDP, DP-RU, and DP-DIS. In Figure 9, we can find that our method could achieve cost savings compared to DP_RU and DP_DIS, as we present a cost-sensitive method for data placement in public cloud.

5. Related Work

Big data needs a huge mass of computing resources and storage resources, to promote the development of cloud technology [19–21]. Data placement in cloud environment has been widely concerned to improve the quality of cloud services.

Data Placement over Cloud. Due to the necessity and importance of data placement, there exist multiple methods to place users' data over multiple clouds [13–15, 22–24]. Fan et al. [13] constructed a tripartite graph in GBDP (genetic based data placement) scheme and demonstrated validation of the scheme. Jiao et al. [14] proposed an optimization approach leveraging graph cuts to optimize multiobjective data placement in multicloud for socially aware services. Yu and Pan [15] showed a location-aware associated data placement scheme to improve the associated data location and the localized data serving and at the same time ensure the balance between nodes. Agarwal et al. [22] presented a system named Volley which can analyze the logs of data center requests and output migration recommendations to address data placement problem. Yu and Pan [23] proposed the sketch-based data placement (SDP) to lower the overhead and keep the benefits of the data placement. Su et al. [24] proposes that better features can be provided by multicloud

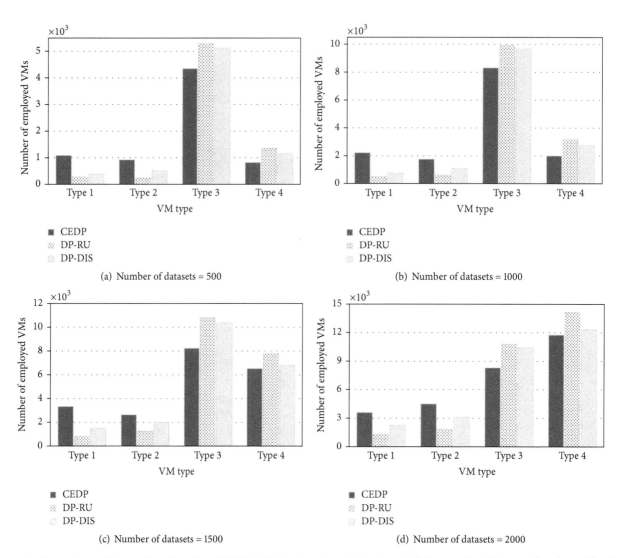

FIGURE 8: Comparison of the number of employed VMs by CEDP, DP-RU, and DP-DIS with different scale of datasets placed in public cloud.

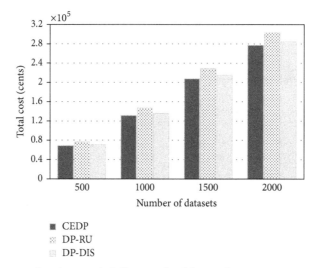

FIGURE 9: Comparison of total cost with different scale of datasets by using CEDP, DP-RU, and DP-DIS.

storage and presented a systematic model Triones to formulate data placement in multiple clouds storage by using erasure coding.

Although cloud computing can provide rich resources of computing and storage and data placement can also maximize the efficiency of cloud usage and expenditure reduction, the data privacy problems become the greatest concern for more and more people [25]. Hybrid cloud that combine public cloud and private cloud can protect user privacy by placing private data on private cloud [26].

Hybrid Cloud. The study of hybrid cloud is also increasing. Mixed cloud on the task scheduling, virtual machine scheduling, privacy, and other related work have made some progress. Some were discussed about separating private data from public data and placing them in trusted private cloud and untrusted public cloud, respectively [27–30]. Zhou et al. [27] presented a set of techniques for privacy-aware data retrieval by splitting data and storing on hybrid cloud. Huang and Du [28] proposed a scheme to achieve image data privacy over hybrid cloud efficiently and proposed a one-to-one mapping function for image encryption. Wang and Jia [29] described several methods about protecting data security in hybrid cloud and discussed an authentication intercloud model. Abrishami et al. [30] presented a scheduling algorithm to protect data privacy while minimizing the cost and satisfying the users' limitation. Tasks, datasets, and virtual machines scheduling in hybrid cloud to maximize the benefits and minimize the cost were studied in [31–34]. Zhou et al. [31] produced a three-stage framework to explore the benefits of uploading applications to hybrid cloud. Qiu et al. [32] described a model for heterogeneous workloads scheduling and an online algorithm for tasks preemptive scheduling. Zinnen and Engel [33] used HGP to estimate task execution times and proved that the former result is the same as optimization with unknown generating distributions. Bakshi [34] introduced a secure hybrid cloud approach and the virtual switching technologies. Although these papers take improving the overall efficiency of the hybrid cloud by scheduling into account, it does not consider the effect of the storage location of the data on overall efficiency when the task has been properly allocated in public and private cloud. Our work considers the impact of data placement in a hybrid cloud environment, paying attention to the energy loss on the private cloud and the rental price on the public cloud.

To the best of our knowledge, there are few works which focus on the data placement problem in the hybrid cloud for privacy-aware applications over big data, considering both the cost in public cloud and the energy consumption in private cloud.

6. Conclusion and Future Work

In the big data era, data placement becomes increasingly important for data accessing and analysis, as the datasets are often too large to host with the computing task. Cloud platforms are proved to be powerful to host the data-intensive tasks. Besides, the data privacy is also a key concern for both academia and industry; thus it is necessary to undergo data placement in the hybrid cloud. In this paper, we propose an energy and cost aware data placement method driven by the requirements of the privacy-aware applications in the hybrid cloud. Our method aims to reduce the energy consumption in the private cloud and save cost for renting the VMs in the public cloud.

For future work, we will try to realize our method for the real-world workflow applications, such as weather forecasting, where the raw data should be stored in the private cloud, and the intermediate data could be stored in the public cloud.

Acknowledgments

This research is supported by the National Science Foundation of China under Grants no. 61702277, no. 61672276, no. 61772283, no. 61402167, and no. 61672290, the Key Research and Development Project of Jiangsu Province under Grants nos. BE2015154 and BE2016120. Besides, this work is also supported by the Startup Foundation for Introducing Talent of NUIST, the Open Project from State Key Laboratory for Novel Software Technology, Nanjing University, under Grant no. KFKT2017B04, the Priority Academic Program Development of Jiangsu Higher Education Institutions (PAPD) fund, Jiangsu Collaborative Innovation Center on Atmospheric Environment and Equipment Technology (CICAEET), and Project "Six Talent Peaks Project in Jiangsu Province" under Grant no. XYDXXJS-040.

References

[1] J. Heidrich, A. Trendowicz, and C. Ebert, "Exploiting big data's benefits," *IEEE Software*, vol. 33, no. 4, pp. 111–116, 2016.

[2] X. Wu, X. Zhu, G.-Q. Wu, and W. Ding, "Data mining with big data," *IEEE Transactions on Knowledge and Data Engineering*, vol. 26, no. 1, pp. 97–107, 2014.

[3] L. Mertz, "What can big data tell us about health? Finding gold through data mining," *IEEE Pulse*, vol. 7, no. 5, pp. 40–44, 2016.

[4] J. Li, Z. Xu, Y. Jiang, and R. Zhang, "The overview of big data storage and management," in *Proceedings of the 13th IEEE International Conference on Cognitive Informatics and Cognitive Computing, ICCI-CC 2014*, pp. 510–513, London, UK, August 2014.

[5] Q. Liu, W. Cai, J. Shen, Z. Fu, X. Liu, and N. Linge, "A speculative approach to spatial-temporal efficiency with multi-objective optimization in a heterogeneous cloud environment," *Security and Communication Networks*, vol. 9, no. 17, pp. 4002–4012, 2016.

[6] E. Chovancová, L. Vokorokos, and M. Chovanec, "Cloud computing system for small and medium corporations," in *Proceedings of the 13th IEEE International Symposium on Applied Machine Intelligence and Informatics, SAMI 2015*, pp. 171–174, svk, January 2015.

[7] K. Peng, R. Lin, B. Huang, H. Zou, and F. Yang, "Link importance evaluation of data center network based on maximum flow," *Journal of Internet Technology*, vol. 18, no. 1, pp. 23–31, 2017.

[8] B. Nelson and T. Olovsson, "Security and privacy for big data: A systematic literature review," in *Proceedings of the 4th IEEE International Conference on Big Data, Big Data 2016*, pp. 3693–3702, usa, December 2016.

[9] S. Yu, "Big Privacy: Challenges and Opportunities of Privacy Study in the Age of Big Data," *IEEE Access*, vol. 4, pp. 2751–2763, 2016.

[10] C. Perera, R. Ranjan, and L. Wang, "End-to-end privacy for open big data markets," *IEEE Cloud Computing*, vol. 2, no. 4, pp. 44–53, 2015.

[11] H. M. Musse and L. A. Alamro, "Cloud Computing: Architecture and Operating System," in *Proceedings of the 2016 Global Summit on Computer & Information Technology (GSCIT)*, pp. 3–8, Sousse, Tunisia, 2016.

[12] A. Sill, "Standards for Hybrid Clouds," *IEEE Cloud Computing*, vol. 3, no. 1, pp. 92–95, 2016.

[13] W. Fan, J. Peng, X. Zhang, and Z. Huang, "Genetic Based Data Placement for Geo-Distributed Data-Intensive Applications in Cloud Computing," in *Advances in Services Computing*, Springer International Publishing, 2016.

[14] L. Jiao, J. Lit, W. Du, and X. Fu, "Multi-objective data placement for multi-cloud socially aware services," in *Proceedings of the 33rd IEEE Conference on Computer Communications, IEEE INFOCOM 2014*, pp. 28–36, Toronto, Canada, May 2014.

[15] B. Yu and J. Pan, "Location-aware associated data placement for geo-distributed data-intensive applications," in *Proceedings of the 34th IEEE Annual Conference on Computer Communications and Networks, IEEE INFOCOM 2015*, pp. 603–611, hkg, May 2015.

[16] X. Xu, W. Dou, X. Zhang, and J. Chen, "EnReal: An Energy-Aware Resource Allocation Method for Scientific Workflow Executions in Cloud Environment," *IEEE Transactions on Cloud Computing*, vol. 4, no. 2, pp. 166–179, 2016.

[17] W. Dou, X. Xu, S. Meng et al., "An energy-aware virtual machine scheduling method for service QoS enhancement in clouds over big data," *Concurrency Computation*, vol. 29, no. 14, Article ID e3909, 2016.

[18] X. Xu, W. Wang, T. Wu, W. Dou, and S. Yu, "A Virtual Machine Scheduling Method for Trade-Offs Between Energy and Performance in Cloud Environment," in *Proceedings of the 4th International Conference on Advanced Cloud and Big Data, CBD 2016*, pp. 246–251, chn, August 2016.

[19] Y. Zhao, Y. Li, S. Lu, I. Raicu, and C. Lin, "Devising a Cloud Scientific Workflow Platform for Big Data," in *Proceedings of the 2014 IEEE World Congress on Services (SERVICES)*, pp. 393–401, Anchorage, AK, USA, June 2014.

[20] L. Qi, X. Xu, X. Zhang et al., "Structural balance theory-based E-commerce recommendation over big rating data," *IEEE Transactions on Big Data*, 2016.

[21] X. Xu, W. Dou, X. Zhang, C. Hu, and J. Chen, "A traffic hotline discovery method over cloud of things using big taxi GPS data," *Software: Practice and Experience*, vol. 47, no. 3, pp. 361–377, 2017.

[22] S. Agarwal, J. Dunagan, N. Jain, S. Saroiu, A. Wolman, and H. Bhogan, "Automated Data Placement for Geo-Distributed Cloud Services. Usenix Symposium on Networked Systems Design and Implementation," in *Proceedings of the NSDI*, pp. 17–32, San Jose, Calif, Usa, 2010.

[23] B. Yu and J. Pan, "Sketch-based data placement among geo-distributed datacenters for cloud storages," in *Proceedings of the 35th Annual IEEE International Conference on Computer Communications, IEEE INFOCOM 2016*, San Francisco, Calif, USA, April 2016.

[24] M. Su, L. Zhang, Y. Wu, K. Chen, and K. Li, "Systematic data placement optimization in multi-cloud storage for complex requirements," *Institute of Electrical and Electronics Engineers. Transactions on Computers*, vol. 65, no. 6, pp. 1964–1977, 2016.

[25] K. Bakshi, "Secure hybrid cloud computing: Approaches and use cases," in *Proceedings of the 2014 IEEE Aerospace Conference*, Big Sky, Mon, USA, March 2014.

[26] L. F. Bittencourt, E. R. M. Madeira, and N. L. S. Da Fonseca, "Scheduling in hybrid clouds," *IEEE Communications Magazine*, vol. 50, no. 9, pp. 42–47, 2012.

[27] Z. Zhou, H. Zhang, X. Du, P. Li, and X. Yu, "Prometheus: privacy-aware data retrieval on hybrid cloud," in *Proceedings of the 32nd IEEE Conference on Computer Communications (IEEE INFOCOM '13)*, pp. 2643–2651, April 2013.

[28] X. Huang and X. Du, "Achieving big data privacy via hybrid cloud," in *Proceedings of the 2014 IEEE Conference on Computer Communications Workshops, INFOCOM WKSHPS 2014*, pp. 512–517, can, May 2014.

[29] J. K. Wang and X. Jia, "Data security and authentication in hybrid cloud computing model," in *Proceedings of the 2012 IEEE Global High Tech Congress on Electronics, GHTCE 2012*, pp. 117–120, chn, November 2012.

[30] H. Abrishami, A. Rezaeian, G. K. Tousi, and M. Naghibzadeh, "Scheduling in hybrid cloud to maintain data privacy," in *Proceedings of the 5th International Conference on Innovative Computing Technology, INTECH 2015*, pp. 83–88, Galicia, Spain, May 2015.

[31] B. Zhou, F. Zhang, J. Wu, and Z. Liu, "Cost Reduction in Hybrid Clouds for Enterprise Computing," in *Proceedings of the 2017 IEEE 37th International Conference on Distributed Computing Systems Workshops (ICDCSW)*, pp. 270–274, Atlanta, GA, USA, June 2017.

[32] X. Qiu, W. L. Yeow, C. Wu, and F. C. M. Lau, "Cost-minimizing preemptive scheduling of mapreduce workloads on hybrid clouds," in *Proceedings of the 2013 IEEE/ACM 21st International Symposium on Quality of Service, IWQoS 2013*, pp. 213–218, Montreal, Canada, June 2013.

[33] A. Zinnen and T. Engel, "Deadline constrained scheduling in hybrid clouds with Gaussian processes," in *Proceedings of the 2011 International Conference on High Performance Computing and Simulation, HPCS 2011*, pp. 294–300, tur, July 2011.

[34] K. Bakshi, "Secure hybrid cloud computing: Approaches and use cases," in *Proceedings of the 2014 IEEE Aerospace Conference*, pp. 1–8, Big Sky, Mon, USA, March 2014.

11

Identification of ICS Security Risks toward the Analysis of Packet Interaction Characteristics Using State Sequence Matching Based on SF-FSM

Jianxin Xu[1,2,3] **and Dongqin Feng**[1,2,3]

[1]*Institute of Cyber-Systems and Control, Zhejiang University, Hangzhou 310027, China*
[2]*National Engineering Laboratory for Safety & Security Technology of Industrial Control System, Zhejiang University, Hangzhou 310027, China*
[3]*State Key Laboratory of Industrial Control Technology, Zhejiang University, Hangzhou 310027, China*

Correspondence should be addressed to Dongqin Feng; dongqinfeng@zju.edu.cn

Academic Editor: Mamoun Alazab

This paper discusses two aspects of major risks related to the cyber security of an industrial control system (ICS), including the exploitation of the vulnerabilities of legitimate communication parties and the features abused by unauthorized parties. We propose a novel framework for exposing the above two types of risks. A state fusion finite state machine (SF-FSM) model is defined to describe multiple request-response packet pair sequence signatures of various applications using the same protocol. An inverted index of keywords in an industrial protocol is also proposed to accomplish fast state sequence matching. Then we put forward the concept of scenario reconstruction, using state sequence matching based on SF-FSM, to present the known vulnerabilities corresponding to applications of a specific type and version by identifying the packet interaction characteristics from the data flow in the supervisory control layer network. We also implement an anomaly detection approach to identifying illegal access using state sequence matching based on SF-FSM. An anomaly is asserted if none of the state sequence signatures in the SF-FSM is matched with a packet flow. Ultimately, an example based on industrial protocols is demonstrated by a prototype system to validate the methods of scenario reconstruction and anomaly detection.

1. Introduction

Industrial control systems (ICS) are widely used at the core of national critical infrastructure and are increasingly exposed to public networks that are at risk from cyber-attacks. The control processes of oil and gas facilities, chemical processing plants, power plants, water treatment plants, traffic control systems, and so forth are becoming more vulnerable to threats originating from external networks [1, 2]. These threats not only affect the confidentiality, integrity, and availability of data but also harm the reliability, stability, and safety of physical devices. However, traditional information security solutions do not consider these situations and security may not effectively protect ICS by preventing abnormal data flows that would disrupt the manufacturing process or cause greater damage. Thus, it is necessary to promote the security level under the precondition that the data flows in the industrial control network remain unaffected and to implement some kind of passive security such as monitoring and an alert mechanism. A typical example of an attack of this nature is Stuxnet, which can be abstracted to general ICS attack process [3, 4]. The attacker firstly gains access to the control network and then, through scanning, accesses control process data. Lastly, the attacker assumes control of the ICS. Thus, the attacker would need to determine how to penetrate the ICS LAN and send instructions by industrial protocols as the key points to complete a successful attack. The research aims to address three problems related to the security of ICS. The first involves determining how to use unidirectional monitoring without affecting the original communication.

The second is to identify the inherent vulnerabilities of ICS applications and devices. The third entails detecting the function responsible for abusing the industrial protocols. Thus, we propose a framework to identify the static and dynamic risks, respectively, caused by application inherent vulnerabilities and the unauthorized behavior of intruders. We use the characteristics of a sequence of industrial protocol packets to identify the communication applications. An SF-FSM model is defined to describe the packet sequence using the state transition sequence. The state transition sequences of all the known applications using the same type of industrial protocol can be fused into one SF-FSM. Thus, we match the packet flows with a state transition sequence of the SF-FSM to identify a legitimate application to determine its vulnerabilities as well as the illegal behavior of an unauthorized application. A novel approach to perform rapid and accurate identification of a sequence of packets is also proposed.

2. Motivation and Contributions

This section presents our analysis of the key issues associated with ICS security and our approach to implementing the solutions. The contributions of this paper are also presented and then an outline is given.

2.1. Challenges and Issues of ICS Security. Because of the characteristics listed below, the implementation of ICS security solutions is highly challenging.

(A) Very few security features capable of withstanding advanced cyber-attacks are incorporated within ICS designs.

(B) Considering the importance of process-critical systems, blocking malicious data may not be a major priority.

(C) A sheer number of manufacturers, brands, series, models, and versions of ICS products with a variety of standards mean there is no unified solution.

(D) Industrial communication protocols generally are of three types: open, half-open, and proprietary. Some manufacturers attempt to promote the security level by nondisclosure protocols [5], but any implicit security protocol can be exploited easily by packet capture and reverse engineering.

(E) Physical safety is more important than information security for an online processing control system [6]. Defense procedures tend to focus on preventing physical damage rather than information leakage.

(F) Even if known vulnerabilities exist in the system, they are not easily patched, because the patches may influence the complex industrial on-site environment in uncertain ways.

(G) ICS has a long-term life cycle [7] measured in decades, after which most online systems are outside of their maintenance period or have been upgraded many times such that it would no longer be possible to integrate the documents and design principles.

(H) ICS is generally distributed in wide or dangerous areas; thus, it is not easy to research on-site data relating to the control process.

Firewalls, intrusion prevention systems, isolation gateways, and other traditional information security solutions are unsuitable given these abovementioned characteristics and risks [8]; therefore, proprietary technology and methods need to be proposed for both industrial security and safety.

Addressing ICS security problems requires the implementation of multiple phases [9] for both offline and online systems, particularly for the latter.

The core of ICS security is to protect physical assets and the production process [10], with the essential part being security-in-process. The main process medium of ICS between communication sites is data; thus, we need to overcome the risks resulting from data flow. In addition, the source and carrier of threats are also data. Therefore, data flow is important in ICS security research.

Current generic methods and ideas for specific ICS able to solve the above problems involve the characteristics of each component [11] of the system as well as discovering vulnerabilities and design flaws of products; however, from the point of view of data security, this method is equivalent to only obtaining static data relating to system security, rather than dynamic data of a system in processing. The current problem is the lack of support for on-site application data in the process of security analysis; thus, while we need to establish a channel for on-site data capturing, we also need to research the characteristics of the on-site data.

The ultimate goal of security implementation of ICS is to completely reinforce the system after exposing the system risk, of which the process is carried out in phases. The first step would entail effectively identifying both the known and unknown risks faced by the target system. The known risks are supposed to identify inherent vulnerabilities and improper configuration of the system, whereas unknown risks require data analysis based on audit, forensic, and other types of analyses to backtrack the source, trace the path, and locate the attack point of the risks, so as to generate a warning and alert mechanism that can provide evidence as motivation to strengthen the security even further.

Figure 1 shows the relationships among the ICS, data, risk, and security. The purpose of monitoring [12–14] is to identify threat behavior. The purpose of preventing is to block the threat behavior. The purpose of probing is to discover the risk.

2.2. Evolution of Security Implementation. ICS is a kind of process-critical system; hence, once the system is in the process of continuously running, usually without stopping for one year or more, even if the system poses risks, it is necessary to avoid or reduce changes to the original operating resources of the system. Therefore, when assessing the security level or attaching protection measures, the first consideration is to ensure that the changes or measures on the system have minimal impact. Additional protection could then be implemented as understanding of the target system intensifies.

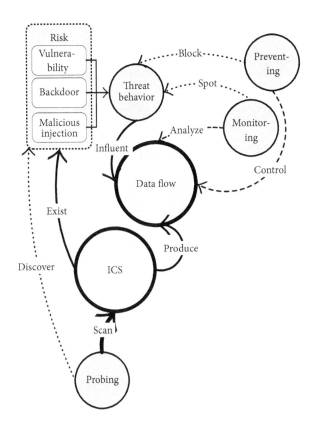

FIGURE 1: Relationships among ICS, data, risk, and security.

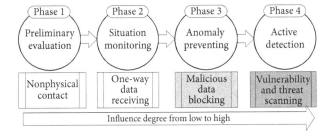

FIGURE 2: Security implementing process and influence on target system.

We divide the process of security implementation into four phases of which the degree of influence ranges from low to high, as shown in Figure 2.

Phase 1: Preliminary Evaluation. This phase evaluates the risks of the system using nonphysical contact in a static way. The risks mainly involve two aspects: inherent vulnerabilities and misconfiguration. The preliminary evaluation phase does not influence the target system.

Phase 2: Situation Monitoring. This phase is mainly based on the structure of the target system remaining unchanged and capturing and collecting network communication data

among hosts on the internal network from data access points that are deployed at key gateways or switches. Then, on the basis of data mining and forensic capability, we can analyze the security situation either manually or in automatic mode and the final result would be presented in the form of a flow statistic or anomaly alert [15]. The situation-monitoring phase only receives one-way data from the target system and therefore does not affect the target system other than deploying some bypass data access points.

Phase 3: Anomaly Preventing. This phase can use some resources and results of the previous phase, including data flow, anomaly warnings, and alerts; however, it prevents intrusion behavior and events in terms of predefined protection rules and policies, which can also be generated by the analysis of historical data and monitoring results and characteristics of situation awareness. The anomaly-preventing phase obtains the communication flow data from either bypass or trunk but needs to block the malicious packets from communication sessions once anomaly events are detected. Thus, we would have to deploy a data blocking point on the trunk that would change the network infrastructure [16] and have an impact on the data stream.

Phase 4: Active Detection. This phase can actively scan and discover potential vulnerabilities and malicious code that exists in the target system by communicating with key components of the system and finally expose risks and threats, with the ultimate ability to take the initiative to defend and repair the system. This process constructs and sends specific packets to the target system. These packets would corrupt software or devices and would be especially harmful for online systems without being tested sufficiently on the processing site. Thus, the impact level of the active detection phase is the highest and can usually be practiced in the process of product development and lifecycle testing.

The most important aspect in ICS security is to understand the risks posed by its own online processing system and to generate alerts in time when threats occur without affecting the system.

As mentioned above, the latter two phases would impact the target system, whereas the former two phases would not. The preliminary evaluation phase can be equated to static analysis as prior knowledge is generally explored manually, whereas the situation-monitoring phase can be equated to the automatic dynamic analysis of data flow. This means that the former two phases can meet the basic needs of ICS security by exposing risks and threats from both internal and external networks.

If these two phases are treated as one input/output system, then the inputs are the target system knowledge and the data flow generated by the system, and the outputs are the system risks and threat events.

2.3. Contributions and Outline. Traditional information security risk assessment [17] considers assets, vulnerabilities, and threats as the essential factors. The qualitative or quantitative risks of a target system are evaluated by analysis and calculation of these three factors. In this paper, a threat is defined as an unknown factor that only presents itself when anomaly events occur. Thus, we treat assets and vulnerabilities as input factors and as system knowledge, which can be acquired through design and deploy documents. However, when the methods in this paper are implemented as a mature product, it usually needs to occur automatically, especially when used in an unknown system; in other words, the assets and vulnerabilities need to be identified without any documents or other supported resources.

In this work, ICS assets are considered to mainly include workstations, servers, network equipment, HMIs, control devices, and field devices according to visible hardware classification, rather than on-site production equipment. The vulnerabilities that are discussed belong to these assets and are harmful to the assets only when exploited by threats.

Data flow is another important form of input to the method proposed in this paper, and it is generated by assets. For one specific system accessed by a monitor product, the only resources that can be obtained are data flow, which can be used for both identification of assets corresponding to vulnerabilities and detection of anomalies.

Overall, in the case of constrained resources, we need to reconstruct the ICS security scenarios including the characteristics of system assets to obtain full understanding of the target based on prior knowledge combined with field data and also monitor the data flow in order to be alerted to unexpected behavior.

The primary index of the reconstruction and detection process is the accuracy of the results, which means an extensive fingerprint library is required. The secondary index is the rate of identification of components and anomalies. Considering the limitation of field resources, an efficient approach needs to be proposed to solve these problems.

In this paper, we consider security risk evaluation and data flow monitoring as one of the major approaches to protect ICS in light of the key points discussed in Section 2 and show the relationships among risks, vulnerabilities, applications, and communication behavior.

A state fusion finite state machine (SF-FSM) model is proposed with the aim of analyzing the packet sequences; it is generally used to identify risks and illegal behavior, which are realized during scenario reconstruction and anomaly detection, respectively.

Several types of packet sequence are also defined and contrasted by the state machine model to describe the characteristics of industrial protocol flow and are regarded as the behavior attributes of the communication component in the software of each application.

An inverted index of keys composing the packets is applied to determine the packet type rapidly, and a set of states to each key is established to easily achieve the state triggered by the packet composed by the chained keys.

The outline of the paper is as follows. The basic communication model of ICS is abstracted and the main risks of ICS in the proposed framework, which illustrates the relationships between risks and data flow in the network of ICS, are highlighted in Section 3. Section 4 contains the data flow analysis model and a detailed description of industrial

protocol packet sequence characteristics with the finite state machine model. An approach to address the accuracy and efficiency of the packet matching is also proposed. The contents and results of scenario reconstruction within the framework and model introduced in the previous sections are provided in Section 5. The criteria of anomaly behavior are discussed in Section 6. Then we demonstrate the monitoring system and the results of an application example in Section 7, followed by the conclusions in Section 8.

3. The Proposed Framework

In this section, we analyze the ICS protocol characteristics and risks in the communication process between control stations and devices. A framework composing scenario reconstruction and anomaly detection to manage risks is described.

3.1. Basic ICS Communication Model. An industrial control system mainly includes workstations, servers, embedded controllers, and other controlling and communication devices as its components and is regarded as hosts in this framework. These hosts set up their communication connections between each other in the supervisory control layer network, which is the primary on-site data source as the main study object.

An industrial protocol is the carrier of processing direction, data flow acquisition, resource scheduling, and distribution and it is initiated by the operating system or application software installed on the host we refer to above. Furthermore, one software program may have multiple functions and can be divided into a few communication components, of which each one performs one communication task using one protocol and sets up a session of the protocol in the operation of the system.

In summary, the ICS has four major parts: host, application, communication component, and network protocol from the point of view of the supervisory control layer network under this framework. Thus, the ICS communication model can be abstracted as in Figure 3.

3.2. Risks to Be Identified. The risks associated with one ICS system include its inherent vulnerabilities and features [18] that could be used by outsiders, often with the help of a violated client or server. A violated client can be used to manipulate the control devices and damage the controlled objects. A violated server can be used to deceive the operators and the HMI with a stealthy attack. Often the server in ICS exists in the form of a controller. This is also one of the main differences with traditional Internet security that treats all business as external untrusted behavior whereas ICS treats all business as internal trusted behavior.

Therefore, our work and aim focus on two aspects. The first is to identify vulnerabilities of the hosts in the communication model and the behavior that can exploit the vulnerabilities [19]. The other is to identify behavior associated with illegal feature utilization. The features in this paper refer to the functions that attackers can use, including directly manipulating the control points of the production

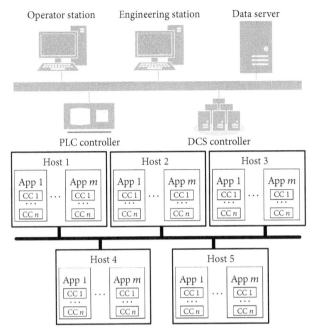

Note: App stands for application software or operating system and CC stands for communication component.

FIGURE 3: ICS supervisory control layer network and abstract model under proposed framework.

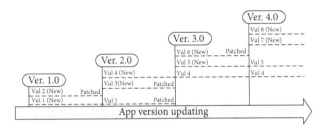

FIGURE 4: Vulnerability evolution with App updating.

equipment, such as read/write parameters from/to the control devices through specific protocol instructions, or indirect control by tampering with the configuration of a control device, such as rewriting the PLC program also through specific protocol instructions. This may not only ruin the integrity of data but also damage the physical equipment.

Vulnerability exists in software and new vulnerabilities will be revealed or be patched along with software updates [20], including those involving applications and the operating system, as shown in Figure 4. Thus, the software version needs to be identified before known vulnerabilities are listed.

Attackers can exploit the vulnerabilities of specific versions of software and can also take advantage of unprotected features to implement attacks on the ICS. Usually these features are applied through communication flows and packets, which require us to distinguish abnormal communication behavior from normal behavior. Figure 5 shows an example of normal and illegal communication behavior by means of excavating the differences between packet pair sequences. In

Figure 5(a), the normal sequence is to read from var1 to var5, whereas in Figure 5(b), the illegal sequence is to read var1 and var5, although there is no limit to this in the standard.

3.3. Rationale of the Framework. Provided the objects and risks that need to be identified have been confirmed, the framework of ICS security can be proposed as in Figure 6.

Firstly, the framework has two phases. The first phase is the identifying phase, namely, the reconstruction of security scenarios in the paper to identify applications and their version on each host. Each communication component of the application generates one or more data flows of one type of protocol that can be matched with the standard protocol. A combination of the matched data flows can be used to confirm the type and version of the application. A vulnerability list is then chosen according to this version. In this way, the scenario reconstruction phase is complete. The second phase is the monitoring phase, namely, anomaly detection to alert the user to anomalous behavior through communication data flow in the network. The anomalous behavior includes two types, that is, packets that exploit the identified vulnerabilities and the abuse of the protocol.

Secondly, the framework has two risk dimensions, including a static dimension that indicates the static risks of application inherent vulnerabilities and a dynamic dimension that indicates the dynamic risks of data flows generated by unexpected access programs or terminals. The static vulnerabilities can also be dynamically exploited by attackers constructing specific packets through the communication channel.

Thirdly, there are three essential libraries in the framework—the vulnerability library, exploitation signature library, and protocol characteristic library. The vulnerability library covers the mapping relationship between the specific version of application and vulnerabilities that need to be reconstructed in the security scenarios. Once the application version is determined, a list of vulnerabilities is selected accordingly. The exploitation signature library provides the signature of packets used by attackers to exploit the host; these signatures help us recognize a malicious packet. The protocol characteristic library maintains a characteristic table of the most common industrial protocols so as to be matched with each data flow generated by the communication component and mark it by attaching a protocol label. However, the construction of the libraries is not discussed in this paper as a prior knowledge referring to other related work.

The proposed framework, as a kind of input/output system, only accepts data flows captured in the network as input and uses applications with version information, vulnerabilities, and intrusion alerts as outputs.

Among the factors of the framework, the packet analysis of each data flow in the network, which is used for both scenario reconstruction and anomaly detection, is the most important and time consuming. This process not only considers the integrity and validity of a single packet but also checks the sequence of a series of packets.

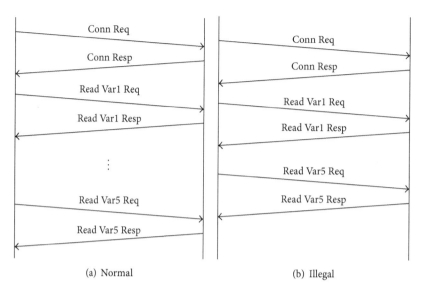

(a) Normal   (b) Illegal

FIGURE 5: Normal and illegal communication interaction sequence.

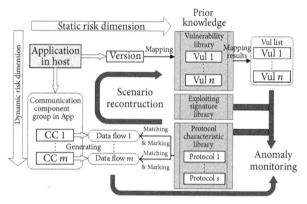

FIGURE 6: Risk identifying and monitoring framework for ICS security.

A finite state machine is a frequently used method to analyze protocol and this paper proposes the SF-FSM model to describe the packet sequence and to manage the update of the industrial protocol version.

4. Model Analysis of Data Flow

This section presents our analysis of the industrial communication process and presents the SF-FSM to describe the characteristics of the industrial protocol and communication process. An SF-FSM state matching method is also proposed to promote the efficiency of packet sequence matching.

4.1. Industrial Protocol Data Flow. Industrial communication protocols [23] and their dynamic data flows have the following characteristics:

(I) The two communicating parties constitute a client/server model, and the messages between them interact in the request/response format. A request-and-response process usually does not rely on other processes.

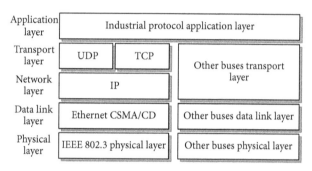

FIGURE 7: General industrial protocol stack structure.

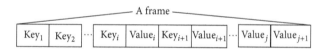

FIGURE 8: Typical industrial protocol packet structure.

(II) Industrial protocols based on Ethernet are normally over TCP/UDP (Figure 7). When using TCP to transport a message, which is generally translated from protocols based on a serial bus such as RS-485, industrial data flow is still transmitted in the form of packets, including a frame as unit instead of a stream, thus supporting compatibility. A frame of an industrial protocol is generally composed of a number of keys and values (Figure 8).

(III) Various versions of protocol standard differ from each other in terms of the addition or removal of functions, service code modification, and so on. In the case of one particular version, manufacturers, third-party developers, and open-source organizations [24] also customize their own communication components to achieve the desired messages.

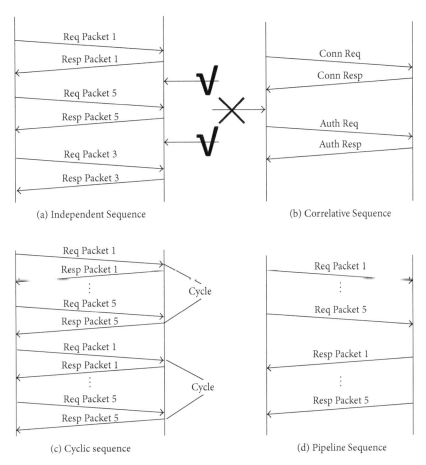

FIGURE 9: Typical sequences in industrial protocol.

(IV) From the perspective of access control, application layer connections, probably including authentication or encryption, are also incorporated in the TCP/UDP sessions.

Overall, a different combination of communication components with a specific version, of which the characteristics reflect those of a request-response packet pair and packet sequence, is used to identify the type and version of the application, whose vulnerabilities are consequently exposed.

Several packet sequences (Figure 9) are used in industrial protocols and can be described as follows:

(i) Independent sequence: an unrelated request-response packet pair, with none of the pairs depending on the other pairs, which means that this type of request-response pair sequence is not rigorously regulated by the protocol standard.

(ii) Correlative sequence: packets are transmitted in a consistent sequence by both communicating parties such as an authenticating sequence and a connection establishing sequence.

(iii) Cyclic sequence: one packet or a serial of packets with the same attributions are periodically transmitted finite or infinite times. This situation is common when reading or writing the I/O supervisory values.

(iv) Pipeline sequence: multiple request packets are continuously sent without waiting for a response packet. Pipeline requests are usually used when configuring the control devices to upload or download the program blocks.

For sequence type (ii) and type (iv), every manufacturer, third-party developer, or open-source organization has to abide by these rules, although they may take advantage of the independence of the pair of packets, for example, type (i) and type (iii), to construct their own facilitated sequences to achieve the expected features without implementing those that are undesired, which leads to the diversity of each application product and can also be used to distinguish illegal applications created by attackers.

Compared to the above scheme, the updated version of the protocol standard may add or remove protocol instructions, modify service codes, and so on, all of which can break the limitation of all sequence types and can also be compatible with the old versions.

To describe the law transforming packet sequences, this paper defines the SF-FSM model to describe the interactive state of the industrial protocol and the transition sequence.

4.2. SF-FSM Model. The finite state machine used for protocol analysis is divided into client state transition and server state transition, which are separately maintained in the client and server components.

In addition, because of characteristic (III) of industrial protocols described in Section 4.1, various components, either clients or servers, and versions implemented by numerous developers may also be given different FSM descriptions.

4.2.1. Baseline SF-FSM and State Transition Condition. The model proposed in this paper can be represented using only one finite state machine to solve the above two problems with state division and state extension.

Definition 1. A protocol packet flow FSM is mathematically modeled in this paper as a quintuple $(\Sigma, S, s_0, \delta, F)$, where

(i) S is a finite, nonempty set of states as

$$S = \{s_i\}, \quad 0 \le i \le N; \tag{1}$$

(ii) Σ is the input packet directory (a finite, nonempty set of packets) as

$$\Sigma = \{p_i\}, \quad 1 \le i \le N; \tag{2}$$

for each state s_i, there is an expected input packet directory as

$$\Sigma_{s_i} = \{p_{s_i,j}\}, \quad 1 \le j \le N,$$
$$\Sigma_{s_i} \subseteq \Sigma; \tag{3}$$

(iii) s_0 is an initial state, an element of S;

(iv) δ is the state transition function, which can be represented by a set of state transition functions from one state to another as

$$\delta = \{\delta_{s_i}(p_{s_i})\}, \quad p_{s_i} \in \Sigma_{s_i}; \tag{4}$$

and the successor state s_{suc} with the input $p_{s_i,j}$ is

$$s_{\text{suc}} = \delta_{s_i}(p_{s_i,j}), \quad p_{s_i,j} \in \Sigma_{s_i}, \ 1 \le j \le N; \tag{5}$$

(v) F is the set of final states, a (possibly empty) subset of S.

The whole state machine processes the data flow as input, of which the packets trigger the state transition. Each state in the FSM has to receive and can accept two inputs, including a request packet and a response packet, both of which are required to meet the state requirement simultaneously to trigger its transition. Thus, one type of state input in the input set Σ can be represented as a packet pair:

$$p_i = (p_{\text{req},i}, p_{\text{resp},i}). \tag{6}$$

As for the condition of accepting only one request packet, we mark the state with a transient state, which becomes a steady state after accepting the response packet, and the

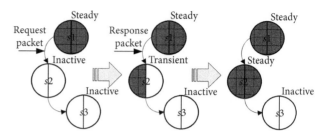

FIGURE 10: Transient and steady state transition.

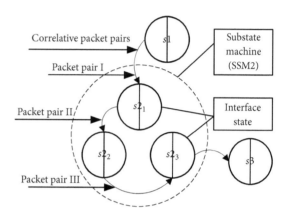

FIGURE 11: Correlative sequence and substate machine.

transition process is illustrated in Figure 10. Thus, we define the state with three substates:

$$s_i = \begin{cases} s_{ua,i}, & p_i = (\text{NULL}, \text{NULL}) \\ s_{tr,i}, & p_i = (p_{\text{req},i}, \text{NULL}) \\ s_{st,i}, & p_i = (p_{\text{req},i}, p_{\text{resp},i}). \end{cases} \tag{7}$$

4.2.2. Sub-FSM and Special State Transition of ICS Protocol. Considering packet sequence type (ii) described in Section 4.1, we propose the nested state machine as shown in Figure 11, in which substate machines are embedded into the master state machine to process the correlative packet pairs. The interface states are the only way the states in the substate machine can transition from or to the master state machine and no other states may contact the master state directly. Correlative packet pairs are input into the substate machine as a whole and each packet pair is regarded as input of the substate. The substate machine can also be integrated as a state of the master state machine and accept correlative packet pairs as state input.

Definition 2. The substate machine is defined as a quintuple:

$$(\Sigma_{\text{sub}}, S_{\text{sub}}, s_{0,\text{sub}}, \delta_{\text{sub}}, F_{\text{sub}}),$$
$$\Sigma_{\text{sub}} \subset \Sigma, \ S_{\text{sub}} \subset S, \ \delta_{\text{sub}} \subset \delta. \tag{8}$$

Obviously, the states $s_{0,\text{sub}}$ and F_{sub} are interface states of the sub-FSM.

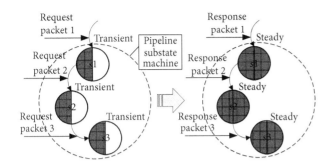

FIGURE 12: Dual state and pipeline state transition.

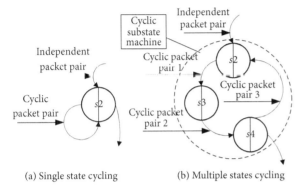

(a) Single state cycling　　　(b) Multiple states cycling

FIGURE 13: Single and multiple cycling state transition.

(1) Pipeline Substate Machine. Using the dual state in Figure 10 and substate machine in Figure 11 enables us to manage the pipeline sequence and regard the packet pairs in the pipeline as input of the substate machine. Each request packet in the pipeline sequence triggers a substate transition to a transient state until all requests are input; then the response packets are input successively and trigger the steady states as shown in Figure 12. Therefore, another type of state input in the input set Σ can be represented as a list of packet pairs given by

$$p_i = \left(\left(p_{\text{req},i1}, p_{\text{req},i2}, \ldots, p_{\text{req},ij} \right), \right.$$
$$\left. \left(p_{\text{resp},i1}, p_{\text{resp},i1}, \ldots, p_{\text{resp},ij} \right) \right). \tag{9}$$

(2) Cyclic Substate Machine. There are two types of cyclic packet sequences, including a single packet pair and multiple packet pairs; namely, each of the sequences, respectively, triggers single state cycling (Figure 13(a)) and multiple state cycling (Figure 13(b)), of which the latter can bundle the cyclic states into a cyclic substate machine in order to be described conveniently.

4.2.3. State Fusion Process. We fuse the FSMs of the protocol communication component with various versions by proposing an extension approach as shown in Figure 14.

Before we construct the FSM, we need to prepare some prior knowledge.

Prior Knowledge 1. The packet sequences of each type and version of communication components composing applications and the differences that are used to distinguish them from

each other are needed in advance. Each client and server may have a different type or version of protocol implementation but they need to be compatible with each other before they can be represented in one FSM.

We first construct the baseline FSM by selecting the original version of the manufacturer applications, including the client and server. To extend the FSM, either a new state is added with new paths or a new path is added using the original states, and so on, as additional FSMs are fused. This happens when the version on either the client side or server side is updated or changed to another type of application. The changes can be summarized as the following aspects and consequently the FSM can be extended.

(A) If the trigger condition of one state to the follow-up state is changed (in other words, the packet pair is changed, mainly because of the content of the request or response being changed), we add a new state and appropriate paths to the FSM as in Figure 14(c).

(B) If an independent packet pair is inserted into an original packet sequence, then we add a new state and appropriate paths to the FSM as in Figure 14(c).

(C) If an independent packet pair is removed from an original packet sequence, then we add a new path from the predecessor to the successor of the removed state as in Figure 14(b).

The FSM extension process is to fuse two or more FSMs essentially.

Definition 3. Consider the case in which two FSMs are fused; we provide the baseline FSM $(\Sigma_b, S_b, s_{b,0}, \delta_b, F_b)$ and the updated FSM $(\Sigma_u, S_u, s_{u,0}, \delta_u, F_u)$. Then for the new SF-FSM $(\Sigma_e, S_e, s_{e,0}, \delta_e, F_e)$, we obtain

$$\Sigma_e = \Sigma_b \cup \Sigma_u, \tag{10}$$

$$S_e = S_b \cup S_u, \tag{11}$$

$$s_{e,0} = s_{b,0} = s_{u,0}, \tag{12}$$

$$\delta_e = \delta_b \cup \delta_u, \tag{13}$$

$$F_e = F_b \cup F_u. \tag{14}$$

Here it should be noted that δ_e in (13) may have two state transition functions δ_{b,s_i} and δ_{u,s_i} for one state s_i if the two functions are inconsistent.

In addition, changes in the states and paths of the substate machine do not affect the master state machine; hence, the substate and master state machines can be fused separately without affecting each other.

4.3. Relationship of States and Components. After the FSMs are constructed and fused, we need to establish the relationship between state sequences and the communication component type and version.

We create a mapping table such as Table 1 to assign a unique identification to each type and version of the communication component, which is associated with the states the

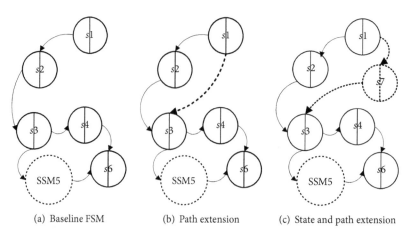

(a) Baseline FSM   (b) Path extension   (c) State and path extension

FIGURE 14: Baseline FSM and extension.

TABLE 1: Mapping of component and identification.

Communication component		Identification
Type	Version	
Own equipment manufacturer client	V1.0	1
	V2.0	2
Own equipment manufacturer server	V1.0	3
Third-party developer client	V1.0	4
Open source server	V1.0	5
⋮	⋮	⋮

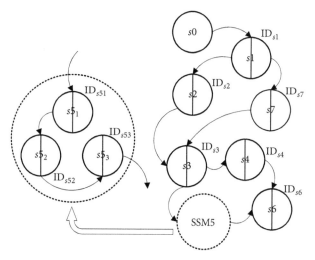

FIGURE 15: States with identification set.

FSM of the component of a specific type or version contains, while each state in the SF-FSM also maintains two sets of identifications mapped separately with the types and versions of the communication client and server.

Through every state transition we obtain two new sets of identifications. We ensure that a unique identification pair of the client and server can be obtained by taking the intersection of all the sets of a state transition sequence until a complete state transition signature sequence is successfully matched by the captured packet flow. The identification, that is, the type and version of the communication component, is not only related to the combination of the states in sequence, but also related to the order in which the states undergo transition; thus we choose the sequence of states as the signatures.

The two sets of identifications for each state are represented as follows:

$$\mathrm{ID}_{\mathrm{cli},s_i} = \left\{ \mathrm{id}_{\mathrm{cli},j} \right\}, \quad 1 \le j \le \max\left(\mathrm{ID}_{\mathrm{cli},s_i} \right),$$
$$\mathrm{ID}_{\mathrm{svr},s_i} = \left\{ \mathrm{id}_{\mathrm{svr},k} \right\}, \quad 1 \le k \le \max\left(\mathrm{ID}_{\mathrm{svr},s_i} \right). \tag{15}$$

Theorem 4. *In an SF-FSM, $\forall id_{cli} \in ID_{cli}$ ($\forall id_{svr} \in ID_{svr}$), there is one and only one state transition signature sequence $C_{id_{cli}} = \overrightarrow{\{s_i\}}$ ($C_{id_{svr}} = \overrightarrow{\{s_i\}}$) mapping with id_{cli} (id_{svr}) and $C_{id_{cli}}$ ($C_{id_{svr}}$) is an ordered set.*

In order to satisfy Theorem 4, we need to assure that each state transition signature sequence is unique after fusing the FSMs.

Theorem 5. *In an SF-FSM, the state transition sequence is a signature only when at least one δ of the sequence exists and does not exist in any other state transition sequence all of which can be mapped with a unique id.*

Actually, through a state transition signature sequence, both id_{cli} and id_{svr} can be confirmed at the same time. Hence, id_{cli} and id_{svr} can be arranged in pairs to each state in a state transition signature sequence as

$$id_{s_i} = \left(id_{cli,s_i}, id_{svr,s_i} \right). \tag{16}$$

So (15) can be replaced with (Figure 15)

$$ID_{s_i} = \left\{ id_{s_i,j} \right\} = \left\{ \left(id_{cli,s_i,j}, id_{svr,s_i,j} \right) \right\},$$
$$1 \le j \le \max\left(ID_{s_i} \right). \tag{17}$$

Moreover, the state transition signature sequence in Theorem 4 can be represented by

$$C_{id} = C_{(id_{cli}, id_{svr})} = \overrightarrow{\{s_i\}}, \quad s_i \in S_e. \tag{18}$$

Similarly, C_{id} is also an ordered set.

Theorem 6. *In an SF-FSM $(\Sigma_e, S_e, s_{e,0}, \delta_e, F_e)$, for a state transition signature sequence $C_{id} = \overrightarrow{\{s_k\}}$, k is the index of s in C_{id} and K is the number of items in C_{id}; then the unique id mapping with the C_{id} is*

$$id = \left(\cdots \left(ID_{s_1} \cap ID_{s_2} \right) \cdots \cap ID_{s_{k-1}} \right) \cap ID_{s_k}, \tag{19}$$

$$1 \le k \le K.$$

4.4. Packet Flow and State Matching. Using the SF-FSM model, we can determine the id of the communication component by matching the packet pair sequence and the state transition signature sequence.

Theorem 7. *Given a packet pair sequence $P = \overrightarrow{\{p_i\}}$ of a specific protocol and the corresponding SF-FSM, if a state transition signature sequence C_{id} is hit by the input P, then id of communication component which generates P is determined.*

Then (19) can be equivalent to

$$id = \left(\cdots \left(ID_{\delta_{s_0}(p_0)} \cap ID_{\delta_{\delta_{s_0}(p_0)}(p_1)} \right) \right.$$

$$\left. \cap ID_{\delta_{\delta_{\delta_{s_0}(p_0)(p_1)}(p_2)}} \cdots \right). \tag{20}$$

If the result is ununique or null, then the matching is considered to have failed.

A number of key words can be taken from the industrial protocol packet with reference to the packet structure in Figure 8. The efficiency of the packet flow matching is improved by constructing an inverted index list of keys to identify packets and the state sequence.

An inverted index is usually used in fast full text searches, of which the keys are not in a predictable position. However, for a packet, the offset of a key is definitely known; thus we can index the keys according to the offset.

In this paper, we are only interested in the packet type, which is determined by the keys composing the packet, rather than the other parts of the packet because we do not inspect the content. We can therefore regard the packet pair as well as the input of the state in SF-FSM as a set of keys.

Definition 8. The packet pair, namely, the expected input $p_i \in \Sigma_e$ of a state in an SF-FSM can be defined as

$$p_i = \left\{ \text{key}_{p_i,1}, \text{key}_{p_i,2}, \ldots, \text{key}_{p_i,j} \right\}$$

$$= \left\{ \left(\text{offset}_{p_i,1}, \text{value}_{p_i,1} \right), \left(\text{offset}_{p_i,2}, \text{value}_{p_i,2} \right), \tag{21} \right.$$

$$\left. \cdots \left(\text{offset}_{p_i,j}, \text{value}_{p_i,j} \right) \right\}, \quad 1 \le j \le N.$$

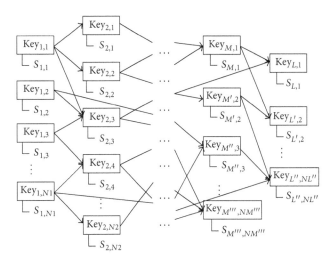

FIGURE 16: Chained inverted index of protocol keys.

For each state, $p_{s_i,j} \in \Sigma_{s_i}$ can be represented by

$$p_{s_i,j} = \left\{ \text{key}_{p_{s_i,j},1}, \text{key}_{p_{s_i,j},2}, \ldots, \text{key}_{p_{s_i,j},k} \right\}. \tag{22}$$

As described above, if all the keys of an input packet pair are matched with (22), then the SF-FSM can be triggered from s_i to the successor state.

Assumption 9. For all $p_i \in \Sigma_e$, any key set of p_i in a specific sequence differs from other sequences.

Prior Knowledge 2. On the basis of Assumption 9, p_i is unique but the key is not unique. Different packets may have the same key at the same offset or different offset and, similarly, the same offset may have a different key.

Theorem 10. *We set up a chained inverted index of keys (Figure 16), of which each one points to the next keys in all p_i and has an attribute of state information, which is represented as $S_{key} = \{s_i\}$, $1 \le i \le N$. From each head key to the tail key through the chain, we can obtain p_i that triggers the SF-FSM from the current state to the next, where the next state is the intersection of S_{key} of all the keys traversed in the chain.*

Normally, if a $\text{key}_{p_{s_i,j},k}$ chain such as that in (22) is matched, then $p_{s_i,j}$ is determined and the next state can be achieved by $s_{\text{suc}} = \delta_{s_i}(p_{s_i,j})$ from (5).

However, referring to Theorem 10, the successor state is

$$s_{suc} = \left(\cdots \left(S_{key_{p_{s_i,j},1}} \cap S_{key_{p_{s_i,j},2}} \right) \cdots \cap S_{key_{p_{s_i,j},k-1}} \right)$$

$$\cap S_{key_{p_{s_i,j},k}}. \tag{23}$$

Thus, we can use the inverted index of keys instead of the transition function to achieve the successor state in the SF-FSM.

Based on all of the above, in the case of a new type or version of the component presented, extension of the current

TABLE 2: Expected results of reconstruction.

Host	Application	Communication component	Vulnerability
H A	App a	CC 1	Vul (1)
			Vul (2)
	App b	CC 2	Vul (3)
H B	App c	CC 3	Vul (4)
		CC 4	Vul (5)
	App d	CC 5	
H C	App e	CC 6	Vul (6)
		CC 7	Vul (7)
			Vul (8)
	App f	CC 8	Vul (9)
			Vul (10)

SF-FSM only requires extension of the set of keys and their link relationships.

5. Scenario Reconstruction

As discussed in Section 3.2, scenario reconstruction aims to identify vulnerabilities of a target industrial control system by analyzing the data flow captured in the supervisory control layer network and the advantages of this method are passive, accurate, and extendable.

The results (Table 2 as an example) of scenario reconstruction mainly include vulnerabilities of applications in every host as illustrated in Figure 3.

Table 2 reveals clear correspondences between the applications and vulnerabilities, whereas there is no correspondence between the communication components and the vulnerabilities. Each combination of components corresponds with an application of determined type and version.

Prior knowledge, including prior knowledge 1 in Section 4.2 and prior knowledge 2 in Section 4.4, is necessary to accomplish the expected security scenarios of a specific ICS.

Prior Knowledge 3. The protocols and the communication components the various applications of ICS use is prior knowledge to identify the applications on the hosts.

Prior Knowledge 4. Each packet structure of the protocol the application uses is prior knowledge and the keys and the key sets used to distinguish the packets are also prior knowledge as the protocol characteristic library in Figure 6. However, how to extract the keys is beyond the range of this paper.

Prior Knowledge 5. The vulnerability lists of the specific type and version of applications are prior knowledge as the vulnerability library in Figure 6. The vulnerability information can be achieved on CVE (Common Vulnerabilities and Exposures) or other databases.

Before reconstruction, we need to make some assumptions to facilitate the process in order to adapt the SF-FSM in Section 4.2.

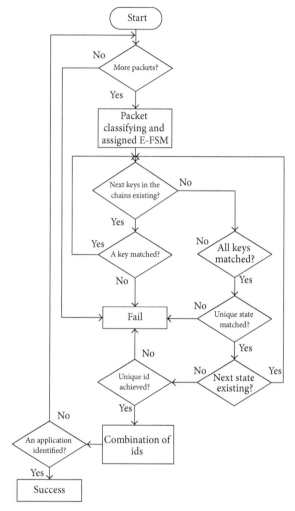

FIGURE 17: Flow chart of scenario reconstruction.

Assumption 11. Each host has an independent function and none of the hosts carry two or more applications for internal communication. This assumption assures that all the data flows exist in the network and can be captured.

Assumption 12. Each session of data flows can be captured from the first packet; in other words, the SF-FSM can be matched from the first state transition.

Assumption 13. Each session of captured data flows can cover a whole packet pair sequence that triggers the state transition and achieves a unique id indicating the component type and version.

Given an integrated packet flow, the process of scenario reconstruction is as shown in Figure 17.

6. Anomaly Detection

After the scenario reconstruction process, the type and version of each application on a host are determined and, accordingly, the list of vulnerabilities (prior knowledge 5) and the expected packet sequence signatures (Theorem 4) are determined. These are the necessary conditions to implement anomaly detection in Section 3.3.

To protect the ICS from potential risks caused by vulnerabilities, we need to know the approach used by the intruder exploiting the vulnerabilities as prior knowledge.

Prior Knowledge 6. The characteristics of packets, often known as PoC (proof of concept), the intruder use to exploit the vulnerabilities are prior knowledge needed as the exploitation signature library in Figure 6.

In this way we obtain the following anomaly criterion.

Theorem 14. *An application of which the type and version have been determined and the exploitation packet signatures are then determined according to prior knowledge 6. An alert is triggered if a captured packet is matched with the exploitation packet signatures.*

We protect the ICS from potential risks caused by abuse of the packet sequence by judging whether the packet flows are legal in terms of the level of expected packet sequence matching.

Theorem 15. *The type and version of an application can be determined after the packet sequence of each of the communication components used by the application is determined according to Theorem 4. Then the key chains are achieved as Figure 16. An alert is triggered if any of the following conditions are met:*

(a) *None of the keys is matched in the chains.*

(b) *None of the next keys in the chains is matched unless the tail of the chain is reached.*

(c) *All the keys in the chains are matched but the state determined by the matched keys is not the expected one in the state transition sequence.*

Ultimately, under the framework proposed in this paper, two aspects of anomalies are monitored:

(a) *Illegal applications, including clients, servers, and abused features, are discovered by analyzing the data flow.*

(b) *Vulnerability exploitation is detected with a lower cost of signature matching for the known existing vulnerabilities without regard to nonexisting ones.*

7. Experiment

In this section, we introduce a monitoring system and demonstrate a few case studies and experiments to verify the availability of the methods in this paper. Attention is fixed on the accuracy of application identification, which is the chief factor affecting the results of scenario reconstruction and anomaly detection.

7.1. Prototype System and Verification Environment. We present a prototype system matching the criteria of the intrusion detection system [25]. The system is connected to the supervisory control layer of an ICS network and access the

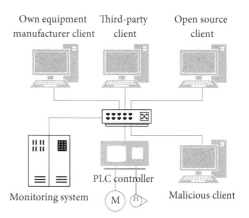

FIGURE 18: Experimental system and environment.

network traffic unidirectionally that can minimize the impact on the target system under monitoring.

The prototype system is based on an industrial controlling computer, on which CentOS, an operating system based on the Linux kernel, is installed. The application software framework is based on ntop [26], which is a monitoring system supporting hundreds of application layer protocols but not industrial protocols. We added some plugin modules of typical industrial protocols. The prototype system provides two interfaces, one for configuration management and for showing the results of monitoring and the other connected to the mirroring-interface of the switch for achieving data flows in the supervisory control layer network.

The prototype system implements the main functions and verifies the methods proposed in this paper as follows.

(a) The communication parties in the network can be identified from the basic session information, including the protocol type, client address, and server address. Then a virtual network relationship model can be constructed.

(b) The type of client can be identified according to packet interaction sequences in the respective session. The types of clients include own equipment manufacturer ones, certified third-party clients, and open source clients. The client version and the type and version of server are not scheduled for evaluation in this section. Then the vulnerabilities of the identified client can be assessed on the vulnerability publishing platform, such as CVE [27] and ICS-CERT [28].

(c) We construct an attack process by developing a client that meets the protocol specification to evaluate the detection capability of the monitoring system.

The structure of the verification environment is shown in Figure 18. We added a motor and a flowmeter as the controlled plant. The validation process includes two steps.

After the monitoring system is linked to the network, the first step is to construct the normal data flows in the network by using each client to configure the PLC controller and upload the configuration of the PLC controller. Then we manipulate the motor by writing the specific output of the

TABLE 3: Multiple types of Ethernet/IP client.

Protocol	Own equipment manufacturer client	Third-party client	Open source client
Ethernet/IP	RSLogix 5000	Molex EIP_Tools [21]	EPICS Tools [22]

I/O module and acquire the flowmeter value by reading the corresponding input of the I/O module. The result of the step is to identify the type of each client by the monitoring system.

The second step links the malicious client to the network and then executes the same operation as the other clients. The result of this step is to identify the malicious client and trigger the alert.

The packets can be captured and saved in the monitoring system to enable us to verify the results.

We provide an example of a typical industrial protocol and construct the circumstance to validate the methods and prototype system in the next two subsections.

7.2. Case Study with Ethernet/IP Protocol. In this circumstance, we provide an example of Ethernet/IP protocol supported by the Open DeviceNet Vendor Association (ODVA) [29]. The clients to be identified are listed in Table 3. The model of the PLC controller is a ControlLogix 1756-L62 and the communication module is 1756-ENBT/A.

Accessing data within the controller by the client using a protocol message typically contains the following address information:

(i) Device network address

(ii) Class ID

(iii) Instance ID

(iv) Attribute ID

(v) Service code (describing the action/service required)

When we download or upload the configurations of the PLC controller, we write or read the value of various combinations of the above address information. Thus for each client, the combinations and sequences of the address information may be different.

7.2.1. Signature Extraction for Client Identification. Before we use the SF-FSM to formalize the packet sequences of the clients, we extract the communication characteristics of each client with the Ethernet/IP protocol in terms of the four types discussed in Section 4.1 and provide one example of each type with the packet captured. The type of sequence in Ethernet/IP is related to the class ID, instance ID, attribute ID, and service code. Figure 19 shows the captured sequences (screenshot from Wireshark) generated by different clients.

(a) Independent Sequence. Most classes (such as Class 0x01, and 0x69) and instances used according to a specific service code (such as 0x03, and 0x52) in Ethernet/IP are independent and thus the client can access any class by an independent

request packet. This characteristic exists in the communication interaction of all the clients. Except for RSLogix 5000, all the independent sequences can be regarded as a list of correlative sequences in the configuration process because the configuration downloading process cannot be segmented into separated steps.

(b) Correlative Sequence. This sequence signature can be regarded as a list of service codes and classes with an independent relationship combined compulsively by the client or the manufacturer customized service codes combination. An example of the latter case is illustrated in Figure 19(a). This sequence is the process of authentication between RSLogix 5000 and 1756-ENBT/A, and the service codes (0x5C, 0x4B, 0x4C) and class ID (0x8E, 0x64) used in this process are also customized by the manufacturer. Thus this sequence can be regarded as a signature of the RSLogix 5000 application.

(c) Cyclic Sequence. If the client needs to keep the linkage with the PLC controller, it would acquire the status of the PLC cyclically. Figure 19(b) shows RSLogix 5000 requiring the status of 1756-L62 using the service code of a multiple service request (0x0A) and multiple class IDs (0x01, 0x69, 0xAC, 0x70, etc.) and the process is repeated constantly until we quit the application. However, the other clients do not need to maintain the connection and do not have this sequence signature.

(d) Pipeline Sequence. Figure 19(c) also shows a case of the RSLogix 5000 signature. The client sends two requests consecutively to start the process of communication. However, the other clients would not respond. Another special type of pipeline sequence in the Ethernet/IP protocol is a multiple service request with the code 0x0A, which is implemented to process a few service requests simultaneously by RSLogix 5000.

Based on the classification of the sequence signatures belonging to different clients, we summarize the minimum set of each type of signature with the specific client in Table 4 and provide examples of the signatures in Table 5. The basic principle is that there is no intersection of signatures among the clients.

7.2.2. Experiment Results. Based on the general communication process of the Ethernet/IP protocol, we constructed the baseline SF-FSM in the monitoring system and extended the SF-FSM with the states that are exclusive for each client according to the respective sequence signature. The key chains of service codes, class IDs, instance IDs, and attribute IDs in the signature sequence packets were also constructed and linked with the state in the SF-FSM.

The experiment network architecture is deployed as shown in Figure 18. The IP address of the PLC (1756-L62) is 192.168.0.1.

We use the three legitimate clients listed in Table 3 to execute the operation of reading an attribute defined in the configuration of the PLC. The IP addresses of the three clients are 192.168.0.2, 192.168.0.3, and 192.168.0.4, respectively.

```
166 Unknown Service (0x5c)
104 Success
403 Unknown Service (0x4b)
104 Partial transfer
106 Unknown Service (0x4b)
104 Partial transfer
106 Unknown Service (0x4b)
234 Success
128 Unknown Service (0x4c)
104 Partial transfer
128 Unknown Service (0x4c)
136 Success
```

(a) Correlative sequence

```
 78 List Services (Req)
 78 List Interfaces (Req)
104 List Services (Rsp), Communications
 80 List Interfaces (Rsp)
 82 Register Session (Req), Session: 0x00000000
 82 Register Session (Rsp), Session: 0x13020500
114 Unconnected Send: Get Attribute All
133 Success
120 Unconnected Send: Get Attribute List
114 Success
114 Unconnected Send: Get Attribute All
190 Success
114 Unconnected Send: Get Attribute All
190 Success
120 Unconnected Send: Get Attribute List
112 Success
```

(c) Pipeline sequence

```
356 Multiple Service Packet,   | Get Attribute List,   | Get Attribute List,   | Get Attribute List,
486 Success,   | Success,   | Success,   | Success,   | Success,   | Success,   | Success,   | Success,
356 Multiple Service Packet,   | Get Attribute List,   | Get Attribute List,   | Get Attribute List,
486 Success,   | Success,   | Success,   | Success,   | Success,   | Success,   | Success,   | Success,
110 Get Attribute List
114 Success
```

(b) Cyclic sequence

FIGURE 19: Sequence types in Ethernet/IP.

TABLE 4: Sequence signatures statistics of clients.

Type of sequence signature	RSLogix 5000	Molex EIP_Tools	EPICS Tools
Independent sequence signature	0	1	1
Correlative sequence signature	3	2	1
Cyclic sequence signature	2	0	0
Pipeline sequence signature	1	0	0

TABLE 5: Examples of signatures.

Type of sequence signature	Examples	Client belonging to
Independent sequence signature	List Identity (Req)	Molex EIP_Tools
Correlative sequence signature	Customized Service 0x5C (Req) Customized Service 0x4B (Req) Customized Service 0x4B (Req) Customized Service 0x4B (Req) Customized Service 0x4C (Req) Customized Service 0x4C (Req)	RSLogix 5000
Cyclic sequence signature	Multiple Service Packet, | Get Attribute List	RSLogix 5000
Pipeline sequence signature	List Services (Req) List Interfaces (Req)	RSLogix 5000

One malicious client developed by Visual studio 2010 was installed on the host with IP address 192.168.0.12. The malicious client was assumed to be used by the attacker who intended to write the attribute value in the configuration of the PLC. The attribute altered by the attacker is used for alias tag definition in 1756-L62. If the alias tag is renamed and quoted by the following code text, the attack could manipulate the desired control point of the physical equipment without affecting the surveillance point, which might be displayed on the HMI, so as to implement a stealth attack.

All the data flows of each client corresponding to the operations were captured and analyzed by the monitoring system; this system then output the results of client identification and anomaly detection.

(1) Effectiveness Analysis. The monitoring results are shown in Figure 20 in the form of logs. Three "Info" level logs were maintained to indicate the legitimate clients, which were marked by the type of application software. These "Info" level logs can be regarded as the results of the scenario reconstruction process. In this experiment, we mainly analyzed the

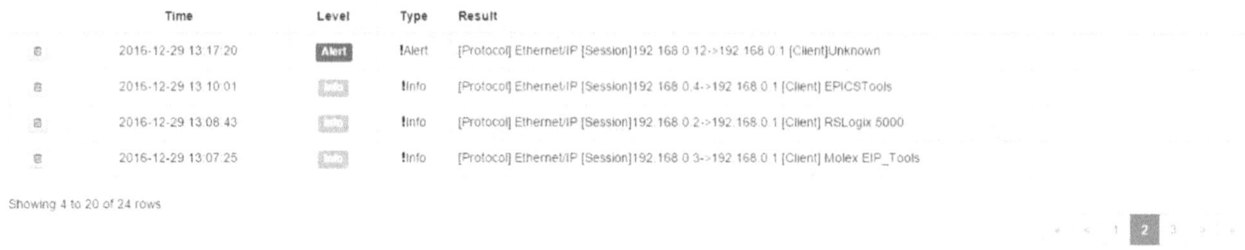

	Time	Level	Type	Result
📄	2016-12-29 13:17:20	Alert	!Alert	[Protocol] Ethernet/IP [Session]192.168.0.12->192.168.0.1 [Client]Unknown
📄	2016-12-29 13:10:01	Info	!Info	[Protocol] Ethernet/IP [Session]192.168.0.4->192.168.0.1 [Client] EPICSTools
📄	2016-12-29 13:08:43	Info	!Info	[Protocol] Ethernet/IP [Session]192.168.0.2->192.168.0.1 [Client] RSLogix 5000
📄	2016-12-29 13:07:25	Info	!Info	[Protocol] Ethernet/IP [Session]192.168.0.3->192.168.0.1 [Client] Molex EIP_Tools

Showing 4 to 20 of 24 rows

« ‹ 1 **2** 3 › »

FIGURE 20: Monitoring results.

client side, so the logs from the server side (namely PLC in the current circumstance) information were filtered out.

One "Alert" level log was maintained to indicate the malicious client, which was marked by unknown type.

The judgement principle of various clients is if all the sequence signatures belonging to each client as shown in Table 4 is hit by the communication session established by client and PLC server.

If none of the sequence signatures is hit by the session, the client can be marked with unknown client. If one or more but not all of the sequence signatures belonging to one client are hit by the session, the client can be marked with unknown client. If two or more sequence signatures belonging to different clients are hit by the session, the client can be marked with unknown client.

The matching hit of each signature is not displayed on the user interface of the monitoring system, but we can access the results through the background interface. We can ensure that the client with IP address 192.168.0.2 hits all the six sequence signatures of RSLogix 5000, the client with IP address 192.168.0.3 hits all the three sequence signatures of Molex EIP_Tools, and the client with IP address 192.168.0.4 hits all the two sequence signatures of EPICSTools. The client with IP address 192.168.0.12, on the other hand, hits two sequence signatures of RSLogix 5000 and one sequence signature of Molex EIP_Tools.

(2) Performance Analysis. The performance of the monitoring system can be measured from two aspects. One is the packet matching efficiency. The other is the client identification efficiency.

The packet matching efficiency is usually evaluated by the average time of packet handling. However, in this experiment, the packet generation rate by the clients is not very high and far below the handling rate of the monitoring system. Therefore, we did not achieve the average time, but we could achieve the average packet handling delay. We added an interface of the monitoring system to output the packets already handled. Then, we employed a PC to capture the input and output packets simultaneously and calculate each packet handling delay. An average delay of 0.132 ms was achieved.

The client identification efficiency depends on the clients' communication execution period. Once the session is finished or all the sequence signatures of one client are hit, the identification result can be generated immediately with the type of matched client. If the sequence signatures of two or more clients are hit, the identification result can also be generated immediately with the type of unknown client.

8. Conclusion

This paper proposed a state fusion finite state machine model in terms of the analysis of the characteristics of industrial data flow. In addition, a packet matching approach to expose the risks of a specific target industrial control system by identifying vulnerabilities and anomalous behavior was also proposed. A framework for the reconstruction of security scenarios and anomaly detection using the SF-FSM model was also conceptualized. A verification system was also developed to demonstrate the examples using the proposed methods in this paper.

In future studies, we aim to attach a larger number of attributes to the state of SF-FSM to promote the accuracy and efficiency of the packet sequence and propose an approach to address the prevention of risks. Further, the storage space of the knowledge libraries should also be considered to conserve hardware resources in the form of embedded systems in practical applications.

Acknowledgments

This work is supported by National Natural Science Foundation of China under Grant 61433006.

References

[1] M. Cheminod, L. Durante, and A. Valenzano, "Review of security issues in industrial networks," *IEEE Transactions on Industrial Informatics*, vol. 9, no. 1, pp. 277–293, 2013.

[2] H. M. Leith and J. W. Piper, "Identification and application of security measures for petrochemical industrial control systems," *Journal of Loss Prevention in the Process Industries*, vol. 26, no. 6, pp. 982–993, 2013.

[3] https://ics-cert.us-cert.gov/content/overview-cyber-vulnerabilities.

[4] https://www.codeproject.com/KB/web-security/StuxnetMalware/Stuxnet_Malware_Analysis_Paper.pdf.

[5] K. Stouffer, J. Falco, and K. Scarfone, "GUIDE to industrial control systems (ICS) security," *NIST Special Publication*, vol. 800, no. 82, p. 16, 2011.

[6] A. Cardenas, S. Amin, B. Sinopoli, A. Giani, A. Perrig, and S. Sastry, "Challenges for securing cyber physical systems," in *Proceedings of the Workshop on Future Directions in Cyber-Physical Systems Security*, p. 5, Newark, NJ, USA, July 2009.

[7] R. Leszczyna, "Approaching secure industrial control systems," *IET Information Security*, vol. 9, no. 1, pp. 81–89, 2015.

[8] INL, *Common Cyber Security Vulnerabilities Observed in Control System Assessments by the INL NSTB Program*, Idaho National Laboratory, Idaho Falls, Idaho, USA, 2008.

[9] R. R. R. Barbosa, R. Sadre, and A. Pras, "Flow whitelisting in SCADA networks," *International Journal of Critical Infrastructure Protection*, vol. 6, no. 3-4, pp. 150–158, 2013.

[10] N. Sayegh, A. Chehab, I. H. Elhajj, and A. Kayssi, "Internal security attacks on SCADA systems," in *Proceedings of the 3rd International Conference on Communications and Information Technology (ICCIT '13)*, pp. 22–27, IEEE, Beirut, Lebanon, June 2013.

[11] T. Vollmer, M. Manic, and O. Linda, "Autonomic intelligent cyber-sensor to support industrial control network awareness," *IEEE Transactions on Industrial Informatics*, vol. 10, no. 2, pp. 1647–1658, 2014.

[12] L. Wang, S. Ren, B. Korel, K. A. Kwiat, and E. Salerno, "Improving system reliability against rational attacks under given resources," *IEEE Transactions on Systems, Man, and Cybernetics: Systems*, vol. 44, no. 4, pp. 446–456, 2014.

[13] C.-W. Ten, G. Manimaran, and C.-C. Liu, "Cybersecurity for critical infrastructures: attack and defense modeling," *IEEE Transactions on Systems, Man, and Cybernetics Part A:Systems and Humans*, vol. 40, no. 4, pp. 853–865, 2010.

[14] H. Janicke, A. Nicholson, S. Webber, and A. Cau, "Runtime-monitoring for industrial control systems," *Electronics*, vol. 4, no. 4, pp. 995–1017, 2015.

[15] P. García-Teodoro, J. Díaz-Verdejo, G. Maciá-Fernández, and E. Vázquez, "Anomaly-based network intrusion detection: techniques, systems and challenges," *Computers and Security*, vol. 28, no. 1-2, pp. 18–28, 2009.

[16] B. Galloway and G. P. Hancke, "Introduction to industrial control networks," *IEEE Communications Surveys and Tutorials*, vol. 15, no. 2, pp. 860–880, 2013.

[17] G. Stoneburner, A. Y. Goguen, and A. Feringa, "Risk management guide for information technology systems," Tech. Rep. SP 800-30, National Institute of Standards & Technology, Gaithersburg, Md, USA, 2002.

[18] S.-J. Kim, D.-E. Cho, and S.-S. Yeo, "Secure model against APT in m-connected SCADA network," *International Journal of Distributed Sensor Networks*, vol. 10, no. 6, Article ID 594652, 2014.

[19] N. Sayegh, I. H. Elhajj, A. Kayssi, and A. Chehab, "SCADA Intrusion Detection System based on temporal behavior of frequent patterns," in *Proceedings of the 17th IEEE Mediterranean Electrotechnical Conference (MELECON '14)*, pp. 432–438, IEEE, Beirut, Lebanon, April 2014.

[20] T. Nelso and M. Chaffin, "Common cybersecurity vulnerabilities in industrial control systems. Control Systems Security Program," Tech. Rep., Idaho National Laboratory, 2011, https://ics-cert.us-cert.gov/sites/default/files/recommended_practices/DHS_Common_Cybersecurity_Vulnerabilities_ICS_2010.pdf.

[21] http://www.molex.com/mx_upload/superfamily/iccc/EtherNet_IPTool.html.

[22] https://github.com/EPICSTools/ether_ip.

[23] J.-D. Decotignie, "Ethernet-based real-time and industrial communications," *Proceedings of the IEEE*, vol. 93, no. 6, pp. 1102–1117, 2005.

[24] A. Mahboob and J. A. Zubairi, "Securing SCADA systems with open source software," in *Proceedings of the 10th International Conference on High Capacity Optical Networks and Emerging/Enabling Technologies (HONET-CNS '13)*, pp. 193–198, December 2013.

[25] V. Jyothsna, V. V. Rama Prasad, and K. Munivara Prasad, "A review of anomaly based intrusion detection systems," *International Journal of Computer Applications*, vol. 28, no. 7, pp. 26–35, 2011.

[26] http://www.ntop.org/.

[27] https://cve.mitre.org.

[28] https://ics-cert.us-cert.gov.

[29] https://www.odva.org/Portals/0/Library/Publications_Numbered/PUB00213R0_EtherNetIP_Developers_Guide.pdf.

12

Relay Selections for Security and Reliability in Mobile Communication Networks over Nakagami-m Fading Channels

Hongji Huang, Wanyou Sun, Jie Yang, and Guan Gui

College of Telecommunication and Information, Nanjing University of Posts and Telecommunications, Nanjing, China

Correspondence should be addressed to Guan Gui; guiguan@njupt.edu.cn

Academic Editor: Guangjie Han

This paper studies the relay selection schemes in mobile communication system over Nakagami-m channel. To make efficient use of licensed spectrum, both single relay selection (SRS) scheme and multirelays selection (MRS) scheme over the Nakagami-m channel are proposed. Also, the intercept probability (IP) and outage probability (OP) of the proposed SRS and MRS for the communication links depending on realistic spectrum sensing are derived. Furthermore, this paper assesses the manifestation of conventional direct transmission scheme to compare with the proposed SRS and MRS ones based on the Nakagami-m channel, and the security-reliability trade-off (SRT) performance of the proposed schemes and the conventional schemes is well investigated. Additionally, the SRT of the proposed SRS and MRS schemes is demonstrated better than that of direct transmission scheme over the Nakagami-m channel, which can protect the communication transmissions against eavesdropping attacks. Additionally, simulation results show that our proposed relay selection schemes achieve better SRT performance than that of conventional direct transmission over the Nakagami-m channel.

1. Introduction

Cognitive radio (CR) [1] is considered as one of the most promising technologies to significantly improve spectrum utilization [2]. According to obtained information in different environments, transmission parameters, such as frequency, transmission power, modulation, and bandwidth, can be adaptively changed in CR networks [3]. Based on the highly dynamic nature existing in architecture of CR networks, however, legitimate CR devices expose themselves to both internal and external attackers. The security problem is urgent to solve in order to devise dependable CR networks. Hence, the security problems of CR network [4–6] have attracted great attention in both academia and industry. Security and reliability are two vital indexes of communication systems, but they fail to have good performance simultaneously in many cases. Therefore, it is of great significance to enhance the security-reliability trade-off (SRT) [7] performance based on the CR network.

Physical-layer security is regarded as one of effective approaches to improve the security of the wireless communications. On the one hand, point-to-point (P2P) transmission

techniques, such as MIMO diversity [8], jamming [9], and beamforming [10], have been developed in order to improve dependable wireless links. Also, since localization provides fundamental support for many location-aware protocols and applications in the communication networks, it is one of the key technologies in wireless sensor networks (WSNs) [11]. For the purpose of improving localization accuracy and energy consumption aspects which are essential factors of designing mobile communication network, a novel algorithm considering the aftermath of disasters based on wireless sensor networks (WSNs) was provided by Han and his colleagues [12]. As observed, in many literatures about physical-layer security, some scholars employ signal processing techniques such as the precoding and beaming to settle relevant issues aiming at obtaining better performance. Recently, an agile confidential transmission strategy combining big data driven cluster and opportunistic beamforming was well investigated [13]. On the other hand, the author in [14] explored a scenario where an eavesdropper appears to tap the transmissions of the source and the relays. Also, node cooperation is employed to overcome eavesdropping without upper layer data encryption

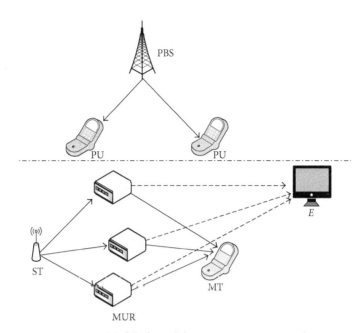

FIGURE 1: Model of a mobile communication network.

and improve the performance of secure wireless communications in the physical-layer security aspect [15]. In addition, relays selection schemes over the Rayleigh fading channel were proposed to improve the SRT performance of the CR networks [16]. However, the Rayleigh channel fails to be corresponding to the characteristics of many actual channels.

The *Nakagami-m* channel is more accordant with channel characteristics in realistic communication systems compared with that of Rayleigh fading channel and Ricean channel. In addition, it is widely used for modeling wireless fading channels, including Rayleigh and the one-sided Gaussian distribution as special cases [17–19]. However, few scholars have employed this kind of channels in SRT analysis. This causes the failure of previous SRT analysis to meet the performance in realistic mobile communication system in general. Motivated by the above considerations, a mobile communication network based on the *Nakagami-m* channel is conducted as a branch of CR networks. This network comprises one primary base station (PBS), eavesdropper (*E*), some primary users (PUs), multiple mobile terminals (MT), multiple relays (MUR), and a secondary transmitter (ST). Different from [16], we propose a scenario that investigates the SRT performance over the *Nakagami-m* channel, which can better capture the characteristics of the physical channel [20–23]. Specifically, relay selection schemes in mobile communication systems over the *Nakagami-m* channel are well investigated, and mathematical SRT analysis of the proposed SRS and MRS schemes over the *Nakagami-m* channel is first provided. Furthermore, simulation results show limpidly that the proposed SRS and MRS schemes over the *Nakagami-m* channel generally outperform the direct transmission scheme in their SRT.

The remainder of this paper is organized as below. Section 2 develops the system model. And the relay selection schemes over the *Nakagami-m* channel and mathematical

analysis are provided in Section 3. In Section 4, simulation results and analysis are presented, which is followed by the conclusions in Section 5.

2. System Model

A typical mobile communication system is considered in Figure 1. As we know, the ST should detect by spectrum sensing whether the PBS occupies the licensed spectrum. In case of this situation, the ST cannot transmit randomly to avoid interference within the PUs. On the contrary, the licensed spectrum is not occupied. Meanwhile, *E* tries to intercept the secondary transmission process. For convenience, we define H_0 and H_1, respectively, as the cases in which the licensed spectrum is unoccupied and occupied by the PBS in a special time slot. Additionally, $\widehat{H}$ represents the status that the licensed spectrum is detected by spectrum sensing. Hence, the status of the spectrum is given as

$$\widehat{H} = \begin{cases} H_0, & \text{unoccupied} \\ H_1, & \text{occupied}, \end{cases} \tag{1}$$

where the probability P_d of the correct detection of the presence of PBS and the associated false alarm probability P_f are noted as $P_d = P(\widehat{H} = H_1 \mid H_1)$ and $P_f = P(\widehat{H} = H_1 \mid H_0)$, respectively. To ensure that the interference exerted on the PUs is below a tolerable level, we set $P_d = 0.99$ and $P_f = 0.01$ according to the IEEE 802.22 standard [14].

3. SRT Analysis over *Nakagami-m* Channel

In this section, we present the SRT analysis about the direct transmission and the SRS and MRS schemes over the *Nakagami-m* channel. As is analyzed in [14], IP and OP, respectively, represent the security and reliability which are experienced by the eavesdropper and destination. Hence, the channel capacities at the destination and eavesdropper are assumed as C_D and C_E and the OP and IP can be expressed as

$$P_{\text{out}} = P\left(C_D < R \mid \widehat{H} = H_0\right) \tag{2}$$

$$P_{\text{int}} = P\left(C_E > R \mid \widehat{H} = H_0\right). \tag{3}$$

3.1. Direct Transmission Scheme. In this section, we consider a conventional direct transmission scheme over the *Nakagami-m* channel. Let P_s and P_R denote the transmit powers of the ST and PBS, respectively. For the licensed spectrum is considered to be unoccupied by the ST (i.e., $\widehat{H} = H_0$), the signal received at the PBS can be expressed as

$$y_{\text{ST}} = h_{\text{MUR}}\sqrt{P_s}\,x_s + h_{\text{PBS}}\sqrt{\alpha P_R}\,x_R + n_0. \tag{4}$$

Here, x_s and x_R represent the random symbols transmitted by the ST and the PBS at a special time instance. Also, without loss of generality, assume that $E[|x_s|^2] = E[|x_R|^2] = 1$, where $E[\cdot]$ is the expected value operator. At the same time, h_{MUR} and h_{PBS} are noted as the fading coefficients of the channel spanning from ST to MT and from PBS to MT, respectively. Furthermore, n_0 is the additive white Gaussian noise (AWGN). Then, the random variable α can be given by

$$\alpha = \begin{cases} 0, & H_0 \\ 1, & H_1. \end{cases} \tag{5}$$

However, for that the wireless medium has a broadcast nature, the signal of the ST which will be overheard by E can be written by

$$y_{\text{SE}} = h_{\text{MT}}\sqrt{P_s}\,x_s + h_E\sqrt{\alpha P_R}\,x_R + n_0. \tag{6}$$

Supposing that a spectrum hole has been detected, from (5), we obtain

$$\begin{aligned} P_{\text{out}}^{\text{direct}} &= P\left(C_{\text{ST}} < R, H_0 \mid \widehat{H} = H_0\right) \\ &\quad + P\left(C_{\text{ST}} < R, H_1 \mid \widehat{H} = H_0\right) \\ &= \lambda_0 P\left(|h_{\text{ST}}|^2 < \Delta\right) \\ &\quad + \lambda_1 P\left(|h_{\text{ST}}|^2 - |h_{\text{PBS}}|^2\gamma_p\Delta < \Delta\right), \end{aligned} \tag{7}$$

where $\Delta = (2^R - 1)/\gamma_s$, $\gamma_s = P_s/N_0$, and $\gamma_p = P_R/N_0$. In (7), $P(|h_{\text{ST}}|^2 < \Delta)$ and $P(|h_{\text{ST}}|^2 - |h_{\text{PBS}}|^2\gamma_p\Delta < \Delta)$ can be obtained as

$$P\left(|h_{\text{ST}}|^2 < \Delta\right)$$

$$= 1 - \sum_{k=1}^{m_1-1} \frac{m_1^{m_1-k}\exp\left(-m_1\Delta\right)}{\Gamma\left(m_1 - k + 1\right)}$$

$$\quad - \exp\left(-m_1\Delta\right) P\left(|h_{\text{ST}}|^2 - |h_{\text{PBS}}|^2\gamma_p\Delta < \Delta\right)$$

$$= 1 + \sum_{k=1}^{m_2-1} \frac{m_2^{m_2-k}\exp\left(m_2/\gamma_p\right)}{\Gamma\left(m_2\right)}$$

$$\quad - \frac{m_2^{m_2}}{\Gamma\left(m_2\right)}\exp\left(-m_1\Delta\right)$$

$$\quad \times \left(m_1\Delta\gamma_p + m_2\right)^{-m_2}\Gamma\left(m_2, \frac{m_1\Delta\gamma_p + m_2}{\gamma_p}\right)$$

$$\quad \times \left(\sum_{k=1}^{m_1-1} \frac{m_1^{m_1-k}}{\Gamma\left(m_1\right)} + 1\right). \tag{8}$$

Furthermore, we can observe from (3) that when the capacity of the ST-E channel exceeds the data rate, an intercept event will occur. Hence, the corresponding IP is given by

$$\begin{aligned} P_{\text{int}}^{\text{direct}} &= \lambda_0 P\left(|h_{\text{MT}}|^2 > \Delta\right) \\ &\quad + \lambda_1 P\left(|h_{\text{MT}}|^2 - |h_{\text{PBS}}|^2\gamma_p\Delta > \Delta\right). \end{aligned} \tag{9}$$

To be specific, $P(|h_{\text{MT}}|^2 > \Delta)$ and $P(|h_{\text{MT}}|^2 - |h_{\text{PBS}}|^2\gamma_p\Delta > \Delta)$ are written as

$$P\left(|h_{\text{MT}}|^2 > \Delta\right)$$

$$= \sum_{k=1}^{m_1-1} \frac{m_1^{m_1-k}\exp\left(-m_1\Delta\right)}{\Gamma\left(m_1 - k + 1\right)}$$

$$\quad + \exp\left(-m_1\Delta\right) P\left(|h_{\text{MT}}|^2 - |h_{\text{PBS}}|^2\gamma_p\Delta > \Delta\right)$$

$$= -\sum_{k=1}^{m_2-1} \frac{m_2^{m_2-k}\exp\left(m_2/\gamma_p\right)}{\Gamma\left(m_2\right)}$$

$$\quad + \frac{m_2^{m_2}}{\Gamma\left(m_2\right)}\exp\left(-m_1\Delta\right)$$

$$\quad \times \left(m_1\Delta\gamma_p + m_2\right)^{-m_2}\Gamma\left(m_2, \frac{m_1\Delta\gamma_p + m_2}{\gamma_p}\right)$$

$$\quad \times \left(\sum_{k=1}^{m_1-1} \frac{m_1^{m_1-k}}{\Gamma\left(m_1\right)} + 1\right). \tag{10}$$

3.2. Single Relay Selection. The SRS scheme over the *Nakagami-m* channel is investigated in this section. Specifically, once the licensed spectrum is deemed to be unoccupied, the ST first broadcasts its signal to the N MUR, which attempts to decode x_s from their received signals. For convenience, Θ is denoted as the set of MUR that succeed in decoding x_s. N MUR are assumed in this network, which consist of 2^N possible subsets Θ, and the sample space of Θ can be formulated as

$$\Theta = \{0, \theta_1, \theta_2, \ldots, \theta_i, \ldots, \theta_{2^N - 1}\}, \tag{11}$$

where 0 and θ_i represent the empty set and the ith nonempty subset of the N relays. If the set Θ is empty, no MUR successfully decodes x_s. By contrast, a specific MUR is selected from Θ to decode the signal and transmit it to the MT. Hence, given that $\widehat{H} = H_0$, we can work out the signal received at a specific MUR-i

$$y_i = h_{Ri} \sqrt{\alpha P_s} x_s + h_{Pi} \sqrt{P_R} x_R + n_0. \tag{12}$$

To make SRT analysis, noting that $\widehat{H} = H_0$, the OP of the cognitive transmission depending on SRS can be denoted as

$$P_{\text{out}}^{\text{single}} = P\left(C_{\text{ST}} < R, \theta = 0 \mid \widehat{H} = H_0\right) + \sum_{n=1}^{2^N - 1} P\left(C_{\text{ST}}\right.$$

$$\left. < R, \theta = \theta_n \mid \widehat{H} = H_0\right) = \lambda_0 \prod_{i=1}^{N} P\left(|h_{Si}|^2 < \Lambda\right)$$

$$+ \lambda_1 \prod_{i=1}^{N} P\left(|h_{Si}|^2 < |h_{Ri}|^2 \gamma_p \Lambda + \Lambda\right)$$

$$+ \lambda_0 \sum_{n=1}^{2^N - 1} \prod_{i \in \Theta} P\left(|h_{Si}|^2 > \Lambda\right)$$

$$\cdot \prod_{j \in \overline{\Theta}} P\left(|h_{Sj}|^2 < \Lambda\right) P\left(\max_{i \in \Theta} |h_{Ri}|^2 < \Lambda\right) \tag{13}$$

$$+ \lambda_1 \sum_{n=1}^{2^N - 1} \prod_{i \in \Theta} P\left(|h_{Si}|^2 > |h_{Ri}|^2 \gamma_p \Lambda + \Lambda\right)$$

$$\cdot \prod_{j \in \overline{\Theta}} P\left(|h_{Sj}|^2 < |h_{Ri}|^2 \gamma_p \Lambda + \Lambda\right) \times P\left(\max_{i \in \Theta} |h_{Ri}|^2\right.$$

$$\left. < |h_{\text{PBS}}|^2 \gamma_p \Lambda + \Lambda\right),$$

where $\Lambda = (2^{2R} - 1)/\gamma_s$. Specifically, (13) consists of the following parts:

$$P\left(|h_{Si}|^2 < \Lambda\right)$$

$$= 1 - \sum_{k=1}^{m_3 - 1} \frac{m_3^{m_3 - k} \exp\left(-m_3 \Lambda\right)}{\Gamma\left(m_3 - k + 1\right)}$$

$$- \exp\left(-m_3 \Lambda\right) P\left(|h_{Si}|^2 - |h_{Ri}|^2 \gamma_p \Lambda < \Lambda\right)$$

$$= 1 + \sum_{k=1}^{m_4 - 1} \frac{m_4^{m_2 - k} \exp\left(m_4/\gamma_p\right)}{\Gamma\left(m_4\right)}$$

$$- \frac{m_4^{m_4}}{\Gamma\left(m_4\right)} \exp\left(-m_3 \Lambda\right) \left(m_3 \Lambda \gamma_p + m_4\right)^{-m_4}$$

$$\times \Gamma\left(m_4, \frac{m_3 \Lambda \gamma_p + m_4}{\gamma_p}\right)$$

$$\times \left(\sum_{k=1}^{m_3 - 1} \frac{m_3^{m_3 - k}}{\Gamma\left(m_3\right)} + 1\right) P\left(\max_{i \in \Theta} |h_{Ri}|^2 < \Lambda\right)$$

$$= \prod_{i \in \Theta} \left[1 - \sum_{k=1}^{m_i - 1} \frac{m_i^{m_i - k} \exp\left(-m_i \Lambda\right)}{\Gamma\left(m_i - k + 1\right)} - \exp\left(-m_i \Lambda\right)\right]. \tag{14}$$

Also, we discuss the IP of the SRS scheme. From (6), the IP can be given by

$$P_{\text{int}}^{\text{single}} = \lambda_0 \sum_{n=1}^{2^N - 1} \prod_{i \in \Theta} P\left(|h_{Si}|^2 > \Lambda\right)$$

$$\cdot \prod_{j \in \overline{\Theta}} P\left(|h_{Sj}|^2 < \Lambda\right) P\left(\max_{i \in \Theta} |h_{\text{best}}|^2 > \Lambda\right)$$

$$+ \lambda_1 \sum_{n=1}^{2^N - 1} \prod_{i \in \Theta} P\left(|h_{Si}|^2 > |h_{Ri}|^2 \gamma_p \Lambda + \Lambda\right) \tag{15}$$

$$\times \prod_{j \in \overline{\Theta}} P\left(|h_{Sj}|^2 < |h_{Ri}|^2 \gamma_p \Lambda + \Lambda\right) \times P\left(|h_{\text{best}}|^2\right.$$

$$\left. > |h_E|^2 \gamma_p \Lambda + \Lambda\right).$$

Here, with the aids of functional analysis theory and multivariate integral theory, we express $P(\max_{i \in \Theta} |h_{Ri}|^2 < |h_{\text{PBS}}|^2 \gamma_p \Lambda + \Lambda)$, $P(\max_{i \in \Theta} |h_{\text{best}}|^2 > \Lambda)$, and $P(\max_{i \in \Theta} |h_{\text{best}}|^2 > |h_{\text{PBS}}|^2 \gamma_p \Lambda + \Lambda)$ as below.

$$P\left(\max_{i \in \Theta} |h_{Ri}|^2 < |h_{\text{PBS}}|^2 \gamma_p \Lambda + \Lambda\right)$$

$$= \prod_{i \in \Theta} \prod_{j \in \Theta} \left\{\left[1 + \sum_{k=1}^{m_j - 1} \frac{m_j^{m_j - k} \exp\left(m_j/\gamma_p\right)}{\Gamma\left(m_j\right)}\right]\right.$$

$$- \frac{m_i^{m_j}}{\Gamma\left(m_j\right)} \exp\left(-m_i \Lambda\right) \times \left(m_i \Lambda \gamma_p + m_j\right)^{-m_j}$$

$$\left. \cdot \Gamma\left(m_j, \frac{m_i \Lambda \gamma_p + m_j}{\gamma_p}\right) \times \left(\sum_{k=1}^{m_i - 1} \frac{m_1^{m_i - k}}{\Gamma\left(m_i\right)} + 1\right)\right\}$$

$$P\left(\max_{i\in\Theta}|h_{\text{best}}|^2 > \Lambda\right) = \prod_{i\in\Theta}\left\{1 - \left[1\right.\right.$$

$$\left.\left. - \sum_{k=1}^{m_i-1}\frac{m_i^{m_i-k}\exp\left(-m_i\Lambda\right)}{\Gamma\left(m_i-k+1\right)} - \exp\left(-m_i\Lambda\right)\right]\right\}$$

$$P\left(\max_{i\in\Theta}|h_{\text{best}}|^2 > |h_{\text{PBS}}|^2\gamma_p\Lambda + \Lambda\right)$$

$$= \prod_{i\in\Theta}\prod_{j\in\Theta}\left\{\left[-1 - \sum_{k=1}^{m_j-1}\frac{m_j^{m_j-k}\exp\left(m_j/\gamma_p\right)}{\Gamma\left(m_j\right)}\right]\right.$$

$$+ \frac{m_i^{m_j}}{\Gamma\left(m_j\right)}\exp\left(-m_i\Lambda\right)\times\left(m_i\Lambda\gamma_p + m_j\right)^{-m_j}$$

$$\left. \cdot\,\Gamma\left(m_j,\frac{m_i\Lambda\gamma_p + m_j}{\gamma_p}\right)\left(\sum_{k=1}^{m_i-1}\frac{m_1^{m_i-k}}{\Gamma\left(m_j\right)} + 1\right)\right\}.$$

$$(16)$$

3.3. Multirelays Selection Scheme.

We provide the SRT analysis which is based on the MRS scheme over the *Nakagami-m* channel in this subsection. Specifically, x_s is first transmitted to N MUR over a detected spectrum hole. As is mentioned in Section 3.2, we denote Θ by the set of SRS with successful decoding. If it is empty, all MUR fail to decode x_s and will not pass the source signal forward, leading to the difficulty in decoding of MT and E. If it is not empty, all MUR within Θ will be utilized for simultaneously transmitting x_s to MT. This is different from the SRS scheme. When it comes to power consumption, a fair comparison with the SRS scheme can be made under the conditions that the overall transmit power across all MUR is constrained to P_s. For the sake of making good use of MRS, we define the weight vector as

$$w = [w_1, w_2, \ldots, w_{|\Theta|}]^T, \quad \|w\| = 1. \tag{17}$$

And the signals received at MT and E are expressed as

$$\begin{aligned} y_D^{\text{multi}} &= \sqrt{P_s}w^T H_D x_s + \sqrt{\alpha P_R}h_{\text{PBS}}x_R + n_0 \\ y_E^{\text{multi}} &= \sqrt{P_s}w^T H_{\text{MT}}x_s + \sqrt{\alpha P_R}h_E x_R + n_0, \end{aligned} \tag{18}$$

where $H_D = [h_{1D}, h_{2D}, \ldots, h_{\Theta D}]$. Then based on the *Nakagami-m* channel, we study the SRT performance of the MRS scheme. Similar to (7), the OP analysis is obtained as

$$P_{\text{out}}^{\text{multi}} = P\left(\theta = 0 \mid \widehat{H} = H_0\right)$$

$$+ \sum_{n=1}^{2^N-1} P\left(C_D^{\text{multi}} < R, \theta = \theta_n \mid \widehat{H} = H_0\right)$$

$$= \lambda_0\prod_{i=1}^{N}P\left(|h_{Si}|^2 < \Lambda\right)$$

$$+ \lambda_1\prod_{i=1}^{N}P\left(|h_{Si}|^2 < |h_{Ri}|^2\gamma_p\Lambda + \Lambda\right)$$

$$+ \lambda_0\sum_{n=1}^{2^N-1}\prod_{i\in\Theta}P\left(|h_{Si}|^2 > \Lambda\right)\prod_{j\in\overline{\Theta}}P\left(|h_{Sj}|^2 < \Lambda\right)$$

$$\cdot P\left(\sum_{i\in\Theta}|h_{Ri}|^2 < \Lambda\right)$$

$$+ \lambda_1\sum_{n=1}^{2^N-1}\prod_{i\in\Theta}P\left(|h_{Si}|^2 > |h_{Ri}|^2\gamma_p\Lambda + \Lambda\right)$$

$$\cdot\prod_{j\in\overline{\Theta}}P\left(|h_{Sj}|^2 < |h_{Ri}|^2\gamma_p\Lambda + \Lambda\right)\times P\left(\sum_{i\in\Theta}|h_{Ri}|^2\right.$$

$$\left. < |h_{\text{PBS}}|^2\gamma_p\Lambda + \Lambda\right). \tag{19}$$

The IP analysis of the MRS scheme can be given as follows:

$$P_{\text{int}}^{\text{multi}} = \lambda_0\sum_{n=1}^{2^N-1}\prod_{i\in\Theta}P\left(|h_{Si}|^2 > \Lambda\right)\prod_{j\in\overline{\Theta}}P\left(|h_{Sj}|^2 < \Lambda\right)$$

$$\times P\left(\frac{|H_{\text{MT}}H_d^H|^2}{|H_D|^2} > \Lambda\right)$$

$$+ \lambda_1\sum_{n=1}^{2^N-1}\prod_{i\in\Theta}P\left(|h_{Si}|^2 > |h_{Ri}|^2\gamma_p\Lambda + \Lambda\right)$$

$$\times\prod_{j\in\overline{\Theta}}P\left(|h_{Sj}|^2 < |h_{Ri}|^2\gamma_p\Lambda + \Lambda\right)$$

$$\cdot P\left(\frac{|H_{\text{MT}}H_d^H|^2}{|H_D|^2} > |h_E|^2\gamma_p\Lambda + \Lambda\right). \tag{20}$$

To find a general closed-form OP and IP expression for the MRS scheme is quite a challenge, and thus we use computer simulations to get the numerical SRT performance of the MRS scheme. Clearly, when h_{Ri} is given as the fading coefficients of the channel spanning from MUR-i to PBS, we have $\sum|h_{Ri}|^2 > \max|h_{Ri}|^2$, $i\in\Theta$. This leads to a performance gain for the MRS over that of SRS in terms of maximizing the legitimate transmission capacity. Furthermore, for a fixed outage requirement, the MRS scheme can, in comparison with the SRS scheme, realize a better intercept performance over the *Nakagami-m* channel. This is due to the fact that an outage reduction achieved by the capacity enhancement of the legitimate transmission relaying on MRS would be converted into an intercept improvement. Meanwhile, in the

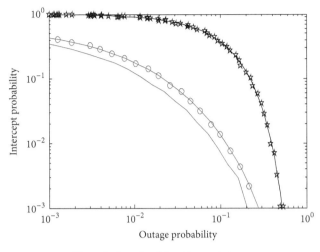

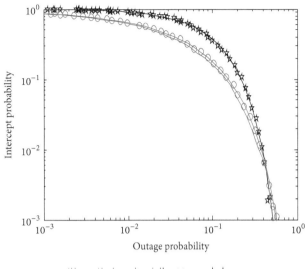

FIGURE 2: OP versus IP when $m = 2$ and $N = 5$ when $P_d = 0.99$ and $P_f = 0.01$.

FIGURE 3: OP versus IP when $m = 2$ and $N = 2$ when $P_d = 0.99$ and $P_f = 0.01$.

MRS scheme, when simultaneously transmitting to MT, it will require a high-complexity symbol-level synchronization for multiple distributed relays, whereas the SRS does not require such a complex synchronization process. Therefore, we can achieve a better performance of MRS over SRS at the expense of a higher implementation.

4. Numerical Results and Discussion

We give a numerical analysis of our expressions using different types of parameters in this section. Specifically, the OP and the IP in the direct transmission schemes, SRS schemes, and MRS schemes are investigated. Theoretical results and the simulation results are presented in the case under different conditions in the *Nakagami-m* channel model. Initially, P_d is set to $P_d = 0.99$, while P_f is 0.01. Also, we set the initial signal-to-noise ratio (SNR) γ_p as 10 dB and data rate is employed as $R = 1$ bit/s/Hz in this simulation.

Figure 2 shows the simulation results when $m = 2$ and $N = 5$, the IP and OP of the direct transmission, along with the SRS and MRS schemes. Here the solid lines and discrete marker symbols each represent the theoretical and simulated results. As is shown in the figure, the proposed SRS and MRS schemes both attain lower OP (reliability) and IP (security) than the direct transmission scheme over the *Nakagami-m* channel. Also, the OP and IP of the MRS are lower than those of SRS scheme. Hence, we can conclude that the SRS and MRS schemes have better SRT performance than the direct transmission scheme. However, considering that the MRS scheme needs to work with very complex and high-cost symbol-level synchronization system, it is inappropriate for us to assert that the MRS scheme outweighs the SRS scheme.

Figure 3 illustrates the simulation results in the case of $m = 2$ and $N = 2$. Compared with the simulation results shown in Figure 2, we can observe that, with the increasing number of the relays, the OP and IP are decreasing. Meanwhile, the performance of the SRS and MRS schemes significantly improves when the number of relays increases. Furthermore, similar to the analysis given in Figure 2, the superiority of the MRS over the SRS shows when elaborate symbol-level synchronization is required among the multiple relays for simultaneously transmitting to the relays or base stations.

In Figure 4, the simulation results under different fading exponents m are presented, in which case $m = 3$ is considered. Figure 4 shows that the proposed SRS and MRS schemes generally outstrip the conventional direct transmission in terms of IP and OP, in the case that $m = 3$. Moreover, compared with the results depicted in Figure 2, the SRT of the SRS and MRS schemes rises as the fading exponent m increases from 2 to 3. Additionally, the MRS schemes outperform the SRS approach in the IP and OP analysis, which further confirms the strength of the MRS for protecting the MUR-PBS links against eavesdropping attacks.

In Figure 5, P_d and P_f are set 0.9 and 0.1, respectively. From Figures 2 and 5, we observe the proposed SRS and MRS schemes perform better than the direct transmission in terms of OP and IP aspect, and the SRT performance improves when $P_d = 0.99$. It illustrates that the SRT performance of the SRS and MRS schemes improves when the correct detection probability increases. Additionally, the MRS schemes outperform the SRS approach in the SRT analysis, which implies the strength of the MRS for protecting the MUR-PBS links against eavesdropping attacks although it needs complex synchronization system.

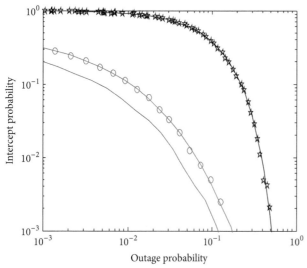

FIGURE 4: OP versus IP when $m = 3$ and $N = 5$ when $P_d = 0.99$ and $P_f = 0.01$.

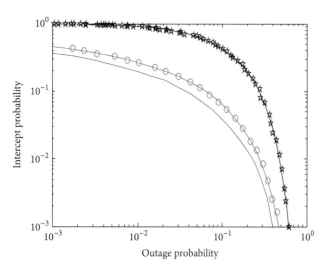

FIGURE 5: OP versus IP when $m = 2$ and $N = 5$ when $P_d = 0.9$ and $P_f = 0.1$.

5. Conclusion

We propose new relay selection schemes over the Nakagami-m channel in the mobile communication system in this paper. SRS and MRS schemes are presented to assess the security and reliability of the communication links. Meanwhile, simulation results indicate a better performance of the SRS and MRS schemes than the direct transmission scheme over the *Nakagami-m* channel. Additionally, with the increasing number of the relays, the SRT performance of both the SRS and the MRS schemes improves remarkably, which demonstrates their benefits in enhancing both the security and reliability of the mobile communication system.

Authors' Contributions

Hongji Huang and Wanyou Sun derived the performance bound and designed the experiments; Hongji Huang and Guan Gui performed the experiments; Hongji Huang and Jie Yang analyzed the data; Hongji Huang and Guan Gui wrote the paper.

Acknowledgments

This work is supported by National Natural Science Foundation of China Grants (no. 61401069, no. 61671252, no. 61471202, and no. 61322112), Jiangsu Specially Appointed Professor Grant (RK002STP16001), high-level talent startup grant of Nanjing University of Posts and Telecommunications (XK0010915026), and "1311 Talent Plan" of Nanjing University of Posts and Telecommunications.

References

[1] G. Han, L. Liu, S. Chan, R. Yu, and Y. Yang, "HySense: a hybrid mobile crowd sensing framework for sensing opportunities compensation under dynamic coverage constraint," *IEEE Communications Magazine*, vol. 55, no. 3, pp. 93–99, 2017.

[2] Y. Zhang, Y. Xie, Y. Liu, Z. Feng, P. Zhang, and Z. Wei, "Outage probability analysis of cognitive relay networks in nakagami-m fading channels," in *Proceedings of the 76th IEEE Vehicular Technology Conference (VTC Fall '12)*, 5, 1 pages, Quebec City, Canada, September 2012.

[3] S. Haykin, "Cognitive radio: brain-empowered wireless communications," *IEEE Journal on Selected Areas in Communications*, vol. 23, no. 2, pp. 201–220, 2005.

[4] J. Mitola and G. Q. Maguire, "Cognitive radio: making software radios more personal," *IEEE Personal Communications*, vol. 6, no. 4, pp. 13–18, 1999.

[5] H. Chen, M. Zhou, L. Xie, and J. Li, "Cooperative spectrum sensing with M-ary quantized data in cognitive radio networks under SSDF attacks," *IEEE Transactions on Wireless Communications*, vol. 16, no. 8, pp. 5244–5257, 2017.

[6] G. Baldini, T. Sturman, A. R. Biswas, R. Leschhorn, G. Gódor, and M. Street, "Security aspects in software defined radio and cognitive radio networks: a survey and a way ahead," *IEEE Communications Surveys and Tutorials*, vol. 14, no. 2, pp. 355–379, 2012.

[7] R. Yin, S. Wei, J. Yuan, X. Shan, and X. Wang, "Tradeoff between reliability and security in block ciphering systems with physical channel errors," in *Proceedings of the IEEE Military Communications Conference (MILCOM '10)*, pp. 2156–2161, San Jose, Claif, USA, November 2010.

[8] J. Huang and A. L. Swindlehurst, "Cooperative jamming for secure communications in MIMO relay networks," *IEEE Transactions on Signal Processing*, vol. 59, no. 10, pp. 4871–4884, 2011.

[9] H. Long, W. Xiang, J. Wang, Y. Zhang, and W. Wang, "Cooperative jamming and power allocation with untrusty two-way relay nodes," *IET Communications*, vol. 8, no. 13, pp. 2290–2297, 2014.

[10] C. Jeong, I.-M. Kim, and D. I. Kim, "Joint secure beamforming design at the source and the relay for an amplify-and-forward MIMO untrusted relay system," *IEEE Transactions on Signal Processing*, vol. 60, no. 1, pp. 310–325, 2012.

[11] G. Han, J. Jiang, C. Zhang, T. Q. Duong, M. Guizani, and G. K. Karagiannidis, "A survey on mobile anchor node assisted localization in wireless sensor networks," *IEEE Communications Surveys & Tutorials*, vol. 18, no. 3, pp. 2220–2243, 2016.

[12] G. Han, X. Yang, L. Liu, M. Guizani, and W. Zhang, "A disaster management-oriented path planning for mobile anchor node-based localization in wireless sensor networks," *IEEE Transactions on Emerging Topics in Computing*, no. 99, article 1, 2017.

[13] S. Han, S. Xu, W. Meng, and C. Li, "An agile confidential transmission strategy combining big data driven cluster and OBF," *IEEE Transactions on Vehicular Technology*, no. 99, article 1, 2017.

[14] Y. Zou, X. Wang, W. Shen, and L. Hanzo, "Security versus reliability analysis of opportunistic relaying," *IEEE Transactions on Vehicular Technology*, vol. 63, no. 6, pp. 2653–2661, 2014.

[15] L. Dong, Z. Han, A. P. Petropulu, and H. V. Poor, "Improving wireless physical layer security via cooperating relays," *IEEE Transactions on Signal Processing*, vol. 58, no. 3, pp. 1875–1888, 2010.

[16] Y. Zou, B. Champagne, W.-P. Zhu, and L. Hanzo, "Relay-selection improves the security-reliability trade-off in cognitive radio systems," *IEEE Transactions on Communications*, vol. 63, no. 1, pp. 215–228, 2015.

[17] H. Lei, C. Gao, I. S. Ansari et al., "Secrecy outage performance of transmit antenna selection for MIMO underlay cognitive radio systems over nakagami-m channels," *IEEE Transactions on Vehicular Technology*, vol. 66, no. 3, pp. 2237–2250, 2017.

[18] Z. Shi, S. Ma, G. Yang, K. Tam, and M. Xia, "Asymptotic outage analysis of HARQ-IR over time-correlated nakagami-m fading channels," *IEEE Transactions on Wireless Communications*, no. 99, article 1, 2017.

[19] M. O. Hasna and M.-S. Alouini, "Outage probability of multihop transmission over Nakagami fading channels," *IEEE Communications Letters*, vol. 7, no. 5, pp. 216–218, 2003.

[20] IEEE 802.22 Working Group, IEEE P802.22/D1.0 draft standard for wireless regional area networks part 22: Cognitive wireless RAN medium access control (MAC) and physical layer (PHY) specifications: Policies and procedures for operation in the TV bands, Apr. 2008.

[21] J. Zhang, Y. Zhang, Y. Yu, R. Xu, Q. Zheng, and P. Zhang, "3-D MIMO: how much does it meet our expectations observed from channel measurements?" *IEEE Journal on Selected Areas in Communications*, vol. 35, no. 8, pp. 1887–1903, 2017.

[22] J. Zhang, P. Tang, L. Tian, Z. Hu, T. Wang, and H. Wang, "6–100 GHz research progress and challenges from a channel perspective for fifth generation (5G) and future wireless communication," *Science China Information Sciences*, vol. 60, no. 8, 2017.

[23] T. S. Rappaport, Y. Xing, G. R. MacCartney, A. F. Molisch, E. Mellios, and J. Zhang, "Overview of millimeter wave communications for fifth-generation (5G) wireless networks-with a focus on propagation models," *IEEE Transactions on Antennas and Propagation*, no. 99, article 1, 2017.

13

A Security and Efficient Routing Scheme with Misbehavior Detection in Delay-Tolerant Networks

Feng Li,[1] Yali Si,[2,3] Ning Lu,[1] Zhen Chen,[2] and Limin Shen[2]

[1]*Computer and Communication Engineering College, Northeastern University at Qinhuangdao, Qinhuangdao, China*
[2]*School of Information Science and Engineering, Yanshan University, Qinhuangdao, China*
[3]*School of Liren, Yanshan University, Qinhuangdao, China*

Correspondence should be addressed to Ning Lu; luning@neuq.edu.cn

Academic Editor: Lianyong Qi

Due to the unique network characteristics, the security and efficient routing in DTNs are considered as two great challenges. In this paper, we design a security and efficient routing scheme, called SER, which integrates the routing decision and the attacks detection mechanisms. In SER scheme, each DTNs node locally maintains a one-dimensional vector table to record the summary information about the contact with other nodes and the trust degree of other nodes. To obtain the global status and the contact relationship among all nodes, the trusted routing table consisting of vectors of all nodes is built in each DTNs node. The method for detecting malicious nodes and selfish nodes is proposed, which exploits the global summary information to analyze the history forwarding behavior of node and judge whether it is a malicious node or selfish node. The routing decision method is proposed based on trust degree of forwarding messages between nodes, which adopts trust degree as relay node selection strategy. Simulation results show that compared with existing schemes SER scheme could detect the attacks behavior of malicious nodes and selfish nodes, at the same time, with higher delivery rate and lower average delivery delay.

1. Introduction

Delay-tolerant networks (DTNs) refer to a new form of self-organizing networks that is envisioned to support communication in case of failure or no preexisting infrastructure, such as interplanetary communication networks in space areas, high-speed vehicular networks that disseminate the city traffic information, and sensor networks in extreme environment [1, 2]. Different from the traditional wireless networks, DTNs are the challenging networks characterized by open medium, long delay and frequent disruption, and lack of fixed and guaranteed end-to-end communication links [3]. DTNs make use of the store-carry-and-forward strategy to forward the message packets (also named bundle) when two nodes appear with contact opportunity. This routing strategy requires that each node in DTNs can cooperate with other nodes and is willing to help with forwarding.

However, DTNs are threatened by various attacks, because some nodes will behave selfishly and may not be willing to help others forward messages in order to conserve their limited resources (e.g., power and buffer), and even some nodes controlled by adversary will behave maliciously and may launch black hole, grey hole, or DoS attacks against the networks by dropping all or part of the received message packets, maliciously tampering message packets, or producing an enormous number of fake message packets [4–7]. The recent researches show that these selfish or malicious nodes would significantly degrade the routing performance of DTNs, resulting in low delivery rate and poor forwarding efficiency of messages and high average delivery delay. Due to the lack of continuous path and centralized management in DTNs, the detection of these attacks is more difficult. Therefore, how to effectively resolve the selfishness problem and defense against attacks of malicious nodes, improving the routing performance, has become a very challenging issue to design security and efficient routing protocol that combines defense technique.

To achieve the better routing performance of DTNs, many routing protocols in DTNs have been proposed in [8–12].

The purpose of routing in DTNs is to select the proper relay nodes to forward messages and improve the routing performance. Most of the existing routing protocols use historical encounter information or social relations as the decision of predicting relay nodes, which can effectively forward the message to the destination node. However, these routing schemes are inefficient in the DTNs environment with malicious or selfish nodes. To mitigate the impact of selfish or malicious nodes on DTNs, some detection attacks schemes are proposed in [3, 6, 7], which make use of the history forwarding evidences and encounter records of each node to analyze its forwarding behavior. However, these detection schemes are independent of specific routing protocols and require more computing capability, network bandwidth, and storage resources to work well. Due to the limited resources (e.g., power, buffer, and bandwidth) and intermittent connectivity in DTNs, we need an efficient routing scheme with misbehavior detection, which could not only improve the routing performance, but also detect malicious nodes and selfish nodes effectively.

In this paper, we propose a security and efficient routing scheme (SER) to improve message forwarding performance and detect malicious attacks. Different from existing routing schemes and malicious attacks detection schemes that work independently, respectively, we integrate the routing decision and attacks detection mechanisms into the trusted routing table. In SER scheme, each DTNs node maintains a one-dimensional vector to record the summary information about the contact with other nodes. The summary information includes the encounter history evidences with other nodes, the evidences of messages of sending to or receiving from other nodes, and trust degree that represents the ability of other nodes to forward messages to it. To form a global view and obtain the contact relationship among all nodes, SER introduces the trusted routing table that consists of vector of each node. In the initial phase, the trusted routing table of each node has only its own vector; when the two nodes meet, they would exchange the trusted routing table with each other and update it by comparing with the received trusted routing table. Therefore, each node could obtain a global view of the previous network connectivity from its trusted routing table. Based on the trusted routing table, we design the routing decision method and malicious attacks detection mechanisms. The main contributions of this paper include the following three parts.

First, we introduce in detail the method of generating and updating the trusted routing table. The proposed method could not only ensure the security and reliability of trusted routing table, but also make the trusted routing table converge quickly to global consistency.

Second, to accurately evaluate the trust degree of the node, we propose a method of forwarding evidence collection based on layered coin model and digital signature mechanism. The forwarding evidences signed by nodes are bound dynamically on message during the relay processes, and the message carries evidences chain to the destination node. The proposed forwarding evidences collection method greatly improves the timeliness and reliability of the evidences collection and effectively reduces the network overhead.

Third, we propose a routing decision method based on trust degree, which could deliver messages to the destination node along the direction of trust gradient increment and improve effectively routing performance of DTNs. Moreover, the malicious attacks detection method is proposed based on the history evidences of trusted routing table, which could detect selfish nodes and malicious nodes effectively.

The remainder of this paper is organized as follows: In Section 2, we present the system model and design goals and some attacker models. In Section 3, we explained in detail the implementation of SER scheme. In Section 4, simulation results and analysis of SER are introduced. Section 5 highlights related work. Finally, we summarize the conclusions of our works in Section 6.

2. System Model and Design Goals

2.1. System Model. In this paper, we adopt the system model similar to the literature [13, 14]. We consider DTN with no trusted authorization center, which is different from [7] in that it exists with a periodically available TA (trusted authority). Each node is equipped with a wireless communication device to communicate with its one-hop neighbor node when the two nodes contact with each other. Each node has a unique ID identifier N_i and the corresponding public/private key pair sk_i/pk_i that is allocated when it first joins the DTNs. When two nodes first encounter, they would exchange their public key certificate. After a period of time, each node in DTNs may obtain public key certificates of the other nodes. We assume that each node is equipped with an independent capacity-limited buffer B_m to store message packets to be forwarded. Each message consists of message header and message content; message header contains a unique message ID m_i, source node ID, destination node ID, and timestamp t that indicates the time of message generation, finite time to live (TTL), maximum number of copies nc, and the signature information to verify the validity of the message, and message content is encrypted by the public key of the destination node. We assume that all nodes in DTNs are loosely synchronized on the local clock.

We adopt the multicopy message forwarding strategy that allows a message to be copied many times; each time only a copy of the message is forwarded to the next relay node, the max number of messages allowed to be copied is set in the header field of the message. The source node sends a message to the destination node via a sequence of intermediate nodes in a multihop manner. When two nodes contact each other, we would detect the behavior of the encounter node and select the most proper next-hop node as a relay node for each message according to the process of Figure 1. If any one copy of the message is delivered to the destination node, the destination node sends an ACK message packet to the network to indicate that the message has been received. The relay node automatically deletes the message from the buffer when the time to live (TTL) of message is in the end or when it received an ACK message from the destination node. When the node generates a new message or receives a message copy from last hop nodes, it first detects whether the remaining buffer space meets the storage requirements. If the remaining

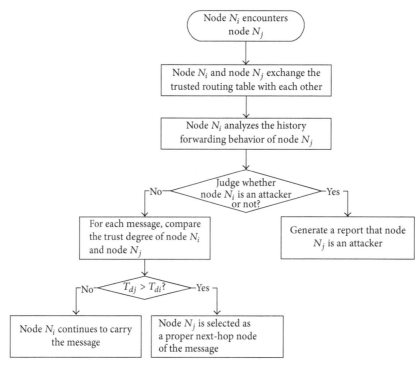

FIGURE 1: A flowchart for SER scheme execution.

buffer space is too small, it will sort the messages according to their TTL and delete the message that its TTL is longest.

2.2. Attacker Model. According to the damage degree of the malicious nodes to the networks, we define two types of attackers as follows.

Definition 1 (selfish attacker). A selfish attacker is a node that often arbitrarily refuses the forwarding message request of the well-behaving nodes, to save the energy, buffer, or computing resources. But selfish attackers may decide to forward the message if they have a good relationship with the source node, the destination node, or last hop relay node. This type of attack is launched by selfish users that only want to profit from network and are not willing to help other users to forward messages.

Definition 2 (malicious attacker). A malicious attacker is a node that often uses the vulnerability of routing scheme to disguise as a relay node to receive a large number of messages from its encounter nodes, then maliciously drops these messages from its buffer, and does not forward these messages to the next-hop node. This type of attack is launched by adversary that wants to degrade or destroy the routing of DTNs.

2.3. Design Goals. Our goals are to design a secure and reliable opportunistic routing protocol that can not only improve the performance of the network, but also effectively restrain the malicious behavior of selfish or malicious node. The specific objectives are as follows.

(1) Improving the Routing Performance of DTNs. The proposed routing scheme should be able to improve the network performance effectively compared with the existing message forwarding methods, that is, higher delivery rate and lower average delivery delay.

(2) Resistance to Malicious and Selfish Attacks. The proposed detection scheme should be able to resist the attacks of malicious and selfish nodes in DTNs. In the process of message delivery, the relay nodes using this scheme could distinguish the malicious nodes and well-behaving nodes and select well-behaving node as the next-hop relay node.

(3) Robustness. The proposed routing scheme should be secure and robust. The formation and evaluation method of node trust degree should be able to resist the attack of malicious nodes. The trusted routing table should not be deleted and modified by malicious nodes.

3. Security and Efficient Routing Scheme Based on Trusted Routing Table

3.1. Basic Idea of Our Scheme. In DTNs, most messages need to be forwarded through multiple intermediate nodes. For example, as shown in Figure 2, the source node N_0 delivers a message to the destination node N_k along the path $N_0 \rightarrow N_1 \rightarrow N_2 \rightarrow N_3 \rightarrow N_k$. Due to those intermediate nodes N_0, N_1, N_2, N_3 successfully participated in forwarding message; according to the regular pattern of periodic movement of nodes, those nodes may deliver messages to the destination node N_k again at some time in the future. If the nodes

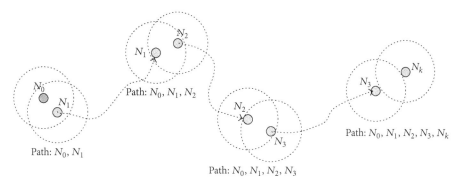

FIGURE 2: Data transmission path.

N_0, N_1, N_2, N_3 often forward messages to node N_k, those nodes would be the best relay nodes when a node delivers a message to node N_k. Moreover, due to the intermittent connectivity of DTNs, only the destination node could know which nodes have successfully participated in delivering message to it. Therefore, the destination node could reward and evaluate these nodes by using trust mechanisms. This means that the more trusted nodes have higher probability of delivering the message to the destination node.

Based on the above observation, we design a security and efficient routing scheme based on trust mechanism. In our scheme, each DTNs node maintains a trusted routing table (TRT), TRT is $n \times n$ two-dimensional matrix, as shown in (1), and n denotes the number of nodes in DTNs. The tuple $Tr_{ij} = \langle E^*_{ij}, T_{ij} \rangle$ generated by node N_i records the summary information about node N_j based on the encounter histories and message forwarding histories, where $E^*_{ij} = E_{ij}, R_{ij}, S_{ij}, \text{sig}_i, \text{sig}_j$ refers to the encounter evidences, receiving and sending messages evidences between node N_i and node N_j, E_{ij} denotes the number of encounters between node N_i and node N_j, R_{ij} and S_{ij} denote the number of messages that node N_i receives from and sends to node N_j respectively, and $\text{sig}_i, \text{sig}_j$ refer to the signature generated by node N_i and node N_j respectively. We will use E_{ij}, R_{ij}, S_{ij} to detect malicious nodes and selfish nodes. T_{ij} denotes the trust value of node N_j evaluated by node N_i based on history message forwarding evidences, which is a real number in the range of $[0, 1]$; the value of T_{ij} denotes the ability of node N_j to deliver the message to node N_i. The larger the trust value T_{ij}, the stronger the ability to deliver message to node N_i. We will use T_{ij} as routing strategy to determine the proper next-hop relay node.

The row vector of matrix $SR_i = (Tr_{i1}, Tr_{i2}, Tr_{i3}, \ldots, Tr_{in})$ represents the summary information that the node N_i reports about other nodes. The node N_i is responsible for maintaining and updating the vector SR_i and periodically updates the latest SR_i in trusted routing table. The column vector $SC_{*i} = (Tr_{1i}, Tr_{2i}, Tr_{3i}, \ldots, Tr_{ni})^T$ represents the summary information that the other nodes report about node N_i. We

can obtain the belief of whether the node N_i is malicious or selfish from the column vector SC_{*i}.

$$\text{TRT} = \begin{bmatrix} Tr_{11} & Tr_{12} & Tr_{13} & \cdots & Tr_{1n} \\ Tr_{21} & Tr_{22} & Tr_{23} & \cdots & Tr_{2n} \\ & & \vdots & & \\ Tr_{i1} & Tr_{i2} & Tr_{i3} & \cdots & Tr_{in} \\ & & \vdots & & \\ Tr_{n1} & Tr_{n2} & Tr_{n3} & \cdots & Tr_{nn} \end{bmatrix}. \tag{1}$$

Therefore, in the routing scheme based on TRT, the relay nodes can determine whether the encountered node is the proper next-hop relay node of the message by using row vector of destination node in the trusted routing table (TRT). The node can determine whether the encounter node is a malicious node or selfish node by using the column vector of encounter node in the trusted routing table.

In Figure 3, we illustrate the message forwarding process based on TRT. Suppose that the node N_1 carries the message m to the destination node N_6, when node N_1 meets node N_2, it first looks up the row vector of node N_2 from TRT to get T_{61}, T_{62}; if $T_{62} > T_{61}$ indicates that the ability of node N_2 to carry messages m to destination node N_6 is greater than that of node N_1, node N_2 is more proper next-hop relay node; therefore node N_1 forwards message m to node N_2. Otherwise, node N_1 continues to carry message m until the destination node is encountered or the next-hop is more reliable. In our scheme, the trust degree of node that it meets is greater than itself as the next-hop relay node. So, the message can be delivered to the destination along the direction of trust gradient increment.

3.2. Collecting Forwarding Evidences. To obtain timely and reliably the forwarding evidences of intermediate nodes, we adopt Captive-Carry mechanism to collect forwarding evidence information. In the message forwarding process, some forwarding evidences information that can prove which nodes have participated in forwarding message is bound

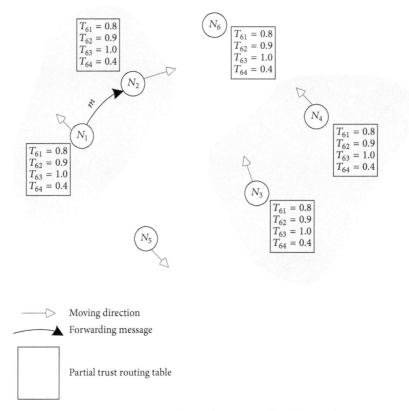

FIGURE 3: Message forwarding process based on trust.

dynamically into message body, carried to the destination node together with the message. After receiving the message, the destination node can obtain a list of intermediate nodes from the forwarding evidence information of message body and validate their authenticity and then reward these intermediate nodes according to the defined evaluation strategy.

To guarantee the security and authenticity of the forwarding evidences and prevent malicious nodes from tampering message and adding fake forwarding evidences, in the implementation, we adopt the layered coin model in the literature [15] to achieve Captive-Carry mechanism and message packet format. A typical layered coin model usually consists of a base layer formed by the source node and multiple endorsed layers formed by the intermediate nodes. If an intermediate node forwards the message to the next-hop relay node, it fists forms an endorsed layer on message and then adds signature information as evidence to the endorsed layer. Figure 3 shows an example of message architecture based on layered coin model; the base layer of message is composed of message header, message content, and endorsed layer 0 formed by the source node, and message header contains six fields: mid, N_0, N_k, t, TTL, nc refer to the identifier of the message, the identifier of the source node, the identifier of the destination node, the timestamp of message created, the time to live, and the max copy number of message, respectively. The message content is only composed of encrypted data; when the source node N_0 wants to send a message to the destination node N_k with the public key pk_k, node N_0 uses the public key pk_k to encrypt the real network data into

$E_{pk_k}(H(N_0 \mid t \mid N_k \mid C))$ to achieve confidentiality, where C denotes real network data and $H(*)$ is a hash function of message properties N_0, t, N_k and network data C to validate message content.

The endorsed layer is formed dynamically by the intermediate node when it wants to forward the message to the next-hop relay node. In Figure 4, for example, when the source node N_0 encounters node N_1 at timestamp ts_0 and has determined that node N_1 is a proper next-hop relay node, node N_0 creates an endorsed layer 0 that contains four fields: sig_0, N_1, ts_0, sig_1, where $sig_0 = SIG_{sk_0}(N_0 \mid mid)$ is its signature over the message identifier mid and node identifier N_0 using its corresponding private key sk_0, N_1 is the identifier of the next-hop relay node, ts_0 is a timestamp indicating the time of message forwarding, $sig_1 = SIG_{sk_1}(H'(N_0 \mid ts_0 \mid N_1))$ is the signature of node N_1 over the content $H'(N_0 \mid ts_0 \mid N_1)$ using its corresponding private key sk_1, and $H'(*)$ is a hash function for generating summary of $N_0 \mid ts_0 \mid N_1$. These four fields used as the forwarding evidence proved that node N_0 has forwarded a message to node N_1 at timestamp ts_0, and the signature sig_1 can prove that node N_1 is willing to receive the message from node N_0 at timestamp ts_0. Other endorsed layers created by relay nodes only include the identifier of the forwarding nodes, timestamp of message forwarding, the identifier of the receiving node, and the signature of the receiving node; for example, in Figure 4, endorsed layer 1 contains N_1, ts_1, N_2, sig_2. The above information is used as forwarding evidence which proved that

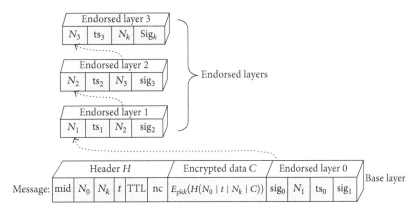

FIGURE 4: Layered coin model based message format.

the message is forwarded to the next-hop relay node. The signature $\text{sig}_1, \text{sig}_2, \ldots$ can witness these nodes that are willing to receive the message.

Overhead of the message is based on layered coin mode. Because the message is added multilayer of evidences information in the forwarding process, the message length is slightly larger than the basic message. Except the signature fields, we assume each field is 2-byte length; then the message header with six fields is 12 bytes, the length of endorsed layer 0 is around $4 + 2 \cdot |\text{sig}|$ bytes, another each endorsed layer is around $6 + |\text{sig}|$ bytes, and then the overhead of a k layered message $\text{Length}_k(m)$ is calculated as follows.

$$\begin{aligned}
\text{Length}_k(m) &= 12 + \left| E_{\text{pk}_k}\left(H\left(N_0 \mid t \mid N_k \mid C\right)\right)\right| + 4 \\
&\quad + 2 \cdot |\text{sig}| + (k-1) \cdot (6 + |\text{sig}|) \text{ bytes} \\
&= 10 + \left| E_{\text{pk}_k}\left(H\left(N_0 \mid t \mid N_k \mid C\right)\right)\right| + 6 \\
&\quad \cdot k + (k+1) \cdot |\text{sig}| \text{ bytes},
\end{aligned} \tag{2}$$

where $\left|E_{\text{pk}_k}(H(N_0 \mid t \mid N_k \mid C))\right|$ denotes the length of encrypted message content; $|\text{sig}|$ denotes the length of signature. Thus, the overhead of a message is mainly composed of message content and additional evidence information. We assume the $|\text{sig}|$ is 20-byte length; then the length of additional evidence is around $L = 26k + 18$ bytes, when $k = 10$, $L \approx 0.25$ kb. Therefore, the additional evidence information is very small, relative to the message content; the overhead of bandwidth and storage is only a little more than the traditional methods.

3.3. Building and Updating Trusted Routing Table.
The tuple $Tr_{ij} = \langle E_{ij}^*, T_{ij} \rangle$ is generated and updated by two processes: encounter process and message receiving process. In encounter process, suppose that node N_i and node N_j meet each other at time t_s; the number of encounters between the two nodes E_{ij}, E_{ji} will be incremented by 1, respectively. Without loss of generality, we assume that node N_i is carrying message that needs to be forwarded to the next-hop nodes. If node N_j is chosen as the next-hop relay of message, node N_i will follow SER routing protocol to forward a message copy to node N_j. After the message copy is successfully

forwarded, S_{ij} will be incremented by 1 to record the number of messages that have been sent to node N_j. In addition, after the node N_j received a message from the node N_i, R_{ji} will also be incremented by 1 to record the number of messages received from node N_i. Similarly, if the node N_i received a message from the node N_j, R_{ij} will be incremented by 1 to record the number of messages received from node N_j, and S_{ji} will also be incremented by 1 to record the number of messages that have been sent to node N_i. The initial value of $E_{ij}, S_{ij}, R_{ij}, E_{ji}, S_{ji}, R_{ji}$ is set to 0. To prevent malicious nodes from forging $E_{ij}, S_{ij}, R_{ij}, E_{ji}, S_{ji}, R_{ji}$ and ensure $E_{ij} = E_{ji}, S_{ij} = R_{ji}, R_{ij} = S_{ji}$, the new evidences $E_{ij}^* = E_{ij}, R_{ij}, S_{ij}, \text{sig}_i, \text{sig}_j$ and $E_{ji}^* = E_{ji}, R_{ji}, S_{ji}, \text{sig}_i, \text{sig}_j$ will be generated by node N_i and node N_j respectively, where $\text{sig}_i = \text{SIG}_{\text{sk}_i}(H'(E_{ij} \mid R_{ij} \mid S_{ij} \mid t_s))$ and $\text{sig}_j = \text{SIG}_{\text{sk}_j}(H'(E_{ji} \mid R_{ji} \mid S_{ji} \mid t_s))$ refer to the signatures generated by node N_i and node N_j, respectively, to show that node N_i and node N_j have accepted these evidences $E_{ij}, S_{ij}, R_{ij}, E_{ji}, S_{ji}, R_{ji}$. Node N_i and node N_j can judge whether $E_{ij} = E_{ji}, S_{ij} = R_{ji}, R_{ij} = S_{ji}$ are established by verifying the signature of the other party. Consequently, malicious nodes have difficulty forging the encounter and forwarding evidences unilaterally.

In message receiving process, if node N_i has received a message m and is the destination node of m, node N_i extracts the forwarding evidences from the multiple endorsed layer of the message m and obtains the intermediate nodes and the message forwarding path as an evidence chain path: $N_0 \xrightarrow{\text{ts}_0} N_1 \xrightarrow{\text{ts}_1} N_2 \xrightarrow{\text{ts}_2} \cdots \to N_j \xrightarrow{\text{ts}_j} \cdots \xrightarrow{\text{ts}_i} N_i$. For each node in the evidence chain, the destination node N_i verifies the validity of their signature $\text{sig}_0, \text{sig}_1, \text{sig}_2, \ldots, \text{sig}_j, \ldots$, and if signature verification for all nodes is correct and valid, those that successfully helped forwarding will be rewarded and trusted. The design of trust reward calculation is the pivot of an efficient routing scheme, which should reflect the ability of the intermediate nodes to forward message to the destination node and the fairness and incentive of trust evaluation. Therefore, we will calculate the trust reward of intermediate nodes based on the principles of reliability and delay.

(1) Reliability Principle. The position of intermediate node in the evidence chain $\text{path}(N_j)$ is closer to the destination node N_i, and the trust reward of this intermediate node should be higher. This is because the larger $\text{path}(N_j)$, the higher the reliability of node N_j to carry a message to the destination node N_i.

(2) Delay Principle. For the message of same link length, if the message delay time $\Delta t = ts_i - t$ is smaller, the intermediate node should get the higher trust reward from the destination node N_i. This is because the smaller Δt is, the quicker those intermediate nodes can deliver the message to the destination node N_i.

Assume that $T_{ij}^{(m)}$ is the trust reward of node N_j evaluated by the destination node N_i based on the received message m. Based on the above principle, we define $T_{ij}^{(m)}$ as

$$T_{ij}^{(m)} = \frac{1}{2} \left(\rho \left(\frac{\Delta t}{\text{TTL}} \right) + f \left(\frac{\text{path}\left(N_j\right)}{|\text{path}\left(m\right)|} \right) \right), \tag{3}$$

where $|\text{path}(m)|$ denotes the length of message m forwarding path in evidence chain; $\rho(x) = e^{-\lambda x}$, $0 < x \leq 1$, is the delay reward function of evidence chain, which has monotonic decreasing character with delay time Δt of the message. The value range of function is $e^{-\lambda} \leq \rho(x) < 1$, $\lambda > 0$ is regulatory factor for the minimum value of the delayed reward, and the larger the parameter λ, the smaller the minimum value of the delayed reward. $\text{path}(N_j)$ denotes the position of intermediate node N_j in the evidence chain, the range is $1 \leq \text{path}(N_j) \leq |\text{path}(m)|$, and $f(y) = \phi + (1 + \phi)y^2$, $0 < y \leq 1$, is a reliability reward function for intermediate node, which has monotone increasing character with the parameter value $\text{path}(N_j)$. The value range of function is $f(y) \in (\phi, 1]$, $0 \leq \phi < 1$ is a regulatory factor for the minimum value of the reliability reward, and the larger the parameter ϕ, the larger the minimum value of the reliability reward. Therefore, the range of $T_{ij}^{(m)}$ is $(e^{-\lambda} + \phi)/2 < T_{ij}^{(m)} < 1$.

The trust degree T_{ij} of node N_i toward node N_j is calculated based on all the messages forwarding evidences in history. The following trust degree calculation is exercised: if no new trust reward is gained in time window Tw, then T_{ij} will decrease with the time; otherwise, T_{ij} will increase based on trust reward $T_{ij}^{(m)}$; that is,

$$T_{ij} = \begin{cases} T'_{ij} \times \zeta\left(t_n, t_o\right) & \text{if } t_n - t_o > \text{Tw \& } N_j \notin \mathfrak{R} \\ T'_{ij} + \left(1 - T'_{ij}\right) \times T_{ij}^{(m)} & \text{otherwise,} \end{cases} \tag{4}$$

where T'_{ij} denotes the old trust degree of node N_i toward node N_j, Tw represents the length of trust update window, and R is the set of nodes that deliver successfully messages to node N_i within the current window, that is, the collection of nodes in the evidence chain received in the current time window. $\zeta \in (1 - \gamma, 1)$ is a time decay function, where t_n, t_0 denote the current time and the latest trust update time, respectively; as

TABLE 1: Trusted routing table TRT_i of node N_i before update.

Destination node	Vector table	TwID	Signature information
N_1	SR_1	1	Sig_1
N_2	SR_2	1	Sig_2
N_i	SR_i	1	Sig_i

TABLE 2: Trusted routing table TRT_j of node N_j before update.

Destination node	Vector table	TwID	Signature information
N_1	SR_1	2	Sig_1
N_3	SR_3	1	Sig_3
N_j	SR_j	1	Sig_j

shown in (5), $0 < \gamma \leq 1$ is a factor of decay rate and minimum; the larger the parameter γ is, the quicker the trust degree value decreases. Therefore, if a node can keep good trust degree continuously, it will have a strong ability to forward message to the node N_i.

$$\zeta\left(t_n, t_o\right) = 1 - \frac{\left(t_n - t_o\right)\gamma}{t_n}. \tag{5}$$

When the encounter process and message receiving process are performed, node N_i will generate or update the tuple $Tr_ij = \langle E_{ij}^*, T_{ij} \rangle$ to record summary information about node N_j. Without loss of generality, node N_i generates the tuple Tr for each DTNs node after multiple cycles of the network operation. Therefore, we adopt vector table $SR_i = (Tr_{i1}, Tr_{i2}, Tr_{i3}, \ldots, Tr_{in})$ to store the summary information that the node N_i reports about other nodes. The trusted routing table (TRT) consists of vector table of each node, but in initial phase, each node's trusted routing table has only its own row vector. To quickly build and update trusted routing table in each DTNs node, when the two nodes meet, they first exchange trusted routing table with each other. When a node received the encounter node's trusted routing table, it compares the received trusted routing table to itself trusted routing table. If there is a new row vector in the received trusted routing table, this node will update its trusted routing table. To prevent malicious nodes from tampering row vector of trusted routing tables, node N_i generates the record information of the row vector $SR_i^* = SR_i$, TwID, Sig_i periodically to update and verify the trusted routing table, where $\text{Sig}_i = \text{SIG}_{sk_i}(H''(SR_i \mid \text{TwID}))$ refers to the signature generated by node N_i on vector table SR_i, $H''(*)$ is a hash function for generating summary of $SR_i \mid \text{TwID}$, and TwID denotes the latest update window of record information SR_i^*.

We use an example to illustrate the update process of the trusted routing table. As shown in Tables 1 and 2, the trusted routing table TRT_i of node N_i contains three row vectors SR_1, SR_2, SR_i, and the trusted routing table TRT_j of node N_j contains three row vectors SR_1, SR_3, SR_j, and when node N_i and node N_j meet, they exchange the trusted routing tables $\text{TRT}_i, \text{TRT}_j$ with each other. After the update operation, as shown in Table 3, the trusted routing tables $\text{TRT}_i, \text{TRT}_j$ of node N_i and node N_j contain five row vectors $SR_1, SR_2, SR_3, SR_i, SR_j$, and SR_1 is the latest vector table in

TABLE 3: Trusted routing table of node N_i and node N_j after update.

destination node	Vector table	TwID	Signature information
N_1	SR_1	2	Sig_1
N_2	SR_2	1	Sig_2
N_3	SR_3	1	Sig_3
N_i	SR_i	1	Sig_i
N_j	SR_j	1	Sig_j

Input: node N_i maintains the vector table
$SR_i = (Tr_{i1}, Tr_{i2}, Tr_{i3}, \cdots, Tr_{in})$; The initial
value of trusted routing table TRT_i contains
only row vectors SR_i;
(1) **if** node N_i updated the vector table SR_i **then**
(2)   generate the new row vector
$SR_i^* = \{SR_i, TwID, Sig_i\}$;
(3)   update row vector SR_i in trusted routing table;
(4)   TwID + +;
(5) **end**
(6) **if** node N_i and node N_j meet each other **then**
(7)   send trusted routing table TRT_i to node N_j;
(8)   receive trusted routing table TRT_j from node N_j;
(9) **end**
(10) **while** $\forall SR_k \in TRT_i \cap TRT_j$ **do**
(11)   **if** $TRT_j \cdot SR_k \cdot TwID > TRT_i \cdot SR_k \cdot TwID$ **then**
(12)   verify the validity of the signature Sig_k;
(13)   **if** Sig_k is valid **then**
(14)   update row vector SR_k in trusted routing
table TRT_i;
(15) $TRT_i \cdot SR_k = TRT_j \cdot SR_k$;
(16) $TRT_i \cdot SR_k \cdot TwID = TRT_j \cdot SR_k \cdot TwID$;
(17) $TRT_i \cdot Sig_k = TRT_j \cdot Sig_k$;
(18)   **end**
(19)   **end**
(20) **end**
(21) **while** $\forall SR_k \in TRT_j$ and $SR_k \notin TRT_j$ **do**
(22)   verify the validity of the signature Sig_k;
(23)   **if** Sig_k is valid **then**
(24)   insert $N_k, SR_k, TwID, Sig_k$ into trusted routing
table TRT_i;
(25)   **end**
(26) **end**

ALGORITHM 1: Building and updating TRT.

node N_j. The detailed update process of trusted routing table is shown in Algorithm 1.

Robustness Analysis. In the building and updating process of the trusted routing table, the malicious node may modify the trusted routing table to forge high trust value and message forwarding ratio. However, this attack can be thwarted in our scheme, since the number of encounters and forwarding message number of malicious node can be verified by well-behaving nodes that encountered malicious node in the past, so the malicious node cannot forge message forwarding ratio. Because each row vector in the trusted routing table has the signature of the corresponding node, if the malicious node

forged high trust value in row vector, then this forged row vector cannot be updated to the trusted routing table of other nodes, because the signature of the node in this forged row vector is incorrect. As a result, the proposed trusted routing table has robustness and nonrepudiation.

3.4. Detecting Malicious Nodes and Selfish Nodes. By analyzing and observing the characteristics of the attacker in Section 2.2, we have the strong belief that can distinguish between well-behaving nodes and malicious nodes through their historical forwarding behavior and trust value, because if a well-behaving node has a high number of encounters with other nodes, it might receive a lot of messages and forward a larger portion of them or all of them; that is, it has higher ratio between forwarded messages and received messages. However, malicious nodes often have high number of encounters and receive a lot of messages from other nodes but only forward a small portion of them or even do not forward any of them, so malicious nodes have lower ratio of forwarded messages over received messages. Different from malicious nodes, selfish nodes receive only a few of messages even if they have high number of encounters with other nodes, but they forward a lot of messages generated by themselves, so selfish nodes have abnormal high ratio between forwarded messages and received messages. Based on the above analysis, we use the column vector in the trusted routing table to define the metrics named malicious behavior ratio, MBR, and selfish behavior ratio, SBR, that can effectively detect malicious nodes and selfish nodes. Suppose the column vector of node N_j is $SC_{*j} = (Tr_{1j}, Tr_{2j}, Tr_{3j}, \ldots, Tr_{nj})^T$, malicious behavior ratio MBR of node N_j can be formulated as

$$MBR = \frac{\left(\sum_{i=1}^{n} Tr_{ij} \cdot R_{ij}\right)^2}{\sum_{i=1}^{n} Tr_{ij} \cdot S_{ij} \times \sum_{i=1}^{n} Tr_{ij} \cdot E_{ij}}, \quad (6)$$

where $\sum_{i=1}^{n} Tr_{ij} \cdot R_{ij}$ is the total number of messages that all DTNs nodes received from node N_j, that is, the total number of messages forwarded by node N_j. $\sum_{i=1}^{n} Tr_{ij} \cdot S_{ij}$ is the total number of messages that all DTNs nodes send to node N_j, that is, the total number of messages received by node N_j. $\sum_{i=1}^{n} Tr_{ij} \cdot E_{ij}$ is the total number of encounters where all DTNs nodes meet node N_j. MBR can potentially reveal malicious behavior of malicious nodes dropping packets frequently, because $\sum_{i=1}^{n} Tr_{ij} \cdot R_{ij}$ is far less than $\sum_{i=1}^{n} Tr_{ij} \cdot S_{ij}$ and $\sum_{i=1}^{n} Tr_{ij} \cdot E_{ij}$, so malicious nodes have lower MBR than the well-behaving nodes.

To effectively detect selfish nodes, selfish behavior ratio SBR can be formulated as

$$SBR = \frac{\sum_{i=1}^{n} Tr_{ij} \cdot R_{ij} \times \sum_{i=1}^{n} Tr_{ij} \cdot E_{ij}}{\left(\sum_{i=1}^{n} Tr_{ij} \cdot S_{ij}\right)^2}, \quad (7)$$

where the meaning of each value and expression is the same as (6), and SBR can potentially reveal behavior of selfish nodes that frequently refuse the request of forwarding message packets, because $\sum_{i=1}^{n} Tr_{ij} \cdot R_{ij}$ and $\sum_{i=1}^{n} Tr_{ij} \cdot E_{ij}$ are greater than $\sum_{i=1}^{n} Tr_{ij} \cdot S_{ij}$, so selfish nodes have abnormal higher SBR than the well-behaving nodes.

Input: Detection node N_j, Th_{MBR}, Th_{SBR}
Output: detection result of node N_j
(1)   get the column vector
       $SC_{*i} = (Tr_{1i}, Tr_{2i}, Tr_{3i}, \ldots, Tr_{ni})^T$ of node N_j from
       trusted routing table;
(2)   calculate malicious behavior ratio MBR of node N_j
       using Eq. (6);
(3)   calculate selfish behavior ratio SBR of node N_j using
       Eq. (7);
(4)   **if** MBR < Th_{MBR} **then**
(5)   return node N_j is a malicious node;
(6)   **else**
(7)   **if** SBR > Th_{SBR} **then**
(8)   return node N_j is a selfish node;
(9)   **else**
(10)   return node N_j is a well-behaving node;
(11)   **end**
(12) **end**

ALGORITHM 2: Detecting malicious and selfish nodes.

Therefore, after obtaining MBR and SBR of node N_j, we compare them with predefined thresholds to judge whether the node N_j is malicious node or not. Th_{MBR} and Th_{SBR} denote threshold of malicious behavior ratio and selfish behavior ratio, respectively, and their value is chosen empirically using simulation. The detailed detection process of malicious and selfish nodes is shown in Algorithm 2.

3.5. Security and Efficient Routing Based on TRT. When node N_I meets node N_j, it triggers Algorithm 3 to perform the following routing steps. Step (1): node N_I first uses Algorithm 2 to judge whether node N_j is a well-behaving node or not; if node N_j is a well-behaving node, it runs to next step. Step (2): node N_i queries messages in its buffer B_m; if there are messages that need to be forwarded, it stores the messages in a temporary set M and then goes to next step. Step (3): for each message $m \in M$, node N_i gets the identity N_d of the destination node from head field of message m and obtains row vector $SR_d = (Tr_{d1}, Tr_{d2}, Tr_{d3}, \ldots, Tr_{dn})$ of node N_d in trusted routing table TRT, then queries the trust value $Tr_{di} \cdot T_{di}, Tr_{dj} \cdot T_{dj}$, of node N_i and node N_j evaluated by node N_d, and goes to next step. Step (4): node N_i forwards the message m to node N_j according to the following strategies.

(1) If $Tr_{di} \cdot T_{di} > Tr_{dj} \cdot T_{dj}$, node N_i will forward a copy of message m with copy number nc_j to node N_j and then updates copy number $nc_i \leftarrow nc_i - nc_j$; otherwise node N_i continues to carry message m until it meets a node with greater trust degree. The copy number of message is divided according to the proportion of trust value, as shown in (8). If the node has higher trust value, it has larger copy number of message.

$$nc_j \leftarrow \left\lceil \frac{Tr_{dj} \cdot T_{dj}}{Tr_{di} \cdot T_{di} + Tr_{dj} \cdot T_{dj}} \cdot nc_i \right\rceil. \qquad (8)$$

(1)   **if** *node N_i meets node N_j* **then**
(2)   node N_i triggers Algorithm 2 and detects behavior of
          node N_j;
(3)   get detection result of node N_j from Algorithm 2;
(4)   **end**
(5)   **if** *node N_j is a well-behavior node and $B_m \neq \phi$* **then**
(6)   sorts messages by the remaining TTL;
(7)   **for** *each message $m \in B_m$* **do**
(8)   get destination node N_d from head field of m;
(9)   get $Tr_{di} \cdot T_{di}, Tr_{dj} \cdot T_{dj}$ of node N_i and node N_j
              from $SR_d = (Tr_{d1}, Tr_{d2}, Tr_{d3}, \ldots, Tr_{dn})$;
(10)   **if** $Tr_{di} \cdot T_{di} > Tr_{dj} \cdot T_{dj}$ **then**
(11)   get copy number nc_i from head field of m;
(12)   calculate nc_j using Eq. (8);
(13)   forwards a copy of m with copy number nc_j
                  to node N_j;
(14)   updates $nc_i \leftarrow nc_i - nc_j$;
(15)   **else**
(16)   **if** $Tr_{di} \cdot T_{di} == 0$ *and* $Tr_{dj} \cdot T_{dj} == 0$ **then**
(17)   calculate $\overline{T}_i, \overline{T}_j$ of node N_i and node N_j;
(18)   **if** $\overline{T}_i == 0$ *and* $\overline{T}_j == 0$ **then**
(19)   forwards a copy of m to node N_j;
(20)   **else**
(21)   **if** $\overline{T}_j > \overline{T}_i$ **then**
(22)   get copy number nc_i from head
                              field of m;
(23)   calculate nc_j using Eq. (9);
(24)   forwards a copy of m with copy
                              number nc_j to node N_j;
(25)   updates $nc_i \leftarrow nc_i - nc_j$;
(26)   **end**
(27)   **end**
(28)   **else**
(29)   **end**
(30) **end**
(31) **end**

ALGORITHM 3: Security and efficient routing algorithm.

(2) In the initial phase, if $Tr_{di} \cdot T_{di}$ and $Tr_{dj} \cdot T_{dj}$ are null values, we use average trust values $\overline{T}_i, \overline{T}_j$ of node N_i and node N_j as the decision for message forwarding, $\overline{T}_i = (1/n)\sum_{x=1}^{n} Tr_{xi} \cdot T_{xi}$ and $\overline{T}_j = (1/n)\sum_{x=1}^{n} Tr_{xj} \cdot T_{xj}$. If $\overline{T}_j = \overline{T}_i = 0$, it shows that the network is in the cold start phase. Therefore, node N_i adopts epidemic algorithm to forward the copy of message m to node N_j and does not divide the copy number of message m.

(3) If $\overline{T}_j > \overline{T}_i$, node N_i will forward a copy of message m with copy number nc_j to node N_j and then updates copy number $nc_i \leftarrow nc_i - nc_j$; otherwise node N_i continues to carry message m until it meets a node with greater trust degree. In this case, the copy number of message is divided as shown in

$$nc_j \leftarrow \left\lceil \frac{\overline{T}_j}{\overline{T}_i + \overline{T}_j} \cdot nc_i \right\rceil. \qquad (9)$$

The proposed routing algorithm only uses the row vectors and column vectors in the local trusted routing table to judge the behavior of encountered node and make forwarding decision. The overhead of the algorithm is low; the maximum time complexity is equal to $O(|M| \times n)$. The algorithm of detecting malicious nodes and selfish nodes can detect the behavior of the encountered node and effectively resist the attacks of malicious and selfish nodes in DTNs. Therefore, the proposed scheme improves the security and reliability of DTNs effectively and achieves the design goal 2 in Section 2.3. In the proposed scheme, a message is delivered to the destination node along the direction of trust gradient increment; only when the condition $Tr_{di} \cdot T_{di} > Tr_{dj} \cdot T_{dj}$ is met, the relay nodes forward the message to the next-hop relay nodes. This scheme makes the probability of the message reaching the destination node get higher and higher and significantly improves the network routing performance, that is, higher delivery ratio and lower average delivery delay and achieves design goal 1 in Section 2.3.

4. Performance Evaluation

4.1. Simulation Setup. We set up the experiment environment with the ONE (opportunistic network environment) simulator, in which we implement our proposed routing algorithm. ONE simulator is designed for evaluating and verifying DTNs routing protocols and includes a variety of movement models, map of Helsinki city, and some typical routing algorithms such as Epidemic, Spray and Wait (SAW), Prophet, and MaxProp. In our experiment, we adopt the map of Helsinki city as the experiment environment and deploy 200 nodes on the map with size of 4500 m to 3400 m. The well-behaving nodes and selfish nodes use shortest path map based movement model to simulate the movement at speed of 0.5 m/s to 1.5 m/s, and malicious nodes move at speed of 2.7 m/s to 13.9 m/s. Messages are generated at the rate of one per 25 to 35 seconds. The simulation time is set to 24 hours, during which 2900 messages are generated. The size of message is 512 kB. Time to live (TTL) is in the range of 30 to 240 minutes. The buffer B_m of each node is in the range of 5 M to 60 M. Delay of reward regulation factor λ is set to 10. Reliability reward regulation factor ϕ is set to 0.3. Time decay factor γ is set to 0.2. The maximum copy number of message nc is set to 10.

We evaluate our scheme in two aspects: effectiveness of malicious attack detection and routing performance. The performance metrics used in the evaluation are (i) detected accuracy, which is the percentage of malicious nodes and selfish nodes that can be detected; (ii) false positive rate, which is the percentage of well-behaving nodes that are falsely judged as malicious nodes and selfish nodes; (iii) delivery rate, which is the percentage of generated messages that are successfully delivered to destination nodes within time to live; (iv) average delivery delay, which is the average time taken for the messages to be delivered from the source nodes to the destination nodes; (v) overhead rate, which is the proportion between the number of relayed messages (excluding the successfully delivered messages) and the number of successfully delivered messages. Both detected accuracy and false positive

rate are used to measure effectiveness of malicious attack detection. Delivery rate, average delivery delay, and overhead rate are used to measure routing performance.

4.2. Simulation Results and Analysis

4.2.1. The Impact of Choosing Different Threshold. First, we evaluate the impact of choosing different threshold Th_{MBR} on malicious behavior detection of SER. The number of malicious nodes is set to 40. The dropping probability of messages is varied from 0.1 to 0.8, which indicates the level of malicious nodes. The threshold of malicious behavior ratio Th_{MBR} is varied from 0.05 to 0.4. Time to live (TTL) of each message is fixed to 30 minutes. The buffer B_m of each node is fixed to 5 M.

Figure 5 presents the detected accuracy and false positive rate of SER with varying thresholds and dropping probability. Figure 5(a) shows that six curves have similar trends, which indicate that the malicious nodes are more likely to be detected when their dropping probability increases. When the dropping probability of messages increases to 0.3, the detected accuracy of SER reaches to 100 percent using four varying thresholds. Even though the dropping probability of messages is lower than 0.1, the detected accuracy of SER is still higher than 70 percent when the threshold is greater than 0.15. This shows that SER could achieve a better detected accuracy. Furthermore, Figure 5(a) also shows that the greater the threshold, the higher the detected accuracy of SER. However, from Figure 5(b), we can obviously find that the greater the threshold, the higher the false positive rate of SER. When the threshold is equal to 0.4, the false positive rate of SER exceeds 14 percent, which is obviously unacceptable even with higher detected accuracy. Therefore, we need to set a threshold tradeoff between detected accuracy and false positive rate. As seen in Figures 5(a) and 5(b), if the threshold is set to 0.1 or 0.15, SER not only has higher detection accuracy, but also has lower false positive rate. That means SER has little effect on well-behaving nodes when we choose the appropriate threshold.

Similarly, we evaluate the impact of choosing different threshold Th_{SBR} on selfish behavior detection of SER. The total number of selfish nodes is varied from 10 to 50. The threshold Th_{SBR} is varied from 1.3 to 3. Figure 6(a) shows that the detected accuracy of SER reaches to 100 percent under all thresholds, when the total number of selfish nodes is less than 20, which implies that the less selfish nodes are easier to be detected. When the number of selfish nodes exceeds 30, the detected accuracy of SER has the drop trends, and the greater the threshold, the more obvious the drop trends. But correspondingly, as shown in Figure 6(b), the false positive rate of SER also has more significant drop trends, when the number of selfish nodes increases. This is because the selfish nodes have more friends and receive more messages from their friends. The result is that some selfish nodes have lower SBR and do not violate the large thresholds. Even though the number of selfish nodes is increased to 50, the detected accuracy of SER is still higher than 94 percent, but the false positive rate of SER is lower than 2 percent when the threshold is equal to 1.3. This means that SER could detect

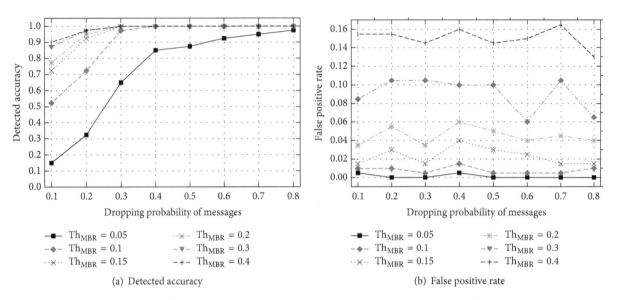

(a) Detected accuracy

(b) False positive rate

FIGURE 5: SER's malicious behavior detection results under varying thresholds Th_{MBR}.

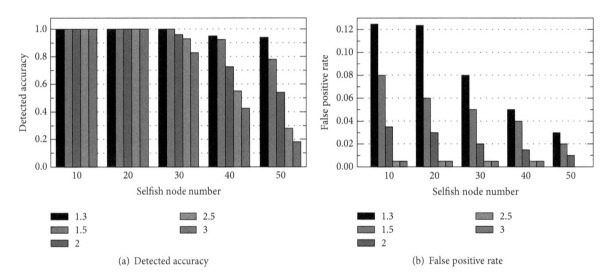

(a) Detected accuracy

(b) False positive rate

FIGURE 6: SER's selfish behavior detection results under varying thresholds Th_{SBR}.

selfish behavior effectively and has a little effect on well-behaving nodes. Therefore, we conclude that if the number of selfish nodes is less than 30, we use the large threshold to detect false positive rate; on the contrary, we use a small threshold.

4.2.2. The Impact of TTL on the Routing Performance. In this section, we compare SER with three classic routing schemes Epidemic, Prophet, and SAW in the routing performance. The buffer B_m of each node is fixed to 5 M. Time to live (TTL) of message is varied from 30 minutes to 240 minutes. Suppose there are no malicious nodes and selfish nodes in DTNs.

Figure 7 shows the performance of four routing schemes under varying TTL. As seen in Figures 7(a) and 7(b), our scheme SER has obvious advantages in delivery rate and average delivery delay compared with other three schemes. From the figure, TTL has little effect on SER. Even though

the TTL is equal to 30 minutes, the delivery rate of SER still reached to 70 percent. When TTL is greater than 120 minutes, the delivery rate of SER reached to 88.5 percent and tends to a steady state. This is because SER adopts the following message forwarding strategy: (1) selecting the more trusted nodes as the next-hop relay nodes and (2) each message having multiple finite copies that are forwarded concurrently along different paths. However, the delivery rates of Epidemic and Prophet have the drop trends when the TTL increases. This is because these two schemes adopt the infinite message copies forwarding strategy; there are many messages that are not forwarded in time, which are deleted by nodes due to buffer capacity limitation and receiving the new messages. Although the delivery rate of SAW approaches SER when the TTL is increased to 240 minutes, SER has greater advantage in the average delivery delay; the other schemes have obvious growth trend with TTL increased. When the TTL is increased

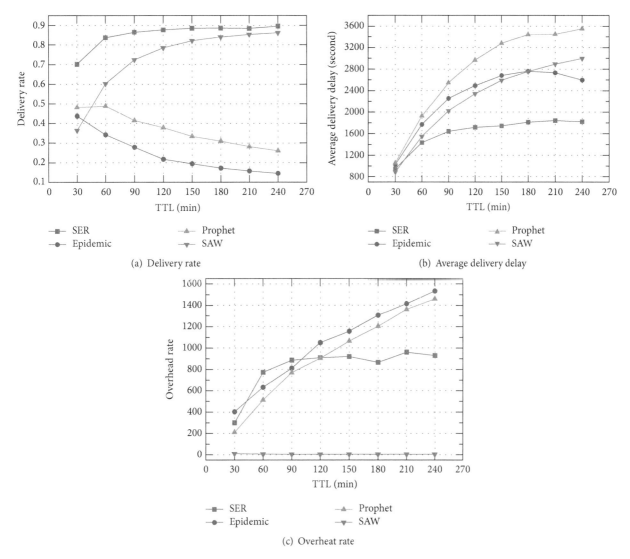

(a) Delivery rate

(b) Average delivery delay

(c) Overheat rate

FIGURE 7: Routing performance under varying TTL.

to 240 minutes, the average delivery delay of SAW exceeds 3000 seconds while SER is only about 1800 seconds. This means that our SER scheme could find a trusted forwarding path with a short delay when the trust mechanism is adopted to forward the message. Figure 7(c) shows that SAW has the most obvious advantage in the overhead rate; this is because SAW adopts the single copy message forwarding strategy. The overheat rate of SER is a little higher than other schemes when TTL is less than 110 minutes.

4.2.3. The Impact of Buffer Capacity on the Routing Performance. Time to live (TTL) of message is fixed to 90 minutes. The buffer B_m of node is varied from 5 M to 60 M. Figure 8 shows the performance of four routing schemes under varying buffer capacity. As seen in Figures 8(a) and 8(b), SER achieves the better performance in the delivery rate and average delivery delay by requiring small buffer. When the buffer capacity is greater than 10 M, the delivery rate of SER exceeds 96 percent and tends to have a steady state,

but, correspondingly, the average delivery delay of SER is less than 1300 seconds. This result indicates that SER has low requirements of the buffer capacity and is suitable for buffer limited DTNs. The delivery rate of Epidemic and Prophet has obvious increasing trends, but, correspondingly, the average delivery delay of Epidemic and Prophet has the dropping trends when the buffer capacity increases. This is because Epidemic and Prophet have enough space to receive the new message and store the messages for long time. This means that Epidemic and Prophet have strong dependence on the buffer capacity and have lower efficiency in buffer limited DTNs. SAW has lower dependency on the buffer capacity than the other three schemes, but the routing performance of SAW is less efficient than SER. Figure 8(c) shows that the overhead rate of SER has the dropping trends with buffer capacity increases. When the buffer capacity is equal to 10 M, the overhead rate of SER is lower than 100 and tends to be in stable state, which indicates that SER could achieve the stable routing performance with varying buffer capacity.

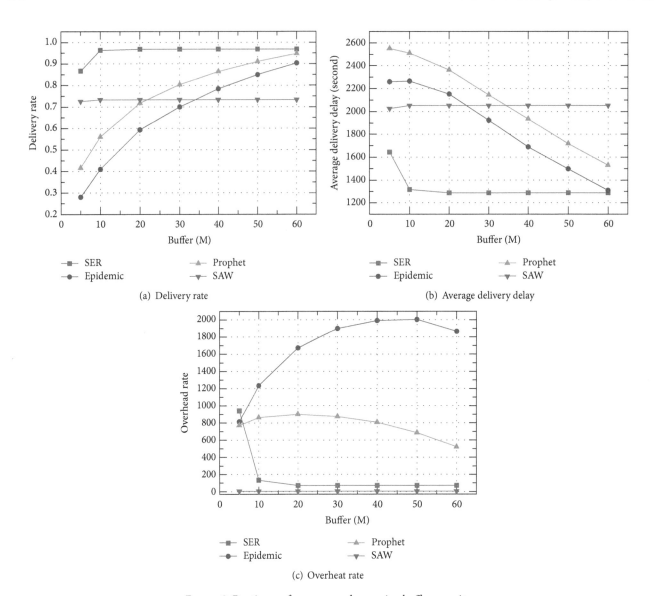

(a) Delivery rate

(b) Average delivery delay

(c) Overheat rate

FIGURE 8: Routing performance under varying buffer capacity.

4.2.4. The Impact of the Number of Malicious Nodes on the Routing Performance. In this experiment, we assume that there are malicious nodes in DTNs. The number of malicious nodes is varied from 0 to 40. The dropping message probability of malicious nodes is fixed to 0.3. The threshold Th_{MBR} on malicious behavior detection of SER is set to 0.15. The buffer B_m of each node is fixed to 10 M. Time to live (TTL) of message is fixed to 60 minutes. We evaluate the routing performance of four schemes under varying number of malicious nodes.

Figure 9(a) shows that the delivery rate of SER has the slight dropping trends, but the delivery rate of other schemes has the obvious dropping trends, when the number of malicious nodes increases. Even though the number of malicious nodes is increased to 40, the delivery rate of SER still exceeds 84 percent that is obviously higher than other schemes. This result indicates that SER has better effect

of resisting malicious behavior by using malicious nodes detection mechanism and the trusted forwarding strategy. However, the average delivery delay of four schemes has obvious rising trends in Figure 9(b); this is because the total number of nodes in the experiment is fixed to 200; if the number of malicious nodes increases, the number of well-behaving nodes would decrease to lead to the increase of average delivery delay. The delivery rate of SAW has the obvious linear dropping trend, which indicates that the malicious nodes have big effect on the single copy strategy. As seen in Figure 9(c), the overhead rate of SER is lower than 100 and close to SAW, which indicates that SER could not only detect the malicious nodes, but also forward the message to the most proper next-hop relay node. The overhead rate of Epidemic and Prophet has the dropping trends, when the number of malicious nodes increases; this is because the total number of copies of the message in DTNs is decreased. As

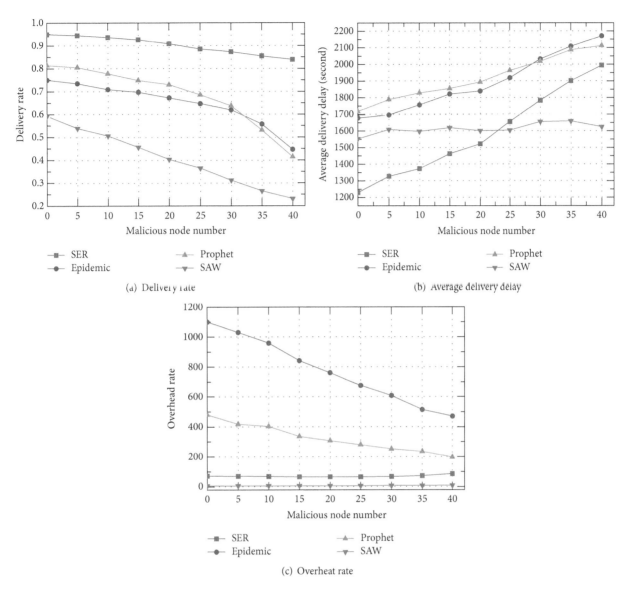

(a) Delivery rate

(b) Average delivery delay

(c) Overheat rate

FIGURE 9: Routing performance under varying of the number of malicious nodes.

a result of the two-hop routing strategy, the overhead rate of SAW is very small; this is because fewer copies of messages are generated in DTNs.

5. Related Work

In recent years, many research works on misbehavior detection and routing in DTNs have been proposed, which are closely related to our SER scheme. In Prophet [11], Lindgren et al. first propose a probabilistic routing protocol for DTNs, which calculates the probability of a node contacting the destination node as the next-hop relay node selection strategies. A node will forward a message to the next-hop node only when the next-hop node has a higher probability of contacting the destination node. MaxProp [8] exploits priority of the transmitted path to schedule the messages to be forwarded and the messages to be dropped and stores a list of previous intermediaries to prevent message from forwarding twice to

the same node. In ERB [12], to minimize overhead in terms of both extra traffic injected into the network and control overhead, ERB adopts historical encounter-based metric for optimization of message forwarding, where each node is only responsible for maintaining the past rate of encounter average to predict future encounter rates. SMART [16], SSAR [10], Bubble Rap [9], and SGBR [17] exploit the various social metrics to select the appropriate next-hop relay node, such as history of interaction, betweenness centrality, and community. Although the routing schemes mentioned above are very effective for improving route performance, they cannot address the security problems in DTNs.

To detect colluding blackhole and greyhole attacks, Pham and Yeo [6] designs a statistical-based detection scheme (SDBG) in which each node locally maintains the encounter records and the meeting summary with other nodes. When the nodes meet each other, they are required to exchange their encounter record histories, based on which other nodes can evaluate their forwarding behaviors. Alajeely et al. [3] present the detection attack and trace back mechanisms based on the Merkle tree, where the legitimate nodes can detect attack based on the received packets and then trace back and identify the malicious nodes. Zhu et al. [7] exploit a trusted authority (TA) to judge the forwarding behavior of nodes based on the collected delegation task evidence, forwarding history evidence, and contact history evidence. Chen et al. [13], Lu et al. [15], Ayday and Fekri [18], Li and Cao [14], Zhao et al. [19], and Chen and Chan [20] adopt the incentive mechanism to motivate selfish nodes to forward messages, which use reputation or credit to represent the forwarding behavior of nodes.

Different from existing routing protocols and misbehavior detection schemes, our proposed SER scheme introduces a trusted routing table (TRT) that contains the behavior history information of each node and the trust degree of forwarding the message to other nodes. We use the trusted routing table not only to analyze the behavior of nodes, but also to make effective routing decisions. Therefore, SER can achieve both the routing performance and the misbehavior detection and only cost the extra resource overhead that maintains the trusted routing table.

6. Conclusions

In this paper, we proposed a security and efficient routing scheme (SER), which has the dual functions of routing decision and malicious attacks detection. Based on the layered coin model and digital signature mechanism, the proposed forwarding evidences collection mechanism can effectively guarantee the security and authenticity of the forwarding evidence. Exploiting the forwarding evidence and historical contact information, we described in detail the build and update process of trusted routing table. By adopting the trusted routing table, the proposed SER scheme can obtain the global view about the contact relationship among all nodes in DTNs. The detailed analysis has shown that the trusted routing table not only is secure and reliable, but also quickly converges to global consistency. The simulation results show that SER could accurately detect the attacks behavior of malicious nodes or selfish nodes by analyzing the history forwarding behavior of node from the global view. In addition, the simulation results also demonstrate that SER has better routing performance compared with the existing algorithms, such as higher delivery rate and lower average delivery delay. For our future work, we will design the hierarchical trusted routing table and further reduce the network resource overhead.

Acknowledgments

This research was supported by National Natural Science Foundation of China (Grant nos. 61300193, 61272125, and 61601107), the Hebei Natural Science Foundation (Grant no. F2015501105, no. F2015501122), and the Fundamental Research Funds for the Central Universities (Grant no. N120323012).

References

[1] N. Chakchouk, "A Survey on Opportunistic Routing in Wireless Communication Networks," *IEEE Communications Surveys and Tutorials*, vol. 17, no. 4, pp. 2214–2241, 2015.

[2] S. Cc, V. Raychoudhury, G. Marfia, and A. Singla, "A survey of routing and data dissemination in Delay Tolerant Networks," *Journal of Network and Computer Applications*, vol. 67, pp. 128–146, 2016.

[3] M. Alajeely, R. Doss, A. Ahmad, and V. Mak-Hau, "Defense against packet collusion attacks in opportunistic networks," *Computers and Security*, vol. 65, pp. 269–282, 2017.

[4] J. Burgess, G. D. Bissias, M. D. Corner, and B. N. Levine, "Surviving attacks on disruption-tolerant networks without authentication," in *Proceedings of the MobiHoc'07: 8th ACM International Symposium on Mobile Ad Hoc Networking and Computing*, pp. 61–70, Canada, September 2007.

[5] F. Li, J. Wu, and A. Srinivasan, "Thwarting blackhole attacks in disruption-tolerant networks using encounter tickets," in *Proceedings of the 28th Conference on Computer Communications, IEEE INFOCOM 2009*, pp. 2428–2436, bra, April 2009.

[6] D. Pham and C. K. Yeo, "Detecting colluding blackhole and greyhole attack in delay tolerant networks," *IEEE Transactions on Mobile Computing*, pp. 1–15, 2015.

[7] H. Zhu, S. Du, Z. Gao, M. Dong, and Z. Cao, "A probabilistic misbehavior detection scheme toward efficient trust establishment in delay-tolerant networks," *IEEE Transactions on Parallel and Distributed Systems*, vol. 25, no. 1, pp. 22–32, 2014.

[8] J. Burgess, B. Gallagher, D. Jensen, and B. N. Levine, "MaxProp: routing for vehicle-based disruption-tolerant networks," in *Proceedings of the 25th IEEE International Conference on Computer Communications (INFOCOM '06)*, April 2006.

[9] P. Hui, J. Crowcroft, and E. Yoneki, "BUBBLE Rap: social-based forwarding in delay-tolerant networks," *IEEE Transactions on Mobile Computing*, vol. 10, no. 11, pp. 1576–1589, 2011.

[10] Q. Li, W. Gao, S. Zhu, and G. Cao, "A routing protocol for socially selfish delay tolerant networks," *Ad Hoc Networks*, vol. 10, no. 8, pp. 1619–1632, 2012.

[11] A. Lindgren, A. Doria, and O. Schelén, "Probabilistic routing in intermittently connected networks," *ACM SIGMOBILE Mobile Computing and Communications Review*, vol. 7, no. 3, pp. 19-20, 2003.

[12] S. C. Nelson, M. Bakht, and R. Kravets, "Encounter-based routing in DTNs," in *Proceedings of the 28th Conference on Computer Communications (INFOCOM '09)*, pp. 846–854, IEEE, April 2009.

[13] I.-R. Chen, F. Bao, M. Chang, and J.-H. Cho, "Dynamic trust management for delay tolerant networks and its application to secure routing," *IEEE Transactions on Parallel and Distributed Systems*, vol. 25, no. 5, pp. 1200–1210, 2014.

[14] Q. Li and G. Cao, "Mitigating routing misbehavior in disruption tolerant networks," *IEEE Transactions on Information Forensics and Security*, vol. 7, no. 2, pp. 664–675, 2012.

[15] R. Lu, X. Lin, H. Zhu, X. Shen, and B. Preiss, "Pi: a practical incentive protocol for delay tolerant networks," *IEEE Transactions on Wireless Communications*, vol. 9, no. 4, pp. 1483–1493, 2010.

[16] T. Zhou, R. R. Choudhury, and K. Chakrabarty, "Diverse routing: Exploiting social behavior for routing in delay-tolerant networks," in *Proceedings of the 2009 IEEE International Conference on Social Computing, SocialCom 2009*, pp. 1115–1122, Canada, August 2009.

[17] T. Abdelkader, K. Naik, A. Nayak, N. Goel, and V. Srivastava, "SGBR: A routing protocol for delay tolerant networks using social grouping," *IEEE Transactions on Parallel and Distributed Systems*, vol. 24, no. 12, pp. 2472–2481, 2013.

[18] E. Ayday and F. Fekri, "An Iterative Algorithm for Trust Management and Adversary Detection for Delay-Tolerant Networks," *IEEE Transactions on Mobile Computing*, vol. 11, no. 9, pp. 1514–1531, 2012.

[19] H. Zhao, X. Yang, and X. Li, "CTrust: trust management in cyclic mobile Ad Hoc networks," *IEEE Transactions on Vehicular Technology*, vol. 62, no. 6, pp. 2792–2806, 2013.

[20] B. B. Chen and M. C. Chan, "MobiCent: a credit-based incentive system for disruption tolerant network," in *Proceedings of the 2010 IEEE INFOCOM*, pp. 1–9, March 2010.

14

Adaptive Security of Broadcast Encryption, Revisited

Bingxin Zhu, Puwen Wei, and Mingqiang Wang

Key Laboratory of Cryptologic Technology and Information Security, Ministry of Education, Shandong University, Jinan, China

Correspondence should be addressed to Puwen Wei; pwei@sdu.edu.cn and Mingqiang Wang; wangmingqiang@sdu.edu.cn

Academic Editor: Paolo D'Arco

We provide a strong security notion for broadcast encryption, called adaptive security in the multichallenge setting (MA-security), where the adversary can adaptively have access to the key generation oracle and the encryption oracle many times (multichallenge). The adversary specially can query for the challenge ciphertexts on different target user sets adaptively, which generalizes the attacks against broadcast encryptions in the real world setting. Our general result shows that the reduction of the adaptive secure broadcast encryption will lose a factor of q in the MA setting, where q is the maximum number of encryption queries. In order to construct tighter MA-secure broadcast encryptions, we investigate Gentry and Water's transformation and show that their transformation can preserve MA-security at the price of reduction loss on the advantage of the underlying symmetric key encryption. Furthermore, we remove the q-type assumption in Gentry and Water's semistatically secure broadcast encryption by using Hofheinz-Koch-Striecks techniques. The resulting scheme instantiated in a composite order group is MA-secure with constant-size ciphertext header.

1. Introduction

Broadcast encryptions (BE), introduced by Fiat and Naor [1], allow a sender to broadcast encrypted messages in such a way that only a specified group of users can decrypt the messages. Such schemes are useful in many applications, for example, pay-TV systems, internet multicasting of video and music, DVD content protection, file system access control, and wireless sensor networks [2]. One basic security requirement for broadcast encryption is the fully collusion resistance, which means that even a coalition of all users outside of target user set S learns nothing about the target plaintext. Naor et al. [3] proposed a fully collusion secure broadcast encryption scheme with the private key overhead $O(\log^2(n))$, where n is the total number of users. Subsequent works [4, 5] reduced the private key size to $O(\log n)$. However, the ciphertexts size of collusion resistant schemes, for example, [3–6], usually grows linearly with either the number of receivers or the number of revoked users. Boneh et al. [7] constructed a fully collusion secure broadcast encryption systems with low ciphertext overhead and short secret keys. But the security of their scheme was proven in a static model, where the adversary needs to choose the target user set before seeing the system parameter. To capture more powerful attacks, Gentry and Waters [8] provided a stronger security model, called adaptive security, where the adversary can compromise users' keys and choose the target user set adaptively. They showed a generic method to construct adaptively secure broadcast encryption scheme by transforming semistatically secure broadcast encryption scheme, while the underlying semistatically secure scheme in [8] is based on a q-type assumption, which is considered to be too strong. By introducing the dual system, Waters [9] presented a broadcast encryption scheme with ciphertext overhead of constant size, and the resulting scheme can be proven adaptively secure under static assumption (non-q-type assumption). Then, Boneh, Waters, and Zhandry [10] made use of multilinear maps to construct a broadcast encryption where ciphertext overhead, private key size, and public key size are all poly-logarithmic in n. Other works [11–15] focus on the improvements of broadcast encryptions with special functionalities, for example, identity-based BE, anonymous BE, and traitor-tracing BE. Recently, Wee [16] presented the first broadcast encryption scheme with constant-size ciphertext overhead, constant-size user secret keys, and linear-size public parameters under static assumptions, while the resulting scheme is proven secure under static security model.

It is worth noting that although adaptive security defined in [8] seems strong enough to capture the security of broadcast encryptions, attacks in the real world are more complex, for example, the adversary may adaptively get multiple challenge ciphertexts instead of only one. Such attacks are described in the so-called multiuser, multichallenge setting. Bellare et al. [17] initiated the study of the formal security in the multiuser setting, which shows that one-user, one-ciphertext security implies security in the multiuser, multichallenge setting. But the reduction loss of the proof is $n_u \cdot n_c$, where n_u and n_c denote the number of users and the number of challenge ciphertexts per user, respectively. However, large reduction loss usually implies large cryptographic parameters, which leads to low efficiency in practice. Recent breakthrough was made by Hofheinz and Jager [18], which provided the first IND-CCA secure PKE in the multiuser/multichallenge setting and the security tightly relates to the decision linear assumption. Here, tight security means that the security loss is a constant. Hofheinz, Koch, and Striecks [19] extended Chen and Wee's proof technique [20] to the multiuser/multichallenge setting and provided an almost tightly secure identity-based encryption (IBE) in the same setting, where the security loss only relies on the security parameter instead of the number of queries or instances of the scheme. Hence, an extension of broadcast encryptions in the multiuser/multichallenge setting is natural. However, the problem of constructing tightly secure broadcast encryptions in the multiuser/multichallenge setting is more subtle.

Our Contribution. We define a stronger notion for broadcast encryption, called the adaptive security in the multichallenge setting (MA-security), where the adversary can not only adaptively have access to the key generation oracle and the encryption oracle many times (multichallenge) but also adaptively query for the challenge ciphertexts on different target user sets instead of only one target set as in previous security model. Since each target user set is actually the combination of different users chosen by the adversary adaptively, it is more challenging for the reduction algorithm to prepare the parameters of broadcast encryptions than that of ordinary PKE or IBE.

Our general result shows that the reduction of the adaptive secure broadcast encryption will lose a factor of q in the MA setting, where q is the maximum number of encryption queries. To achieve tighter MA-security, we investigate the following two methods. The first method is from Gentry and Waters transformation [8] mentioned above. By exploring the random self-reducibility of BDHE assumption, we show that their transformation still holds in terms of MA-security, but at the cost of reduction loss q on the advantage of underlying symmetric key encryption. We emphasize that the resulting broadcast encryption scheme's security depends on both the BDHE assumption and the security of the symmetric key encryption. The reduction loss on the underlying symmetric key encryption is q, while the reduction on BDHE is tight due to the random self-reducibility of BDHE assumption, which is not implied by the general result of [17]. To remove the BDHE assumption, our second method applies the Hofheinz-Koch-Striecks techniques [19] to Gentry-Waters' semistatic secure broadcast encryption. The resulting scheme is essentially the Hofheinz-Koch-Striecks IBE scheme instantiated in a composite order group, while the user's decryption

key of broadcast encryption is expressed in a different way from that of [19]. Both methods can turn Gentry-Waters' semistatically secure broadcast encryption into a MA-secure one with constant-size ciphertext header.

Note that the public key size of both schemes is linear with the number of users. An interesting problem is how to reduce the public key size of a MA-secure broadcast encryption under standard assumptions while preserving constant ciphertext header size.

2. Preliminaries

Notations. Let $[1, n] := \{1, \ldots, n\}$, where $n \in \mathbb{N}$. For a finite set $\mathcal{S}$, we denote by $x \xleftarrow{R} \mathcal{S}$ the fact that x is picked uniformly at random from $\mathcal{S}$. S can be denoted as a binary string; that is, $S = s_1 \cdots s_n$, where $s_i \in \{0, 1\}$ for $i \in [1, n]$. We write vectors in bold font; for example, $\mathbf{K} = (K_0, \ldots, K_{2n})$ for a vector of length $2n + 1$. $\mathsf{SD}(X; Y)$ denotes the statistical distance of X and Y, where X and Y are random variables. We say X and Y are ε-close if $\mathsf{SD}(X; Y) \leq \varepsilon$.

2.1. Bilinear Map. Let $\mathbb{G}$ and $\mathbb{G}_T$ be two groups of prime order p, and let g be a generator of $\mathbb{G}$. $e : \mathbb{G} \times \mathbb{G} \to \mathbb{G}_T$ is a bilinear map with the following properties.

(1) Bilinearity: for all $u, v \in \mathbb{G}$ and $a, b \in \mathbb{Z}$, $e(u^a, v^b) = e(u, v)^{ab}$.

(2) Nondegeneracy: $e(g, g) \neq 1$.

(3) Computability: there exists an efficient algorithm to compute $e(u, v)$, for any $u, v \in \mathbb{G}$.

2.2. Assumptions

Decisional BDHE Problem [8]. Let $(\mathbb{G}, \mathbb{G}_T, e, p)$ be the description of the group parameter which is the output of group generator $\mathscr{G}(\lambda)$, where λ is the security parameter. Choose $b \xleftarrow{R} \{0, 1\}$ and given $2n + 2$ elements

$$\left(g^s, g, g^a, g^{a^2}, \ldots, g^{a^n}, g^{a^{n+2}}, \ldots, g^{a^{2n}} \right) \in \mathbb{G}^{2n+1}, \qquad (1)$$
$$Z \in \mathbb{G}_T,$$

where $a, s \xleftarrow{R} \mathbb{Z}_p^*$, $Z \leftarrow e(g^s, g^{a^{n+1}})$ if $b = 0$ and $Z \xleftarrow{R} \mathbb{G}_T$ if $b = 1$. The problem is to guess b.

The decisional BDHE assumption states that for any PPT adversary $\mathscr{A}$ which takes as inputs the description of $(\mathbb{G}, \mathbb{G}_T, e)$ and the above elements and outputs b^*, the advantage

$$\mathsf{Adv}_{\mathscr{G}, \mathscr{A}}^{\mathrm{BDHE}}(\lambda) := \left| \Pr[b = b^*] - \frac{1}{2} \right| \qquad (2)$$

is negligible in λ.

2.3. Broadcast Encryption Systems. A broadcast encryption system consists of four randomized algorithms described below.

TABLE 1: MA experiment.

$\mathrm{Exp}_{\mathcal{A},\mathrm{BE}}^{\mathrm{MA}}(\lambda)$
$(\mathrm{PK},\mathrm{SK}) \longleftarrow \mathrm{Setup}\,(n,\ell)$;
$b \xleftarrow{R} \{0,1\}$;
$b' \longleftarrow \mathcal{A}^{\mathscr{O}_{\mathrm{KeyGen}}(\cdot,\mathrm{SK}),\mathscr{O}_{\mathrm{Enc}}(\cdot,\mathrm{PK})}$;
If $b' = b$, return 1; otherwise, 0.

TABLE 2: MS experiment.

$\mathrm{Exp}_{\mathcal{A},\mathrm{BE}}^{\mathrm{MS}}(\lambda)$
$S^* \longleftarrow \mathcal{A}$;
$(\mathrm{PK},\mathrm{SK}) \longleftarrow \mathrm{Setup}\,(n,\ell)$;
$b \xleftarrow{R} \{0,1\}$;
$b' \longleftarrow \mathcal{A}^{\mathscr{O}_{\mathrm{KeyGen}}(\cdot,\mathrm{SK}),\mathscr{O}_{\mathrm{Enc}}(\cdot,\mathrm{PK})}$;
If $b' = b$, return 1; otherwise, 0.

Setup(n,ℓ). Take as input the number of users n and the maximal size $\ell \leq n$ of a broadcast recipient group and output a public/secret key pair (PK, SK). (The security parameter λ is taken as parts of the input implicitly.)

KeyGen(i, SK). Take as input a user index $i \in [1, n]$ and the secret key SK and output a private key d_i.

Enc(S, PK). Take a user set $S \subseteq [1, n]$ and the public key PK as input. It outputs a pair (Hdr, K), where Hdr is the header and $K \in \mathscr{K}$ is the message encryption key from a key space $\mathscr{K}$.

Dec(S, i, d_i, Hdr, PK). Take as input a user set $S \subseteq [1, n]$, a user index $i \in [1, n]$, and the corresponding private key d_i for user i, a header Hdr, and the public key PK. If $i \in S$, then the algorithm outputs the message encryption key $K \in \mathscr{K}$.

3. Adaptive Security in the Multichallenge Setting (MA-Security)

In this section, we define the adaptive security of broadcast encryption in the multichallenge setting. Let BE = (Setup, KeyGen, Enc, Dec) be a broadcast encryption scheme. The experiment for BE is described in Table 1.

During the experiment, the adversary $\mathcal{A}$ takes λ and the description of BE including PK as inputs and $\mathcal{A}$ can have access to the following two kinds of oracles.

(i) $\mathscr{O}_{\mathrm{KeyGen}}(\cdot, \mathrm{SK})$ is the secret key generation oracle which takes a user index i as input and outputs KeyGen(i, SK). Note that $\mathcal{A}$ cannot make i as the key generation query if $i \in S_j$, where S_j has been queried to the encryption oracle. Suppose the adversary can make q_{key} key generation queries at most.

(ii) $\mathscr{O}_{\mathrm{Enc}}(\cdot, \mathrm{PK})$ is the encryption oracle which takes S_j as input and outputs the challenge ciphertext $C_j = (Hdr_j^*, K_{b,j})$, where $(Hdr_j^*, K_{0,j}) \leftarrow \mathrm{Enc}(S_j, \mathrm{PK})$, $K_{1,j} \xleftarrow{R} \mathscr{K}$. The restriction on encryption query is that S_j can not include any user index i which has been queried to $\mathscr{O}_{\mathrm{KeyGen}}$. Suppose that the adversary $\mathcal{A}$ can only query encryption oracle $\mathscr{O}_{\mathrm{Enc}}(\cdot, \mathrm{PK})$ at most q_{Enc} times.

A broadcast encryption scheme BE is adaptively secure in the multichallenge setting (MA-secure) if, for any PPT adversary $\mathcal{A}$, the advantage

$$\mathrm{Adv}_{\mathcal{A},\mathrm{BE}}^{\mathrm{MA}}(\lambda) := \left| \Pr\left[\mathrm{Exp}_{\mathcal{A},\mathrm{BE}}^{\mathrm{MA}}(\lambda) = 1 \right] - \frac{1}{2} \right| \qquad (3)$$

is negligible in λ.

Remark 1. The main difference between our MA-security and the adaptive security defined in [8] is the encryption queries. In MA-security experiment, the adversary can not only adaptively have access to the encryption oracle many times but also query for the challenge ciphertexts on different target user sets, while the adversary can make only one encryption query for one target user set in adaptive security experiment $\mathrm{Exp}_{\mathcal{A},\mathrm{BE}}^{\mathrm{A}}$ [8], where the related advantage of $\mathrm{Exp}_{\mathcal{A},\mathrm{BE}}^{\mathrm{A}}$ is denoted as $\mathrm{Adv}_{\mathcal{A},\mathrm{BE}}^{\mathrm{A}}(\lambda) := |\Pr[\mathrm{Exp}_{\mathcal{A},\mathrm{BE}}^{\mathrm{A}}(\lambda) = 1] - 1/2|$.

To investigate Gentry and Waters transformation in the multichallenge setting, we also need to extend semistatic security defined in [8] to the multichallenge setting, which is called semistatic security in the multichallenge setting (MS-security). The MS-security is defined in a similar way as that of MA-security, where the adversary also takes λ and the description of BE including PK as inputs and can have access to $\mathscr{O}_{\mathrm{KeyGen}}(\cdot, \mathrm{SK})$ and $\mathscr{O}_{\mathrm{Enc}}(\cdot, \mathrm{PK})$ as defined in MA-security. But additional restrictions in MS-security are that $\mathcal{A}$ has to choose a target user set S^* at the beginning of the experiment and encryption queries S_j are such that $S_j \subseteq S^*$. Details of MS experiment are shown in Table 2

A broadcast encryption scheme BE is semistatically secure in the multichallenge setting (MS-secure) if, for any PPT adversary $\mathcal{A}$, the advantage

$$\mathrm{Adv}_{\mathcal{A},\mathrm{BE}}^{\mathrm{MS}} := \left| \Pr\left[\mathrm{Exp}_{\mathcal{A},\mathrm{BE}}^{\mathrm{MS}}(\lambda) = 1 \right] - \frac{1}{2} \right| \qquad (4)$$

is negligible in λ.

4. MA-Secure Broadcast Encryption

First we give a general result on the reduction loss of an adaptive secure broadcast encryption in the MA setting. Then, to derive a tighter reduction, we show how to extend Gentry-Waters transformation to the multichallenge setting and construct a concrete MA-secure broadcast encryption based on BDHE assumption.

4.1. General Construction

Theorem 2. *For any PPT adversary $\mathcal{A}$ which can make at most $q_{key} = q_{key}(\lambda)$ key generation queries and $q_{Enc} = q_{Enc}(\lambda)$ encryption queries with running time t', there exists an algorithm $\mathcal{B}$ with about the same running time as $\mathcal{A}$, such that*

$$\mathrm{Adv}_{\mathcal{A},\mathrm{BE}}^{\mathrm{MA}}(\lambda) \leq q_{\mathrm{Enc}} \cdot \mathrm{Adv}_{\mathcal{B},\mathrm{BE}}^{\mathrm{A}}(\lambda). \qquad (5)$$

Proof. The proof proceeds via the following games.

(i) Game_0: Game_0 is the real MA experiment except the following differences. When the adversary adaptively makes encryption query for set S_j, the challenger responds with $\text{Enc}(S_j, \text{PK}) = (Hdr_j, K_{0,j})$, where $j \in [1, q_{\text{Enc}}]$.

(ii) Game_1: Game_1 is identical to Game_0 except that the challenger replies the encryption queries with $(Hdr_j, K_{1,j})$ for $j \in [1, q_{\text{Enc}}]$, where $(Hdr_j, K_{0,j}) \leftarrow \text{Enc}(S_j, \text{PK})$, $K_{1,j} \xleftarrow{R} \mathcal{K}^*$ and $\mathcal{K}^*$ denotes the key space.

Now we construct a series of subgames $0, \iota$ for $\iota = 0, \ldots, q_{\text{Enc}}$ to prove the indistinguishability between Game_0 and Game_1.

(i) $\text{Game}_{0,1}$. $\text{Game}_{0,1}$ is the same as Game_0 except that the challenger chooses $K_{1,1} \xleftarrow{R} \mathcal{K}^*$ to construct challenge $(Hdr_1, K_{1,1})$ for the first encryption query S_1.

(ii) $\text{Game}_{0,\iota}$. $\text{Game}_{0,\iota}$ is the same as $\text{Game}_{0,\iota-1}$ except that the challenger chooses $K_{1,\iota} \xleftarrow{R} \mathcal{K}^*$ to construct challenge $(Hdr_\iota, K_{1,\iota})$ for the ιth encryption query S_ι, where $\iota \in [1, q_{\text{Enc}}]$.

Let $\text{Game}_{0,\iota} = 1$ denote the event that the adversary outputs 1 in $\text{Game}_{0,\iota}$. Note that $\text{Game}_{0,0}$ and $\text{Game}_{0,q_{\text{Enc}}}$ are identical to Game_0 and Game_1, respectively. Thus,

$$\text{Adv}_{\mathcal{A},\text{BE}}^{\text{MA}}(\lambda) := \left| \Pr\left[\text{Exp}_{\mathcal{A},\text{BE}}^{\text{MA}}(\lambda) = 1\right] - \frac{1}{2}\right| = \left|\frac{1}{2}\right|$$

$$\cdot \Pr\left[\text{Exp}_{\mathcal{A},\text{BE}}^{\text{MA}}(\lambda) = 0 \mid b = 0\right] + \frac{1}{2}$$

$$\cdot \Pr\left[\text{Exp}_{\mathcal{A},\text{BE}}^{\text{MA}}(\lambda) = 1 \mid b = 1\right] - \frac{1}{2}\right| = \frac{1}{2}$$

$$\cdot \left| \Pr\left[\text{Exp}_{\mathcal{A},\text{BE}}^{\text{MA}}(\lambda) = 1 \mid b = 1\right] - \left(1\right.\right.$$

$$\left.\left. - \Pr\left[\text{Exp}_{\mathcal{A},\text{BE}}^{\text{MA}}(\lambda) = 0 \mid b = 0\right]\right)\right| = \frac{1}{2}$$

$$\cdot \left| \Pr\left[\text{Exp}_{\mathcal{A},\text{BE}}^{\text{MA}}(\lambda) = 1 \mid b = 1\right]\right.$$

$$\left. - \Pr\left[\text{Exp}_{\mathcal{A},\text{BE}}^{\text{MA}}(\lambda) = 1 \mid b = 0\right]\right| = \frac{1}{2} \tag{6}$$

$$\cdot \left| \Pr\left[\text{Game}_1 = 1\right] - \Pr\left[\text{Game}_0 = 1\right]\right| = \frac{1}{2}$$

$$\cdot \left| \Pr\left[\text{Game}_{0,q_{\text{Enc}}} = 1\right] - \Pr\left[\text{Game}_{0,0} = 1\right]\right| = \frac{1}{2}$$

$$\cdot \left| \Pr\left[\text{Game}_{0,q_{\text{Enc}}} = 1\right] - \Pr\left[\text{Game}_{0,q_{\text{Enc}}-1} = 1\right]\right.$$

$$+ \Pr\left[\text{Game}_{0,q_{\text{Enc}}-1} = 1\right] - \Pr\left[\text{Game}_{0,q_{\text{Enc}}-2} = 1\right]$$

$$\left. + \cdots + \Pr\left[\text{Game}_{0,1} = 1\right] - \Pr\left[\text{Game}_{0,0} = 1\right]\right| \le \frac{1}{2}$$

$$\cdot \sum_{\iota=1}^{q_{\text{Enc}}} \left| \Pr\left[\text{Game}_{0,\iota} = 1\right] - \Pr\left[\text{Game}_{0,\iota-1} = 1\right]\right|.$$

Next, we show that $|\Pr[\text{Game}_{0,\iota} = 1] - \Pr[\text{Game}_{0,\iota-1} = 1]|$ is negligible, for $\iota \in [1, q_{\text{Enc}}]$. That is, if there exists a PPT adversary $\mathcal{A}_1$ which can distinguish the adjacent games for

some ι, we can construct a PPT algorithm $\mathcal{B}$ which can break the adaptive security of the underlying scheme.

Claim ($\text{Game}_{0,\iota-1}$ to $\text{Game}_{0,\iota}$). For any PPT adversary $\mathcal{A}_1$ which can make at most $q_{\text{key}} = q_{\text{key}}(\lambda)$ key generation queries and $q_{\text{Enc}} = q_{\text{Enc}}(\lambda)$ encryption queries with running time t', there exists algorithm $\mathcal{B}$ with about the same running time as $\mathcal{A}_1$, such that

$$\frac{1}{2} \cdot \left| \Pr\left[\text{Game}_{0,\iota} = 1\right] - \Pr\left[\text{Game}_{0,\iota-1} = 1\right]\right| \tag{7}$$

$$= \text{Adv}_{\mathcal{B},\text{BE}}^{\text{A}}(\lambda).$$

Proof. $\mathcal{B}$ simulates the experiment as follows.

(i) The challenger runs $\text{Setup}(n, \ell)$ and sends PK to $\mathcal{B}$ which will send PK to $\mathcal{A}_1$.

(ii) $\mathcal{A}_1$ adaptively makes key generation queries for user index i.

(iii) $\mathcal{B}$ sends user index i to the challenger which runs $\text{KeyGen}(i, \text{SK})$ and sends back the secret key d_i for user i. Then $\mathcal{B}$ sends d_i to $\mathcal{A}_1$.

(iv) $\mathcal{A}_1$ adaptively makes encryption queries for S_j, where j denotes the jth query.

(a) If $j \in [1, \iota - 1]$, $\mathcal{B}$ runs $\text{Enc}(S_j, \text{PK}) = (Hdr_j, K_{0,j})$ and chooses $K_{1,j} \xleftarrow{R} \mathcal{K}^*$ and sends $(Hdr_j, K_{1,j})$ to $\mathcal{A}_1$.

(b) If $j \in [\iota + 1, q_{\text{Enc}}]$, $\mathcal{B}$ runs $\text{Enc}(S_j, \text{PK}) = (Hdr_j, K_{0,j})$ and sends $(Hdr_j, K_{0,j})$ to $\mathcal{A}_1$.

(c) If $j = \iota$, $\mathcal{B}$ sends S_ι to the challenger which then chooses $b \xleftarrow{R} \{0, 1\}$ and sends back $C_\iota^* = (Hdr_\iota, K_{b,\iota})$ where $K_{1,\iota} \xleftarrow{R} \mathcal{K}^*$, $(Hdr_\iota, K_{0,\iota}) \leftarrow \text{Enc}(S_\iota, \text{PK})$. Next $\mathcal{B}$ sends C_ι^* to $\mathcal{A}_1$.

(v) $\mathcal{A}_1$ outputs b'. If $b' = b$, $\mathcal{B}$ outputs 1, otherwise, 0.

Observe that if $b = 1$, $\mathcal{A}_1$'s view is identical to that of $\text{Game}_{0,\iota}$. Otherwise $\mathcal{A}_1$'s view is identical to that of $\text{Game}_{0,\iota-1}$. Thus

$$\text{Adv}_{\mathcal{B},\text{BE}}^{\text{A}} := \left| \Pr\left[\text{Exp}_{\mathcal{B},\text{BE}}^{\text{A}}(\lambda) = 1\right] - \frac{1}{2}\right| = \left|\frac{1}{2}\right|$$

$$\cdot \Pr\left[\text{Exp}_{\mathcal{B},\text{BE}}^{\text{A}}(\lambda) = 1 \mid b = 1\right] + \frac{1}{2}$$

$$\cdot \Pr\left[\text{Exp}_{\mathcal{B},\text{BE}}^{\text{A}}(\lambda) = 0 \mid b = 0\right] - \frac{1}{2}\right| = \frac{1}{2}$$

$$\cdot \left| \Pr\left[\text{Exp}_{\mathcal{B},\text{BE}}^{\text{A}}(\lambda) = 1 \mid b = 1\right]\right.$$

$$\left. - \left(1 - \Pr\left[\text{Exp}_{\mathcal{B},\text{BE}}^{\text{A}}(\lambda) = 0 \mid b = 0\right]\right)\right| = \frac{1}{2} \tag{8}$$

$$\cdot \left| \Pr\left[\text{Exp}_{\mathcal{B},\text{BE}}^{\text{A}}(\lambda) = 1 \mid b = 1\right]\right.$$

$$\left. - \Pr\left[\text{Exp}_{\mathcal{B},\text{BE}}^{\text{A}}(\lambda) = 1 \mid b = 0\right]\right| = \frac{1}{2}$$

$$\cdot \left| \Pr\left[\text{Game}_{0,\iota} = 1\right] - \Pr\left[\text{Game}_{0,\iota-1} = 1\right]\right|.$$

Hence we have

$$\text{Adv}_{\mathcal{A},\text{BE}}^{\text{MA}}(\lambda) \le q_{\text{Enc}} \cdot \text{Adv}_{\mathcal{B},\text{BE}}^{\text{A}}(\lambda), \qquad (9)$$

which completes the proof of Theorem 2. $\qquad \square$

4.2. MS-Secure Broadcast Encryption Based on BDHE Assumption. To reduce the reduction loss, we investigate Gentry-Waters broadcast encryption [8] in the MA setting. First we briefly recall the semistatically secure broadcast encryption scheme in [8]. Let $\mathscr{G}(\lambda, n)$ be a PPT algorithm which takes as input the security parameter λ and the number of users n and generates the description of group parameter $(\mathbb{G}, \mathbb{G}_T, e, p)$, where $\mathbb{G}, \mathbb{G}_T$ denotes the group of prime order $p = p(\lambda, n)$ and e is the bilinear map.

Setup(n). $(\mathbb{G}, \mathbb{G}_T, e) \overset{R}{\leftarrow} \mathscr{G}(\lambda, n)$, $g, h_1, \ldots, h_n \overset{R}{\leftarrow} \mathbb{G}^{n+1}$, where $g, h_1, \ldots, h_n$ are generators of $\mathbb{G}$ and $\alpha \overset{R}{\leftarrow} \mathbb{Z}_p$. Set

$$\text{PK} = \left(\mathbb{G}, \mathbb{G}_T, e; g, e\left(g, g\right)^{\alpha}, h_1, \ldots, h_n \right), \qquad (10)$$

$$\text{SK} = g^{\alpha}. \qquad (11)$$

Output (PK, SK).

KeyGen(i, SK). Choose $r_i \overset{R}{\leftarrow} \mathbb{Z}_p$ and output user i's private key

$$\begin{aligned} d_i &= (d_{i,0}, d_{i,1}, \ldots, d_{i,i-1}, d_{i,i}, d_{i,i+1}, \ldots, d_{i,n}) \\ &= (g^{-r_i}, h_1^{r_i}, \ldots, h_{i-1}^{r_i}, g^{\alpha} h_i^{r_i}, h_{i+1}^{r_i}, \ldots, h_n^{r_i}). \end{aligned} \qquad (12)$$

Enc(S, PK). Choose $t \overset{R}{\leftarrow} \mathbb{Z}_p$ and compute $C_1 = g^t, C_2 = (\prod_{j \in S} h_j)^t$. Set

$$Hdr = \left(g^t, \left(\prod_{j \in S} h_j \right)^t \right), \qquad (13)$$

$$K = e\left(g, g\right)^{\alpha \cdot t}. \qquad (14)$$

Output (Hdr, K).

Dec(S, i, d_i, Hdr, PK). If $i \in S$, parse d_i as $(d_{i,0}, \ldots, d_{i,n})$ and Hdr as (C_1, C_2) and output

$$K = e\left(d_{i,i} \cdot \prod_{j \in S \setminus \{i\}} d_{i,j}, C_1 \right) \cdot e\left(d_{i,0}, C_2 \right). \qquad (15)$$

Theorem 3. *For any PPT adversary $\mathcal{A}$ which can make at most $q_{key} = q_{key}(\lambda)$ key generation queries, $q_{Enc} = q_{Enc}(\lambda)$ encryption queries with running time t', there exists*

an algorithm $\mathcal{B}$ with about the same running time as $\mathcal{A}$, such that

$$\text{Adv}_{\mathcal{A},\text{BE}}^{\text{MS}}(\lambda) = \text{Adv}_{\mathscr{G},\mathcal{B}}^{\text{BDHE}}(\lambda). \qquad (16)$$

The proof is similar to that of [8] except that we have to deal with multiple challenges in the simulation. Furthermore, to derive a tighter reduction, we need the following lemma which makes use of the random self-reducibility of BDHE.

Lemma 4. *There exists an efficient algorithm that takes as input $(g^s, g, g^a, g^{a^2}, \ldots, g^{a^n}, g^{a^{n+2}}, \ldots, g^{a^{2n}}, Z)$ for $Z = e(g^{a^n}, g^c)$ and generates many tuples of the form*

$$\left(g^{s_j}, g, g^a, g^{a^2}, \ldots, g^{a^n}, g^{a^{n+2}}, \ldots, g^{a^{2n}}, Z_j \right), \qquad (17)$$

where $Z_j = e(g^{a^n}, g^{c_j})$ and $s_j, c_j \in \mathbb{Z}_p$.

Proof. Compute $g^{s_j} = (g^s)^{v_j} \cdot g^{u_j}$ and $Z_j = Z^{v_j} \cdot e(g^{a^n}, g^a)^{u_j}$, where $u_j, v_j \overset{R}{\leftarrow} \mathbb{Z}_p$. Let $e = c - as \bmod p$. We implicitly set

$$\begin{aligned} s_j &= s \cdot v_j + u_j \bmod p, \\ c_j &= as_j + ev_j \bmod p. \end{aligned} \qquad (18)$$

Hence, we have

$$Z_j = \begin{cases} e\left(g^{a^n}, g^{as_j}\right) & \text{if } c = as \bmod p \\ e\left(g^{a^n}, g^{as_j + ev_j}\right) & \text{if } c \ne as \bmod p. \end{cases} \qquad (19)$$

If $e = 0$, namely, $c = as$, then $c_j = as_j$. If $e \ne 0$, namely, $c \ne as$, then $c_j = as_j + ev_j$. Since ev_j are uniformly distributed, we have c_j uniformly distributed over $\mathbb{Z}_p$. $\qquad \square$

Next, more details of the concrete proof of Theorem 3 can be found in Appendix A.

4.3. Transforming MS-Security to MA-Security. In this section, we show that Gentry-Waters transformation still holds in the multichallenge setting, but at the cost of reduction loss q_{Enc} in the advantage of underlying symmetric encryption scheme. First, we briefly recall Gentry-Waters transformation [8]. Let $\text{BE}_{\text{MS}} = (\text{Setup}_{\text{MS}}, \text{KeyGen}_{\text{MS}}, \text{Enc}_{\text{MS}}, \text{Dec}_{\text{MS}})$ be a MS-secure broadcast system and $\Pi_{\text{sym}} = (\text{SymSetup}, \text{SymEnc}, \text{SymDec})$ be a symmetric encryption scheme with key space $\mathscr{K}'$.

Setup(n). Run $\text{Setup}_{\text{MS}}(2n) \to (PK', SK')$. Let $s \overset{R}{\leftarrow} \{0, 1\}^n$ and s_i denotes ith bit of s. Let $\text{PK} = PK'$ and $\text{SK} = (SK', s)$. Output (PK, SK).

KeyGen(i, SK). Run $\text{KeyGen}_{\text{MS}}(2i - s_i, SK') \to d_i'$. Set $d_i = (d_i', s_i)$. Output private key d_i.

TABLE 3: IND-CPA experiment.

$\mathrm{Exp}_{\mathscr{A},\Pi_{\mathrm{sym}}}^{\mathrm{CPA}}(\lambda)$

$b \xleftarrow{R} \{0,1\}$;

$k \longleftarrow \mathrm{SymSetup}\left(1^\lambda\right)$;

$b' \longleftarrow \mathscr{A}^{\mathscr{O}_{\mathrm{Enc}}(k,\cdot)}$;

If $b' = b$, return 1; otherwise, 0.

$Enc(S, PK)$. Generate random $|S|$ bits: $t \leftarrow \{t_i \xleftarrow{R} \{0,1\} : i \in S\}$ and $K \xleftarrow{R} \mathscr{K}$. Set

$$S_0 \longleftarrow \{2i - t_i : i \in S\},$$

$$\mathrm{Enc}_{\mathrm{MS}}\left(S_0, PK'\right) \longrightarrow (Hdr_0, \kappa_0),$$

$$\mathrm{SymEnc}\left(\kappa_0, K\right) \longrightarrow C_0;$$

$$S_1 \longleftarrow \{2i - (1 - t_i) : i \in S\}, \qquad (20)$$

$$\mathrm{Enc}_{\mathrm{MS}}\left(S_1, PK'\right) \longrightarrow (Hdr_1, \kappa_1),$$

$$\mathrm{SymEnc}\left(\kappa_1, K\right) \longrightarrow C_1;$$

$$Hdr \longleftarrow \left(Hdr_0, Hdr_1, C_0, C_1, t\right).$$

Output (Hdr, K).

$Dec(S, i, d_i, Hdr, PK)$. Parse Hdr as $(Hdr_0, Hdr_1, C_0, C_1, t)$ and d_i as (d_i', s_i). Set S_0 and S_1 as above. Run

$$\kappa_{s_i \oplus t_i} \longleftarrow \mathrm{Dec}_{\mathrm{MS}}\left(S_{s_i \oplus t_i}, i, d_i', Hdr_{s_i \oplus t_i}, PK'\right),$$

$$K \longleftarrow \mathrm{SymDec}\left(\kappa_{s_i \oplus t_i}, C_{s_i \oplus t_i}\right). \qquad (21)$$

Output K.

Theorem 5. *For any PPT adversary $\mathscr{A}$ which can make at most $q_{key} = q_{key}(\lambda)$ key generation queries and $q_{Enc} = q_{Enc}(\lambda)$ encryption queries with running time t', there exist algorithms $\mathscr{A}_1, \mathscr{A}_2, \mathscr{A}_3,$ and $\mathscr{A}_4$, each with about the same running time as $\mathscr{A}$, such that*

$$\mathrm{Adv}_{\mathscr{A},\mathrm{BE},n}^{\mathrm{MA}}(\lambda) \leq \mathrm{Adv}_{\mathscr{A}_1,\mathrm{BE},2n}^{\mathrm{MS}}(\lambda) + \mathrm{Adv}_{\mathscr{A}_2,\mathrm{BE},2n}^{\mathrm{MS}}(\lambda)$$

$$+ q_{Enc} \cdot \mathrm{Adv}_{\mathscr{A}_3,\Pi_{\mathrm{sym}}}^{\mathrm{CPA}}(\lambda) + q_{Enc} \qquad (22)$$

$$\cdot \mathrm{Adv}_{\mathscr{A}_4,\Pi_{\mathrm{sym}}}^{\mathrm{CPA}}(\lambda).$$

Notice that $\mathrm{Adv}_{\mathscr{B},\Pi_{\mathrm{sym}}}^{\mathrm{CPA}}(\lambda)$ denotes the advantage of $\Pi_{\mathrm{sym}} =$ (SymSetup, SymEnc, SymDec), which is defined by the following one-time symmetric key IND-CPA experiment described in Table 3.

During the experiment, $\mathscr{A}$ takes the security parameter and the description of Π_{sym} as input and can make only one encryption query to encryption oracle $\mathscr{O}'_{\mathrm{Enc}}(k, \cdot)$. More precisely, A chooses a pair of plaintexts (m_0, m_1) of the same

length as the query and $\mathscr{O}'_{\mathrm{Enc}}(k, \cdot)$ returns $\mathrm{SymEnc}(k, m_b)$ as the challenge ciphertext.

We say the symmetric key encryption scheme Π_{sym} is one-time CPA-secure if, for any PPT adversary $\mathscr{A}$, the advantage

$$\mathrm{Adv}_{\mathscr{A},\Pi_{\mathrm{sym}}}^{\mathrm{CPA}} := \left| \mathrm{Pr}\left[\mathrm{Exp}_{\mathscr{A},\Pi_{\mathrm{sym}}}^{\mathrm{CPA}}(\lambda) = 1\right] - \frac{1}{2}\right| \qquad (23)$$

is negligible in λ, where the probability is taken over the random coins used in the experiment, as well as the random coins used by $\mathscr{A}$.

Proof of Sketch. The main idea of the proof is similar to that of [8] except that we need to deal with multiple challenges, which incurs a reduction loss in the advantage of symmetric key encryption scheme. More precisely, we need to prove the indistinguishability of the following games

(i) Game_0 is identical to $\mathrm{Exp}_{\mathscr{A},\mathrm{BE}}^{\mathrm{MA}}(\lambda)$.

(ii) Game_1 is the same as Game_0 except that for each encryption query the challenger chooses $\kappa_{0,j} \xleftarrow{R} \mathscr{K}'$ to construct $C_{0,j} = \mathrm{SymEnc}(\kappa_{0,j}, K_{0,j})$, where $K_{0,j} = K_{1,j}$.

(iii) Game_2 is the same as Game_1 except that for each encryption query the challenger chooses $\kappa_{1,j} \xleftarrow{R} \mathscr{K}'$ to construct $C_{1,j} = \mathrm{SymEnc}(\kappa_{1,j}, K_{1,j})$, where $K_{0,j} = K_{1,j}$.

(iv) Game_3 is the same as Game_2 except that the challenger chooses $K_{0,j} \xleftarrow{R} \mathscr{K}$ to construct $C_{0,j} = \mathrm{SymEnc}(\kappa_{0,j}, K_{0,j})$.

(v) Game_4 is the same as Game_3 except that the challenger chooses $K_{1,j} \xleftarrow{R} \mathscr{K}$ to construct $C_{1,j} = \mathrm{SymEnc}(\kappa_{1,j}, K_{1,j})$.

The indistinguishability among Game_0, Game_1, and Game_2 relies on the MS-security of BE. By using hybrid arguments, we show the indistinguishability between Game_2 and Game_3 (Game_3 and Game_4), which relies on the one-time CPA security of the underlying symmetric key encryption. It is easy to check that the adversary has no advantage in Game_4. More details are shown in Appendix B.

5. Remove q-Type Assumption

In this section, we show how to remove the q-type assumption of the MS-secure Gentry-Waters scheme in Section 4 by using Hofheinz-Koch-Striecks techniques [19], where the original Gentry-Waters scheme is lifted to composite order groups.

Let $\mathscr{G}(\lambda, 4)$ be a composite-order group generator which generates group parameters $(G, G_T, N, e, g, g_1, g_2, g_3, g_4)$, where $e : G \times G \rightarrow G_T$ is a nondegenerate bilinear map and G, G_T are cyclic groups of order N and N is the product of different primes $p_1, p_2, p_3,$ and p_4, and let g be the generator of group G and g_i, for $i \in [1, 4]$, be the random generators of subgroups $G_{p_1}, G_{p_2}, G_{p_3}, G_{p_4}$ of orders p_1, p_2, p_3, p_4, respectively.

Let $\mathcal{UH}$ be a family of universal hash functions $\mathsf{H} : G_T \rightarrow \{0,1\}^\tau$ with the property that for any nontrivial subgroup $G_T' \subseteq G_T$ and for $\mathsf{H} \leftarrow \mathcal{UH}$, $X \leftarrow G_T'$ and $U \leftarrow \{0,1\}^\tau$, we have $\mathsf{SD}((\mathsf{H}, \mathsf{H}(X)), (\mathsf{H}, U)) = \mathbf{O}(2^{-\tau})$. In addition, the resulting scheme relies on the following assumptions [19].

Dual System Assumption 1 (DS1). For any PPT adversary $\mathcal{A}$, the advantage function

$$
\begin{aligned}
&\mathsf{Adv}_{\mathcal{A}}^{\mathrm{DS1}}(\lambda) \\
&\quad := \left| \Pr\left[\mathcal{A}\left(D, T_0\right) = 1 \right] - \Pr\left[\mathcal{A}\left(D, T_1\right) = 1 \right] \right|
\end{aligned}
\tag{24}
$$

is negligible in λ, where

$$
\begin{aligned}
&(G, G_T, N, e, g, (g_i)_i) \longleftarrow \mathcal{G}(\lambda, 4); \\
&D := \left(G, G_T, N, e, g, g_1, g_3, g_4\right); \\
&T_0 \xleftarrow{R} G_{p_1}, \\
&T_1 \xleftarrow{R} G_{p_1 p_2}.
\end{aligned}
\tag{25}
$$

Dual System Assumption 2 (DS2). For any PPT adversary $\mathcal{A}$, the advantage function

$$
\begin{aligned}
&\mathsf{Adv}_{\mathcal{A}}^{\mathrm{DS2}}(\lambda) \\
&\quad := \left| \Pr\left[\mathcal{A}\left(D, T_0\right) = 1 \right] - \Pr\left[\mathcal{A}\left(D, T_1\right) = 1 \right] \right|
\end{aligned}
\tag{26}
$$

is negligible in λ, where

$$
\begin{aligned}
&(G, G_T, N, e, g, (g_i)_i) \longleftarrow \mathcal{G}(\lambda, 4); \\
&D := \left(G, G_T, N, e, g, g_1, g_4, g_{\{1,2\}}, g_{\{2,3\}}\right); \\
&g_{\{1,2\}} \xleftarrow{R} G_{p_1 p_2}, \\
&g_{\{2,3\}} \xleftarrow{R} G_{p_2 p_3}; \\
&T_0 \xleftarrow{R} G_{p_1 p_2}, \\
&T_1 \xleftarrow{R} G_{p_1 p_3}.
\end{aligned}
\tag{27}
$$

Dual System Assumption 3 (DS3). For any PPT adversary $\mathcal{A}$, the advantage function

$$
\begin{aligned}
&\mathsf{Adv}_{\mathcal{A}}^{\mathrm{DS3}}(\lambda) \\
&\quad := \left| \Pr\left[\mathcal{A}\left(D, \hat{T}_0, \tilde{T}_0\right) = 1 \right] - \Pr\left[\mathcal{A}\left(D, \hat{T}_1, \tilde{T}_1\right) = 1 \right] \right|
\end{aligned}
\tag{28}
$$

is negligible in λ, where

$$
\begin{aligned}
&(G, G_T, N, e, g, (g_i)_i) \longleftarrow \mathcal{G}(\lambda, 4); \\
&D := \left(G, G_T, N, e, g, (g_i)_i, g_2^x \hat{X}_4, g_2^y \hat{Y}_4, g_3^x \tilde{X}_4, g_3^y \tilde{Y}_4\right); \\
&\hat{X}_4, \tilde{X}_4, \hat{Y}_4, \tilde{Y}_4 \xleftarrow{R} G_{p_4}, \\
&x, y \longleftarrow \mathbb{Z}_N^*, \gamma' \longleftarrow \mathbb{Z}_N^*; \\
&\hat{T}_0 = g_2^{xy}, \\
&\hat{T}_1 = g_2^{xy+\gamma'}; \\
&\tilde{T}_0 = g_3^{xy}, \\
&\tilde{T}_1 = g_3^{xy+\gamma'}.
\end{aligned}
\tag{29}
$$

Dual System Bilinear DDH Assumption (DS-BDDH). For any PPT adversary $\mathcal{A}$, the advantage function

$$
\begin{aligned}
&\mathsf{Adv}_{\mathcal{A}}^{\mathrm{DS\text{-}BDDH}}(\lambda) \\
&\quad := \left| \Pr\left[\mathcal{A}\left(D, T_0\right) = 1 \right] - \Pr\left[\mathcal{A}\left(D, T_1\right) = 1 \right] \right|
\end{aligned}
\tag{30}
$$

is negligible in λ, where

$$
\begin{aligned}
&(G, G_T, N, e, g, (g_i)_i) \longleftarrow \mathcal{G}(\lambda, 4); \\
&D := \left(G, G_T, N, e, g, (g_i)_i, g_1^a, g_2^a, g_2^b, g_{\{2,4\}}, g_{\{2,4\}}^b, g_{\{2,4\}}^c\right); \\
&T_0 = e\left(g_2, g_2\right)^{abc}, \\
&T_1 = e\left(g_2, g_2\right)^z;
\end{aligned}
\tag{31}
$$

$$
g_{\{2,4\}} \xleftarrow{R} G_{p_2 p_4}, \quad a, b, c, z \longleftarrow \mathbb{Z}_N^*.
$$

5.1. Construction

Setup(n, n). Generate $\alpha, \omega_1, \ldots, \omega_{2n} \xleftarrow{R} \mathbb{Z}_N$ and compute $(g_1, g_1^{\omega_1}, \ldots, g_1^{\omega_{2n}}) \in G_{p_1}^{2n+1}$. Set $h \xleftarrow{R} G_N$, generate $(R_{4,1}, \ldots, R_{4,2n}) \xleftarrow{R} G_{p_4}^{2n}$, and compute $(h_1, \ldots, h_{2n}) = (h^{\omega_1} \cdot R_{4,1}, \ldots, h^{\omega_{2n}} \cdot R_{4,2n})$. Set

$$
\begin{aligned}
&\mathsf{mpk} \\
&\quad = \left(g_1, g_1^{\omega_1}, \ldots, g_1^{\omega_{2n}}, g_4, h, e\left(g_1, h\right)^\alpha, h_1, \ldots, h_{2n}\right),
\end{aligned}
\tag{32}
$$

$$
\mathsf{msk} = h^\alpha.
\tag{33}
$$

Output $(\mathsf{mpk}, \mathsf{msk})$.

KeyGen(u, msk). Take an index $u \in [1, n]$ and the master key msk as input. Set $r_u \xleftarrow{R} \mathbb{Z}_N$, generate $(R_{4,1}', \ldots, R_{4,2n}') \xleftarrow{R} G_{p_4}^{2n}$, and compute $K_0 = h^{r_u}$, $K_1 = h_1^{r_u} \cdot R_{4,1}', \ldots, K_{2n} = h_{2n}^{r_u} \cdot R_{4,2n}'$

and output a user secret key

$$sk_u = (K_0, K_1, \ldots, \text{msk} \cdot K_{2u-1}, K_{2u+1}, \ldots, K_{2n})$$

$$= \left(h^{r_u}, h_1^{r_u} \cdot R'_{4,1}, \ldots, \text{msk} \cdot h_{2u-1}^{r_u} \cdot R'_{4,2u-1}, h_{2u+1}^{r_u} \right. \qquad (34)$$

$$\left. \cdot R'_{4,2u+1}, \ldots, h_{2n}^{r_u} \cdot R'_{4,2n}\right).$$

Note that K_{2u} is not used in sk_u.

$Enc(S, \text{mpk})$. Take a set $S \subseteq [1, n]$ as well as a master public key mpk as input. We denote S as a binary string; that is, $S = s_1 \cdots s_n$, where $s_u \in \{0, 1\}$ and $u \in [1, n]$. That is, $s_u = 1$ if user u is in S. Otherwise, $s_u = 0$. Generate $t \xleftarrow{R} \mathbb{Z}_N$ and output

$$Hdr = (C_0, C_1) = \left(g_1^t, \left(\prod_{j=1}^n g_1^{\omega_{2j-s_j}}\right)^t\right), \qquad (35)$$

$$K = \mathsf{H}\left(e\left(g_1, h\right)^{\alpha t}\right). \qquad (36)$$

$Dec(S, u, sk_u, Hdr, \text{mpk})$. If $u \in S$, parse sk_u as $(K_0, K_1, \ldots, \text{msk} \cdot K_{2u-1}, K_{2u+1}, \ldots, K_{2n})$ and Hdr as (C_0, C_1) and output

$$K = \mathsf{H}\left(\frac{e\left(C_0, \text{msk} \cdot \prod_{j=1}^n K_{2j-s_j}\right)}{e\left(C_1, K_0\right)}\right). \qquad (37)$$

Correctness.

$$\frac{e\left(C_0, \text{msk} \cdot \prod_{j=1}^n K_{2j-s_j}\right)}{e\left(C_1, K_0\right)}$$

$$= \frac{e\left(g_1^t, \text{msk} \cdot \prod_{j=1}^n h_{2j-s_j}^{r_u} \cdot R'_{4,2j-s_j}\right)}{e\left(\prod_{j=1}^n g_1^{\omega_{2j-s_j}}, h\right)^{t \cdot r_u}}$$

$$= \frac{e\left(g_1^t, h^\alpha\right) \cdot e\left(g_1, \prod_{j=1}^n h_{2j-s_j}\right)^{t \cdot r_u}}{e\left(\prod_{j=1}^n g_1^{\omega_{2j-s_j}}, h\right)^{t \cdot r_u}} \qquad (38)$$

$$= \frac{e\left(g_1, h\right)^{\alpha t} \cdot e\left(g_1, \prod_{j=1}^n h^{\omega_{2j-s_j}}\right)^{t \cdot r_u}}{e\left(\prod_{j=1}^n g_1^{\omega_{2j-s_j}}, h\right)^{t \cdot r_u}} = e\left(g_1, h\right)^{\alpha t}.$$

5.2. Security Proof

Theorem 6. *For any PPT adversary $\mathcal{A}$ which can make at most $q_{key} = q_{key}(\lambda)$ key generation queries and $q_{Enc} = q_{Enc}(\lambda)$ encryption queries with running time t', there exist algorithm $\mathcal{B}_1$ on DS1, $\mathcal{B}_2$ on DS2, $\mathcal{B}_3$ on DS3, and $\mathcal{B}_4$ on DS-BDDH with running time $t' + \mathbf{O}(n\lambda^c(q_{key} + q_{Enc}))$, respectively, for some constant $c \in \mathbb{N}$, such that*

$$\text{Adv}_{\mathcal{A}, \text{BE}}^{\text{MA}}(\lambda) \leq \text{Adv}_{\mathcal{B}_1}^{\text{DS1}}(\lambda) + 2n \cdot \text{Adv}_{\mathcal{B}_2}^{\text{DS2}}(\lambda) + n$$

$$\cdot \text{Adv}_{\mathcal{B}_3}^{\text{DS3}}(\lambda) + \text{Adv}_{\mathcal{B}_4}^{\text{DS-BDDH}} + q_{\text{Enc}} \qquad (39)$$

$$\cdot \mathbf{O}\left(2^{-\tau}\right).$$

The proof follows that of [19] and proceeds via a series of games described in Appendix C, where the user set S is considered as a special kind of identity *id*.

The main difference between games is presented in Table 4. Random function families, auxiliary secret key generation, auxiliary encryption function, semifunctional user secret keys, pseudo-normal ciphertexts, and semifunctional ciphertexts are defined as follows. More details can be found in Table 4.

(i) Random Function Families. In our scheme each user index $u \in [1, n]$ is interpreted as n-bit binary string $u = 0 \cdots 010 \cdots 0$, where only u-th bit is 1. Both user index u and user set S are denoted as identity *id*. Let $id|_i := id_1 \cdots id_i$ be i-bit prefix of *id* and denote $\text{ID}|_i := \{0, 1\}^i$. For $i \in [0, n]$, define two random functions as follows.

(a) $\widehat{\mathsf{RF}}_i(id|_i) : \text{ID}|_i \to G_{p_2} G_{p_4}; id|_i \mapsto (g_2 g_4)^{\widehat{\gamma}_i(id|_i)};$

$$\widehat{\gamma}_i(id|_i) : \text{ID}|_i \to \mathbb{Z}_{p_2 p_4}^*; id|_i \mapsto \widehat{\gamma}_i, \text{ where } \widehat{\gamma}_i \xleftarrow{R} \mathbb{Z}_{p_2 p_4}^*.$$

(b) $\widetilde{\mathsf{RF}}_i(id|_i) : \text{ID}|_i \to G_{p_3} G_{p_4}; id|_i \mapsto (g_3 g_4)^{\widetilde{\gamma}_i(id|_i)};$

$$\widetilde{\gamma}_i(id|_i) : \text{ID}|_i \to \mathbb{Z}_{p_3 p_4}^*; id|_i \mapsto \widetilde{\gamma}_i, \text{ where } \widetilde{\gamma}_i \xleftarrow{R} \mathbb{Z}_{p_3 p_4}^*.$$

(ii) Auxiliary Secret Key Generation

$$\overline{\text{KeyGen}}(u, \text{msk}, \mathbf{K})$$

$$= (K_0, K_1, \ldots, \text{msk} \cdot K_{2u-1}, K_{2u+1}, \ldots, K_{2n}), \qquad (40)$$

where $\mathbf{K} = (K_0, K_1, K_2, \ldots, K_{2n}) \in G_N^{2n+1}$.

(iii) Auxiliary Encryption Function

$$\overline{\text{Enc}}(S^*, \text{mpk}, \mathbf{g}_1, \text{msk}) = (Hdr; K)$$

$$= \left(g_1^t, \left(\prod_{j=1}^n g_1^{\omega_{2j-s_j}}\right)^t; \mathsf{H}\left(e\left(g_1, \text{msk}\right)^t\right)\right), \qquad (41)$$

where $\mathbf{g}_1 = (g_1^t, g_1^{\omega_1 t}, \ldots, g_1^{\omega_{2n} t})$.

(iv) Semi-Functional Type-i User Secret Keys

$$\overline{\text{KeyGen}}\left(u, \text{msk} \cdot \widehat{\mathsf{RF}}_i\left(id|_i\right) \cdot \widetilde{\mathsf{RF}}_i\left(id|_i\right), \mathbf{K}\right)$$

$$= \left(K_0, K_1, \ldots, \text{msk} \cdot \widehat{\mathsf{RF}}_i\left(id|_i\right) \cdot \widetilde{\mathsf{RF}}_i\left(id|_i\right) \qquad (42)\right.$$

$$\left. \cdot K_{2u-1}, K_{2u+1}, \ldots, K_{2n}\right),$$

where user $u = id_1 \cdots id_n$ is denoted as *id*.

TABLE 4: Sequence of games, where a dash(–) means the same as in the previous game. Note that user set S^* and user identity u are interpreted as id^* and id, respectively.

Game	Challenge ciphertexts for identity S^*	User secret keys for identity $u \in [1, n]$
0	$\mathsf{Enc}(S^*, \mathsf{mpk})$	$\mathsf{KeyGen}(u, \mathsf{msk})$
1	$\overline{\mathsf{Enc}}(S^*, \mathsf{mpk}, \mathbf{g}_{\{1,2\}}, \mathsf{msk})$	$\overline{\mathsf{KeyGen}}(u, \mathsf{msk}, \mathbf{K})$
2, i, 0	$\overline{\mathsf{Enc}}(-, -, \mathbf{g}_{\{1,2\}}, \mathsf{msk} \cdot \widehat{\mathsf{RF}}_{i-1}(id^*\|_{i-1}))$	$\overline{\mathsf{KeyGen}}(u, \mathsf{msk} \cdot \widehat{\mathsf{RF}}_{i-1}(id\|_{i-1}) \cdot \widetilde{\mathsf{RF}}_{i-1}(id\|_{i-1}), \mathbf{K})$
2, i, 1	if $id_i^* = 0$: $\overline{\mathsf{Enc}}(-, -, \mathbf{g}_{\{1,2\}}, \mathsf{msk} \cdot \widehat{\mathsf{RF}}_{i-1}(id^*\|_{i-1}))$ if $id_i^* = 1$: $\overline{\mathsf{Enc}}(-, -, \mathbf{g}_{\{1,3\}}, \mathsf{msk} \cdot \widehat{\mathsf{RF}}_{i-1}(id^*\|_{i-1}))$	$\overline{\mathsf{KeyGen}}(u, \mathsf{msk} \cdot \widehat{\mathsf{RF}}_{i-1}(id\|_{i-1}) \cdot \widetilde{\mathsf{RF}}_{i-1}(id\|_{i-1}), \mathbf{K})$
2, i, 2	if $id_i^* = 0$: $\overline{\mathsf{Enc}}(-, -, \mathbf{g}_{\{1,2\}}, \mathsf{msk} \cdot \widehat{\mathsf{RF}}_i(id^*\|_i))$ if $id_i^* = 1$: $\overline{\mathsf{Enc}}(-, -, \mathbf{g}_{\{1,3\}}, \mathsf{msk} \cdot \widehat{\mathsf{RF}}_i(id^*\|_i))$	$\overline{\mathsf{KeyGen}}(u, \mathsf{msk} \cdot \widehat{\mathsf{RF}}_i(id\|_i) \cdot \widetilde{\mathsf{RF}}_i(id\|_i), \mathbf{K})$
3	$\overline{\mathsf{Enc}}(-, -, \mathbf{g}_{\{1,2\}}, \mathsf{msk} \cdot \widehat{\mathsf{RF}}_n(id^*))$	$\overline{\mathsf{KeyGen}}(u, \mathsf{msk} \cdot \widehat{\mathsf{RF}}_n(id) \cdot \widetilde{\mathsf{RF}}_n(id), \mathbf{K})$
4	$\overline{\mathsf{Enc}}(-, -, \mathbf{g}_{\{1,2\}}, \mathsf{msk} \cdot \widehat{\mathsf{RF}}_n(id^*)), K_b \xleftarrow{R} \{0, 1\}^\tau$	$\overline{\mathsf{KeyGen}}(u, \mathsf{msk} \cdot \widehat{\mathsf{RF}}_n(id) \cdot \widetilde{\mathsf{RF}}_n(id), \mathbf{K})$

(v) Pseudo-Normal Ciphertexts

$$
\overline{\mathsf{Enc}}\left(S^*, \mathsf{mpk}, \mathbf{g}_{\{1,2\}}, \mathsf{msk}\right) = (Hdr; K) = \left(g_{\{1,2\}}^t, \right.
$$

$$
\left. \left(\prod_{j=1}^{n} \left(g_{\{1,2\}}\right)^{\omega_{2j-s_j}}\right)^t ; \mathsf{H}\left(e\left(g_{\{1,2\}}, \mathsf{msk}\right)^t\right) \right), \tag{43}
$$

where $\mathbf{g}_{\{1,2\}} = (g_{\{1,2\}}^t, g_{\{1,2\}}^{\omega_1 t}, \ldots, g_{\{1,2\}}^{\omega_{2n} t})$.

(vi) Semi-Functional Type-$(\wedge, i)$ Ciphertexts

$$
\overline{\mathsf{Enc}}\left(S^*, \mathsf{mpk}, \mathbf{g}_{\{1,2\}}, \mathsf{msk} \cdot \widehat{\mathsf{RF}}_i\left(id\|_i\right) \cdot \widetilde{\mathsf{RF}}_i\left(id\|_i\right)\right)
$$

$$
= (Hdr; K) = \left(g_{\{1,2\}}^t, \left(\prod_{j=1}^{n} g_{\{1,2\}}^{\omega_{2j-s_j}}\right)^t ; \right.
$$

$$
\left. \mathsf{H}\left(e\left(g_{\{1,2\}}, \mathsf{msk} \cdot \widehat{\mathsf{RF}}_i\left(id\|_i\right)\right) \cdot \widetilde{\mathsf{RF}}_i\left(id\|_i\right)^t\right) \right) \tag{44}
$$

$$
= \left(g_{\{1,2\}}^t, \left(\prod_{j=1}^{n} g_{\{1,2\}}^{\omega_{2j-s_j}}\right)^t ; \right.
$$

$$
\left. \mathsf{H}\left(e\left(g_{\{1,2\}}, \mathsf{msk} \cdot \widehat{\mathsf{RF}}_i\left(id\|_i\right)\right)^t\right) \right),
$$

where $\mathbf{g}_{\{1,2\}} = (g_{\{1,2\}}^t, g_{\{1,2\}}^{\omega_1 t}, \ldots, g_{\{1,2\}}^{\omega_{2n} t})$ and id denotes $S^* = s_1 \cdots s_n$.

(vii) Semi-Functional Type-$(\sim, i)$ Ciphertexts

$$
\overline{\mathsf{Enc}}\left(S^*, \mathsf{mpk}, \mathbf{g}_{\{1,3\}}, \mathsf{msk} \cdot \widehat{\mathsf{RF}}_i\left(id\|_i\right) \cdot \widetilde{\mathsf{RF}}_i\left(id\|_i\right)\right)
$$

$$
= (Hdr; K) = \left(g_{\{1,3\}}^t, \left(\prod_{j=1}^{n} g_{\{1,3\}}^{\omega_{2j-s_j}}\right)^t ; \right.
$$

$$
\left. \mathsf{H}\left(e\left(g_{\{1,3\}}, \mathsf{msk} \cdot \widehat{\mathsf{RF}}_i\left(id\|_i\right) \cdot \widetilde{\mathsf{RF}}_i\left(id\|_i\right)\right)^t\right) \right) \tag{45}
$$

$$
= \left(g_{\{1,3\}}^t, \left(\prod_{j=1}^{n} g_{\{1,3\}}^{\omega_{2j-s_j}}\right)^t ; \right.
$$

$$
\left. \mathsf{H}\left(e\left(g_{\{1,3\}}, \mathsf{msk} \cdot \widetilde{\mathsf{RF}}_i\left(id\|_i\right)\right)^t\right) \right),
$$

where $\mathbf{g}_{\{1,3\}} = (g_{\{1,3\}}^t, g_{\{1,3\}}^{\omega_1 t}, \ldots, g_{\{1,3\}}^{\omega_{2n} t})$ and id denotes $S^* = s_1 \cdots s_n$.

Appendix

A. Proof of Theorem 3

Proof. If there exists a PPT adversary $\mathscr{A}$ which can break the MS-security of the broadcast encryption, then we show how to construct a PPT algorithm $\mathscr{B}$ to break BDHE assumption.

Upon receiving the BDHE problem instance, which consists of $(g^s, g, g^a, g^{a^2}, \ldots, g^{a^n}, g^{a^{n+2}}, \ldots, g^{a^{2n}})$ and Z, $\mathscr{B}$ simulates the experiment $\mathsf{Exp}_{\mathscr{A}, \mathsf{BE}}^{\mathsf{MS}}(\lambda)$ for $\mathscr{A}$ as follows.

(i) $\mathscr{A}$ chooses a set $S^* \subseteq [1, n]$.

(ii) Setup. $\mathscr{B}$ generates $y_0, \ldots, y_n \xleftarrow{R} \mathbb{Z}_p$ and sets

$$h_i = g^{y_i} \quad \text{if } i \in S^*,$$
$$h_i = g^{y_i + a^i} \quad \text{if } i \notin S^*. \tag{A.1}$$

Since $g^{a^{n+1}}$ is unknown, we implicitly set $\alpha = y_0 \cdot a^{n+1}$ and $e(g, g)^\alpha$ can be computed as $e(g^a, g^{a^n})^{y_0}$. Now the public key is

$$\text{PK} = \left(\mathbb{G}, \mathbb{G}_T, e; g, e(g, g)^\alpha, h_1, \ldots, h_n \right). \tag{A.2}$$

$\mathscr{B}$ sends PK to $\mathscr{A}$.

(iii) Key generation queries: for $i \in [1, n] \setminus S^*$, $\mathscr{B}$ chooses $z_i \xleftarrow{R} \mathbb{Z}_p$ and computes $r_i = z_i - y_0 \cdot a^{n+1-i}$ and outputs

$$d_i = (d_{i,0}, d_{i,1}, \ldots, d_{i,i-1}, d_{i,i}, d_{i,i+1}, \ldots, d_{i,n})$$
$$= (g^{-r_i}, h_1^{r_i}, h_2^{r_i}, \ldots, h_{i-1}^{r_i}, g^\alpha h_i^{r_i}, h_{i+1}^{r_i}, \ldots, h_n^{r_i}), \tag{A.3}$$

where $d_{i,i} = g^\alpha h_i^{r_i} = g^{y_0 \cdot a^{n+1} + (y_i + a^i)(z_i - y_0 \cdot a^{n+1-i})} = g^{y_i r_i + a^i \cdot z_i}$.

(iv) Encryption queries: $\mathscr{A}$ adaptively makes subset $S_j \subseteq S^*$ as encryption query. $\mathscr{B}$ runs the algorithm of Lemma 4 to generate (g^{s_j}, Z_j) for $j \in [1, q_{\text{Enc}}]$ and set $Hdr_j^* = (C_{1,j}, C_{2,j}) = (g^{s_j}, (\prod_{i \in S_j} h_i)^{s_j}) = (g^{s_j}, (g^{s_j})^{\sum_{i \in S_j} y_i})$, $K_j = Z_j^{y_0}$. Return (Hdr_j^*, K_j) as the answer to S_j.

Eventually, $\mathscr{A}$ outputs a bit b' which is also the output of $\mathscr{B}$. It is easy to check that $\mathscr{B}$ perfectly simulates $\text{Exp}_{\mathscr{A}, \text{BE}}^{\text{MS}}(\lambda)$. Therefore, $\mathscr{B}$'s advantage in deciding the BDHE instance is precisely $\mathscr{A}$'s advantage against the MS-security of the broadcast encryption scheme, which completes the proof. $\quad\square$

B. Proof of Theorem 5

Proof. Let $\text{Game}_i = 1$ denote the event that the adversary outputs 1 in Game_i.

Game_0. This is the real game which is identical to experiment $\text{Exp}_{\mathscr{A}, \text{BE}}^{\text{MA}}$. Thus,

$$\text{Adv}_{\mathscr{A}, \text{BE}, n}^{\text{MA}}(\lambda) = \left| \Pr[\text{Game}_0 = 1] - \frac{1}{2} \right|. \tag{B.1}$$

(Game_1 *to* Game_0). Game_1 is identical to Game_0 except that the challenge ciphertext $C_{0,j}$ for $j \in [1, q_{\text{Enc}}]$ is computed as follows: $\kappa_{0,j} \xleftarrow{R} \mathscr{K}'$ and $C_{0,j} \leftarrow \text{SymEnc}(\kappa_{0,j}, K_j)$.

For any PPT adversary $\mathscr{A}$ which can distinguish Game_1 from Game_0, there exists an algorithm $\mathscr{A}_1$ which can break the MS-security of BE_{MS} scheme. Suppose q_{Enc} is the maximal number of encryption queries that adversary can make. $\mathscr{A}_1$ acts as follows:

(i) Choose $b^* \xleftarrow{R} \{0, 1\}$.

(ii) Choose $s \xleftarrow{R} \{0, 1\}^n$ and generate $S^* \leftarrow \{2i - (1 - s_i) : i \in [1, n]\}$, where s_i denotes ith bit of s. $\mathscr{A}_1$ sends S^* to the challenger. Notice that $S^* \subseteq [1, 2n]$.

(iii) The challenger runs Setup_{MS} to obtain (PK', SK') and sends PK' to $\mathscr{A}_1$. Then $\mathscr{B}_1$ sets $\text{PK} \leftarrow \text{PK}'$ and sends PK to $\mathscr{A}$.

(iv) $\mathscr{A}$ adaptively makes key generation queries for $i' \in [1, n]$. Then $\mathscr{A}_1$ sends $2i' - s_{i'}$ to the challenger of the MS experiment.

(v) The challenger runs $\text{KeyGen}_{\text{MS}}(2i' - s_{i'}, \text{SK}')$ to obtain $d_{i'}'$ and sends $d_{i'}'$ to $\mathscr{A}_1$, which returns $d_{i'} \leftarrow (d_{i'}', s_{i'})$ to $\mathscr{A}$.

(vi) $\mathscr{A}$ adaptively makes encryption queries S_j. Then $\mathscr{A}_1$ sets $T_j = \{t_i = 1 - s_i : i \in S_j\}$, $S_{0,j} = \{2i - t_i : i \in S_j\}$, $S_{1,j} = \{2i - (1 - t_i) : i \in S_j\}$ and sends $S_{0,j}$ for $j \in [1, q_{\text{Enc}}]$ to the challenger. Notice that $S_{0,j} \subseteq S^*$.

(vii) The challenger sends back $(Hdr_{0,j}, \kappa_{0,j}^{(b)})$, where $(Hdr_{0,j}, \kappa_{0,j}^{(0)}) \leftarrow \text{Enc}_{\text{MS}}(S_{0,j}, \text{PK}')$ and $\kappa_{0,j}^{(1)} \xleftarrow{R} \mathscr{K}'$. Note that $b \leftarrow \{0, 1\}$ has been chosen by the challenger at the beginning of the experiment.

(viii) $\mathscr{A}_1$ sets $(Hdr_{1,j}, \kappa_{1,j}) \leftarrow \text{Enc}_{\text{MS}}(S_{1,j}, \text{PK}')$ and generates $K_{0,j}, K_{1,j} \xleftarrow{R} \mathscr{K}$. Then it sets $C_{0,j} \leftarrow \text{SymEnc}(\kappa_{0,j}^{(b)}, K_{0,j})$, $C_{1,j} \leftarrow \text{SymEnc}(\kappa_{1,j}, K_{0,j})$, and $Hdr_j^* \leftarrow (Hdr_{0,j}, C_{0,j}, Hdr_{1,j}, C_{1,j}, T_j)$ and sends $(Hdr_j^*, K_{b^*, j})$ to adversary $\mathscr{A}$.

(ix) $\mathscr{A}$ outputs a bit b'. If $b^* = b'$, $\mathscr{A}_1$ outputs 0, otherwise, 1.

Notice that if $b = 0$, $\mathscr{A}$'s view is identical to that of Game_0. Otherwise, $\mathscr{A}$'s view is identical to that of Game_1. Hence, we have

$$\left| \Pr[\text{Game}_0 = 1] - \Pr[\text{Game}_1 = 1] \right|$$
$$\leq \text{Adv}_{\mathscr{A}_1, \text{BE}, 2n}^{\text{MS}}(\lambda). \tag{B.2}$$

(Game_2 *to* Game_1). Game_2 is identical to Game_1 except that for each encryption query the challenger chooses $\kappa_{1,j} \xleftarrow{R} \mathscr{K}'$ to construct $C_{1,j} = \text{SymEnc}(\kappa_{1,j}, K_{0,j})$. The proof of the indistinguishability between Game_2 and Game_1 is similar to that of Game_1 and Game_0. So we have

$$\left| \Pr[\text{Game}_1 = 1] - \Pr[\text{Game}_2 = 1] \right|$$
$$\leq \text{Adv}_{\mathscr{A}_2, \text{BE}, 2n}^{\text{MS}}(\lambda). \tag{B.3}$$

(Game_3 *to* Game_2). Game_3 is identical to Game_2 except that for each encryption query the challenger chooses $K_{0,j} \xleftarrow{R} \mathscr{K}$ to construct $C_{0,j} \xleftarrow{R} \text{SymEnc}(\kappa_{0,j}, K_{0,j})$ for $j \in [1, q_{\text{Enc}}]$.

We construct a series of subgame 2, ι for $\iota = 1, \ldots, q_{\text{Enc}}$, to prove the indistinguishability between Game 2 and Game 3.

(i) $\text{Game}_{2,1}$. $\text{Game}_{2,1}$ is identical to Game_2 except that the challenger chooses $K_{0,1} \xleftarrow{R} \mathcal{K}$ to construct $C_{0,1} \xleftarrow{R} \text{SymEnc}(\kappa_{0,1}, K_{0,1})$.

(ii) $\text{Game}_{2,\iota}$. $\text{Game}_{2,\iota}$ is identical to $\text{Game}_{2,\iota-1}$ except that the challenger chooses $K_{0,\iota} \xleftarrow{R} \mathcal{K}$ to construct $C_{0,\iota} \xleftarrow{R} \text{SymEnc}(\kappa_{0,\iota}, K_{0,\iota})$.

Note that Game_3 is identical to $\text{Game}_{2,q_{\text{Enc}}}$.

Claim ($\text{Game}_{2,\iota-1}$ *to* $\text{Game}_{2,\iota}$). For any PPT adversary $\mathcal{M}$ which can make at most $q_{\text{key}} = q_{\text{key}}(\lambda)$ key generation queries and $q_{\text{Enc}} = q_{\text{Enc}}(\lambda)$ encryption queries with running time $\tilde{t}$, there exists an algorithm $\mathscr{A}_3$ with running about the same time as $\mathcal{M}$, such that

$$\left| \Pr[\text{Game}_{2,\iota-1} = 1] - \Pr[\text{Game}_{2,\iota} = 1] \right| \leq \text{Adv}_{\mathscr{A}_3, \Pi_{\text{sym}}}^{\text{CPA}}(\lambda). \tag{B.4}$$

Proof. $\mathscr{A}_3$ chooses $b^* \xleftarrow{R} \{0,1\}$ and simulates the experiment as follows.

(i) $\mathscr{A}_3$ runs $\text{Setup}(n,\ell)$ and $\text{KeyGen}(i',\text{SK})$ as in Game_2.

(ii) $\mathcal{M}$ adaptively makes encryption queries for S_j, where j denotes jth query. If $j \in [1, \iota-1]$, $\mathscr{A}_3$ returns the answer as in $\text{Game}_{2,\iota-1}$. If $j \in [\iota+1, q_{\text{Enc}}]$, $\mathscr{A}_3$ returns the answer as in Game_2. If $j = \iota$, $\mathscr{A}_3$ chooses $K_{0,\iota}, K_{1,\iota} \xleftarrow{R} \mathcal{K}$ and sends $(K_{0,\iota}, K_{1,\iota})$ to the challenger. The challenger chooses $b \xleftarrow{R} \{0,1\}$ and returns $C_{0,\iota} = \text{SymEnc}(\kappa, K_{b,\iota})$. Then $\mathscr{A}_3$ chooses $\kappa_{1,\iota} \xleftarrow{R} \mathcal{K}'$, computes $C_{1,\iota} = \text{SymEnc}(\kappa_{1,\iota}, K_{1,\iota})$, and returns $(C_{0,\iota}, C_{1,\iota})$.

(iii) $\mathcal{M}$ outputs b'. If $b^* = b'$, $\mathscr{A}_3$ outputs 0, otherwise, 1.

Observe that if $b = 1$, $\mathcal{M}$'s view is identical to that of $\text{Game}_{2,\iota-1}$. Otherwise, $\mathcal{M}$'s view is identical to that of $\text{Game}_{2,\iota}$. Thus

$$\left| \Pr[\text{Game}_{2,\iota-1} = 1] - \Pr[\text{Game}_{2,\iota} = 1] \right| \leq \text{Adv}_{\mathscr{A}_3, \Pi_{\text{sym}}}^{\text{CPA}}(\lambda), \tag{B.5}$$

which concludes the proof of the Claim.

Due to the Claim, we have

$$\left| \Pr[\text{Game}_2 = 1] - \Pr[\text{Game}_3 = 1] \right| \leq q_{\text{Enc}} \cdot \text{Adv}_{\mathscr{A}_3, \Pi_{\text{sym}}}^{\text{CPA}}(\lambda). \tag{B.6}$$

(Game_4 *to* Game_3). Game_4 is identical to Game_3 except that the challenger sets $K_{1,j} \xleftarrow{R} \mathcal{K}$ to construct $C_{1,j} = \text{SymEnc}(\kappa_{1,j}, K_{1,j})$ for $j \in [1, q_{\text{Enc}}]$. The proof of the indistinguishability between Game_4 and Game_3 is similar to that of Game_3 and Game_2. So we have

$$\left| \Pr[\text{Game}_3 = 1] - \Pr[\text{Game}_4 = 1] \right|$$
$$\leq q_{\text{Enc}} \cdot \text{Adv}_{\mathscr{A}_4, \Pi_{\text{sym}}}^{\text{CPA}}(\lambda). \tag{B.7}$$

In Game_4, all $\kappa_{0,j}, \kappa_{1,j}, K_{0,j}, K_{1,j}$ for $j \in [1, q_{\text{Enc}}]$ are chosen at random and Hdr_j^* is independent of $K_{b,j}$. Hence, the adversary has no advantage. That is,

$$\left| \Pr[\text{Game}_4 = 1] - \frac{1}{2} \right| = 0. \tag{B.8}$$

Hence, we have

$$\text{Adv}_{\mathscr{A},\text{BE},n}^{\text{MA}}(\lambda) \leq \text{Adv}_{\mathscr{A}_1,\text{BE},2n}^{\text{MS}}(\lambda) + \text{Adv}_{\mathscr{A}_2,\text{BE},2n}^{\text{MS}}(\lambda)$$
$$+ q_{\text{Enc}} \cdot \text{Adv}_{\mathscr{A}_3,\Pi_{\text{sym}}}^{\text{CPA}}(\lambda) + q_{\text{Enc}} \tag{B.9}$$
$$\cdot \text{Adv}_{\mathscr{A}_4,\Pi_{\text{sym}}}^{\text{CPA}}(\lambda).$$

$\square$

C. Proof of Theorem 6

Game Sequence

(i) Game_0 is the real experiment $\text{Exp}_{\mathscr{A},\text{BE}}^{\text{MA}}$.

(ii) Game_1 is the same as Game_0 except that all the challenge ciphertexts are pseudo-normal.

(iii) $\text{Game}_{2,i,0}$ is the same as Game_1 except that all user secret keys are semifunctional of type-$(i-1)$, while the challenge ciphertexts are semifunctional of type-$(\wedge, i-1)$ for $i \in [1, n]$.

(iv) $\text{Game}_{2,i,1}$ is the same as $\text{Game}_{2,i,0}$ except that if ith bit of a challenge identity id^* is 0 (i.e., $id_i^* = 0$), then the corresponding challenge ciphertexts are semifunctional of type-$(\wedge, i-1)$. Otherwise, the corresponding challenge ciphertexts are semifunctional of type-$(\sim, i-1)$.

(v) $\text{Game}_{2,i,2}$ is the same as $\text{Game}_{2,i,1}$ except that if ith bit of a challenge identity id^* is 0 (i.e., $id_i^* = 0$), then the corresponding challenge ciphertexts are semifunctional of type-$(\wedge, i)$. Otherwise, the corresponding challenge ciphertexts are semifunctional of type-$(\sim, i)$.

(vi) Game_3 is the same as $\text{Game}_{2,n,0}$ except that all the challenge ciphertexts and user secret keys are semifunctional of type-$(\wedge, n)$ and semifunctional of type-n, respectively.

(vii) Game_4 is the same as Game_3 except that the challenge keys K_b output by oracle $\mathcal{O}_{\text{Enc}}(\cdot, \text{mpk})$ are uniform bitstrings over $\{0,1\}^\tau$.

Lemma C.1 (Game_0 to Game_1). *For any PPT adversary $\mathscr{A}$ with at most $q_{\text{key}} = q_{\text{key}}(\lambda)$ key generation queries, $q_{\text{Enc}} = q_{\text{Enc}}(\lambda)$ encryption queries, and running time $\tilde{t}$, there exists an* algorithm $\mathcal{B}_1$ on DS1 with running time $t_1 \approx \tilde{t} + \mathbf{O}(n\lambda^c(q_{key} + q_{Enc}))$, for some constant $c \in \mathbb{N}$, such that

$$|\Pr[\mathsf{Game}_0 = 1] - \Pr[\mathsf{Game}_1 = 1]| \leq \mathsf{Adv}^{DS1}_{\mathcal{B}_1}(\lambda). \quad (C.1)$$

Proof. $\mathcal{B}_1$ receives the instance $(G, G_T, N, e, g, g_1, g_3, g_4, T)$ from the challenger, where $T \xleftarrow{R} G_{p_1}$ or $T \xleftarrow{R} G_{p_1 p_2}$, and simulates the experiment for $\mathcal{A}$ as follows.

Setup. Choose a bit $b \leftarrow \{0,1\}$. Pick $\alpha, \omega_1, \ldots, \omega_{2n} \xleftarrow{R} \mathbb{Z}_N$ and compute $(g_1, g_1^{\omega_1}, \ldots, g_1^{\omega_{2n}}) \in G_{p_1}^{2n+1}$. Let $h = g \in G_N$, $r_\mu \xleftarrow{R} \mathbb{Z}_N^*, R_{4,\mu} = g_4^{r_\mu}$ for $\mu \in [1, 2n]$. Compute $h_\mu = h^{\omega_\mu} \cdot R_{4,\mu}$ for $\mu \in [1, 2n]$. Set

mpk

$$= \left(g_1, g_1^{\omega_1}, \ldots, g_1^{\omega_{2n}}, g_4, h, e(g_1, h)^\alpha, h_1, \ldots, h_{2n}\right), \quad (C.2)$$

$$\mathsf{msk} = h^\alpha.$$

Key Generation Queries. To answer key generation queries $u \in [1, n]$, set $r'_\mu \xleftarrow{R} \mathbb{Z}_N^*$ and compute $R'_{4,\mu} = g_4^{r'_\mu}$ for $\mu \in [1, 2n]$ and generate $\mathbf{K} = (K_0, K_1, K_2, \ldots, K_{2n}) = (h^t, h_1^t \cdot R'_{4,1}, \ldots, h_{2n}^t \cdot R'_{4,2n}) \in G_N^{2n+1}$, where $t \xleftarrow{R} \mathbb{Z}_N^*$, and return $\overline{\mathsf{KeyGen}}(u, \mathsf{msk}, \mathbf{K})$.

Encryption Queries. $\mathcal{A}$ can adaptively make encryption queries S_l at most $q_{Enc} = q_{Enc}(\lambda)$ times. $\mathcal{B}_1$ sets

$$\mathsf{Enc}(S_l, \mathsf{mpk}) = \left(T^{t_l}, \prod_{j=1}^n T^{t_l \cdot \omega_{2j-s_j}}, \mathsf{H}\left(e(T^{t_l}, \mathsf{msk})\right)\right) \quad (C.3)$$

$$= \left(Hdr_l^*, K_{l,0}^*\right),$$

where $t_l \xleftarrow{R} \mathbb{Z}_N^*, l \in [1, q_{Enc}]$ and returns $(Hdr_l^*, K_{l,b}^*)$, where $K_{l,1}^* \leftarrow \{0,1\}^\tau$.

Finally, $\mathcal{A}$ outputs a guess b'. $\mathcal{B}_1$ outputs 1 if $b' = b$, otherwise, 0.

The distribution of the master public key and user secret keys that $\mathcal{A}$ requests are identical to those in Game_0 as well as in Game_1. If $T \xleftarrow{R} G_{p_1}$, the distribution of challenge ciphertexts is identical to that of Game_0, while if $T \xleftarrow{R} G_{p_1 p_2}$, the distribution of challenge ciphertexts is identical to that of Game_1. Therefore, we have (C.1). $\square$

Lemma C.2 (Game_1 to $\mathsf{Game}_{2,1,0}$). *For any PPT adversary $\mathcal{A}$ with at most $q_{key} = q_{key}(\lambda)$ key generation queries, $q_{Enc} = q_{Enc}(\lambda)$ encryption queries, and running time $\tilde{t}$, we have*

$$\Pr[\mathsf{Game}_1 = 1] = \Pr[\mathsf{Game}_{2,1,0} = 1]. \quad (C.4)$$

Proof. As shown in Table 4, $\mathsf{msk} \leftarrow G_N$ in Game_1, while $\mathsf{msk}' = \mathsf{msk} \cdot \widehat{\mathsf{RF}}_0(\varepsilon) \cdot \widetilde{\mathsf{RF}}_0(\varepsilon)$ in $\mathsf{Game}_{2,1,0}$ is also uniform in G_N, where $id|_0$ denotes the empty string ε. Since the distribution of msk and $\mathsf{msk} \cdot \widehat{\mathsf{RF}}_0(\varepsilon) \cdot \widetilde{\mathsf{RF}}_0(\varepsilon)$ is identical, (C.4) holds. $\square$

Lemma C.3 ($\mathsf{Game}_{2,i,0}$ to $\mathsf{Game}_{2,i,1}$). *For any PPT adversary $\mathcal{A}$ with at most $q_{key} = q_{key}(\lambda)$ key generation queries, $q_{Enc} = q_{Enc}(\lambda)$ encryption queries, and running time $\tilde{t}$, there exists an algorithm $\mathcal{B}_2$ on DS2 with running time $t_2 \approx \tilde{t} + \mathbf{O}(n\lambda^c(q_{key} + q_{Enc}))$, for some constant $c \in \mathbb{N}$, such that*

$$|\Pr[\mathsf{Game}_{2,i,0} = 1] - \Pr[\mathsf{Game}_{2,i,1} = 1]|$$
$$\leq \mathsf{Adv}^{DS2}_{\mathcal{B}_2}(\lambda). \quad (C.5)$$

Proof. $\mathcal{B}_2$ receives the instance $(G, G_T, N, e, g, g_1, g_4, g_{\{1,2\}}, g_{\{2,3\}}, T)$ from the challenger, where $T \xleftarrow{R} G_{p_1 p_2}$ or $T \xleftarrow{R} G_{p_1 p_3}$ and chooses $b \xleftarrow{R} \{0,1\}$. Then $\mathcal{B}_2$ can use the parameter to generate $\mathsf{msk}, \mathsf{mpk}$ as in the proof of Lemma C.1 and define a truly random function $\mathsf{RF} : \{0,1\}^{i-1} \to G_{p_2 p_3 p_4}$.

Key Generation Queries. Next, it can answer the secret key queries for $u \in [1, n]$ as $\overline{\mathsf{KeyGen}}(u, \mathsf{msk} \cdot \mathsf{RF}(id|_{i-1}), \mathbf{K})$, where $\mathsf{RF}(id|_{i-1}) : id|_{i-1} \to (g_{\{2,3\}} g_4)^{\gamma_{i-1}(id|_{i-1})}, \gamma_{i-1}(id|_{i-1}) : id|_{i-1} \mapsto \gamma_{i-1}$, and $\gamma_{i-1} \xleftarrow{R} \mathbb{Z}_N^*$.

Encryption Queries. Upon receiving encryption queries S_l^*, $\mathcal{B}_2$ chooses $t_l \xleftarrow{R} \mathbb{Z}_N^*$, $l \in [1, q_{Enc}]$ and returns

$$\overline{\mathsf{Enc}}\left(S_l^*, \mathsf{mpk}, \mathbf{g}_{\{1,2\}}^{t_l}, \mathsf{msk} \cdot \mathsf{RF}\left(id_l^*|_{i-1}\right)\right)$$

$$\text{if } (id_l^*)_i = 0, \quad (C.6)$$

$$\overline{\mathsf{Enc}}\left(S_l^*, \mathsf{mpk}, T^{t_l}, \mathsf{msk} \cdot \mathsf{RF}\left(id_l^*|_{i-1}\right)\right)$$

$$\text{if } (id_l^*)_i = 1.$$

Finally, $\mathcal{A}$ outputs a guess bit b'. $\mathcal{B}_2$ outputs 1 if $b' = b$; otherwise 0.

Note that $\mathbf{g}_{\{1,2\}}^{t_l}$ is distributed uniformly over $G_{p_1 p_2}$. If $T \xleftarrow{R} G_{p_1 p_2}$, the challenge ciphertexts are distributed identically as in $\mathsf{Game}_{2,i,0}$. Otherwise, the distribution is the same as in $\mathsf{Game}_{2,i,1}$. Hence (C.5) holds. $\square$

Lemma C.4 ($\mathsf{Game}_{2,i,1}$ to $\mathsf{Game}_{2,i,2}$). *For any PPT adversary $\mathcal{A}$ with at most $q_{key} = q_{key}(\lambda)$ key generation queries, $q_{Enc} = q_{Enc}(\lambda)$ encryption queries, and running time $\tilde{t}$, there exists an algorithm $\mathcal{B}_3$ on DS3 with running time $t_3 \approx \tilde{t} + \mathbf{O}(n\lambda^c(q_{key} + q_{Enc}))$, for some constant $c \in \mathbb{N}$, such that*

$$|\Pr[\mathsf{Game}_{2,i,1} = 1] - \Pr[\mathsf{Game}_{2,i,2} = 1]|$$
$$\leq \mathsf{Adv}^{DS3}_{\mathcal{B}_3}(\lambda). \quad (C.7)$$

Proof. $\mathcal{B}_3$ gets the instance (D, T), where $T = (\hat{T}, \widetilde{T})$ is either (g_2^{xy}, g_3^{xy}) or $(g_2^{xy+\gamma'}, g_3^{xy+\gamma'})$ for

$$D = \left(G, G_T, N, e, g, g_1, g_2, g_3, g_4, g_2^x \widehat{X}_4, g_2^y \widehat{Y}_4, g_3^x \widetilde{X}_4, \right.$$
$$\left. g_3^y \widetilde{Y}_4\right), \quad (C.8)$$

$$\widehat{X}_4, \widehat{Y}_4, \widetilde{X}_4, \widetilde{Y}_4 \xleftarrow{R} G_{p_4}, x, y, \gamma' \longleftarrow \mathbb{Z}_N^*. \quad (C.9)$$

Setup. $\mathcal{B}_3$ chooses $b \leftarrow \{0,1\}$ and $(\alpha, \omega_1, \ldots, \omega_{2n}) \in \mathbb{Z}_N^{2n+1}$, computes $(g_1^{\omega_1}, \ldots, g_1^{\omega_{2n}}) \in G_{p_1}^{2n}$, and generates $r, \hat{r}, \tilde{r} \xleftarrow{R} \mathbb{Z}_N^*$ and sets

$$h = (g_1 g_2 g_3 g_4)^r \in G_N,$$

$$\hat{h} = (g_2 g_4)^{\hat{r}} \in G_{p_2 p_4}, \qquad \text{(C.10)}$$

$$\tilde{h} = (g_3 g_4)^{\tilde{r}} \in G_{p_3 p_4}.$$

Next $\mathcal{B}_3$ generates $r_\mu \xleftarrow{R} \mathbb{Z}_N^*$ for $\mu \in [1, 2n]$ and $(R_{4,1}, \ldots, R_{4,2n}) = (g_4^{r_1}, \ldots, g_4^{r_{2n}}) \in G_{p_4}^{2n}$ and sets

$$(h_1, \ldots, h_{2i-1}, h_{2i}, \ldots, h_{2n}) = \left(h^{\omega_1} \cdot R_{4,1}, \ldots, h^{\omega_{2i-1}} \right.$$
$$\cdot \left(g_2^y \hat{Y}_4 \right)^r \cdot R_{4,2i-1}, h^{\omega_{2i}} \cdot \left(g_3^y \tilde{Y}_4 \right)^r \cdot R_{4,2i}, \ldots, h^{\omega_{2n}}$$
$$\left. \cdot R_{4,2n} \right), \qquad \text{(C.11)}$$

$$\mathsf{mpk} = \left(g_1, g_1^{\omega_1}, \ldots, g_1^{\omega_{2n}}, g_4, h, e(g_1, h)^\alpha, h_1, \ldots, h_{2n} \right).$$

Key Generation Queries. During the experiment $\mathcal{B}_3$ can answer key generation queries for identity id_ℓ for $\ell \in [1, q_{\mathsf{key}}]$ as follows.

By running the algorithm in Lemma 6 of [20] (or algorithm in [19]) which takes as input $(1^{q_{\mathsf{key}}}, (g_2, g_4, g_2^x \hat{X}_4, g_2^y \hat{Y}_4), \hat{T})$ and $(1^{q_{\mathsf{key}}}, (g_3, g_4, g_3^x \tilde{X}_4, g_3^y \tilde{Y}_4), \tilde{T})$, $\mathcal{B}_3$ can generate the following tuples:

$$\left(g_2^{\hat{r}_\ell} \hat{X}_{4,\ell}, \hat{T}_\ell \right)_{\ell=1}^{q_{\mathsf{key}}},$$
$$\left(g_3^{\tilde{r}_\ell} \tilde{X}_{4,\ell}, \tilde{T}_\ell \right)_{\ell=1}^{q_{\mathsf{key}}}, \qquad \text{(C.12)}$$

respectively, where

$$\hat{T}_\ell = \begin{cases} g_2^{\hat{r}_\ell y} \cdot \hat{Y}_{4,\ell}, & \text{if } \hat{T} = g_2^{xy} \\ g_2^{\hat{r}_\ell y} \cdot \hat{Y}_{4,\ell} \cdot g_2^{\hat{\gamma}_\ell'}, & \text{if } \hat{T} = g_2^{xy+\gamma'}, \end{cases}$$

$$\tilde{T}_\ell = \begin{cases} g_3^{\tilde{r}_\ell y} \cdot \tilde{Y}_{4,\ell}, & \text{if } \tilde{T} = g_3^{xy} \\ g_3^{\tilde{r}_\ell y} \cdot \tilde{Y}_{4,\ell} \cdot g_3^{\tilde{\gamma}_\ell'}, & \text{if } \tilde{T} = g_3^{xy+\gamma'}. \end{cases} \qquad \text{(C.13)}$$

Then $\mathcal{B}_3$ generates $r_\ell' \leftarrow \mathbb{Z}_N^*$, $(g_4^{t_{\ell,1}}, \ldots, g_4^{t_{\ell,2n}}) = (R_{\ell,1}, \ldots, R_{\ell,2n}) \in G_{p_4}^{2n}$, where $(t_{\ell,1}, \ldots, t_{\ell,2n}) \xleftarrow{R} (\mathbb{Z}_N^*)^{2n}$, and sets

$$K_0 = h^{r_\ell'} \cdot g_2^{\hat{r}_\ell} \hat{X}_{4,\ell} \cdot g_3^{\tilde{r}_\ell} \tilde{X}_{4,\ell},$$

$$K_1 = K_0^{\omega_1} \cdot R_{\ell,1},$$

$$\vdots$$

$$K_{2j-1} = K_0^{\omega_{2j-1}} \cdot \left(g_2^y \hat{Y}_4 \right)^{r_\ell' \cdot r} \cdot \hat{T}_\ell \cdot R_{\ell,2j-1}, \qquad \text{(C.14)}$$

$$K_{2j} = K_0^{\omega_{2j}} \cdot \left(g_3^y \tilde{Y}_4 \right)^{r_\ell' \cdot r} \cdot \tilde{T}_\ell \cdot R_{\ell,2j},$$

$$\vdots$$

$$K_{2n} = K_0^{\omega_{2n}} \cdot R_{\ell,2n}.$$

Thus $\mathbf{K}_\ell = (K_0, K_1, \ldots, K_{2j-1}, K_{2j}, \ldots, K_{2n})$. For identity id_ℓ and $\ell \in [1, q_{\mathsf{key}}]$, $\mathcal{B}_3$ defines the random functions below:

$$\widehat{\mathsf{RF}}_i \left(id_\ell |_i \right) = \widehat{\mathsf{RF}}_{i-1} \left(id_\ell |_{i-1} \right),$$

$$\widetilde{\mathsf{RF}}_i \left(id_\ell |_i \right) = \widetilde{\mathsf{RF}}_{i-1} \left(id_\ell |_{i-1} \right) \cdot \left(\tilde{h} \right)^{\tilde{\gamma}_\ell}$$
$$\text{if } (id_\ell)_i = 0,$$

$$\widetilde{\mathsf{RF}}_i \left(id_\ell |_i \right) = \widetilde{\mathsf{RF}}_{i-1} \left(id_\ell |_{i-1} \right),$$

$$\widehat{\mathsf{RF}}_i \left(id_\ell |_i \right) = \widehat{\mathsf{RF}}_{i-1} \left(id_\ell |_{i-1} \right) \cdot \left(\hat{h} \right)^{\hat{\gamma}_\ell}$$
$$\text{if } (id_\ell)_i = 1, \qquad \text{(C.15)}$$

where $\tilde{\gamma}_\ell, \hat{\gamma}_\ell \leftarrow \mathbb{Z}_N^*$. Next $\mathcal{B}_3$ answers ℓ-th secret key generation query for identity id_ℓ with prefix $id_\ell |_i$ that is not a prefix of an already queried identity as

$$\overline{\mathsf{KeyGen}} \left(u_\ell, \mathsf{msk} \cdot \widehat{\mathsf{RF}}_i \left(id_\ell |_i \right) \cdot \widetilde{\mathsf{RF}}_{i-1} \left(id_\ell |_{i-1} \right), \mathbf{K}_\ell \right)$$
$$\text{if } (id_\ell)_i = 0,$$

$$\overline{\mathsf{KeyGen}} \left(u_\ell, \mathsf{msk} \cdot \widehat{\mathsf{RF}}_{i-1} \left(id_\ell |_{i-1} \right) \cdot \widetilde{\mathsf{RF}}_i \left(id_\ell |_i \right), \mathbf{K}_\ell \right)$$
$$\text{if } (id_\ell)_i = 1. \qquad \text{(C.16)}$$

For an identity prefix $id_\ell |_i$ that is a prefix of an already queried identity, we rerandomize the element of $\mathbf{K}_\ell$.

Encryption Queries. Upon receiving encryption queries S_l^*, $\mathcal{B}_3$ chooses $t_l \xleftarrow{R} \mathbb{Z}_N^*$ and returns

$$\overline{\mathsf{Enc}} \left(S_l^*, \mathsf{mpk}, (\mathbf{g}_1 \mathbf{g}_2)^{t_l}, \mathsf{msk} \cdot \widehat{\mathsf{RF}}_i \left(id_l^* |_i \right) \right)$$
$$\text{if } (id_l^*)_i = 0,$$

$$\overline{\mathsf{Enc}} \left(S_l^*, \mathsf{mpk}, (\mathbf{g}_1 \mathbf{g}_3)^{t_l}, \mathsf{msk} \cdot \widetilde{\mathsf{RF}}_i \left(id_l^* |_i \right) \right)$$
$$\text{if } (id_l^*)_i = 1, \qquad \text{(C.17)}$$

where $\mathbf{g}_1 \mathbf{g}_2 = ((g_1 g_2)^{t^*}, (g_1 g_2)^{\omega_1 t^*}, \ldots, (g_1 g_2)^{\omega_{2n} t^*})$, $\mathbf{g}_1 \mathbf{g}_3 = ((g_1 g_3)^{\hat{t}}, (g_1 g_3)^{\omega_1 \hat{t}}, \ldots, (g_1 g_3)^{\omega_{2n} \hat{t}})$, $t^*, \hat{t} \xleftarrow{R} \mathbb{Z}_N^*$.

Finally, $\mathcal{A}$ outputs a guess bit b'. $\mathcal{B}_3$ outputs 1 if $b' = b$, otherwise 0. If $T = (g_2^{xy}, g_3^{xy})$ (i.e., $T_\ell = (g_2^{\hat{r}_\ell y} \cdot \hat{Y}_{4,\ell}, g_3^{\tilde{r}_\ell y} \cdot \tilde{Y}_{4,\ell})$), then the secret keys are distributed identically as in $\mathsf{Game}_{2,i,1}$. If $T = (g_2^{xy+\gamma'}, g_3^{xy+\gamma'})$ (i.e., $T_\ell = (g_2^{\hat{r}_\ell y} \cdot \hat{Y}_{4,\ell} \cdot g_2^{\hat{r}_\ell'}, g_3^{\tilde{r}_\ell y} \cdot \tilde{Y}_{4,\ell} \cdot g_3^{\tilde{r}_\ell'})$), we have

$$\left(\hat{h}, g_2^{\hat{r}_\ell} \cdot \hat{Y}_{4,\ell} \right),$$

$$\left(\hat{h}, \left(\hat{h} \right)^{\hat{r}_\ell} \cdot \hat{Y}_{4,\ell} \right)$$

$$\left(\tilde{h}, g_3^{\tilde{r}_\ell} \cdot \tilde{Y}_{4,\ell} \right), \qquad \text{(C.18)}$$

$$\left(\tilde{h}, \left(\tilde{h} \right)^{\tilde{r}_\ell} \cdot \tilde{Y}_{4,\ell} \right)$$

identically distributed, respectively. Therefore, in this case, the distribution is the same as in $\mathsf{Game}_{2,i,2}$. Besides, the distribution of the challenge ciphertexts is identical in these two games. Hence, (C.7) holds. □

Lemma C.5 ($\mathsf{Game}_{2,i-1,2}$ to $\mathsf{Game}_{2,i,0}$). *For any PPT adversary $\mathscr{A}$ with at most $q_{key} = q_{key}(\lambda)$ key generation queries, $q_{Enc} = q_{Enc}(\lambda)$ encryption queries, and running time $\widetilde{t}$, there exists an algorithm $\mathscr{B}_2$ on DS2, with running time $t_2 \approx \widetilde{t} + \mathbf{O}(n\lambda^c(q_{key} + q_{Enc}))$, for some constant $c \in \mathbb{N}$, such that*

$$\left| \Pr\left[\mathsf{Game}_{2,i-1,2} = 1\right] - \Pr\left[\mathsf{Game}_{2,i,0} = 1\right]\right|$$
$$\leq \mathsf{Adv}^{DS2}_{\mathscr{B}_2}(\lambda). \tag{C.19}$$

Lemma C.6 ($\mathsf{Game}_{2,n,2}$ to Game_3). *For any PPT adversary $\mathscr{A}$ with at most $q_{key} = q_{key}(\lambda)$ key generation queries, $q_{Enc} = q_{Enc}(\lambda)$ encryption queries, and running time $\widetilde{t}$, there exists an algorithm $\mathscr{B}_2$ on DS2, with running time $t_2 \approx \widetilde{t} + \mathbf{O}(n\lambda^c(q_{key} + q_{Enc}))$, for some constant $c \in \mathbb{N}$, such that*

$$\left| \Pr\left[\mathsf{Game}_{2,n,2} = 1\right] - \Pr\left[\mathsf{Game}_3 = 1\right]\right|$$
$$\leq \mathsf{Adv}^{DS2}_{\mathscr{B}_2}(\lambda). \tag{C.20}$$

In $\mathsf{Game}_{2,i,0}$ all the challenge ciphertexts are semifunctional of type-$(\wedge, i - 1)$, while in $\mathsf{Game}_{2,i-1,2}$ if ith bit of challenge identity id is 0 (i.e., $id_i = 0$), the challenge ciphertexts are totally identical to those in $\mathsf{Game}_{2,i,0}$. Otherwise, the challenge ciphertexts are semifunctional of type-$(\sim, i - 1)$. Actually, the proof of ($\mathsf{Game}_{2,i-1,2}$ to $\mathsf{Game}_{2,i,0}$) and ($\mathsf{Game}_{2,n,2}$ to Game_3) is similar to that in Lemma C.3 and thus omitted.

Lemma C.7 (Game_3 to Game_4). *For any PPT adversary $\mathscr{A}$ with at most $q_{key} = q_{key}(\lambda)$ key generation queries, $q_{Enc} = q_{Enc}(\lambda)$ encryption queries, and running time $\widetilde{t}$, there exists an algorithm $\mathscr{B}_4$ on DS-BDDH with running time $t_4 \approx \widetilde{t} + \mathbf{O}(n\lambda^c(q_{key} + q_{Enc}))$, for some constant $c \in \mathbb{N}$ such that*

$$\left| \Pr\left[\mathsf{Game}_3 = 1\right] - \Pr\left[\mathsf{Game}_4 = 1\right]\right|$$
$$\leq \mathsf{Adv}^{DS\text{-}BDDH}_{\mathscr{B}_4}(\lambda) + q_{Enc} \cdot \mathbf{O}\left(2^{-\tau}\right). \tag{C.21}$$

Proof. $\mathscr{B}_4$ is provided with the instance (D, T) where T is either $e(g_2, g_2)^{abc}$ or $e(g_2, g_2)^z$, for

$$D = \left(G, G_T, N, e, g, (g_i)_i, g_1^a, g_2^a, g_2^b, g_{\{2,4\}}, g_{\{2,4\}}^b, g_{\{2,4\}}^c\right), \tag{C.22}$$

where $a, b, c, z \leftarrow \mathbb{Z}_N^*$.

Setup. $\mathscr{B}_4$ chooses $(\alpha, \omega_1, \ldots, \omega_{2n}) \xleftarrow{R} \mathbb{Z}_N^{2n+1}$ and computes $(g_1^{\omega_1}, \ldots, g_1^{\omega_{2n}}) \in G_{p_1}^{2n}$. Set $h = g \in G_N$, $(r_1, r_2, \ldots, r_{2n}) \xleftarrow{R} (\mathbb{Z}_N^*)^{2n}$ and compute $(R_{4,1}, \ldots, R_{4,2n}) = (g_4^{r_1}, \ldots, g_4^{r_{2n}}) \in G_{p_4}^{2n}$. Thus

$$(h_1, \ldots, h_{2n}) = (h^{\omega_1} \cdot R_{4,1}, \ldots, h^{\omega_{2n}} \cdot R_{4,2n});$$

$$\mathsf{mpk} = \left(g_1, g_1^{\omega_1}, \ldots, g_1^{\omega_{2n}}, h, e(g_1, h)^{\alpha}, h_1, \ldots, h_{2n}\right), \tag{C.23}$$

$$\mathsf{msk} = h^{\alpha}.$$

Key Generation Queries. $\mathscr{B}_4$ defines a truly random function $\mathsf{RF}' : \{0,1\}^n \to G_{p_2 p_4}$. Next it can answer the secret key generation queries for identity $u \in [1, n]$ as

$$\overline{\mathsf{KeyGen}}\left(u, \mathsf{msk} \cdot \mathsf{RF}'(id), \mathbf{K}\right), \tag{C.24}$$

where $\mathsf{RF}' : id \mapsto (g_{\{2,4\}})^{\gamma'(id)}$, $\gamma'(id) : id \mapsto \gamma'$ for $\gamma' \xleftarrow{R} \mathbb{Z}_N^*$, and $\mathbf{K} = (h^{\widehat{t}}, h_1^{\widehat{t}} \cdot R'_{4,1}, \ldots, h_{2n}^{\widehat{t}} \cdot R'_{4,2n})$ for $\widehat{t} \xleftarrow{R} \mathbb{Z}_N^*$, $(R'_{4,1}, \ldots, R'_{4,2n}) = (g_4^{r'_1}, \ldots, g_4^{r'_{2n}})$, where $(r'_1, \ldots, r'_{2n}) \xleftarrow{R} (\mathbb{Z}_N^*)^{2n}$.

Encryption Queries. Upon receiving encryption queries S_l^* for some $l \in [1, q_{Enc}]$, $\mathscr{B}_4$ sets

$$\mathbf{g} = \left(g_1^s, g_1^{s\omega_1}, \ldots, g_1^{s\omega_{2n}}\right),$$

$$\mathbf{g}^a = \left(g_1^{sa}, g_1^{s\omega_1 a}, \ldots, g_1^{s\omega_{2n} a}\right);$$

$$\widehat{\mathbf{g}} = \left(g_2^{\widehat{s}}, g_2^{\widehat{s}\omega_2}, \ldots, g_2^{\widehat{s}\omega_{2n}}\right), \tag{C.25}$$

$$\widehat{\mathbf{g}}^a = \left(g_2^{\widehat{s}a}, g_2^{\widehat{s}\omega_2 a}, \ldots, g_2^{\widehat{s}\omega_{2n} a}\right);$$

$$\left(g_2^{\widehat{s}}\right)^b, g_{\{2,4\}}^b, g_{\{2,4\}}^c,$$

where $s, \widehat{s} \xleftarrow{R} \mathbb{Z}_N^*$. Then $\mathscr{B}_4$ runs the algorithm $\mathsf{Rerand}_{abc}(N, \mathbf{g}, \mathbf{g}^a, \widehat{\mathbf{g}}, \widehat{\mathbf{g}}^a, (g_2^{\widehat{s}})^b, g_{\{2,4\}}, g_{\{2,4\}}^b, g_{\{2,4\}}^c, T)$ in [19] and outputs $(\mathbf{g}^{a_l}, \widehat{\mathbf{g}}^{a_l}, (g_2^{\widehat{s}})^{b_l}, g_{\{2,4\}}^{b_l}, g_{\{2,4\}}^{c_l}, T_{abc}^l)$, where

$$\mathbf{g}^{a_l} = \left(g_1^{sa_l}, g_1^{s\omega_1 a_l}, \ldots, g_1^{s\omega_{2n} a_l}\right) = \left((g_1^{sa})^{r_1}\right.$$
$$\left. \cdot (g_1^s)^{t_1}, (g_1^{s\omega_1 a})^{r_1} \cdot (g_1^{s\omega_1})^{t_1}, \ldots, (g_1^{s\omega_{2n} a})^{r_1}\right.$$
$$\left. \cdot (g_1^{s\omega_{2n}})^{t_1}\right),$$

$$\widehat{\mathbf{g}}^{a_l} = \left(\widehat{g}_2^{\widehat{s}a_l}, \widehat{g}_2^{\widehat{s}\omega_1 a_l}, \ldots, \widehat{g}_2^{\widehat{s}\omega_{2n} a_l}\right) = \left((\widehat{g}_2^{\widehat{s}a})^{r_1}\right.$$
$$\left. \cdot (\widehat{g}_2^{\widehat{s}})^{t_1}, (\widehat{g}_2^{\widehat{s}\omega_1 a})^{r_1} \cdot (\widehat{g}_2^{\widehat{s}\omega_1})^{t_1}, \ldots, (\widehat{g}_2^{\widehat{s}\omega_{2n} a})^{r_1}\right.$$
$$\left. \cdot (\widehat{g}_2^{\widehat{s}\omega_{2n}})^{t_1}\right), \tag{C.26}$$

$$\left(g_2^{\widehat{s}}\right)^{b_l} = \left(g_2^{\widehat{s}b}\right)^{r_2} \cdot \left(g_2^{\widehat{s}}\right)^{t_2} = \left(g_2^{\widehat{s}}\right)^{br_2 + t_2},$$

$$g_{\{2,4\}}^{b_l} = \left(g_{\{2,4\}}^b\right)^{r_2} \cdot g_{\{2,4\}}^{t_2} = g_{\{2,4\}}^{br_2 + t_2},$$

$$g_{\{2,4\}}^{c_l} = \left(g_{\{2,4\}}^c\right)^{r_3} \cdot g_{\{2,4\}}^{t_3} = g_{\{2,4\}}^{cr_3 + t_3},$$

$$T_{abc}^l = e\left(g_2^{\widehat{s}}, g_{\{2,4\}}\right)^{z_{abc}},$$

where $r_1, r_2, r_3, t_1, t_2, t_3 \xleftarrow{R} \mathbb{Z}_N^*$, $z_a = zr_1 + bct_1$; $z_{ab} = z_a r_2 + a_l ct_2$, $z_{abc} = z_{ab} r_3 + a_l b_l t_3$. It is easy to check that a_l, b_l, c_l

are uniformly distributed in $\mathbb{Z}_N$. If $z = abc$, then $z_a = a_l bc$, $z_{ab} = a_l b_l c$, $z_{abc} = a_l b_l c_l$ and $T_{abc}^l = T^{a_l b_l c_l}$. For the case $z \neq abc$, since $a, b, c, z, r_1, t_1, r_2, t_2, r_3, t_3 \leftarrow \mathbb{Z}_N^*$ and a_l, b_l, c_l are uniformly distributed over $\mathbb{Z}_N$, we have z_a, z_{ab}, z_{abc} all uniformly distributed in $\mathbb{Z}_N$ and $T_{abc}^l = e(\widehat{g}_2^{\widehat{s}}, g_{\{2,4\}})^{z_{abc}}$.

(i) If the challenge identity was not queried before, then $\mathcal{B}_4$ computes

$$\left(\mathbf{g}^{a_l}, \widehat{\mathbf{g}}^{a_l}, \left(g_2^{\widehat{s}} \right)^{b_l}, g_{\{2,4\}}^{b_l}, g_{\{2,4\}}^{c_l}, T_{abc}^l \right)$$

$$\leftarrow \text{Rerand}_{abc} \left(N, \mathbf{g}, \mathbf{g}^a, \widehat{\mathbf{g}}, \widehat{\mathbf{g}}^a, \left(g_2^{\widehat{s}} \right)^b, g_{\{2,4\}}, g_{\{2,4\}}^b, \quad (\text{C}.27) \right.$$

$$\left. g_{\{2,4\}}^c, T \right)$$

and returns

$$\left(\left(g_1^s \widehat{g}_2^{\widehat{s}} \right)^{a_l}, \left(\prod_{j=1}^{n} \left(g_1^s \widehat{g}_2^{\widehat{s}} \right)^{\omega_{2j-s_j}} \right)^{a_l}, \mathsf{H} \left(e \left(\left(g_1^s \widehat{g}_2^{\widehat{s}} \right)^{a_l}, \mathsf{msk} \right) \cdot T_{abc}^l \right) \right). \qquad (\text{C}.28)$$

(ii) If the challenge identity was queried before, then $\mathcal{B}_4$ uses the algorithm Rerand_a in [19] to compute

$$\left(\mathbf{g}^{a_l'}, \widehat{\mathbf{g}}^{a_l'}, \left(g_2^{\widehat{s}} \right)^{b_l}, g_{\{2,4\}}^{b_l}, g_{\{2,4\}}^{c_l}, T_l' \right) \leftarrow \text{Rerand}_a \left(N, \right.$$

$$\left. \mathbf{g}, \mathbf{g}^{a_l}, \widehat{\mathbf{g}}, \widehat{\mathbf{g}}^{a_l}, \left(g_2^{\widehat{s}} \right)^{b_l}, g_{\{2,4\}}, g_{\{2,4\}}^{b_l}, g_{\{2,4\}}^{c_l}, T_{abc}^l \right) \qquad (\text{C}.29)$$

and returns

$$\left(\left(g_1^s \widehat{g}_2^{\widehat{s}} \right)^{a_l'}, \left(\prod_{j=1}^{n} \left(g_1^s \widehat{g}_2^{\widehat{s}} \right)^{\omega_{2j-s_j}} \right)^{a_l'}, \right.$$

$$\left. \mathsf{H} \left(e \left(\left(g_1^s \widehat{g}_2^{\widehat{s}} \right)^{a_l'}, \mathsf{msk} \right) \cdot T_l' \right) \right). \qquad (\text{C}.30)$$

The distribution of mpk and the requested user secret keys are identical to the real scheme.

If $T = e(g_2, g_2)^{abc} = e((g_1 g_2)^a, g_{\{2,4\}})^{bc}$ and the challenge identity was not queried before,

$$\left(\left(g_1^s \widehat{g}_2^{\widehat{s}} \right)^{a_l}, \left(\prod_{j=1}^{n} \left(g_1^s \widehat{g}_2^{\widehat{s}} \right)^{\omega_{2j-s_j}} \right)^{a_l}, \right.$$

$$\mathsf{H} \left(e \left(\left(g_1^s \widehat{g}_2^{\widehat{s}} \right)^{a_l}, \mathsf{msk} \right) \cdot T_{abc}^l \right) \right) = \left(\left(g_1^s \widehat{g}_2^{\widehat{s}} \right)^{a_l}, \right.$$

$$\left(\prod_{j=1}^{n} \left(g_1^s \widehat{g}_2^{\widehat{s}} \right)^{\omega_{2j-s_j}} \right)^{a_l}, \qquad (\text{C}.31)$$

$$\left. \mathsf{H} \left(e \left(\left(g_1^s \widehat{g}_2^{\widehat{s}} \right)^{a_l}, \mathsf{msk} \cdot \left(g_{\{2,4\}} \right)^{b_l c_l} \right) \right) \right).$$

Note that the exponents a, b, c, and z are required to be uniformly distributed in $\mathbb{Z}_N^*$, but when we reuse the outputs

of Rerand_a and Rerand_b, a_l, b_l are uniformly distributed in $\mathbb{Z}_N$. Since the uniform distribution in $\mathbb{Z}_N$ is statistically indistinguishable from the uniform distribution in $\mathbb{Z}_N^*$, we have that the distribution of challenge ciphertexts are $\mathbf{O}(2^{-\tau})$-close to that of Game_3. Note that we implicitly set $\widehat{\gamma}_l = b_l c_l$. For the challenge identity queried before, we can just rerandomize the previously used query value a_l.

If $T = e(g_2, g_2)^z$, then

$$\left(\left(g_1^s \widehat{g}_2^{\widehat{s}} \right)^{a_l}, \left(\prod_{j=1}^{n} \left(g_1^s \widehat{g}_2^{\widehat{s}} \right)^{\omega_{2j-s_j}} \right)^{a_l}, \right.$$

$$\mathsf{H} \left(e \left(\left(g_1^s \widehat{g}_2^{\widehat{s}} \right)^{a_l}, \mathsf{msk} \right) \cdot T_{abc}^l \right) \right) = \left(\left(g_1^s \widehat{g}_2^{\widehat{s}} \right)^{a_l}, \right.$$

$$\left(\prod_{j=1}^{n} \left(g_1^s \widehat{g}_2^{\widehat{s}} \right)^{\omega_{2j-s_j}} \right)^{a_l}, \qquad (\text{C}.32)$$

$$\left. \mathsf{H} \left(e \left(\left(g_1^s \widehat{g}_2^{\widehat{s}} \right)^{a_l}, \mathsf{msk} \cdot \left(g_{\{2,4\}} \right)^{z_{abc} \cdot a_l^{-1}} \right) \right) \right).$$

Since a_l, z_{abc} are uniformly distributed over $\mathbb{Z}_N$. So $e((g_1^s \widehat{g}_2^{\widehat{s}})^{a_l}, \mathsf{msk} \cdot (g_{\{2,4\}})^{z_{abc} \cdot a_l^{-1}})$ is statically close to the uniform distribution of subgroup of G_T. Due to the property of universal hash function we have $\mathrm{SD}((\mathsf{H}, \mathsf{H}(e((g_1^s \widehat{g}_2^{\widehat{s}})^{a_l}, \mathsf{msk} \cdot (g_{\{2,4\}})^{z_{abc} \cdot a_l^{-1}}))); (\mathsf{H}, U)) = \mathbf{O}(2^{-\tau})$ for $U \leftarrow \{0,1\}^\tau$. Thus the challenge ciphertexts are distributed $\mathbf{O}(2^{-\tau})$-close to that of Game_4. Hence (C.21) holds.

Finally, we have

$$\mathsf{Adv}_{\mathcal{A},\mathsf{BE}}^{\mathsf{MA}}(\lambda) \leq \mathsf{Adv}_{\mathcal{B}_1}^{\mathsf{DS1}}(\lambda) + 2n \cdot \mathsf{Adv}_{\mathcal{B}_2}^{\mathsf{DS2}}(\lambda) + n$$

$$\cdot \mathsf{Adv}_{\mathcal{B}_3}^{\mathsf{DS3}}(\lambda) + \mathsf{Adv}_{\mathcal{B}_4}^{\mathsf{DS\text{-}BDDH}} + q_{\mathsf{Enc}} \qquad (\text{C}.33)$$

$$\cdot \mathbf{O} \left(2^{-\tau} \right),$$

which completes the proof of Theorem 6. $\qquad \square$

Disclosure

Parts of this paper are presented at Inscrypt 2016.

Acknowledgments

All authors were funded by National 973 Grant 2013CB834205, NSFC Grant 61672019, and The Fundamental Research Funds of Shandong University Grant 2016JC029. Puwen Wei was also funded by NSFC Grant 61502276.

References

[1] A. Fiat and M. Naor, "Broadcast encryption," in *Advances in Cryptology—(CRYPTO '93)*, D. R. Stinson, Ed., vol. 773 of *Lecture Notes in Computer Science*, pp. 480–491, Springer, Berlin, Germany, 1993.

[2] I. Kim and S. O. Hwang, "An optimal identity-based broadcast encryption scheme for wireless sensor networks," *IEICE Transactions on Communications*, vol. E96-B, no. 3, pp. 891–895, 2013.

[3] D. Naor, M. Naor, and J. Lotspiech, "Revocation and tracing schemes for stateless receivers," in *Proceedings of the Advances in Cryptology—(CRYPTO '01), 21st Annual International Cryptology Conference*, pp. 41–62, Springer, Berlin, Germany.

[4] D. Halevy and A. Shamir, "The LSD broadcast encryption scheme," in *Advances in Cryptology—(CRYPTO '02)*, M. Yung, Ed., vol. 2442 of *Lecture Notes in Computer Science*, pp. 47–60, Springer, Berlin, Germany, 2002.

[5] M. T. Goodrich, J. Z. Sun, and R. Tamassia, "Efficient tree-based revocation in groups of low-state devices," in *Advances in Cryptology—(CRYPTO '04)*, M. K. Franklin, Ed., vol. 3152 of *Lecture Notes in Computer Science*, pp. 511–527, Springer, Berlin, Germany, 2004.

[6] Y. Dodis and N. Fazio, "Public key broadcast encryption for stateless receivers," in *Security and Privacy in Digital Rights Management, ACM CCS-9 Workshop*, J. Feigenbaum, Ed., vol. 2696 of *Lecture Notes in Computer Science*, pp. 61–80, Springer, Berlin, Germany, 2003.

[7] D. Boneh, C. Gentry, and B. Waters, "Collusion resistant broadcast encryption with short ciphertexts and private keys," in *Advances in Cryptology—(CRYPTO '05)*, V. Shoup, Ed., vol. 3621 of *Lecture Notes in Computer Science*, pp. 258–275, Springer, Berlin, Germany, 2005.

[8] C. Gentry and B. Waters, "Adaptive security in broadcast encryption systems (with short ciphertexts)," in *Advances in Cryptology—(EUROCRYPT '09)*, A. Joux, Ed., vol. 5479 of *Lecture Notes in Computer Science*, pp. 171–188, Springer, Berlin, Germany, 2009.

[9] B. Waters, "Dual system encryption: realizing fully secure IBE and HIBE under simple assumptions," in *Advances in Cryptology—(CRYPTO '2009)*, S. Halevi, Ed., vol. 5677 of *Lecture Notes in Computer Science*, pp. 619–636, Springer, Berlin, Germany, 2009.

[10] D. Boneh, B. Waters, and M. Zhandry, "Low overhead broadcast encryption from multilinear maps," in *Advances in Cryptology—(CRYPTO '14)*, J. A. Garay and R. Gennaro, Eds., vol. 8616 of *Lecture Notes in Computer Science*, pp. 206–223, Springer, Berlin, Germany, 2014.

[11] D. Boneh and B. Waters, "A fully collusion resistant broadcast, trace, and revoke system," in *Proceedings of CCS 2006: 13th ACM Conference on Computer and Communications Security*, pp. 211–220, Alexandria, Virginia, USA, November 2006.

[12] J. H. Han, J. H. Park, and D. H. Lee, "Transmission-efficient broadcast encryption scheme with personalized messages," *IEICE Transactions on Fundamentals of Electronics, Communications and Computer Sciences*, vol. E96-A, no. 4, pp. 796–806, 2013.

[13] M. Zhang, B. Yang, Z. Chen, and T. Takagi, "Efficient and adaptively secure broadcast encryption systems," *Security and Communication Networks*, vol. 6, no. 8, pp. 1044–1052, 2013.

[14] J. Kim, W. Susilo, M. H. Au, and J. Seberry, "Adaptively secure identity-based broadcast encryption with a constant-sized ciphertext," *IEEE Transactions on Information Forensics and Security*, vol. 10, no. 3, pp. 679–693, 2015.

[15] S. H. Islam, M. K. Khan, and A. M. Al-Khouri, "Anonymous and provably secure certificateless multireceiver encryption without bilinear pairing," *Security and Communication Networks*, vol. 8, no. 13, pp. 2214–2231, 2015.

[16] H. Wee, "Déjà Q: Encoreé un petit IBE," in *Theory of Cryptography—13th International Conference, TCC 2016-A*, E. Kushilevitz and T. Malkin, Eds., vol. 9563 of *Lecture Notes in Computer Science*, pp. 237–258, Springer, Berlin, Germany, 2016.

[17] M. Bellare, A. Boldyreva, and S. Micali, "Public-key encryption in a multi-user setting: security proofs and improvements," in *Advances in Cryptology—(EUROCRYPT '2000)*, B. Preneel, Ed., vol. 1807 of *Lecture Notes in Computer Science*, pp. 259–274, Springer, Berlin, Germany, 2000.

[18] D. Hofheinz and T. Jager, "Tightly secure signatures and public-key encryption," *Designs, Codes and Cryptography. An International Journal*, vol. 80, no. 1, pp. 29–61, 2016.

[19] D. Hofheinz, J. Koch, and C. Striecks, "Identity-based encryption with (almost) tight security in the multi-instance, multi-ciphertext setting," in *Public-key cryptography—(PKC '15)*, J. Katz, Ed., vol. 9020 of *Lecture Notes in Computer Science*, pp. 799–822, Springer, Berlin, Germany, 2015.

[20] J. Chen and H. Wee, "Fully, (almost) tightly secure IBE and dual system groups," in *Advances in Cryptology—(CRYPTO '13)*, R. Canetti and J. A. Garay, Eds., vol. 8043 of *Lecture Notes in Computer Science*, pp. 435–460, Springer, Berlin, Germany, 2013.

15

A Comparative Evaluation of Algorithms in the Implementation of an Ultra-Secure Router-to-Router Key Exchange System

Nishaal J. Parmar and Pramode K. Verma

Telecommunications Engineering Program, School of Electrical and Computer Engineering, University of Oklahoma, Tulsa, OK 74135, USA

Correspondence should be addressed to Nishaal J. Parmar; nishaal.parmar@ou.edu

Academic Editor: Vincente Martin

This paper presents a comparative evaluation of possible encryption algorithms for use in a self-contained, ultra-secure router-to-router communication system, first proposed by El Rifai and Verma. The original proposal utilizes a discrete logarithm-based encryption solution, which will be compared in this paper to RSA, AES, and ECC encryption algorithms. RSA certificates are widely used within the industry but require a trusted key generation and distribution architecture. AES and ECC provide advantages in key length, processing requirements, and storage space, also maintaining an arbitrarily high level of security. This paper modifies each of the four algorithms for use within the self-contained router-to-router environment system and then compares them in terms of features offered, storage space and data transmission needed, encryption/decryption efficiency, and key generation requirements.

1. Introduction

With the rise of globalization, microelectronics, and the information age, the need for rapid, long-distance transmission of unconditionally secure information has never been greater. Whether dealing with military intelligence, corporate secrets shared between two (or more) company offices, remote control of vital national infrastructure components such as power and traffic control systems, or mechanical instructions transmitted to off-site medical devices for telesurgery, device updates, and health reports, there are many situations where the rapid, accurate, and secure transmission of information between two parties is a basic necessity. In extreme cases, alteration or even decryption of this information by unauthorized parties may result in damages of billions of dollars and the lives of others.

Historically, only two encryption schemes have been proposed which offer unconditional security, both unsuitable for practical telecommunications. The first, the one-time pad, proposed by Gilbert Vernam in 1919 [1], utilizes a single-use encryption key equal to the message length which both the sending and receiving parties may use to encrypt and decrypt the message. The disadvantages of this system in a long-term high data rate communication system are obvious,

with each message requiring a preshared key equal to the message length. The second, recently proposed unconditional cryptographic system is quantum cryptography, where security is achieved through the laws of quantum mechanics, which allow for very accurate determination of eavesdroppers along a quantum channel, as well as the simultaneous determination of small shared and secure random values. Currently available quantum encryption protocols include BB84, proposed in 1984 by Bennett and Brassard [2], the variant SARG04 [3], and the later-developed B92 [4]. All three solutions, while unconditionally secure, possess severe limitations which make them unsuitable for general commercial use, including reliance on single-photon generators (greatly limiting practical data rate) and, most importantly, the presence of a physical, well characterized quantum channel between endpoints, with a maximum practical distance of a few hundred km. While some research has been proposed in the use of multiphoton quantum sources [5] and channel extension [6], this technology remains extremely expensive and unfeasible for general commercial use.

While unconditional security may be an unachievable goal, it may be realized to an arbitrarily high level via existing symmetric and asymmetric encryption systems. Currently, the most widely used form of global network communication between two distant parties relies on public key, asymmetric key cryptography such as RSA for transferring symmetric keys. Symmetric encryption systems then use these keys to encrypt the information being transferred. Noteworthy corporations offering SSL certificates with Elliptic Curve Cryptography (ECC), RSA, and DSA support include Symantec (formerly Verisign), GoDaddy, and Comodo.

Although presenting a viable and widely used solution to secure communication, allowing for message encryption and authentication, the security certificate system requires the presence of a trusted third party for the verification of the identity and legitimacy of certificate owners. The compromise of or loss of trust in such a third party, or the inability to contact the distribution network at need, may result in a large-scale breakdown of reliable and secure communications [7]. Furthermore, the increasingly large RSA key length requirements of public certificates to guarantee secure communication may be a barrier to practical implementation on limited-resource devices.

A novel proposal [9] for a secure communication system not requiring a third party for key generation and distribution involves instead a system of paired routers, communicating securely on any standard classical channel. Each router pair would be factory-initialized with a shared secret, enabling direct secure communication between the two regardless of network distance or security, with shared transmitted data on each end decrypted and used as the basis of further secure key generation as necessary. While the original system uses a variant of the discrete logarithm problem to introduce the nonlinearity necessary in a secure encryption system, nonlinearity introduced via other encryption methods offers alternative advantages. This paper first examines the originally proposed discrete logarithm-based encryption system and then proposes and compares other more commonly used encryption systems which may be used in this entirely self-contained environment, including RSA, ECC, and AES based encryption.

2. Related Work: Discrete Logarithm

The encryption system initially proposed in [9] is a variant of the discrete logarithm problem. This problem states that for the equation $b = a^i \mod(p)$ if a user knows a, I, and p, computing b is computationally trivial. If, however, only b and a are known (and p), then there is no efficient algorithm to compute i.

Under the proposed encryption system, the sender, Alice, and the receiver, Bob, choose a large prime p and its primitive root a. These values may be public. Additionally, Alice secretly chooses two random positive numbers $x, i_1 < p$, Bob secretly chooses one random positive number $i_2 < p$, and both Alice and Bob know a shared secret random number R.

(1) Alice calculates $K = a^x \mod(p)$ and $L_1 = a^{Ri_1} \mod(p)$ and sends L_1 to Bob.

(2) Bob, knowing the value of R but not i_1, calculates $L_2 = a^{R(i_1+i_2)} \mod(p)$ and sends L_2 to Alice.

(3) Alice, who knows the value of i_1 and R but not i_2, calculates $L_3 = a^{R(x+i_2)} \mod(p)$ and sends L_3 to Bob.

(4) Bob, who knows the value of i_2, may easily recover x from L_3 and use it to calculate Alice's chosen key $K = a^x \mod(p)$, which is used to encrypt further communications.

As these 3 transmitted equations involve a total of 4 unknowns to any intercepting party (R, x, i_1, i_2), determining the key for anyone who is not Alice or Bob is a nontrivial task, equivalent to finding the exponential of a discrete log problem.

Although initialization of the system requires shared public values of p and a and a shared secret random value R, once a key has been used for a certain length of time, decrypted data transmitted between Alice and Bob may be used by both parties in an algorithm to determine a new R value, and Alice or Bob may propose a new key exchange. With each iteration in a cycle, new values of x, i_1, and i_2 are arbitrarily chosen, while R is partially updated with a shared algorithm applied to the decrypted data transmissions of the previous iteration. With each complete cycle, the R value chosen will be completely replaced from the same iteration of the previous cycle. Further details may be found in [9].

If the key transfer protocol is not completed successfully, whether due to data loss or due to malicious interference, it may be necessary to reinitialize the system via use of another preshared secret R.

Storage requirements for this system involve a preshared secret of length R. Although no minimum length is required for R, for increased security, it should be assumed that R is relatively large, at a minimum approaching the approximate length of p. p itself should be a large prime, in order to deter brute force attacks. Processing time for this encryption system for both encryption and decryption is relatively trivial, involving multiple multiplication, exponentiation, and mod operations. As both endpoints share a common key K, this system does not allow for external message authentication or differentiation between messages originating from Alice or Bob.

The most efficient attack currently used on the general case of the discrete logarithm problem is the number field sieve [10], arriving at a solution for a prime number n in $L_p[1/3; 3^{2/3}]$ (this is approximately $e^{(2.08+O(1))(\log n)^{1/3}(\log \log n)^{2/3}}$). The security provided may thus be directly compared to that of RSA, which also may be most efficiently defeated via the general number field sieve, although discrete logarithms offer slightly more protection for a given key size. A quantum system, once it exists, may use Shor's algorithm to solve this problem in polynomial time [11].

3. Alternative I: RSA

The RSA algorithm has the advantage of being one of the most widely used and studied encryption methods today and is extremely elegant, simple, and well-tested. As the default algorithm used by many SSL providers, as well as the basic public key encryption scheme most others are compared to, RSA is used here as a baseline for the comparison of other encryption methods, even though it is not as storage-efficient or processing-efficient as other algorithms studied and requires the use of longer key lengths for equivalent security. Current commonly used RSA key lengths include 1024 and 2048 bits.

The basic principle of RSA security rests on the theory that it is extremely difficult to factor the product of two large prime numbers into its constituent factors. Each individual in the RSA network must create 2 complimentary keys, commonly referred to as a public key and a private key, with each key able to decrypt messages enciphered using its compliment. To create this key pair, Alice and Bob must each do the following [1]:

(1) Choose two similar large prime numbers p and q, which are within a few digits of each other in length. p and q are multiplied together to form a modulus n.

(2) An integer e is chosen such that $e < (\varphi(n))$ and e and $\varphi(n)$ are coprime. $(\varphi(n) = n - p - q + 1)$. A common value of e is 65,537 ($2^{16} + 1$). The public key consists of n and e (modulus and public key exponent).

(3) The modular multiplicative inverse of $e \bmod(\varphi(n))$, $d \equiv e^{-1}(\bmod(\varphi(n)))$ is calculated, and the private key consists of n and d (modulus and private key exponent).

(4) Message encryption may then be expressed, using the one key, as $C = (m^{K1})(\bmod n)$, while decryption uses the other key as $p = C^{K2}(\bmod n)$.

Typically, as the sending party must know the recipient's public key, as well as their own private key, RSA is not used within a self-contained system. Key generation for large primes may also be time consuming and resource intensive. Instead, third-party organizations must exist and are trusted to verify that a given public key corresponds to the stated owner's private key. Issued certificates linking a public key and verification of its owner's identity are generally valid for a set length of time, after which a new key must be generated and a new certificate request verifying the key's owner must be submitted to the central verification authority.

As our proposed router system must be self-contained after initial manufacture, this third-party verification method is not feasible, and we cannot rely on external communication for the identity verification of new public key data, requiring a slight modification of the standard RSA system. Instead, Alice's router will need to be initialized with prestored values for Alice's private key and Bob's public key, and Bob's will have Alice's public key and his own private key. In this scenario, it is not necessary for either party to know their own public key, and all 4 keys are kept private within the network.

Encryption and decryption function as standard RSA operations, with Alice encrypting data with Bob's public key and Bob decrypting data with his private key, and vice versa. After a data threshold is exceeded, Alice and Bob will both calculate new RSA key pairs and encrypt and send their new public keys using the old keys, with this encryption further

acting as identity verification previously requiring a third party. For example, Alice's new public key would be encrypted first with her old private key for authentication and identity verification and then with Bob's old public key for security; then it will be sent to Bob. Bob would decrypt data using his own old private key and then Alice's old public key. Once both parties have received the new keys, all data will be transmitted using these. This system would allow for the use of RSA indefinitely, with rapid key updates, without the necessity of a third party. In the event of a communication failure due to data loss or malicious action, it may be necessary to switch to a new preshared certificate pair and begin the process again.

Storage requirements for an n-bit RSA system are comparatively large, as larger key lengths are needed to assure equivalent security. Specifically, each router using this n-bit RSA algorithm will need to store 1 public and 1 private key, each consisting of an n-bit modulus and a smaller exponent (also of maximum length about n) for maximum total requirement of $4n$ bits per router. Processing time for RSA is also comparatively long, due to the larger key lengths and exponentiation operations required. The security of RSA is based upon the difficulty of the factorization problem. As with the discrete logarithm attack, the current approach to integer factorization involves the general number field sieve algorithm [12], which for an integer n will arrive at a solution in $L_p[1/3; 1.923]$, that is, $(e^{(1.923+O(1))(\log n)^{1/3}(\log \log n)^{2/3}})$. A quantum computer, should it ever exist, may factor large integers in polynomial time [11].

Although it is obvious that RSA offers several disadvantages when compared to other symmetric and asymmetric ciphers, it also offers at least one key advantage when compared to the other algorithms herein: message authentication. Unlike discrete logarithm, ECC, or AES encryption, since neither Alice nor Bob knows the other individual's private key, it would be possible for a third-party external audit, given hardware access to both router keys and all traffic sent, to determine the sender of all encrypted data. Using the other encryption systems, given the encrypted data alone, it is possible to determine that either Alice or Bob sent a message, but not to authenticate which one encrypted the data.

4. Alternative II: AES

AES, based upon the Rijndael cipher, was announced by the National Institute of Standards and Technology in 2001 and was shortly thereafter approved as an accepted encryption standard by the United States Federal Government. AES, similar to its predecessor, DES, is a symmetric block cipher, using a shared secret key to encrypt a data stream one block at a time. In AES, each 128-bit data block undergoes 10–14 rounds (depending on key length) of permutations, substitutions, and additions [1]. AES is an extensively used and studied algorithm and like most symmetric ciphers offers advantages in terms of required processing power, processing time, and key length when compared to asymmetric ciphers such as RSA and ECC. The simplicity of each round enables simple and rapid implementation on any 8-bit processor, while the chaining of multiple rounds per block provides excellent security. The AES algorithm itself is quite straightforward to implement within hardware, and hardware AES optimization is currently already present in many modern, commercially available processors, including current processors from Intel, AMD, and Qualcomm, making this an excellent algorithm choice for use with existing components.

To modify AES for use in our closed system, Alice and Bob's routers will both require a single preshared AES key and a reliable PRNG. Initial communication will be made using the preshared key. After a data threshold has been reached, similar to the discrete logarithm system, Alice and Bob will input the decrypted data into an algorithm (such as a cryptographic hash function) to generate a random value R. This value will be used as a PRNG seed on both systems to generate identical intermediate keys of the desired AES key length. To compensate for any bias in the data used to generate R (similar data between data cycles may lead to a smaller PRNG seed pool), the intermediate key may be XOR'd with the previous AES key to generate a new, random shared secret key by which further communication will be encrypted.

As mentioned earlier, AES offers efficient processing time, and the storage requirements for this system are minimal, requiring a single preshared key to be saved on each of the two end routers, much shorter than a security-equivalent RSA key pair. No effective cryptanalytic attacks are currently known against AES, with the current best attacks only a few orders of magnitude above the worst-case brute force scenario and requiring infeasibly large amounts of storage space [13]. Unlike asymmetric encryption algorithms, AES is likely resistant to attacks by theoretical future quantum computers. In the event of a communication failure due to data loss or malicious action, it may be necessary to switch to a new preshared key and begin the process again.

5. Alternative III: ECC

Elliptic Curve Cryptography (ECC) is an asymmetric cryptographic system, which uses a variant of the discrete logarithm problem as applied to points in an elliptic curve group as the core of its security. Many consumers have recently begun adopting ECC as an alternative to RSA, due to its efficiency in both key size and processing requirements. Careful choice of the ECC curve is necessary to avoid potential security hazards.

In Elliptic Curve Cryptography, first a curve is chosen, with variables and coefficients restricted over either the finite field $GF(2^m)$ of the form $y^2+xy = x^3+ax^2+b$ or a prime curve over Z_p and modulo p where variables and coefficients range from 0 to $(p-1)$ of the form $y^2 \bmod p = (x^3 + ax + b)\bmod p$.

In the prime curve case, there are a limited number of nonnegative integer points between $(0,0)$ and $(p-1, p-1)$ which satisfy any given elliptic curve values for a and b. Similarly, for the finite field case, there will be a limited number of (x, y) integer values that lie on the curve for any given values of a and b.

These points are used to define a finite abelian group, with rules for addition defined specifically for the abelian group, similar to modular multiplication in conventional algorithms. Likewise, multiple additions are preformed similarly to modular exponentiation. Using abelian group rules, given two points M and N, $M = kN$ is easily calculated given k and N but difficult to calculate given M and N, forming the one-way trapdoor function at the basis of elliptic cryptography.

Generally, the curve parameter values of a, b and z, C and n are made public and often correspond to one of several well-studied elliptic curves. a and b are the coefficients discussed earlier, forming the curve $E_z(a, b)$, where z is an integer in the finite field 2^m (finite field curve) or a large prime number (prime curve). A base point C is picked such that the smallest positive integer n that satisfies $nC = 0$ is very large. With all curve parameters defined, Alice and Bob may begin the key selection process [1].

(1) Alice and Bob both choose secret integers I_A and I_B less than n as their private keys.

(2) Public keys are generated according to $p_A = I_A \times C$ and $p_B = I_B \times C$ and shared with each other.

(3) A common secret key is generated my multiplying the known private key with the opposite public key, with $I_A \times p_B = I_B \times p_A$.

(4) To encrypt or decrypt data, the data is first encoded as a point M on the elliptic curve and then sent as a ciphertext message as a pair of points $(kC, M + kp)$ with k as any chosen positive integer and decrypted with the matching private key using $(M_x I - M_y)$.

Modifying this system to function in our self-contained router environment involves a process similar to that used for RSA. All curve parameters are assumed to be publicly known, and use of a known secure curve is assumed. Each router must be initialized with secret data corresponding to its own private key and the public key of the other router. Again, it is not strictly necessary for each party to know or retain its own public key, and, in any case, all 4 key values are kept secret within the network.

Encryption and decryption function as standard ECC operations, with Alice encrypting data with Bob's public key and Bob decrypting data with his private key, and vice versa. After a data threshold is exceeded, Alice and Bob will both calculate new public and private ECC keys, choosing new secret integers, and encrypt and send each other their new public keys using their old private keys. Once both parties have received the new keys, all data will be transmitted using these. This system would allow for the use of ECC indefinitely, with rapid key updates, without the necessity of a third party. In the event of a communication failure due to data loss or malicious action, it may be necessary to switch to a new preshared certificate pair and begin the process again. Unlike in RSA, the use of a common secret key prevents message authentication via external audit.

Storage requirements for ECC involve two large integers of size n or smaller, corresponding to the public and private keys, on each router, for a total maximum storage capacity of $2n$ per shared secret per router. Key lengths used are much shorter than those needed for equivalent RSA or discrete logarithm security levels, about double the size of that found in symmetric encryption systems. Likewise, while not quite as processing-efficient as a symmetric cryptosystem, ECC offers large performance gains when compared to RSA. The best known attack to ECC is Pollard's Rho [14] which may be paralyzed and needs relatively little memory but is nevertheless not computationally feasible for currently used curve parameters. As with other public key protocols, ECC is expected to be vulnerable to attack by quantum computers, once such exist.

6. Algorithm Comparison

The RSA, ECC, AES, and discrete logarithm protocols may each provide an arbitrary level of security, determined by the length of the encryption keys used for each algorithm [8]. Figure 1 visually illustrates the required key length needed by various encryption algorithms in order to achieve a level of security comparable to a specified RSA key length (e.g., to achieve the same level of security provided by 2048-bit RSA encryption, AES requires only a 112-bit key). In the case of the discrete logarithm method, the equivalent key length of the prime p used was determined using the general number field algorithm as compared to RSA key lengths and was found to be approximately equal in requirement with RSA key N equivalent to a discrete log key $0.84N$ (less than one-bit difference). ECC and AES hold clear advantages here over RSA and discrete log methods, as key sizes for the latter two increase rapidly as increased security is needed, while the key length : security ratio remains relatively linear for ECC and AES. The longer key lengths of RSA and discrete log will also require additional bandwidth for public key transfer, compared to shorter ECC public keys, and no additional bandwidth overhead is required for AES.

Storage requirements for preshared secret data per router (ignoring overhead and indexing values), as outlined by the modified algorithms described earlier, are as follows:

(1) n-bit RSA requires a maximum of $4n$ bits per secret.

(2) n-bit ECC requires a total of $2n$ bits per secret.

(3) n-bit AES requires a single stored n-bit key.

(4) n-bit discrete log method involves a preshared secret R, assumed to be of maximum length n.

Using these values, in combination with the key length requirements illustrated in Figure 1, it is possible to calculate the minimum storage requirements of each router for pre-shared secret data. For example, from Figure 1, we see that a 2048-bit RSA or discrete logarithm key is the equivalent of a 224-bit ECC key, or a 112-bit AES key. Each shared secret stored by the router at this security level would thus require a maximum of $(2048 * 4) = 8192$ bits for RSA and 2048 bits for discrete log but only $(224 * 2) = 448$ bits for ECC, or 112 bits for AES. Using these calculations, Figure 2 illustrates the total number of preshared secrets which may be stored per gigabyte of memory for any given security level and encryption algorithm (e.g., $8,000,000,000/8192 = 976,562$ shared secrets per GB for 2048-bit RSA, or over 70 million shared secrets per GB for the equivalent 112-bit AES).

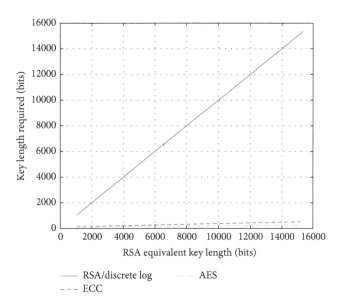

FIGURE 1: Key length versus security for AES, ECC, RSA, and discrete log. Data source: National Security Agency, Central Security Service [8].

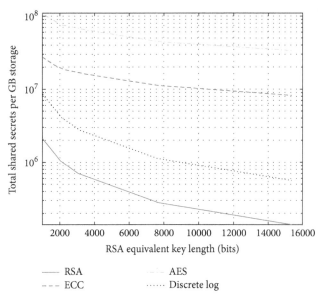

FIGURE 2: Router preshared secret storage requirements.

As calculated in Figure 2, a single GB of router secret data storage allocation may hold hundreds of thousands of shared secrets even when using the inefficient RSA algorithm at the 7680-bit security level. When using AES, millions of shared secrets may be stored in this space. Regardless of algorithm choice, shared secret storage space is unlikely to be a limiting factor in practical router implementation.

Encryption and decryption performance for the various algorithms are difficult to measure and are heavily influenced by system architecture and software/hardware optimizations. Generally, however, symmetric key ciphers such as AES will offer the fastest encryption and decryption times. ECC offers dramatically superior key pair generation performance compared to RSA, with the large primes generated for RSA requiring several orders of magnitude more time when compared to a much smaller ECC key, especially at RSA bit lengths of 2048 and above. In router systems with frequent key refreshes this could be a potential issue. Additionally, manufacturing hardware may struggle to fill even a modestly sized storage chip with unique preshared RSA keys (even a 1 GB sized chip may be able to hold hundreds of thousands of preshared RSA certificates!), while even millions of shared symmetric encryption keys would simply involve filling the same chip pair with identical random data. RSA encryption is generally slightly faster than ECC, while ECC decryption may be several times faster than RSA, although both are generally efficient enough not to provide a practical system bottleneck [15, 16]. The discrete log method is assumed to offer a similar processing time as RSA due to similarities in algorithm implementation but will likely take longer due to the multiple exchanges involved.

7. Practical Implementations

The primary limitation on this router-to-router encryption system is the necessity for each router to be factory-manufactured containing shared secret information, enabling secure communication only with its matched counterpart.

This limitation may be partially mitigated by offering routers containing several small storage chip expansion slots. These storage chips would be manufactured in pairs, with each pair stamped with a matching serial number and containing a number of matching shared secret keys. Although each chip should be clearly labeled with its identical match, the actual matching data therein should not be retained after generation by the manufacturer, preventing compromise of manufacturer records from affecting system security.

A single router could thus be configured to securely communicate with a number of endpoints, with each endpoint sharing a unique inserted security chip pair, easily installable and replaceable as needed. Given the low cost of solid-state storage, under any proposed encryption scheme, the number of shared initial secret keys on a single chip would well exceed the lifetime of the router itself, even in a scenario where high data loss over a connection prevents the easy determination of additional keys before another shared hardware key is needed.

8. Conclusion and Future Work

Ultimately, algorithm choice will likely be determined by system needs and the availability of supporting hardware. Whatever algorithm is chosen, it will be necessary to provide preshared secret data to factory-paired communication devices, either built directly into each router pair or provided as paired insertable expansion chips with pregenerated shared encryption keys. Once the initial key is shared, a combination of PRNG values, prior secret data, and decrypted current communication may be used to generate new secure keys on demand, ensuring a regular refresh of the currently used key. While advances in modern solid-state storage make

it unlikely that shared secret storage space is ever a practical limitation of the proposed router-to-router key exchange system, algorithm processing efficiency, data efficiency, and key generation time may have a much larger impact on system design.

While discrete logarithm, RSA, ECC, and AES may each be used to provide the necessary nonlinearity for the establishment of a self-contained secure communication channel between two paired hardware devices, RSA and AES offer the most features and most efficient functionality, respectively. If authentication is needed, RSA, the weakest algorithm in terms of key generation and processing efficiency, is the clear choice. The use of RSA will, however, require a great deal of additional key generation time on the router manufacturing end. If, however, authentication is not needed, then symmetric key systems such as the AES exchange proposed offer the most efficient alternative and the only choice which offers more resistance to quantum computing attacks. AES hardware optimization is both extremely efficient and widely available in many currently used commercial processors, resulting in superior encryption, decryption, and processing times. AES key pair data, consisting effectively of a random bitstream, may be much more rapidly generated and preloaded onto devices than RSA, ECC, or discrete logarithm key pairs and provide greater security than equivalent-length asymmetric ciphers. Alternatively, a hybrid of both systems may be used, offering on-demand authentication when needed and efficient nonauthenticated secure communication otherwise.

As a final consideration, as with any digital security, any encryption system is vulnerable to physical hardware compromise. If an attacker is able to gain access to the shared secret data stored on the router's security hardware, even the most secure encryption framework will be compromised, and care must be taken during hardware manufacture and distribution to ensure that these keys are not copied or prematurely accessed.

Competing Interests

The authors declare that they have no competing interests.

References

[1] W. Stallings, *Cryptography and Network Security: Principles and Practice*, Prentice Hall, 6th Edition, 2014, 2011, 2006, pp. 47-48, pp. 264–278, pp. 130–173, pp. 303-304.

[2] C. H. Bennet and G. Brassard, "Quantum cryptography: public key distribution and coin tossing," in *Proceedings of the IEEE International Conference on Computer System and Signal Processing*, Bangalore, India, December 1984.

[3] V. Scarani, A. Acín, G. Ribordy, and N. Gisin, "Quantum cryptography protocols robust against photon number splitting attacks for weak laser pulse implementations," *Physical Review Letters*, vol. 92, no. 5, Article ID 057901, 4 pages, 2004.

[4] C. H. Bennett, "Quantum cryptography using any two non-orthogonal states," *Physical Review Letters*, vol. 68, no. 21, pp. 3121–3124, 1992.

[5] S. Mandal, G. Macdonald, M. El Rifai et al., "Implementation of secure quantum protocol using multiple photons for communication," https://arxiv.org/abs/1208.6198.

[6] Z. Zhao, T. Yang, Y.-A. Chen, A.-N. Zhang, and J.-W. Pan, "Experimental realization of entanglement concentration and a quantum repeater," *Physical Review Letters*, vol. 90, no. 20, Article ID 207901, 2003.

[7] J. Menn, "Key internet operator VeriSign hit by hackers," *Reuters*, 2012.

[8] "The Case for Elliptic Curve Cryptography," National Security Agency—Central Security Service, Jan 2009, http://web.archive .org/web/20150627183730/https://www.nsa.gov/business/pro- grams/elliptic_curve.shtml.

[9] P. K. Verma and M. El Rifai, "An Ultra-secure Router-to-router Spontaneous Key Exchange System," *International Journal of Computer Network and Information Security*, vol. 7, no. 7, pp. 1–9, 2015.

[10] D. M. Gordon, "Discrete logarithms in GF(P) using the number field sieve," *SIAM Journal on Discrete Mathematics*, vol. 6, no. 1, pp. 124–138, 1993.

[11] P. W. Shor, "Polynomial-time algorithms for prime factorization and discrete logarithms on a quantum computer," *SIAM Review*, vol. 41, no. 2, pp. 303–332, 1999.

[12] D. Coppersmith, "Modifications to the number field sieve," *Journal of Cryptology*, vol. 6, no. 3, pp. 169–180, 1993.

[13] A. Bogdanov, D. Khovratovich, and C. Rechberger, "Biclique cryptanalysis of the full AES," in *Advances in Cryptology— ASIACRYPT 2011: 17th International Conference on the Theory and Application of Cryptology and Information Security, Seoul, South Korea, December 4–8, 2011. Proceedings*, vol. 7073 of *Lecture Notes in Computer Science*, pp. 344–371, Springer, Berlin, Germany, 2011.

[14] J. W. Bos, M. E. Kaihara, T. Kleinjung, A. K. Lenstra, and P. L. Montgomery, "On the security of 1024-bit RSA and 160-bit elliptic curve cryptography," Tech. Rep. EPFL-REPORT-164549, 2009.

[15] M. Savari, M. Montazerolzohour, and Y. E. Thiam, "Comparison of ECC and RSA algorithm in multipurpose smart card application," in *Proceedings of the International Conference on Cyber Security, Cyber Warfare and Digital Forensic (CyberSec '12)*, IEEE, 2012.

[16] K. Maletsky, "RSA vs ECC comparison for embedded systems," Atmel, 2015, http://www.atmel.com/images/atmel-8951-cryp- toauth-rsa-ecc-comparison-embedded-systems-whitepaper.pdf.

16

Improving an Anonymous and Provably Secure Authentication Protocol for a Mobile User

Jongho Moon,[1] **Youngsook Lee,**[2] **Jiye Kim,**[3] **and Dongho Won**[4]

[1]*Department of Electrical and Computer Engineering, Sungkyunkwan University, 2066 Seobu-ro, Jangan-gu, Suwon-si,*
 Gyeonggi-do 16419, Republic of Korea
[2]*Department of Cyber Security, Howon University, 64 Howondae 3-gil, Impi-myeon, Gunsan-si,*
 Jeonrabuk-do 54058, Republic of Korea
[3]*Department of Mobile Internet, Daelim University College, 29 Imgok-ro, Dongan-gu, Anyang-si, Gyeonggi-do 13916, Republic of Korea*
[4]*Department of Computer Engineering, Sungkyunkwan University, 2066 Seobu-ro, Jangan-gu, Suwon-si,*
 Gyeonggi-do 16419, Republic of Korea

Correspondence should be addressed to Dongho Won; dhwon@security.re.kr

Academic Editor: Hongxin Hu

Recently many authentication protocols using an extended chaotic map were suggested for a mobile user. Many researchers demonstrated that authentication protocol needs to provide key agreement, mutual authentication, and user anonymity between mobile user and server and resilience to many possible attacks. In this paper, we cautiously analyzed chaotic-map-based authentication scheme and proved that it is still insecure to off-line identity guessing, user and server impersonation, and on-line identity guessing attacks. To address these vulnerabilities, we proposed an improved protocol based on an extended chaotic map and a fuzzy extractor. We proved the security of the proposed protocol using a random oracle and AVISPA (Automated Validation of Internet Security Protocols and Applications) tool. Furthermore, we present an informal security analysis to make sure that the improved protocol is invulnerable to possible attacks. The proposed protocol is also computationally efficient when compared to other previous protocols.

1. Introduction

Given recent developments in mobile telecommunications and the rapid spread of mobile devices, there is a growing importance of wireless and wired networking services that utilize bygone and current positional information from users carrying mobile devices with location tracking capabilities [1]. Remote user authentication schemes typically verify registered credentials using stored databases. Since Lamport [2] presented the first authentication scheme based on passwords in 1981, various remote user authentication schemes [3, 4] based on passwords have been proposed. However, since a server under a password-based remote user authentication protocol needs to store a verification table, which stores the password to determine the credentials of a remote user, the server arranges for extra storage for the verification table.

Furthermore, several studies have shown that password-based remote user authentication protocols are insecure against some attacks, including off-line password guessing or stolen smart card attacks [5–7]. The problem with password-based authentication scheme is that it can be easily stolen or lost and making it difficult to remember on a regular basis. For these reasons, many researchers have presented new remote user authentication protocols that use biometrics. A major characteristic of biometrics is it uniqueness. Other advantage is that it cannot be guessed or stolen. Biological characteristics have been used in numerous remote user authentication schemes [8–13].

To design a secure authentication scheme, some cryptographic algorithms are also used, such as an RSA cryptosystem [14, 15], elliptic curve cryptography [16, 17], hash function [18, 19], and chaos-based cryptography [20–22].

Recently, many chaos-based authentication protocols have been suggested. Xiao et al. [23] first presented a user authentication protocol using a chaotic map and claimed that their protocol is useful and suitable for serviceable implementations. Unfortunately, many attacks were demonstrated by Han [31]. To overcome these vulnerabilities in [23], Han et al. [24] presented an enhanced user authentication protocol using chaos and asserted that their protocol resists all possible attacks. After that, Niu and Wang [32] proved that Han et al.'s protocol is vulnerable against an insider attack. Furthermore, Yoon [33] demonstrated that Niu and Wang's protocol does not resist a denial-of-service (DoS) attack. After that, Xue and Hong [34] proposed an improved authentication and key agreement protocol using a chaotic map to improve the security to some possible attacks. Unfortunately, Tan [35] found that Xue and Hong's protocol does not resist a man-in-the-middle attack. Lee et al. [25] presented an improved chaotic map-based authentication protocol, and He et al. [29] proved that Lee et al.'s protocol does not resist DoS and insider attacks. To enhance the functionality and security, Lin [26] proposed a new authentication and key agreement protocol using a chaotic map and dynamic identity. Unfortunately, Islam et al. [27] found that Lin's protocol cannot resist well-known attacks, and proposed an enhanced authentication protocol. However, we found that Islam et al.'s protocol is still insecure against off-line identity guessing, impersonation, and on-line identity guessing attacks.

The remainder of this paper is organized as follows. We briefly introduce the Chebyshev chaotic maps, threat assumptions, and fuzzy extractor that we adopt in the proposed protocol in Section 2. In Sections 3 and 4, we, respectively, review and cryptanalyze Islam et al.'s protocol. In Section 5, we propose an improved authentication and key agreement protocol for a mobile user. In Section 6, we present a security analysis of the proposed protocol. Section 7 explains the functionality and performance analyses comparing the proposed protocol to previous protocols. The conclusions are presented in Section 8.

1.1. Our Contribution. To address the security vulnerabilities in Islam et al.'s authentication protocol and obtain the required performance, we propose a security-improved scheme. The primary contribution of this paper are described below.

(i) First, we prove that Islam et al.'s protocol is still vulnerable to some attacks, and we show how an adversary can impersonate a legitimate user or server.

(ii) Second, we suggest an improved biometrics-based authentication and key agreement protocol on Islam et al.'s protocol. The improved protocol is designed to be secure to well-known attacks.

(iii) Third, we analyze that the proposed protocol has better robustness and a lower computational cost with a performance analysis.

2. Preliminaries

We briefly introduce the Chebyshev chaotic maps [28, 36], threat assumptions, and fuzzy extractor.

2.1. Chebyshev Chaotic Maps. The Chebyshev polynomial $T_k(v)$ is a v polynomial of degree k.

Definition 1. Let k be a whole number and w be a real number from the round $[-1, 1]$; the Chebyshev polynomial of degree k is then defined as $T_k(v) = \cos(k \cdot \arccos(v))$.

Definition 2 (CMDLP). Given the two parameters $v, w \in Z_n^*$, the Chaotic Maps Discrete Logarithm Problem is whether integer k can be found such that $w = T_k(v)$. The probability of $\mathscr{E}$ being able to address the CMDLP is defined as $\Pr[\mathscr{E}(v, w) = k : k \in Z_n^*, w = T_k(v) \bmod n]$.

Definition 3 (CMDHP). Given the three elements $v, T_j(v)$, and $T_k(v)$, the Chaotic Maps Diffie-Hellman Problem is whether $T_{jk}(v)$ can be computed such that $T_{jk}(v) = T_j(T_k(v)) = T_k(T_j(v))$.

2.2. Threat Assumptions. We introduce some threat model [37, 38] and consider constructing the threat assumptions described as follows:

(i) Adversary $\mathscr{E}$ can be both a user or server. Any registered mobile user can act as an adversary.

(ii) $\mathscr{E}$ can intercept all messages in a public channel, thereby capturing any message exchanged between a user or server.

(iii) $\mathscr{E}$ has the ability to modify, reroute, or delete the captured message.

(iv) Stored parameters can be extracted from the mobile device.

2.3. Fuzzy Extractor. In this subsection, we describe the basis for a biometric-based fuzzy extractor that converts biometric information data into a random value. Based on [39–41], the fuzzy extractor is operated through two procedures (Gen, Rep), demonstrated as

(i) Gen(BIO) → ⟨α, β⟩,

(ii) Rep(BIO*, β) = α if BIO* is reasonably close to BIO.

Gen is a probabilistic generation function for which the biometrics BIO returns an "extracted" string $\alpha \in \{0, 1\}^k$ and auxiliary string $\beta \in \{0, 1\}^*$, and Rep is a deterministic reproduction function that enables the recovery of α from β and any vector BIO* close to BIO. Detailed information of the fuzzy extractor can be found in [42].

3. Review of Islam et al.'s Protocol

We review Islam et al.'s protocol. Their protocol consists of registration, login, verification, and password change phases and uses an extended chaotic maps. The term $T_k(a)$ is the chaotic map computation that is calculated with respect to "mod n" and $a \in (-\infty, +\infty)$. The notations of this paper are illustrated in the Notations.

3.1. Registration Phase

(i) User U_i selects the identity ID_i and password PW_i and inputs these values into the mobile devices MD_i. MD_i then chooses a random number t, calculates $W_i = PW_i \oplus t$, and sends $\langle ID_i, W_i \rangle$ to server S over an insecure channel.

(ii) Upon receiving $\langle ID_i, W_i \rangle$, server S computes $H_i = h(s, ID_i)$ and $n_i = h(W_i, ID_i) \oplus (H_i, T_s(H_i))$ and sends $\langle n_i \rangle$ to user U_i by using a secure channel.

(iii) Upon receiving $\langle n_i \rangle$, MD_i retrieves $N_i = n_i \oplus h(W_i, ID_i) \oplus h(ID_i, PW_i)$, $(H_i, T_s(H_i)) = N_i \oplus h(ID_i, PW_i)$, and $X_i = h(h(ID_i, PW_i) \parallel (H_i \parallel T_s(H_i))$ and stores $\langle N_i, X_i \rangle$ into MD_i.

3.2. Login Phase

(i) User U_i enters ID_i and PW_i into MD_i.

(ii) MD_i computes $(H_i \parallel T_s(H_i)) = N_i \oplus h(ID_i, PW_i)$ and $X_i' = h(h(ID_i, PW_i) \parallel (H_i \parallel T_s(H_i)))$. MD_i then checks whether X_i' is equal to X_i. If this holds, MD_i executes the following stage; otherwise, MD_i rejects the login request.

(iii) MD_i chooses a random number k and then computes $Z_i = T_k(T_s(H_i))$ and $CID_i = ID_i \oplus (H_i \parallel T_1 \parallel Z_i)$, where $C_i = T_k(H_i)$, $R_i = H_i \oplus Z_i$, $V_i = h(CID_i, Z_i, H_i, R_i, T_1)$, and T_1 is the current timestamp. MD_i sends $\langle CID_i, C_i, V_i, R_i, T_1 \rangle$ to server S by using a public channel.

3.3. Verification Phase

(i) When receiving the request message $\langle CID_i, C_i, V_i, R_i, T_1 \rangle$ from user U_i, server S verifies freshness of timestamp T_1 and terminates the session if $(T_2 - T_1) \leq \Delta T$ is false; otherwise, server S continues the next stage.

(ii) S computes $Z_i = T_s(C_i)$, $H_i = R_i \oplus Z_i$, $ID_i = CID_i \oplus (H_i \parallel T_1 \parallel Z_i)$, and $V_i' = h(CID_i, Z_i, H_i, R_i, T_1)$. S then rejects the session if $V_i' \neq V_i$; otherwise, server S continues the following stage.

(iii) S randomly chooses a number l and computes the session key $\lambda = h(H_i, T_1, T_2, T_l(C_i))$, and $V_s = h(\lambda, H_i, T_1, T_2)$. S then sends the response messages $\langle V_s, T_2, T_l(H_i) \rangle$ over an insecure channel.

(iv) After receiving the response message $\langle V_s, T_2, T_l(H_i) \rangle$ from server S at time T_3, MD_i checks the freshness of T_2 and terminates the session if $(T_3 - T_2) \leq \Delta T$ is false; otherwise, MD_ie then computes $\lambda = h(H_i, T_1, T_2, T_k(T_l(H_i)))$, and $V_s' = h(\lambda, H_i, T_1, T_2)$. MD_i next checks whether $V_s' \stackrel{?}{=} V_s$. If this holds, MD_i accepts λ as the session key and authenticates server S; otherwise, MD_i rejects the session.

3.4. Password Change Phase

(i) User U_i inputs ID_i and PW_i into the mobile device MD_i.

(ii) MD_i computes $(H_i \parallel T_s(H_i)) = N_i \oplus h(ID_i, PW_i)$ and $X_i' = h(h(ID_i, PW_i) \parallel (H_i \parallel T_s(H_i)))$. MD_i then checks whether X_i' is the same to X_i. If this holds, the mobile device asks the new identity and password to U_i; otherwise, MD_i rejects the password change request.

(iii) U_i inputs a new ID_i^* and PW_i^* into MD_i. MD_i then computes $N_i^* = N_i \oplus h(ID_i, PW_i) \oplus h(ID_i^*, PW_i^*)$ and $X_i^* = h(h(ID_i^*, PW_i^*) \parallel (H_i \parallel T_s(H_i)))$ and replaces $\langle N_i, X_i \rangle$ by $\langle N_i^*, X_i^* \rangle$ into MD_i.

4. Cryptanalysis of Islam et al.'s Protocol

We cryptanalyze the security problems in Islam et al.'s protocol [27]. Islam et al. analyzed the protocol by Lin et al. and improved it to support an improved security functionality. However, we found that Islam et al.'s protocol was vulnerable to some possible attacks. These attacks are based on the threat assumptions that an adversary $\mathscr{E}$ was entirely monitored through the public channel connecting U_i and S in the login and verification phases and that $\mathscr{E}$ obtained the mobile device. Therefore, $\mathscr{E}$ can insert, modify, eavesdrop on, or delete any message transmitted over a public network. We now reveal further details of these problems.

4.1. Violation of the Identity. Let $\mathscr{E}$ be an active adversary who is a legitimate user and owns a mobile device to extract information $\langle N_{\mathscr{E}}, X_{\mathscr{E}} \rangle$ and suppose that an adversary $\mathscr{E}$ eavesdrops on the communication messages $\langle CID_i, C_i, V_i, R_i, T_1, V_s, T_2, T_l(H_i) \rangle$ between user U_i and server S. $\mathscr{E}$ can then easily obtain the identity of user U_i. The details are described as follows:

(i) Adversary $\mathscr{E}$ calculates $(H_{\mathscr{E}} \parallel T_s(H_{\mathscr{E}})) = N_{\mathscr{E}} \oplus h(ID_{\mathscr{E}}, PW_{\mathscr{E}})$.

(ii) Using [43], the adversary computes $s' = (\arccos(T_s(H_{\mathscr{E}})) + 2k'\pi) / \arccos(H_{\mathscr{E}})$, $\forall k \in Z$.

(iii) $\mathscr{E}$ can then compute $Z_i' = T_{s'}(C_i)$, $H_i' = R_i \oplus Z_i$, and $ID_i = CID_i \oplus (H_i' \parallel T_1 \parallel Z_i')$.

4.2. On-Line Identity Guessing and User Impersonation Attack. Let $\mathscr{E}$ be an active adversary who is a legitimate user and owns a mobile device to extract information $\langle N_{\mathscr{E}}, X_{\mathscr{E}} \rangle$. $\mathscr{E}$ can then easily guess the identity of any user U_i and impersonate U_i as follows.

(i) Adversary $\mathscr{E}$ computes $(H_{\mathscr{E}} \parallel T_s(H_{\mathscr{E}})) = N_{\mathscr{E}} \oplus h(ID_{\mathscr{E}}, PW_{\mathscr{E}})$.

(ii) $\mathscr{E}$ generates a random number k, computes $Z_{\mathscr{E}} = T_k(T_s(H_{\mathscr{E}}))$, guesses any identity ID_i, and then computes $CID_i = ID_i \oplus (H_{\mathscr{E}} \parallel T_1 \parallel Z_{\mathscr{E}})$, where $C_{\mathscr{E}} = T_k(H_{\mathscr{E}})$, $R_{\mathscr{E}} = H_{\mathscr{E}} \oplus Z_{\mathscr{E}}$, $V_i = h(CID_i, Z_{\mathscr{E}}, H_{\mathscr{E}}, R_{\mathscr{E}}, T_1)$, and T_1 is the current time stamp. MD_i sends $\langle CID_i, C_{\mathscr{E}}, V_i, R_{\mathscr{E}}, T_1 \rangle$ to server S over an insecure network.

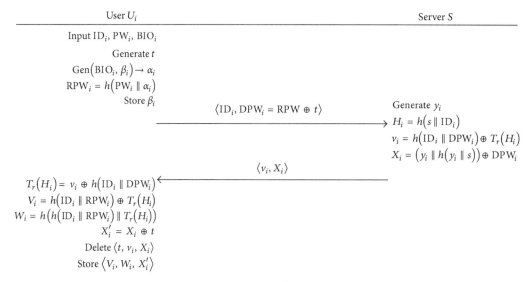

FIGURE 1: Registration phase of the proposed scheme.

(iii) Upon receiving the login request message $\langle CID_i, C_\mathscr{E},$ $V_i, R_\mathscr{E}, T_1 \rangle$ from the adversary $\mathscr{E}$, server S verifies the freshness of the timestamp T_1 and terminates the session if $(T_2 - T_1) \leq \Delta T$ is false; otherwise, server S continues the next stage.

(iv) S computes $Z_\mathscr{E} = T_s(C_\mathscr{E})$, $H_\mathscr{E} = R_\mathscr{E} \oplus Z_\mathscr{E}$, $ID_i = CID_i \oplus (H_\mathscr{E} \parallel T_1 \parallel Z_\mathscr{E})$, and $V_i' = h(CID_i, Z_\mathscr{E}, H_\mathscr{E}, R_\mathscr{E}, T_1)$. S then rejects the session if $V_i' \neq V_i$; otherwise, server S continues the following stage.

(v) S randomly chooses a number l and computes the session key $\lambda = h(H_\mathscr{E}, T_1, T_2, T_l(C))$, and $V_s = h(\lambda, H_\mathscr{E}, T_1, T_2)$. S then sends the response messages $\langle V_s, T_2, T_l(H_\mathscr{E}) \rangle$ over an insecure channel.

(vi) After receiving the response messages $\langle V_s, T_2, T_l(H_\mathscr{E}) \rangle$ from server S at time T_3, the mobile device checks the freshness of T_2 and terminates the session if $(T_3 - T_2) \leq \Delta T$ is false; otherwise, MD_i then computes $\lambda = h(H_\mathscr{E}, T_1, T_2, T_k(T_l(H_\mathscr{E})))$. Finally, $\mathscr{E}$ and S "successfully" conclude on the session key λ. However, server S faultily decides that he/she is communicating with user U_i.

4.3. Server Impersonation Attack.
Let $\mathscr{E}$ be an active adversary who is a legitimate user and owns a mobile device to extract information $\langle N_\mathscr{E}, X_\mathscr{E} \rangle$. $\mathscr{E}$ can then easily impersonate S as follows.

(i) Adversary $\mathscr{E}$ computes $(H_\mathscr{E} \parallel T_s(H_\mathscr{E})) = N_\mathscr{E} \oplus h(ID_\mathscr{E}, PW_\mathscr{E})$.

(ii) Using [43], the adversary computes $s' = (\arccos(T_s(H_\mathscr{E})) + 2k'\pi)/ \arccos(H_\mathscr{E})$, $\forall k \in Z$.

(iii) When receiving the login request message $\langle CID_i, C_i, V_i, R_i, T_1 \rangle$ from user U_i, $\mathscr{E}$ computes $Z_i' = T_{s'}(C_i)$ and $H_i = R_i \oplus Z_i'$.

(iv) Adversary $\mathscr{E}$ randomly chooses a number l and computes the session key $\lambda = h(H_i, T_1, T_2, T_l(C_i))$,

and $V_s = h(\lambda, H_i, T_1, T_2)$. The $\mathscr{E}$ then sends the response messages $\langle V_s, T_2, T_l(H_i) \rangle$ to user U_i over an insecure channel.

(v) After receiving the response message $\langle V_s, T_2, T_l(H_i) \rangle$ from adversary $\mathscr{E}$ at time T_3, the mobile device checks the freshness of T_2 and terminates the session if $(T_3 - T_2) \leq \Delta T$ is false; otherwise, MD_i then computes $\lambda = h(H_i, T_1, T_2, T_k(T_l(H_i)))$, and $V_s' = h(\lambda, H_i, T_1, T_2)$. The mobile device next checks whether $V_s' = V_s$. If this holds, the mobile device accepts λ as the session key. However, server S faultily decides that he/she is communicating with U_i.

4.4. Violation of the Session Key.
Assume that any adversary $\mathscr{E}$ eavesdrops on the communication messages $\langle CID_i, C_i, V_i, R_i, T_1, V_s, T_2, T_l(H_i) \rangle$ between user U_i and server S. $\mathscr{E}$ can then easily calculate the session key between U_i and S.

(i) $\mathscr{E}$ calculates $(H_\mathscr{E} \parallel T_s(H_\mathscr{E})) = N_\mathscr{E} \oplus h(ID_\mathscr{E}, PW_\mathscr{E})$.

(ii) Using [43], the adversary computes $s' = (\arccos(T_s(H_\mathscr{E})) + 2k'\pi)/ \arccos(H_\mathscr{E})$, $\forall k \in Z$.

(iii) $\mathscr{E}$ can compute $Z_i' = T_{s'}(C_i)$ and $H_i = R_i \oplus Z_i'$.

(iv) Using [43], the adversary computes $k' = (\arccos(C_i) + 2k'\pi)/ \arccos(H_i)$, $\forall k \in Z$.

(v) $\mathscr{E}$ can then compute the session key $\lambda = h(H_i, T_1, T_2, T_{k'}(T_l(H_i)))$.

5. The Proposed Protocol

We will propose an improved biometric-based authentication protocol using the fuzzy extractor. The proposed protocol is also two members, user U_i and server S, and consists of four phases such as registration, login, verification, and password change. Figures 1 and 2 are the registration and login and verification phases of the proposed scheme.

User U_i Server S

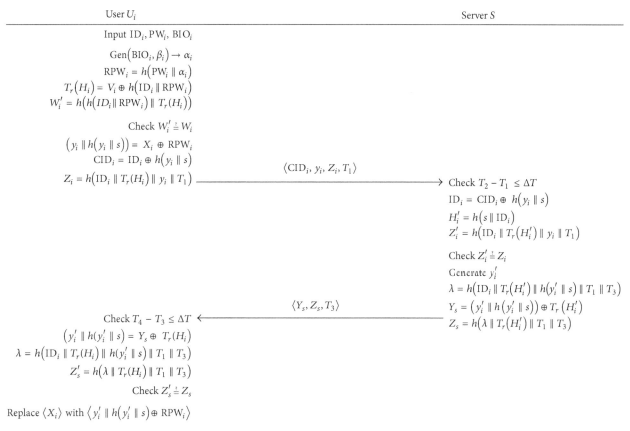

FIGURE 2: Login and verification phases of the proposed protocol.

5.1. Registration Phase

(i) U_i gives one's biometrics BIO_i at the mobile device MD_i. The MD_i then scans BIO_i, pulls out two random strings (α_i, β_i) from the computation $Gen(BIO_i) \rightarrow (\alpha_i, \beta_i)$, and stores β_i in storage. U_i enters the identity ID_i and password PW_i, and MD_i then calculates $RPW_i = h(PW_i \parallel \alpha_i)$. Finally, MD_i generates a random number t, stores t in the storage, and sends user registration request message $\langle ID_i, DPW_i = RPW_i \oplus t \rangle$ to server S by using a secure communication channel.

(ii) Upon receiving the request message for registration, S randomly chooses a number y_i and calculates $H_i = h(s \parallel ID_i)$, $v_i = h(ID_i \parallel DPW_i) \oplus T_r(H_i)$, and $X_i = (y_i \parallel h(y_i \parallel s)) \oplus DPW_i$, where r is a fixed random positive integer and s is the master key of server S.

(iii) S sends $\langle v_i, X_i \rangle$ to the MD_i.

(iv) After receiving the registration response message $\langle v_i, X_i \rangle$, MD_i computes $T_r(H_i) = v_i \oplus h(ID_i \parallel DPW_i)$, $V_i = h(ID_i \parallel RPW_i) \oplus T_r(H_i)$, $W_i = h(h(ID_i \parallel RPW_i) \parallel T_r(H_i))$, and $X_i' = X_i \oplus t = (y_i \parallel h(y_i \parallel s)) \oplus RPW_i$ and stores $\langle V_i, W_i, X_i' \rangle$ into storage after deleting t, v_i, and X_i.

5.2. Login Phase

(i) U_i enters ID_i and PW_i and gives BIO_i^* into the mobile device MD_i.

(ii) MD_i scans BIO_i^* and recovers α_i from the computation $Rep(BIO_i^*, \beta_i) \rightarrow \alpha_i$.

(iii) MD_i then computes $RPW_i = h(PW_i \parallel \alpha_i)$, $T_r(H_i) = V_i \oplus h(ID_i \parallel RPW_i)$, and $W_i' = h(h(ID_i \parallel RPW_i) \parallel T_r(H_i))$, and checks whether W_i' is the same to the stored W_i. If this holds, MD_i performs the next stage; otherwise, MD_i rejects the login request.

(iv) MD_i calculates $(y_i \parallel h(y_i \parallel s)) = X_i \oplus RPW_i$, $CID_i = ID_i \oplus h(y_i \parallel s)$, and $Z_i = h(ID_i \parallel T_r(H_i) \parallel y_i \parallel T_1)$, where T_1 is the current timestamp.

(v) Finally, MD_i sends the request message $\langle CID_i, y_i, Z_i, T_1 \rangle$ for login to server S.

5.3. Verification Phase

(i) When receiving the request message $\langle CID_i, y_i, Z_i, T_1 \rangle$ from MD_i, server S checks whether $T_2 - T_1 \leq \Delta T$ is valid, where ΔT is the minimum acceptable time interval and T_2 is the actual arrival time of login request. If this holds, S continues to proceed to the next stage; otherwise, S rejects the request.

(ii) S then calculates $\text{ID}_i = \text{CID}_i \oplus h(y_i \parallel s)$, $H_i = h(s \parallel \text{ID}_i)$, and $Z_i' = h(\text{ID}_i \parallel T_r(H_i) \parallel y_i \parallel T_1)$ and checks whether Z_i' is the same to the received Z_i. If this holds, the S continues to proceed to the next stage; otherwise, S terminates this session.

(iii) S randomly chooses a number y_i' and calculates the session key $\lambda = h(\text{ID}_i \parallel T_r(H_i) \parallel h(y_i' \parallel s) \parallel T_1 \parallel T_3)$, $Y_s = (y_i' \parallel h(y_i' \parallel s)) \oplus T_r(H_i)$, and $Z_s = h(\lambda \parallel T_r(H_i) \parallel T_1 \parallel T_3)$. S then sends the login response message $\langle Y_s, Z_s, T_3 \rangle$ where T_3 is the current timestamp.

(iv) After receiving the response message $\langle Y_s, Z_s, T_3 \rangle$ from server S, MD_i checks whether $T_4 - T_3 \le \Delta T$ is valid, where ΔT is the minimum acceptable time interval and T_4 is the actual arrival time of response message. If this holds, MD_i continues to the next stage; otherwise, MD_i terminates this session.

(v) MD_i computes $y_i' \parallel h(y_i' \parallel s) = Y_s \oplus T_r(H_i)$ and the session key $\lambda = h(\text{ID}_i \parallel T_r(H_i) \parallel h(y_i' \parallel s) \parallel T_1 \parallel T_3)$ and $Z_s' = h(\lambda \parallel T_r(H_i) \parallel T_1 \parallel T_3)$ and verifies whether Z_s' is the same to the received Z_s. If this holds, MD_i continues to the next stage; otherwise, MD_i terminates current session.

(vi) Finally, MD_i replaces $\langle X_i \rangle$ by $\langle (y_i' \parallel h(y_i' \parallel s)) \oplus \text{RPW}_i \rangle$ into storage.

5.4. Password Change Phase

(i) User U_i inputs ID_i and PW_i and gives BIO_i^* into the mobile device MD_i.

(ii) MD_i scans BIO_i^* and recovers α_i from the computation $\text{Rep}(\text{BIO}_i^*, \beta_i) \to \alpha_i$.

(iii) MD_i then computes $\text{RPW}_i = h(\text{PW}_i \parallel \alpha_i)$, $T_r(H_i) = V_i \oplus h(\text{ID}_i \parallel \text{RPW}_i)$, and $W_i' = h(h(\text{ID}_i \parallel \text{RPW}_i) \parallel T_r(H_i))$ and checks whether W_i' is the same to the stored W_i. If this holds, MD_i performs the next stage; otherwise, MD_i rejects the password change request.

(iv) U_i inputs a new password PW_i^* into MD_i. MD_i then computes $\text{RPW}_i^* = h(\text{PW}_i^* \parallel \alpha_i)$, $V_i^* = h(\text{ID}_i \parallel \text{RPW}_i^*) \oplus T_r(H_i)$, $W_i^* = h(h(\text{ID}_i \parallel \text{RPW}_i^*) \parallel T_r(H_i))$, and $X_i^* = X_i \oplus \text{RPW}_i \oplus \text{RPW}_i^*$.

(v) Finally, MD_i replaces $\langle V_i, W_i, X_i \rangle$ by $\langle V_i^*, W_i^*, X_i^* \rangle$ into storage.

6. Security Analysis of the Improved Protocol

The proposed protocol, which retains the advantages of Islam et al.'s protocol, is demonstrated, and it can resist some possible attacks and supports all security properties. The analysis of the improved protocol was organized with the threat assumptions made in Preliminaries.

6.1. Formal Security Analysis. A random oracle-based formal analysis is demonstrated here, and its security is shown. First, the following hash function is defined [44]:

Definition 4. A collision-resistance and one-way hash function $h : \{0, 1\}^* \to \{0, 1\}^k$ receives an input as a binary string of arbitrary length $v \in \{0, 1\}^*$, returns a binary string of fixed length $h(v) \in \{0, 1\}^k$, and gratifies the following conditions:

(i) Given $w \in W$, it is computationally impracticable to find a $v \in V$ such that $w = h(v)$.

(ii) Given $v \in V$, it is computationally impracticable to find another $v' \ne v \in V$, such that $h(v') = h(v)$.

(iii) It is computationally impracticable to find a pair $(v', v) \in V' \times V$, with $v' \ne v$, such that $h(v') = h(v)$.

Theorem 5. *According to the assumptions if hash function $h(\cdot)$ similarly acts like an random oracle, then the improved protocol is clearly secure to an adversary $\mathscr{E}$ to protect sensitive information, including identity ID_i, semigroup property $T_r(H_i)$, common session key λ, and master secret key s.*

Proof. Formal proof of the proposed protocol is similar in [40, 45], and it uses the oracle to construct $\mathscr{E}$, which will have the ability to extract ID_i, $T_r(H_i)$, λ, and s. □

Reveal. Random oracle can extract input value a from hash value $n = h(a)$ without failing. Adversary $\mathscr{E}$ now executes the experimental algorithm shown in Algorithm 1, $\text{EXP}_{\text{HASH,A}}^{\text{BBSMK}}$ for the proposed scheme as BBSMK, for example. Let us then define the probability of success for $\text{EXP}_{\text{HASH,A}}^{\text{BBSMK}}$ as $\text{Success}_{\text{HASH,A}}^{\text{BBSMK}} = |\text{Pr}[\text{EXP}_{\text{HASH,A}}^{\text{BBSMK}} = 1] - 1|$, where $\text{Pr}(\cdot)$ means the probability of $\text{EXP}_{\text{HASH,A}}^{\text{BBSMK}}$. The advantage function for this algorithm then defines $\text{Adv}_{\text{HASH,A}}^{\text{BBSMK}}(t, q_R) = \max_{\text{Success}}$, where t and q_R are the execution time and number of queries. We then discuss the algorithm in Algorithm 1 for $\mathscr{E}$. If $\mathscr{E}$ has the capability to address the problem of hash function given in Definition 4, then he/she can immediately retrieve ID_i, $T_r(H_i)$, λ, and s. In that case, $\mathscr{E}$ will detect the complete connections between U_i and S; however, the inversion of the input from a given hash result is not possible computationally; that is, $\text{Adv}_{\text{HASH,A}}^{\text{BBSMK}}(t) \le \epsilon$, for all $\epsilon > 0$. Thus, $\text{Adv}_{\text{HASH,A}}^{\text{BBSMK}}(t, q_R) \le \epsilon$, since $\text{Adv}_{\text{HASH,A}}^{\text{BBSMK}}(t, q_R)$ depends on $\text{Adv}_{\text{HASH,A}}^{\text{BBSMK}}(t)$. In conclusion, there is no method for $\mathscr{E}$ to detect the complete connections between U_i and S, and the proposed protocol is distinctly invulnerable to an adversary $\mathscr{E}$ to retrieve $(\text{ID}_i, T_r(H_i), \lambda, s)$.

6.2. Simulation Result Using AVISPA. We perform to simulate the improved protocol for formal analysis using the widely accepted AVISPA. The main contribution of the simulation is to prove that the improved protocol is invulnerable to man-in-the-middle and replay attacks. AVISPA tool consists of four back-ends: (1) On-the-Fly Model Checker (OFMC); (2) Constraint-Logic-Based Attack Searcher; (3) SAT-Based Model Checker; and (4) Tree Automata Based on Automatic Approximations for the Analysis of Security Protocols. In the AVISPA, the protocol is implemented in High-Level Protocol Specification Language (HLPSL) [44], which is based on the roles: the basic roles for representing each entity role and composition roles for representing the scenarios of the basic

(1)   Eavesdrop the login request message $\{\text{CID}_i, y_i, Z_i, T_1\}$
(2)   Call the Reveal oracle. Let $\langle \text{ID}_1', T_r(H_i)' \rangle \leftarrow \text{Reveal}(Z_i)$
(3)   Eavesdrop the authentication response message $\{Y_s, Z_s, T_3\}$
(4)   Use the Reveal oracle. Let $\langle \lambda', T_r(H_i)'' \rangle \leftarrow \text{Reveal}(Z_s)$
(5)   **if** $(T_r(H_i)' = T_r(H_i)'')$ **then**
(6)   Compute $y_i' \parallel h(y_i' \parallel s) = Y_s \oplus T_r(H_i)'$
(7)   Call the Reveal oracle. Let $\langle \text{ID}_i'' \rangle \leftarrow \text{Reveal}(\lambda')$
(8)   **if** $(\text{ID}_i' == \text{ID}_i'')$ **then**
(9)   Compute $h(y_i \parallel s) = \text{CID}_i \oplus \text{ID}_i'$
(10)   Call the Reveal oracle. Let $\langle s' \rangle \leftarrow \text{Reveal}(M_1 = h(y_i \parallel s))$
(11)   Call the Reveal oracle. Let $\langle s'' \rangle \leftarrow \text{Reveal}(M_2 = h(y_i' \parallel s))$
(12)   **if** $(s' == s'')$ **then**
(13)   Accept $\text{ID}_i', T_r(H_i)', \lambda', s'$ as the correct $\text{ID}_i, T_r(H_i), \lambda, s$, respectively.
(14)   **return** 0 (Success)
(15)   **else**
(16)   **return** 0 (Failure)
(17)   **else**
(18)   **return** 0 (Failure)
(19) **else**
(20)   **return** 0 (Failure)
(21) **end if**

ALGORITHM 1: Algorithm $\text{EXP}_{\text{HASH},A}^{\text{BBSMK}}$.

roles. The fundamental types available in the HLPSL are [46] as follows:

- (i) agent: it means a primary name. The intruder always has the special identifier i.

- (ii) symmetric_key: it is the key using the symmetric-key cryptosystem.

- (iii) text: the text values are applied for messages. They are often used as nonces.

- (iv) nat: the nat is used for meaning the natural numbers in nonmessage contexts.

- (v) const: it is the type for representing constants.

- (vi) hash_func: the basic type hash_func expresses collision-resistance secure one-way hash functions.

The role of the initiator, user U_i, is shown in Algorithm 2. U_i first receives the signal for starting and modifies its state variable from 0 to 1. This state variable is retained by the variable *state*. Similar to user, the roles of server S are implemented and shown in Algorithm 3. The specifications in HLPSL for the roles of environment, session, and goal are described in Algorithm 4. The result for the formal security verification of the improved protocol using OMFC is provided in Algorithm 5. It is clear that the improved protocol is invulnerable to passive and active attacks including the two attacks.

6.3. Informal Security Analysis

6.3.1. Mutual Authentication. Not only does the proposed scheme guarantee security as the other biometric-based schemes, but also U_i and S authenticate each other. S authenticates U_i by checking whether Z_i is valid or not, because only a

legitimate user can compute a valid $h(\text{ID}_i \parallel T_r(H_i) \parallel y_i \parallel T_1)$ using a chaotic map. U_i then authenticates S by checking Z_s, which only S can compute using the long-term key s and timestamp T_3.

6.3.2. User Anonymity. To compromise the anonymity of user U_i, adversary $\mathscr{E}$ must be able to compute $h(y_i \parallel s)$. The value s is the master secret key of server S, and the random value y_i changes every session. Thus, the login request message changes every session. Even if adversary $\mathscr{E}$ eavesdrops on the login request message of a user U_i, $\mathscr{E}$ does not know ID_i. The proposed protocol provides user anonymity.

6.3.3. User Impersonation Attack. Suppose that an adversary $\mathscr{E}$ steals the mobile device MD_i of user U_i and extracts the parameters $\{V_i, W_i, y_i, \beta_i, X_i\}$ from MD_i. To make the login request message $\langle \text{CID}_i, y_i, Z_i, T_1 \rangle$, where $\text{CID}_i = \text{ID}_i \oplus h(y_i \parallel s)$ and $Z_i = h(\text{ID}_i \parallel T_r(H_i) \parallel y_i \parallel T_1)$, the server's master key s is needed. Without the master secret key s from server S, $\mathscr{E}$ cannot compute Z_i. The proposed protocol can therefore resist a user impersonation attack.

6.3.4. Privileged Insider Attack. In the proposed protocol, user U_i sends the login request message $\langle \text{ID}_i, \text{DPW}_i = \text{RPW}_i \oplus t \rangle$. Even if the privileged insider adversary $\mathscr{E}$ obtains these values $\langle \text{ID}_i, \text{DPW}_i = \text{RPW}_i \oplus t \rangle$, $\mathscr{E}$ does not know RPW_i and cannot impersonate user U_i. The proposed protocol can therefore resist a privileged insider attack.

6.3.5. Lost Mobile Device Attack. Suppose that user U_i's mobile device MD_i has been stolen or lost and any adversary $\mathscr{E}$ obtains it. $\mathscr{E}$ then tries to login to server S using MD_i; however, $\mathscr{E}$ does not know the correct password PW_i. To

```
role user (Ui, AS: agent,
SKuas: symmetric_key,
H, F: function,
SND, RCV: channel (dy))

played_by Ui def=

local State: nat,
IDi, PWi, BIOi, RPWi, DPWi, T, Ai: text,
Hi, Vi, VVi, R, S, Xi, Yi, Wi: text,
CIDi, Zi, T1, T3, SK, Y2, Ys, Zs: text
const as_ui_y2,
sc1, sc2, sc3, sc4: protocol_id

init State := 0

transition

(1) State = 0 ∧ RCV(start) =|>
State' := 1 ∧ T' := new()
∧ RPWi' := H(PWi.Ai)
∧ DPWi' := xor(RPWi',T')
∧ secret({PWi.Ai}, sc1, Ui)
∧ secret(IDi, sc2, {Ui,AS})
∧ SND({IDi.DPWi'}_SKuas)

(2) State = 2 ∧ RCV({ xor(H(IDi.xor(H(PWi.Ai),T')),F(R.H(S.IDi))).xor((Yi'.H(Yi'.S)),
xor(H(PWi.Ai),T')) }_SKuas) =|>
State' := 4 ∧ secret(R, S, sc3, AS)
∧ secret(F(R.H(S.IDi)), sc4, Ui, AS)
∧ VVi' := xor(H(IDi.H(PWi.Ai)), F(R.H(S.IDi)))
∧ Wi' := H(H(IDi.H(PWi.Ai)).F(R.H(S.IDi)))
∧ Xi' := xor((Yi'.H(Yi'.S)),H(PWi.Ai))
∧ CIDi' := xor(IDi, H(Yi'.S))
∧ T1' := new()
∧ Zi' := H(IDi.F(R.H(S.IDi)).Yi'.T1')
∧ SND(CIDi'.Yi'.Zi'.T1')

(3) State = 6 ∧ RCV(xor((Y2'.H(Y2'.S)),F(R.H(S.IDi))).H(SK.F(R.H(S.IDi)).T1'.T3').T3') =|>
State' := 8 ∧ SK' := H(IDi.F(R.H(S.IDi)).H(Y2'.S).T1'.T3')
∧ Xi' := xor((Y2'.H(Y2'.S)),H(PWi.Ai))
∧ request(Ui, AS, as_ui_y2, Y2')

end role
```

ALGORITHM 2: Role specification for user U_i.

login to S, the biometrics BIO_i is also needed. The proposed protocol can therefore resist a lost mobile device attack.

6.3.6. Replay Attack. One of the best solutions to prevent replay attack is to use a timestamp technique. The proposed protocol also uses timestamps. Even if any adversary $\mathscr{E}$ eavesdrops on any user's login request message and sends it to the server S, the server S checks the freshness of the timestamp and rejects the request. Furthermore, an adversary E cannot compute Z_i without ID_i and y_i. The proposed protocol can therefore resist a replay attack.

6.3.7. Off-Line Password Guessing Attack. To obtain a password of user U_i, the biometrics BIO_i is needed. Biometrics is

uniquene and it cannot be guessed or stolen. The proposed protocol can therefore resist an off-line password guessing attack.

6.3.8. Stolen Verifier Attack. In the proposed protocol, a server S does not store any information related to the user's identity or password. The proposed protocol can therefore resist a stolen verifier attack.

6.3.9. Session Key Forward Security. One important objective of any user authentication protocols is to constitute a session key between user U_i and server S. The forward secrecy can protect previous and future session keys from adversary $\mathscr{E}$ if the master secret key of S is exposed. Suppose that the master

```
role applicationserver (Ui, AS: agent,
SKuas: symmetric_key,
H, F: function,
SND, RCV: channel(dy))

played_by AS def=

local State: nat,
IDi, PWi, BIOi, RPWi, DPWi, T, Ai: text,
Hi, Vi, VVi, R, S, Xi, Yi, Wi: text,
CIDi, Zi, T1, T3, SK, Y2, Ys, Zs: text
const as_ui_y2,
sc1, sc2, sc3, sc4: protocol_id

init State:= 1

transition

(1) State = 1 ∧ RCV(IDi.xor(H(PWi.Ai),T')) –|>
State' := 3 ∧ Hi' := H(S.IDi)
∧ Vi' := xor(H(IDi.xor(H(PWi.Ai),T')),F(R.H(S.IDi)))
∧ Yi' := new()
∧ Xi' := xor((Yi'.H(Yi'.S)),xor(H(PWi.Ai),T'))
∧ secret(F(R.H(S.IDi)), sc4, {Ui, AS})
∧ SND({Vi'.Xi'}_SKuas)

(2) State = 5 ∧ RCV(xor(IDi,H(Yi'.S).Yi'.H(IDi.F(R.H(S.IDi).Yi'.T1')).T1')) =|>
State' := 7 ∧ Hi' := H(S.IDi)
∧ Y2' := new()
∧ T3' := new()
∧ SK' := H(IDi.F(R.H(S.IDi))).H(Y2'.S).T1'.T3')
∧ Ys' := xor((Y2'.H(Y2'.S)),F(R.H(S.IDi)))
∧ Zs' := H(SK'.F(R.H(S.IDi)).T1'.T3')
∧ SND(Ys'.Zs'.T3')
∧ witness(AS, Ui, as_ui_y2, Y2')

end role
```

ALGORITHM 3: Role specification for application server AS.

secret key s of S is known to $\mathscr{E}$. However, $\mathscr{E}$ does not know $T_r(H_i)$. Thus, the session key $\lambda = h(ID_i \parallel T_r(H_i) \parallel h(y_i' \parallel s) \parallel T_1 \parallel T_3)$ of the improved protocol is still undiscovered to $\mathscr{E}$. Therefore, forward secrecy is retained in the proposed protocol.

7. Comparison of Functionality and Performance

This section presents comparisons of the functionality between the improved protocol and related protocols [23–28], and the computational spending between the improved protocol and the other protocols [25–30] is also compared here.

7.1. Functionality Analysis. Table 1 compares the security features provided by the proposed protocol with previous protocols. The results indicate that the proposed protocol

is distinctly invulnerable and achieves all of the avoidance requirements.

7.2. Performance Analysis. We demonstrated the computational cost of the improved protocol against previous protocols in terms of the computational cost. According to the simulations obtained in [34], we found that $T_c \approx 32.40$ ms and $T_h \approx 0.20$ ms, respectively, with a system using Pentium IV 3.2 G (CPU) with a 3.0 GB (RAM). According to [47], the computational cost of the fuzzy extractor technique T_f is nearly identical to ECC multiplication. Kilinc and Yanik [48] has gauged the execution time of some cryptographic algorithms by using the Pairing-Based Cryptography Library (version 0.5.12) [49] in the OS: 32-bit Ubuntu 12.04.1, 2.2 G (CPU), and 2.0 G (RAM). They demonstrated that the cost to perform an elliptic curve point multiplication T_e is nearly 2.226 ms. In addition, they proved that the cost of a bitwise XOR operation is negligible. In Table 2, we presented the

TABLE 1: Functionality comparison of the improved protocol with others.

Property	[23]	[24]	[25]	[26]	[27]	[28]	The proposed
Mutual authentication	×	×	×	×	√	×	√
User anonymity	×	×	×	×	√	√	√
Impersonation attack	×	×	×	×	×	×	√
Insider attack	×	×	√	√	√	×	√
DoS attack	√	√	×	√	√	√	√
Replay attack	×	√	×	√	√	√	√
Off-line password guessing attack	×	√	×	×	√	×	√
Stolen verifier attack	×	√	√	√	√	√	√
Session key attack	×	×	×	×	×	×	√
Provable security	×	×	×	×	√	×	√

```
    role session (Ui, AS: agent,
    SKuas: symmetric_key,
    H, F: function)

def=
local H1, H2, R1, R2: channel (dy)
composition

    user (Ui, AS, SKuas, H, F, H1, R1)
    ∧ applicationserver (Ui, AS, SKuas, H, F, H2, R2)

    end role

    role environment() def=

    const ui, as: agent,
    skuas: symmetric_key,
    h, f: function,
    cidi, yi, zi, tl, ys, zs, t3: text,
    as_ui_y2,
    sc1, sc2, sc3, sc4: protocol_id

    intruder_knowledge = ui, as, h, f, cidi, yi, zi, tl, ys, zs, t3

    composition

    session(ui, as, skuas, h, f)
    ∧ session(i, as, skuas, h, f)
    ∧ session(ui, i, skuas, h, f)

    end role

    goal

    secrecy_of sc1, sc2, sc3, sc4
    authentication_on as_ui_y2

    end goal

    environment()
```

ALGORITHM 4: Role specification for session, goal, and environment.

```
    % OFMC
    % Version of 2006/02/13
    SUMMARY
    SAFE

    DETAILS
    BOUNDED_NUMBER_OF_SESSIONS

    PROTOCOL
    /home/span/span/testsuite/results/testrv3.if

    GOAL
    as_specified

    BACKEND
    OFMC

    COMMENTS
    STATISTICS
    parseTime: 0.00 s
    searchTime: 0.03 s
    visiteNodes: 4 nodes
    depth: 2 piles
```

ALGORITHM 5: The result of simulation using OFMC backends.

computational cost of the improved protocol for each phase and execution time (millisecond) with the related schemes. Compared to Islam et al.'s protocol, the improved protocol performs seven further hash functions and two fuzzy-extract operations. However, we reduce four extended chaotic operations. The improved protocol therefore is more effective than Islam et al.'s protocol.

8. Conclusion

Recently, Islam et al. demonstrated the security vulnerabilities in Lin et al.'s protocol and presented an improved authentication protocol using extended chaotic map. Islam

TABLE 2: Performance comparison of the improved protocol with others.

	[25]	[29]	[26]	[27]	[28]	[30]	The proposed
Registration	$3T_h$	$4T_h$	$4T_h + T_c$	$6T_h + T_c$	$4T_h$	$3T_h + T_c$	$7T_h + T_c + T_f$
Login	$5T_h + T_c$	$3T_h + 2T_c$	$2T_h + 2T_c$	$3T_h + 2T_c$	$5T_h + 2T_c$	$2T_h + 3T_c$	$3T_h + T_f$
Verification	$6T_h + 5T_c$	$6T_h + 4T_c$	$6T_h + T_c$	$6T_h + T_c$	$7T_h + 4T_c$	$6T_h + 2T_c$	$8T_h + 1T_c$
Total	$14T_h + 6T_c$	$13T_h + 6T_c$	$14T_h + 4T_c$	$15T_h + 4T_c$	$16T_h + 6T_c$	$11T_h + 6T_c$	$18T_h + 2T_c + 2T_f$
Time (ms)	≈197.2	≈197.0	≈132.4	≈132.6	≈197.6	≈196.6	≈72.9

et al. also asserted that their authentication protocol is more secure than Lin et al.'s protocol and that it guarantees user anonymity. However, Islam et al.'s protocol is still insecure against some types of attacks, such as on-line identity guessing and user impersonation. To overcome these security weaknesses, in the current paper, we suggest an improved user authentication protocol using a fuzzy extractor that preserves the advantages of Islam et al.'s protocol and contributes to inclusive security properties. The formal and informal analyses of this work clarify why the improved protocol is more efficient and secure.

Notations

U_i:	Mobile user
MD_i:	Mobile device of user
ID_i:	Identity of user
PW_i:	Password of user
BIO_i:	Biometrics of user
S:	Remote server
x:	Real number chosen set $[-1, 1]$
$T_k(x)$:	Chebyshev polynomial of degree k
s:	Master secret key of server S
r:	Positive random integer generated server S
$h(\cdot)$:	Cryptographic hash function
9 α_i, β_i:	U_i's nearly random binary and auxiliary binary strings
λ:	Session key
T:	Timestamp
$\|$:	Concatenation operator
$\oplus$:	Bitwise XOR operator.

Conflicts of Interest

The authors declare that they have no conflicts of interest.

Acknowledgments

This research was supported by Basic Science Research Program through the National Research Foundation of Korea (NRF) funded by the Ministry of Education (NRF-2010-0020210).

References

[1] N. Park, H. W. Kim, S. Kim, and D. Won, "Open location-based service using secure middleware infrastructure in web services," in *Proceedings of the International Conference on Computational Science and Its Applications - ICCSA 2005*, pp. 1146–1155, sgp, May 2005.

[2] L. Lamport, "Password authentication with insecure communication," *Communications of the ACM*, vol. 24, no. 11, pp. 770–772, 1981.

[3] M. Kumar, "On the weaknesses and improvements of an efficient password based remote user authentication scheme using smart cards," *IACR Cryptology ePrint Archive*, pp. 163–174, 2004.

[4] H. Lin, "Efficient mobile dynamic ID authentication and key agreement scheme without trusted servers," *International Journal of Communication Systems*, vol. 30, no. 1, Article ID e2818, 2017.

[5] M. Khan and J. Zhang, "Improving the security of "a flexible biometrics remote user authentication scheme"," *Computer Standards and Interfaces*, vol. 29, no. 1, pp. 82–85, 2007.

[6] W. Jeon, J. Kim, J. Nam, Y. Lee, and D. Won, "An enhanced secure authentication scheme with anonymity for wireless environments," *IEICE Transactions on Communications*, vol. 95, no. 7, pp. 2505–2508, 2012.

[7] D. He, N. Kumar, M. K. Khan, and J.-H. Lee, "Anonymous two-factor authentication for consumer roaming service in global mobility networks," *IEEE Transactions on Consumer Electronics*, vol. 59, no. 4, pp. 811–817, 2013.

[8] D. Mishra, A. Das, and S. Mukhopadhyay, "A secure user anonymity-preserving biometric-based multi-server authenticated key agreement scheme using smart cards," *Expert Systems with Applications*, vol. 41, no. 18, pp. 8129–8143, 2014.

[9] R. Amin, S. Islam, G. Biswas, M. Khan, and N. Kumar, "A robust and anonymous patient monitoring system using wireless medical sensor networks," *Future Generation Computer Systems*, 2015.

[10] R. Amin, R. Sherratt, D. Giri, S. Islam, and M. Khan, "A software agent enabled biometric security algorithm for secure file access in consumer storage devices," *IEEE Transactions on Consumer Electronics*, vol. 63, no. 1, pp. 53–61, 2017.

[11] P. Mohit, R. Amin, and G. Biswas, "Design of authentication protocol for wireless sensor network-based smart vehicular system," *Vehicular Communications*, vol. 9, pp. 64–71, 2017.

[12] A. Chaturvedi, D. Mishra, S. Jangirala, and S. Mukhopadhyay, "A privacy preserving biometric-based three-factor remote user authenticated key agreement scheme," *Journal of Information Security and Applications*, vol. 32, pp. 15–26, 2017.

[13] D. Mishra, S. Kumari, M. Khan, and S. Mukhopadhyay, "An anonymous biometric-based remote user-authenticated key agreement scheme for multimedia systems," *International Journal of Communication Systems*, vol. 30, no. 1, Article ID e2946, 2017.

[14] S. Park, S. Kim, and D. Won, "ID-based group signature," *Electronics Letters*, vol. 33, no. 19, pp. 1616-1617, 1997.

[15] R. Amin and G. Biswas, "An Improved RSA Based User Authentication and Session Key Agreement Protocol Usable in TMIS," *Journal of Medical Systems*, vol. 39, no. 8, article no. 79, 2015.

[16] J. Nam, M. Kim, J. Paik, Y. Lee, and D. Won, "A provably-secure ECC-based authentication scheme for wireless sensor networks," *Sensors*, vol. 14, no. 11, pp. 21023–21044, 2014.

[17] R. Amin, S. Islam, G. Biswas, M. Khan, and N. Kumar, "An Efficient and Practical Smart Card Based Anonymity Preserving User Authentication Scheme for TMIS using Elliptic Curve Cryptography," *Journal of Medical Systems*, vol. 39, no. 11, article no. 180, 2015.

[18] C. Chen, D. He, S. Chan, J. Bu, Y. Gao, and R. Fan, "Lightweight and provably secure user authentication with anonymity for the global mobility network," *International Journal of Communication Systems*, vol. 24, no. 3, pp. 347–362, 2011.

[19] H. Debiao, C. Jianhua, and Z. Rui, "A more secure authentication scheme for telecare medicine information systems," *Journal of Medical Systems*, vol. 36, no. 3, pp. 1989–1995, 2012.

[20] S. Wu, Y. Zhu, and Q. Pu, "Robust smart-cards-based user authentication scheme with user anonymity," *Security and Communication Networks*, vol. 5, no. 2, pp. 236–248, 2012.

[21] P. Gong, P. Li, and W. Shi, "A secure chaotic maps-based key agreement protocol without using smart cards," *Nonlinear Dynamics. An International Journal of Nonlinear Dynamics and Chaos in Engineering Systems*, vol. 70, no. 4, pp. 2401–2406, 2012.

[22] J. Moon, Y. Choi, J. Kim, and D. Won, "An Improvement of Robust and Efficient Biometrics Based Password Authentication Scheme for Telecare Medicine Information Systems Using Extended Chaotic Maps," *Journal of Medical Systems*, vol. 40, no. 3, article no. 70, pp. 1–11, 2016.

[23] D. Xiao, X. Liao, and S. Deng, "A novel key agreement protocol based on chaotic maps," *Information Sciences. An International Journal*, vol. 177, no. 4, pp. 1136–1142, 2007.

[24] S. Han, H. Tseng, R. Jan, and W. Yang, "A chaotic maps-based key agreement protocol that preserves user anonymity," in *Proceedings of the IEEE International Conference on Communications (ICCâ09, pp. 1–6, Dresden, Germany, 2009.

[25] C. Lee, C. Chen, C. Wu, and S. Huang, "An extended chaotic maps-based key agreement protocol with user anonymity," *Nonlinear Dynamics. An International Journal of Nonlinear Dynamics and Chaos in Engineering Systems*, vol. 69, no. 1-2, pp. 79–87, 2012.

[26] H. Lin, "Chaotic map based mobile dynamic ID authenticated key agreement scheme," *Wireless Personal Communications*, vol. 78, no. 2, pp. 1487–1494, 2014.

[27] S. Islam, M. Obaidat, and R. Amin, "An anonymous and provably secure authentication scheme for mobile user," *International Journal of Communication Systems*, vol. 29, no. 9, pp. 1529–1544, 2016.

[28] C. Lee and C. Hsu, "A secure biometric-based remote user authentication with key agreement scheme using extended chaotic maps," *Nonlinear Dynamics. An International Journal of Nonlinear Dynamics and Chaos in Engineering Systems*, vol. 71, no. 1-2, pp. 200–211, 2013.

[29] D. He, Y. Chen, and J. Chen, "Cryptanalysis and improvement of an extended chaotic maps-based key agreement protocol," *Nonlinear Dynamics. An International Journal of Nonlinear Dynamics and Chaos in Engineering Systems*, vol. 69, no. 3, pp. 1149–1157, 2012.

[30] D. Guo, Q. Wen, W. Li, H. Zhang, and Z. Jin, "Analysis and Improvement of 'Chaotic Map Based Mobile Dynamic ID Authenticated Key Agreement Scheme," *Wireless Personal Communications*, vol. 83, no. 1, pp. 35–48, 2015.

[31] S. Han, "Security of a key agreement protocol based on chaotic maps," *Chaos, Solitons & Fractals*, vol. 38, no. 3, pp. 764–768, 2008.

[32] Y. Niu and X. Wang, "An anonymous key agreement protocol based on chaotic maps," *Communications in Nonlinear Science and Numerical Simulation*, vol. 16, no. 4, pp. 1986–1992, 2011.

[33] E. Yoon, "Efficiency and security problems of anonymous key agreement protocol based on chaotic maps," *Communications in Nonlinear Science and Numerical Simulation*, vol. 17, no. 7, pp. 2735–2740, 2012.

[34] K. Xue and P. Hong, "Security improvement of an anonymous key agreement protocol based on chaotic maps," *Communications in Nonlinear Science and Numerical Simulation*, vol. 17, no. 7, pp. 2969–2977, 2012.

[35] Z. Tan, "A chaotic maps-based authenticated key agreement protocol with strong anonymity," *Nonlinear Dynamics. An International Journal of Nonlinear Dynamics and Chaos in Engineering Systems*, vol. 72, no. 1-2, pp. 311–320, 2013.

[36] C. Li, C. Lee, and C. Weng, "An extended chaotic maps based user authentication and privacy preserving scheme against DoS attacks in pervasive and ubiquitous computing environments," *Nonlinear Dynamics. An International Journal of Nonlinear Dynamics and Chaos in Engineering Systems*, vol. 74, no. 4, pp. 1133–1143, 2013.

[37] D. Dolev and A. Yao, "On the security of public key protocols," *Institute of Electrical and Electronics Engineers. Transactions on Information Theory*, vol. 29, no. 2, pp. 198–208, 1983.

[38] J. Moon, Y. Choi, J. Jung, and D. Won, "An improvement of robust biometrics-based authentication and key agreement scheme for multi-server environments using smart cards," *PLoS ONE*, vol. 10, no. 12, Article ID e0145263, 2015.

[39] Y. Dodis, B. Kanukurthi, J. Katz, and A. Smith, "Robust fuzzy extractors and authenticated key agreement from close secrets," *IEEE Transactions on Information Theory*, vol. 58, no. 9, pp. 6207–6222, 2012.

[40] A. Das, "A secure and effective biometric-based user authentication scheme for wireless sensor networks using smart card and fuzzy extractor," *International Journal of Communication Systems*, vol. 30, no. 1, Article ID e2933, 2017.

[41] C. Wang, X. Zhang, and Z. Zheng, "Cryptanalysis and improvement of a biometric-based user authentication scheme for wireless sensor networks using smart card and fuzzy extractor," in *PLoS One*, vol. 11, pp. 25-25, 2016.

[42] Y. Dodis, L. Reyzin, and A. Smith, "Fuzzy extractors: how to generate strong keys from biometrics and other noisy data," in *Advances in cryptology—EUROCRYPT 2004*, vol. 3027 of *Lecture Notes in Comput. Sci.*, pp. 523–540, Springer, Berlin, 2004.

[43] P. Bergamo, P. D'Arco, A. De Santis, and L. Kocarev, "Security of public-key cryptosystems based on Chebyshev polynomials," *IEEE Transactions on Circuits and Systems. I. Regular Papers*, vol. 52, no. 7, pp. 1382–1393, 2005.

[44] A. Das, "A secure and effective user authentication and privacy preserving protocol with smart cards for wireless communication," in *Networking Science*, vol. 2, pp. 12–27, 2, 2013.

[45] Y. Lu, L. Li, X. Yang, and Y. Yang, "Robust biometrics based authentication and key agreement scheme for multi-server environments using smart cards," *PLoS ONE*, vol. 10, no. 5, Article ID 0126323, 2015.

[46] von Oheimb D. The high-level protocol specification language hlpsl developed in the eu project avispa. In Proceedings of the Applied Semantics 2005 Workshop, Frauenchiemsee, Germany, 12–15 September 2005; pp. 1–17.

[47] M. Wazid, A. K. Das, S. Kumari, X. Li, and F. Wu, "Design of an efficient and provably secure anonymity preserving three-factor user authentication and key agreement scheme for TMIS," *Security and Communication Networks*, vol. 9, no. 13, pp. 1983–2001, 2016.

[48] H. Kilinc and T. Yanik, "A survey of SIP authentication and key agreement schemes," *IEEE Communications Surveys and Tutorials*, vol. 16, no. 2, pp. 1005–1023, 2014.

[49] Lynn B. Pairing-based cryptography library, available at http://crypto.stanford.edu/pbc/.

Permissions

List of Contributors

Changsheng Wan
School of Information Science and Engineering, Southeast University, Nanjing, Jiangsu 210096, China
Nanjing University, Nanjing, Jiangsu 210093, China
Key Lab of Information Network Security of Ministry of Public Security of China, Shanghai 201204, China

Juan Zhang
Nanjing University, Nanjing, Jiangsu 210093, China

Daoli Huang
Key Lab of Information Network Security of Ministry of Public Security of China, Shanghai 201204, China

Murat Dener
Graduate School of Natural and Applied Sciences, Gazi University, Besevler, Ankara, Turkey

Omer Faruk Bay
Department of Electronics and Computer, Gazi University, Besevler, Ankara, Turkey

Zheng Zhao, Fenlin Liu and Daofu Gong
Zhengzhou Science and Technology Institute, Zhengzhou 450002, China

Chenyu Wang and Guoai Xu
School of CyberSpace Security, Beijing University of Posts and Telecommunications, Beijing 100876, China

Ivan Vaccari, Enrico Cambiaso and Maurizio Aiello
National Research Council (CNR), IEIIT Institute, Via De Marini 6, 16149 Genova, Italy

Chun-Juan Ouyang, Ming Leng, Jie-Wu Xia and Huan Liu
Key Laboratory of Watershed Ecology and Geographical Environment Monitoring of NASG, Jinggangshan University, Ji'an 343009, China
School of Electronics and Information Engineering, Jinggangshan University, Ji'an 343009, China

Yujia Liu, Weiming Zhang and Nenghai Yu
University of Science and Technology of China, Hefei, China

Chalee Vorakulpipat, Soontorn Sirapaisan, Ekkachan Rattanalerdnusorn and Visut Savangsuk
National Electronics and Computer Technology Center, 112Thailand Science Park, Phahonyothin Road, Khlong 1,Khlong Luang, PathumThani 12120,Thailand

Shuai Han and Lin Lyu
Department of Computer Science and Engineering, Shanghai Jiao Tong University, Shanghai 200240, China
State Key Laboratory of Cryptology, Beijing 100878, China

Shengli Liu
Department of Computer Science and Engineering, Shanghai Jiao Tong University, Shanghai 200240, China
State Key Laboratory of Cryptology, Beijing 100878, China
Westone Cryptologic Research Center, Beijing 100070, China

Wei Tian
School of Computer and Software, Nanjing University of Information Science and Technology, Nanjing, China
Jiangsu Engineering Centre of Network Monitoring, Nanjing University of Information Science and Technology, Nanjing, China

Xiaolong Xu
School of Computer and Software, Nanjing University of Information Science and Technology, Nanjing, China
Jiangsu Engineering Centre of Network Monitoring, Nanjing University of Information Science and Technology, Nanjing, China
State Key Laboratory for Novel Software Technology, Nanjing University, Nanjing, China

Wanchun Dou, Xuan Zhao and Jie Zhang
State Key Laboratory for Novel Software Technology, Nanjing University, Nanjing, China

Alex X. Liu
Department of Computer Science and Engineering, Michigan State University, East Lansing, MI, USA

Feng Ruan
School of Information and Control, Nanjing University of Information Science and Technology, Nanjing, China

Jianxin Xu and Dongqin Feng
Institute of Cyber-Systems and Control, Zhejiang University, Hangzhou 310027, China

National Engineering Laboratory for Safety & Security Technology of Industrial Control System, Zhejiang University, Hangzhou 310027, China
State Key Laboratory of Industrial Control Technology, Zhejiang University, Hangzhou 310027, China

Hongji Huang, Wanyou Sun, Jie Yang and Guan Gui
College of Telecommunication and Information, Nanjing University of Posts and Telecommunications, Nanjing, China

Feng Li and Ning Lu
Computer and Communication Engineering College, Northeastern University at Qinhuangdao, Qinhuangdao, China

Zhen Chen and Limin Shen
School of Information Science and Engineering, Yanshan University, Qinhuangdao, China

Yali Si
School of Information Science and Engineering, Yanshan University, Qinhuangdao, China
School of Liren, Yanshan University, Qinhuangdao, China

Bingxin Zhu, Puwen Wei and Mingqiang Wang
Key Laboratory of Cryptologic Technology and Information Security, Ministry of Education, Shandong University, Jinan, China

Nishaal J. Parmar and Pramode K. Verma
Telecommunications Engineering Program, School of Electrical and Computer Engineering, University of Oklahoma, Tulsa, OK 74135, USA

Jongho Moon
Department of Electrical and Computer Engineering, Sungkyunkwan University, 2066 Seobu-ro, Jangan-gu, Suwon-si, Gyeonggi-do 16419, Republic of Korea

Youngsook Lee
Department of Cyber Security, Howon University, 64 Howondae 3-gil, Impi-myeon, Gunsan-si, Jeonrabuk-do 54058, Republic of Korea

Jiye Kim
Department ofMobile Internet,DaelimUniversity College, 29 Imgok-ro,Dongan-gu, Anyang-si, Gyeonggi-do 13916, Republic of Korea

Dongho Won
Department of Computer Engineering, Sungkyunkwan University, 2066 Seobu-ro, Jangan-gu, Suwon-si, Gyeonggi-do 16419, Republic of Korea

Index